FICTION'S JOURNEY

50 Stories

FICTION'S JOURNEY

50 Stories

BARBARA McKENZIE

University of Georgia

HARCOURT BRACE JOVANOVICH, INC.

New York   San Diego   Chicago   San Francisco   Atlanta

ISBN: 0-15-527320-5

Library of Congress Catalog Card Number: 77-83621

Printed in the United States of America

Cover photo by Harry W. Rinehart

ACKNOWLEDGMENTS

For permission to use the selections reprinted in this book, the author is grateful to the following publishers and copyright holders:

A. S. BARNES & COMPANY, INC. For "The Old Lion and the Fox" and "The Crow and the Fox" from *Aesop Without Morals,* edited by Lloyd W. Daly. Reprinted by permission of A. S. Barnes & Company, Inc.

THE BODLEY HEAD For "The Story-Teller" from *Beasts and Superbeasts* by Saki. Reprinted by permission of The Bodley Head.

THOMAS Y. CROWELL COMPANY, INC. For "The Man Who Was Almost a Man" from *Eight Men* by Richard Wright. Copyright © 1940, 1961 by Richard Wright. Originally published by World Publishing. Used with permission of Thomas Y. Crowell Company, Inc., publisher.

DOUBLEDAY & COMPANY, INC. For "Lost in the Funhouse," copyright © 1967 By The Atlantic Monthly Company. From *Lost in the Funhouse* by John Barth; for "The Only Way to Make It in New York" by Rosellen Brown from *Street Games,* copyright © 1974 by Rosellen Brown; and for "My Kinsman, Major Molineux" from *The Complete Short Stories of Nathaniel Hawthorne* by Nathaniel Hawthorne. All are reprinted by permission of Doubleday & Company, Inc.

Acknowledgments continue on page 539, an extension of the copyright page.

for Clark Emery
    who guided my journey into fiction

Preface

Fiction's Journey is both an anthology and a handbook of short fiction. The use of the term short *fiction* rather than short stories is deliberate, for stories existed long before the mid-nineteenth century when the short story came into being as a distinct literary genre. Accordingly, a story from Homer's *Odyssey* begins this collection. Also included are other examples of early narrative art— the Characters of Theophrastus, the fables of Aesop, and a Grimm fairy tale. The past enriches our sense of self by telling us where we have been, but it also fascinates us by the persistence with which it informs the present. Thus, Thurber's fables appear with Aesop's, a tall tale of Faulkner's is included with one of Mark Twain's, and Theophrastus is echoed not only in Addison's character sketches but in the portrait of an American in Brautigan's "The World War I Los Angeles Airplane."

The past also informs the present in the persistence of fictional techniques. The Cyclops' cave is described with realistic detail no less precise than the cottage in Updike's "The Day of the Dying Rabbit," and Odysseus is as complex and ambiguous a character as the revolutionary leader in Hawthorne's "My Kinsman, Major Molineux" or Kaph in Le Guin's "Nine Lives."

Stories from fiction's past and present share similar themes as well as techniques, most often because the experience they reflect is so universal and inescapable that time and place fade or disappear. The theme of initiation, for example, is expressed not only in "My Kinsman" but in Joyce's "Araby," Wright's "The Man Who Was Almost a Man," and Barth's "Lost in the Funhouse." Sometimes the past informs a contemporary story through specific reference to earlier authors and conventions, as in "Uncle Tom's Cabin: Alternate Ending" by LeRoi Jones and "A Conversation with My Father" by Grace Paley.

The Jones and Paley relate thematically to another group of stories in their use of fiction-making as subject matter. Sometimes this takes the form of a character who is a writer by profession, as in James' "The Middle Years" and Cheever's "The Jewels of the Cabots." At other times, plot or language is used as subject matter, as in Cortazar's "Continuity of Parks," Barthelme's "Sentence," and Borges's "Theme of the Traitor and the Hero." Stories about fiction-making facilitate discussion of the elements of fiction because their content leads inevitably to the process of fiction itself.

Useful as such stories are to students of literature, an anthology that included only serious stories—whether about fiction-making or about pain, misery, and death—would be unrepresentative of the rich variety of short fiction. For there should be delight as well as instruction in the stories, and for this reason many comic stories—such as Parker's "You Were Perfectly Fine," Welty's "Why I Live at the P.O.," and Apple's "The Oranging of America"—are included. Not that serious stories don't yield pleasure too, but it is a different kind of pleasure, a kind students may not be able to experience at the beginning of their journey into fiction but perhaps will have learned to experience toward the end. Laughter remains, however, a necessary corrective for the tragic vision that dominates so much of our literature.

Fiction's Journey is arranged according to the elements of fiction—point of view, plot, setting, style, and tone. The extensive introduction discusses the fifty stories in terms of these categories; this arrangement is simply one way of organizing the collection into a coherent whole, however, for every story of course includes all categories. The arrangement is not intended to be an inflexible itinerary, for inflexibility precludes discovery, and discovery is the point of a journey. Those who use this book are encouraged to plot their own route and to choose among the stories, for there are probably too many here for a semester's reading.

These are some of the principles that influenced the form and content of this book. But there is one last consideration: journeys have a way of ending where they began, either literally or figuratively. "Lost in the Funhouse" exemplifies the cyclic nature of fiction's journey, and for this reason it ends the anthology. Inherent to any journey, however, are the changes to the self that result from the discoveries it allows. The Instructor's Manual and the questions following each story are intended as roadside markers for teacher and student respectively. But the most helpful guideposts are embedded in the fiction itself and await only recognition and interpretation.

I would like to thank Natalie Bowen and Eben W. Ludlow for their help in organizing and shaping the content of this book, and Harry W. Rinehart for giving that content an imaginative visual form.

Barbara McKenzie

Contents

50 STORIES

FICTION'S JOURNEY
50 Stories

Then who that will have the very understanding of this matter . . . must oft and many times read in this book. . . . And for them that understandeth it, it shall be right joyous, pleasant, and profitable.

—William Caxton, 1481

Introduction

WHAT A STORY IS

In the Beginning

Fiction's journey begins in obscurity. No single country claims its origination. No specific year marks its birthdate. And certainly no individual stands apart as the first storyteller. For stories were told long before written language came into being. Stories making plausible the mysteries of birth and death, recounting the glories and anguish of war and the hunt, preserving the genealogies of families, and incorporating the customs of a people—their laws, their medicine, their rituals—became the shared property of the ruled and the ruling, told by one generation and remembered by the next to be retold . . . and retold . . . in a seemingly endless chain. So it went, for thousands and thousands of years, until 6000 B.C., when written language first emerged. And, paradoxically, so it goes, for the oral tradition of storytelling persists into the present, and not only in primitive societies.

Our study begins in Greece around 800 B.C. The storyteller is Homer, and his story is of the wanderings of Odysseus—including Odysseus's encounter with the Lotus-eaters and the Cyclops, the episode reprinted here. But India with its *Ocean of the Streams of Story* would have served our purpose just as well. Or Persia and the stories told by Scheherazade in *The Thousand Nights and a Night*—a compendium of magical tales and historical accounts, preachy morality tales and bawdy comedies of low life. Or Judea and Syria and the Old Testament stories of Abraham and Isaac, of the prodigal son, of Daniel, of Jonah, and of Job. Or Rome and the *Metamorphoses* of Ovid. Or Italy and the *Decameron* by Boccaccio. Or England and Chaucer's *The Canterbury Tales*. These or other collections and cycles too numerous to mention would have provided an equally suitable place to begin our inquiry. For what is at stake is not the fiction of any one country but the oral tradition represented by the folk tale as it appears and reappears in written literature. The folk tale is basic to each of these literary works as it is to the *Odyssey*. The story of Odysseus becomes, then, a suitable place to launch fiction's journey—to describe *what a story is*.

W. H. D. Rouse, who translated the *Odyssey* into the prose version reprinted in this collection, has called it "the best story ever written." Readers

3

"who like thrillers and detective novels" will discover ample excitement, and those who like psychology will find plenty to entertain them in the characters, both gods and men, and particularly in the wonderful picture of Odysseus himself. . . ." Rouse's praise is not misdirected: the *Odyssey* may well be the best story ever written. Maybe not after a laborious first reading in high school English—or a frantic skimming in an abbreviated study guide. But read more casually, episode by episode, for surely that was how its first audiences heard these stories. And viewed not as a "classic" but as a story which, like most stories, is intended to delight and to instruct.

Like most fiction and drama, the *Odyssey* combines both fantasy and historical fact. The frame story—Odysseus's wanderings and reception at Ithaca—is the folk tale of the Returning Hero, a popular story found in the traditional literature of many countries. Odysseus, however, is believed to have been an actual person who fought in the Trojan War. As both stories circulated in the repertoire of bards, history and fantasy merged, with the real-life Odysseus becoming the archetypal Returning Hero. Homer was the inheritor of this merger as he was of the long history of oral poetry.

The episode included here takes place at the Court of the Phaiacian King. Odysseus is in the tenth year of his wanderings. Shipwrecked without comrades or possessions at Phaiacia, he is treated hospitably by the king. During a court banquet, the royal minstrel entertains with stories of famous men, beginning with Odysseus and his participation in the Trojan War. The minstrel's song causes Odysseus to weep. Noticing his distress, the king asks the bard to end the song and his guest to reveal his identity. Odysseus complies, after which he tells the first of his adventures on leaving Troy—his encounter with the Lotus-eaters and the Cyclops. Three levels of storytelling are involved at this point: the *Odyssey* considered as a whole; the minstrel's story of Odysseus's adventures, a tale within a tale; and the story told by Odysseus, another tale within a tale. Examined in this manner, the *Odyssey* is like a box that when opened contains another box that when opened . . . This doubling and turning inward is characteristic of much fiction. Through the centuries storytellers have enjoyed letting their own characters tell stories within the larger context of the fictional narrative. Saki (H. H. Munro), William Faulkner, Jorge Luis Borges, John Barth, and Grace Paley (whose stories are represented in this collection) are among the inheritors of this tradition.

Odysseus uses all the ingredients of the storyteller's art to relate his adventures. There are characters aplenty, ranging from the seemingly harmless Lotus-eaters to the mighty Cyclops—"savage, knowing neither justice nor law." Pitted against these opponents is Odysseus—crafty, strong, brave, foolhardy, proud, boastful, and stubborn. Every story has a narrator; in this instance Odysseus acts as a first-person narrator, thus establishing a particular point of view. The encounter with the Cyclops is heavy on action of a most dramatic kind. Lots of blood and guts are spilled. And a puzzle is solved. How are Odysseus and his men going to escape from the cave? The solution is worthy of the most ingenious detective hero—replete with a play on words, disguise, and violence. The plot takes place against various settings: the ever-changing sea, the country of the Lotus-eaters, the magnificently fecund island where Odysseus and his men camp, and the Cyclops' cave.

The action is narrated in language both folksy and metaphoric. Rouse chose to translate Homer's dactylic hexameter into idiomatic English prose because he found prose closer to the language Homer employed than translations "filled with affectation and attempts at poetic language which Homer himself is quite free from." Figures of speech do heighten the language, however, as when Odysseus describes the Cyclops as a "wonderful monster, not like a mortal man who eats bread, but rather like a mountain peak with trees on the top standing up alone in the highlands." The size of the Cyclops is stressed again when Odysseus recounts the gouging of the giant's eye:

> As a man bores a ship's timber with an auger, while others at the lower part keep turning it with a strap which they hold at each end, and round and round it runs: so we held the fire-sharpened pole and turned it, and the blood bubbled about its hot point. . . . As a smith plunges an axe or an adze in cold water, for that makes the strength of steel, and it hisses loud when he tempers it, so his eye sizzled about the pole of olive-wood.

Alliteration lends emphasis and rhythm to the language. So do periodic sentences and the use of inversion, as in "Glad indeed our friends were to see us, all of us that were left alive." Further, because we see Odysseus as both brave and foolish, our reaction to him is ambivalent. And in so far as our sympathies are engaged, we react to his story with emotions ranging from admiration to repulsion. Most good literature is affective—that is, it speaks to the heart as well as to the mind.

Like all lasting fictions, the *Odyssey* can be read on more than one level. The actual journey of Odysseus is also a figurative journey that ends in a spiritual as well as a physical reconciliation for the hero. But is the *Odyssey* about one man or about humankind? The inclusion of the Lotus-eaters and the Cyclops points toward a symbolic interpretation of at least this portion of the journey. Is Odysseus telling a literal story or are his adventures with these fabulous creatures intended to be taken as metaphors for experience—as a way of saying, this is what my wanderings have been like? The Lotus-eaters with their honeyed fruit may be symbolic of a state of moral torpor that causes persons to forget their homeland and, therefore, to lose a deeply embedded instinct—the desire to go home. The cave of the lawless Cyclops may well be only another dark trap that Odysseus in his greed and pride has wandered into. Serious literature almost always demands interpretation; its meaning is seldom found on the surface, and often more than one interpretation is possible. For human experience is seldom simple, and truth almost never single. In such a way does this episode from the *Odyssey* reveal *what a story is*. Fiction's journey has had a good beginning.

Short fiction, as noted earlier, existed long before the time of Homer and long after, surviving through the Middle Ages and into the eighteenth century as fable and romance, character sketch and morality tale, adventure story and dream vision, folk tale and fairy tale. Not until the early nineteenth century did the *short story* emerge as a literary genre separate from short fiction. Its first practitioners were not Europeans but the Americans Nathaniel Hawthorne and Edgar Allan Poe, who both wrote not only stories but prefaces and reviews that established the short story as a distinctive literary form. The most significant and far-reaching theoretical discussion of the short story is Poe's review of Hawthorne's *Twice-Told Tales* (1842). The esthetic of the "short prose narrative" described by Poe in this essay provided the basic definition of the modern short story.

In praising Hawthorne for fashioning the events of his stories to accommodate his thoughts, Poe says of the short story:

> In the whole composition there should be no word written, of which the tendency, direct or indirect, is not to the one preestablished design. And by such means, with such care and skill, a picture is at length painted which leaves in the mind of him who contemplates it with a kindred art, a sense of the fullest satisfaction. . . . Truth is often, and in some very great degree, the aim of the tale.

Poe's insistence on unity and on a preconceived effect brought tension, a desirable characteristic of poetry, to the short story. This same dictum has led generations of later writers and critics to place a high value on stories that are *well made.* As Poe did, they have admired stories in which "not only is all done that should be done, but (what perhaps is an end with more difficulty attained) there is nothing done which should not be. Every word *tells,* and there is not a word that does not tell. . . ." The concept of the well-made story does not presuppose a formulaic approach to storytelling (although it can lead to that), but it does suggest an adherence to a formalistic structure—one with a beginning, a middle, and an end; with recognizable characters engaged in recognizable actions; with involvement in a world that bears some resemblance to the readers' own; with truth or revelation as its principal aim.

Asked to define a short story, Flannery O'Connor (in the Winter 1959 issue of *Esprit*) described the question as "inspired by the devil who tempts textbook publishers" and then acknowledged,

> The best I can do is tell you what a story is not.
>
> 1. It is not a joke.
> 2. It is not an anecdote.
> 3. It is not a lyric rhapsody in prose.
> 4. It is not a case history.
> 5. It is not a reported incident.
>
> It is none of these things because it has an extra dimension and I think this extra dimension comes about when the writer puts us in the middle of some human action and shows it as it is illuminated and outlined by mystery.

By indirection, O'Connor's list of negative characteristics tells us a great deal about what a story is. Implicit in it are these assumptions: that a story illuminates the human action it depicts (in distinction to the anecdote and the joke which are intended primarily to entertain and amuse), that it has a plot and characters (unlike the lyric rhapsody), that it is a work of the imagination (separating it from the case history), that it possesses a formal structure (differentiating it from the reported incident). Each of these assumptions is compatible with the definition proposed by Poe.

The well-made story has counterparts in the novel, drama, painting, and film. Yet in each of these arts there also exists a parallel tradition that uses and abuses the conventions of the established genre, resulting in works that turn the tenets of the conventional art-form inside out. Though somewhat stronger in these other arts, this unconventional approach is found even in the short story (the most conservative of literary genres), where it results in stories that *appear* to be no more than reported incidents, case histories, lyric rhapsodies, anecdotes, jokes, or some wild and unruly combination of some or all of these "nonstories." In dealing with such stories in this collection, the reader should remember that appearances are often deceiving and that thus it is the reader's job to see through the deceptions and discover the "extra dimension" that unites conventional and experimental works of fiction.

Accordingly, the scope of this introduction is threefold: its first and largest task is to describe the principal elements of fiction and to explain the conventions of the well-made story; its second, to describe the techniques found most frequently in experimental stories; and its third, to suggest something of the circular route of fiction's journey. Because the well-made story is more abundant historically, it is predominant in this collection. And because conventional elements and processes underlie experimental stories—even to the point of becoming subject matter in some—the bulk of this introduction will deal with the technical aspects of traditional fiction. Reversing this emphasis would place the innovation before the standard, the exception before the rule.

This introduction will emphasize throughout that the writing of fiction is a craft, a process, a human activity and that awareness of the tools of this craft and the stages of this process permit the reader to comprehend the complex possibilities of the short story and to judge the success or failure of a story in demonstrating those possibilities. Axiomatic is the assumption that insight into the process of fiction increases one's appreciation of the substance of fiction. Thus, hopefully, as specific examples are drawn from the stories in this collection, the introduction and stories will serve to illuminate each other.

Readers should be forewarned, however, that no amount of technical knowledge will provide an understanding of a story if they are unwilling to commit themselves to it—to contemplate it "with a kindred art." Living in a Gutenberg galaxy, we daily confront a mass of printed matter, from which we attempt to extract information. Of necessity, we learn to skim so that we can, for example, tell someone else "what a story is about." But serious literature requires us to read three-dimensionally, as it were—to cut through the resistant and lulling surfaces of prose. This in-depth reading demands that readers willingly involve themselves in the human action of a story—an involvement that is a first step to experiencing the "extra dimension" of fiction.

Words as the Base Metal of Fiction

Language is to the writer what paint is to the painter, marble to the sculptor, or musical tones to the composer. Through language, the human action that serves as subject matter is depicted. If the writer is skilled, the words that appear in a particular story and the form in which they are cast achieve a lasting significance. Like paint, marble, or musical tones, language offers its user a set of "conditions"—a certain body of privileges and restrictions.

An obvious limitation that confronts the story writer is the proliferation and banality of words. Indeed, every art involves a substance common to daily, unheightened existence. There is nothing *exclusive* about paint, marble, or musical tones—each may be used by anyone to express anything or nothing. The writer is like other creative artists who must overcome and put to individual use the ordinariness of their material. The writer's refusal to take words for granted can result in the innovative use of language. As Eudora Welty has said (in "The Reading and Writing of Short Stories"), "The words in the story we are writing now might as well never have been used before. . . . Stories are *new* things, stories make words new; that is one of their illusions and part of their beauty." In turn, this "newness" may move the reader to unaccustomed responses.

Language is not only commonplace; it is also elusive, its flexibility warring against precise formulation and the communication of single, uncontestable meanings. Once again, a consideration of various materials reveals that each in its own way resists the artist's efforts to give hitherto unshaped substances expressive form. Take, for example, the amorphous quality of paint, or the hardness of marble or bronze. For the writer, however, the elusiveness of words is a mixed blessing. On the one hand, connotative words permit the creation of highly textured prose that is rich in imagery, associations, and multiple meanings. On the other hand, the suggestiveness of language allows readers to bring their own experiences and associations to what they read. Accordingly, the writer's intended meaning is often misinterpreted by "public" readers who have their own "private" connotations and responses.

Still another condition affecting the use of language is its symbolic nature. Like the brush strokes on a canvas or the planes in a statue, a word is never the object or emotion itself but a conventional mark or sound that stands for or suggests the referent. Like the completed canvas or sculpture, the story (as a structure) is also symbolic. It is a representation of characters, events, and objects—a grouping of words arranged sequentially so as to stand for a certain pattern of human action. Thus, the story writer is always at a symbolic remove from the human activity that acts as referent. Paradoxically, the writer's success lies in making us feel the immediacy and intensity of that fictional, symbolic world.

A final disadvantage for the fiction writer is the tendency of language to lend itself to explanation—to *explain* rather than to *present*. Much of our pleasure in reading fiction comes from the intensity of rendered experience in a story—an intensity achieved in part by the writer's ability to *show,* to present us with a situation so that we perceive it immediately and directly rather than to *tell* us about the same set of circumstances.

Undeniably, part of the enjoyment of literature derives from our recognizing the resistances of the medium. Observing that words are commonplace, we delight in their heightened usage. Understanding that words are imprecise, we respond favorably to the aptly chosen word and to the intentional employment of ambiguity; we take pleasure in the imaginative use of the flexibility of language. Recognizing that words lack immediacy, we appreciate a writer's ability to achieve a seemingly tangible reality.

The Story as Narration

If words provide the base metal of fiction, narration is the form into which they are cast. At its most fundamental level, the purpose of narration is to relate an event or succession of events. Thus, narration—whether oral or written, in verse (epic, ballad, or metrical romance) or prose (parable, fable, tale, story, or novel)—involves people or animals *(characters)* who act and are acted upon *(plot)* and who exist in a certain place and at a certain time *(setting)*. Furthermore, narration requires a *narrator,* the *events* related by this narrator, and a *listener* or *reader*.

Narration can be classified as either simple or sophisticated. Anecdotes, case histories, reported incidents, and (usually) jokes are simple narratives—the kind of narration engaged in daily and informally by anyone recounting an incident or series of incidents to anyone else. Simple narration is lucid, entertaining, and often informative. Events follow each other in chronological order. Characters are neatly described and categorized. The "moral" is clearly stated. In contrast, most of the stories in this collection are sophisticated narratives—narratives that rearrange the order of events to suit the purposes of theme; that yield layers of meaning; that utilize devices not needed and therefore not found in simple narration; and that, in the case of the experimental stories, manage either to conceal their narrative origins or to turn the conventions of narrative art into subject matter.

Like all narratives, the story is a temporal art (rather than a spatial art like sculpture) and is cumulative in its effects. The unity and final meaning of a story depend on seeing how its individual sentences relate to the structure as a whole. Yet this kind of understanding is nearly impossible. "Nothing, no power, will keep a book steady and motionless before us, so that we may have time to examine its shape and design," Percy Lubbock acknowledges in *The Craft of*

Fiction. "As quickly as we read it, it melts and shifts in the memory; even at the moment when the last page is turned, a great part of the book, its finer detail, is already vague and doubtful." Less cumulative than the novel only in that it is shorter, even the shortest story resists any attempts to "fix" its moving parts.

The brevity of the story accounts for two significant traits—unity and intensity. The restricted scope of the story allows the author to arrange the material to create a single effect, if so desired, and thus grants the story a structural and thematic unity nearly unattainable in a longer, more diffuse narrative. Because the story is short enough to be read at one sitting, it benefits (as Poe also notes in his review) from the "immense force derivable from totality," achieving an intensity lacking in a work that is read piecemeal. Brevity also accounts for other attributes of the story: it encourages the depiction of a single aspect of experience, which the story seeks to illuminate rather than to resolve; it prohibits the author from covering great periods of time in copious detail; and it makes natural a focus on one or two characters.

In sophisticated narratives and some simple narratives, the narrator as *teller* of the tale and the author as *creator* are separate entities. Only in certain kinds of simple narration do the narrator and teller possess a single identity. For example, if you tell someone about your summer travels—either actual or imaginary— you are both the creator of the "story" you relate and the teller or narrator. If, however, you describe your travels to someone who relates them to a third party, you have, in essence, established a narrator who is separate from yourself. If you have chosen a narrator congenial to your aims and values, your travels can be made to sound exciting. But an unfriendly narrator can represent these same events as dull and pointless meanderings. A narrator to whom you have given an incomplete account will, of course, give the listener only a partial reckoning. Other relationships between you and your narrator induce other interpretations of these same events. Out of these different relationships comes much of the complexity of interpretive fiction.

Various literary critics have pointed to still another presence in narrative— the author's second self or, to use Wayne C. Booth's term, the *implied author*. According to Booth, the implied author is the image of an author derived by a reader from the author's written works and must not be confused with the historical or "actual" author, that is, the person who wrote the story or novel. Thus the implied author is an illusion, created anew within the mind of each reader by each new book.

Frequently, the implied author and the historical author do not "match," a disparity that leaves the historical author open to an unfair charge of insincerity. Consider, for example, what would happen were a reader to confuse the implied author of "Hills Like White Elephants" with the actual Hemingway. The protagonist is shallow, unimaginative, and unloving, but the actual Hemingway was complex, imaginative, and, as recent biographies reveal, a loving, if emotionally troubled, father and husband.

When writers draw heavily on events of their own lives for the material of fiction, they seem, like Hemingway, intent on merging these two identities—on forcing us to consider the actual or historical self. If an obvious connection exists between the fictional and actual events, readers legitimately may investigate the background of the historical author. But this inquiry should be limited to questions that relate to the practice of fiction—what actual events the writer used, how they were transformed, and what prompted a preoccupation with autobiographical detail.

Even the presence of seemingly untransformed portions of autobiography should not make readers forget that the author they "know" is the implied author. Accordingly, they should be guided in the analysis of fiction by the values of the consciousness that is directing the behavior of the fictional characters and controlling the events of that world. Often—especially in modern fiction, and most noticeably in the work of the experimentalists—the reader identifies less with the characters and narrator of a novel or short story than with the implied author—the intelligence that superintends the fictional events. Sometimes, identification with the implied author stems from the implicit breadth of the perspective, which, by extending beyond the events of the story, is capable of "correcting" the lopsided world so frequently conveyed by the characters and narrators of modern fiction.*

Certainly, recognition of the separate existence of the historical author, the implied author, and the narrator is a first step in understanding the art of fiction—in understanding, for example, that writers choose the kind and placement of a narrator in any given work and may create a narrator who is totally different in character from themselves, and that this narrator, in turn, helps to create our sense of the implied author. The separation of the historical and implied authors from the narrator is also responsible for a major structural device in all interpretive fiction—point of view.

THE ELEMENTS OF FICTION

Point of View

In his essay "Technique as Discovery," the critic Mark Schorer observes, "The difference between content, or experience, and achieved content, or art, is technique." According to Schorer, "When we speak of technique . . . we speak of nearly everything. . . . Technique is the only means he [the writer] has of discovering, exploring, developing his subject, of conveying its meaning, and, finally, of evaluating it." Since technique gives a story its "form" or shape, and insofar as form *is* meaning, technique embraces more than technical devices or

---

*For additional comments on the function of the implied author, see Chapter 3 of Wayne C. Booth's *The Rhetoric of Fiction* (Chicago: University of Chicago Press, 1961).

technical proficiency. By controlling the manner in which the story material is communicated to the reader—a process that makes content *achieved* content—technique determines meaning.

The fiction writer's chief structural resource is *point of view*—at its most fundamental level, the physical vantage point occupied by the narrator in a story or novel and the device by which the writer establishes the "authority" for the fiction. For the writer, point of view is the basic means of ordering and unifying material. Once the position and, further, the disposition of the narrator have been decided (choices that are often partly unconscious), all other ingredients of the work must relate to this decision. For readers, point of view, by affecting the shape of the story, determine how the story material reaches them and how, therefore, they perceive the fictional events.

The narrator can occupy a variety of different positions in regard to the characters and action of a story. Perhaps the easiest approach to understanding the very complex behavior of the narrator is to consider to what degree the narrator calls attention to himself*—that is, whether the author has chosen to make the narrator's presence felt or not. It is possible to think of narrators as occuyping various places on a scale relative to their presence or visibility within the frame of the story. Looked at in this manner, four basic kinds of narrator can be distinguished:

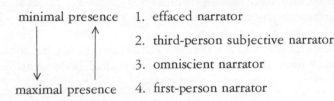

minimal presence   1. effaced narrator

2. third-person subjective narrator

3. omniscient narrator

maximal presence   4. first-person narrator

While these major categories of narrators permit distinctions useful in describing and understanding point of view, they represent a simplification. In actual practice subtle variations sometimes occur that modulate the narrative voice slightly, or even cause the narrator to change roles so that a story that starts out with one type of narrator may end up with another.

It must be remembered, too, that all art is based on the principle of selection so that when a narrator creates the impression that he is revealing "everything" about a character, action, or scene, the facts of fiction-making belie the "all-knowingness" that is attributed to him. The quantity of information we receive from any narrator is both limited and relative. The world outside the

---

*A narrator, of course, can be either a male or a female, but to avoid the constant repetition of "he or she" and "him or her" this text will use masculine pronouns throughout when referring to unspecified narrators.

fiction is always larger and more infinitely varied than the fiction itself: the writer makes finite only a small portion of that variousness.

In addition to ascertaining the effects of each narrative perspective and disposition, the critical reader must pay attention to the matter of "open" and "closed" consciousnesses and their relation to point of view. A character whose inner thoughts are revealed to the reader has an *open consciousness.* Frequently, the author depicts setting or action through the perceptions of such a character. A character whose inner thoughts are hidden has a *closed consciousness.* The reader must view that character through such externals as physical action, dialogue, personal appearance, and the reaction of other characters. Ultimately, the reader must see how point of view, as Mark Schorer contends, serves as *a mode of thematic definition* (as a way of conveying meaning) as well as *a mode of dramatic definition* (as a determiner of structure).

EFFACED NARRATOR

The effaced narrator communicates almost no sense of his own presence, has no individuality, has either an extremely limited access or no access to the consciousnesses of the characters (and therefore does not, strictly speaking, adopt their perspective), and offers little description (much less analysis or interpretation) of events and characters. In stories with an effaced narrator, the events seem to unfold automatically and the characters reveal themselves directly, through dialogue and action.

Fiction employing the effaced narrator resembles drama in structure. Usually, the narrator is noticeable at the beginning of the story, when he sets the scene and introduces the characters, and on those subsequent occasions when the narrative embraces a new character or a change in location. As in drama, dialogue supplies exposition, characterizes the speakers, and advances most of the action. Thus, while the omniscient narrator tends to explain and to summarize, the natural bent of the effaced narrator is to present and to dramatize action.

The effaced narrator affords objectivity and immediacy; the reader is present at the action, watching the characters move about and listening to them talk. The story-illusion is not disrupted by intrusions that divert attention to the narrator. The chief limitation of this narrator is that he cannot offer overt analyses without violating his "invisibility." At times, however, if the author's intended meaning is to be made clear, the reader needs explicit interpretation of events and characters.

Two stories in this collection, "You Were Perfectly Fine" by Dorothy Parker and "Hills Like White Elephants" by Ernest Hemingway, are told from the point of view of the effaced narrator. The action and characters of "You Were Perfectly Fine" are presented almost entirely through dialogue that reveals, to the embarrassment of the young man, that his conduct the previous evening was not "perfectly fine" but atrocious. Not only had he flirted with another man's wife, picked a fight with a stranger, fallen on an icy sidewalk but, in his drunkenness, he had proposed to the "clear-eyed girl" who smiles "brightly at him" during their conversation. Having sworn off liquor forever at the beginning of the story, at the story's end, he is asking weakly for another drink.

"You Were Perfectly Fine" resembles a joke in structure, and the point of view, by keeping us and the young man in partial ignorance, heightens the punch line. But is this story only a cute joke? Certainly the story lacks the depth of feeling of many stories in this collection. The action is trivial; the characters superficial and affected. But here, as elsewhere, point of view is related to meaning as well as to structure. In personality, neither character is particularly sympathetic; the point of view discourages intimacy by failing to provide "inside" views. We might feel momentarily sorry for the young man but our sympathies are not deeply affected. The irony of the situation contributes to our sense of aloofness, for irony of this sort is the product of mind, not heart. The point of view does not permit us to discover why the young man drank so much and probably will continue to do so, nor why the young woman chose to ignore his inebriation. These are one-dimensional figures, mannequins with voice boxes. Yet the implication—all that is left unstated about this relationship—is frightening.

"Hills Like White Elephants" is also about a relationship between a man and a woman. As in the previous story, with the exception of brief descriptions of scenery or physical action, the story is told through dialogue. In this story, however, the relationship is more intimate and more profound than in "You Were Perfectly Fine." The two characters in the Hemingway story have lost more in the failure of their relationship than the couple in the Parker story seems capable of obtaining. As in the previous story, we are told nothing about the background of the characters and so we must fill in missing details by conjecture. The absence of specific facts causes us to pay close attention not only to what is said but how it is said. The bleakness of the dialogue parallels the emotional bleakness of the characters; the impending abortion becomes a symbol for lives that have become reduced to "looking at things" and trying "new drinks." The woman's speech is, at times, ironical and metaphorical; the man's, placating and hypocritical. The last line, "There's nothing wrong with me. I feel fine," echoes the young woman's repeated reassurances in "You Were Perfectly Fine." Only this time an evening's drunkenness is not at stake; the issue here is a paradise that was within reach but never gained.

The link between point of view and meaning is clear. As in the Parker story, neither the woman nor the man is a sympathetic character. Point of view and the absence of background information or access to the characters' thoughts and feelings act once again as distancing agents. Hemingway lets us draw our own conclusions as does Dorothy Parker. Both stories concern alienation and misunderstanding. The point of view offers nothing to cushion these two very somber views of contemporary life—nothing to soften the barrenness and vacuity of the relationship in "Hills Like White Elephants," nothing to make us feel better about the flip desperateness in "You Were Perfectly Fine."

THIRD-PERSON SUBJECTIVE NARRATOR

The effaced narrator is like the butler who sets the table and serves the food and then disappears, letting the assembled guests talk and eat, reappearing only to clear away empty dishes (old characters) or bring new ones. The third-person subjective narrator uses reverse tactics to minimize his presence. Rather than disappear, the subjective narrator becomes a disembodied presence at the dinner table. He is not a guest for he is *not* a character in the story, but he uses the consciousness of one of the guests as his narrative focus.

If this narrator has a counterpart in real life, it would be the use of the subjective camera in filmmaking. In this cinematic technique, the camera becomes the eyes of one of the characters, causing the audience to see events as that character sees them but in a manner determined by the director or filmmaker who has chosen that particular perspective. In the case of fiction, the "camera" not only sees but records and interprets the thought processes as well as the actions of the character. Unless the character's perceptions and thoughts are reproduced directly in dialogue or interior monologue, descriptions and analysis are in the narrator's own language—regardless of the amount of detail filtered through the character's perception or how much the narrator uses language that approaches the character's own idiom.

The most thorough analysis and practice of the third-person subjective narrator can be found in the critical writing and fiction of Henry James. "The great chroniclers," James wrote, have "always either placed a mind of some sort—in the sense of a reflecting and coloring medium—in possession of the general adventure . . . or else paid signally, as to the interest created, for their failure to do so." Fictional characters are interesting to James only "in proportion as they feel their respective situations," and events or plot only when they are mirrored in an engaged consciousness. The use of a "mirroring consciousness" gives fiction a tightly controlled focus that provides a structural unity and an intensity—advantages sought after by James and by generations of subsequent writers.

James advocated that the "reflector" (or "register") have intelligence and sensibility and be "finely aware and richly responsible." For such persons get the most "out of all that happens to them and . . . in so doing enable us, as readers of their record, as participators by a fond attention, also to get most. Their being finely aware—as Hamlet and Lear, say, are finely aware—*makes* absolutely the intensity of their adventure, gives the maximum of sense to what befalls them."

"The Middle Years" provides a good example not only of third-person subjective narration but of James' use of a "reflector" who is "finely aware and richly responsible." Dencombe, the protagonist, is a man of great sensibility and intellect. As such, he serves James' purposes in this story well. For "The Middle

Years" is less about the last few weeks of a man's life than about the relationship of art to life. The drama in this story is less a drama of events than a drama of consciousness.

> What he saw so intensely today, what he felt as a nail driven in, was that only now, at the very last, had he come into possession. His development had been abnormally slow. . . . It had taken too much of his life to produce too little of his art. The art had come, but it had come after everything else.

Dencombe longs for a "second age"—an "extension." But neither art nor life offers a second chance.

> "A second chance—*that's* the delusion," Dencombe says as he lies dying. "There never was to be but one. We work in the dark—we do what we can—we give what we have. Our doubt is our passion and our passion is our task. The rest is the madness of art."

In the character of Dencombe, James has a perfect vehicle for the transmission of both feeling and thought. Because of this, everything in the story comes from Dencombe's perspective although, as always with the subjective narrator, descriptions and action are given with third-person pronouns and in the narrator's own language. The restricted point of view reinforces the story's concern with the contribution of a single artist: "It *is* glory—to have been tested, to have had our little quality and cast our little spell. The thing is to have made somebody care."

Not every writer who uses the third-person subjective narrator has adopted James' theory that the reflector be "finely aware and richly responsible." Subsequent writers have discovered that considerable tension can be created by a reflector who, in some way, is incapable of subtle analysis or full comprehension of the situation. Alan Paton uses the consciousness of an unidentified man, presumably a middle-aged laborer, in "The Waste Land."

> It was too late to run after the bus; it went down the dark street like an island of safety in a sea of perils. Though he had known of his danger only for a second, his mouth was already dry, his heart was pounding in his breast, something within him was crying out in protest against the coming event.

The danger the man senses is represented by the "young men" who wait to rob him. But the protagonist's specific situation remains ambiguous. Neither city nor country is specified. The waste land with its abandoned car bodies is undifferentiated from similar dumping grounds that blight the urban landscape of industrialized nations everywhere. No explanation for the young men's excessively violent behavior is offered. No hope for public assistance is implied.

As the man outwits his attackers, the reader learns that on this desolate battleground loyalties are not to family but to self; the man saves his life through murder. His victim may have been his son, but this identification is not explicit:

> He turned on his side, so that he would not need to touch the body of the young man. He buried his face in his arms, and said to himself in the idiom of his own language. "People, arise! The world is dead." Then he arose himself, and went heavily out of the waste land.

Paton's use of a mirroring consciousness that avoids explanation raises questions of interpretation at the same time that it propels the story toward allegory. Much of the impact of this very brief story comes from the curious resonance of its ambiguity. The violence may spring from an unjust economic system that turns human beings against each other, or the violence may be a reenactment of the conflict between generations and the need of the young to establish a new order. The absence of explanation in this story is baffling and terrifying. But then so is wanton violence.

The character who serves as reflector is not always the protagonist. Sometimes, as in some of the stories and novels of Henry James, the narrative perspective is that of a "witness or reporter, some person who contributes to the case mainly a certain amount of criticism and interpretation of it." The reader should be aware of this possibility. The reader should recognize, too, that on occasion even Henry James acknowledged the necessity of "successive centers as reflectors"—a "represented community of vision between several parties to the action." But, he cautioned, "I understand no breaking-up of the register, no sacrifice of the recording consistency, that doesn't rather scatter and weaken."

OMNISCIENT NARRATOR

While the third-person subjective narrator disappears into the woodwork of the story, so to speak, the omniscient narrator can be heard hammering the house together and can be observed, on occasion, moving the furniture around. The omniscient narrator has no counterpart in everyday life. As children, we may have granted omniscience to parents, teachers, or policemen. But not now! We know too much. Accordingly, we have to resort to fantasy to find a counterpart. The figure that comes to mind is a superindefatigable news commentator—a monumental Walter Cronkite who is backed up by teams of researchers and experts in various recondite fields of knowledge and a network that encourages the dissemination of information and opinion.

The omniscient narrator is the most flexible of all narrators and possesses considerable freedom of statement: he is at liberty to summarize, interpret, speculate, and judge, and to do this overtly in the guise of his own persona. Able to open the consciousness of any character, the omniscient narrator can disclose the attitudes and feelings of characters separated in time and place or even antagonistic to each other, as Stephen Crane does in "The Bride Comes to

Yellow Sky." Because an omniscient narrator is not locked into a single point of view, he has freedom of movement: he can use his panoramic view to describe and analyze events from a distance, or he can descend momentarily to the level of action within the story and open the consciousnesses of selected characters, revealing action from their isolated vantage points for brief periods of time. In fact, in "My Kinsman, Major Molineux," Hawthorne's omniscient narrator hoists himself into the heavens and gives us the moon's reaction to the "congregated mirth" of the townspeople. Because of his flexibility, the omniscient narrator is not aligned in sympathy or knowledge with any character or group of characters, unless the author wishes him to be.

Most eighteenth- and nineteenth-century novelists used this point of view. Its obvious advantage (particularly to the novel) is that the author and narrator are able to cover great stretches of time and space. But the maneuverings, transitional assists, and interpretive comments of the omniscient narrator can disrupt the "recording consistency" and break the illusion of reality engendered by the people and action. At such times, the machinery of narration calls attention to itself and to the story as artifice—an effect only occasionally desirable as a narrative technique.

Because this mode of narration lends itself to explanation and summary, stories related by an omniscient narrator are sometimes weak in "specification," or memorable scenes—the charge James leveled against William Thackeray. In such instances, large portions of the story come through the wealth of information possessed by the narrator and not through character action and dialogue. In "My Kinsman, Major Molineux," however, Hawthorne uses his omniscient narrator with discretion. Although the narrator does call attention to his presence (as in the opening paragraph), the story is clearly Robin's: much description and most of the action come to us through the perceptions of the bewildered youth as he encounters the unexpectedly hostile townspeople and the unfamiliar town. Point of view here, as in other stories, reinforces theme. In this story, as elsewhere, Hawthorne is exploring the dark Puritanism of the New England colonies. The omniscient narrator, by giving us a sense of historical perspective, lends authenticity to a bizarre setting and a frightening incident. Yet by using Robin as narrative focus, Hawthorne can dramatize the boy's initiation into adulthood—a corollary theme in this story.

"The Story-Teller" by Saki illustrates a more limited use of the omniscient narrator. Since the plot consists mainly of a story narrated by the children's aunt and one told in retaliation by the bachelor, much of Saki's story is told in dialogue. Nonetheless the presence of the omniscient narrator can be observed, particularly in the opening paragraph and when he tells us what the aunt and the bachelor are thinking. Throughout, the consciousnesses of the children remain closed.

The encounter of the aunt and her talkative charges and the bachelor is, of course, a chance happening—a casual meeting of strangers on a train. At no point in the story do we know more about the aunt and the bachelor than they know about each other. But the humor in their situation is there for the observing; the irony is there for the seeing. The effect of the story lies in the contrast between the tale told by the aunt and that told by the bachelor and the children's reactions to each. Saki presents no heavy message in this story; its chief virtues are concision, humorous dialogue, vivid character interaction, and the wry comment it makes about human nature.

Some critics differentiate between omniscient narrators who give us inside information about only two or three characters and minimal background information and interpretation, and those narrators who are "fully" omniscient: the former are described as *selective* or *limited* omniscient narrators. The omniscient narrator is best approached in the same way that other narrators are approached—by understanding that each narrative perspective permits degrees of adherence to the basic definition. On the graduated scale presented earlier, "The Story-Teller" stands fairly close to the effaced point of view represented by "You Were Perfectly Fine," while "My Kinsman, Major Molineux" stands close to stories told by third-person subjective narrators.

FIRST-PERSON NARRATOR

First-person narration is the oldest manner of storytelling, the mode used in conversation to relate a personal experience. This narrative mode lifts its method directly from life. Three types of first-person narrators can be differentiated: 1) the narrator as protagonist of the story; 2) the narrator as one who plays an important part in the action but who is a secondary character; and 3) the narrator as a witness whose active role is tangential to the story he is telling. In fiction as in life, whenever the first-person narrator (also referred to as the *dramatized narrator*) describes his own activities or thoughts, he calls attention to his presence.

As Odysseus's story illustrates, the most obvious advantage of the first-person narrator is the immediate authority it conveys: readers are predisposed to believe what the "I" is telling them. In part, this results from the apparent artlessness of the dramatized narrator, an artlessness that prompted Henry James to call this narrative method "that accurst autobiographical form which puts a premium on the loose, the improvised, the cheap and the easy." Unlike the omniscient point of view, first-person narration causes events to be viewed through a narrow rather than a wide-angle lens. Often, much background is omitted. In third-person subjective narration, because the character and the narrator are separate, the narrator can tell us more than the character could possibly know. The only information that the dramatized narrator has access to is what the "I" can legitimately know. And what the "I" knows best—or *thinks* he knows best—are his own thoughts and feelings. His understanding of other characters' motivation is always fragmentary—even when he is telling their own story. Thus, he stands opposite the omniscient narrator who can open the minds of as many fictional characters as he wishes. Also, the dramatized narrator has an even greater problem than the subjective narrator in giving an account of simultaneous happenings or dissociated scenes. Yet by narrowing the perspective, dramatized narration provides the writer with a facile means of ordering the material.

"The Day of the Dying Rabbit" by John Updike provides a good example of a first-person narrator who is the principal character. The narrator is surrounded by people—wife, children, friends, friends' children, strangers. The story reflects their presence but the metaphors, predominantly about photography, and the interpretation of experience are clearly his. The dying rabbit allows Updike to dramatize the diverse personalities of the narrator's children, but the theme of the story lies in the meaning of the rabbit's death for the narrator. His insight into the fragility of life and the need for gallantry in the face of this fragility is an adult recognition: "This day was singular in its, let's say, gallantry: between the cat's gallant intentions and my son's gallantly calm warning, the dying rabbit sank like film in the developing pan, and preserved us all."

Dr. Watson in "A Scandal in Bohemia" by Arthur Conan Doyle illustrates a first-person narrator who is a secondary character. In this, as in other Sherlock Holmes stories, Dr. Watson serves the detective well by feeding him questions, admiring his ingenuity, and following his directions.

> The lamps had been lit, but the blinds had not been drawn, so that I could see Holmes as he lay upon the couch. I do not know whether he was seized with compunction at that moment for the part he was playing, but I know that I never felt more heartily ashamed of myself in my life.... And yet it would be the blackest treachery to Holmes to draw back now from the part which he had intrusted to me. I hardened my heart, and took the smoke-rocket from under my ulster.

Since Watson as narrator is ignorant of Holmes' plans for solving a mystery, so are we as readers until, at the conclusion, the detective enlightens us both. Watson draws us into the action through his participation, but his incomplete knowledge keeps us on the outside as a baffled audience to the brilliant drama of Holmes' mind. The first-person narrator provides Arthur Conan Doyle with an excellent link between the reader and his detective hero.

Like Dr. Watson, the first-person narrator of another detective story, Edgar Allan Poe's "The Purloined Letter," is a listener with a knack for asking the right questions, but unlike Watson he is *only* a listener—a witness and faithful "biographer." Poe's detective, C. Auguste Dupin, needs no accomplice to execute his plan. But he does need a friend to be in his presence so that conversations between him and the Prefect of the Parisian police can be recounted legitimately and so that his solution can be explained at length, fortified with literary, historical, and mathematical allusions and parallels. As these stories make clear, first-person narration represents a very legitimate way for the author to withhold information and therefore build suspense.

Faulkner's narrator in "Spotted Horses" is a persuasive and colorful storyteller. A traveling sewing-machine salesman, he is a shrewd judge of people and tolerant of most of them. But neither the narrator nor the townspeople prove a match for the tight-lipped and unscrupulous Flem Snopes:

He skun me in two trades, myself, and the fellow that can do that, I just hope he'll get rich before I do; that's all.

Flem's refusal to discuss his business dealings means that the narrator and everyone else—including the reader—can only speculate about his involvement with the Texan and the spotted horses.

> . . . nobody knowed yet if Flem had ere a interest in them horses or not. So finally I come right out and asked him. "Flem's done skun all of us so much," I says, "that we're proud of him. Come on, Flem," I says, "how much did you and that Texas man make offen them horses? . . . "
>
> They was all whittling, not looking at Flem, making like they was studying. But you could a heard a pin drop. . . . Flem finished cutting the sliver offen his stick. He spit across the porch, into the road. "Twarn't none of my horses," he says.
>
> I. O. cackled, like a hen, slapping his legs with both hands. "You boys might just as well quit trying to get ahead of Flem," he said.

Flem's past history and subsequent "charity" to Mrs. Armstid belie his denial of complicity. But his involvement is never proved. Much of the tension in this story is generated by the narrator's imperfect knowledge.

The first-person narrator, like the third-person subjective narrator, is well-suited to the short story and, in particular, to the modern story. The reasons are chiefly esthetic: the brevity of the form encourages the exploration of particular moments in time and the consciousness of a single person, and the narrator's position inside the action of the story ensures an immediacy and authority that heighten the illusion of reality. But the predominance of inside views in the contemporary short story has additional bases. Like the writer, modern readers are particularly aware that their vision is limited, fragmented, immediate, and egocentric. And, like the first-person narrator, readers, in real life, are bound within a particular frame of action, similarly restricted to the perspective of a single consciousness or "community" of consciousnesses.

To many writers, the modern world—with its tremendous movements and forces—seems beyond human control and understanding. The fictional point of view that collapses the perspective of a "know-it-all" narrator and fosters the intimacy of a world restricted to the thoughts and feelings of one character offers, among its other advantages, a means of dealing with the external world through an ordering of experience based on the interior lives of individual persons. Also, this inner life has been made more accessible by the findings of Sigmund Freud, Carl Jung, Otto Rank, and the other investigators of the subconscious. Not surprisingly, modern writers have used these insights as the form and substance of their fiction.

RELIABLE AND UNRELIABLE NARRATORS

Frequently, the writer who adopts the inside point of view not only relinquishes the ability to transcend the limits of a particular scene but chooses a perspective that is untrustworthy. Many stories told from the inside come from narrators who are incapable of giving a reliable report. Even when such narrators can get the "facts" straight, their analyses and judgments are often unacceptable. Wayne C. Booth has observed (in *The Rhetoric of Fiction*) that if we discuss point of view in relation to "literary effects," whether the narrator is omniscient or subjective, or referred to as "I" or "he," can be less important than his moral and intellectual qualities. "If he is discovered to be untrustworthy, then the total effect of the work he relays to us is transformed." In Booth's analysis, a *reliable narrator* "speaks for or acts in accordance with the norms of the work." An *unreliable narrator* speaks and acts against these norms.

The norms of any narrative are the explicit and implicit attitudes and values that help shape the theme, or view of life, that a literary work suggests. Integrally related, then, to meaning, the norms of a work derive from and, in turn, aid in establishing the implied author. By speaking or acting in accord with these attitudes and values, the reliable narrator necessarily stands close to the implied author.

Surprisingly, among the four categories of narrators, the first-person narrator is the least reliable, often standing at a considerable distance from the implied author and hampered by an emotional and physical involvement in the action the narrator not only describes but frequently interprets. In Eudora Welty's "Why I Live at the P.O.," for example, the narrator's jealousy of her younger sister is obvious to the reader as soon as the postmistress opens her mouth:

> I was getting along fine with Mama, Papa-Daddy and Uncle Rondo until my sister Stella-Rondo just separated from her husband and came back home again. Mr. Whitaker! Of course I went with Mr. Whitaker first, when he first appeared here in China Grove, taking "Pose Yourself" photos, and Stella-Rondo broke us up. Told him I was one-sided. Bigger on one side than the other, which is a deliberate, calculated falsehood: I'm the same. Stella-Rondo is exactly twelve months to the day younger than I am and for that reason she's spoiled.

Convinced that Stella-Rondo has set the rest of the family against her, the narrator rationalizes her decision to live at the post office. She claims that she is comfortable in her new situation, but the reader suspects that she is as unhappy in her alienation as she is curious to learn intimate details of Stella-Rondo's life with Mr. Whitaker:

> Some of the folks here in town are taking up for me and some turned against me. I know which is which. There are always people who will quit buying stamps just to get on the right side of Papa-Daddy.
> But here I am, and here I'll stay. I want the world to know I'm happy.
> And if Stella-Rondo should come to me this minute, on bended knees, and *attempt* to explain the incidents of her life with Mr. Whitaker, I'd simply put my fingers in both my ears and refuse to listen.

The narrator's one-sided account dramatizes her pettiness and the comic provincialism of her family and the small Mississippi town they inhabit. Because of the discrepancy between the narrative surface and the reader's penetration of that surface, a tension is created, an ephemeral realm in which truth flourishes.

Third-person subjective narrators can be as unreliable as first-person narrators if they fail to correct the misconceptions or limited perspective of the character who serves as their focus. In "The Man Who Was Almost a Man" by Richard Wright, the center of interest is the consciousness of the young black boy who is the protagonist. The story opens with Dave walking across the fields,

> looking homeward through paling light. Whut's the use talkin wid em niggers in the field? Anyhow, his mother was putting supper on the table. Them niggers can't understan nothing. One of these days he was going to get a gun and practice shooting, then they couldn't talk to him as though he were a little boy.

The narrator thus takes us directly into Dave's consciousness, letting us see the jumble of his thoughts and his false equation of possessing a gun with becoming a man. The rest of the story concerns the consequences of this false assumption. The discrepancy between Dave's apprehension of reality and the reader's sense of the character's situation reveals the terrible illogic of the boy's reasoning as well as the enviormental forces that nurtured that illogic.

The narrator of Rosellen Brown's "The Only Way to Make It in New York" is similarly unreliable in that no perspective other than the woman's is offered to correct her distorted assessment of reality. In this story, a burglar is treated like a guest: the woman wants to know his name, and then invites him to stay and have a beer. The reader gradually realizes, however, that the woman is "'very upset. Coming apart, kind of,'" as she explains to the burglar. Her vision is haunted by the memory of an earthquake she and her family survived in California. Her obsessive nightmare of an apocalyptic landslide merges into the man-made horrors of New York City:

> "Robberies," she said, smiling bitterly. "Muggings." Rapes.
> She would not tell him how she was closed up by it, cauterized. Here and there her skin puckered with memory. She got through the day. She got through the night.

The woman's view of contemporary American existence is disturbing. But it can be dismissed because she is mildly insane. Or is she insane? Is her "insanity" a way of coping with an increasingly hostile environment for which California and New York City serve as metaphors? The narrator supplies no answers. Instead we are left inside the woman's consciousness to share her vision of emptiness and to "spread the word."

Unlike subjective narrators, the omniscient narrator is usually reliable. His vantage point and "knowledge" allow him to report and interpret accurately and thereby to support the norms of the work. In Crane's "The Bride Comes to Yellow Sky," the narrator provides all the information we need. We do not feel that important facts are being withheld or that we are getting an unbalanced view. The narrator, like the implied author, has sympathy for both bridegroom and "bad guy," or so we feel as a result of character portrayal and the story's resolution; the confrontation between Jack Potter and Scratchy Wilson is a mutual defeat that signals the end of a way of life.

In stories told by an effaced narrator, where insight into the characters comes chiefly from what they say and how they act, the narrator is neither reliable nor unreliable—he is neutral. That is, the question of reliability is beside the point because we accept the convention that we see the action *directly,* without the narrator acting as a middleman. Obviously, however, descriptions (no matter how minimal), transitions, and the juxtaposition of scenes indicate that a story like "Hills Like White Elephants" has a narrator as much as a story like "My Kinsman, Major Molineux," and that this narrator influences (however subtly) our interpretation of characters and actions. Because of his detachment, however, the effaced narrator is trustworthy to the extent that neither his presence nor his comments interferes with the action from which the reader must derive norms.

At this point, a reader might wonder why a writer should choose an unreliable narrator. There are two principal advantages. First, the discrepancy between the reader's conception of a character and that character's self-image can be esthetically and thematically effective, as in "The Man Who Was Almost a Man." Our awareness of how wrong Dave's values are makes us painfully aware of the dominant white culture that inculcated those false values. A variant of this discrepancy occurs in "Why I Live at the P.O." The longer the narrator talks, the more we distrust her assessment of Stella-Rondo, and to the degree that our distrust grows, so does our emotional involvement in the story. Second, the unreliable narrator gives the writer a way of bringing the reader into the action of the story. Rather than handing out neatly packaged "correct" interpretations, the unreliable narrator engages the reader by raising questions about the validity of the information and judgments being received.

Characters

In fiction, the view of life a work suggests—its theme—arises from the human action that is its substance. Because ideas are seen in the context of characters involved with each other and their environment, the reader is made to feel the *human* implications of hitherto impersonal abstractions. In "The Waste Land," for example, fear is made terrifyingly concrete: "His fear was great and instant, and the smell of it went from his body to his nostrils. . . . So trapped was he that he was filled suddenly with strength and anger. . . ." On a more public level, the story dramatizes an historical abstraction: the unchecked violence signals a moral and political anarchy. In "Lullaby" by Leslie Silko, the end of a traditional way of life is made concrete by the imminent death of Chato and his wife Ayah. Chiefly through the characters, the norms of a work are emotive as well as rational.

As readers, we may be intrigued by a writer's style, awed by the wisdom of the implied author, or fascinated by the skillful handling of point of view. But the great emotional appeal of fiction lies in its characters, whose lives are displayed before us to engender some emotional response—admiration, scorn, envy, or dislike. Thus, for Henry James as for many other writers, fiction has its "starting-point in character." Character, said James, is "action, and action is plot, and any plot which hangs together, even if it pretend to interest us only in the fashion of a Chinese puzzle, plays upon our emotion, our suspense, by means of personal references. We care what happens to people only in proportion as we know what people are."

It is instructive to compare the ways we get to know "what people are" in fiction with the ways we get to know them in real life. Whereas the physical reality of the actual people we encounter is never in question, one of the writer's principal tasks is to make the characters "real" to us. As E. M. Forster notes in *Aspects of the Novel,* characters become real when they live according to the laws of fiction that govern their existence. They are convincing when they appear credible within the achieved content of a story or novel. In both life and fiction, we pay attention to a person's behavior, appearance, speech, gestures, and mannerisms. We take stock of surroundings, especially objects like clothes and cars and furniture; we listen to what other people say about this person and we evaluate his or her friends and enemies. But, in fiction, these matters come to us from a narrator. That is, we *hear about* a character's house or apartment, clothes, friends, and so forth. Thus, we are always in the position of seeing a character through the eyes of someone else—the narrator—and, ultimately, of judging that character in a way predetermined by the author.

Consequently, the most obvious distinction between the two modes of knowing is also the most significant one for the study of fiction: a character is an imaginary creation who possesses only those qualities, capacities, thoughts, and responses that a creator has granted. Further, no matter how well we know a person in real life, we are never *inside* that person's mind as we can be in fiction through certain narrative perspectives. The supreme law of fiction has to do with the role of the narrator and his ability to open the consciousnesses of selected characters. In real life we imperfectly understand the people we encounter; in fiction we can understand a character completely if the author so desires. In real life many attributes of a person are objectively, immediately, and randomly evident, while other qualities may never be recognized by observers or even by that person. In fiction the writer determines what qualities the character has, the order and manner of presentation of those qualities, their relative importance, and even their place within the author's own value system.

In real life our knowledge about other people depends on their proximity and the nature of our relationship to them. Similarly, in fiction, point of view and the choice of narrator control our relationship to the character and that character's accessibility to us. For example, first-person narrators sometimes let us into their minds more readily and openly than do our acquaintances in ordinary life; we also become very close to the character whose intelligence serves the third-person subjective narrator as focus. Similarly, the omniscient narrator may give us some description and some action from the inside perspective of characters in the story. On the other hand, the effaced narrator limits us to exterior views of the characters.

STATIC AND DYNAMIC CHARACTERS

The *kinds* of characters writers create not only alert us to their intentions but also carry much of the story's meaning. One useful classification distinguishes between static and dynamic characters. A *static character* is one whose essential nature does not change in the course of the story. A *dynamic character* is one whose experiences cause a change in attitude which in turn modifies behavior, so that this character emerges a different person at the conclusion of the work.

Most protagonists in novels are dynamic characters, since the length of the novel allows portrayal of character changes over a logical course of time. Yet even in the more limited scope of the short story, some characters undergo spiritual transformations significant enough to alter their behavior. "Nine Lives," by Ursula K. Le Guin, provides a good example of a dynamic character. The time is the distant future; the setting a distant planet. Cloning, the reproduction of human life from a single body cell, has become standard practice. Into the insular world of the Libra Exploratory Mission Base, inhabited by two individual men, Martin and Pugh, comes a ten-person clone: five men and five women. "They were all tall, with bronze skin, black hair, high-bridged noses, epicanthic fold, the same face." But the genetic identity that is their strength is also their undoing. During the earthquake, the clone looks to each other for help rather than signaling for assistance from Martin and Pugh. Only one member, Kaph, survives the disaster, and he wants to die:

> Kaph spoke with clarity and precision: "I am nine-tenths dead. There is not enough of me left alive."
> That precision convinced Pugh, and he fought the conviction. "No," he said, peremptorily. "They are dead. The others. Your brothers and sisters. You're not them, you're alive. You are John Chow. Your life is in your own hands."
> The young man lay still, looking into a darkness that was not there.

The remainder of the story traces Kaph's painful and slow metamorphosis into a single human being who, like all persons, must learn "how you go it alone" and how you "hold your hand out in the dark" to another person.

In many stories, a character undergoes experiences that potentially could change behavior, but the story ends before the character has a chance to act on the new insights. The implication is that the young boy in "Araby" and Harry Bendiner in "Old Love" will act differently in the future, but the narrative does not take us into that future. Often such stories end with an epiphany, a theological term applied to literature by James Joyce to describe an instantaneous and significant revelation—a sudden flash of recognition into the essential nature of an object, event, or character that discloses a previously hidden truth. The darkened bazaar causes the young protagonist in "Araby" to experience an epiphany. "Gazing up into the darkness I saw myself as a creature driven and derided by vanity; and my eyes burned with anguish and anger." "Old Love" ends with Harry Bendiner's impossibly "adventurous idea"—that he will "fly to British Columbia, find the young woman in the wilderness, comfort her, be a father to her, and perhaps try to meditate together with her on why a man is born and why he must die." In neither story is the concluding insight acted upon.

Frequently the short-story writer makes the protagonist a static character. Examples include the bachelor and the aunt in "The Story-Teller," the postmistress in "Why I Live at the P.O.," Dave in "The Man Who Was Almost a Man," and the prisoner in "Daydreams." In both the novel and the short story, minor characters are almost always static.

If a writer wishes, information about a new character can be presented in one or several paragraphs of extended description. The remainder of the story plays against the expectations aroused by the *set piece,* as this method of character depiction has been called. If the writer chooses to reveal a character sequentially, the set piece is avoided and the cumulative nature of fiction is used to let actions, speech, thoughts, and feelings depict the character to us gradually as the story unfolds.

The relationship between point of view and the way a character becomes known to the reader is significant. An omniscient narrator often provides a set piece, as in "Daydreams," where the two constables are described in the opening paragraph and their prisoner in the second paragraph:

> The man they are escorting does not at all fit the usual conception of a tramp. He is a puny little man, feeble and sickly, with small, colorless, extremely blurred features. His eyebrows are scanty, his expression gentle and submissive; he has hardly a trace of a mustache, although he is over thirty. He moves timidly, a hunched figure. . . .

Since an effaced narrator portrays characters through action and dialogue, the characters are necessarily revealed sequentially. Most often, the third-person subjective narrator offers information about a character in bits and pieces, letting the puzzle of personality fall into place gradually, as in "The Only Way to Make It in New York." A first-person narrator may begin with autobiographical information, as in "Zakhar-the-Pouch." In this story, a narrative device known as a *frame* conveys this information. A frame encloses the action of a story by establishing a situation that prompts the telling of a story or series of stories. Usually, the story ends with a return to the initial situation—or frame. More commonly, however, first-person narrators become known to the reader sequentially, as in "The Day of the Dying Rabbit" and "The Jewels of the Cabots."

FLAT CHARACTERS

Static characters are almost always *flat* as opposed to *round*—an additional way of classifying characters. Flat characters are useful when a writer wishes to emphasize ideas because their one-dimensionality keeps interest away from them as people and focused on the abstraction they represent. In Greece, around 320 B.C., Theophrastus popularized a literary genre called the Character, in which the flat character is used as technique and subject matter. In its purest form, the Character is a brief description of a person who represents some specific trait: insincerity, greed, officiousness, absent-mindedness, etc. What typifies this person is stressed; traits that run counter to the dominant quality are ignored. Literary portraiture in the Character is unequivocally flat, as in Theophrastus's "The Offensive Man" and "The Oligarchical Man." But as these sketches show, Theophrastus had a good eye for realistic detail and a preference, like Homer, for depicting character through description and action rather than through analysis. Specific references to everyday places and events, direct quotation, and a sense of movement are fictional techniques that contribute to the immediacy and appeal of the sketches.

The Character became popular in seventeenth-century England and France following the publication of a Latin translation of Theophrastus's *Ethical Characters.* The *Spectator,* an early eighteenth-century English periodical published by Joseph Addison and Sir Richard Steele, improved and extended the form by using dialogue as well as direct quotation, inventing continuing characters like Sir Roger de Coverly, localizing and expanding the settings as in the use of Sir Roger's country estate, and putting more emphasis on what is idiosyncratic about a person rather than on generic qualities. As a "younger Brother of a Great Family," Will Wimble represents a class of persons and thereby belongs to the pure Character, fully deserving of the moral attached to his type. By individualizing the type, however, Addison gives Will a particularity that brings him close to the characters that appeared a few decades later in the novels of Defoe, Richardson, Smollett, and Fielding.

Since the proficient writer can create convincing, even memorable, flat characters in a few sentences, this kind of character is well suited to the short story. The characters of fairy tales are always flat, as illustrated by "Cinderella." Magic and chance rule their world; the play of the intellect is less important than the toss of dice that governs their fate. Cinderella is totally good; the stepmother and her two daughters are totally evil; the prince is totally charming. The one-dimensionality of these characters makes credible their exaggerated traits, magical powers, and startling metamorphoses.

Typically, *comic* characters are flat, lending themselves to comic portrayal because they exhibit only a single facet or passion and because they are unchanged by experience, for example, the young man in "You Were Perfectly Fine" and the postmistress in "Why I Live at the P.O." We laugh at distortion and incongruity, and we laugh when we see a certain character mechanically

repeating the same foolish actions and suffering the same inevitable consequences. The flatness of comic characters ensures our viewing them as *objects*
rather than *identifying* with them as *subjects,* the way we do with rounded
protagonists. Henry Armstid in "Spotted Horses" is a comic character because
of his inane persistence—initially in buying the horse at the rigged auction, and
subsequently in attempting to catch the terrified and untamed animal. Desperately poor, Henry can ill afford the five dollars he paid for the horse yet refuses
the auctioneer's offer of a refund. Not once does he engage our sympathies—
not even when he is trampled by the horses. The narrator offers a possible
explanation:

> I says, "Well, if a man can't take care of himself in a trade, he can't blame the man
> that trims him."
>   Flem never said nothing, trimming at the stick. . . . "Yes, sir," I says. "A fellow
> like Henry Armstid ain't got nobody but hisself to blame."
>   "Course he ain't," I. O. says. . . . "Henry Armstid's a born fool. Always is been.
> If Flem hadn't a got his money, somebody else would."

Foolishness in itself is not funny; injury less so. Yet because Faulkner shows us
only Armstid's foolishness unredeemed by any glint of intelligence or kindness,
Henry is incapable of causing us to feel pity. The same is true for the narrator of
"Journalism in Tennessee." The journalist suffers incredible injury: a bullet
nicks his ear; another takes off his finger; an explosion knocks out a few teeth; a
brick hits him on the back—and so on. But since Mark Twain offers no
information about his first-person narrator that makes him anything but an
unfortunate cartoon figure, we view the physical punishment he receives with
about the same emotion with which we watch cars being knocked about in a
demolition derby.

    As a result, flat characters serve the writer whose purpose is satiric, for
satire exposes human folly and in so doing makes fun of it. Distortion is one of
the satirist's chief weapons. The flat character and his generic qualities are useful
to the satirical writer. In "The Oranging of America," for example, Howard
Johnson and Millie are satirical characters. The description of Mr. HJ's Cadillac,
his method of testing new ice-cream flavors, his relief map with its orange and
white dots marking existing and future "HJ houses," and above all his infallible
instinct in locating sites for new HJs satirize the man with keen yet kind humor.

> Howard knew the land, Mildred thought, the way the Indians must have known
> it. . . . [He] had a sixth sense that would sometimes lead them from the main roads
> to, say, a dark green field in Iowa or Kansas. . . . Before the emergency brake had
> settled into its final prong, Howard Johnson was into the field and after the
> scent. . . . Sometimes he would sit down, disappearing in a field of long and tangled
> weeds. . . . She had actually seen him chew the grass, getting down on all fours like
> an animal and biting the tops without pulling the entire blade from the soil.

In this story, Howard Johnson is not presented historically as a flesh-and-blood character but as a caricature—a person whose individual qualities have been exaggerated and distorted for humorous effects. In similar ways, Addison distorted the character of Ned Softly, seizing on all that was foolish and egocentric about the man to reveal his pretensions as a poet. Completely self-absorbed, Ned Softly accepts insults as compliments and good-natured ridicule as heartfelt advice.

ROUND CHARACTERS

In an essay on Honoré de Balzac, Henry James says that

> with Balzac the whole person springs into being at once; the character is never left shivering for its fleshly envelope, its face, its figure, its gestures, its tone, its costume, its name, its bundle of antecedents. . . . Behind Balzac's figures we feel a certain heroic pressure that drives them home to our credence—a contagious illusion on the author's own part. . . . They seem to proceed from a sort of creative infinite and they help each other to be believed in.

James is describing, of course, the great appeal of *round characters* in fiction. Despite the brevity of the story as a form, many writers are able to create round characters—characters in whom several traits blend and fight for supremacy. "It is only round people," says E. M. Forster, "who are fit to perform tragically for any length of time and can move us to any feelings except humor and appropriateness." The husband and wife in "Lappin and Lapinova," Larry in "The Girl Who Sang With the Beatles," Harry Bendiner in "Old Love," and Dencombe in "The Middle Years" are among the round characters in this anthology, depicted so as to surprise us by their behavior and to arouse feelings of pity and, perhaps, fear. In a curious way, the brevity of the short story can be used to enhance the impression of roundness because it allows an author to sustain an intensity and carry the action through at a high pitch. During the time these characters exist before us, they do so very vividly.

In "The Middle Years," when Dencombe is thinking about the strange trio of Dr. Hugh, the Countess, and Miss Vernham, he reflects

> that there would still be work to do in a world in which such odd combinations were presented. It wasn't true, what he had tried for renunciation's sake to believe, that all the combinations were exhausted. They weren't by any means—they were infinite: the exhaustion was in the miserable artist.

Dencombe, the fictional novelist, is speaking for James, the actual novelist. For the characters of fiction can be as numerous and varied as persons in real life. And paired or combined by the writer's imagination or by life, the possibilities are "infinite." As with any ingredient in narration, the kinds of characters a writer creates are appropriate if they serve the purpose of the fiction. When this happens and when a writer creates characters able to stir our curiosity and concern about their destinies, characters in fiction are truly memorable, whether they be static or dynamic, flat or round, minor or major.

Plot, Form, and Time

PLOT

Plot is most simply defined as a series of interrelated actions. Because narration is sequential, plot is fundamental to narrative art. And because actors participate in the actions, plot is linked to characterization. In fact, one mark of serious fiction is the degree to which the action arises from and reflects the traits of the characters, thereby involving the reader in the values and judgments they bring into play. Henry James was concerned with this issue when he asked, "What is character but the determination of incident? What is incident but the illustration of character?" In this general and theoretical sense, plot includes not only physical but metaphysical action—that is, the intellectual and emotional responses of the characters.

Plot is generally set in motion by *conflict,* which, in serious fiction, is both external and internal. External conflict concerns the struggles of the protagonist against an objectified antagonist such as another individual ("The Bride Comes to Yellow Sky"), the setting ("The Man Who Was Almost a Man"), "fate" ("A Hunger Artist"), or a combination of all three forces ("My Kinsman, Major Molineux"). If the conflict is also internal, as it is in most of the stories in this collection, the action takes place at another level—within the mind of the character who is torn frequently between contrasting loyalties and ways of life ("The Girl Who Sang With the Beatles") or between two aspects of the self, usually one that is "idealized" and one that is "real" ("Araby").

A conventional way of looking at plot is to see the action of a story moving through five basic stages:

1. *exposition:* explanation of essential information, usually about events that have occurred prior to the narrative present
2. *complication* (or rising action): events that follow the initiation of the conflict by the inciting force
3. *crisis* (or climax): the turning point to which the incidents that constitute the complication have been leading
4. *falling action:* the less intense action that comes about as a result of the turning point
5. *resolution* (or denouement): the resolving or unknotting of the situation.

"Cinderella" provides a good example of a conventionally plotted story. The plot is as simple and stereotypical as the characters:

1. *exposition:* death of Cinderella's mother and father's remarriage; first appearance of the magical bird
2. *rising action:* announcement and preparation for the King's festival; the ball where Cinderella meets the prince who falls in love with her
3. *crisis*: successful search for the real Cinderella
4. *falling action*: the marriage of the prince and Cinderella
5. *resolution:* the stepsisters are punished.

As in many conventionally plotted stories, poetic justice prevails in that goodness is rewarded, and evil punished. In the version printed in this anthology, two white doves blind the stepsisters by pecking out their eyes. "And thus, for their wickedness and falsehood, they were punished with blindness as long as they lived."* Poetic justice is especially satisfying in the world of the fairy tale because it has little place in the real world where the good do not always win and the evil too often escape punishment.

Stephen Crane structures the action of "The Bride Comes to Yellow Sky" along similarly conventional lines. In this story, however, the rising action takes place in two separate locations and concerns two characters who converge later in the story. The marriage of the marshal and his arrival with his bride in Yellow Sky comprises one part of the rising action. The appearance of Scratchy Wilson on the streets of Yellow Sky comprises the other part. The turning point occurs when the two men meet. The falling action and the surprise ending come quickly and develop naturally from the characters and their setting.

Most detective stories follow a conventional plot structure although in "The Purloined Letter" and, to a lesser degree, in "A Scandal in Bohemia" the action may be buried under a lot of talk. The first few sentences of "The Purloined Letter" establish the somber and contemplative mood that prevails in the "little back library" of C. Auguste Dupin's apartment. The complication ensues with the arrival of the Prefect of the Parisian police who describes the case of the missing letter and the inability of the police to solve the crime. The climax occurs when Dupin produces the purloined letter, and the falling action consists of Dupin's lengthy explanation to the narrator of how he retrieved it. The detective's final literary revenge on the Minister D——, the official who had stolen the letter, comprises the resolution. In Poe's story, the only direct action occurs in the opening scene and in the two visits of the Prefect. The rest of the action is conveyed through conversation.

"A Scandal in Bohemia" is similar to "The Purloined Letter" in structure. In both stories, the detective is asked to retrieve an object that has been hidden. The concealed object is to be used to blackmail a person of exalted position.

---

*In the version most American children know, poetic justice occurs only to the extent that Cinderella is rewarded by marriage to the prince; rather than being punished, the stepsisters are forgiven by Cinderella, who arranges their marriages to "two rich gentlemen of the Court." This less bloody and less vindictive version is credited to Charles Perrault. The Margaret Hunt translation printed in this anthology is faithful to the German original as it appears in *Grimm's Household Tales.*

Each detective uses the ploy of an arranged disturbance to help him carry out his plan. In both stories, the detective and the criminal are persons of high intelligence. And, in both stories, much of the action is "explained." That "A Scandal in Bohemia" should parallel "A Purloined Letter" in so many ways is not surprising, for the basic strategy of the detective story is found in Poe's tales of ratiocination and many writers, including Arthur Conan Doyle, have borrowed from him freely.

The puzzle that lies at the heart of these narratives has a history that pre-dates the detective story as a literary genre. For the puzzle is basic to human activity—deciphering the meanings hidden behind commonplace phenomena, attaining seemingly impossible goals, and inventing strategies of war and peace. Odysseus escapes from the Cyclops' cave because he treats his imprisonment like a puzzle and works out an appropriate solution. The art of detection lies at the heart of many of Aesop's fables, including "The Old Lion and the Fox." The wily fox's decision *not* to visit the lion is based on the application of common-sense logic to observable phenomena. Many fairy tales use puzzles (word games as in "Rumpelstiltskin") and strategies (the disguise in "Little Red Riding Hood" and the trail of crumbs in "Hansel and Gretel"). In "Cinderella," the love-smitten prince devises an ingenious plan to discover the young girl's identity:

> The King's son had, however, used a strategem, and had caused the whole staircase to be smeared with pitch, and there, when she ran down, had the maiden's left slipper remained sticking. The King's son picked it up, and it was small and dainty, and all golden.

Poe's detective, C. Auguste Dupin, solves the puzzle of the missing letter through analogous acts of detection. For nineteenth-century readers, the logic of Dupin's reasoning was immensely appealing. The description of the methods and tools employed by the Paris police amazed Poe's contemporaries in the same way we are amazed by new surveillance systems or by the engineering and machinery behind explorations of outer space. For twentieth-century readers who take the scientific method of Dupin's strategy for granted, "The Purloined Letter" may seem a bit obvious. The drama of this story is the drama of the reasoning mind. The detective story in the hands of Poe's successors became a drama of body as well as mind.

Throughout John Barth's "Lost in the Funhouse," the narrator interrupts the "story" proper to discuss problems of authorship and conventions of nine-teenth-century fiction—among them the "action of conventional dramatic narra-tive" with its exposition, rising action, turning point, and resolution. The narrator observes:

> While there is no reason to regard this pattern as an absolute necessity, like many other conventions it became conventional because great numbers of people over many years learned by trial and error that it was effective; one ought not to forsake

it, therefore, unless one wishes to forsake as well the effect of drama or has clear cause to feel that deliberate violation of the "normal" pattern can better can better effect that effect.

The narrator's lengthy discussions and concern about plot only serve, of course, to remind us of the absence of action in this story.

Not all writers are as willing to forego the "effect of drama" as Barth, although many contemporary authors have taken liberties with conventional plot structure. Like Rosellen Brown in "The Only Way to Make It in New York," they tend to omit or modify exposition and to minimize resolution in the sense of providing any clear-cut "resolving" or "unknotting." The opening sentence of this story plunges the reader into present action and establishes the nature of the conflict: "She had caught him going through her jewelry." The woman's thoughts as she watches the burglar appraise her jewelry provide minimal background information: we learn that she has been robbed before, that she has a child named Wendy, that she lives with a man named Martin. Husband? Lover? Brother? We do not know yet. Gradually, through the conversation that ensues, we discover that Martin is her husband and that they had lived in California. The conversation constitutes the rising action; the burglar's exit, the turning point. But the climax is strangely muted and necessitates no falling action. The resolution is enigmatic, a surreal vision appropriate to the surreal non-events of the story proper.

Several stories in this collection have narrative structures similar to that of "The Only Way to Make It in New York"—among them "The Waste Land," "The Girl Who Sang With the Beatles," "Sanchez," "Lullaby," and "Old Love." These stories bring us quickly into the rising action, letting us pick up background information through dialogue, flashbacks, reflection on the part of characters, and occasional statements by the narrator. Their resolutions are ambiguous and frequently subdued. Often, their last sentences are centrifugal, lifting the concluding action away from specific, finite meaning into the freer realm of metaphor and myth. The conclusion of "Sanchez" provides a good example:

> In the dark morning the people of the town were awakened by the blaze of fire that was the house of Juan Sanchez. Believing that he had perished in the flames, several of the townspeople placed a marker next to the grave of his wife with his name on it. But, of course, on that score they were mistaken. Juan Sanchez had simply gone home.

All fiction represents a selection of incidents. Because the short story is brief, the story writer must be especially selective in choosing plot details, omitting certain incidents entirely and summarizing others. When long periods of time need to be condensed, action is related through narrative statement or summary. If a particular incident needs to be described at length, dialogue in addition to detailed description of physical action is used. Whether a writer relies heavily on summary or presents action directly depends on the point of view and the chronological time encompassed by the action. The omniscient narrator in "A Hunger Artist" uses narrative summary to condense long periods of time:

> The fine placards grew dirty and illegible, they were torn down; the little notice board telling the number of fast days achieved, which at first was changed carefully every day, had long stayed at the same figure, for after the first few weeks even this small task seemed pointless to the staff; and so the artist simply fasted on and on, as he had once dreamed of doing, and it was no trouble to him, just as he had always foretold, but no one counted the days, no one, not even the artist himself, knew what records he was already breaking, and his heart grew heavy.

Since the effaced narrator avoids exposition, action in stories told from this point of view comes to us through dialogue. First-person narrators, like Watson in "A Scandal in Bohemia," and third-person subjective narrators, like the narrator in "The Middle Years," are at liberty to summarize action as well as to involve us in the direct presentation of incidents.

As writers strive to make their characters convincing within the laws of fiction, so must they make plot—an artificial ordering of events—convincing. Quite obviously, life is more random than that reflected in fiction, events are less casually connected than those in a story. Consequently, the writer must use chance and coincidence with discretion. *Chance*—an occurrence resulting from unknown or unconsidered forces—is always unanticipated, stemming from neither past action nor the disposition of the characters. *Coincidence* is the accidental coming together of two events that have a particular correspondence. In "The Middle Years," Dencombe's meeting with Dr. Hugh [and the two strangers] happens by chance. However, it is coincidence that Dr. Hugh is reading an advance copy of Dencombe's novel at the precise moment that he meets its author. Although chance and coincidence both occur in ordinary life, their presence in fiction calls attention to the story as fabrication by heightening the "unnaturalness" of its plot. Truth is often stranger than fiction, but successful fiction may seldom be stranger than truth.

Because plot is based on selection and arrangement, the writer is able to employ *foreshadowing* by hinting at subsequent developments through narrative comment, dialogue, setting, atmosphere, imagery, and symbols. Thus, foreshadowing is the writer's chief means of evoking *suspense*—a sense of mystification and anticipation. Too much foreshadowing, however, decreases suspense by making the outcome predictable. In "My Kinsman, Major Molineux," Hawthorne uses foreshadowing to hint that Robin's meeting with his kinsman will be unpleasant. The unfamiliar town with its "crooked and narrow streets" is foreboding. The boy's questions about the Major are greeted with hostility or laughter by the unfriendly townspeople. Twice he is threatened with punishment in the stocks. He converses with a stranger who is grotesquely terrifying:

> Robin gazed with dismay and astonishment on the unprecedented physiognomy of the speaker. The forehead with its double prominence, the broad hooked nose, the

shaggy eyebrows, and fiery eyes were those which he had noticed at the inn, but the man's complexion had undergone a singular, or, more properly, a twofold change. One side of the face blazed an intense red, while the other was black as midnight.

These and other details make Robin's long vigil suspenseful. Like him, we are mystified and prepared for an unusual occurrence. But the ending of the story is shocking despite the portentousness of the setting and the events leading to the story's climax. Hawthorne builds suspense by keeping us an outsider like Robin, instead of using his omniscient narrator to open the consciousnesses of the townspeople or reveal their private conversations. In both the novel and short story, point of view can be instrumental in determining the nature and degree of the reader's mystification.

FORM

In stories with a conventional plot we admire the way in which the author has ordered the interrelated sequence of events to produce a certain effect. For example, we admire the surprise ending of "The Bride Comes to Yellow Sky" and the careful building to a crisis in "The Man Who Was Almost a Man." But in other stories, like "The Only Way to Make It in New York," we are responding more to an intuitive ordering of events than we are to their causality or their rational progression. In these stories we are responding more to *form* than we are to plot.

In 1924, Sherwood Anderson complained, "There was a notion that ran through all storytelling in America, that stories must be built about a plot and that absurd Anglo-Saxon notion that they must point a moral, uplift the people, make better citizens, etc." The notion of plot, said Anderson, seemed "to poison all story-telling. What was wanted I thought was form, not plot, an altogether more elusive and difficult thing to come at." *Form* refers to the manner in which the ingredients of a story have been ordered so as to give the narrative a distinguishing shape. In this sense, every story has a form: indeed, plot can be one of the means of achieving form. But in some stories, form alone provides the esthetic cohesiveness that allows an otherwise random collection of incidents and observations to be recognizable as verbal art.

In "Lost in the Funhouse," the narrator disrupts the story proper to discuss the absence of plot in his story:

The function of the *beginning* of a story is to introduce the principal characters, establish their initial relationships, set the scene for the main action, expose the background of the situation if necessary, plant motifs and foreshadowings where appropriate, and initiate the first complication or whatever of the "rising action." Actually, if one imagines a story called "The Funhouse," or "Lost in the Funhouse," the details of the drive to Ocean City don't seem especially relevant. The *beginning* should recount the events between Ambrose's first sight of the funhouse early in the afternoon and his entering it with Magda and Peter in the evening. The *middle* would narrate all relevant events from the time he goes in to the time he loses his way; middles have the double and contradictory function of delaying the climax while at the same time preparing the reader for it and fetching him to it. Then the *ending* would tell what Ambrose does while he's lost, how he finally finds his way out, and what everybody makes of the experience. So far there's been no real dialogue, very little sensory detail, and nothing in the way of a *theme.* And a long time has gone by already without anything happening; it makes a person wonder.

In many contemporary stories a "long time" goes by "without anything happening." "'I always Wanted You to Admire My Fasting'; or, Looking at Kafka" is a good example. Roth's story can be interpreted as a modern analogue to "A Hunger Artist," itself a conventionally plotted story despite the lack of immediacy occasioned by the omniscient narrator who, informed and generous in his sympathies, describes the plight of the hunger artist in a conversational style that approaches the essay. Roth explains that he wrote the story when he was teaching at the University of Pennsylvania and trying to get his students

> to read Kafka's fiction without becoming Biblical exegesists in the process. Sometimes serious students of literature tend to read Kafka as though he had written his stories on Mars, or in graduate school, instead of in Prague. On a recent trip I made to Prague I found it reminded me of nothing so much as the Newark in which I'd grown up in the thirties and forties, a shabby, impoverished provincial capital under the cloud of war. . . . Out of this trip, then, and my teaching, and my own long-standing interest in Kafka's work, this piece arose.

The first half of the story is an eloquent essay on Franz Kafka that weaves the events of Kafka's life into the substance of his fiction and into a future imagined by Roth. Roth describes Kafka's face:

> sharp and skeletal, a burrower's face. . . . There is a familiar Jewish flare in the bridge of the nose, the nose itself is long and weighted slightly at the tip—the nose of half the Jewish boys who were my friends in high school. Skulls chiseled like this one were shoveled by the thousands from the ovens; had he lived, his would have been among them, along with the skulls of his three younger sisters.

Roth explores Kafka's relationship to his father and to the women in his life. And then the historical Kafka disappears and the other Kafka takes his place—a fictional character named Dr. Kafka, the narrator's Hebrew-school teacher in the Newark of Roth's boyhood. The parallels between the real Franz Kafka and Roth's Dr. Kafka become increasingly obvious: both are the same age, both are Jewish, both are from Prague, both are celibate, both are tubercular. The real-life Kafka has become the immigrant Hebrew teacher of Roth's fiction. This fictional portrait is what Roth imagines Kafka would have been like had he survived into the 1930s and lived to see Germany under Nazi rule. But there is a difference. Dr. Kafka "leaves no books: no *Trial,* no *Castle,* no 'Diaries.'" The story ends with a quotation from "A Hunger Artist" and Roth's parallels between the hunger artist and Franz Kafka and between Franz Kafka and Dr. Kafka:

"Well, clear this out now!" said the overseer, and they buried the hunger artist, straw and all. No, it simply is not in the cards for Kafka ever to become *the* Kafka—why, that would be stranger even than a man turning into an insect. No one would believe it, Kafka least of all.

In such a way is Kafka's fiction defined by his life and by Roth's fictional recreation of an analogous life. While the narrative of Dr. Kafka has a beginning, middle, and ending, the two-part structure of the story and the insistence with which the real-life Kafka appears in the fiction "makes a person wonder," to borrow again from "Lost in the Funhouse."

Sometimes stories composed of seemingly random incidents are strengthened through imagery and symbolism ("The Day of the Dying Rabbit"), or through the unity and intensity of flashbacks used to round out the present action ("The Jewels of the Cabots"). Frequently a writer combines these ways of achieving form, as in the John Cheever story, which is unified by imagery, symbolism, and flashbacks as well as by the psychological wholeness of the protagonists's thoughts.

TIME

A story that is not dependent on causality for its narrative flow is frequently close to our notions of inner time—a perception of time that has little correspondence to objective time. Psychological time as well as historical or actual time is what is being explored in "The Jewels of the Cabots." In this story, present time moves easily into past events. The story begins with Amos Cabot's funeral, which the narrator attends as an adult, and then shifts to the narrator's boyhood when Molly Cabot was his girlfriend:

> It was long ago, so long ago that the foliage of elm trees was part of the summer night. (It was so long ago that when you wanted to make a left turn you cranked down the car window and *pointed* in that direction. Otherwise you were not allowed to point. Don't point, you were told. I can't imagine why, unless the gesture was thought to be erotic.) The dances—the Assemblies—were formal and I would be wearing a tuxedo handed down from my father to my brother and from my brother to me like some escutcheon or sumptuary torch. I took Molly in my arms.

The dance shifts to the narrator's experiences at a camp on Cape Cod that summer and from there to "an early winter afternoon" when "Mrs. Cabot washed her diamonds and hung them out to dry" and returned to find them and her older daughter missing:

> Geneva had packed a bag, gathered the diamonds, and taken the last train out of town: the 4:37. How thrilling it must have been. The diamonds were meant to be stolen. They were a flagrant snare and she did what she was meant to do.

And so the narrative goes, weaving boyhood memories of Sunday dinners with description of the town's run-down East Bank and then switching to Rome and next to America and finally, after a long last memory of the day Geneva absconded with her mother's diamonds, to a visit with Geneva and her husband on the Upper Nile. As the plastic arts have moved away from representation, so modern fiction has moved away from objective chronological continuity. Further, stories that do not resolve, but rather dissolve (such as "The Only Way to Make It in New York") reinforce our notions of irresolution, of continuance— our awareness that the past continuously and inescapably influences the present and that in life there are no conclusive endings except death.

Setting

Setting is the representation in fiction of the place and time that constitute the environment of the action. Incorporating the tangible and spiritual aspects of physical locations and historical eras, setting includes the depiction of objects and institutions peculiar to certain places and periods—the wigs and lanterns of "My Kinsman, Major Molineux," the tape-recorded messages in "August 2026: There Will Come Soft Rains," the monument in "Zakhar-the-Pouch."

Closely related to characterization, setting enhances the credibility of the characters by providing a visible context for them. Setting is seldom an extraneous ingredient to the action and is almost always more than interior decoration in serious fiction. In some stories, setting fuses into plot so that it becomes part of the action, as in "Nine Lives." Le Guin personifies the setting, giving the planet Libra human characteristics:

> She was alive inside, but dead outside, her face a black and dun net of wrinkles, tumors, cracks. She was bald and blind. The tremors that crossed Libra's face were mere quiverings of corruption: underneath, in the black corridors, the halls beneath the skin, there were crepitations in darkness, ferments, chemical nightmares that went on for centuries.

The crisis in the story is occasioned by the setting, for without warning the hostile planet erupts. The resulting earthquake causes the mine to collapse, killing nine members of the clone and leaving only Kaph to confront the human condition of aloneness.

In Ray Bradbury's "August 2026: There Will Come Soft Rains," setting is the action: the story has no characters unless the inanimate objects in the deserted house can be considered characters. And the story has no plot unless the gradual annihilation of the house can be considered a plot. An atomic holocaust has destroyed a California town, killing its inhabitants and leaving only this one house standing. The mechanized house is unaware of its emptiness, and so the tape-recorded messages continue to play and the automated cooking and cleaning equipment continues to function:

> The garden sprinklers whirled up in golden founts, filling the soft morning air with

scatterings of brightness. . . . The entire west face of the house was black, save for five places. Here the silhouette in paint of a man mowing a lawn. Here, as in a photograph, a woman bent to pick flowers. Still farther over, their images burned on wood in one titanic instant, a small boy, hands flung into the air; higher up, the image of a thrown ball, and opposite him a girl, hands raised to catch a ball which never came down.

The five spots of paint—the man, the woman, the children, the ball—remained. The rest was a thin charcoaled layer.

The gentle sprinkler rain filled the garden with falling light.

In other stories, setting has a less noticeable part, but its force is always felt. Sometimes it is a shaping influence on the lives of the characters, like the Dublin of "Araby," or the New England of "The Jewels of the Cabots"; sometimes it is part of the story's meaning, like the post office in "Why I Live at the P.O."; or sometimes it is the impulse for the fiction itself, like the Newark of Philip Roth's boyhood in "Looking at Kafka."

Like the richly varied characters of fiction, settings are similarly diverse. The writer may invent a place and time, creating fanciful landscapes sustained only by imagination and putting the action forward into a visionary future, as Ursula K. Le Guin and Ray Bradbury have done. Or the writer may put the action into the historical past, re-creating a place and time, as Nathaniel Hawthorne and Jorge Luis Borges have done. Other writers have chosen to write about their own time and to use a "real" setting or one closely resembling an actual location. Thus, "A Scandal in Bohemia" takes place in the London of Arthur Conan Doyle; "The Girl Who Sant With the Beatles" in contemporary New York City; and "Old Love" in Miami Beach.

By setting a story in a "real" location or in one resembling an actual place, the writer releases a host of associations in the reader. The Babylon of F. Scott Fitzgerald's "Babylon Revisited" is Paris; the time is early 1931; and the protagonist, Charles Wales, is revisiting the city where he and so many Americans spent time and money so freely during the 1920s. But the city Charlie revisits is muted and empty: "the stillness in the Ritz bar was strange and portentous. It was not an American bar any more—he felt polite in it, and not as if he owned it. It had gone back to France." Later that evening he visits Montmartre:

Zelli's was closed, the bleak and sinister cheap hotels surrounding it were dark; up in the Rue Blanche there was more light and a local, colloquial French crowd. The Poet's Cave had disappeared, but the two great mouths of the Cafe of Heaven and the Cafe of Hell still yawned—even devoured, as he watched, the meager contents of a tourist bus. . . .

So much for the effort and ingenuity of Montmartre. All the catering to vice and waste was on an utterly childish scale, and he suddenly realized the meaning of the word "dissipate"—to dissipate into thin air; to make nothing out of something.

Fitzgerald can take advantage of the reader's knowledge of Paris and history—that the "city of lights" that Americans found romantic and enticing in the 1920s had been stripped of some of its glamor by the harsh reality of the stock market crash of 1929. Thus the reader can sympathize with Charlie who, remembering drunken evenings when he had given an orchestra a thousand-franc note to play a single number and a doorman a hundred-franc note to call a cab, remembers also:

> But it hadn't been given for nothing.
> It had been given, even the most wildly squandered sum, as an offering to destiny that he might not remember the things most worth remembering, the things that now he would always remember—his child taken from his control, his wife escaped to a grave in Vermont.

Despite the fact that different readers view a city like Paris differently, owing to their subjective experiences with the actual place, the general effect of specifying a "real" location is the active engagement of the reader's imagination. The writer can also assume that the reader's notions about Paris will make the setting visible without copious description.

By establishing a "real" setting, the writer can manipulate the reader's knowledge in still another way—by choosing to confirm preconceptions about a particular place or to reverse those expectations. A host of associations have grown up around Paris: that the city is charming and beautiful and cosmopolitan, that the city permits a freedom to live as one chooses, that the city is decadent—that "people's moral scheme *does* break down in Paris," as Henry James noted. "Babylon Revisited" supports these traditional images.

Settings, like characters, can be viewed as flat or round. For example, Alan Paton does not particularize the setting of "The Waste Land." The violent attack by the young men could occur on the outskirts of any industrial city anywhere in the world. In this story, particularities of location are less important than the debasement of human relationships symbolized by the urban waste land. On the other hand, a writer may suggest the complexity of a particular setting, as F. Scott Fitzgerald does in "Babylon Revisited," in which the objective and most obvious aspects of Paris are undercut by the subjective and intangible qualities of Charles Wales' memories of earlier experiences there.

Like every other aspect of fiction, setting is affected by point of view. In stories told by an effaced narrator, description of setting is customarily objective and brief, with the narrator providing only those details necessary to convey a minimal sense of place. In contrast, there is often copious description in stories related by an omniscient narrator, who is at liberty to depict setting either through his own perceptions or through those of his characters, as in "My Kinsman, Major Molineux."

In general, the third-person subjective narrator depicts setting dramatically and subjectively through the perceptions of the "mirroring consciousness," as in "Babylon Revisited" and "Old Love." The first-person narrator always reveals setting through his own perceptions. Thus, the narrator in "Zakhar-the-Pouch" describes Kulikova Field as he experiences it, mixing visual description with historical vision:

> Suddenly the crops came to an end and the hillside became even more like a reservation, a piece of fallow land overgrown with tough rye-grass instead of the usual feather-grass. We paid homage to this ancient place in the best way possible—just by breathing the pure air. One look around, and behold!—there in the light of sunrise the Mongol chief Telebei is engaged in single combat with Prince Peresvet, the two leaning against each other like two sheaves of wheat; the Mongolian cavalry are shooting their arrows and brandishing their spears; with faces contorted with blood lust, they trample on the Russian infantry, breaking through the core of their formation and driving them back to where a milky cloud of mist has risen from the Nepriadva and the Don.

The narrator's imagination and his knowledge of Russian history transfigures the setting so that the historical site becomes more than a poorly maintained and desolate state park: the sense of the past emanating from "this wild field" fills the narrator with a profound spirituality:

> Night set in, with a full moon. . . . Not one aeroplane flew overhead; no motorcar rumbled by, no train rattled past in the distance. By moonlight the pattern of the nearby fields was no longer visible. Earth, grass, and moonlit solitude were as they had been in 1380. The centuries stood still, and as we wandered over the field we could evoke the whole scene—the campfires and the troops of dark horses. From the river Nepriadva came the sound of swans, just as Blok had described.
>   We wanted to understand the battle of Kulikovo in its entirety, grasp its inevitability, ignore the infuriating ambiguities of the chronicles. . . .

Setting is related to mood as well as to point of view. *Mood* refers to the atmosphere that surrounds and helps to define the world in which the characters move. Thus mood involves the feeling that emanates from certain locales or accrues from particular actions, like the sense of Russian history that pervades "Zakhar-the-Pouch." Although intangible, mood affects our response to a story, as in real life we are affected by the atmosphere of certain places. In "My Kinsman, Major Molineux," the meandering streets through which Robin wanders, the darkness that causes the "forms of distant objects" to recede "with almost ghostly indistinctness, just as his eye appeared to grasp them," the "murmur of voices" from the tavern and the "wild and confused laughter of the crowd" create a sense of mystery, frustration, and unrest. In this story, as in others (like "Nine Lives"), the physical setting, by its creation of a dominant mood, sends out nonphysical signals that foreshadow subsequent events. In "Daydreams," the somber mood of the place clashes with the joyous mood created by the little tramp's fantasies of plenitude and underscores the childishness of his daydreams. Similarly the frozen landscape in "Lullaby" establishes a mood of desolation and of death itself, against which the tattered Army blanket is insufficient protection. In "The Day of the Dying Rabbit," the commonplace setting establishes a mood of tranquility and uneventfulness: the four-room cottage, the path "full of poison ivy," the sand dunes, and the "salt-pimpled aluminum screen door" create a mood of ordinariness, of homeyness—a very different atmosphere from either the weary cosmopolitanism of "Babylon Revisited" or the small-minded provincialism of "Why I Live at the P.O."

The objects in a story play an integral part in creating and enhancing the authenticity of the setting and characters. But possessions also reveal inner qualities about a character that contribute to the story's meaning. In "Lappin and Lapinova," Rosalind is an outsider to her husband's family, "a mere drop among all those Thorburns." At the golden wedding anniversary, her gift reveals her emotional separation:

> Holding her present in her hand she advanced toward her mother-in-law sump-tuous in yellow satin; and toward her father-in-law decorated with a rich yellow carnation. All round them on tables and chairs there were golden tributes, some nestling in cotton wool; others branching resplendent—candlesticks; cigar boxes; chains; each stamped with the goldsmith's proof that it was solid gold, hall-marked, authentic. But her present was only a little pinchbeck box pierced with holes; an old sand caster, an eighteenth-century relic, once used to sprinkle sand over wet ink. Rather a senseless present she felt—in an age of blotting paper. . . .

At the dinner party, "everything was gold." Only Rosalind, "in her white wedding dress peering ahead of her with her prominent eyes seemed insoluble as an icicle." Next to the prolific, gregarious, hearty Thorburns, Rosalind stands alone: fragile, sensitive, childless, passive, given to fantasies.

In "The Girl Who Sang With the Beatles," objects also carry some of the story's meaning. On one level, the furniture that Larry and Cynthia buy shows the impermanence of faddish enthusiasms:

> They agreed on all of it—the worn (but genuine) Oriental rugs; the low carved Spanish tables; the dusky colors, grays and mauve and rose; the damask sofa with its down pillows; and, in the bedrooms, the twin beds, nearly joined but held separate by an ornate brass bedstead.

To Cynthia, the apartment is "pure *Sunset Boulevard*"—the imagery coming from her infatuation with thirties movies. But in less than two years, the newly purchased furniture displeases them:

> Everyone was buying Spanish now, and there was too much around in the cheap stores. Larry and Cynthia found themselves in a dowdy apartment full of things that looked as if they had been there since the twenties. It was depressing.

The furniture, bought on impulse and because Larry believed that he shared Cynthia's preference for objects and activities of the popular culture, objectifies the instability of their marriage:

> How was Larry to tell her the truth without making her think he was either a snob or a fool? There was no way. The thing was, he said, that when they met he *did* like what she liked, period. Just because she liked it. What was wrong with that? He

wanted to see her enjoying herself, so they did what she wanted to do. . . . Forget the things he liked if she didn't—foreign movies and chamber music and walks in Central Park, all that.

A democracy, such as ours, grants freedom of speech; a capitalistic society, freedom to purchase: a steak on every barbeque grill, a riding lawn mower in every two-car garage. A good writer is able to reveal the human feelings we invest in the objects we purchase.

Integrally related to action and characters, setting helps to shape the story's meaning. Sometimes, as in "Sanchez" and "Zakhar-the-Pouch," for example, the setting *is* the meaning. The meaning of "Sanchez" lies in the father's reverence for the "high white cold of the California mountains." He tries unsuccessfully to show his son the "loveliness of the Sierra Nevada, to instruct him toward true manhood." But the boy is indifferent to the mountains and prefers the city and a job at the Flotill Cannery. To the father the city is a plague that spreads its destruction as cruelly as the harsh land he knew as a boy in Mexico. The father and son talk:

> "They are tearing down the old buildings," Jesus explained. "Redevelopment," he pronounced. "Even my building is to go someday."
> Juan looked at his son. "And what of the men?" he asked. "Where do the men go when there are no buildings?"

The father looks at a vacant lot next to his son's hotel:

> The hole which was left had that recent, peculiar look of uprootedness. There were the remains of the foundation, the broken flooring, and the cracked bricks of tired red to which the gray blotches of mortar clung like dried phlegm. But the ground had not yet taken on the opaqueness of wear that the air and sun give it. It gleamed dully in the light and held to itself where it had been torn, as earth does behind a plow.

In the end, the father's love for the mountains transcends a specific geographical place and reaches out to include all nature and the divine forces of the natural world.

> For a truth had come upon him after the years of waiting, the ultimate truth. . . . There was another kind of love, a very profound, embracing love that he had felt of late blowing across the mountains from the south and that, he knew now, had always been there from the beginning of his life, disguised in the sun and wind. In this love there was blood and earth and yes, even God, some kind of god, at least the power of a god.

But love for the specific, beautiful "created or made thing" embodied by the Sierra Nevada had to come first as a necessary step to this larger spiritual oneness with the universe.

"Zakhar-the-Pouch" is about history, or more specifically the neglect of tradition in modern Russia as represented by Kulikova Field and Zakhar, its caretaker:

> As we walked along, we were wondering why it was in this state. This was, after all, a historic spot. What happened here was a turning point in the fate of Russia. For our invaders have not always come from the West. . . . Yet this place is spurned, forgotten.

The caretaker of Kulikova Field, like the field itself, is ill-clothed and ill-kept. His patched, "long-skirted" coat is the color "you read about in folk tales— somewhere between grey, brown, red, and purple." His homemade shirt hangs out "from underneath his jacket." His canvas boots are frayed at the top; his officer's breeches are second-hand. On two occasions, however, setting fuses into character and character into meaning. Once, the narrator sees Zakhar lying on the grass: "the way he was sprawled across the ground was very touching. He went perfectly with the field. They should cast an iron figure like that and place it here." Another time, the narrator sees the bedraggled and dedicated Zakhar as the battleground's "tutelary spirit":

> He had spent the night in the haycock, in the bone-chilling cold. Why? Was it anxiety or was it devotion to the place that had made him do it?
> Immediately our previous attitude of amused condescension vanished. Rising out of the haycock on that frosty morning, he was no longer the ridiculous Keeper but rather the Spirit of the Field, a kind of guardian angel who never left the place.

Tradition has been left for Zakhar to guard in the only way he knows: protectively and intuitively, acting not from education but instinct. But perhaps he is closer in spirit to the fourteenth-century Russians who died on that battlefield than to a more learned and sophisticated curator.

In an essay titled "How I Write," Eudora Welty observed, "Like a good many other writers, I am myself touched off by place. The place where I am and the place I know, and other places that familiarity with and love for my own make strange and lovely and enlightening to look into, are what set me to writing my stories." In addition, she describes place as "one of the most simple and obvious and direct sources of the short story." But, if the "source" is simple, the substance is usually complex. As these stories attest, the physical and spiritual qualities of setting provide a great and intricate reality.

Style

Most great authors have been great prose stylists, having created styles suitable to their purposes, and having stamped upon language their own originality and vision. Because characters, incidents, and setting—as well as ideas— can be conveyed only through language, *style* is the visible and invisible manifestation of the writer's intentions. Capable of unifying the separate aspects and segments of a narrative, style relates to the way the historical author views life and to that author's conception of the story as a whole.

Style can be loosely conceived as applying to everything in a story, for everything in it involves the writer's use of language. But it is possible to define *style* in a narrower sense on the basis of certain technical aspects of language— specifically, the kinds of words a writer uses *(diction)*, how words are combined in sentences *(syntax)*, the auditory appeals of language *(rhythm* and *sound)*, and the nature and uses of spoken language *(dialogue)*. Style also embraces those aspects of language that allow the writer to extend the impact and significance of a narrative—*imagery* and *symbolism.*

Because writers create narrators who speak in a manner appropriate to their position and disposition, style—like the other aspects of fiction—is related to point of view. For example, in "The Day of the Dying Rabbit," John Updike submerges his voice into that of the first-person narrator and tells the story in a style appropriate to the experiences and sensibility of the father; in "Spotted Horses," Wiliam Faulkner uses the countrified speech patterns and idioms of the sewing-machine salesman who serves as narrator. In "The Only Way to Make It in New York," Rosellen Brown adapts her writing to the vernacular of the woman through whose fragmented consciousness the story is revealed.

DICTION AND SYNTAX

As noted earlier, diction refers to the kinds of words a writer uses. Although every writer is bound by the limits and preferences of a personal vocabulary, words from various levels of usage may be employed to accommo- date the point of view, the characters, and the setting. A writer may use the informal language of everyday speech ("The Girl Who Sang With the Beatles"), a more esoteric vocabulary ("The Middle Years"), or language so lyrical as to approach the poetic ("The Death of Sun"). The words of a story may be predominantly flat and factual ("Hills Like White Elephants") or richly connota- tive ("Araby"). The language may be heavily Latinate (leaning toward abstrac- tion) or predominantly Anglo-Saxon (which tends toward concrete depiction). But while the choice of words is directly influenced by the particular needs in a story, these needs are directly influenced by the larger social environment within which the writer lives. If, as John Updike suggests, we live in "an age of nuance, of ambiguous gestures and psychological jockeying," those qualities are bound to find expression in modern literature. Updike's own prose style attests to their presence.

Because *how* something is said affects *what* is said, syntax—the arrange- ment of words into sentences—helps determine meaning and tone. *Loose* sen- tences, in which the most important idea occurs early in the sentence, mirror the spoken language, suggesting artlessness and honesty that contrast with the deliberateness or artifice implied by *balanced* and *periodic* sentences. Consider the effects of these three sentences from "My Kinsman, Major Molineux":

loose:

> "*He now became entangled* in a succession of crooked and narrow streets, which crossed each other, and meandered at no great distance from the water-side."

balanced:

> "The annals of Massachusetts Bay will inform us, that of six governors in the space of about forty years from the surrender of the old charter, under James II, *two were imprisoned* by a popular insurrection; *a third,* as Hutchinson inclines to believe, *was driven* from the province by the whizzing of a musket-ball; *a fourth,* in the opinion of the same historian, *was hastened* to his grave by continual bickerings with the House of Representatives; and the *remaining two,* as well as their successors, till the Revolution, *were favored* with few and brief intervals of peaceful sway."

periodic:

> "There the torches blazed like the brightest, there the moon shone out like day, and there, in tar-and-feather dignity, *sat his kinsman, Major Molineux!*"

In each sentence, the main clause(s) or idea(s) is italicized here for illustrative purposes. As these examples show, balanced and periodic sentences depend on equating or paralleling ideas and on withholding information in an effort to stress a point or to create suspense. But even the loose sentence contains an adjective clause (modifying "streets") with a compound verb ("crossed" and "meandered"). Generally, stories like "My Kinsman, Major Molineux," with many periodic and symmetrical sentences, appear more contrived because the prose is more controlled than in stories like "The Girl Who Sang With the Beatles," which contain a preponderance of asymmetrical loose sentences and natural-sounding dialogue. In addition, the reader should observe how the structure and arrangement of sentences affect the general pace of a story. For example, short and relatively simple sentences make the pace of "The Waste Land" rapid, as opposed to the slower place of "The Middle Years."

RHYTHM AND SOUND

Unlike the regular rhythm of the conventional poetic line, the rhythm of prose is less regular and more expensive. It depends upon individual stress groups and large intonational patterns—the succession of pitches that occur in the speaking of such larger units as clauses and sentences—rather than upon the repetition of identical metrical feet, as in traditional poetry. In the following passage from "The Death of Sun," the diagonal lines indicate the stress groups— groups of words that contain a unit of meaning and one or more stressed syllables:

And so Sun would sit with the same God dignity and decorous finality with which he had emerged / —then once more without seeming volition / ride the crest of an updraft above Indian Country on six-foot wings / to settle again on his throne aerie in awful splendor, / admonitory, / serene / —regal and doomed.

In this passage as elsewhere, rhythm is related to meaning; here the strong cadences heighten the emotionality of the subject matter. Pauses, parallel constructions, and the alternation of stressed and unstressed syllables suggest the flight of the magnificent bird—settling momentarily on his aerie, and then riding the crest of an updraft once again. The effect is very similar to that created by Gerard Manley Hopkins in his poem "The Windhover":

> I caught this morning morning's minion, king-
> dom of daylight's dauphin, dapple-dawn-drawn Falcon, in his riding
> Of the rolling level underneath him steady air, and striding
> High there, how he rung upon the rein of a wimpling wing
> In his ecstasy! then off, off forth on swing,
> As a skate's heel sweeps smooth on bow-bend: the hurl and gliding
> Rebuffed the big wind. My heart in hiding
> Stirred for a bird, —the achieve of, the mastery of the thing!

Other elements of a writer's style also contribute to prose rhythm, particularly the effect achieved by alteration between description and dialogue; by changes in scene; and by flashbacks, which switch the action to historical or psychological time.

Related to rhythm is the sound of individual syllables, words, and sentences. Words that contain a preponderance of harsh consonants, such as *c, t, s, p, d, g, k, b, x,* are cacophonous. For example, the following passage (again from "The Death of Sun") describes the beginning of the helicopter chase:

> Ira Osmun allowed the chopper to spurt up and away to tilt off at a weird angle so that it clawed its way sideways like a crab that flew, a piece of junk, of tin and chrome and gaudy paint, alien and obscene in the perfect pure blue New Mexican sky, an intruder in the path of sun. Now the chopper clawed its way to the aerie of Sun.

In this description, the harsh consonants predominate, drowning out the softer consonants, *l, r, w, m, n, j,* and the vowel sounds, and underscoring the narrator's repugnance for the cruelty of this vicious act. In contrast, another passage describes a civilization before the advent of the white man and his machines. Here vowels and vowel sounds predominate:

> Like the Indians, the ancestors of Sun had one time roamed a virgin continent abloom with the glory of life, alive with fresh flashing streams, a smogless sky, all the world a sweet poem of life where all was beginning. Nothing ever ended. Now it was all ending.

The long vowels are mellifluous and enhance this evocation of the natural world. In contrast, the *n* and *d* sounds of the last two sentences have a deadening effect that negates this pastoral vision.

Onomatopoeia refers to the use of words that are directly imitative of sounds. In "The Death of Sun," the Indians in the schoolhouse can hear "the *whack-whack-whack* of the huge rotor blades of the copter." Wilson Drago, the helicopter's gunner, pumps a shell into the shotgun with a "*solid slam*." Mary-Forge sees Ira Osmun's "M-16 *quicking* out *nicks* of flame." The Indians blast away at the "*zooming*-in copter." These words are onomatopoetic in that they sound like the actions they describe. The reader should notice also the presence and effect of alliteration and assonance. *Alliteration* refers to the repetition of consonant sounds, particularly in accented syllables and at the beginnings of words; *assonance* refers to the repetition of vowel sounds in neighboring words. In the following passage, notice how alliteration (the repeated *g, s, w, b, m* sounds, for example) and assonance (the repeated long *e* and *o* and long and short *a* and *i*, for example) heighten the lyricism and meaning of the description:

> The golden eagle called Sun spiraled upward again, its wings steady, wild, sure, in the glorious and rapt quietude of the blue, blue, blue New Mexico morning, a golden eagle against the blue, a kind of heliograph, and a flashing jewel in the perfect and New Mexico sea of sky. The gold eagle, recapitulent, lost then found as it twirled steady and upward in the shattered light, followed by the tin bird.

Used effectively, rhythm and sound underscore the denotative and connotative meanings of words by communicating moods and attitudes that exist beneath the level of conscious verbal exchange. In prose, these devices serve the writer when they emphasize the meaning and enhance the tonal quality; they work against the writer if they call attention to themselves in undesirable ways—if they break the illusion of "reality," for example, in a story that relies on a highly conversational style for its effect.

DIALOGUE

Since dialogue is basic to fiction, the degree and kind of dialogue in a story is an important aspect of prose style. The reader should observe whether the dialogue is appropriate to the social class, psychic state, and region of the speaker; whether it is stilted or natural, witty or dull; and whether it serves to advance the action by revealing thoughts, feelings, and plot details. Dialogue contributes to the informality and naturalness of Brown's style in "The Only Way to Make It in New York" and to the formality and precision of the prose in Henry James's "The Middle Years":

> The young man blushed a little, but turned it off. "Oh never mind the Countess!"

> "You told me she was very exacting."
> Doctor Hugh had a wait. "So she is."
> "And Miss Vernham's an *intrigante.*"
> "How do you know that?"
> "I know everything. One *has* to, to write decently!"
> "I think she's mad," said limpid Doctor Hugh.

In other stories, such as William Eastlake's "The Death of Sun," the dialogue is intentionally unrealistic. Indians and school teachers do not talk the way Mary-Forge and her Navajo students talk; neither do helicopter pilots and gunmen, as the following passage between Ira Osmun and Drago illustrates:

> "Do you want eagles to take over the country?
> "I don't know."
> "Eagles and Indians at one time controlled this whole country, Drago; you couldn't put out a baby or a lamb in my grandfather's time without an Indian or an eagle would grab it. Now we got progress. Civilization. That means a man is free to go about his business."
> "It does?"
> "Yes, now that we got them on those ropes we can't let them go, Drago."
> "We can't?"
> "No, that would be letting civilized people down. It would be letting my grandfather down. What would I say to him?"
> "Are you going to see your grandfather?"
> "No, he's dead."

In Richard Wright's "The Man Who Was Almost a Man," the Southern dialect of the characters is rendered phonetically:

> Shucks, Ah ain scareda them even ef they are biggern me! Aw, Ah know whut Ahma do. Ahm going by ol Joe's sto n git that Sears Roebuck catlog n look at them guns. Mebbe Ma will lemme buy one when she gits mah pay from ol man Hawkins. Ahma beg her t gimme some money. Ahm old ernough to hava gun. Ahm seventeen.

In "Spotted Horses," Faulkner conveys the Southern dialect of his characters less through phonetic spellings than through word choice, idiomatic expressions, and speech patterns:

> "He said Saturday," she says, "that he wouldn't sell Henry no horse. He said I could get the money from you."
> Flem looked up. The knife never stopped. It went on trimming off a sliver same as if he was watching it. "He taken that money off with him when he left," Flem says.
> Mrs. Armstid never looked at nothing. We never looked at her, neither, except that boy of Eck's. He had a half-et cracker in his hand, watching her, chewing.

"He said Henry hadn't bought no horse," Mrs. Armstid says. "He said for me to get the money from you today."

"I reckon he forgot about it," Flem said. "He taken that money off with him Saturday." He whittled again.

The problem of interpretation is more difficult if a writer relies heavily on phonetic spellings because of the unfamiliar shape and combinations of the words.

In "The Girl Who Sang With the Beatles," dialogue is interspersed with paraphrase, as in the following passage:

"I thought you gave all that up," Cynthia said. "I thought you'd changed."

"I thought you *would* change," Larry said. "I thought you wanted to. I thought if you wanted to marry me you must want to change."

"Be an *intellectual?*" Cynthia said. "You must be kidding."

No, he was serious. Why didn't she get bored with the stuff she watched and the junk she read? *He* did. When you had seen three Perry Masons, you had seen them all, and that went for Doris Day movies, the eleven-o'clock news, and "What's My Line?"

"I know all that," Cynthia said. She *liked* to be bored. God, you couldn't keep thinking about *reality* all the time. You'd go out of your mind. She liked stories and actors that she knew, liked movies she had seen a dozen times and books she could read over and over again. Larry took his reading so seriously. As if reading were *life.*

Indirect quotation depicts the fundamental differences between Cynthia and Larry through a form of dramatized summary. Paraphrase here acts as a literary shorthand that allows their philosophic disagreement to be conveyed in a short amount of space while keeping the level of tension high. At no place in the story does the reader lose sight of the issues that separate the characters.

As in "The Girl Who Sang With the Beatles," Hemingway's "Hills Like White Elephants" concerns a man and a woman whose differing sensibilities and needs threaten their relationship. Although the absence of paraphrase gives Hemingway's story the appearance of artlessness and makes his manner of revealing personality seem direct and spontaneous, the actual dialogue between the pair is elliptical, oblique, and artful. In the following passage, "it" refers both to abortion, and to the possibility of having a child.

"You've got to realize," he said, "that I don't want you to do it if you don't want to. I'm perfectly willing to go through with it if it means anything to you."

"Doesn't it mean anything to you? We could get along."

"Of course it does. But I don't want anybody but you. I don't want any one else. And I know it's perfectly simple."

"Yes, you know it's perfectly simple."

"It's all right for you to say that, but I do know it."

"Would you do something for me now?"

"I'd do anything for you."

"Would you please please please please please please please stop talking?"

The woman's words and attitude are mocking and ironical. But her cynicism does a poor job of covering up her desire to have a child. The man's attempt to flatter her belies his underlying selfishness. So does his insistence on the simpleness of the operation. The man's words are as empty as his emotions and the life they have been leading: the woman's attempt to find meaning within that life is as stillborn as the life within her is destined to be.

Dialogue is a clue to a character's social class as well as to his or her temperament, ranging as it does from the vacuous rationalizations of the post-mistress in "Why I Live at the P.O." to the erudite logic of C. Auguste Dupin and Sherlock Holmes; from the pious unanchored speech of the prisoner in "Daydreams" to the clipped jargon of the clones in "Nine Lives"; from the outbursts of the unruly children in "The Storyteller" to the intricate fantasies of Rosalind and Ernest in "Lappin and Lapinova." The world around us is full of talk; the talented writer is able to reproduce that talk—imitating in fiction the many voices of actual life or using dialogue to approach the suggestiveness of poetry as William Eastlake has done.

IMAGERY

Imagery may be either literal or figurative. *Literal imagery* refers to the verbal representation of sense experience—that is, to words and phrases that identify, describe, or evoke sensory responses. Accordingly, literal imagery extends to the representation of auditory, tactile, gustatory, olfactory, and kinetic sensations as well as visual, often blending several senses in a single image (like the word *dripping* in the following passage from "Araby"):

> When the short days of winter came dusk fell before we had well eaten our dinners. When we met in the street the houses had grown somber. The space of sky above us was the color of ever-changing violet and towards it the lamps of the street lifted their feeble lanterns. The cold air stung us and we played till our bodies glowed. Our shouts echoed in the silent street. The career of our play brought us through the dark muddy lanes behind the houses where we ran the gauntlet of the rough tribes from the cottages, to the back doors of the dark dripping gardens where odors arose from the ashpits, to the dark odorous stables where a coachman smoothed and combed the horse or shook music from the buckled harness.

By allowing the reader to experience the sensuous qualities of places, events, and characters, literal imagery aids the writer in creating and sustaining the illusion of reality.

While literal imagery seeks to represent the sensation or object as directly as possible, *figurative imagery* is associative and involves saying one thing in terms of another. A figurative image likens an object, place, event, animal, or human being to something else, which may or may not be in the same category. In fiction, the most common types of figurative images are *simile,* which describes or identifies by explicit analogy; *metaphor,* which describes or identifies by implicit analogy; and *personification,* which describes or identifies by attributing human qualities to animals, inanimate objects, or abstractions. As the following examples from "Araby" show, figurative imagery is often sensory, in that the thing being compared, or what it is compared to, or both, can evoke sensory responses, like the auditory, tactile, and kinetic senses appealed to in the simile below:

simile:
"But my body was like a harp and her words and gestures were like fingers running upon the wires."

metaphor:
"Her image accompanied me even in places the most hostile to romance. On Saturday evenings when my aunt went marketing I had to go to carry some of the parcels. We walked through the flaring streets, jostled by drunken men and bargaining women. . . . These noises converged in a single sensation of life for me: I imagined that I bore my chalice safely through a throng of foes."

personification:
"The other houses of the street, conscious of decent lives within them, gazed at one another with brown imperturbable faces."

In "The Day of the Dying Rabbit," photography occurs and reoccurs as simile, metaphor, and as actual and remembered event. The story begins with a metaphor that likens the taking of a picture to the apparent randomness of life itself: "The shutter clicks, and what is captured is mostly accident—that happy foreground diagonal, the telling expression forever pinned in mid-flight between the two plateaus of vacuity." The narrator explains: "Margaret and I didn't exactly intend to have six children. At first, we were trying until we got a boy." For the dramatized narrator, who is a professional photographer, photography is a way not only of making a living but of apprehending reality. The viewfinder of a camera becomes a frame of reference; the lens a way of focusing and making sharp and clear what he sees; the film a way of making permanent the images of everyday life. For John Updike, photography becomes a way of unifying his story. So insistently and consistently does this metaphor occur that photography becomes a leitmotif (German for "leading-motive")—a term applied to literature but taken from music and art to describe a recurring melodic phrase, or a prevailing design in the plastic arts.

Closely related to figurative imagery is the *allusion,* a detailed or general reference to persons, places, events, eras, and objects that exist beyond the framework of the story. Mythology, literature, the Bible, history, and geography are the writer's chief sources of allusions. The conversation of the young man in

"You Were Perfectly Fine" contains various allusions to literature: his hangover makes him think that his head is "something that used to belong to Walt Whitman"; his slipping on the icy sidewalk invokes a reference to Louisa May Alcott. In "The Death of Sun," the Indians and Mary-Forge talk of Feodor Dostoevski, Søren Kierkegaard, and Sigmund Freud. In "The Purloined Letter," ,the erudite Dupin draws on various fields of human knowledge for analogies. Concerning the commissioner of the Paris police, he observes: "A certain set of highly ingenious resources are, with the Prefect, a sort of Procrustean bed, to which he forcibly adapts his designs." In Greek mythology, Procrustes was a giant who either stretched or shortened his captives to fit his iron beds.

In "My Kinsman, Major Molineux," Hawthorne alludes to historical personages and events—to Thomas Hutchinson who wrote a history of the Massachusetts Bay colony, to the "original charters," which had been revoked almost fifty years prior to the historical present of the story; to Fast Day sermons, delivered every spring on the day the governor set aside for fasting and penance. There are references to Shakespeare's *A Midsummer Night's Dream* and to the Bible (1 Timothy 4:4) to explain the colonists' "Predilection for the Good Creature in some of its various shapes"—in this instance liquor.

"Theme of the Traitor and the Hero" by Jorge Luis Borges is replete with allusions to history and literature. In fact, the entire story is about an imagined historical event concerning an imaginary hero/traitor. The epigraph is from W. B. Yeats; the first paragraph invokes the English journalist, poet, and mystery writer G. K. Chesterton and the German mathematician-philosopher Gottfried Wilhelm von Leibniz. The second paragraph mentions the "verses of Browning and Hugo"—the English poet Robert Browning and the French writer Victor Hugo. And, of course, the plot revolves around an analogy between the facts of Borges's imagined story and two of Shakespeare's tragedies—*Julius Caesar* and *Macbeth.* Borges's protagonist, Ryan, is a researcher accumulating data on his hero Kilpatrick, and finding parallels between the Irish patriot and Shakespeare's Julius Caesar. This analogy causes Ryan

> to suppose the existence of a secret form of time, a pattern of repeated lines. He thinks of the decimal history conceived by Condorcet, of the morphologies proposed by Hegel, Spengler and Vico, of Hesiod's men, who degenerate from gold to iron. He thinks of the transmigration of souls, a doctrine that lends horror to Celtic literature and that Caesar himself attributed to the British druids.

The contemporary writer Marshall McLuhan has popularized the notion that the content of one medium is always another medium. The use of analogies makes clear that in addition to being an imitation of life, fiction draws from many disciplines: from history, philosophy, psychology, poetry, drama, mythology, from the accounts of travelers and the findings of scientists, from painting and music and, of course, from fiction itself. In very few stories, however, do allusions form the substance of the story, as they do in "Theme of the Traitor and the Hero."

SYMBOLISM

In the short story or novel, a *symbol* is an object, setting, action, or character that suggests a meaning larger than itself. For example, the Army blanket in "Lullaby" is a symbol of the usurpation of the white culture. In this story, the tattered green blanket is insufficient to protect either the old Indian woman, Ayah, or her husband against the snow and bitter cold. Ayah's remembrances of the past comprise much of the substance of the story; at one point, she remembers her girlhood and combing wool for her grandmother to spin and her mother to weave:

> Her mother worked at the loom with yarns dyed bright yellow and red and gold. She watched them dye the yarn in boiling black pots full of beeweed petals, juniper berries, and sage. The blankets her mother made were soft and woven so tight that rain rolled off them like birds' feathers. Ayah remembered sleeping warm on cold windy nights, wrapped in her mother's blankets on the hogan's sandy floor.

The handmade blankets with their traditional colors and designs had provided protection against the rain and cold; the Army blanket offers neither art nor lasting warmth. Machine-made, it was used by soldiers in a war that had taken the life of her oldest child.

Symbolism provides the writer with ways of suggesting abstract qualities, attitudes, and ideas through specific, concrete depiction of objects and people in the visible world. By utilizing the symbolic potential of the elements of fiction, the writer can imply a theme without making explicit statements, as most essayists would. "Lullaby" is about the decline of a traditional culture—this is its controlling idea, to borrow a phrase from rhetoric handbooks. But through the characters and the rich suggestiveness of the blanket, the impending death of a traditional way of life becomes part of the reader's *felt* experience: the annihilation of a culture is no longer only an idea or abstraction—nor, for the sensitive reader, will it ever be again.

Like simile and metaphor, a symbol is suggestive. But unlike these figures of speech, the symbol does not openly compare two objects by describing one in terms of the other; rather, the symbol is a single entity, like the blanket, with an objective reality separate from the additional meanings its presence suggests. To function effectively, however, the symbolic entity must either typify or recall (by possession of similar qualities or by association real or imagined) the meaning(s) it suggests.

In "Lost in the Funhouse," the narrator points out that the diving could be used as a literary symbol:

> To go off the high board you had to wait in a line along the poolside and up the ladder. Fellows tickled girls and goosed one another and shouted to the ones at the top to hurry up, or razzed them for bellyfloppers. Once on the springboard some took a great while posing or clowning or deciding on a dive or getting up their

nerve; others ran right off. Especially among the younger fellows the idea was to strike the funniest pose or do the craziest stunt as you fell, a thing that got harder to do as you kept on and kept on. But whether you hollered *Geronimo!* or *Sieg heil!*, held your nose or "rode a bicycle," pretended to be shot or did a perfect jacknife or changed your mind halfway down and ended up with nothing, it was over in two seconds, after all that wait.

The symbolism embodied by the diving, while unexplained by the narrator, is of course, comprehensible to the reader: (1) the clownishness of the divers is a microcosm of the larger carnival atmosphere of the amusement park, (2) the innocent and overt acrobatics on the diving board symbolize the covert sexual acrobatics for which, as Ambrose realizes, "the restaurants and dance halls and test-your-strength machines" are "preparation and intermission," and (3) the variety of attitudes toward the diving symbolizes the variety of responses to life itself. The boardwalk, too, functions symbolically. On the boardwalk, where Ambrose walks with his family, frivolity and propriety mingle; under the boardwalk, where Ambrose ventures alone, are matchbook covers, cigar butts, Coca-Cola caps, cardboard lollipop sticks, "grainy other things," and a man and woman engaged in a sexual embrace. The boardwalk symbolizes the dichotomy between the exterior, visible world of genteel traditions and the interior, mysterious, dark underside of human sexuality.

Symbols can be classified as either created or conventional. A *created symbol* achieves its suggestiveness from the specific context in which it appears rather than from traditional associations. For example, in "The Girl Who Sang With the Beatles," the headphones are a created symbol. In themselves, the headphones are only electronic gadgets, extensions of the television and stereo set. In the story, however, the headphones are a symbol of Cynthia and Larry's relationship:

> "That isn't it," he said. "You know what it is? It's the noise. All the things you like make *noise*."
> "I read."
> "Sure. With the radio or the stereo or the TV on. I can't. I have to do one thing at a time," Larry said. "What if I want to sit home at night and read a book?"
> "So read."
> "When you have these programs you quote have to watch unquote?"
> "Get me headphones. That's what my first husband did when he stopped talking to me. Or go in the bedroom and shut the door. I don't mind."

Initially, the headphones are emblematic of Cynthia and Larry's separateness. In an unexpected way, however, they serve as a strange symbol of unity at the conclusion of the story. In neither instance has the physical reality of the headphones changed—only their associated meanings in the specific context of this particular story.

In "Lullaby," the freezing night is a *conventional symbol;* cold has long been associated with barrenness and sterility and, at its most extreme, with death. The bitterly cold night has this symbolic function in "Lullaby": the freezing cold will claim the lives of the old Indian couple in the same way that the white civilization has claimed the traditional ways of the Navajo. In "My Kinsman, Major Molineux," the darkness that shrouds the town is a conventional symbol. In diverse cultures, night and blackness are equated with the unknown and with evil: vampires flee with the coming of dawn; the black cat who crosses a person's path brings bad luck. Black is associated with death: mourning clothes, hearses—even some carrion eaters—are black. In literature, black is symbolic of deceit (the mysterious dark lady of Shakespeare's sonnets) while fairness of hair and skin is emblematic of purity (Dante's Beatrice in *The Divine Comedy*). In Hawthorne's story, the riotous, pagan procession takes place under cover of darkness. Here the darkness symbolizes both Robin's ignorance and the evilness of the proceedings.

Many conventional symbols can be classified as archetypes, a term that has come into literary criticism chiefly through the work of Carl Jung. Jung postulated the existence of a collective unconscious—a storehouse of racial memories we all carry about as part of our psychic inheritance, memories that extend even to pre-human experience. These primordial images, or universal symbols, are termed *archetypes*. In literature, archetypes are embodied in particular images, plot patterns, and character types. Because of the recurrent associations of darkness with evil in the literature and ritual celebrations of widely separated cultures, blackness is not only a conventional symbol but an archetype, and thus reflects something fundamental and shared about human experience.

Close familial relationships are the substance of many archetypal patterns. For example, in the Western world, the relationship between Cain and Abel is the archetypal relationship between brothers. The question Cain evasively and defensively asks after slaying Abel—"Am I my brother's keeper?"—signals that, in the world view represented in the Bible, a key element in the relationship between brothers is responsibility. In the development of Western thought, the meaning of the story has sometimes included the responsibility of each human being for all human beings. Any writer who depicts a situation in which persons must act responsibly toward each other establishes automatic, and perhaps unwanted, connections with an awesome, archetypal layer of meaning accessible through the reader's awareness of the Cain-Abel story. A simple narrative can thereby take on some of the attributes of a biblical story—its grandeur, its universality, or its concern with morality. Le Guin draws on the Cain-Abel archetype in "Nine Lives." Pugh is going out to rescue Martin after a second earthquake has occurred. Kaph, the only surviving member of the clone, tries to stop him, telling the "singleton" that he is taking an unnecessary risk. But Pugh is acting not from common sense but from human instinct. Later, after Martin's rescue, Kaph asks:

"Do you love Martin?"

Pugh looked up with angry eyes: "Martin is my friend. We've worked together, he's a good man." He stopped. After a while he said, "Yes, I love him. Why did you ask that?"

Kaph said nothing, but he looked at the other man. His face was changed, as if he were glimpsing something he had not seen before; his voice too was changed. "How can you . . . ? How do you . . . ?"

But Pugh could not tell him. "I don't know," he said, "it's practice, partly. I don't know. We're each of us alone, to be sure. What can you do but hold your hand out in the dark?"

At the story's conclusion, Kaph has progressed toward the inevitable humanization that will allow him to be his brother's keeper when the situation makes this demand.

Another dominant archetypal pattern centers on the initiation ceremony. Initiation rites have been part of the tribal or religious life in almost every primitive and sophisticated culture of every age and every country and continue to exert a powerful force in contemporary society. The initiation usually concerns an adolescent boy, less typically a young girl, who undergoes a prescribed spiritual and physical ordeal and emerges as an adult, having shed the former self and acquired new attributes of manliness or womanliness. The universality of the initiation rite suggests that it reveals a very significant truth about the nature of humanness. That many authors draw on the rites of passage for theme and narrative structure is not surprising. "The Man Who Was Almost a Man" depicts a particularly violent initiation into what Dave assumes is manhood. Important to this initiation is the acquisition of a weapon traditionally associated with authority. At the conclusion of "My Kinsman, Major Molineux," Robin is no longer the innocent country boy he is at the story's beginning: he has been introduced to the relativity of good and evil.

In "Araby," the boy learns that the material goods sold at the bazaar are unable to satisfy the exalted requirements of his idealized love. The boy recognizes the foolishness of his quest and experiences the frustration of his hope: this sad but profound recognition is his initiation into adult reality. Other stories in this collection embody other archetypal patterns: the Contest ("The Bride Comes to Yellow Sky"), the Hero ("Theme of the Traitor and the Hero"), the Trickster ("Spotted Horses"), the Scapegoat ("A Hunger Artist"), the Quest ("Babylon Revisited"), to name only a few. Writers that use archetypes either consciously or unconsciously are drawing upon a very rich shared heritage; such stories may often affect readers emotionally in ways not obvious until they understand that they are responding to an element in the story that is as old as the human race itself.

Because the recognition of symbols provides intellectual enjoyment and because symbols add to the meaning of a story, some readers tend to see symbols in whatever they read. But "symbol-hunting" has its dangers. The most obvious of these is the possibility of the reader's manufacturing symbols where none occur in the narrative or assigning personal and irrelevant meanings to symbols that are clearly present. Frequently, in pursuing the symbolic significance of a work, the reader overlooks the fact that a short story is basically empirical—a narrative woven from the materials of human existence. Without characters and the interest and meaning inherent in their actions, symbolic meanings are only ornament. The literary symbol is significant only as it enlarges the concerns of a specific story. Given these cautionary remarks, however, the reader of this book should be aware of the importance of symbols in literature. Through their use, the short-story writer, like the novelist, achieves a scope and depth that stretch the boundaries of narrative.

"Style in a writer is a policy about life, not a stunt," Herbert Gold has said in *Fiction of the Fifties*. Because style is the personal mark and signal of an author's involvement, style reveals a good deal about the underlying attitudes and values in a story, at times overriding such aspects as characters, plot, and setting and even, one suspects, the author's conscious intentions. For example, an "elegant" and highly symbolic style cannot hide the vacuousness of a story centered around a cliché; neither can a deliberately folksy style conceal the dishonesty of a story that, in some way, falsifies a crucial issue. In the largest sense, as Gold has observed, style *is* the writer's "moral stance."

Tone

Tone is the most general and elusive aspect in the criticism of fiction, a concept, like style, that embraces the story as a whole. In the most widely accepted meaning of the term, *tone* refers to the author's attidude toward the subject—an attitude that reveals itself not only through explicit statement but implicitly, through all the elements of fiction and all the matters of technique discussed so far—point of view, narrators, characters, plot, form, time, setting, and style. Undeniably, how an author views a subject affects how that subject is depicted. Accordingly, every fictional ingredient, every narrative decision—to use the scenic point of view in "Hills Like White Elephants," to make the dramatized narrator of "The Day of the Dying Rabbit" a commercial photographer, to let the postmistress in "Why I Live at the P.O." tell her own story in her own words, to create a Dr. Watson as friend and "biographer" of Sherlock Holmes, to use indirect quotation in "The Girl Who Sang With the Beatles," to include both an actual and a fictional biography in "'I Always Wanted You to Admire My Fasting'; or, Looking at Kafka"—and *all* similar choices relate to tone.

Since serious fiction involves values and judgments, becoming aware of tone helps readers to discover their relationship to the values represented in the work. Of all the elements of fiction, tone is related most directly to meaning or theme.

IRONY

A recurrent tone in modern fiction is the ironic. *Irony* always traffics in disparity, whether it is *verbal irony* (a statement that says one thing but means something else), *irony of situation* (a circumstance in which the outcome is unexpected or inappropriate), or *cosmic irony* (a sense that despite people's best intentions, fate prevents their success). Linked to point of view and to the manipulation of plot, *dramatic irony* occurs only when the reader possesses knowledge that the characters do not have—information that allows the outcome or resolution to be anticipated or predicted. Dramatic irony can be easily achieved in stories that use the omniscient narrator, whose broad perspective permits giving the reader more information than the characters possess. The reader is then in a better position than the characters to predict the conclusion. But in many stories, like "My Kinsman, Major Molineux," the omniscient narrator is chary with the information he releases in order to sustain suspense and ensure that the specific events of the resolution are a surprise. In stories like "The Only Way to Make It in New York," however, dramatic irony is noticeably absent because the reader has access only to the consciousness of the woman. The reader's ignorance of the burglar's thoughts and feelings prevents predicting what will happen.

Irony of tone is more pervasive than the accumulated effects of the various forms of irony. In the largest sense, *irony of tone* is the author's acknowledgment that existence is a mass of contradictions, that there is no absolute truth, and that to commit oneself to a single belief is an untenable simplification. To communicate this vision, such a writer uses the doubleness of irony. Recognizing that words often conceal the truth ("You Were Perfectly Fine"); that appearances frequently deceive ("A Scandal in Bohemia"); that expectations are forever being stymied ("Araby" and "Old Love"); that the truths of history are sometimes falsehoods ("Theme of the Traitor and the Hero"), the author adopts an attitude and rhetoric that allows these incongruities to be displayed. The reader who fails to recognize when an author is being ironic takes everything literally instead of perceiving the doubleness of the vision. The reader should, therefore, be alert to the devices that signal the presence of irony: verbal techniques such as understatement, overstatement, and paradox; the use of situations that are paradoxical or involve the operation of cosmic irony; and discrepancies between the events of the story and the manner in which they are related.

Inevitably, the presence of irony in fiction establishes a tension within the work. In literature, as in life, tension is a force resulting from the interplay of contrary stresses. The Greek philosopher Heraclitus observed, "As with the bow and the lyre, so with the world: it is the tension of opposing forces that makes the structure one." Thus tension, in literature, is a desirable, unifying, esthetically satisfying quality accruing from any number of opposing forces: characters who oppose each other, the conflict basic to plot, the clash between psychological time and chronological time, and the opposition basic to irony.

If the writer uses understatement, overstatement, or paradox, a tension is set up between what is said and what is meant. Irony of situation and cosmic irony create a tension derived from what should happen and what does happen. Dramatic irony establishes a tension between the reader's knowledge and that of the characters—between the reader's awareness of the outcome and the limited, often fragmentary action unfolding in the story.

At its worst, an author can allow "an all-pervasive 'un-earned' irony to substitute for an honest discrimination among his materials," Booth notes. At its best, irony represents a writer's involvement with the subject, dramatizing not only the disparities of existence but the consequences of disparity, as evidenced by "Theme of the Traitor and the Hero."

The title holds the key to the principal irony in this story—rather than being the martyred hero of history book and legend Kilpatrick is a traitor to his cause and his people. But is he a traitor to be maligned now that his true role has been revealed, or is he, viewed in another light, a hero? For his "deliberately dramatic" death abets the cause of revolution. Kilpatrick did a grand job of acting in a grand and ennobling drama. His performance in this theater piece rather than his actions in real life is his final definition.

And here are other ironies. Nolan is both the agent of Kilpatrick's death and his salvation. Appointed by Kilpatrick to discover the traitor in their midst, Nolan reveals Kilpatrick, who is forced to sign his own death sentence. But the drama of the assassination is Nolan's invention. Accordingly he saves Kilpatrick by allowing him to die young, heroic, beautiful, and revered.

The concluding irony occurs in the final paragraph. Ryan perceives that "he too forms part of Nolan's plot" in that Nolan wanted someone to uncover the facts of Kilpatrick's treachery. But because Ryan sees Kilpatrick's double role, "he resolves to keep his discovery silent. He publishes a book dedicated to the hero's glory; this too, perhaps, was foreseen."

CYNICISM

"Know then thyself, presume not God to scan, the proper study of mankind is man," wrote Alexander Pope, the foremost poet of England's Age of Reason. Well-praised and well-paid (an unusual combination in the early eighteenth century) for his translations of Homer's *Iliad* and *Odyssey,* Pope's own poetry is steeped in the classical tradition. Like his contemporaries, including Addison and Steele, Pope argued for "reasonableness" and drew from the literature of Greece and Rome for examples and analogies.

Introspection seldom proved a joyous exercise to the Greek; the labyrinth of the self revealed too many pockets of self-pride and blind alleys of hypocrisy and deceit. The outer view, as the sketches of Theophrastus show, was similarly discouraging. Failure to find either virtue or self-control in the conduct of most persons led to the formulation of Cynicism as a major philosophy. The best-known Greek Cynic is the philosopher Diogenes, who carried his lantern about in a fruitless search for "an honest man." Cynicism as a formal philosophy no longer commands much attention, but cynicism as an attitude has long enjoyed a wide and diverse popular following. Today the term denotes a denial of the doctrine that human beings are innately good. The cynic doubts accepted social standards and ideals and is scornful of the motives or virtues of others.

The fables of Aesop take their special quality from their deeply embedded cynicism. They are a peculiar and very human response to the proper study of mankind. For how much easier it is to recreate the deceits, frailties, and shortcomings of human beings in the characters of animals than to dramatize those same weaknesses in human characters. And the device of talking animals who display human weaknesses and predilections is funny—if not to the Greeks at least to twentieth-century readers, as James Thurber recognized. The beast fable as a literary form has had a long and lasting popular appeal. Its application has not been limited to the anecdote but has been used in longer works, including the story of Chanticleer and Pertelote told by the Nun's Priest in *The Canterbury Tales*; an anonymous epic-length beast fable, *The History of Reynard the Fox,* from the Middle Ages; and *Animal Farm,* George Orwell's famous short novel.

The cynicism in Aesop's fables is easily observable and usually overpowers the moralistic strain. The moral that acts as a conclusion is often so generalized as to constitute a non sequitur. A good example is the fable of "The Crow and the Fox." Here the clever fox triumphs through flattery. How easily the crow is duped by the praise heaped on him by the hungry fox! How quickly he opens his mouth to display his voice! As a result, the victorious fox has his meat and eats it too: the last words are his—a reprimand to the foolish crow. Vividly and economically presented, the talk and antics of the animals impress themselves in the reader's memory. In contrast, the moral is unspecific and anticlimactic: "The tale is appropriate for a senseless person."

In the fables of James Thurber the morals are punchy "one-liners." In fact, Thurber has made the whole fable form much funnier. In his retelling of "The Fox and the Crow," Thurber draws on Aesop and then reverses the anticipated turning point. In this instance, the crow does not succumb initially to the flattery of the fox and does not drop the cheese he holds in his beak. So the fox resorts to another strategy and asks the crow to talk about himself. Unable to refuse an invitation to vaunt his superiority to other animals, the crow willingly gives the fox the larger portion of the cheese and then sings his own praises. The fox eats, listens, and then departs, after thanking the crow for giving him the "'lion's share of what I know you could not spare.'" Thurber's moral is more pointed: "'Twas true in Aesop's time and La Fontaine's, and now, no one else can praise thee quite so well as thou."

Cynicism is not restricted to the beast fable or other talking-animal forms. It is an attitude that permeates the moral outlook of many writers who use human characters in their fictions. At its worst, like irony, an all-pervasive cynicism can be substituted for "an honest discrimination" among a writer's "materials" so that the possibility of any goodness in any person or institution is automatically rejected. At its best, cynicism provides an author with a moral outlook that counterbalances a too facile optimism. Cynicism is useful if it counteracts the platitudes of moral goodness that blind a person to the ambiguities of everyday living. In this anthology, cynicism is most apparent in "The Storyteller," "You Were Perfectly Fine," and "Hills Like White Elephants." A cynical attitude usually prevails in detective fiction, beginning with Poe's Monsieur Dupin, for the detective's survival and success depends upon a distrust of appearances.

Cynicism often disguises fear, as it does for Harry Bendiner in "Old Love." At the age of eighty-two, Harry lives alone in a condominium in Miami Beach. He has little to do with his neighbors and avoids both the pool and tenants' meetings:

> Men and women greeted him in the elevator and at the supermarket, but he didn't know who any of them were. From time to time someone asked him, "How are you, Mr. Bendiner?" And he usually replied, "How *can* you be at my age? Each day is a gift."

He acknowledges to himself that "his life made no sense whatever," but finds that his neighbors' lives are equally meaningless. His wealth is a source of envy and speculation for the other tenants who are full of questions and advice:

> Why didn't he settle in Israel? Why didn't he go to a hotel in the mountains during the summer? Why didn't he get married? Why didn't he hire a secretary? He had acquired the reputation of a miser. . . . Everyone tried in one way or another to get something out of him, but no one would have given him a penny if he needed it.

Cynicism is an old man's protection from a world that he sees as motivated by self-interest, vanity, and greed, but suspicion is a double-edged sword. It protects him from other people but in no way reduces his vulnerability or assuages his loneliness. It also makes him unable, at first, to recognize the genuine kindness of a new neighbor:

> "She wants something; she has some ulterior motive," Harry told himself. He recalled what he had read in the newspapers about female cheats who swindled fortunes out of men and out of other women, too. The main thing was to promise nothing, to sign nothing, not to hand over even a single penny.

But cynicism gives way to acceptance and acceptance to love. Although the woman's suicide ends his dream of intimacy and warmth, their brief encounter awakens him to the possibilities of love and of sharing his life once again. At the story's conclusion, he is both more trusting and more vulnerable.

SATIRE

Because the beast fable depicts the foolishness of human beings, it serves as a vehicle for satire. In literature, satire takes many forms: poetry, drama, fiction, the essay, literary and dramatic criticism—even the proto-short story as represented by the character sketches of Theophrastus and of Addison and Steele. What unites these diverse forms is their common intention of ridiculing and reforming some aspect of society and human behavior. As the Aesopic fables illustrate, satire claims a moralistic purpose, so that ridicule is not an end in itself but a means to bring about desirable change through laughter. Literary critics differentiate between two types of satire, named after two Roman poets, Juvenal and Horace. Juvenalian satire is bitter and angry and attacks the baser aspects of man. Rabelais and Jonathan Swift are Juvenalian satirists. Horatian satire is restrained and attacks man's foolishness, like the beast fables of Aesop and the Characters of Theophrastus. "Ned Softly the Poet," "Journalism in Tennessee," and "The Oranging of America" are Horatian although each represents a different aspect of the satirist's art. Addison's "Ned Softly" is directed against the foolish and vain poet who reads his abominable verse to Bickerstaff and then is impervious to his captive listener's devastating criticism. The target of Addison's satire is "pretty" poetry and "easy lines"—poetry ornamented with "epigrammatical conceits, turns, points, and quibble" rather than poetry "after the manner of the ancients" that succeeds because of the "simplicity of its natural beauty and perfection." Ned's contemporary counterparts can be found in numerous places today—in bars, in coffee houses, on the pages of home-town weekly newspapers, and in university classrooms and faculty lounges.

The target of "Journalism in Tennessee" is local journalistic practices, and Twain's hyperbolic prose style in this short satire matches the subject; he wins his point by energy rather than elegance. The first-person narrator is a Yankee who has been told that living in the South would improve his health. Accordingly he moves to Tennessee and accepts a job on the *Morning Glory and Johnson County War-Whoop*. The narrator's first article is rejected by the *War-Whoop's* editor as being "gruel"; to show his new employee proper journalistic style the editor rewrites the Yankee's article, filling it with invective, misinformation, and other libelous matters. While this rewriting is going on, irate readers attacked in previous issues use the editor and his new associate for target practice—bullets fly, hand grenades and bricks are thrown, a duel occurs. The narrator and the editor suffer incredibly gruesome wounds. For, after all, Twain is not telling a realistic story; this is a tall tale full of physical humor and ironic understatement as the conclusion of the warfare in the *War-Whoop's* office illustrates:

People were shot, probed, dismembered, blown up, thrown out of the window. There was a brief tornado of murky blasphemy, with a confused and frantic war-dance glimmering through it, and then all was over. In five minutes there was silence, and the gory chief and I sat alone and surveyed the sanguinary ruin that strewed the floor around us.

He said, "You'll like this place when you get used to it."

The narrator's gracious leave-taking is made more humorous because it follows the bloody scene previously described:

> "Vigorous writing is calculated to elevate the public, no doubt, but then I do not like to attract so much attention as it calls forth. I can't write with comfort when I am interrupted so much as I have been to-day. I like this berth well enough, but I don't like to be left here to wait on the customers."

The target of satire in both these sketches is the misuse of language. But while Twain's story is vigorous, provincial, and smacks of frontier humor, Addison's sketch is controlled, urban, and looks to the classics for standards. Twain uses two brawny fists to ridicule the Tennessee press; Addison satirizes "pretty" poetry with an iron fist in a velvet glove. Twain wins by a knock-out; Addison by a decision.

"The Oranging of America" (its title a parody of Charles Reich's *The Greening of America* with its compliant optimism) is a satire on Howard Johnson—the man and his establishments. But it is more that that; its source is the popular culture of which Howard Johnson franchises are only small orange dots on the greenness of America. Max Apple writes his story as though it were an historical account. The fictional Howard Johnson is in his late sixties and is "chairman emeritus of the board." Young men, including his son, have taken over the company. He is left with Mildred Bryce, his ailing business associate, companion and mistress; Otis Brighton his chauffeur; and his 1964 Cadillac. The Cadillac is a masterstroke of the satiric imagination:

> From the outside it looked like any ordinary 1964 Cadillac limousine. In the expensive space between the driver and passengers, where some installed bars or even bathrooms, Mr. Howard Johnson kept a tidy ice cream freezer in which there were always at least eighteen flavors on hand, though Mr. Johnson ate only vanilla.

In another passage, the narrative takes on biblical overtones and Mr. HJ's vocation is described with Old Testament grandeur. A relief map of the United States has been taped onto the plexiglass divider in the limousine. Existing HJ restaurants and motels are marked by orange dots, future sites by white dots:

> Nothing gave the ice cream king greater pleasure than watching Mildred with her fine touch, and using the original crayon, turn an empty white dot into an orange fulfillment.
>
> "It's like a seed grown into a tree, Millie," Mr. HJ liked to say at such moments when he contemplated the map and saw that it was good.

Not even Howard Johnson's godlike omiscience and omnipotence can vanquish illness and death, but the "host of the highways" makes a valiant try. His solution is worthy of his vocation. This story is as American as Twain's; it is a fictional history that turns one of our institutions into myth; it is fantasy and the product of a rich imagination; it is a light-hearted spoof and poignant human drama. And finally it is very good satire.

THE COMIC VOICE

The classification of literature into genres is arbitrary, like the separation of points of view, and more useful to the critic than to the writer. If traditional definitions of satire insist that even Horatian satire must ridicule in order to reform, then "The Oranging of America" is not satire. Perhaps it is a fantasy with satirical elements, or perhaps simply a comic story. For comedy claims no reason for its existence: it exists for its own sake—to entertain and delight.

Comedy in narrative and dramatic literature has had a long but not altogether respectable history. The comic spirit sees humanity as created less in the image of God than in that of more earth-bound counterparts and finds one source of its humor in the anatomy, digestive system, and instinctual drives of the human body. In short fiction, ribald tales abound in *The Thousand Nights and a Night,* the *Decameron,* and *The Canterbury Tales;* in dramatic literature, the comedies of Aristophanes, of Shakespeare, of Wycherley and the other Restoration dramatists are full of sexual play and interplay. In our own time, many authors, such as John Barth, Philip Roth, and Grace Paley, write with comic exuberance and eloquence about sexual adventure and its inevitable complications.

But the human body and sexual encounters are not the only source of humor in imaginative literature. Running a close second is physical violence, provided that the consequences cause no permanent damage. A primary source of comedy in "Journalism in Tennessee" and "Spotted Horses" is the physical abuse heaped on the major characters. Another (and related) source of humor in these stories is exaggeration: the more preposterous the better; the wilder the action the more comic the reaction. Also, as these stories illustrate, another person's discomfort is often amusing. The young man's physical and emotional depletion in "You Were Perfectly Fine" is humorous. So is the aunt's distress in "The Story-Teller," which makes the reader relish the bachelor's smugness about his victory.

The unexpected also causes comic reaction. The conclusion of "The Bride Comes to Yellow Sky" is humorous because the resolution is unanticipated. "The Only Way to Make It in New York" has comic moments because of the incongruity of the burglar being treated as a guest. As that story shows, even in serious stories, there are often moments of comic relief. Sometimes dialogue is responsible for a story's humorous content: in "Why I Live at the P.O.," for example, the narrator's language accounts for much of the comedy. In this passage printed here, she and her mother have been discussing Shirley-T, Stella-Rondo's child:

> "Mama," I says, "can that child talk?" I simply had to whisper! "Mama, I wonder if that child can be—you know—in any way? Do you realize," I says, "that she hasn't spoken one single, solitary word to a human being up to this minute? This is the way she looks," I says, and I looked liked this.

The child not only can talk but she can sing and tap dance—much to the narrator's chagrin:

> And in a minute the loudest Yankee voice I ever heard in my life yells out, "OE'm Pop-OE the Sailor-r-r-r Ma-a-an!" and then somebody jumps up and down in the upstairs hall. In another second the house would of fallen down.

The humor in this passage is, of course, more devastating when read in the context of the story as a whole. But even out of context, the comedy is evident: the false gentility behind the narrator's unwillingness to say that Shirley-T is *retarded;* her silent miming of the child as if the reader could see the face she makes; the unexpected demonstration of Shirley-T's vocal talents. Having refused to apologize to Stella-Rondo, the narrator returns to the kitchen "helpless" to defend herself.

> So that made Mama, Papa-Daddy and the baby all on Stella-Rondo's side.
> Next, Uncle Rondo.
> I must say that Uncle Rondo has been marvellous to me at various times in the past and I was completely unprepared to be made to jump out of my skin, the way it turned out.

The narrator then relates the events that led Uncle Rondo to throw firecrackers into her bedroom. And the cycle of revenge continues in its petty and comic way.

In "The Death of Sun," a story tragic in its implication, dialogue provides moments of comic relief beginning with the conversation between Mary-Forge and the Indian students, and including the absurdist discussion between Ira Osmun and Drago that leads to the gunner's being pushed from the helicopter. Here word play abounds, including puns. A portion of dialogue will have to suffice for the whole of this rather extended narrative segment:

> The Indians on the ground were amazed to see the white man come down. Another Dropout. "Poor old Wilson Drago. We knew him well. Another man who couldn't take progress—civilization."

The conversation continues as the Indians look at what remains of Drago's body:

"The last time I saw him drunk in Gallup I thought he was coming apart, but this is a surprise."

"I knew he had it in him, but I never expected it to come out all at once."

"I can't find his scalp. What do you suppose he did with it? Did he hide it?"

The literal truth expressed in figurative and comic language brings up another point about comedy—that it often conceals the truth.

Wit is akin to comedy but is more allied with wisdom or the intellect than to the physical. The humor in "The Only Way to Make It in New York," "The Story-Teller" and "The Death of Sun" is both physical and intellectual, bearing out the truth of the observation that humor is nature, while wit is art—or to quote from Alexander Pope again: "True wit is nature to advantage dressed, what oft was thought, but ne'er so well express'd." The dialogue in these three stories is skillful, employing puns, epigrams, words that have different (and usually opposing) meanings for speaker and listener, allusions, and keen and incisive phraseology. Other stories in which wit contributes to meaning and to the story's corroboration of everyday actuality include "You Were Perfectly Fine," "The Girl Who Sang With the Beatles," "A Scandal in Bohemia," and "The Jewels of the Cabots."

Another characteristic of comedy—probably revealed in this discussion—is that it resists analysis. Gloom and misery are more easily dissectible. In fact, they seem to spread and deepen and become even gloomier when analyzed, while the comic spirit seems to dissipate into airy nothingness and even to disappear. Another problem with stories intended as humorous is that they either are trivial or appear to be trivial when compared to "serious" stories. "You Were Perfectly Fine" *is* trivial compared with "Babylon Revisited." But certainly, in this anthology as in our lives, we need the comic voice regardless of how lightweight, ephemeral, and faddish it may be. Gloom and misery are not everywhere despite their seeming pervasiveness in the modern short story.

THE LONELY VOICE

In *The Lonely Voice: A Study of the Short Story,* Frank O'Connor contends that the short story reveals "an intense awareness of human loneliness," that while the novel adheres "to the classical concept of civilized society, of man as an animal who lives in a community, . . . the short story remains by its very nature remote from the community—romantic, individualistic, and intransigent." Although the stories in this collection occur within a generalized social context, many convey little sense of community—that is, of a group of individuals related to each other by common interests, working for a common good. For example, the drama of the protagonist's struggle in "The Waste Land" is more terrifying because of his aloneness. Similarly, Sanchez's great capacity for love is made more poignant because of his isolation from the other inhabitants of Twin Pines: "Though the town would never accept them as equals, it came that summer to tolerate their presence." To know that you are tolerated rather than accepted is a harsh and lonely truth.

In "The Girl Who Sang With the Beatles," Larry and Cynthia's relationship to New York City is limited to its commercial aspects: bars, the Orpheum theater, Radio City Music Hall, Basin Street. The headphones Larry buys for Cynthia and for himself represent their estrangement not only from each other but from other people. Cynthia's fantasy that she is the fifth Beatle is not only a retreat from reality but from her husband. Later, by joining her fantasy world, Larry aligns himself with his wife once again but symbolically suggests their mutual withdrawal from the outside world.

In stories that do convey a sense of community, the protagonist frequently stands at odds to it rather than at one within it. In "Lappin and Lapinova," for example, Rosalind's marriage to Ernest Thorburn provides a "community," but she is an outsider to her husband's family:

> She felt bitterly that she was an only child and an orphan at that; a mere drop among all those Thorburns assembled in the great drawing-room with the shiny satin wallpaper and the lustrous family portraits. The living Thorburns much resembled the painted; save that instead of painted lips they had real lips; out of which came jokes; jokes about schoolrooms, and how they had pulled the chair from under the governess; jokes about . . . .

Rosalind's reaction to her psychological alienation is to create a fantasy world in which Ernest is King Lappin, a bold rabbit with great skill as a hunter; she is Queen Lapinova, a small, silver-gray hare. Lappin's domain is "the busy world of rabbits"; Rosalind's territory, which she roams "mostly by moonlight," is mysterious and desolate. Their fantasy allows the young couple to possess

> a private world, inhabited, save for the one white hare, entirely by rabbits. No one guessed that there was such a place, and that of course made it all the more amusing. It made them feel, more even than most young married couples, in league together against the rest of the world. . . . Without that world, how, Rosalind wondered, that winter could she have lived at all?

In time, the fantasy of King Lappin and Queen Lapinova collapses, but it had become so woven into Rosalind's actual marriage and so compelling as a private world that its demise signals "the end of that marriage."

In part, the brevity of the short story accounts for the writer's neglect of community. Describing the short-story writer, Frank O'Connor observes, "Because his frame of reference can never be the totality of a human life, he must be forever selecting the point at which he can approach it, and each selection he makes contains the possibility of a new form as well as the possibility of a complete fiasco." The use of inside points of view also contributes to the absence of community, to the "lonely voice" of the short story. The dramatized narrator or the third-person subjective narrator underscores the selectivity of the writer's vision by remaining inside the consciousness of a single character and, often, within a single physical space. "Old Love" provides a good illustration. By letting us see the world through Harry Bendiner's eyes, we experience his loneliness, his temporary release from it, and his inevitable return to a solitary existence. The choice of point of view is a substantiation of Harry's alienation: the reader knows that Harry's frail health will not permit his traveling to find the woman's daughter, and that once the old man acknowledges the impossibility of his "adventurous idea," he must resign himself to meditate alone "on why a man is born and why he must die."

In still another way, the absence of community in the short story explains the relative scarcity of comic stories in modern literature. If laughter needs an echo, community is its sounding board. This point is well illustrated by "Spotted Horses." For it is the sense of community that heightens the humorous action of that comic yarn. Through his narrator, Faulkner links past with present, supplying a partial history of Flem Snopes (in this instance, Flem's first appearance as Jody Varner's clerk):

> One morning about ten years ago, the boys was just getting settled down on Varner's porch for a little talk and tobacco, when here come Flem out from behind the counter, with his coat off and his hair all parted, like he might have been clerking for Varner for ten years already. Folks all knowed him; it was a big family of them about five miles down the bottom. That year, at least. Share-cropping. They never stayed on any place over a year.

Further, the characters in the story *act* as members of a community. They are knowledgeable about each other's present activities and concerned for each other's welfare, even for someone as doltish as Henry Armstid. In the sense that the community as a whole is duped by Flem, the jokes—the "deals" that he pulls—are at the expense of the community at large. As a group, the "boys" on Varner's porch can laugh at their own collective naiveté and stupidity in being, forever, the hapless victims of Flem's schemes. The comic action is played against this recognition and thereby heightened. A recognizable social milieu affords an enclosure for an isolated action that gives the action something to bounce against. By being greater than the characters and events of the story, such a frame of reference offers a necessary sense of resonance.

The absence of laughter or laughter-producing situations in contemporary short stories is not surprising, for laughter implies superiority: we frequently laugh *at* something—at incongruity, distortion, or repetition. In the main, however, not only do we find ourselves sympathetic to most of the characters in these stories but we also sense that the authors themselves view their characters sympathetically, having created them out of respect and concern. For it is through the fictional personages that the author represents the profundity and baffling complexity of human experience. Even when there are moments of comedy, as in "The Death of Sun," there is often the larger vein of concern—of awareness of the moral ambiguities of society, or of impending disaster, rendering the comedy subordinate to the tragic implications of the cumulative action.

The content of contemporary experience, too, militates against laughter. The fragmentary nature of existence means that readers do not bring to fiction a shared body of experiences and values that would provide an implicit sounding board. Also, the post-Hiroshima world—the world reflected and refracted in many of these stories—is not a pervasively joyous place. Buchenwald, Hiroshima, the Berlin Wall, Dallas-Memphis-Los Angeles, Watergate, stand as natural symbols of the post-World War II world. What they suggest is horrifying and, because they share a fundamental irrationality, absurd.

Yet the reader must not confuse the "lonely voice" of the short story with nihilism. Stories like "The Death of Sun" do not represent a death of the human spirit but a questioning of it—a dramatization of where human beings have been and the marks they have left. Even the ending of this story is reasonably optimistic, for Sun has been replaced by Star—an eagle that

> sailed in one beginning night to reclaim the country of Sun. . . . Then he, the great eagle Star, settled on his throne aerie in awful and mimic splendor, and again admonitory, serene—regal and doomed?

Doomed? Perhaps not—not, at least, if human beings submit to the continuity and balance of life implicit in the natural order. Although readers may initially decide that despair is the dominant tone of many stories in this collection, they will discover that this response is simplistic, for the tones of serious fiction are rich and complex, signifying most often not negation but an affirmation of life.

SYMPATHY AND ESTHETIC DISTANCE

A strong emotive appeal of fiction derives from the reader's sympathetic involvement with the characters. In general, *sympathy* depends on identification. We sympathize with characters when we understand why they behave as they do and when, by displaying traits that resemble our own or those of acquaintances, they stir our sense of what it is to be human. Because the writer is able to manipulate our sympathies to accord with personal attitudes and feelings about the characters, sympathy is linked with tone. For by recognizing those characters with whom the writer *wants* us to sympathize, we gain insight into the author's implicit evaluation of the subject.

Sympathy is closely related to point of view and to open and closed consciousnesses. Since we tend to sympathize with the characters whom we know best, the author controls our sympathies by allowing us to see into the minds of certain characters and by excluding us from the consciousnesses of others. For example, by revealing "Babylon Revisited" through the consciousness of Charlie Wales, F. Scott Fitzgerald makes sure that we align ourselves with Wales. Had Fitzgerald opened or revealed the consciousnesses of Marion Peters, of the bartender at the Ritz, or of Lorraine Quarrles, we would not only be separated from Charlie but forced to view him in a less favorable light. Certainly, any other perspective or any combination of perspectives would weaken our belief in his moral reform. Because the action comes to us through Charlie's perceptions, we admire his lonely battle to regain custody of his daughter, and we hope that Marion will forgive him for his dissolute behavior in the past. Wayne C. Booth's discussion of John Marcher in Henry James' story "The Beast in the Jungle" is enlightening: "By seeing the whole thing through the isolated sufferer's vision we are forced to feel it through his heart. And it is our sense of his isolation, of vulnerability in a world where no one can set him straight, that contributes most to this sympathy."

Closely allied to sympathy is the concept of *esthetic distance*: the degree to which the writer succeeds in objectifying an experience or emotion in a story, and the degree to which the reader is separated from the narrative. To be successful, the writer must use the technical devices that allow experience to be turned into "achieved content." For example, from many of F. Scott Fitzgerald's stories and articles, we learn that he shared some of Charlie Wales' weaknesses and experiences. Like his protagonist, Scott and Zelda Fitzgerald lived in Paris in the 1920s; like Charlie and Helen, the Fitzgeralds drank heavily and partied frequently—squandering money and time and talent. In "Babylon Revisited," Lorraine Quarrles sends Charlie a note in which she recalls two drunken escapades:

> "We *did* have such good times that crazy spring, like the night you and I stole the butcher's tricycle, and the time we tried to call on the president and you had the old derby rim and the wire cane."

Charlie's initial response to the note is "one of awe that he had actually, in his mature years, stolen a tricycle and pedaled Lorraine all over the Étoile between the small hours and dawn." In *Exiles from Paradise,* Sara Mayfield's biography of Fitzgerald, she recounts a brief visit to Paris where she met

> two friends of the Fitzgeralds who had been to Ciro's with them the night before and were frank to say that if you got involved with them these days you did so at your own peril. Scott had ended the evening by taking a baker boy's tricycle and pedaling up and down the Champs Elysées, thwacking with a long loaf of bread the gold-braided Russian doormen in front of the night clubs. . . .

There are differences, of course, between Fitzgerald and his characters. Zelda did not die in the months following the Wall Street crash of 1929, although her neurosis intensified during their prolonged visits to Paris, causing her to enter a sanitarium in April 1930. From that point on, she was in and out of sanitariums for the remainder of her life. Unlike Charlie Wales, Fitzgerald did not lose custody of his only child, a daughter; but he feared that his wife's family might initiate such an action. Also, since Fitzgerald was a writer and not a businessman, he was not hurt financially by the crash. But he has Wales admit that although he lost a lot of money in the crash, he had lost everything he wanted in the boom years:

> Again the memory of those days swept over him like a nightmare—the people they had met travelling; then people who couldn't add a row of figures or speak a coherent sentence.

In "Echoes of the Jazz Age," Fitzgerald expresses a similar sentiment. After describing the violent deaths of several friends, he explains: "These are not catastrophes that I went out of my way to look for—these were my friends; moreover, these things happened not during the depression but during the boom."

From the standpoint of the story a key question is whether Fitzgerald, as a writer of fiction, was able to give his own experiences and emotions an objective, esthetic form. If there is too little esthetic distance between the author and his or her story, the effect of the story as an art form is diminished—the author's subjectivity muddies the tone and distorts the meaning. Most critics agree that in "Babylon Revisited" Fitzgerald transformed portions of autobiography into a short story remarkable for its truthfulness and artistry.

The second aspect of esthetic distance (sometimes identified separately as psychic distance) concerns the separation between the reader and the narrative and the degree of involvement that a writer wishes to elicit from the reader. These considerations include the problem of "over-distancing" and "under-distancing"—highly personal relationships that vary among readers according to their experiences, attitudes, and sensitivity to the nature of narrative art. *Over-distancing* occurs when the reader cannot identify with the story. If the work seems improbable, trivial, antithetical to personal values, or too erudite in its allusions or too convoluted in its form, the reader will stand at too great a distance from it and be unaffected, finding the story "meaningless" or "weird." Possibly "You Were Perfectly Fine," "The Only Way to Make It in New York," or "The Death of Sun" could have this effect on some readers, who might find the language too artificial, the characters too neurotic or "unreal," and the action too bizarre to allow identification.

Under-distancing occurs when the reader becomes too emotionally involved in the work—too subjectively enmeshed in the action and characters to respond esthetically. The narrative is not viewed as a work of art. In all probability, a reader familiar with Philip Roth's life may not recognize that the childhood created in "'I Always Wanted You to Admire my Fasting'" is fiction. If so, part of the story's meaning will be lost. Similarly, readers must recognize that "The Oranging of America" is fiction and not fact. The meaning of the story lies in its being pseudo-history—in its content deriving "entirely from Max Apple's imagination," as a disclaimer at the end of the story verifies. Over-distancing and under-distancing are related to tone: if readers are too removed from a story, they may miss its underlying attitudes and significance; and if esthetic distance is too slight, readers may lose themselves in the work for their own reasons.

Point of view affects both kinds of esthetic distance. Some points of view make it relatively easy to objectify experiences and emotions—in particular, the effaced narrator permits great objectivity. Similarly, the omniscient narrator allows a detachment that is harder to achieve in stories told from the subjective points of view unless authors dramatize the consciousnesses of characters vastly different from themselves, and very obviously at odds with the norms of the story. Such a work often becomes ironic, as in "Why I live at the P.O." Because inside points of view tend to shorten the distance between the reader and the story, this perspective affects psychic distance by forcing the reader and the story together, especially if the subject matter lends itself to this kind of emotional proximity.

Being able to see beyond subject matter to attitude involves establishing the proper esthetic distance—one that permits enough identification so that the stories have a meaning, yet one that prevents an emotional involvement so subjective that the stories cannot be viewed as art but only as accounts of catastrophe, of breakdowns on a private and public scale, comparable to those reported daily in newspapers and newscasts. That is, the reader must understand that these stories are a representation of life—verbal structures that involve a heightening and a patterning, that permit esthetic pleasure and offer an interpretation of the action they present. As should be evident by now, the serious author is conveying attitudes about life through narrative. This is the province of tone. The most inclusive element of fiction—the one that unifies a work and communicates impressions and attitudes that we are asked to absorb—tone brings the reader closest to grasping the story as a whole.

THE ELEMENTS OF FICTION AS FICTION

In the *Poetics,* Aristotle describes tragedy as being "an imitation, not of men as such, but of action and life, of happiness and misery"; and, for centuries, imitation, or mimesis, has been as basic to the novel and short story as it has been to drama. Indeed, the contention that a novelist should *show* events or characters in action rather than *tell* us about them stems from a belief in art as mimesis. Mimetic art attempts to hid artists' hands behind their creations and, at the same time, to make the creation disappear as the "life" it represents takes over in our consciousnesses. The conventions of traditional fiction, as represented by the well-made story or novel, aid the writer in achieving this goal: by minimizing the fiction as literary construct they help the writer convince us that we are experiencing "reality."

But some modern writers of fiction want us not only to see their hands at work but to continuously acknowledge their creations as literary fabrications. One way in which they prompt this acknowledgment is by having their works call attention to the fiction-making process itself—either by making the protagonist a very self-conscious writer or by using the elements and process of fiction as subject matter. In *Bech: A Book,* John Updike does both: his hero is a writer who comments frequently on the episodes in which he appears. "I wonder if it *is* me, enough me, purely me," the fictional Bech complains to Updike:

> My childhood seems out of Alex Portnoy and my ancestral past out of I. B. Singer, I get a whiff of Malamud in your city breezes, and am I paranoid to feel my "block" an ignoble version of the more or less noble renunciations of H. Roth, D. Fuchs, and J. Salinger? Withal, something Waspish, theological, scared, and insulatingly ironical that derives, my wild surmise is, from you.

Characters in conventional fiction almost never call attention to themselves as invented personages; indeed, the author's intention ordinarily is to convince us of the reality of the characters—not to remind us that they are inventions. By reversing these conventional principles in *Bech: A Book,* Updike undercuts its fiction as mimesis. In varying degrees, all the stories in this section contain assaults on illusion, the most deliberately anti-realist being "The World War I Los Angeles Airplane," "Uncle Tom's Cabin: Alternate Ending," "Continuity of Parks," "Sentence," and "I Am Donald Barthelme."

The attack on illusion is nothing new to fiction. Homer's audience in ancient Greece may have viewed Odysseus's encounter with the Cyclops not as history but as metaphor, as mentioned earlier in this introduction. In *The Thousand Nights and a Night* the illusion of reality so carefully evoked by Scheherazade to engage the imagination of the king is broken by the interruption that ends each night's storytelling. Beast fables are not realistic. Neither is the fairy tale. And from the first, the novel has called attention to itself as fiction. *Don Quixote* (1605) pretends to be a translation from the historian Cid Hamete Benengeli and to depict the adventures of an actual knight, but the subject matter of Cervantes's novel is actually other books—in this instance the "vain and empty books of chivalry" so popular in his day. The great eighteenth-century writers—most notably Henry Fielding and Lawrence Sterne—wrote anti-realist fiction; Fielding's *Joseph Andrews* was conceived as a spoof on Samuel Richardson's *Pamela* and Sterne's *Tristram Shandy* is full of devices that call attention to the author and to the fiction as artifice. And despite the brilliance of characterization in Thackeray's *Vanity Fair* (1847) and the vividness of scenes like the ball that preceded the Battle of Waterloo, the author intrudes frequently into the novel, disrupting the narrative flow:

> But as we are to see a great deal of Amelia, there is no harm in saying, at the outset of our acquaintance, that she was a dear little creature; and a great mercy it is, both in life and in novels, which (and the latter especially) abound in villains of the most sombre sort, that we are to have for a constant companion, so guileless

and good-natured a person. As she is not a heroine, there is no need to describe her person. . . .

Although Thackeray's purpose was to write a realistic novel of manners about upper-middle-class London society, his style is as conversational and his observations about individuals as trenchant as those of the eighteenth-century essayists Addison and Steele, his literary forebears. Like all writers, Thackeray is an inheritor, and like them free to use earlier styles and to re-dress old genres in new clothes.

Yet fiction is faddish, even serious fiction; and whether serious or "popular" it is attuned to the marketplace, which itself is attuned to government, science, and industry. Almost all the stories discussed in the previous section are mimetic in that they try to persuade us of the reality of their characters and events—even recent stories like "The Girl Who Sang With the Beatles" and "The Jewels of the Cabots." The explanation for the preponderance of conventional stories over anti-realist short fiction lies partially in history, for the short story came of age during the middle of the nineteenth century—the great period of realism in fiction—in England the age not only of Thackeray but of George Meredith and George Eliot; in America of William Dean Howells, Theodore Dreiser, and Stephen Crane; in France of Honoré de Balzac, Emile Zola, and Gustave Flaubert. And so the short story, which gained respectability as a genre of artistic merit late in the history of fiction, was simply following a literary fashion dictated by the realism of the longer form of the novel.

But while artifice in fiction fell temporarily from grace, art never did—as the many well-made stories in this collection attest. And while the popularity of the short story made it appeal to writers more interested in the money offered by the mass-circulation magazines than by Poe's claim that the story belongs to the "highest region of Art," short fiction survived the hack writers and the formula stories they produced. F. Scott Fitzgerald wrote numerous pot-boilers but he also produced "Babylon Revisited." Other writers like James Joyce refused the easy money of "marketable" fiction and wrote to suit themselves and a small but appreciative group of readers.

In time, the mass-circulation magazines that carried short fiction began to disappear—replaced largely by television, which not only appeals to a mass audience with its formulaic dramatic and comedy series but reproduces reality more immediately, vividly, and believably than fiction can. As a result many writers turned away from the well-made story with its mimetic impulse and began to write deliberately non-mimetic stories.

The stories included in this section comprise only a fraction of either the styles or content of contemporary experimental stories. Each is linked by a common theme—fiction-making: illusion opposed to reality, artifice contrasted with imitation, and with the recognition that these "opposites" are often mutually supportive. Since understanding and analyzing these stories depends on comprehending their subject matter—the nature of fiction—this section can be considered a review of the theory of fiction as well as an introduction to contemporary anti-mimetic fiction.

Although a common thread of reflexivity unites these stories, they none-theless illustrate some of the major types of stories being written by the experimentalists. Not unexpectedly, many of the experimental writers have looked backward, making use of older literary genres. One genre that has been reworked toward contemporary ends is the gothic tale, represented in this collection by Joyce Carol Oates's "The Girl." The tall tale and "put-on" are part of our literary tradition, as Twain's "Journalism in Tennessee" illustrates, but the experimentalists have also enjoyed the put-on—such as Charles Nicol's parody "I Am Donald Barthelme." Some experimentalists have turned to allegory, like LeRoi Jones in "Uncle Tom's Cabin: Alternate Ending." Other contemporary writers have used the materials of modern existence to create myths appropriate to our time and place. Despite the conventionality of technique in "The Oranging of America," Max Apple is reworking ancient myth—the story of Howard Johnson has its roots in the creation myths; and in adding a new mythology to existing legends and stories that concern mortality—the invention of Millie's cryonic vault.

Readers interested in experimental fiction should explore the writing of Vladimir Nabokov, Samuel Beckett, Nathalie Sarraute, Alain Robbe-Grillet, Italo Calvino, John Fowles, John Hawkes, William Gass, Heinrich Böll, Robert Coover, Stanley Elkin, Cynthia Ozick, Kurt Vonnegut, Jr., Ishmael Reed, and John Gardner. But the stories represented here should serve as a challenging introduction to fiction that is experimental in technique.

Since the techniques of conventional fiction appear—however hidden and distorted—in the fiction of the experimentalists, the elements of the well-made story will be discussed again—but this time, only as they relate to experimental writing. Experimental stories are neither better than nor inferior to well-made stories. Experimental stories are only *different* from fiction that places more emphasis on mimesis—and not always even radically different.

Point of View

Consistency of point of view is basic to fiction in which mimesis is accorded a high value. Violations of the established point of view call attention to themselves and therefore disrupt the illusion that we are experiencing reality. Indeed, in realistic fiction we admire an author's ability to conceal himself or herself in a narrator and the narrator's "ability" to conceal himself in the character (by adopting the character's perspective, idiom, and so on). These disappearances aid our suspension of disbelief by allowing us to overlook the story as fabrication. Therefore, writers who want us to be consciously aware of their fiction as a made object are likely to deny the convention and fashion a narrator who is both noticeable and inconsistent. In portions of "Lost in the Funhouse," John Barth appears to have created an omniscient narrator; in fact, his recounting of history is stylistically similar to the brief history of the Massachusetts Bay Colony summarized in "My Kinsman, Major Molineux." Eventually, however, as the clues in Barth's story become clearer, we realize that

Ambrose is a dramatized narrator telling his own story in the third person and, in the process, using and discussing the conventions of traditional fiction— including that of the omniscient narrator.

The narrative voice of "Uncle Tom's Cabin: Alternate Ending" is varied and complex. At first the narrator stands apart from the teacher: the boy's answer "seemed to irritate Miss Orbach." But in the second paragraph the narrator moves inside the teacher's consciousness only to return to an omniscient point of view in the third paragraph ("Ellen, Eileen, Evelyn . . . Orbach. She could be any of them. Her personality was one of theirs."), and then, in that same paragraph, to let us into the consciousness of the schoolteacher once again:

> She would have loved to do something really dirty. But nothing she had ever heard of was dirty enough. So she contented herself with good, i.e., purity, as a refuge from mediocrity.

At other times the narrative voice becomes self-consciously epigrammatic. Later in the story the point of view switches to the first person:

> I would have said "No, boy, shut up and sit down. You are wrong. You don't know anything. Get out of here and be very quick. Have you no idea what you're getting involved in? My God . . . you nigger, get out of here and save yourself, while there's time. Now beat it." But those people had already been convinced.

After which the omniscient narrator reappears—this time in a parenthetical statement:

> [The psychological and the social. The spiritual and the practical. Keep them together and you profit, maybe, someday, come out on top. Separate them, and you go along the road to the commonest of Hells. The one we westerners love to try to make art out of.]

The constant switching of narrative voice breaks the illusion of reality, so that the story is to be interpreted not as an imitation of a single action but as a parable or allegory about the complex relationship between blacks and whites in our society.

Many experimentalists favor the first-person narrator, who appears in "The World War I Los Angeles Airplane," "A Conversation With My Father," "Sentence," "I Am Donald Barthelme," and "The Girl." The drama in "The Girl" is that of the narrator's consciousness. "'Place the center of the subject in the young woman's own consciousness,'" Henry James wrote, "'and you get as interesting and as beautiful a difficulty as you could wish.'" Joyce Carol Oates followed James' advice but employed a significant variation; instead of using a third-person "reflector," she used the first-person narrator's consciousness. But the girl is incapable of telling her story in a way that is either straightforward or reliable. The traumatic events she tries to describe are almost inaccessible to her conscious mind and therefore to the reader. It is as though she were a witness rather than a victim of the brutalizing experience she attempts to reconstruct. The following passage is typical of the fragmented quality of the narrative voice in this story:

> Came by with a truck, The Director and Roybay and a boy I didn't know. Roybay leaned out the window, very friendly. I got in and we drove around for a while. The Director telling us about his movie-vision, all speeded-up because his friend, his contact, had lent him the equipment from an educational film company in town, and it had to be back Sunday P.M. The Director said: "It's all a matter of art and compromise." He was very excited. I knew him from before, a few days before; his name was DePinto or DeLino, something strange, but he was called The Director. He was in the third person most of the time.

The fact that the violence is implied rather than described in literal detail makes its viciousness incredibly dramatic.

"Sentence" is an extended monologue—a direct address to the reader. The narrator in this story is a voice using the editorial *we,* addressing the reader as *you,* and referring to himself as *I:*

> even though it is true that in our young manhood we were taught that short, punchy sentences were best (but what did he mean? doesn't 'punchy' mean punch-drunk? I think he probably intended to say "short, *punching* sentences," meaning sentences that lashed out at you, bloodying your brain if possible, and looking up the word just now I came across the nearby "punkah," which is a large fan suspended from the ceiling in India, operated by an attendant pulling a rope—that is what I want for my sentence, to keep it cool!) we are mature enough now to stand the shock of learning that much of what we were taught in our youth was wrong, or improperly understood by those who were teaching it . . .

Throughout the story the voice speaks to us in this fashion—revealing his thoughts and associations and feelings as they come into his consciousness; as such he is the accumulation of the words that he uses. Carried to its furthest extreme, the narrator *is* the sentence itself.

Various writers, including Alain Robbe-Grillet and Nathalie Sarraute, have argued that the concept of character in contemporary fiction is outmoded and that great novels of character, such as *Anna Karenina* or *Madame Bovary,* belong to an earlier age—to an age when individualism as a philosophy was historically valid. John Barth acknowledges that in a mass society "the novel of character is a kind of anachronism." His solution is to use the first person, as he tells Joe David Bellamy in *The New Fiction:*

> You and I still imagine ourselves to be characters, and our lives are influenced by other people around us whom we see as characters and our relations to whom we perceive in a dramatic, in a dramatical, way. . . . Now, if you write a novel with an "I" narrator, none of these things that Robbe-Grillet objects to as being obsolete or

anarchonistic can be charged against the *author,* because they only reflect the anachronistic presuppositions of a first-person narrator, who is no more responsible for them than the rest of us are as we go through our lives.

Barth's explanation may well explain the prevalence of first-person narration not only in the work of the experimentalists but in the fiction of other contemporary writers as well. Certainly the dramatized narrator allows Joyce Carol Oates and Grace Paley to write stories in which character is central to the emotional and conceptual meaning of their fiction.

Characters

In Grace Paley's "A Conversation With My Father," the first-person narrator and her father talk about storytelling. Fiction takes its impulse from life, so their conversation reveals contrasting views on the meaning of human existence. Their gentle conflict stems from the father's recognition of his impending death and his daughter's unwillingness to look "tragedy . . . in the face." Their disagreement about storytelling comes from the father's preference for conventional fiction and the daughter's insistence on another kind of realism. The old man, bed-ridden but alert mentally, asks his daughter

> "to write a simple story just once more . . . the kind de Maupassant wrote, or Chekhov, the kind you used to write. Just recognizable people and then write down what happened to them next."

The daughter obliges her father and constructs a well-made story based on an actual occurrence. But the father objects to its brevity and to what has been omitted. "You left everything out. Turgenev wouldn't do that. Chekhov wouldn't do that." The old man wants to know what the characters look like and what their backgrounds are:

> "What were her parents like, her stock? That she became such a person. It's interesting, you know."
> "From out of town. Professional people. The first to be divorced in the county. How's that? Enough?" I asked.
> "With you, it's all a joke," he said. "What about the boy's father? Why didn't you mention him? Who was he? Or was the boy born out of wedlock?"

The questions continue and the narrator supplies descriptions missing from the fiction she has told. She then writes a second longer version, but this reworking also fails to satisfy the old man:

> "Jokes," he said. "As a writer that's your main trouble. You don't want to recognize it. Tragedy! Plain tragedy! Historical tragedy! No hope. The end."

Paley's main purpose is to call attention to the act and art of storytelling, but she also creates a memorable portrait of a proud and independent old man.

> He had been a doctor for a couple of decades and then an artist for a couple of decades and he's still interested in details, craft, technique.

The verbal exchange between father and daughter is eloquent and full of wisdom. Inevitably, the daughter, like her father, must learn to accept the "truth" of human mortality.

The creation of identifiable flesh-and-blood characters is less important in the other experimental stories included here and, in fact, it is antithetical to the meaning of some. In "The World War I Los Angeles Airplane," Brautigan writes about the death of his wife's father. The first-person narrator tells the reader that he has done "a lot of thinking about what his death means to all of us." Yet the story offers no explanation of the death—only a presentation of events in a man's life. The social and physical mobility of the man and the role of chance give his life a typicalness. The numbered series of events fails to explain the significance of a man's life. Obviously, Brautigan's intention was not to create a round character but a symbolic one. By reducing the fullness of a human life to an outline, the narrator's father-in-law appears as a prototypical American, a contemporary Everyman.

In "The Girl," characterization is deliberately vague. Characters are identified in the girl's mind by the parts they play in the film: the Director, the Motorcyclist, the Cop. Biographical information is blurred and ambiguous. The girl refers to Roybay as "my closest friend of all of them" but admits later that perhaps his name was Robbie, or maybe Roy Bean, or "sometimes just Roy or Ray. Said he came over from Trinidad, Colorado—I think. Or someone else his size said that, some other day." She admits that she could describe the Santa Monica Freeway better than the men who had beaten her. The fuzziness of characterization contributes to the impersonality of the violence. To the girl, the violence and degradation are justified by the act of film-making, which takes precedence over everything else; the director's vision, distorted and perverted, transcends and justifies the cruel reality. By withholding biographical information and by telling the story through the girl's narrative perspective, Oates dramatizes the absence of cause-and-effect relationships, the randomness of violence, the casualness of meetings with strangers, and the near tragic endings such meetings may have.

The principal character of "Sentence" is also a first-person narrator, but he is a "voice" rather than a flesh-and-blood character. We learn about some of his activities and preferences—floating sheets of Reynolds Wrap around the room, listening to FM radio, inventing fantastic stories—but if he engages our sympathy at all it is because his predicament makes a comment on a pattern of contemporary urban life. "I Am Donald Barthelme" is not only a parody of a Donald Barthelme story but a spoof on the "real-life" author. Like the narrator of "Sentence," the first-person narrator in Nicol's story is a voice who claims to be the genuine Donald Barthelme because of his spiritual affinity with the Barthelme stories he has read. Disproving the claims of spurious Barthelmes, the narrator establishes his own "identity" in a parodic story that is a tribute to the real-life author.

In "Uncle Tom's Cabin: Alternate Ending," Jones' many-faceted narrators describe characters who are representative types: the upwardly mobile black family, the repressed white teacher, the "exotically liberal" female principal. The author provides enough details so that his fictional personages are realistic, but they resemble the Characters of Theophrastus and Addison more than they do the round characters of mimetic fiction.

The creation of unrealistic fictional characters is not the exclusive province of contemporary experimental writers, as Aesop's and Thurber's beast fables illustrate. Talking birds and animals have always been part of the fairy tale. And, as in "A Conversation With My Father," the characters of antimimetic fiction may be identifiable as flesh-and-blood creations. But when writers give up sympathetic, round characters with whom the reader can identify in favor of nonrealistic characters, they are relinquishing pathos, a dependable ingredient in most successful conventional stories. Much of learning what experimental fiction is about concerns discovering what its authors have chosen as substitutes for proven ingredients.

Plot, Form, and Time

The "simple story" requested by the father in "A Conversation With My Father" requires not only "recognizable people" but a clearly defined beginning, middle, and end. Although the narrator dislikes the causality inherent in writing "what happened to them next," she wants to please her father:

> I *would* like to try to tell such a story, if he means the kind that begins: "There was a woman . . ." followed by plot, the absolute line between two points which I've always despised. Not for literary reasons, but because it takes all hope away. Everyone, real or invented, deserves the open destiny of life.

The significance the father places on believable characters supports not only his preference for conventional fiction but a view of life in which character *is* destiny. Accordingly, the father sees the woman's life in his daughter's story as fixed in place and refuses to accept a second, more optimistic, ending that reflects her belief in an "open destiny." Two views of fiction, two views of "why a man is born and why he must die."

Like Grace Paley, most experimental writers opt for stories in which form and time are more significant than plot. "The World War I Los Angeles Airplane" treats birth, maturation, and death. But Brautigan's concern is with form rather than plot, as he reveals by his use of a list. The private events of the man's life fuse with public events: World War I, the stock market crash of 1929, the Depression, the rise of the automobile industry, the advent of afternoon television. But the effect of the public events is not analyzed, only itemized; the meaning of the private events is unexplored. The causality of plot is missing:

> 32. Once he had been followed by a rainbow across the skies of France while flying a World War I airplane carrying bombs and machine guns.
> 33. "Your father died this afternoon."

Item number thirty-three returns the reader to the opening sentence of the story and, by so doing, emphasizes cyclicalness rather than progression.

The plot of "Sentence" is the construction of a sentence. But notice that Barthelme's story begins in the middle: the first word, *or,* is a coordinating conjunction suggesting grammatically that something has gone before. And the story ends without a period, suggesting an infinite continuance. "Sentence" does contain action of sorts; there are digressions and conjectures and even a description of a woman whom the narrator examines as though he were a doctor in a Marx Brothers movie, but the events are clearly the narrator's thoughts as he constructs a story that has modern life as its referent but fiction-making as its subject.

While Barthelme uses the construction of a sentence as subject matter, Julio Cortazar uses plot as content. The plot of "Continuity of Parks" brings the reader directly into the problem of the story's meaning. Does the action the man reads about in the novel occur to him in real life? Or are the events in the novel so vividly depicted that they take on a life in his imagination, thus blurring the distinction between the vicarious experience of reading and the physical reality of actual events? The title supports both possibilities. The simpler explanation is that the facts of fiction fuse into the facts of everyday life—so that the "park" described in the novel becomes the park depicted in the short story, and the man who is reading is the murderer's victim.

Without plot to lend narrative causality, the form of many experimental stories comes from other elements: from diction, imagery, syntax, irony, and tone; from an intuitive "felt" patterning; from a sensibility that shapes the whole; from the story's calling attention to itself. By not involving us in action that purports to be a representation of life and by not arousing our curiosity about what happens next, the writer relinquishes elements of conventional fiction that appeal to most readers. For physical action, the experimental writer often substitutes philosophical conjecture or psychological repercussions; for surprise and explanation, the itemization of a man's life into thirty-three events; for "realistic" action we often get allegory, as in "Uncle Tom's Cabin: Alternate Ending"; and instead of causality, the illogic of "Sentence" and the playfulness of "I Am Donald Barthelme."

Perhaps plot in the sense of destiny belongs to an earlier age when people could see life steadily and see it whole—to a period represented by the father in

Grace Paley's story in which character was a strong determiner of action and therefore of fate. But action, however nonphysical and altered in appearance, and time, however curiously arranged, are staple ingredients of all fiction— conventional or experimental.

Setting

Since the characters in experimental fiction are not obliged to be believable, the settings in which they are placed need not enhance their credibility. And most often they do not. In "Continuity of Parks," however, the realistically described setting makes the transition from fiction into actuality believable. Or, if the experiences of the man in that story are only vicarious, the specifically described setting makes his imaginative involvement plausible. In "Uncle Tom's Cabin: Alternate Ending," the fifth-grade classroom "in a grim industrial complex of northeastern America; about 1942" makes credible not only the literal events in the story but their social and symbolic significance.

The setting of "The Girl" merges effortlessly into the action of the story. In the popular imagination California and the movie culture are one. The girl seems to fit the stereotype of "the California girl" perpetuated by advertisers, television, and the movies:

> The Director said: "Oh Jesus honey your tan, your tanned legs, your feet, my God even your feet your toes, are tan, tanned, you're so lovely. . . ."

The particular beach used as location for the film is unimportant to the girl. She is asked:

> "Which stretch of beach? Where? How far up the coast? Can't you identify it, can't you remember? We need your cooperation, can't you cooperate?"
> On film, any stretch of beach resembles any stretch of beach. They called it The Beach.

The anonymity of place corresponds to the namelessness of the characters and the girl's inability to remember the specific violence of the action. Moreover, to The Director, the deserted beach is upsetting; the rocks and dunes "'hobbling to the eye'":

> He had wanted the movie to take place in the real world. "Really wanted Venice Beach on a Sunday, packed, but room for the motorcycle, and the whole world crowded in . . . a miscellaneous flood of people, souls, to represent the entire world. . . ."

The natural innocence and beauty of the beach contrasts with the perverseness of The Director's "vision."

"The World War I Los Angeles Airplane" is also set in California—at least the beginning and conclusion. But the man's life has the mobility of place and occupation so indigenous to America: a farm in South Dakota, Europe during World War I, a sheep ranch in Idaho, and then California where he moved in the midst of the Depression. His last job was as a school janitor, and after retirement he became a sweet-wine alcoholic:

> 30. He used sweet wine in place of life because he didn't have any more life to use.
> 31. He watched afternoon television.

The physical setting for "A Conversation With My Father" is unimportant. The story is set in the house of a parent, so there is an intimacy that the usual sequestering of an invalid in a hospital room would have vitiated. But the real setting of this story, as in "Sentence" and "I Am Donald Barthelme," is the stage of the mind. It is there the jokes are spun, the speculations raised, the cries let loose, the battles fought, and the stories told.

In experimental writing, as in all fiction, the setting should match the characters and action. In some stories, the match is good if the setting initiates some of the action, as in "Uncle Tom's Cabin: Alternate Ending." In stories with overt physical action, setting serves a double purpose if it acts as a symbolic equivalent of the action, as in "The Girl." Minimal physical settings are appropriate when the action is interior, as in "Sentence."

Style

At the conclusion of "Sentence," Barthelme introduces a new character who had been trained as an "expert on sentence construction" at the Bauhaus— an institute established after World War I in Weimar, Germany, for the study of art, design, and architecture. The narrator hopes that Ludwig will use "the improved ways of thinking developed in Weimar" in order "to cure the sentence's sprawl." But the German explains that the Bauhaus is defunct and that he has been "reduced" to writing examination review books for policemen. The meaning of Ludwig's inability to restore the "infected sentence" to health is that the stern functionalism advocated by the Bauhaus is of little use in the eclecticism of the present and to an author like Barthelme. But Ludwig's disappearance "into the history of man-made objects" does serve to remind the narrator and us

> that the sentence itself is a man-made object, not the one we wanted of course, but still a construction of man, a structure to be treasured for its weakness, as opposed to the strength of stones.

"Sentence" is an extravagant collage—a collection of anecdotes, analogies, side-trips, remembrances, puns, doubts, and hopes—strung together so that its rambling self-consciousness reflects the frail stubbornness of the human spirit. "The point of collage," Barthelme has explained,

> is that unlike things are stuck together to make, in the best case, a new reality. This new reality, in the best case, may be or imply a comment on the other reality from which it came, and may be also much else. It's an *itself,* if it's successful. . . .*

Applying this description to "Sentence," the reader can infer that "Sentence" is not only a comment on fiction-making but an entity in itself without any outside experiential meaning. The words are meant to be enjoyed for their own peculiar evoking of the way ideas and emotions, events and people tumble into our brains, and for their own sake simply as *words.*

In his novella *Snow White,* Barthelme defends the manufacturing of plastic buffalo humps:

> They are "trash," and what in fact could be more useless or trashlike? It's that we want to be on the leading edge of this trash phenomenon, the everted sphere of the future, and that's why we pay particular attention, too, to those aspects of language that may seem as a model of the trash phenomenon.

"Sentence" is filled with sense and no-sense, with treasures and trash: particularly "trashy" are the doctor-patient scene with the "electric toe caddy" that wards off pneumonia and the "permanent press white hospital gown"; and the scene in which the narrator reflects on the future of his sentence in the "run-mad skimble-skamble of information sickness" and mentions as encouragement to continue "an erotic advertisement which begins, 'How to Make Your Mouth a Blowtorch of Excitement' (but wouldn't that overtax our mouthwashes?)." Experimental writers like Barthelme respond to the unprecedented pervasiveness of the mass culture by syphoning off its energies and gestures; in doing so, they hope to make the popular culture reveal something about itself. This, however, is a very difficult task. Popular culture is a hard act for the fiction writer to follow, particularly when both reader and author are engulfed in it: familiarity tends to breed imperceptiveness; nearness blinds.

In describing how she writes, Joyce Carol Oates has stated:

> At times my head seems crowded; there is a kind of pressure inside it, almost a frightening physical sense of confusion, fullness, dizziness. Strange people appear in my thoughts and define themselves slowly to me: first their faces, then their personalities and quirks and personal histories, then their relationships with other people, who very slowly appear, and a kind of "plot" then becomes clear to me as I figure out how all these people came together and what they are doing.†

A well-made story, like "The Bride Comes to Yellow Sky" is an orderly affair. An experimental story, like "The Girl," is disorderly, or so it seems on the

*Interview in *The New Fiction* by Joe David Bellamy (University of Illinois Press, 1974), pp. 51–52.
†Interview in *The New Fiction,* p. 21.

surface because its order is taken from the girl's fragmented and disturbed consciousness. The story has a specific beginning, middle, and end. But the reader must fit the pieces together in much the same way as the girl does, or as the police and doctors try to do.

Also characteristic of much experimental fiction are frequent and cataclysmic shifts in style and mood, as in "Uncle Tom's Cabin: Alternate Ending." In this story, the style ranges from the literal to the symbolic, from the lyrical to the epigrammatic, from the humorous to the prophetic. Similarly, Brautigan in his itemization of a man's life mixes the lyrical with the flatly realistic. The enchanted moment when a rainbow follows the young aviator "through the skies of France for part of an afternoon" precedes a starkly literal encounter":

> 6. When the war was over he got out a captain and he was traveling on a train through Texas when the middle-aged man sitting next to him and with whom he had been talking for about three hundred miles said, "If I was a young man like you and had a little extra cash, I'd go up to Idaho and start a bank. There's a good future in Idaho banking."
> 7. That's what her father did.

Some experimental writers have adopted the parody—a genre that the experimentalist shares with poets, dramatists, and writers of well-made stories alike. "I am Donald Barthelme" is a parody of not only a Barthelme story but of the many stories written in the manner of Barthelme, who has been described as the most imitated author of our time. The experimentalist often makes the parody extremely complicated, however, as Charles Nicol has done. Nicol's parody does not stop with Barthelme; for in it are the literary tricks and puzzles of Jorge Luis Borges—in particular of "Pierre Menard, Author of the *Quixote*" and "Borges and Myself"—and of Miguel de Cervantes, creator of *Don Quixote*.

Joyce Carol Oates has also borrowed from the past as suggested by the titles of some of her stories. "The Dead," "The Lady With the Pet Dog," and "The Turn of the Screw" are "reimaginings" of famous stories—these being reinventions of stories with the same titles by James Joyce, Anton Chekhov, and Henry James respectively. As she explains, "These stories are meant to be autonomous stories, yet they are also testaments of my love and extreme devotion to these other writers; I imagine a kind of spiritual 'marriage' between myself and them. . . .*

The best fiction has never been formulaic, and it is as easy for an experimental writer to write according to a formula as for the writer of the well-made story. There has been a host of Barthelme imitations, as Charles Nicol's parody makes clear. And, as in every other time and place, writers have reworked the literature of past generations, as Oates has done. But like the truly great writers of the well-made story, the talented experimentalists will separate themselves from their less talented counterparts—from the "spurious" Bar-

*The New Fiction, p. 22.

thelmes. For in experimental writing as elsewhere, style is not decoration: rather, considerations of style lead to examination of the author's underlying attitudes and values, which are the province of tone.

Tone

The most dominant attitude that emerges from the experimental stories collected here is a concern for the elements of fiction and thus for fiction itself, and an accompanying interest in the relation of fiction to life. Writing fiction in the middle of the twentieth century has created special problems, according to Philip Roth:

> The American writer . . . has his hands full in trying to understand, and then describe, and then make *credible* much of the American reality. It stupefies, it sickens, it infuriates, and finally it is even a kind of embarrassment to one's own meager imagination.*

The difficulty for Roth and other contemporary writers has been in fabricating narrative forms capable of serving as fictional equivalents for an actuality that consistently outdoes the talents of the most gifted writer, and a culture that "tosses up figures almost daily that are the envy of any novelist" (Roth). Yet, as stories like "A Conversation With My Father," "Uncle Tom's Cabin: Alternate Ending," "The World War I Los Angeles Airplane," and "Sentence" illustrate, the concern for the elements of fiction is also a concern for life itself. The verbal and structural tricks the experimentalist pulls, the modifications of form, the retelling of old myths and stories, and the reappearance of Gothicism, parody, and fable, should not conceal, for the enlightened reader, the writer's concern for literature as an expression of the intellect and the imagination. Lucian Stryk, editor of *TriQuarterly,* expresses this concept:

> . . . politically man is a beast, incapable of the kind of love leading to universal harmony, yet individually he has it in him to become a saint. Literature, wherever it occurs in the world, is meant not for the political animal but for the human— mostly unhappy, sometimes well disposed, usually hoping for something slightly bigger than himself, the vision of which is offered by, among only a few other things, books. Which are valuable only to the rare, those able to experience in the way that all good things are experienced: with the senses and the engaged imagination.†

The experimentalists' interest in the elements of fiction as fiction has led to a self-consciousness about their craft and their own identities that is not always becoming. But the sin is one of degree rather than kind, for the literature of

*"Writing American Fiction," *Commentary* (March 1961), p. 224.
†*TriQuarterly,* 31, Fall 1974, p. 5.

every age reveals a self-absorption in the craft (Homer in the *Odyssey*) and a self-interest implicit in descriptions of the social organization (the Characters of Theophrastus). Some experimentalists are simply excess.ve in the degree to which they have turned the elements of fiction into the subj:ct of fiction. But we live in a society that is increasingly infatuated with itself and its own processes; the experimentalists, like all artists, are responding to a dominant attitude in the general culture. Where nonfiction uses the survey as mirror, the experimentalist uses the elements of fiction.

Although self-consciousness is a prevailing attitude in these stories, other more traditional attitudes that determine tone in more conventional fiction can also be found: irony ("A Conversation With My Father," and "Uncle Tom's Cabin: Alternate Ending"); cynicism and satire ("Uncle Tom's Cabin: Alternate Ending," "Sentence," and "I Am Donald Barthelme"); the comic voice ("A Conversation With My Father," "Sentence," and "I Am Donald Barthelme"); and the lonely voice ("The World War I Los Angeles Airplane," and "Continuity of Parks").

Experimental stories, as well as conventional fiction, incur problems of sympathy and esthetic distance. The narrator in "Sentence," for example, is so much a voice and so minimally a three-dimensional character that most readers have very little emotional reaction to him although they may experience admiration for the virtuosity of Barthelme's writing. On the other hand, "The Girl," and "A Conversation With My Father" are basically melodramatic; if they had been written more conventionally, the reader could be pulled too closely into the story, at the expense of esthetic distance. In Paley's story, additionally, the general toughness of its prose and the gentle irony of its conversation give the story an insistent philosophical tone that minimizes the possibility of under-distancing.

Another persistent determinant of tone is energy—particularly in "A Conversation With My Father," "The World War I Los Angeles Airplane," and "Sentence." Still another determinant is a sense of honesty or integrity, as in "Uncle Tom's Cabin: Alternate Ending." Jones depicts the McGhee family as being upwardly mobile: Louise McGhee is college educated; Eddie Jr. is intelligent and is treated as an equal by his classmates; the war years had brought prosperity to the

> thriving urban lower middle classes. Postmen's sons and factory-worker debutantes. Making a great run for America, now prosperity and the war had silenced for a time the intelligent cackle of tradition.

Yet the meaning of Jones' story lies in the author's underlying antagonism to the white society and in his belief that American capitalism is doomed to failure. Accordingly blacks, like the McGhee family who were being admitted into the dominant society, "would die when the rest of the dream died not even understanding that they, like Ishmael, should have been the sole survivors. But now they were being tricked." The narrator urges Eddie Jr. and others like him to stop behaving like Uncle Toms and to get out and save themselves when their salvation was still possible. "But those people had already been convinced. Read Booker T. Washington one day, when there's time. What that led to. The 6½'s moved for power . . . and there seemed no other way." The "6½'s" in this story are the Eddie Jrs., who give the correct answers and whose fate is not to question the values of the white society but to join it proudly.

The ending of Harriet Beecher Stowe's *Uncle Tom's Cabin* describes the enlightened George Shelby freeing his slaves. He tells the assembled throng that it was on the grave of Uncle Tom that he resolved, with God as his witness, never to own another slave:

> that nobody, through me, should ever run the risk of being parted from home and friends, and dying on a lonely plantation, as he died. So, when you rejoice in your freedom, think that you owe it to that good old soul, and pay it back in kindness, to his wife and children. Think of your freedom, every time you see Uncle Tom's Cabin; and let it be a memorial to put you all in mind to follow in his steps, and be as honest and faithful and Christian as he was.

The alternate ending of the Jones story describes the school teacher's sudden release from her repression. Hostility toward blacks has been replaced by acceptance; fear by friendship. The story ends:

> When Miss Orbach got to the principal's office and pushed open the door she looked directly into Louise McGhee's large brown eyes, and fell deeply and hopelessly in love.

The ending parallels *Uncle Tom's Cabin*—only this time the position of power has been reversed—at least temporarily, at least in fiction. But neither Louise McGhee nor Miss Orbach—nor by implication the societal groups they represent—is free.

On the whole, experimental stories evince a playfulness noticeably absent in fiction in which the characters and events are closer to "real life" counterparts. Generally, the experimentalist takes pleasure in word games, in verbal jests, in artifices, in imagizing absurdity and then triumphing over it through the form the story takes, as in "Sentence." But playfulness should not disguise seriousness about the life represented in experimental fiction. Nor should it conceal the seriousness of experimentalists toward their craft and the reader's recognition that a story is, after all, the work of a human being, something "to be treasured for its weakness, as opposed to the strength of stones."

The attempt to create new forms and to use old forms in new ways—the hallmark of experimental fiction—is an honorable task. So are the reader's efforts to avoid preconceptions about what fiction should be and to see its possibilities in the strange, if not brave new world of the decades that have followed World War II.

WHAT A STORY IS (AGAIN)

Words as the Base Metal of Fiction

When asked about the subject of a painting, the contemporary nonrepresentational artist often explains that the act of painting is itself the subject of the painting. In the same way, experimental writers often maintain that words are the subject of their stories, novels, or plays. In many experimental plays—such as Harold Pinter's *Old Times,* for example—the action of the drama lies mainly in words; the play itself is not an imitation of action, as in conventional drama. Similarly, in stories like "Sentence," words are what the story is about; the surface of the prose demands attention in the same way that the surface of an abstract painting demands scrutiny—and appreciation. In "Sentence," the careful reader will notice that several transformations occur; the narrator begins by addressing the reader as "you"—a coequal, someone caught as he is in the tentativeness and muted satisfaction of contemporary existence. But then the narrator turns into a weird doctor investigating the mystery of "your smile." The reader-patient engages in a series of mock doctor-patient rituals that end when the doctor asks his patient to "lay down her arms" ·so that he can "lie down in them," and

> permit themselves a bit of the old slap and tickle, she wearing only her Mr. Christopher medal, on its silver chain, and he (for such is the latitude granted the professional classes) worrying about the sentence, about its thin wires of dramatic tension, which have been omitted, about whether we should write down some natural events occurring in the sky (birds, lightning bolts), and about a possible coup d'etat within the sentence, whereby its chief verb would be—but at this moment a messenger rushes into the sentence, bleeding from a hat of thorns he's wearing, and cries out: "You don't know what you're doing! Stop making this sentence, and begin instead to make Moholy-Nagy cocktails, for those are what we really need, on the frontiers of bad behavior!" and then he falls to the floor, and a trap door opens under him. . . .

Following the disappearance of the messenger, the narrator-doctor, having apparently forgotten his reader-patient-girlfriend, imagines

> a better sentence, worthier, more meaningful, like those in the Declaration of Independence . . . a statement summing up the unreasonable demands that you make on life, and one that also asks the question, if you can imagine these demands, why are they not routinely met, tall fool?

But then the narrator acknowledges that his "infected sentence" had not started out to answer that question but to answer "some other query that we shall some day discover the nature of. . . ."

Clearly Barthelme is using language differently from the way Chekhov or contemporary writers such as Eudora Welty or Robert Hemenway use it. A writer like Welty takes full advantage of the symbolic meanings invested in words, while Barthelme and other experimentalists tend to minimize their symbolic value and to use words as self-contained entities that refer inward to the nonaction of the story rather than outward to a physical reality. In "Sentence," the occasional "real life" touches supplied by Barthelme serve mainly to remind us how self-contained the rest of the story is.

In *Snow White,* Barthelme describes the men who live with Snow White as reading

> books that have a lot of *dreck* in them, matter which presents itself as not wholly relevant (or indeed, at all relevant) but which, carefully attended to, can supply a kind of "sense" of what is going on. This "sense" is not to be obtained by reading between the lines (for there is nothing there in those white spaces) but by reading the lines themselves.

Because of its emphasis on "reading the lines themselves," experimental fiction has been described as a return to a more verbal kind of writing. John Barth expresses this concept in "Dunyazadiad" when Scheherazade tells her sister (Dunyazade):

> It's in words that the magic is—Abracadabra, Open Sesame, and the rest—but the magic words in one story aren't magical in the next. The real magic is to understand which words work, and when, and for what; the trick is to learn the trick.

"Dunyazadiad," which Barth subtitles "the second greatest story ever told," is a complicated retelling of *The Thousand Nights and a Night,* in which Barth introduces a twentieth-century counterpart for Scheherazade—a writer of "artful fiction" who bears a physical and spiritual resemblance to the author himself. In Barth's retelling, Scheherazade and the writer-friend conspire to outwit the king, for both understand that the magic of fiction lies in the particular words of a story:

> And those words are made from the letters of our alphabet: a couple-dozen squiggles we can draw with this pen. This is the key, Doony! And the treasure, too, if we can only get our hands on it! It's as if—as if the key to the treasure is the treasure!"

Scheherazade's discovery—that words not only unlock the treasure but are the treasure—lies at the heart of all successful fiction. This is more than saying that form is content or that structure is meaning, because it acknowledges the primitive power of language itself, a power that is particularly important to the experimentalist.

The primacy of words in experimental fiction is enhanced by fiction calling attention to itself as artifice. In a sense, experimental writers are doing what poets have done from time immemorial—they are using the force of words to stimulate the imagination rather than to create replicas of the "real" world. The power of words to engage the imagination in flights of nonmimetic fantasy brings us back to the beginnings of narration: to the legends and myths that attempted to explain such phenomena as the rising of the sun and the quarter-ings of the moon and the strangest creature of the unpeaceable kingdom—the human being, to whom the gift or curse of language was given. It also brings us back to ancient Greece and the oral tradition of epic poetry, to the "earth-minstrel" Demodocos, singing of the great heroes of the Trojan war and causing one of his listeners to weep as he heard the exploits of his life recounted. Barth acknowledges the significance of the oral tradition to storytelling in the Author's Note to *Lost in the Funhouse,* his collection of short stories:

> . . . While some of these pieces were composed expressly for print, others were not. . . . "Night-Sea Journey" was meant for either print or recorded authorial voice, but not for live or non-authorial voice; "Glossolalia" will make no sense unless heard in live or recorded voices, male and female, or read as if so heard; "Echo" is intended for monophonic authorial recording, either disc or tape. . . .

The oral tradition forces us to hear the sound of words, and by paying attention to the sound of words to pay attention to the words themselves. Words are the base metal of all narrative, but to the experimentalist they are the design and patina as well.

The Story as Narration

The magic of words, as Scheherazade observed, is to be found not only in the words themselves but in their juxtaposition, their successiveness, the singu-larity of their placement: "the magic words in one story aren't magical in the next." The selection and arrangement of words in a story lie at the heart of narrative art: "every word *tells,* and there is not a word that does not tell" (Poe). For the nature of fiction is cumulative, words building on words to create mystery or suspense and to bring about "the one preestablished design." As E. M. Forster noted in *Aspects of the Novel:*

> Scheherazade avoided her fate because she knew how to wield the weapon of suspense—the only literary tool that has any effect upon tyrants and savages. Great novelist though she was—exquisite in her descriptions, tolerant in her judgments, ingenious in her incidents, advanced in her morality, vivid in her delineations of character, expert in her knowledge of three Oriental capitals—it was yet on none of these gifts that she relied when trying to save her life. . . . She only survived because she managed to keep the king wondering what would happen next.

As this collection of short stories reveals, however, many writers, both past and present, pay little heed to suspense or to narrative causality—that is, to explaining *why* a specific event occurs. Their interest is on the arrangement of words to create a particular form or design. But the particular conditions of fiction come from its being a temporal art rather than a spatial one. The temporality of narration with its inherent linearity ensures a certain amount of action—even if the action is created only by the movement of words across the printed page.

Another common denominator to the various genres and subgenres of narration is, of course, a narrator. So all stories, no matter how wild or eccentric their form, have narrators that describe events no matter how ambiguous ("The Girl") or how minimal ("The Sentence"). Narration, like all art, has created a set of conditions that writers can adopt literally, or modify, or abuse, or use as subject matter, but never ignore, as even the most unconventional stories illustrate.

In talking about the convolutions and twists of literary fashions, John Barth draws an analogy between painting and photography:

> Just as painting in a certain period of history defines itself against still photography, so it may be that the particular aspects of literature that can't be duplicated in any other medium (especially the cinema), such as its linearity, for example, and its visual verbality, and its translation of all sense stimuli into signs, are precisely the ones that we should pay the most attention to. That is, instead of trying to defeat time . . . perhaps we should *accept* the fact that writing and reading are essentially linear activities and devote our attention as writers to those aspects of experience that can best be rendered linearly . . . instead of trying to force the medium into things that are not congenial to it. I say this with all sorts of reservations, because I *am* interested in formal experimentation.*

Fiction is a congenial and accommodating medium, and some writers will continue to experiment with narrative forms that match the absurdity and nonevents of actuality while others will continue to write stories that use the linearity of fiction in more conventional ways.

Countless readers and writers have found delight and instruction in *The Thousand Nights and a Night.* For Jorge Luis Borges, the particular fascination of this collection of tales comes from the fact that Scheherazade and her sister, who are fictional characters in their own right, become listeners or authors of their own stories. The interplay of the fictional frame with the continuous fictions that Scheherazade invents brings into question the "reality" of the "real" world by reminding us that it may be only a dream, the product of our own invention. Like Borges, Barth's fascination with Scheherazade lies not only in the stories she tells but in her character and situation, for reasons that will be made clear in the following discussion of "Lost in the Funhouse."

---

*The New Fiction, p. 4.

Back to the Beginning

Fiction's journey began, for us, with the story of Odysseus's encounter with the Cyclops and ends with John Barth's story of an American family's excursion to an amusement park. Ambrose, the adolescent protagonist of "Lost in the Funhouse," bears little resemblance to the worldly-wise Odysseus, and Fat May and the funhouse are only mildly terrifying counterparts of the lawless Cyclops and his vast, barbarous cave. But beneath the narrative surface—at the deeper level of structure and myth—Ambrose and Odysseus, Homer and Barth, are separated only by chronology and geography, not by psychology and purpose.

The family outing that is Barth's avowed subject is mundane and identifiable; Ocean City, Maryland, is a 1940s' version of Disney World or Six Flags Over Texas which, in turn, are twentieth-century counterparts of the Oriental bazaar and the Greek and Roman marketplace. The amusement park or bazaar blends entertainment and magic, commercialism and sexuality. Like Odysseus, Ambrose encounters and then rejects sexual involvement. His name links him with the gods of Greek mythology, for ambrosia was the food of the gods and was thought to impart immortality. Like Odysseus, therefore, Ambrose is differentiated from ordinary mortals; yet, like the Greek hero, the adolescent boy is mortal—his character flawed, his fears universal, his ignorance justified by his inexperience. Both protagonists undertake journeys, but Ambrose's journey occupies a single day rather than ten years. And, unlike Odysseus, whose journey begins in spiritual and physical alienation and ends in reconciliation, Ambrose is alienated only spiritually from his family. Both heroes lose their identity temporarily; in Barth's story, however, the setting is not the wine-dark sea, with its alien islands and hostile shores, but a funhouse whose labyrinthian interior Ambrose must explore on his journey from partial ignorance to partial knowledge.

Like the *Odyssey* and all lasting fictions, "Lost in the Funhouse" can be read at more than one level. The literal story is the frame story—the family excursion to the seashore on the Fourth of July. Concerning this story, Barth has written:

> I meant it to look back—at the narrator Ambrose's earlier youth, . . . and at some classical manners and concerns of the conventional realist-illusionist short story— and also "forward," to some less conventional narrative matters and concerns as well as to some future, more mythic avatars of the narrator. Finally, I meant it to be accessible, entertaining, perhaps moving; for I have no use for merely cerebral inventions, merely formalistic tours de force, and the place and time—tidewater Maryland, World War Twotime—are pungent in my memory.

Barth succeeds in making "Lost in the Funhouse" appeal to the reader at the level of entertainment and emotion because Ambrose engages the reader's imagination and sympathy. The adolescent boy emerges as a fully rounded character: self-conscious, awkward, uncertain, given to digressions and fantasies, yet courageous and tenacious. Barth provides enough time-honored ingredients of conventional fiction to make his character and situation identifiable. But supplying sufficient details to create a character who is believable, a setting that is visible, and action that is comprehensible does not fully account for the emotional impact of this story. For that we must look deeper—to the universality of the experience Ambrose undergoes, to its roots in archetype and in myth.

The journey to Ocean City prefigures and parallels symbolically Ambrose's wanderings inside the funhouse. Like the car ride during which Ambrose is obsessed with Magda's physical presence, both the amusement park and the funhouse are laden with sexual implications for the boy:

> Under the boardwalk, matchbook covers, grainy other things. What is the story's theme? Ambrose is ill. He perspires in the dark passages; candied apples-on-a-stick, delicious-looking, disappointing to eat. Funhouses need men's and ladies' rooms at intervals. Others perhaps have also vomited in corners and corridors; may even have had bowel movements liable to be stepped on in the dark. The word *fuck* suggests suction and/or and/or flatulence.

Later in the story, Ambrose realizes that sex is "the whole point" of the funhouse. Moreover,

> If you looked around, you noticed that almost all the people on the boardwalk were paired off into couples except the small children; in a way, that was the whole point of Ocean City! If you had X-ray eyes and could see everything going on at that instant under the boardwalk and in all the hotel rooms and cars and alleyways, you'd realize that all that normally *showed,* like restaurants and dance halls and clothing and test-your-strength machines, was merely preparation and intermission.

Among the members of his party, only Ambrose has avoided the funhouse on previous occasions; the others "had been through it before." Terrified yet intrigued, he thinks that his father should take him into his confidence and explain the secrets of this particular initiation. He imagines his father as saying:

> "There is a simple secret to getting through the funhouse, as simple as being first to see the Towers. Here it is. Peter does not know it; neither does your Uncle Karl. You and I are different. Not surprisingly, you've often wished you weren't. Don't think I haven't noticed how unhappy your childhood has been! But you'll understand, when I tell you, why it had to be kept secret until now. And you won't regret not being like your brother and your uncle. *On the contrary!*"

But this initiation, like most rites of passage, must be undertaken alone and without explicit instruction. Even "whispered advice from an old-timer" proves erroneous.

At the level of archetype, the various aspects of the funhouse take on mythic significance. Fat May, the guardian at its portal, is excessively female:

> Larger than life, Fat May mechanically shook, rocked on her heels, slapped her thighs while recorded laughter—uproarious, female—came amplified from a hidden loudspeaker. It chuckled, wheezed, wept; tried in vain to catch its breath; tittered, groaned, exploded raucous and anew.

Fat May is a giant earth mother, a mechanized Venus Urania, a laugh-track custodian of the "Devil's-mouth entrance." Inside the funhouse, the mirror-maze and the dark corridors become the fabled labyrinth of Crete. According to Greek legend, the intricate maze concealed the Minotaur, a man-eating monster slain by Theseus who, with the aid of Ariadne, penetrated the labyrinth and returned victorious. But no monsters other than those created by Ambrose's fantasies and fears exist inside the funhouse. Unlike Theseus, Ambrose must wander around like most mortals, stumbling in the dark, bumping into people and walls, taking wrong turns until, despite his doubts, he emerges safely. But his experiences have changed him:

> He wishes he had never entered the funhouse. But he has. Then he wishes he were dead. But he's not. Therefore he will construct funhouses for others and be their secret operator—though he would rather be among the lovers for whom funhouses are designed.

Ambrose's decision to construct funhouses leads to Barth's other concern in this story—fiction-making. The amusement park and the funhouse in particular are metaphors for fiction. "In a perfect funhouse," Ambrose conjectures, "you'd be able to go only one way, like the divers off the high board; getting lost would be impossible; the doors and halls would work like minnow traps or the valves in veins." The "perfect funhouse" is the physical and metaphorical equivalent of the well-made story. In conventionally plotted stories like "The Story-Teller" and "The Bride Comes to Yellow Sky," "getting lost" is difficult because the narrative is constructed so that actions follow each other logically and chronologically.

Barth acknowledges the traditions of the well-made story through digressions about conventional techniques of fiction-making:

> Description of physical appearance and mannerisms is one of several standard methods of characterization used by writers of fiction.

> To say that Ambrose's and Peter's mother was *pretty* is to accomplish nothing; the reader may acknowledge the proposition, but his imagination is not engaged.

> The more closely an author identifies with the narrator, literally or metaphorically, the less advisable it is, as a rule, to use the first-person narrative viewpoint.

Barth's intentions in this story are obviously antimimetic, as these intrusions into the narrative interrupt the plot at its literal level. Accordingly, the funhouse Ambrose imagines serves as the equivalent of the experimental story:

He envisions a truly astonishing funhouse, incredibly complex yet utterly controlled from a great central switchboard like the console of a pipe organ. Nobody had enough imagination. He could design such a place himself, wiring and all, and he's only thirteen years old. He would be its operator: panel lights would show what was up in every cranny of its cunning of its multifarious vastness; a switch-flick would ease this fellow's way, complicate that's, to balance things out; if anyone seemed lost or frightened, all the operator had to do was.

Ambrose's "astonishing funhouse" parallels "Lost in the Funhouse" itself. Barth has constructed an "incredibly complex yet utterly controlled" story for readers to get lost in—forcing them to retrace their steps, sort fantasy from reality, examine the conventions of the "realist-illusionist short story," experience the reversals of antimimetic narrative, and see that fiction and fact may be simultaneous in their equal "reality."

Inevitably, the designer of astonishing funhouses or the writer of experimental fiction is different from other people. Ambrose reflects on his isolation:

People don't know what to make of him, he doesn't know what to make of himself, he's only thirteen, *athletically and socially inept,* not astonishingly bright, but there are antennae; he has . . . some sort of receivers in his head; things speak to him, he understands more than he should, the world winks at him through its objects, grabs grinning at his coat. Everybody else is in on some secret he doesn't know; they've forgotten to tell him.

The secret of people like his brother Peter and Uncle Karl lies in their literal acceptance of events (like baptisms) and objects (like funhouses). Ambrose's vision is transcendent: traditional rituals leave him unaffected, and an amusement park is more terrifying than amusing. For Ambrose, objects and events are always different from what they seem:

Nothing was what it looked like. Every instant, under the surface of the Atlantic Ocean, millions of living animals devoured one another. Pilots were falling in flames over Europe; women were being forcibly raped in the South Pacific.

Ambrose recognizes that "there was some simple, radical difference about him" which he hopes is "genius" but fears is "madness." What Ambrose must learn is that his condition is the writer's condition—and, more than that, the condition of all persons who are creators. *What* is created—funhouses, fiction, nations—is relatively unimportant; what is crucial is the *act* of creation. The decision to engage in the struggle inherent in any creative effort sets Ambrose apart from other people. A similar destiny separated Odysseus from his fellow men. Indeed, in one of his fantasies about the funhouse, Ambrose likens himself to the Greek hero. Imagining that he finds another person who was also lost in the dark, Ambrose speculates: "They'd match their wits together against the funhouse, struggle like Ulysses past obstacle after obstacle, help and encourage each other."*

The story of Odysseus has done more than provide a useful starting point in our study of narrative art. For the *Odyssey* has figured prominently in almost every epoch of Western literature, beginning with the Greek dramatists Sophocles *(Ajax)* and Euripides *(Hecuba* and *Iphigenia in Aulis)*, reappearing in the works of the Roman poets Virgil *(Aeneid)* and Ovid *(Metamorphoses)* and the dramatist Seneca *(Troades)*, and emerging centuries later in Dante's *Divine Comedy*. English writers who have used Homer as source and resource include Shakespeare *(Troilus and Cressida)*, Nicholas Rowe *(Ulysses, a tragedy)*, Charles Lamb *(Adventures of Ulysses)*, and Tennyson in the dramatic monologue *Ulysses*. In the twentieth century, the *Odyssey* has been interpreted by the German poet-dramatist Gerhart Hauptmann *(The Bow of Odysseus)*, the French dramatist Jean Giraudoux *(Tiger at the Gates)*, and the Greek writer Nikos Kazantzakis, whose *The Odyssey: A Modern Sequel*, published in 1938, is three times as long as Homer's poem.

But the greatest interpreter and re-creator of the *Odyssey* is James Joyce, whose *Ulysses* serves as a literary reference for Ambrose. Early in the story, Ambrose mentions Joyce's description of the sea:

> The Irish author James Joyce, in his unusual novel entitled Ulysses, now available in this country, uses the adjectives *snot-green* and *scrotum-tightening* to describe the sea. Visual, auditory, tactile, olfactory, gustatory.

Later, Ambrose remembers an experience that occurred when he was alone on the seawall near his house. At that time he was transported beyond himself:

> The grass was alive! The town, the river, himself, were not imaginary; time roared in his ears like wind; the world was *going on!* This part ought to be dramatized. The Irish author James Joyce once wrote. Ambrose M—— is going to scream.

This moment of transcendence frightens him because his sense of oneness with the universe occurred not during his baptism but during a solitary communion with nature. His epiphany is the stronger for being unanticipated.

It is not coincidence that is responsible for Ambrose's likening himself to Ulysses, for the boy is a precocious reader. Nor is it coincidence that Barth refers to James Joyce, for Joyce's technical innovations with language, his use of epiphany as structure and theme, and his adaptation of myth are important in the history of contemporary literature. As Homer was the inheritor of not only the epic but the folk tales of his people, so modern writers like Barth are inheritors of a vast and imposing literary tradition. Some have created structures of conventional design, but others have elected to construct funhouses.

---

*(Ulysses is the Latin name for Odysseus.)

Fiction's journey is impossible to chart with precision. Much has been lost in the vagaries of time, or never recorded in the thousands of centuries when the human race had no written alphabet. And there have been uncounted side trips and stopovers and back-trackings. In addition, the territory is vast and amorphous. The pattern of narrative art is not linear and sequential, but its development is not without design. Like many journeys, fiction's journey is circular: each convolution overlaps and incorporates what has gone before, continuously adds onto itself, tries new forms and new directions, but never moves far from the original source of narrative—the primacy of words and the delight in creating fictional forms capable of embodying experience and aspiration, reality and dream.

And, finally, what is true of all journeys is also true of fiction's journey: in the end, the journey *is* the teacher. That is the truth implicit in the design of this book.

50 Stories

What a Story Is

HOMER

The Odyssey

Book 9: How Odysseus Visited
the Lotus-eaters and the Cyclops

Translation by W. H. D. Rouse

Homer's Odyssey *consists of more than 12,000 lines of poetry, divided into 24 sections, or books. In Book 9, reprinted here in a modern prose translation, the Greek warrior Odysseus has been shipwrecked off one of the Phaiacian islands and is being honored at a royal banquet. Odysseus has been away from his native Ithaca for almost twenty years—ten of them spent fighting in Troy; the remaining ten in his arduous journey home, a journey marked by enchantment and catastrophe. Book 9 can be considered a flashback, occasioned by the Phaiacian king's request that Odysseus identify himself, describe his travels, and explain his grief at the minstrel's song about the Trojan war. Reluctantly Odysseus begins his "sad story," telling of his departure from Troy almost ten years ago and the first of his adventures.*

Then Odysseus began his tale:

"What a pleasure it is, my lord," he said, "to hear a singer like this, with a divine voice! I declare it is just the perfection of gracious life: good cheer and good temper everywhere, rows of guests enjoying themselves heartily and listening to the music, plenty to eat on the table, wine ready in the great bowl, and the butler ready to fill your cup whenever you want it. I think that is the best thing men can have.—But you have a mind to hear my sad story, and make me more unhappy than I was before. What shall I begin with, what shall I end with? The lords of heaven have given me sorrow in abundance.

"First of all I will tell you my name, and then you may count me one of your friends if I live to reach my home, although that is far away. I am Odysseus Laërtiadês, a name well known in the world as one who is ready for any event. My home is Ithaca, that bright conspicuous isle, with Mount Neriton rising clear out of the quivering forests. Round it lie many islands clustering close, Dulichion and Samê and woody Zacynthos. My island lies low, last of all in the sea to westward, the others away towards the dawn and the rising sun. It is rough, but a nurse of good lads; I tell you there is no sweeter sight any man can see than his own country. Listen now: a radiant goddess Calypso tried to keep me by her in her cave, and wanted me for a husband; Circê also would have had me stay in her mansion, and a clever creature she was, and she also wanted me for a husband, but she never could win my heart. How true it is that nothing is sweeter than home and kindred, although you may have a rich house in a foreign land far away from your kindred! Ah well, but you are waiting to hear of my journey home, and all the sorrows which Zeus laid upon me after I left Troy.

"From Ilion the wind carried me to Ismaros of the Ciconians. There I destroyed the city and killed the men. We spared the women and plenty of cattle and goods, which we divided to give each man a fair share. I told the men we must show a light heel and be off, but the poor fools would not listen. Plenty of wine was drunk, plenty of sheep were killed on that beach, and herds of cattle! Meanwhile some of the enemy got away and shouted to other Ciconians, neighbors of their inland, more men and better men, who knew how to fight from the chariot against a foe, and on foot if need be.

"A multitude of these men swarmed down early in the morning, as many as leaves and flowers in the season of the year. Surely Zeus sent us a hard fate that day, to bring trouble on a lot of poor devils! They drew up near the ships, and then came volleys on both sides. All through the morning while the day grew stronger we stood our ground and held them off, although they outnumbered us; but when the sun began to change course, about ox-loosing time,[1] the Ciconians got the upper hand and bent our line. Six men-at-arms from each vessel were killed; and the rest of us were saved alive.

"From that place we sailed onward much discouraged, but glad to have escaped death, although we had lost good companions. Yet we did not let the galleys go off, until we had called thrice on the name of each of our hapless comrades who died in that place. But Zeus Cloudgatherer sent a norwester upon our fleet with a furious tempest, bringing clouds over land and sea; and night rushed down from the sky. The ships were blown plunging along, the sails were split into shreds and tatters by the violence of the wind. We let down the sails in fear of death, and rowed the bare hulls to shore. There we lay two days and two nights on end, eating out our hearts with hardship and anxiety. But when the third day showed welcome streaks of light, we stept the masts and hoisted new sails, and sat still, while the wind drove us on and the steersman held the way. Then I might have come safe to my native land, but the sea and the

[1]About noon, when the day's plowing is done.

current and the north-west wind caught me as I was doubling Cape Malea, and drifted me outside Cythera.

"Nine days after that I was beaten about on the sea by foul winds, and on the tenth day we made land in the country of the lotus-eaters, who get their food from flowers.[1] We went ashore and took in water, and the men made their meal on the spot close to the ships. When we had eaten and drunk, I sent some of them to find out who the natives were: two picked men with a speaker. Before long they came across some of the lotus-eaters. However, they did no harm to the men, only gave them some of their lotus to eat. As soon as they tasted that honey-sweet fruit, they thought no more of coming back to us with news, but chose rather to stay there with the lotus-eating natives, and chew their lotus, and goodbye to home. I brought them back to the ships by main force, grumbling and complaining, and when I had them there, tied them up and stowed them under the benches. Then I ordered the rest to hurry up and get aboard, for I did not want them to have a taste of lotus and say good-bye to home. They were soon on board and sitting on their benches, and rowing away over the sea.

"From that place we sailed on in low spirits. We came next to the Cyclopians, the Goggle-eyes, a violent and lawless tribe. They trust to providence, and neither plant nor plow, but everything grows without sowing or plowing; wheat and barley and vines, which bear grapes in huge bunches, and the rain from heaven makes them grow of themselves. These Cyclopians have no parliament for debates and no laws, but they live on high mountains in hollow caves; each one lays down the law for wife and children, and no one cares for his neighbors.

"Now a low flat island lies across their harbor, not very near the land and not very far, covered with trees. In this are an infinite number of wild goats, for no man walks there to scare them away, and no hunters frequent the place to follow their toilsome trade in the forests and the hills. So it has neither flocks nor tillage; but unsown and unplowed, untrodden of men, it feeds the bleating goats. For the Goggle-eyes have no ships with their crimson cheeks, and no shipwrights among them, to build boats for them to row in and visit the cities of the world, like men who traverse the seas on their lawful occasions. Such craftsmen might have civilized the island: for it is not a bad island. It could produce all the kindly fruits of the earth; there are meadows along the shore, soft land with plenty of water; there might be no end of grapes. There is smooth land for the plow; the soil is very rich, and they might always stack a good harvest in the season of the year. There is a harbor with easy riding; no cable is wanted, no anchor-stones or stern-hawsers. You just beach your ship, and stay till the sailors have a fancy to go and the wind blows fair. Moreover, at the head of the harbor there is glorious water, a spring running out of a cave, with poplars growing all round.

"Some providence guided us in through the dark night, with not a thing to be seen; for a thick mist was about our ships, and the moon showed no light

[1] Not the lotus grass, but some kind of berry like a small date or poppy-pod.

through the clouds. At that time we did not catch a glimpse of the island: indeed we saw no long breakers rolling towards the land, before our ships ran up on the beach. When they were safe there, we lowered the sails and got out on the shore, and slept heavily until the dawn.

"As soon as dawn gleamed through the mist, we roamed about and admired the island. Then those kindly daughters of Zeus, the Nymphs, sent down goats from the hills to give us all a good meal. We lost no time, got our bows and long spears out of the ships, divided into three bands, and let fly at the quarry. Very soon God gave us as much as we wanted. I had twelve ships with me, and nine goats were given to each by lot, but ten were picked out for me alone. So all day long we sat there feasting, with plenty of meat and delicious wine. For the good red wine was not all used up yet, but some was left; when we took the Ciconian city, each crew had supplied themselves with plenty in large two-handled jars. We gazed at the country of the Goggle-eyes, which was quite close; we could see the smoke and hear the bleating of sheep and goats. When the sun set and darkness came, we lay down on the beach to sleep.

"But with the first rosy streaks of the dawn, I called a meeting and made a speech to the men. 'My good fellows,' I said, 'the rest of you stay here, while I take my ship and crew and see who these people are; whether they are wild savages who know no law, or hospitable men who know right from wrong.'

"So I went aboard and told my crew to cast loose; they were soon in their places and rowing along. The land was not far off, and when we reached it we saw a cave there on a headland close by the sea, high and shaded with laurels, in which numbers of animals were housed by night, both sheep and goats. Outside was an enclosure with high walls round it, made of great stones dug into the earth and the trunks of tall pines and spreading oaks. These were the night-quarters of a monstrous man, who was then tending his flocks a long way off by himself; he would not mix with the others, but kept apart in his own lawless company. Indeed he was a wonderful monster, not like a mortal man who eats bread, but rather like a mountain peak with trees on the top standing up alone in the highlands.

"Then I told the rest of my men to wait for me and look after the ship, but I picked out twelve of the best men I had, and we set out. I took with me a goatskin of ruby wine, delicious wine, which I had from Maron Euanthidês, priest of Apollo who was the protecting god of Ismaros. We had saved him and his wife and child out of reverence, because he lived in the sacred grove of Phoibos Apollo. I had glorious gifts from him: he gave me seven talents' weight of worked gold, he gave me a mixing-bowl of solid silver, but besides that, he gave me great jars of wine, a whole dozen of them, delicious wine, not a drop of water in it, a divine drink! Not a soul knew about this wine, none of the servants or women, except himself and his own wife and one cellarer. When they drank of this wine, he used to pour one cup of it into twenty measures of water, and a sweet scent was diffused abroad from the mixer, something heavenly; no one wanted to be an abstainer then! I had filled a skin with this wine, and brought it with me, also a bag of provisions; for from the first I had a foreboding that I should meet a man of mighty strength, but savage, knowing neither justice nor law.

"We walked briskly to the cave, but found him not at home; he was tending his fat flocks on the pasture. So we entered the cave and took a good look all round. There were baskets loaded with cheeses, there were pens stuffed full of lambs and kids. Each lot was kept in a separate place; firstlings in one, middlings in another, yeanlings in another. Every pot and pan was swimming with whey, all the pails and basins into which he did the milking. The men begged me first to let them help themselves to the cheeses and be off; next they wanted to make haste and drive the kids and lambs out of the pens and get under sail. But I would not listen—indeed it would have been much better if I had! but I wanted to see himself and claim the stranger's gift. As it turned out, he was destined to be anything but a vision of joy to my comrades.

"So we lit a fire and made our thank-offering, and helped ourselves to as many cheeses as we wanted to eat; then we sat inside till he should come back with his flocks. At last in he came, carrying a tremendous load of dry wood to give light for supper. This he threw down inside the cave with a crash that terrified us, and sent us scurrying into the corners. Then he drove his fat flocks into the cave, that is to say, all he milked, leaving the rams and billy-goats outside the cave but within the high walls of the enclosure. Then he picked up a huge great stone and placed it in the doorway: not two and twenty good carts with four wheels apiece could have lifted it off the ground,[1] such was the size of the precipitous rock which he planted in front of the entrance. Then he sat down and milked the goats and ewes, bleating loudly, all in order, and put her young under each. Next he curdled half of the white milk and packed it into wicker baskets, leaving the other half to stand in bowls, that he might have some to drink for supper or whenever he wanted. At last after all this busy work, he lighted the fire and saw us.

" 'Who are you?' he called out. 'Where do you come from over the watery ways? Are you traders, or a lot of pirates ready to kill and be killed, bringing trouble to foreigners?'

"While he spoke, our hearts were wholly broken within us to see the horrible monster, and to hear that beastly voice. But I managed to answer him:

" 'We are Achaians from Troy, driven out of our course over the broad sea by all the winds of heaven. We meant to sail straight home, but we have lost our way altogether: such was the will of Zeus, I suppose. We have the honor to be the people of King Agamemnon Atreidês, whose fame is greatest of all men under the sky, for the strong city he sacked and the many nations he conquered. But we have found you, and come to your knees, to pray if you will give us the stranger's due or anything you may think proper to give to a stranger. Respect the gods, most noble sir; see, we are your suppliants! Strangers and suppliants have their guardian strong, God walks with them to see they get no wrong.'

---

[1]This is a parody of the common phrase which describes how "two good men" could not have lifted a certain stone. So with "precipitous rock," used of cliffs and mountains.

"He answered me with cruel words: 'You are a fool, stranger, or you come from a long way off, if you expect me to fear gods. Zeus Almighty be damned and his blessed gods with him. We Cyclopians care nothing for them, we are stronger than they are. I should not worry about Zeus if I wanted to lay hands on you or your companions. But tell me, where did you moor your ship—far off or close by? I should be glad to know that.'

"He was just trying it on, but I knew something of the world, and saw through it; so I answered back, 'My ship was wrecked by Poseidon Earthshaker, who cast us on the rocks near the boundary of your country; the wind drove us on a lee shore. But I was saved with these others.'

"The cruel monster made no answer, but just jumped up and reached out towards my men, grabbed two like a pair of puppies and dashed them on the ground: their brains ran out and soaked into the earth. Then he cut them up limb by limb, and made them ready for supper. He devoured them like a mountain lion, bowels and flesh and marrow-bones, and left nothing. We groaned aloud, lifting our hands to Zeus, when we saw this brutal business; but there was nothing to be done.

"When Goggle-eye had filled his great belly with his meal of human flesh, washed down with a draught of milk neat, he lay and stretched himself among the sheep. But I did not lose heart. I considered whether to go near and draw my sharp sword and drive it into his breast; I could feel about till I found the place where the midriff encloses the liver. But second thoughts kept me back. We should have perished ourselves in that place, dead and done for; we could never have moved the great stone which he had planted in the doorway. So we lay groaning and awaited the dawn.

"Dawn came. He lit the fire, milked his flocks, all in order, put the young under each, then he grabbed two more men and prepared his breakfast. That done, he drove out the fat flocks, moving away the great stone with ease; but he put it back again, just as you fit cover to quiver. With many a whistle Goggle-eye turned his fat flocks to the hills; but I was left brooding and full of dark plans, longing to have my revenge if Athena would grant my prayer.

"Among all my schemes and machinations, the best plan I could think of was this. A long spar was lying beside the pen, a sapling of green olive-wood; Goggle-eye had cut it down to dry it and use as a staff. It looked to us about as large as the mast of a twenty-oar ship, some broad hoy that sails the deep sea; it was about that length and thickness. I cut off a fathom of this, and handed it over to my men to dress down. They made it smooth, then I sharpened the end and charred it in the hot fire, and hid it carefully under the dung which lay in a great mass all over the floor. Then I told the others to cast lots who should help me with the pole and rub it into his eye while he was sound asleep. The lot fell on those four whom I would have chosen myself, which made five counting me.

"In the evening, back he came with his flocks. This time he drove them all into the cave, and left none outside in the yard; whether he suspected something, or God made him do it, I do not know. Then he lifted the great stone and set it in place, sat down and milked his ewes and nannies bleating loudly, all in order, put her young under each, and when all this was done, grabbed two more men and made his meal.

"At this moment I came near to Goggle-eye, holding in my hand an ivy-wood cup full of the red wine, and I said:

"'Cyclops, here, have a drink after that jolly meal of mansmutton! I should like to show you what drink we had on board our ship. I brought it as a drink-offering for you, in the hope that you might have pity and help me on my way home. But you are mad beyond all bearing! Hard heart, how can you expect any other men to pay you a visit? For you have done what is not right.'

"He took it and swallowed it down. The good stuff delighted him terribly, and he asked for another drink:

"'Oh, please give me more, and tell me your name this very minute! I will give you a stranger's gift which will make you happy! Mother earth does give us wine in huge bunches, even in this part of the world, and the rain from heaven makes them grow; but this is a rivulet of nectar and ambrosia!'

"Then I gave him a second draught. Three drinks I gave him; three times the fool drank. At last, when the wine had got into his head, I said to him in the gentlest of tones:

"'Cyclops, do you ask me my name? Well, I will tell you, and you shall give me the stranger's due, as you promised. Noman is my name; Noman is what mother and father call me and all my friends.'

"Then the cruel monster said, 'Noman shall be last eaten of his company, and all the others shall be eaten before him! that shall be your stranger's gift.'

"As he said this, down he slipped and rolled on his back. His thick neck drooped sideways, and all-conquering sleep laid hold on him; wine dribbled out of his gullet with lumps of human flesh, as he belched in his drunken slumbers. Then I drove the pole deep under the ashes to grow hot, and spoke to hearten my men that no one might fail me through fear.

"As soon as the wood was on the point of catching fire, and glowed white-hot, green as it was, I drew it quickly out of the fire while my men stood round me: God breathed great courage into us then. The men took hold of the stake, and thrust the sharp point into his eye; and I leaned hard on it from above and turned it round and round. As a man bores a ship's timber with an auger, while others at the lower part keep turning it with a strap which they hold at each end, and round and round it runs: so we held the fire-sharpened pole and turned it, and the blood bubbled about its hot point. The fumes singed eyelids and eyelashes all about as the eyeball burnt and the roots crackled in the fire. As a smith plunges an axe or an adze in cold water, for that makes the strength of steel, and it hisses loud when he tempers it, so his eye sizzled about the pole of olive-wood.

"He gave a horrible bellow till the rocks rang again, and we shrank away in fear. Then he dragged out the post from his eye dabbled and dripping with blood, and threw it from him, wringing his hands in wild agony, and roared aloud to the Cyclopians who lived in caves round about among the windy hills.

They heard his cries, and came thronging from all directions, and stood about the cave, asking what his trouble was:

"'What on earth is the matter with you, Polyphemos?' they called out. 'Why do you shout like this through the night and wake us all up? Is any man driving away your flocks against your will? Is any one trying to kill you by craft or main force?'

"Out of the cave came the voice of mighty Polyphemos: 'O my friends, Noman is killing me by craft and not by main force!'

"They answered him in plain words:

"'Well, if no man is using force, and you are alone, there's no help for a bit of sickness when heaven sends it; so you had better say your prayers to Lord Poseidon your father!'

"With these words away they went, and my heart laughed within me, to think how a mere nobody had taken them all in with my machinomanations!

"But the Cyclops, groaning and writhing in agony, fumbled about with his hands until he found the stone and pushed it away from the entrance. There he sat with his hands outspread to catch any one who tried to go out with the animals. A great fool he must have thought me! But I had been casting about what to do for the best, if I could possibly find some escape from death for my comrades and myself. All kinds of schemes and machinations I wove in my wits, for it was life or death, and perdition was close by. The plan that seemed to me best was this. The rams were well grown, large and fine, with coats of rich dark wool. In dead silence I tied them together with twisted withies, which the monster used for his bed. I tied them in threes, with a man under the middle one, while the two others protected him on each side. So three carried each of our fellows; but for myself—there was one great ram, the finest of the whole flock; I threw my arms over his back, and curled myself under his shaggy belly, and there I lay turned upwards, with only my hands to hold fast by the wonderful fleece in patience. So we all waited anxiously for the dawn.

"At last the dawn came. The rams and billies surged out to pasture, but the nannies and ewes unmilked went bleating round the pens; for their udders were full to bursting. Their master still tormented with pain felt over the backs of all the animals as they passed out; but the poor fool did not notice how my men were tied under their bellies. Last of all the great ram stalked to the door, cumbered with the weight of his wool and of me and my teeming mind. Polyphemos said as he pawed him over:

"'Hullo, why are you last to-day, you lazy creature? It is not your way to let them leave you behind! No, no, you go first by a long way to crop the fresh grass, stepping high and large, first to drink at the river, first all eagerness to come home in the evening; but now last! Are you sorry perhaps for your master's eye, which a damned villain has blinded with his cursed companions, after he had fuddled me with wine? Noman! who hasn't yet escaped the death in store for him, I tell him that! If you only had sense like me, if you could only speak, and tell me where the man is skulking from my vengeance! Wouldn't I beat his head on the ground, wouldn't his brains go splashing all over the place! And then I should have some little consolation for the trouble which this nobody of a Noman has brought upon me!'

"So he let the ram go from him out of the cave. A little way from the cave and its enclosure, I shook myself loose first from under my ram; then I freed my companions, and with all speed we drove the fat animals trotting along, often looking round, until we reached our ship. Glad indeed our friends were to see us, all of us that were left alive; they lamented the others, and made such a noise that I had to stop it, frowning at them and shaking my head. I told them to look sharp and throw on board a number of the fleecy beasts, and get away. Soon they were in their places paddling along; but when we were about as far off from the shore as a man can shout, I called out in mockery:

"'I say, Cyclops! He didn't turn out to be such a milksop after all, did he, when you murdered his friends, and gobbled them up in your cave? Your sins were sure to find you out, you cruel brute! You had no scruple to devour your guests in your own house, therefore vengeance has fallen upon you from Zeus and the gods in heaven!'

"This made him more furious than ever. He broke off the peak of a tall rock and threw it; the rock fell in front of the ship; the sea splashed and surged up as it fell; it raised a wave which carried us back to the land, and the rolling swell drove the ship right upon the shore. I picked up a long quant and pushed her off, and nodded to the men as a hint to row hard and save their lives. You may be sure they put their backs into it! When we were twice as far as before, I wanted to shout again to Goggle-eye, although my comrades all round tried to coax me not to do it—

"'Foolhardy man! Why do you want to provoke the madman? Just now he threw something to seaward of us and drove back the ship to land, and we thought all was up with us. And if he had heard one of us speaking or making a sound, he would have thrown a jagged rock and smashed our timbers and our bones to smithereens! He throws far enough!'

"But I was determined not to listen, and shouted again in my fury:

"'I say, Cyclops! if ever any one asks you who put out your ugly eye, tell him your blinder was Odysseus, the conqueror of Troy, the son of Laërtês, whose address is in Ithaca!'

"When he heard this he gave a loud cry, and said, 'Upon my word, this is the old prophecy come true! There was a soothsayer here once, a fine tall fellow, Telemos Eurymedês, a famous soothsayer who lived to old age prophesying amongst our people. He told me what was to happen, that I should lose my sight at the hands of Odysseus. But I always expected that some tall handsome fellow would come this way, clothed in mighty power. Now a nobody, a weakling, a whippersnapper, has blinded my eye after fuddling me with wine! Come to me, dear Odysseus, and let me give you the stranger's gift, let me beseech the worshipful Earthshaker to grant you a happy voyage! For I have the honour to be his son, and he declares he is my father. He will cure me, if he chooses, all by himself, without the help of blessed gods or mortal man.

"I answered at once, 'I wish I could kill you and send you to hell as surely as no one will ever unblind your eye, not even the Earthshaker!'

"At this he held out his hand to heaven, and prayed to Lord Poseidon:

"'Hear me, Poseidon Earthholder Seabluehair! If I am truly thy son, and thou art indeed my father, grant that Odysseus the conqueror of Troy—the son of Laërtês—whose address is in Ithaca, may never reach his home![1] But if it is his due portion to see his friends and come again to his tall house and his native land, may he come there late and in misery, in another man's ship, may he lose all his companions, and may he find tribulation at home!'

"This was his prayer, and Seabluehair heard it. Then once again he lifted a stone greater than the other, and circled it round his head, gathering all his vast strength for the blow,[2] and flung it; down it fell behind our ship, just a little, just missed the end of the steering-oar. The sea splashed and surged up as it fell, and the wave carried her on and drove her to shore on the island.

"When we came safe to the island, where the other ships were waiting for us, we found our companions in great anxiety, hoping against hope. We drew up our ship on the sand, and put the sheep of old Goggle-eye ashore, and divided them so as to give every one a fair share. But by general consent the great ram was given to me. I sacrificed him on the beach to Zeus Cronidês; clouds and darkness are round about him, and he rules over all. I made my burnt-offering, but Zeus regarded it not; for as it turned out, he intended that all my tight ships and all my trusty companions should be destroyed.

"We spent the rest of the day until sunset in feasting, eating full and drinking deep; and when the sun set and darkness came on, we lay to rest on the seashore. Then at dawn I directed the men in all haste to embark and throw off the moorings. They were soon aboard and rowing away in good fettle over the sea.

"So we fared onwards, thankful to be alive, but sorrowing for our comrades whom we had lost."

QUESTIONS

1. Odysseus refers to himself as "well known in the world as one who is ready for any event." How do his encounters with the Ciconians and lotus-eaters support this description?

2. Why, on two occasions, does Odysseus reject advice offered by his men? What does this action reveal about Odysseus? Would you describe him as round? flat? static? dynamic? sympathetic? unsympathetic?

3. Odysseus lies to Polyphemos twice. Was each falsehood justified by the situa-

---

[1] Odysseus introduced himself in the proper Greek way, name, family, and address; the reader will notice how carefully the Cyclops repeats it to his divine father, that there may be no mistake. . . .
[2] The movements of putting the weight.

tion? What do these lies reveal about Odysseus's character? Do they advance the plot?

4. Why does Odysseus choose to blind Polyphemos rather than to kill him?

5. How important is setting to this story?

6. Describe the role of irony in Odysseus's encounter with Polyphemos.

7. Who is Poseidon? Why does Poseidon answer Polyphemos's prayer? Who is Zeus?

8. Odysseus's encounter with the Cyclops has enthralled generations of readers. What aspects of the storyteller's art contribute to its universal appeal?

Point of View

SAKI
(H. H. MUNRO)

The Story-Teller

It was a hot afternoon, and the railway carriage was correspondingly sultry, and the next stop was at Templecombe, nearly an hour ahead. The occupants of the carriage were a small girl, and a smaller girl, and a small boy. An aunt belonging to the children occupied one corner seat, and the further corner seat on the opposite side was occupied by a bachelor who was a stranger to their party, but the small girls and the small boy emphatically occupied the compartment. Both the aunt and the children were conversational in a limited, persistent way, reminding one of the attentions of a housefly that refused to be discouraged. Most of the aunt's remarks seemed to begin with "Don't," and nearly all of the children's remarks began with "Why?" The bachelor said nothing out loud.

"Don't, Cyril, don't," exclaimed the aunt, as the small boy began smacking the cushions of the seat, producing a cloud of dust at each blow.

"Come and look out of the window," she added.

The child moved reluctantly to the window. "Why are those sheep being driven out of that field?" he asked.

"I expect they are being driven to another field where there is more grass," said the aunt weakly.

"But there is lots of grass in that field," protested the boy; "there's nothing else but grass there. Aunt, there's lots of grass in that field."

"Perhaps the grass in the other field is better," suggested the aunt fatuously.

"Why is it better?" came the swift, inevitable question.

"Oh, look at those cows!" exclaimed the aunt. Nearly every field along the

116

line had contained cows or bullocks, but she spoke as though she were drawing attention to a rarity.

"Why is the grass in the other field better?" persisted Cyril.

The frown on the bachelor's face was deepening to a scowl. He was a hard, unsympathetic man, the aunt decided in her mind. She was utterly unable to come to any satisfactory decision about the grass in the other field.

The smaller girl created a diversion by beginning to recite "On the Road to Mandalay." She only knew the first line, but she put her limited knowledge to the fullest possible use. She repeated the line over and over again in a dreamy but resolute and very audible voice; it seemed to the bachelor as though some one had had a bet with her that she could not repeat the line aloud two thousand times without stopping. Whoever it was who had made the wager was likely to lose his bet.

"Come over here and listen to a story," said the aunt, when the bachelor had looked twice at her and once at the communication cord.

The children moved listlessly towards the aunt's end of the carriage. Evidently her reputation as a story-teller did not rank high in their estimation.

In a low, confidential voice, interrupted at frequent intervals by loud, petulant questions from her listeners, she began an unenterprising and deplorably uninteresting story about a little girl who was good, and made friends with every one on account of her goodness, and was finally saved from a mad bull by a number of rescuers who admired her moral character.

"Wouldn't they have saved her if she hadn't been good?" demanded the bigger of the small girls. It was exactly the question that the bachelor had wanted to ask.

"Well, yes," admitted the aunt lamely, "but I don't think they would have run quite so fast to her help if they had not liked her so much."

"It's the stupidest story I've ever heard," said the bigger of the small girls, with immense conviction.

"I didn't listen after the first bit, it was so stupid," said Cyril.

The smaller girl made no actual comment on the story, but she had long ago recommenced a murmured repetition of her favorite line.

"You don't seem to be a success as a story-teller," said the bachelor suddenly from his corner.

The aunt bristled in instant defense at this unexpected attack.

"It's a very difficult thing to tell stories that children can both understand and appreciate," she said stiffly.

"I don't agree with you," said the bachelor.

"Perhaps *you* would like to tell them a story," was the aunt's retort.

"Tell us a story," demanded the bigger of the small girls.

"Once upon a time," began the bachelor, "there was a little girl called Bertha, who was extraordinarily good."

The children's momentarily-aroused interest began at once to flicker; all stories seemed dreadfully alike, no matter who told them.

"She did all that she was told, she was always truthful, she kept her clothes clean, ate milk puddings as though they were jam tarts, learned her lessons perfectly, and was polite in her manners."

"Was she pretty?" asked the bigger of the small girls.

"Not as pretty as any of you," said the bachelor, "but she was horribly good."

There was a wave of reaction in favor of the story; the word *horrible* in connection with goodness was a novelty that commended itself. It seemed to introduce a ring of truth that was absent from the aunt's tales of infant life.

"She was so good," continued the bachelor, "that she won several medals for goodness, which she always wore, pinned on to her dress. There was a medal for obedience, another medal for punctuality, and a third for good behavior. They were large metal medals and they clicked against one another as she walked. No other child in the town where she lived had as many as three medals, so everybody knew that she must be an extra good child."

"Horribly good," quoted Cyril.

"Everybody talked about her goodness, and the Prince of the country got to hear about it, and he said that as she was so very good she might be allowed once a week to walk in his park, which was just outside the town. It was a beautiful park, and no children were ever allowed in it, so it was a great honor for Bertha to be allowed to go there."

"Were there any sheep in the park?" demanded Cryil.

"No," said the bachelor, "there were no sheep."

"Why weren't there any sheep?" came the inevitable question arising out of that answer.

The aunt permitted herself a smile, which might almost have been described as a grin.

"There were no sheep in the park," said the bachelor, "because the Prince's mother had once had a dream that her son would either be killed by a sheep or else by a clock falling on him. For that reason the Prince never kept a sheep in his park or a clock in his palace."

The aunt suppressed a gasp of admiration.

"Was the Prince killed by a sheep or by a clock?" asked Cyril.

"He is still alive so we can't tell whether the dream will come true," said the bachelor unconcernedly; "anyway, there were no sheep in the park, but there were lots of little pigs running all over the place."

"What color were they?"

"Black with white faces, white with black spots, black all over, gray with white patches, and some were white all over."

The story-teller paused to let a full idea of the park's treasures sink into the children's imaginations; then he resumed:

"Bertha was rather sorry to find that there were no flowers in the park. She had promised her aunts, with tears in her eyes, that she would not pick any of the kind Prince's flowers, and she had meant to keep her promise, so of course it made her feel silly to find that there were no flowers to pick."

"Why weren't there any flowers?"

"Because the pigs had eaten them all," said the bachelor promptly. "The gardeners had told the Prince that you couldn't have pigs and flowers, so he decided to have pigs and no flowers."

There was a murmur of approval at the excellence of the Prince's decision; so many people would have decided the other way.

"There were lots of other delightful things in the park. There were ponds with gold and blue and green fish in them, and trees with beautiful parrots that said clever things at a moment's notice, and humming birds that hummed all the popular tunes of the day. Bertha walked up and down and enjoyed herself immensely, and thought to herself: 'If I were not so extraordinarily good I should not have been allowed to come into this beautiful park and enjoy all that there is to be seen in it,' and her three medals clinked against one another as she walked and helped to remind her how very good she really was. Just then an enormous wolf came prowling into the park to see if it could catch a fat little pig for its supper."

"What color was it?" asked the children, amid an immediate quickening of interest.

"Mud-color all over, with a black tongue and pale gray eyes that gleamed with unspeakable ferocity. The first thing that it saw in the park was Bertha; her pinafore was so spotlessly white and clean that it could be seen from a great distance. Bertha saw the wolf and saw that it was stealing towards her, and she began to wish that she had never been allowed to come into the park. She ran as hard as she could, and the wolf came after her with huge leaps and bounds. She managed to reach a shrubbery of myrtle bushes and she hid herself in one of the thickest of the bushes. The wolf came sniffing among the branches, its black tongue lolling out of its mouth and its pale gray eyes glaring with rage. Bertha was terribly frightened, and thought to herself: 'If I had not been so extraordinarily good I should have been safe in the town at this moment.' However, the scent of the myrtle was so strong that the wolf could not sniff out where Bertha was hiding, and the bushes were so thick that he might have hunted about in them for a long time without catching sight of her, so he thought he might as well go off and catch a little pig instead. Bertha was trembling very much at having the wolf prowling and sniffing so near her, and as she trembled the medal for obedience clinked against the medals for good conduct and punctuality. The wolf was just moving away when he heard the sound of the medals clinking and stopped to listen; they clinked again in a bush quite near him. He dashed into the bush, his pale gray eyes gleaming with ferocity and triumph, and dragged Bertha out and devoured her to the last morsel. All that were left of her were her shoes, bits of clothing, and the three medals for goodness."

"Were any of the little pigs killed?"

"No, they all escaped."

"The story began badly," said the smaller of the small girls, "but it had a beautiful ending."

"It is the most beautiful story that I ever heard," said the bigger of the small girls, with immense decision.

"It is the *only* beautiful story I have ever heard," said Cyril.

A dissentient opinion came from the aunt.

"A most improper story to tell to young children! You have undermined the effect of years of careful teaching."

"At any rate," said the bachelor, collecting his belongings preparatory to leaving the carriage, "I kept them quiet for ten minutes, which was more than you were able to do."

"Unhappy woman!" he observed to himself as he walked down the platform of Templecombe station; "for the next six months or so those children will assail her in public with demands for an improper story!"

QUESTIONS

1. Are the aunt and the bachelor flat or round characters? static or dynamic? Are either the aunt or the bachelor sympathetic characters?

2. Discuss the function of setting. Can you imagine another setting that would be equally appropriate? If so, why?

3. Explain the children's and the bachelor's objections to the aunt's story. Are these objections valid? Why do you suppose Saki chose to summarize the aunt's story rather than to let her tell it in its entirety?

4. Explain why the aunt finds the bachelor's story "a most improper story to tell to young children." What elements in the bachelor's story appeal to the children? Examine the role of irony in the story as a whole.

5. Which mode of story telling do you prefer? Is the bachelor's story more truthful than the aunt's? Explain, making specific reference to the triumph or failure of poetic justice.

6. What point of view is employed in this story? Does the narrator provide any exposition? If so, where? What information is revealed? Would additional background information about the characters make the story more effective? How does the point of view affect the story's meaning?

7. Discuss the significance of the last paragraph. Is it fair to say that the bachelor's observations provide insight into Saki's role as a storyteller and therefore help to establish tone?

DOROTHY PARKER

You Were Perfectly Fine

The pale young man eased himself carefully into the low chair, and rolled his head to the side, so that the cool chintz comforted his cheek and temple.

"Oh, dear," he said. "Oh, dear, oh, dear, oh, dear. Oh."

The clear-eyed girl, sitting light and erect on the couch, smiled brightly at him.

"Not feeling so well today?" she said.

"Oh, I'm great," he said. "Corking, I am. Know what time I got up? Four o'clock this afternoon, sharp. I kept trying to make it, and every time I took my head off the pillow, it would roll under the bed. This isn't my head I've got on now. I think this is something that used to belong to Walt Whitman. Oh, dear, oh, dear, oh, dear."

"Do you think maybe a drink would make you feel better?" she said.

"The hair of the mastiff that bit me?" he said. "Oh, no thank you. Please never speak of anything like that again. I'm through. I'm all, all through. Look at that hand; steady as a humming-bird. Tell me, was I very terrible last night?"

"Oh, goodness," she said, "everybody was feeling pretty high. You were all right."

"Yeah," he said. "I must have been dandy. Is everybody sore at me?"

"Good heavens, no," she said. "Everyone thought you were terribly funny. Of course, Jim Pierson was a little stuffy, there for a minute at dinner. But people sort of held him back in his chair, and got him calmed down. I don't think anybody at the other tables noticed it at all. Hardly anybody."

"He was going to sock me?" he said. "Oh, Lord. What did I do to him?"

"Why, you didn't do a thing," she said. "You were perfectly fine. But you know how silly Jim gets, when he thinks anybody is making too much fuss over Elinor."

"Was I making a pass at Elinor?" he said. "Did I do that?"

"Of course you didn't," she said. "You were only fooling, that's all. She thought you were awfully amusing. She was having a marvelous time. She only got a little tiny bit annoyed just once, when you poured the clam-juice down her back."

"My God," he said. "Clam-juice down that back. And every vertebra a little Cabot. Dear God. What'll I ever do?"

"Oh, she'll be all right," she said. "Just send her some flowers, or something. Don't worry about it. It isn't anything."

"No, I won't worry," he said. "I haven't got a care in the world. I'm sitting pretty. Oh, dear, oh, dear. Did I do any other fascinating tricks at dinner?"

"You were fine," she said. "Don't be so foolish about it. Everybody was crazy about you. The maître d'hôtel was a little worried because you wouldn't stop singing, but he really didn't mind. All he said was, he was afraid they'd close the place again, if there was so much noise. But he didn't care a bit, himself. I think he loved seeing you have such a good time. Oh, you were just singing away, there, for about an hour. It wasn't so terribly loud, at all."

"So I sang," he said. "That must have been a treat. I sang."

"Don't you remember?" she said. "You just sang one song after another. Everybody in the place was listening. They loved it. Only you kept insisting that you wanted to sing some song about some kind of fusiliers or other, and everybody kept shushing you, and you'd keep trying to start it again. You were wonderful. We were all trying to make you stop singing for a minute, and eat something, but you wouldn't hear of it. My, you were funny."

"Didn't I eat any dinner?" he said.

"Oh, not a thing," she said. "Every time the waiter would offer you something, you'd give it right back to him, because you said that he was your long-lost brother, changed in the cradle by a gypsy band, and that anything you had was his. You had him simply roaring at you."

"I bet I did," he said. "I bet I was comical. Society's Pet, I must have been. And what happened then, after my overwhelming success with the waiter?"

"Why, nothing much," she said. "You took a sort of dislike to some old man with white hair, sitting across the room, because you didn't like his necktie and you wanted to tell him about it. But we got you out, before he got really mad."

"Oh, we got out," he said. "Did I walk?"

"Walk! Of course you did," she said. "You were absolutely all right. There was that nasty stretch of ice on the sidewalk, and you did sit down awfully hard, you poor dear. But good heavens, that might have happened to anybody."

"Oh, sure," he said. "Louisa Alcott or anybody. So I fell down on the sidewalk. That would explain what's the matter with my—Yes. I see. And then what, if you don't mind?"

"Ah, now, Peter!" she said. "You can't sit there and say you don't remember what happened after that! I did think that maybe you were just a little tight at dinner—oh, you were perfectly all right, and all that, but I did know you were feeling pretty gay. But you were so serious, from the time you fell down— I never knew you to be that way. Don't you know, how you told me I had never seen your real self before? Oh, Peter, I just couldn't bear it, if you didn't remember that lovely long ride we took together in the taxi! Please, you do remember that, don't you? I think it would simply kill me, if you didn't.

"Oh, yes," he said. "Riding in the taxi. Oh, yes, sure. Pretty long ride, hmm?"

"Round and round and round the park," she said. "Oh, and the trees were shining so in the moonlight. And you said you never knew before that you really had a soul."

"Yes," he said. "I said that. That was me."

"You said such lovely, lovely things," she said. "And I'd never known, all this time, how you had been feeling about me, and I'd never dared to let you see how I felt about you. And then last night—oh, Peter dear, I think that taxi ride was the most important thing that ever happened to us in in our lives."

"Yes," he said. "I guess it must have been."

"And we're going to be so happy," she said. "Oh, I just want to tell everybody! But I don't know—I think maybe it would be sweeter to keep it all to ourselves."

"I think it would be," he said.

"Isn't it lovely?" she said.

"Yes," he said. "Great."

"Lovely!" she said.

"Look here," he said, "do you mind if I have a drink? I mean, just medicinally, you know. I'm off the stuff for life, so help me. But I think I feel a collapse coming on."

"Oh, I think it would do you good," she said. "You poor boy, it's a shame you feel so awful. I'll go make you a whiskey and soda."

"Honestly," he said, "I don't see how you could ever want to speak to me again, after I made such a fool of myself, last night. I think I'd better go join a monastery in Tibet."

"You crazy idiot!" she said. "As if I could ever let you go away now! Stop talking like that. You were perfectly fine."

She jumped up from the couch, kissed him quickly on the forehead, and ran out of the room.

The pale young man looked after her and shook his head long and slowly, then dropped it in his damp and trembling hands.

"Oh, dear," he said. "Oh, dear, oh, dear, oh, dear."

QUESTIONS

1. Identify the point of view and discuss its effect on suspense.

2. Although the events described by the young woman are presented chronologically, each builds upon the other psychologically and emotionally. Identify the turning point. Why does Peter want another drink? Is the ending happy, unhappy, or inconclusive?

3. Discuss irony as a source of comedy in this story, citing examples of verbal irony, dramatic irony, and irony of situation.

4. How does dialogue help characterize the young man? In particular, discuss his diction and his probable tone of voice. What do his literary allusions and play on words tell you about him? How does dialogue help characterize the young woman? Do you think she is being intentionally ironical or do you think she condones Peter's conduct?

5. Does the story have an underlying theme of philosophical significance or is it only a mildly amusing anecdote intended as light reading?

6. Are the characters, their situation, and their language so outdated that the story is a period piece, or do you find the story meaningful? Can you imagine a contemporary incident that would be analogous?

WILLIAM FAULKNER

Spotted Horses

Yes, sir. Flem Snopes has filled that whole country full of spotted horses. You can hear folks running them all day and all night, whooping and hollering, and the horses running back and forth across them little wooden bridges ever now and then kind of like thunder. Here I was this morning pretty near half way to town, with the team ambling along and me setting in the buckboard about half asleep, when all of a sudden something come swurging up outen the bushes and jumped the road clean, without touching hoof to it. It flew right over my team, big as a billboard and flying through the air like a hawk. It taken me thirty minutes to stop my team and untangle the harness and the buckboard and hitch them up again.

That Flem Snopes. I be dog if he ain't a case, now. One morning about ten years ago, the boys was just getting settled down on Varner's porch for a little talk and tobacco, when here come Flem out from behind the counter, with his coat off and his hair all parted, like he might have been clerking for Varner for ten years already. Folks all knowed him; it was a big family of them about five miles down the bottom. That year, at least. Share-cropping. They never stayed on any place over a year. Then they would move on to another place, with the chap or maybe the twins of that year's litter. It was a regular nest of them. But Flem. The rest of them stayed tenant farmers, moving ever year, but here come Flem one day, walking out from behind Jody Varner's counter like he owned it. And he wasn't there but a year or two before folks knowed that, if him and Jody was both still in that store in ten years more, it would be Jody clerking for Flem Snopes. Why, that fellow could make a nickel where it wasn't but four cents to begin with. He skun me in two trades, myself, and the fellow that can do that, I just hope he'll get rich before I do; that's all.

All right. So here Flem was, clerking at Varner's, making a nickel here and there and not telling nobody about it. No, sir. Folks never knowed when Flem got the better of somebody lessen the fellow he beat told it. He'd just set there in the store-chair, chewing his tobacco and keeping his own business to hisself, until about a week later we'd find out it was somebody else's business he was keeping to hisself—provided the fellow he trimmed was mad enough to tell it. That's Flem.

We give him ten years to own ever thing Jody Varner had. But he never waited no ten years. I reckon you-all know that gal of Uncle Billy Varner's, the youngest one; Eula. Jody's sister. Ever Sunday ever yellow-wheeled buggy and curried riding horse in that country would be hitched to Bill Varner's fence, and the young bucks setting on the porch, swarming around Eula like bees around a honey pot. One of these here kind of big, soft-looking gals that could giggle richer than plowed new-ground. Wouldn't none of them leave before the others, and so they would set there on the porch until time to go home, with some of them with nine and ten miles to ride and then get up tomorrow and go back to the field. So they would all leave together and they would ride in a clump down to the creek ford and hitch them curried horses and yellow-wheeled buggies and get out and fight one another. Then they would get in the buggies again and go on home.

Well, one day about a year ago, one of them yellow-wheeled buggies and one of them curried saddle-horses quit this country. We heard they was heading for Texas. The next day Uncle Billy and Eula and Flem come in to town in Uncle Bill's surrey, and when they come back, Flem and Eula was married. And on the next day we heard that two more of them yellow-wheeled buggies had left the country. They mought have gone to Texas, too. It's a big place.

Anyway, about a month after the wedding, Flem and Eula went to Texas, too. They was gone pretty near a year. Then one day last month, Eula come back, with a baby. We figgered up, and we decided that it was as well-growed a three-months-old baby as we ever see. It can already pull up on a chair. I reckon Texas makes big men quick, being a big place. Anyway, if it keeps on like it started, it'll be chewing tobacco and voting time it's eight years old.

And so last Friday here come Flem himself. He was on a wagon with another fellow. The other fellow had one of these two-gallon hats and a ivory-handled pistol and a box of ginger snaps sticking out of his hind pocket, and tied to the tail-gate of the wagon was about two dozen of them Texas ponies, hitched to one another with barbed wire. They was colored like parrots and they was quiet as doves, and ere a one of them would kill you quick as a rattlesnake. Nere a one of them had two eyes the same color, and nere a one of them had ever see a bridle, I reckon; and when that Texas man got down offen the wagon and walked up to them to show how gentle they was, one of them cut his vest clean offen him, same as with a razor.

Flem had done already disappeared; he had went on to see his wife, I reckon, and to see if that ere baby had done gone on to the field to help Uncle

Billy plow, maybe. It was the Texas man that taken the horses on to Mrs. Littlejohn's lot. He had a little trouble at first, when they come to the gate, because they hadn't never see a fence before, and when he finally got them in and taken a pair of wire cutters and unhitched them and got them into the barn and poured some shell corn into the trough, they durn nigh tore down the barn. I reckon they thought that shell corn was bugs, maybe. So he left them in the lot and he announced that the auction would begin at sunup to-morrow.

That night we was setting on Mrs. Littlejohn's porch. You-all mind the moon was nigh full that night, and we could watch them spotted varmints swirling along the fence and back and forth across the lot same as minnows in a pond. And then now and then they would all kind of huddle up against the barn and rest themselves by biting and kicking one another. We would hear a squeal, and then a set of hoofs would go Bam! against the barn, like a pistol. It sounded just like a fellow with a pistol, in a nest of cattymounts, taking his time.

II

It wasn't ere a man knowed yet if Flem owned them things or not. They just knowed one thing: that they wasn't never going to know for sho if Flem did or not, or if maybe he didn't just get on that wagon at the edge of town, for the ride or not. Even Eck Snopes didn't know, Flem's own cousin. But wasn't nobody surprised at that. We knowed that Flem would skin Eck quick as he would ere a one of us.

They was there by sunup next morning, some of them come twelve and sixteen miles, with seed-money tied up in tobacco sacks in their overalls, standing along the fence, when the Texas man come out of Mrs. Littlejohn's after breakfast and clumb onto the gate post with that ere white pistol butt sticking outen his hind pocket. He taken a new box of gingersnaps outen his pocket and bit the end offen it like a cigar and spit out the paper, and said the auction was open. And still they was coming up in wagons and a horse- and mule-back and hitching the teams across the road and coming to the fence. Flem wasn't nowhere in sight.

But he couldn't get them started. He begun to work on Eck, because Eck holp him last night to get them into the barn and feed them that shell corn. Eck got out just in time. He come outen that barn like a chip on the crest of a busted dam of water, and clumb into the wagon just in time.

He was working on Eck when Henry Armstid come up in his wagon. Eck was saying he was skeered to bid on one of them, because he might get it, and the Texas man says, "Them ponies? Them little horses?" He clumb down offen the gate post and went toward the horses. They broke and run, and him following them, kind of chirping to them, with his hand out like he was fixing to catch a fly, until he got three or four of them cornered. Then he jumped into them, and then we couldn't see nothing for a while because of the dust. It was a big cloud of it, and them blare-eyed, spotted things swoaring outen it twenty foot to a jump, in forty directions without counting up. Then the dust settled and there they was, that Texas man and the horse. He had its head twisted clean around like a owl's head. Its legs was braced and it was trembling like a new bride and groaning like a saw mill, and him holding its head wrung clean around on its neck so it was snuffing sky. "Look it over," he says, with his heels dug too and that white pistol sticking outen his pocket and his neck swole up like a spreading adder's until you could just tell what he was saying, cussing the horse and talking to us all at once: "Look him over, the fiddle-headed son of fourteen fathers. Try him, buy him; you will get the best—" Then it was all dust again, and we couldn't see nothing but spotted hide and mane, and that ere Texas man's boot-heels like a couple of walnuts on two strings, and after a while that two-gallon hat come sailing out like a fat old hen crossing a fence.

When the dust settled again, he was just getting outen the far fence corner, brushing himself off. He come and got his hat and brushed it off and come and clumb onto the gate post again. He was breathing hard. He taken the gingersnap box outen his pocket and et one, breathing hard. The hammer-head horse was still running round and round the lot like a merry-go-ground at a fair. That was when Henry Armstid come shoving up to the gate in them patched overalls and one of them dangle-armed shirts of hisn. Hadn't nobody noticed him until then. We was all watching the Texas man and the horses. Even Mrs. Littlejohn; she had done come out and built a fire under the wash-pot in her back yard, and she would stand at the fence a while and then go back into the house and come out again with a arm full of wash and stand at the fence again. Well, here come Henry shoving up, and then we see Mrs. Armstid right behind him, in that ere faded wrapper and sunbonnet and them tennis shoes. "Git on back to that wagon," Henry says.

"Henry," she says.

"Here, boys," the Texas man says; "make room for missus to git up and see. Come on, Henry," he says; "here's your chance to buy that saddle-horse missus has been wanting. What about ten dollars, Henry?"

"Henry," Mrs. Armstid says. She put her hand on Henry's arm. Henry knocked her hand down.

"Git on back to that wagon, like I told you," he says.

Mrs. Armstid never moved. She stood behind Henry, with her hands rolled into her dress, not looking at nothing. "He hain't no more despair than to buy one of them things," she says. "And us not five dollars ahead of the pore house, he hain't no more despair." It was the truth, too. They ain't never made more than a bare living offen that place of theirs, and them with four chaps and the very clothes they wears she earns by weaving by the firelight at night while Henry's asleep.

"Shut your mouth and git on back to that wagon," Henry says. "Do you want I taken a wagon stake to you here in the big road?"

Well, that Texas man taken one look at her. Then he begun on Eck again, like Henry wasn't even there. But Eck was skeered. "I can git me a snapping turtle or a water moccasin for nothing. I ain't going to buy none."

So the Texas man said he would give Eck a horse. "To start the auction, and because you holp me last night. If you'll start the bidding on the next horse," he says, "I'll give you that fiddle-head horse."

I wish you could have seen them, standing there with their seed-money in their pockets, watching that Texas man give Eck Snopes a live horse, all fixed to call him a fool if he taken it or not. Finally Eck says he'll take it. "Only I just starts the bidding," he says. "I don't have to buy the next one lessen I ain't overtopped." The Texas man said all right, and Eck bid a dollar on the next one, with Henry Armstid standing there with his mouth already open, watching Eck and the Texas man like a mad-dog or something. "A dollar," Eck says.

The Texas man looked at Eck. His mouth was already open too, like he had started to say something and what he was going to say had up and died on him. "A dollar?" he says. "One dollar? You mean, *one* dollar, Eck?"

"Durn it," Eck says; "two dollars, then."

Well, sir, I wish you could a seen that Texas man. He taken out that gingersnap box and held it up and looked into it, careful, like it might have been a diamond ring in it, or a spider. Then he throwed it away and wiped his face with a bandanna. "Well," he says. "Well. Two dollars. Two dollars. Is your pulse all right, Eck?" he says. "Do you have ager-sweats at night, maybe?" he says. "Well," he says, "I got to take it. But are you boys going to stand there and see Eck get two horses at a dollar a head?"

That done it. I be dog if he wasn't nigh as smart as Flem Snopes. He hadn't no more than got the words outen his mouth before here was Henry Armstid, waving his hand. "Three dollars," Henry says. Mrs. Armstid tried to hold him again. He knocked her hand off, shoving up to the gate post.

"Mister," Mrs. Armstid says, "we got chaps in the house and not corn to feed the stock. We got five dollars I earned my chaps a-weaving after dark, and him snoring in the bed. And he hain't no more despair."

"Henry bids three dollars," the Texas man says. "Raise him a dollar, Eck, and the horse is yours."

"Henry," Mrs. Armstid says.

"Raise him, Eck," the Texas man says.

"Four dollars," Eck says.

"Five dollars," Henry says, shaking his fist. He shoved up right under the gate post. Mrs. Armstid was looking at the Texas man too.

"Mister," she says, "if you take that five dollars I earned my chaps a-weaving for one of them things, it'll be a curse onto you and yourn during all the time of man."

But it wasn't no stopping Henry. He had shoved up, waving his fist at the Texas man. He opened it; the money was in nickels and quarters, and one dollar bill that looked like a cow's cud. "Five dollars," he says. "And the man that raises it'll have to beat my head off, or I'll beat hisn."

"All right," the Texas man says. "Five dollars is bid. But don't you shake your hand at me."

III

It taken till nigh sundown before the last one was sold. He got them hotted up once and the bidding got up to seven dollars and a quarter, but most of them went around three or four dollars, him setting on the gate post and picking the horses out one at a time by mouth-word, and Mrs. Littlejohn pumping up and down at the tub and stopping and coming to the fence for a while and going back to the tub again. She had done got done too, and the wash was hung on the line in the back yard, and we could smell supper cooking. Finally they was all sold; he swapped the last two and the wagon for a buckboard.

We was all kind of tired, but Henry Armstid looked more like a mad-dog than ever. When he bought, Mrs. Armstid had went back to the wagon, setting in it behind them two rabbit-sized, bone-pore mules, and the wagon itself looking like it would fall all to pieces soon as the mules moved. Henry hadn't even waited to pull it outen the road; it was still in the middle of the road and her setting in it, not looking at nothing, ever since this morning.

Henry was right up against the gate. He went up to the Texas man. "I bought a horse and I paid cash," Henry says. "And yet you expect me to stand around here until they are all sold before I can get my horse. I'm going to take my horse outen that lot."

The Texas man looked at Henry. He talked like he might have been asking for a cup of coffee at the table. "Take your horse," he says.

Then Henry quit looking at the Texas man. He begun to swallow, holding onto the gate. "Ain't you going to help me?" he says.

"It ain't my horse," the Texas man says.

Henry never looked at the Texas man again, he never looked at nobody. "Who'll help me catch my horse?" he says. Never nobody said nothing. "Bring the plowline," Henry says. Mrs. Armstid got outen the wagon and brought the plowline. The Texas man got down offen the post. The woman made to pass him, carrying the rope.

"Don't you go in there, missus," the Texas man says.

Henry opened the gate. He didn't look back. "Come on here," he says.

"Don't you go in there, missus," the Texas man says.

Mrs. Armstid wasn't looking at nobody, neither, with her hands across her middle, holding the rope. "I reckon I better," she says. Her and Henry went into the lot. The horses broke and run. Henry and Mrs. Armstid followed.

"Get him into the corner," Henry says. They got Henry's horse cornered finally, and Henry taken the rope, but Mrs. Armstid let the horse get out. They hemmed it up again, but Mrs. Armstid let it get out again, and Henry turned and hit her with the rope. "Why didn't you head him back?" Henry says. He hit her again. "Why didn't you?" It was about that time I looked around and see Flem Snopes standing there.

It was the Texas man that done something. He moved fast for a big man. He caught the rope before Henry could hit the third time, and Henry whirled and made like he would jump at the Texas man. But he never jumped. The Texas man went and taken Henry's arm and led him outen the lot. Mrs. Armstid come behind them and the Texas man taken some money outen his pocket and he give it into Mrs. Armstid's hand. "Get him into the wagon and take him on home," the Texas man says, like he might have been telling them he enjoyed his supper.

Then here come Flem. "What's that for, Buck?" Flem says.

"Thinks he bought one of them ponies," the Texas man says. "Get him on away, missus."

But Henry wouldn't go. "Give him back that money," he says. "I bought that horse and I aim to have him if I have to shoot him."

And there was Flem, standing there with his hands in his pockets, chewing, like he had just happened to be passing.

"You take your money and I take my horse," Henry says. "Give it back to him," he says to Mrs. Armstid.

"You don't own no horse of mine," the Texas man says. "Get him on home, missus."

Then Henry seen Flem. "You got something to do with these horses," he says. "I bought one. Here's the money for it." He taken the bill outen Mrs. Armstid's hand. He offered it to Flem. "I bought one. Ask him. Here. Here's the money," he says, giving the bill to Flem.

When Flem taken the money, the Texas man dropped the rope he had snatched outen Henry's hand. He had done sent Eck Snope's boy up to the store for another box of gingersnaps, and he taken the box outen his pocket and looked into it. It was empty and he dropped it on the ground. "Mr. Snopes will have your money for you to-morrow," he says to Mrs. Armstid. "You can get it from him to-morrow. He don't own no horse. You get him into the wagon and get him on home." Mrs. Armstid went back to the wagon and got in. "Where's that ere buckboard I bought?" the Texas man says. It was after sundown then. And then Mrs. Littlejohn come out on the porch and rung the supper bell.

IV

I come on in and et supper. Mrs. Littlejohn would bring in a pan of bread or something, then she would go out to the porch a minute and come back and tell us. The Texas man had hitched his team to the buckboard he had swapped them last two horses for, and him and Flem had gone, and then she told that the rest of them that never had ropes had went back to the store with I. O. Snopes to get some ropes, and wasn't nobody at the gate but Henry Armstid, and Mrs. Armstid setting in the wagon in the road, and Eck Snopes and that boy of hisn. "I don't care how many of them fool men gets killed by them things," Mrs. Littlejohn says, "but I ain't going to let Eck Snopes take that boy into that lot again." So she went down to the gate, but she come back without the boy or Eck neither.

"It ain't no need to worry about that boy," I says. "He's charmed." He was right behind Eck last night when Eck went to help feed them. The whole drove of them jumped clean over that boy's head and never touched him. It was Eck that touched him. Eck snatched him into the wagon and taken a rope and frailed the tar outen him.

So I had done et and went to my room and was undressing, long as I had a long trip to make next day; I was trying to sell a machine to Mrs. Bundren up past Whiteleaf; when Henry Armstid opened that gate and went in by hisself.

They couldn't make him wait for the balance of them to get back with their ropes. Eck Snopes said he tried to make Henry wait, but Henry wouldn't do it. Eck said Henry walked right up to them and that when they broke, they run clean over Henry like a hay-mow breaking down. Eck said he snatched that boy of hisn out of the way just in time and that them things went through that gate like a creek flood and into the wagons and teams hitched side the road, busting wagon tongues and snapping harness like it was fishing-line, with Mrs. Armstid still setting in their wagon in the middle of it like something carved outen wood. Then they scattered, wild horses and tame mules with pieces of harness and single trees dangling offen them, both ways up and down the road.

"There goes ourn, paw!" Eck says his boy said. "There it goes, into Mrs. Littlejohn's house." Eck says it run right up the steps and into the house like a boarder late for supper. I reckon so. Anyway, I was in my room, in my underclothes, with one sock on and one sock in my hand, leaning out the window when the commotion busted out, when I heard something run into the melodeon in the hall; it sounded like a railroad engine. Then the door to my room come sailing in like when you throw a tin bucket top into the wind and I looked over my shoulder and see something that looked like a fourteen-foot pinwheel a-blaring its eyes at me. It had to blare them fast, because I was already done jumped out the window.

I reckon it was anxious, too. I reckon it hadn't never seen barbed wire or shell corn before, but I know it hadn't never seen underclothes before, or maybe it was a sewing-machine agent it hadn't never seen. Anyway, it swirled and turned to run back up the hall and outen the house, when it met Eck Snopes and that boy just coming in, carrying a rope. It swirled again and run down the hall and out the back door just in time to meet Mrs. Littlejohn. She had just gathered up the clothes she had washed, and she was coming onto the back porch with a armful of washing in one hand and a scrubbing-board in the other, when the horse skidded up to her, trying to stop and swirl again. It never taken Mrs. Littlejohn no time a-tall.

"Git outen here, you son," she says. She hit it across the face with the scrubbing-board; that ere scrubbing-board split as neat as ere a axe could have done it, and when the horse swirled to run back up the hall, she hit it again with what was left of the scrubbing-board, not on the head this time. "And stay out," she says.

Eck and that boy was half-way down the hall by this time. I reckon that horse looked like a pinwheel to Eck too. "Git to hell outen here, Ad!" Eck says. Only there wasn't time. Eck dropped flat on his face, but the boy never moved. The boy was about a yard tall maybe, in overhalls just like Eck's; that horse swoared over his head without touching a hair. I saw that, because I was just coming back up the front steps, still carrying that ere sock and still in my underclothes, when the horse come onto the porch again. It taken one look at me and swirled again and run to the end of the porch and jumped the banisters and the lot fence like a hen-hawk and lit in the lot running and went out the gate again and jumped eight or ten upside-down wagons and went on down the road.

It was a full moon then. Mrs. Armstid was still setting in the wagon like she had done been carved outen wood and left there and forgot.

That horse. It ain't never missed a lick. It was going about forty miles a hour when it come to the bridge over the creek. It would have had a clear road, but it so happened that Vernon Tull was already using the bridge when it got there. He was coming back from town; he hadn't heard about the auction; him and his wife and three daughters and Mrs. Tull's aunt, all setting in chairs in the wagon bed, and all asleep, including the mules. They waked up when the horse hit the bridge one time, but Tull said the first he knew was when the mules tried to turn the wagon around in the middle of the bridge and he seen that spotted varmint run right twixt the mules and run up the wagon tongue like a squirrel. He said he just had time to hit it across the face with his whip-stock, because about that time the mules turned the wagon around on that ere one-way bridge and that horse clumb across one of the mules and jumped down onto the bridge again and went on, with Vernon standing up in the wagon and kicking at it.

Tull said the mules turned in the harness and clumb back into the wagon too, with Tull trying to beat them out again, with the reins wrapped around his wrist. After that he says all he seen was overturned chairs and womenfolks' legs and white drawers shining in the moonlight, and his mules and that spotted horse going on up the road like a ghost.

The mules jerked Tull outen the wagon and drug him a spell on the bridge before the reins broke. They thought at first that he was dead, and while they was kneeling around him, picking the bridge splinters outen him, here come Eck and that boy, still carrying the rope. They was running and breathing a little hard. "Where'd he go?" Eck says.

V

I went back and got my pants and shirt and shoes on just in time to go and help get Henry Armstid outen the trash in the lot. I be dog if he didn't look like he was dead, with his head hanging back and his teeth showing in the moonlight, and a little rim of white under his eyelids. We could still hear them horses, here and there; hadn't none of them got more than four—five miles away yet, not knowing the country, I reckon. So we could hear them and folks yelling now and then: "Whooey. Head him!"

We toted Henry into Mrs. Littlejohn's. She was in the hall; she hadn't put down the armful of clothes. She taken one look at us, and she laid down the busted scrubbing-board and taken up the lamp and opened a empty door. "Bring him in here," she says.

We toted him in and laid him on the bed. Mrs. Littlejohn set the lamp on the dresser, still carrying the clothes. "I'll declare, you men," she says. Our shadows was way up the wall, tiptoeing too; we could hear ourselves breathing. "Better get his wife," Mrs. Littlejohn says. She went out, carrying the clothes.

"I reckon we had," Quick says. "Go get her, somebody.

"Whyn't you go?" Winterbottom says.

"Let Ernest git her," Durley says. "He lives neighbors with them."

Ernest went to fetch her. I be dog if Henry didn't look like he was dead. Mrs. Littlejohn come back, with a kettle and some towels. She went to work on Henry, and then Mrs. Armstid and Ernest come in. Mrs. Armstid come to the foot of the bed and stood there, with her hands rolled into her apron, watching what Mrs. Littlejohn was doing, I reckon.

"You men get outen the way," Mrs. Littlejohn says. "Git outside," she says. "See if you can't find something else to play with that will kill some more of you."

"Is he dead?" Winterbottom says.

"It ain't your fault if he ain't," Mrs. Littlejohn says. "Go tell Will Varner to come up here. I reckon a man ain't so different from a mule, come long come short. Except maybe a mule's got more sense."

We went to get Uncle Billy. It was a full moon. We could hear them, now and then, four mile away: "Whooey. Head him." The country was full of them, one on ever wooden bridge in the land, running across it like thunder: "Whooey. There he goes. Head him."

We hadn't got far before Henry begun to scream. I reckon Mrs. Littlejohn's water had brung him to; anyway, he wasn't dead. We went on to Uncle Billy's. The house was dark. We called to him, and after a while the window opened and Uncle Billy put his head out, peart as a peckerwood, listening. "Are they still trying to catch them durn rabbits?" he says.

He come down, with his britches on over his night-shirt and his suspenders dangling, carrying his horse-doctoring grip. "Yes, sir," he says, cocking his head like a woodpecker; "they're still a-trying."

We could hear Henry before we reached Mrs. Littlejohn's. He was going Ah-Ah-Ah. We stopped in the yard. Uncle Billy went on in. We could hear Henry. We stood in the yard, hearing them on the bridges, this-a-way and that: "Whooey, Whooey."

"Eck Snopes ought to caught hisn," Ernest says.

"Looks like he ought," Winterbottom said.

Henry was going Ah-Ah-Ah steady in the house; then he begun to scream. "Uncle Billy's started," Quick says. We looked into the hall. We could see the light where the door was. Then Mrs. Littlejohn come out.

"Will needs some help," she says. "You, Ernest. You'll do." Ernest went into the house.

"Hear them?" Quick said. "That one was on Four Mile bridge." We could hear them; it sounded like thunder a long way off; it didn't last long:

"Whooey."

We could hear Henry: "Ah-Ah-Ah-Ah-Ah."

"They are both started now," Winterbottom says. "Ernest too."

That was early in the night. Which was a good thing, because it taken a long night for folks to chase them things right and for Henry to lay there and holler, being as Uncle Billy never had none of this here chloryfoam to set

Henry's leg with. So it was considerate in Flem to get them started early. And what do you reckon Flem's com-ment was?

That's right. Nothing. Because he wasn't there. Hadn't nobody see him since that Texas man left.

VI

That was Saturday night. I reckon Mrs. Armstid got home about daylight, to see about the chaps. I don't know where they thought her and Henry was. But lucky the oldest one was a gal, about twelve, big enough to take care of the little ones. Which she did for the next two days. Mrs. Armstid would nurse Henry all night and work in the kitchen for hern and Henry's keep, and in the afternoon she would drive home (it was about four miles) to see the chaps. She would cook up a pot of victuals and leave it on the stove, and the gal would bar the house and keep the little ones quiet. I would hear Mrs. Littlejohn and Mrs. Armstid talking in the kitchen. "How are the chaps making out?" Mrs. Little-john says.

"All right," Mrs. Armstid says.

"Don't they git skeered at night?" Mrs. Littlejohn says.

"Ina May bars the door when I leave," Mrs. Armstid says. "She's got the axe in bed with her. I reckon she can make out."

I reckon they did. And I reckon Mrs. Armstid was waiting for Flem to come back to town; hadn't nobody seen him until this morning; to get her money the Texas man said Flem was keeping for her. Sho. I reckon she was.

Anyway, I heard Mrs. Armstid and Mrs. Littlejohn talking in the kitchen this morning while I was eating breakfast. Mrs. Littlejohn had just told Mrs. Armstid that Flem was in town. "You can ask him for that five dollars," Mrs. Littlejohn says.

"You reckon he'll give it to me?" Mrs. Armstid says.

Mrs. Littlejohn was washing dishes, washing them like a man, like they was made out of iron. "No," she says. "But asking him won't do no hurt. It might shame him. I don't reckon it will, but it might."

"If he wouldn't give it back, it ain't no use to ask," Mrs. Armstid says.

"Suit yourself," Mrs. Littlejohn says. "It's your money."

I could hear the dishes.

"Do you reckon he might give it back to me?" Mrs. Armstid says. "That Texas man said he would. He said I could get it from Mr. Snopes later."

"Then go and ask him for it," Mrs. Littlejohn says.

I could hear the dishes.

"He won't give it back to me," Mrs. Armstid says.

"All right," Mrs. Littlejohn says. "Don't ask him for it, then."

I could hear the dishes; Mrs. Armstid was helping. "You don't reckon he would, do you?" she says. Mrs. Littlejohn never said nothing. It sounded like she was throwing the dishes at one another. "Maybe I better go and talk to Henry about it," Mrs. Armstid says.

"I would," Mrs. Littlejohn says. I be dog it it didn't sound like she had two plates in her hands, beating them together. "Then Henry can buy another five-dollar horse with it. Maybe he'll buy one next time that will out and out kill him. If I thought that, I'd give you back the money, myself."

"I reckon I better talk to him first," Mrs. Armstid said. Then it sounded like Mrs. Littlejohn taken up all the dishes and throwed them at the cook-stove, and I come away.

That was this morning. I had been up to Bundren's and back, and I thought that things would have kind of settled down. So after breakfast, I went up to the store. And there was Flem, setting in the store chair and whittling, like he might not have ever moved since he come to clerk for Jody Varner. I. O. was leaning in the door, in his shirt sleeves and with his hair parted too, same as Flem was before he turned the clerking job over to I. O. It's a funny thing about them Snopes: they all looks alike, yet there ain't ere a two of them that claims brothers. They're always just cousins, like Flem and Eck and Flem and I. O. Eck was there too, squatting against the wall, him and that boy, eating cheese and crackers outen a sack; they told me that Eck hadn't been home a-tall. And that Lon Quick hadn't got back to town, even. He followed his horse clean down to Samson's Bridge, with a wagon and a camp outfit. Eck finally caught one of hisn. It run into a blind lane at Freeman's and Eck and the boy taken and tied their rope across the end of the lane, about three foot high. The horse come to the end of the lane and whirled and run back without ever stopping. Eck says it never seen the rope a-tall. He says it looked just like one of these here Christmas pinwheels. "Didn't it try to run again?" I says.

"No," Eck says, eating a bite of cheese offen his knife blade. "Just kicked some."

"Kicked some?" I says.

"It broke its neck," Eck says.

Well, they was squatting there, about six of them, talking, talking at Flem; never nobody knowed yet if Flem had ere a interest in them horses or not. So finally I come right out and asked him. "Flem's done skun all of us so much," I says, "that we're proud of him. Come on, Flem," I says, "how much did you and that Texas man make offen them horses? You can tell us. Ain't nobody here but Eck that bought one of them; the others ain't got back to town yet, and Eck's your own cousin; he'll be proud to hear, too. How much did you-all make?"

They was all whittling, not looking at Flem, making like they was studying. But you could a heard a pin drop. And I. O. He had been rubbing his back up and down on the door, but he stopped now, watching Flem like a pointing dog. Flem finished cutting the sliver offen his stick. He spit across the porch, into the road. "Twarn't none of my horses," he says.

I. O. cackled, like a hen, slapping his legs with both hands. "You boys might just as well quit trying to get ahead of Flem," he said.

Well, about that time I see Mrs. Armstid come outen Mrs. Littlejohn's gate, coming up the road. I never said nothing. I says, "Well, if a man can't take care of himself in a trade, he can't blame the man that trims him."

Flem never said nothing, trimming at the stick. He hadn't seen Mrs. Armstid. "Yes, sir," I says. "A fellow like Henry Armstid ain't got nobody but hisself to blame."

"Course he ain't," I. O. says. He ain't seen her, neither. "Henry Armstid's a born fool. Always is been. If Flem hadn't a got his money, somebody else would."

We looked at Flem. He never moved. Mrs. Armstid come on up the road.

"That's right," I says. "But, come to think of it, Henry never bought no horse." We looked at Flem; you could a heard a match drop. "That Texas man told her to get that five dollars back from Flem next day. I reckon Flem's done already taken that money to Mrs. Littlejohn's and give it to Mrs. Armstid."

We watched Flem. I. O. quit rubbing his back against the door again. After a while Flem raised his head and spit across the porch, into the dust. I. O. cackled, just like a hen. "Ain't he a beating fellow, now?" I. O. says.

Mrs. Armstid was getting closer, so I kept on talking, watching to see if Flem would look up and see her. But he never looked up. I went on talking about Tull, about how he was going to sue Flem, and Flem setting there, whittling his stick, not saying nothing else after he said they wasn't none of his horses.

Then I. O. happened to look around. He seen Mrs. Armstid. "Psssst!" he says. Flem looked up. "Here she comes!" I. O. says. "Go out the back. I'll tell her you done went in to town to-day."

But Flem never moved. He just set there, whittling, and we watched Mrs. Armstid come up onto the porch, in that ere faded sunbonnet and wrapper and them tennis shoes that made a kind of hissing noise on the porch. She come onto the porch and stopped, her hands rolled into her dress in front, not looking at nothing.

"He said Saturday," she says, "that he wouldn't sell Henry no horse. He said I could get the money from you."

Flem looked up. The knife never stopped. It went on trimming off a sliver same as if he was watching it. "He taken that money off with him when he left," Flem says.

Mrs. Armstid never looked at nothing. We never looked at her, neither, except that boy of Eck's. He had a half-et cracker in his hand, watching her, chewing.

"He said Henry hadn't bought no horse," Mrs. Armstid says. "He said for me to get the money from you today."

"I reckon he forgot about it," Flem said. "He taken that money off with him Saturday." He whittled again. I. O. kept on rubbing his back, slow. He licked his lips. After a while the woman looked up the road, where it went on up the hill, toward the graveyard. She looked up that way for a while, with that boy of Eck's watching her and I. O. rubbing his back slow against the door. Then she turned back toward the steps.

"I reckon it's time to get dinner started," she says.

"How's Henry this morning, Mrs. Armstid?" Winterbottom says.

She looked at Winterbottom; she almost stopped. "He's resting, I thank you kindly," she says.

Flem got up, outen the chair, putting his knife away. He spit across the porch. "Wait a minute, Mrs. Armstid," he says. She stopped again. She didn't look at him. Flem went on into the store, with I. O. done quit rubbing his back now, with his head craned after Flem, and Mrs. Armstid standing there with her hands rolled into her dress, not looking at nothing. A wagon come up the road and passed; it was Freeman, on the way to town. Then Flem come out again, with I. O. still watching him. Flem had one of these little striped sacks of Jody Varner's candy; I bet he still owns Jody that nickel, too. He put the sack into Mrs. Armstid's hand, like he would have put it into a hollow stump. He spit again across the porch. "A little sweetening for the chaps," he says.

"You're right kind," Mrs. Armstid says. She held the sack of candy in her hand, not looking at nothing. Eck's boy was watching the sack, the half-et cracker in his hand; he wasn't chewing now. He watched Mrs. Armstid roll the sack into her apron. "I reckon I better get on back and help with dinner," she says. She turned and went back across the porch. Flem set down in the chair again and opened his knife. He spit across the porch again, past Mrs. Armstid where she hadn't went down the steps yet. Then she went on, in that.ere sunbonnet and wrapper all the same color, back down the road toward Mrs. Littlejohn's. You couldn't see her dress move, like a natural woman walking. She looked like a old snag still standing up and moving along on a high water. We watched her turn in at Mrs. Littlejohn's and go outen sight. Flem was whittling. I. O. begun to rub his back on the door. Then he begun to cackle, just like a durn hen.

"You boys might just as well quit trying," I. O. says. "You can't git ahead of Flem. You can't touch him. Ain't he a sight, now?"

I be dog if he ain't. If I had brung a herd of wild cattymounts into town and sold them to my neighbors and kinfolks, they would have lynched me. Yes, sir.

QUESTIONS

1. Identify the point of view and discuss its effect on believability. What other devices contribute to the story's credibility? Were you reminded at any point that Flem Snopes and the Armstids are fictional characters who are as fictitious as the narrator?

2. Is the narrator the story's main character? Give a thumbnail sketch of the narrator. Discuss the ways in which the narrator's personality is revealed.

3. Do you find the narrator an engaging storyteller? Is his way of speaking integral to his success as a storyteller? Do you think it makes him fail as a storyteller?

4. What is the narrator's attitude to Henry Armstid? to Mrs. Armstid? Do you agree with his judgment?

5. What is the narrator's attitude to Flem Snopes? Do you agree with his judgment?

6. How is the auctioneer different from Flem Snopes? What scene most clearly reveals their differences?

7. A characteristic of the first-person narrator is his incomplete knowledge of other people. Discuss the incompleteness of the narrator's information. What is the effect of his guessing at the "truth" of the situation that is the basis of his story?

8. This story has the flavor of a tall tale. Explain, discussing the narrator as a yarn-spinner and citing examples of exaggeration and physical humor.

EUDORA WELTY

Why I Live at the P.O.

I was getting along fine with Mama, Papa-Daddy and Uncle Rondo until my sister Stella-Rondo just separated from her husband and came back home again. Mr. Whitaker! Of course I went with Mr. Whitaker first, when he first appeared here in China Grove, taking "Pose Yourself" photos, and Stella-Rondo broke us up. Told him I was one-sided. Bigger on one side than the other, which is a deliberate, calculated falsehood: I'm the same. Stella-Rondo is exactly twelve months to the day younger than I am and for that reason she's spoiled.

She's always had anything in the world she wanted and then she'd throw it away. Papa-Daddy gave her this gorgeous Add-a-Pearl necklace when she was eight years old and she threw it away playing baseball when she was nine, with only two pearls.

So as soon as she got married and moved away from home the first thing she did was separate! From Mr. Whitaker! This photographer with the popeyes she said she trusted. Came home from one of those towns up in Illinois and to our complete surprise brought this child of two.

Mama said she like to made her drop dead for a second. "Here you had this marvelous blonde child and never so much as wrote your mother a word about it," says Mama. "I'm thoroughly ashamed of you." But of course she wasn't.

Stella-Rondo just calmly takes off this *hat,* I wish you could see it. She says, "Why, Mama, Shirley-T.'s adopted, I can prove it."

"How?" says Mama, but all I says was, "H'm!" There I was over the hot stove, trying to stretch two chickens over five people and a completely unexpected child into the bargain, without one moment's notice.

"What do you mean—'H'm!'?" says Stella-Rondo, and Mama says, "I heard that, Sister."

I said that oh, I didn't mean a thing, only that whoever Shirley-T. was, she was the spit-image of Papa-Daddy if he'd cut off his beard, which of course he'd never do in the world. Papa-Daddy's Mama's papa and sulks.

Stella-Rondo got furious! She said, "Sister, I don't need to tell you you got a lot of nerve and always did have and I'll thank you to make no future reference to my adopted child whatsoever."

"Very well," I said. "Very well, very well. Of course I noticed at once she looks like Mr. Whitaker's side too. That frown. She looks like a cross between Mr. Whitaker and Papa-Daddy."

"Well, all I can say is she isn't."

"She looks exactly like Shirley Temple to me," says Mama, but Shirley-T. just ran away from her.

So the first thing Stella-Rondo did at the table was turn Papa-Daddy against me.

"Papa-Daddy," she says. He was trying to cut up his meat. "Papa-Daddy!" I was taken completely by surprise. Papa-Daddy is about a million years old and's got this long-long beard. "Papa-Daddy, Sister says she fails to understand why you don't cut off your beard."

So Papa-Daddy l-a-y-s down his knife and fork! He's real rich. Mama says he is, he says he isn't. So he says, "Have I heard correctly? You don't understand why I don't cut off my beard?"

"Why," I says, "Papa-Daddy, of course I understand, I did not say any such of a thing, the idea!"

He says, "Hussy!"

I says, "Papa-Daddy, you know I wouldn't any more want you to cut off your beard than the man in the moon. It was the farthest thing from my mind! Stella-Rondo sat there and made that up while she was eating breast of chicken."

But he says, "So the postmistress fails to understand why I don't cut off my beard. Which job I got you through my influence with the government. 'Bird's nest'—is that what you call it?"

Not that it isn't the next to smallest P.O. in the entire state of Mississippi.

I says, "Oh, Papa-Daddy," I says, "I didn't say any such of a thing, I never dreamed it was a bird's nest, I have always been grateful though this is the next to smallest P.O. in the state of Mississippi, and I do not enjoy being referred to as a hussy by my own grandfather."

But Stella-Rondo says, "Yes, you did say it too. Anybody in the world could of heard you, that had ears."

"Stop right there," says Mama, looking at *me.*

So I pulled my napkin straight back through the napkin ring and left the table.

As soon as I was out of the room Mama says, "Call her back, or she'll starve to death," but Papa-Daddy says, "This is the beard I started growing on the Coast when I was fifteen years old." He would of gone on till nightfall if Shirley-T. hadn't lost the Milky Way she ate in Cairo.

So Papa-Daddy says, "I am going out and lie in the hammock, and you can all sit here and remember my words: I'll never cut off my beard as long as I live, even one inch, and I don't appreciate it in you at all." Passed right by me in the hall and went straight out and got in the hammock.

It would be a holiday. It wasn't five minutes before Uncle Rondo suddenly appeared in the hall in one of Stella-Rondo's flesh-colored kimonos, all cut on the bias, like something Mr. Whitaker probably thought was gorgeous.

"Uncle Rondo!" I says. "I didn't know who that was! Where are you going?"

"Sister," he says, "get out of my way, I'm poisoned."

"If you're poisoned stay away from Papa-Daddy," I says. "Keep out of the hammock. Papa-Daddy will certainly beat you on the head if you come within forty miles of him. He thinks I deliberately said he ought to cut off his beard after he got me the P.O., and I've told him and told him and told him, and he acts like he just don't hear me. Papa-Daddy must of gone stone deaf."

"He picked a fine day to do it then," says Uncle Rondo, and before you could say "Jack Robinson" flew out in the yard.

What he'd really done, he'd drunk another bottle of that prescription. He does it every single Fourth of July as sure as shooting, and it's horribly expensive. Then he falls over in the hammock and snores. So he insisted on zigzagging right on out to the hammock, looking like a half-wit.

Papa-Daddy woke up with this horrible yell and right there without moving an inch he tried to turn Uncle Rondo against me. I heard every word he said. Oh, he told Uncle Rondo I didn't learn to read till I was eight years old and he didn't see how in the world I ever got the mail put up at the P.O., much less read it all, and he said if Uncle Rondo could only fathom the lengths he had gone to to get me that job! And he said on the other hand he thought Stella-Rondo had a brilliant mind and deserved credit for getting out of town. All the time he was just lying there swinging as pretty as you please and looping out his beard, and poor Uncle Rondo was *pleading* with him to slow down the hammock, it was making him as dizzy as a witch to watch it. But that's what Papa-Daddy likes about a hammock. So Uncle Rondo was too dizzy to get turned against me for the time being. He's Mama's only brother and is a good case of a one-track mind. Ask anybody. A certified pharmacist.

Just then I heard Stella-Rondo raising the upstairs window. While she was married she got this peculiar idea that it's cooler with the windows shut and locked. So she has to raise the window before she can make a soul hear her outdoors.

So she raises the window and says, *"Oh!"* You would have thought she was mortally wounded.

Uncle Rondo and Papa-Daddy didn't even look up, but kept right on with what they were doing. I had to laugh.

I flew up the stairs and threw the door open! I says, "What in the wide world's the matter, Stella-Rondo? You mortally wounded?"

"No," she says, "I am not mortally wounded but I wish you would do me the favor of looking out that window there and telling me what you see."

So I shade my eyes and look out the window.

"I see the front yard," I says.

"Don't you see any human beings?" she says.

"I see Uncle Rondo trying to run Papa-Daddy out of the hammock," I says. "Nothing more. Naturally, it's so suffocating-hot in the house, with all the windows shut and locked, everybody who cares to stay in their right mind will have to go out and get in the hammock before the Fourth of July is over."

"Don't you notice anything different about Uncle Rondo?" asks Stella-Rondo.

"Why, no, except he's got on some terrible looking flesh-colored contraption I wouldn't be found dead in, is all I can see," I says.

"Never mind, you won't be found dead in it, because it happens to be part of my trousseau, and Mr. Whitaker took several dozen photographs of me in it," says Stella-Rondo. "What on earth could Uncle Rondo *mean* by wearing part of my trousseau out in the broad open daylight without saying so much as 'Kiss my foot,' *knowing* I only got home this morning after my separation and hung my negligee up on the bathroom door, just as nervous as I could be?"

"I'm sure I don't know, and what do you expect me to do about it?" I says. "Jump out the window?"

"No, I expect nothing of the kind. I simply declare that Uncle Rondo looks like a fool in it, that's all," she says. "It makes me sick to my stomach."

"Well, he looks as good as he can," I says. "As good as anybody in reason could." I stood up for Uncle Rondo, please remember. And I said to Stella-Rondo, "I think I would do well not to criticize so freely if I were you and came home with a two-year-old child I had never said a word about, and no explanation whatever about my separation."

"I asked you the instant I entered this house not to refer one more time to my adopted child, and you gave me your word of honor you would not," was all Stella-Rondo would say, and started pulling out every one of her eyebrows with some cheap Kress tweezers.

So I merely slammed the door behind me and went down and made some green-tomato pickle. Somebody had to do it. Of course Mama had turned both the niggers loose; she always said no earthly power could hold one anyway on the Fourth of July, so she wouldn't even try. It turned out that Jaypan fell in the lake and came within a very narrow limit of drowning.

So Mama trots in. Lifts up the lid and says, "H'm! Not very good for your Uncle Rondo in his precarious condition, I must say. Or poor little adopted Shirley-T. Shame on you!"

That made me tired. I says, "Well, Stella-Rondo had better thank her lucky stars it was her instead of me came trotting in with that very peculiar-looking child. Now if it had been me that trotted in from Illinois and brought a peculiar-looking child of two, I shudder to think of the reception I'd of got, much less controlled the diet of an entire family."

"But you must remember, Sister, that you were never married to Mr. Whitaker in the first place and didn't go up to Illinois to live," says Mama, shaking a spoon in my face. "If you had I would of been just as overjoyed to see you and your little adopted girl as I was to see Stella-Rondo, when you wound up with your separation and came on back home."

"You would not," I says.

"Don't contradict me, I would," says Mama.

But I said she couldn't convince me though she talked till she was blue in the face. Then I said, "Besides, you know as well as I do that that child is not adopted."

"She most certainly is adopted," says Mama, stiff as a poker.

I says, "Why, Mama, Stella-Rondo had her just as sure as anything in this world, and just too stuck up to admit it."

"Why, Sister," said Mama. "Here I thought we were going to have a pleasant Fourth of July, and you start right out not believing a word your own baby sister tells you!"

"Just like Cousin Annie Flo. Went to her grave denying the facts of life," I remind Mama.

"I told you if you ever mentioned Annie Flo's name I'd slap your face," says Mama, and slaps my face.

"All right, you wait and see," I says.

"I," says Mama, "*I* prefer to take my children's word for anything when its humanly possible." You ought to see Mama, she weighs two hundred pounds and has real tiny feet.

Just then something perfectly horrible occurred to me.

"Mama," I says, "can that child talk?" I simply had to whisper! "Mama, I wonder if that child can be—you know—in any way? Do you realize," I says, "that she hasn't spoken one single, solitary word to a human being up to this minute? This is the way she looks," I says, and I looked like this.

Well, Mama and I just stood there and stared at each other. It was horrible!

"I remember well that Joe Whitaker frequently drank like a fish," says Mama. "I believed to my soul he drank *chemicals*." And without another word she marches to the foot of the stairs and calls Stella-Rondo.

"Stella-Rondo? O-o-o-o-o! Stella-Rondo!"

"What?" says Stella-Rondo from upstairs. Not even the grace to get up off the bed.

"Can that child of yours talk?" asks Mama.

Stella-Rondo says, "Can she what?"

"Talk! Talk!" says Mama. "Burdyburdyburdyburdy!"

So Stella-Rondo yells back, "Who says she can't talk?"

"Sister says so," says Mama.

"You didn't have to tell me, I know whose word of honor don't mean a thing in this house," says Stella-Rondo.

And in a minute the loudest Yankee voice I ever heard in my life yells out, "OE'm Pop-OE the Sailor-r-r-r Ma-a-an!" and then somebody jumps up and down in the upstairs hall. In another second the house would of fallen down.

"Not only talks, she can tap-dance!" calls Stella-Rondo. "Which is more than some people I won't name can do."

"Why, the little precious darling thing!" Mama says, so surprised. "Just as smart as she can be!" Starts talking baby talk right there. Then she turns on me. "Sister, you ought to be thoroughly ashamed! Run upstairs this instant and apologize to Stella-Rondo and Shirley-T."

"Apologize for what?" I says. "I merely wondered if the child was normal, that's all. Now that she's proved she is, why, I have nothing further to say."

But Mama just turned on her heel and flew out, furious. She ran right upstairs and hugged the baby. She believed it was adopted. Stella-Rondo hadn't done a thing but turn her against me from upstairs while I stood there helpless over the hot stove. So that made Mama, Papa-Daddy and the baby all on Stella-Rondo's side.

Next, Uncle Rondo.

I must say that Uncle Rondo has been marvelous to me at various times in the past and I was completely unprepared to be made to jump out of my skin, the way it turned out. Once Stella-Rondo did something perfectly horrible to him—broke a chain letter from Flanders Field—and he took the radio back he had given her and gave it to me. Stella-Rondo was furious! For six months we all had to call her Stella instead of Stella-Rondo, or she wouldn't answer. I always thought Uncle Rondo had all the brains of the entire family. Another time he sent me to Mammoth Cave, with all expenses paid.

But this would be the day he was drinking that prescription, the Fourth of July.

So at supper Stella-Rondo speaks up and says she thinks Uncle Rondo ought to try to eat a little something. So finally Uncle Rondo said he would try a little cold biscuits and ketchup, but that was all. So *she* brought it to him.

"Do you think it wise to disport with ketchup in Stella-Rondo's flesh-colored kimono?" I says. Trying to be considerate! If Stella-Rondo couldn't watch out for her trousseau, somebody had to.

"Any objections?" asks Uncle Rondo, just about to pour out all the ketchup.

"Don't mind what she says, Uncle Rondo," says Stella-Rondo. "Sister has been devoting this solid afternoon to sneering out my bedroom window at the way you look."

"What's that?" says Uncle Rondo. Uncle Rondo has got the most terrible temper in the world. Anything is liable to make him tear the house down if it comes at the wrong time.

So Stella-Rondo says, "Sister says, 'Uncle Rondo certainly does look like a fool in that pink kimono!'"

Do you remember who it was really said that?

Uncle Rondo spills out all the ketchup and jumps out of his chair and tears off the kimono and throws it down on the dirty floor and puts his foot on it. It had to be sent all the way to Jackson to the cleaners and re-pleated.

"So that's your opinion of your Uncle Rondo, is it?" he says. "I look like a fool, do I? Well, that's the last straw. A whole day in this house with nothing to do, and then to hear you come out with a remark like that behind my back!"

"I didn't say any such of a thing, Uncle Rondo," I says, "and I'm not saying who did, either. Why, I think you look all right. Just try to take care of yourself and not talk and eat at the same time," I says. "I think you better go lie down."

"Lie down my foot," says Uncle Rondo. I ought to of known by that he was fixing to do something perfectly horrible.

So he didn't do anything that night in the precarious state he was in—just played Casino with Mama and Stella-Rondo and Shirley-T. and gave Shirley-T. a nickel with a head on both sides. It tickled her nearly to death, and she called him "Papa." But at 6:30 A.M. the next morning, he threw a whole five-cent package of some unsold one-inch firecrackers from the store as hard as he could into my bedroom and they every one went off. Not one bad one in the string. Anybody else, there'd be one that wouldn't go off.

Well, I'm just terribly susceptible to noise of any kind, the doctor has always told me I was the most sensitive person he had ever seen in his whole life, and I was simply prostrated. I couldn't eat! People tell me they heard it as far as the cemetery, and old Aunt Jep Patterson, that had been holding her own so good, thought it was Judgment Day and she was going to meet her whole family. It's usually so quiet here.

And I'll tell you it didn't take me any longer than a minute to make up my mind what to do. There I was with the whole entire house on Stella-Rondo's side and turned against me. If I have anything at all I have pride.

So I just decided I'd go straight down to the P.O. There's plenty of room there in the back, I says to myself.

Well! I made no bones about letting the family catch on to what I was up to. I didn't try to conceal it.

The first thing they knew, I marched in where they were all playing Old Maid and pulled the electric oscillating fan out by the plug, and everything got real hot. Next I snatched the pillow I'd done the needlepoint on right off the the davenport from behind Papa-Daddy. He went "Ugh!" I beat Stella-Rondo up the stairs and finally found my charm bracelet in her bureau drawer under a picture of Nelson Eddy.

"So that's the way the land lies," says Uncle Rondo. There he was, piecing on the ham. "Well, Sister, I'll be glad to donate my army cot if you got any place to set it up, providing you'll leave right this minute and let me get some peace." Uncle Rondo was in France.

"Thank you kindly for the cot and 'peace' is hardly the word I would select if I had to resort to firecrackers at 6:30 A.M. in a young girl's bedroom," I says back to him. "And as to where I intend to go, you seem to forget my position as postmistress of China Grove, Mississippi," I says. "I've always got the P.O."

Well, that made them all sit up and take notice.

I went out front and started digging up some four-o'clocks to plant around the P.O.

"Ah-ah-ah!" says Mama, raising the window. "Those happen to be my four-o'clocks. Everything planted in that star is mine. I've never known you to make anything grow in your life."

"Very well," I says. "But I take the fern. Even you, Mama, can't stand there and deny that I'm the one watered that fern. And I happen to know where I can send in a box top and get a packet of one thousand mixed seeds, no two the same kind, free."

"Oh, where?" Mama wants to know.

But I says, "Too late. You 'tend to your house, and I'll 'tend to mine. You hear things like that all the time if you know how to listen to the radio. Perfectly marvelous offers. Get anything you want free."

So I hope to tell you I marched in and got that radio, and they could of all bit a nail in two, especially Stella-Rondo, that it used to belong to, and she well knew she couldn't get it back, I'd sue for it like a shot. And I very politely took the sewing-machine motor I helped pay the most on to give Mama for Christmas back in 1929, and a good big calendar, with the first-aid remedies on it. The thermometer and the Hawaiian ukulele certainly were rightfully mine, and I stood on the stepladder and got all my watermelon-rind preserves and every fruit and vegetable I'd put up, every jar. Then I began to pull the tacks out of the bluebird wall vases on the archway to the dining room.

"Who told you you could have those, Miss Priss?" says Mama, fanning as hard as she could.

"I bought 'em and I'll keep track of 'em," I says. "I'll tack 'em up one on each side the post office window, and you can see 'em when you come to ask me for your mail, if you're so dead to see 'em."

"Not I! I'll never darken the door to that post office again if I live to be a hundred," Mama says. "Ungrateful child! After all the money we spent on you at the Normal."

"Me either," says Stella-Rondo. "You can just let my mail lie there and *rot,* for all I care. I'll never come and relieve you of a single, solitary piece."

"I should worry," I says. "And who you think's going to sit down and write you all those big fat letters and postcards, by the way? Mr. Whitaker? Just because he was the only man ever dropped down in China Grove and you got him—unfairly—is he going to sit down and write you a lengthy correspondence after you come home giving no rhyme nor reason whatsoever for your separation and no explanation for the presence of that child? I may not have your brilliant mind, but I fail to see it."

So Mama says, "Sister, I've told you a thousand times that Stella-Rondo simply got homesick, and this child is far too big to be hers," and she says, "Now, why don't you all sit down and play Casino?"

Then Shirley-T. sticks out her tongue at me in this perfectly horrible way. She has no more manners than the man in the moon. I told her she was going to cross her eyes like that some day and they'd stick.

"It's too late to stop me now," I says. "You should have tried that yesterday. I'm going to the P.O. and the only way you can possibly see me is to visit me there."

So Papa-Daddy says, "You'll never catch me setting foot in that post office, even if I should take a notion into my head to write a letter some place." He says, "I won't have you reachin' out of that little old window with a pair of shears and cuttin' off any beard of mine. I'm too smart for you!"

"We all are," says Stella-Rondo.

But I said, "If you're so smart, where's Mr. Whitaker?"

So then Uncle Rondo says, "I'll thank you from now on to stop reading all the orders I get on postcards and telling everybody in China Grove what you think is the matter with them," but I says, "I draw my own conclusions and will continue in the future to draw them." I says, "If people want to write their inmost secrets on penny postcards, there's nothing in the wide world you can do about it, Uncle Rondo."

"And if you think we'll ever *write* another postcard you're sadly mistaken," says Mama.

"Cutting off your nose to spite your face then," I says. "But if you're all determined to have no more to do with the U.S. mail, think of this: What will Stella-Rondo do now, if she wants to tell Mr. Whitaker to come after her?"

"Wah!" says Stella-Rondo. I knew she'd cry. She had a conniption fit right there in the kitchen.

"It will be interesting to see how long she holds out," I says. "And now—I am leaving."

"Good-bye," says Uncle Rondo.

"Oh, I declare," says Mama, "to think that a family of mine should quarrel on the Fourth of July, or the day after, over Stella-Rondo leaving old Mr. Whitaker and having the sweetest little adopted child! It looks like we'd all be glad!"

"Wah!" says Stella-Rondo, and has a fresh conniption fit.

"*He* left *her*—you mark my words," I says. "That's Mr. Whitaker. I know Mr. Whitaker. After all, I knew him first. I said from the beginning he'd up and leave her. I foretold every single thing that's happened."

"Where did he go?" asks Mama.

"Probably to the North Pole, if he knows what's good for him," I says.

But Stella-Rondo just bawled and wouldn't say another word. She flew to her room and slammed the door.

"Now look what you've gone and done, Sister," says Mama. "You go apologize."

"I haven't got time, I'm leaving," I says.

"Well, what are you waiting around for?" asks Uncle Rondo.

So I just picked up the kitchen clock and marched off, without saying "Kiss my foot" or anything, and never did tell Stella-Rondo good-bye.

There was a nigger girl going along on a little wagon right in front.

"Nigger girl," I says, "come help me haul these things down the hill, I'm going to live in the post office."

Took her nine trips in her express wagon. Uncle Rondo came out on the porch and threw her a nickel.

And that's the last I've laid eyes on any of my family or my family laid eyes on me for five solid days and nights. Stella-Rondo may be telling the most horrible tales in the world about Mr. Whitaker, but I haven't heard them. As I tell everybody, I draw my own conclusions.

But oh, I like it here. It's ideal, as I've been saying. You see, I've got everything cater-cornered, the way I like it. Hear the radio? All the war news. Radio, sewing machine, book ends, ironing board and that great big piano lamp—peace, that's what I like. Butter-bean vines planted all along the front where the strings are.

Of course, there's not much mail. My family are naturally the main people in China Grove, and if they prefer to vanish from the face of the earth, for all the mail they get or the mail they write, why, I'm not going to open my mouth. Some of the folks here in town are taking up for me and some turned against me. I know which is which. There are always people who will quit buying stamps just to get on the right side of Papa-Daddy.

But here I am, and here I'll stay. I want the world to know I'm happy.

And if Stella-Rondo should come to me this minute, on bended knees, and *attempt* to explain the incidents of her life with Mr. Whitaker, I'd simply put my fingers in both my ears and refuse to listen.

QUESTIONS

1. Is the first-person narrator reliable or unreliable? Is she a sympathetic character? Are any of the characters sympathetic? Discuss the presence of psychic distance in this story, paying particular attention to its effect on comedy.

2. Much of the humor comes from the illogic of the narrator's reasoning. Find at least three examples of her convoluted logic.

3. Using this story as evidence, defend or attack Henry James' charge that the first-person narrator places a premium on "the loose, the improvised, the cheap and the easy."

4. When the narrator leaves, she takes certain household objects that are hers. What are these objects? How do they help to characterize the narrator and her family?

5. What national holiday serves as background for most of the events of the story? How does this holiday heighten the tension?

6. Is Shirley-T adopted, as Stella-Rondo insists, or is the narrator correct in implying that the child is Stella-Rondo's? Why does the mother choose to believe Stella-Rondo rather than the narrator? Is Stella-Rondo as jealous of the narrator as the latter is of her and Shirley-T? (Who is the famous person for whom Shirley-T is an abbreviation?)

7. How long has the narrator been living at the post office at the time she tells her story? Do you think she will return to her family soon? If so, why?

8. A critic has observed: "A great deal of the Southern writer's work is done for him before he begins, because our history lives in our talk. In one of Eudora Welty's stories a character says, 'Where I come from, we use fox for yard dogs and owls for chickens, but we sing true.' Now there is a whole book in that one sentence; and when the people of your section can talk like that, and you ignore it, you're just not taking advantage of what's yours." Find at least three sentences that reflect a strong sense of place and personality.

9. There's a saying that if you give people enough rope they will hang themselves. Does this proverb apply to the narrator?

ALAN PATON

The Waste Land

The moment that the bus moved on he knew he was in danger, for by the lights of it he saw the figures of the young men waiting under the tree. That was the thing feared by all, to be waited for by the young men. It was a thing he had talked about, now he was to see it for himself.

It was too late to run after the bus; it went down the dark street like an island of safety in a sea of perils. Though he had known of his danger only for a second, his mouth was already dry, his heart was pounding in his breast, something within him was crying out in protest against the coming event.

His wages were in his purse, he could feel them weighing heavily against his thigh. That was what they wanted from him. Nothing counted against that. His wife could be made a widow, his children made fatherless, nothing counted against that. Mercy was the unknown word.

While he stood there irresolute he heard the young men walking towards him, not only from the side where he had seen them, but from the other also. They did not speak, their intention was unspeakable. The sound of their feet came on the wind to him. The place was well chosen, for behind him was the high wall of the Convent, and the barred door that would not open before a man was dead. On the other side of the road was the waste land, full of wire and iron and the bodies of old cars. It was his only hope, and he moved towards it; as he did so he knew from the whistle that the young men were there too.

His fear was great and instant, and the smell of it went from his body to his nostrils. At that very moment one of them spoke, giving directions. So trapped was he that he was filled suddenly with strength and anger, and he ran towards the waste land swinging his heavy stick. In the darkness a form loomed up at him, and he swung the stick at it, and heard it give a cry of pain. Then he plunged blindly into the wilderness of wire and iron and the bodies of old cars.

Something caught him by the leg, and he brought his stick crashing down on it, but it was no man, only some knife-edged piece of iron. He was sobbing and out of breath, but he pushed on into the waste, while behind him they pushed on also, knocking against the old iron bodies and kicking against tins and buckets. He fell into some grotesque shape of wire; it was barbed and tore at his clothes and flesh. Then it held him, so that it seemed to him that death must be near, and having no other hope, he cried out, "Help me, help me!" in what should have been a great voice but was voiceless and gasping. He tore at the wire, and it tore at him too, ripping his face and his hands.

Then suddenly he was free. He saw the bus returning, and he cried out again in the great voiceless voice, "Help me, help me!" Against the lights of it he could plainly see the form of one of the young men. Death was near him, and for a moment he was filled with the injustice of life, that could end thus for one who had always been hardworking and law-abiding. He lifted the heavy stick and brought it down on the head of his pursuer, so that the man crumpled to the ground, moaning and groaning as though life had been unjust to him also.

Then he turned and began to run again, but ran head first into the side of an old lorry which sent him reeling. He lay there for a moment expecting the blow that would end him, but even then his wits came back to him, and he turned over twice and was under the lorry. His very entrails seemed to be coming into his mouth, and his lips could taste sweat and blood. His heart was like a wild thing in his breast, and seemed to lift his whole body each time that it beat. He tried to calm it down, thinking it might be heard, and tried to control the noise of his gasping breath, but he could not do either of these things.

Then suddenly against the dark sky he saw two of the young men. He thought they must hear him; but they themselves were gasping like drowning men, and their speech came by fits and starts.

Then one of them said, "Do you hear?"

They were silent except for their gasping, listening. And he listened also, but could hear nothing but his own exhausted heart.

"I heard a man . . . running . . . on the road," said one. "He's got away . . . let's go."

Then some more of the young men came up, gasping and cursing the man who had got away.

"Freddy," said one, "your father's got away."

But there was no reply.

"Where's Freddy?" one asked.

One said "Quiet!" Then he called in a loud voice, "Freddy."

But still there was no reply.

"Let's go," he said.

They moved off slowly and carefully, then one of them stopped.

"We are saved," he said, "here is the man."

He knelt down on the ground, and then fell to cursing.

"There's no money here," he said.

One of them lit a match, and in the small light of it the man under the lorry saw him fall back.

"It's Freddy," one said, "he's dead."

Then the one who had said "Quiet" spoke again.

"Lift him up," he said. "Put him under the lorry."

The man under the lorry heard them struggling with the body of the dead young man, and he turned once, twice, deeper into his hiding-place. The young men lifted the body and swung it under the lorry so that it touched him. Then he heard them moving away, not speaking, slowly and quietly, making an occasional sound against some obstruction in the waste.

He turned on his side, so that he would not need to touch the body of the young man. He buried his face in his arms, and said to himself in the idiom of his own language, "People, arise! The world is dead." Then he arose himself, and went heavily out of the waste land.

QUESTIONS

1. The setting functions on both a literal and symbolic level. Explain, making reference to the title.

2. The third-person subjective narrator limits descriptions to what the protagonist sees and experiences, but the language is clearly the narrator's. Explain.

3. Are you convinced that the father has killed his son? What makes you sure? If you are not sure, explain why.

4. Discuss the story as allegory. If the author's purpose is allegorical, why is a third-person subjective narrator a better choice than a first-person narrator?

5. In the concluding paragraph, the protagonist, using "the idiom of his own language," says, "'People, arise! The world is dead.'" What is the narrator's language? Is national identity important to this story? What is the meaning of the protagonist's statement?

6. With only a few words, Paton vividly conveys the protagonist's fear. Where and how does he do so?

HENRY JAMES

The Middle Years

The April day was soft and bright, and poor Dencombe, happy in the conceit of reasserted strength, stood in the garden of the hotel, comparing, with a deliberation in which however there was still something of languor, the attractions of easy strolls. He liked the feeling of the south so far as you could have it in the north, he liked the sandy cliffs and the clustered pines, he liked even the colorless sea. "Bournemouth as a health-resort" had sounded like a mere advertisement, but he was thankful now for the commonest conveniences. The sociable country postman, passing through the garden, had just given him a small parcel which he took out with him, leaving the hotel to the right and creeping to a bench he had already haunted, a safe recess in the cliff. It looked to the south, to the tinted walls of the Island, and was protected behind by the sloping shoulder of the down. He was tired enough when he reached it, and for a moment was disappointed; he was better of course, but better, after all, than what? He should never again, as at one or two great moments of the past, be better than himself. The infinite of life was gone, and what remained of the dose a small glass scored like a thermometer by the apothecary. He sat and stared at the sea, which appeared all surface and twinkle, far shallower than the spirit of man. It was the abyss of human illusion that was the real, the tideless deep. He held his packet, which had come by book-post, unopened on his knee, liking, in the lapse of so many joys—his illness had made him feel his age—to know it was there, but taking for granted there could be no complete renewal of the pleasure, dear to young experience, of seeing one's self "just out." Dencombe, who had a reputation, had come out too often and knew too well in advance how he should look.

His postponement associated itself vaguely, after a little, with a group of three persons, two ladies and a young man, whom, beneath him, straggling and seemingly silent, he could see move slowly together along the sands. The gentleman had his head bent over a book and was occasionally brought to a stop by the charm of this volume, which, as Dencombe could perceive even at a distance, had a cover alluringly red. Then his companions, going a little further, waited for him to come up, poking their parasols into the beach, looking around them at the sea and sky and clearly sensible of the beauty of the day. To these things the young man with the book was still more clearly indifferent; lingering, credulous, absorbed, he was an object of envy to an observer from whose connection with literature all such artlessness had faded. One of the ladies was large and mature; the other had the spareness of comparative youth and of a social situation possibly inferior. The large lady carried back Dencombe's imagination to the age of crinoline; she wore a hat of the shape of a mushroom, decorated with a blue veil, and had the air, in her aggressive amplitude, of clinging to a vanished fashion or even a lost cause. Presently her companion produced from under the folds of a mantle a limp portable chair which she stiffened out and of which the large lady took possession. This act, and something in the movement of either party, at once characterized the performers— they performed for Dencombe's recreation—as opulent matron and humble dependent. Where, moreover, was the virtue of an approved novelist if one couldn't establish a relation between such figures? the clever theory for instance that the young man was the son of the opulent matron and that the humble dependent, the daughter of a clergyman or an officer, nourished a secret passion for him. Was that not visible from the way she stole behind her protectress to look back at him?—back to where he had let himself come to a full stop when his mother sat down to rest. His book was a novel, it had the catchpenny binding; so that while the romance of life stood neglected at his side he lost himself in that of the circulating library. He moved mechanically to where the sand was softer and ended by plumping down in it to finish his chapter at his ease. The humble dependent, discouraged by his remoteness, wandered with a martyred droop of the head in another direction, and the exorbitant lady, watching the waves, offered a confused resemblance to a flying-machine that had broken down.

When his drama began to fail Dencombe remembered that he had after all another pastime. Though such promptitude on the part of the publisher was rare he was already able to draw from its wrapper his "latest," perhaps his last. The cover of "The Middle Years" was duly meretricious, the smell of the fresh pages the very odor of sanctity; but for the moment he went no further—he had become conscious of a strange alienation. He had forgotten what his book was about. Had the assault of his old ailment, which he had so fallaciously come to. Bournemouth to ward off, interposed under blankness as to what had preceded it? He had finished the revision of proof before quitting London, but his subsequent fortnight in bed had passed the sponge over color. He couldn't have chanted to himself a single sentence, couldn't have turned with curiosity or confidence to any particular page. His subject had already gone from him, leaving scarce a superstition behind. He uttered a low moan as he breathed the chill of this dark void, so desperately it seemed to represent the completion of a sinister process. The tears filled his mild eyes; something precious had passed away. This was the pang that had been sharpest during the last few years—the sense of ebbing time, of shrinking opportunity; and now he felt not so much that his last chance was going as that it was gone indeed. He had done all he should ever do, and yet hadn't done what he wanted. This was the laceration—that practically his career was over: it was as violent as a grip at his throat. He rose from his seat nervously—a creature hunted by a dread; then he fell back in his weakness and nervously opened his book. It was a single volume; he preferred single volumes and aimed at a rare compression. He began to read and, little by little, in this occupation, was pacified and reassured. Everything came back to him, but came back with a wonder, came back above all with a high and magnificent beauty. He read his own prose, he turned his own leaves, and had as he sat there with the spring sunshine on the page an emotion peculiar and intense. His career was over, no doubt, but it was over, when all was said, with *that*.

He had forgotten during his illness the work of the previous year; but what he had chiefly forgotten was that it was extraordinarily good. He dived once more into his story and was drawn down, as by a siren's hand, to where, in the dim underworld of fiction, the great glazed tank of art, strange silent subjects float. He recognized his motive and surrendered to his talent. Never probably had that talent, such as it was, been so fine. His difficulties were still there, but what was also there, to his perception, though probably, alas! to nobody's else, was the art that in most cases had surmounted them. In his surprised enjoyment of this ability he had a glimpse of a possible reprieve. Surely its force wasn't spent—there was life and service in it yet. It hadn't come to him easily, it had been backward and roundabout. It was the child of time, the nursling of delay; he had struggled and suffered for it, making sacrifices not to be counted, and now that it was really mature was it to cease to yield, to confess itself brutally beaten? There was an infinite charm for Dencombe in feeling as he had never felt before that diligence *vincit omnia*. The result produced in his little book was somehow a result beyond his conscious intention: it was as if he had planted his genius, had trusted his method, and they had grown up and flowered with this sweetness. If the achievement had been real, however, the process had been painful enough. What he saw so intensely to-day, what he felt as a nail driven in, was that only now, at the very last, had he come into possession. His development had been abnormally slow, almost grotesquely gradual. He had been hindered and retarded by experience, he had for long periods only groped his way. It had taken too much of his life to produce too little of his art. The art had come, but it had come after everything else. At such a rate a first existence was too short—long enough only to collect material; so that to fructify, to use the material, one should have a second age, an extension. This extension was what poor Dencombe sighed for. As he turned the last leaves of his volume he murmured "Ah for another go, ah for a better chance!"

The three persons drawing his attention to the sands had vanished and then reappeared; they had now wandered up a path, an artificial and easy ascent, which led to the top of the cliff. Dencombe's bench was halfway down, on a sheltered ledge, and the large lady, a massive heterogeneous person with bold black eyes and kind red cheeks, now took a few moments to rest. She wore dirty gauntlets and immense diamond ear-rings; at first she looked vulgar, but she contradicted this announcement in an agreeable off-hand tone. While her companions stood waiting for her she spread her skirts on the end of Dencombe's seat. The young man had gold spectacles, through which, with his finger still in his red-covered book, he glanced at the volume, bound in the same shade of the same color, lying on the lap of the original occupant of the bench. After an instant Dencombe felt him struck with a resemblance; he had recognised the gilt stamp on the crimson cloth, was reading "The Middle Years" and now noted that somebody else had kept pace with him. The stranger was startled, possibly even a little ruffled, to find himself not the only person favored with an early copy. The eyes of the two proprietors met a moment, and Dencombe borrowed amusement from the expression of those of his competitor, those, it might even be inferred, of his admirer. They confessed to some resentment—they seemed to say: "Hand it, has he got it *already?* Of course he's a brute of a reviewer!" Dencombe shuffled his copy out of sight while the opulent matron, rising from her repose, broke out: "I feel already the good of this air!"

"I can't say I do," said the angular lady. "I find myself quite let down."

"I find myself horribly hungry. At what time did you order luncheon?" her protectress pursued.

The young person put the question by. "Doctor Hugh always orders it."

"I ordered nothing to-day—I'm going to make you diet," said their comrade.

"Then I shall go home and sleep. *Qui dort dine!*"

"Can I trust you to Miss Vernham?" asked Doctor Hugh of his elder companion.

"Don't I trust *you?*" she archly inquired.

"Not too much!" Miss Vernham, with her eyes on the ground, permitted herself to declare. "You must come with us at least to the house," she went on while the personage on whom they appeared to be in attendance began to mount higher. She had got a little out of ear-shot; nevertheless Miss Vernham became, so far as Dencombe was concerned, less distinctly audible to murmur to the young man: "I don't think you realize all you owe the Countess!"

Absently, a moment, Doctor Hugh caused his gold-rimmed spectacles to shine at her. "Is that the way I strike you? I see—I see!"

"She's awfully good to us," continued Miss Vernham, compelled by the lapse of the other's motion to stand there in spite of his discussion of private matters. Of what use would it have been that Dencombe should be sensitive to shades hadn't he detected in that arrest a strange influence from the quiet old convalescent in the great tweed cape? Miss Vernham appeared suddenly to become aware of some such connection, for she added in a moment: "If you want to sun yourself here you can come back after you've seen us home."

Doctor Hugh, at this, hesitated, and Dencombe, in spite of a desire to pass for unconscious, risked a covert glance at him. What his eyes met this time, as happened, was, on the part of the young lady, a queer stare, naturally vitreous, which made her remind him of some figure—he couldn't name it—in a play or a novel, some sinister governess or tragic old maid. She seemed to scan him, to challenge him, to say out of general spite: "What have you got to do with us?" At the same instant the rich humor of the Countess reached them from above: "Come, come, my little lambs; you should follow your old *bergère!*" Miss Vernham turned away for it, pursuing the ascent, and Doctor Hugh, after another mute appeal to Dencombe and a minute's evident demur, deposited his book on the bench as if to keep his place, or even as a gage of earnest return, and bounded without difficulty up the rougher part of the cliff.

Equally innocent and infinite are the pleasures of observation and the resources engendered by the trick of analyzing life. It amused poor Dencombe, as he dawdled in his tepid air-bath, to believe himself awaiting a revelation of something at the back of a fine young mind. He looked hard at the book on the end of the bench, but wouldn't have touched it for the world. It served his purpose to have a theory that shouldn't be exposed to refutation. He already felt better of his melancholy; he had, according to his old formula, put his head at the window. A passing Countess could draw off the fancy when, like the elder of the ladies who had just retreated, she was as obvious as the giantess of a caravan. It was indeed general views that were terrible; short ones, contrary to an opinion sometimes expressed, were the refuge, were the remedy. Doctor Hugh couldn't possibly be anything but a reviewer who had understandings for early copies with publishers or with newspapers. He reappeared in a quarter of an hour with visible relief at finding Dencombe on the spot and the gleam of white teeth in an embarrassed but generous smile. He was perceptibly disappointed at the eclipse of the other copy of the book; it made a pretext the less for speaking to the quiet gentleman. But he spoke notwithstanding; he held up his own copy and broke out pleadingly: "*Do* say, if you have occasion to speak of it, that it's the best thing he has done yet!"

Dencombe responded with a laugh: "Done yet" was so amusing to him, made such a grand avenue of the future. Better still, the young man took *him* for a reviewer. He pulled out "The Middle Years" from under his cape, but instinctively concealed any telltale look of fatherhood. This was partly because a person was always a fool for insisting to others on his work. "Is that what you're going to say yourself?" he put to his visitor.

"I'm not quite sure I shall write anything. I don't, as a regular thing—I enjoy in peace. But it's awfully fine."

Dencombe just debated. If the young man had begun to abuse him he would have confessed on the spot to his identity, but there was no harm in drawing out any impulse to praise. He drew it out with such success that in a few moments his new acquaintance, seated by his side, was confessing candidly that the works of the author of the volumes before them were the only ones he could read a second time. He had come the day before from London, where a friend of his, a journalist, had lent him his copy of the last, the copy sent to the office of the journal and already the subject of a "notice" which, as was pretended there—but one had to allow for "swagger"—it had taken a full quarter of an hour to prepare. He intimated that he was ashamed for his friend, and in the case of a work demanding and repaying study, of such inferior manners; and, with his fresh appreciation and his so irregular wish to express it, he speedily became for poor Dencombe a remarkable, a delightful apparition. Chance had brought the weary man of letters face to face with the greatest admirer in the new generation of whom it was supposable he might boast. The admirer in truth was mystifying, so rare a case was it to find a bristling young doctor—he looked like a German physiologist—enamored of literary form. It was an accident, but happier than most accidents, so that Dencombe, exhilarated as well as confounded, spent half an hour in making his visitor talk while he kept himself quiet. He explained his premature possession of "The Middle Years" by an allusion to the friendship of the publisher, who, knowing he was at Bournemouth for his health, had paid him this graceful attention. He allowed he had been ill, for Doctor Hugh would infallibly have guessed it; he even went so far as to wonder if he mightn't look for some hygienic "tip" from a personage combining so bright an enthusiasm with a presumable knowledge of the remedies now in vogue. It would shake his faith a little perhaps to have to take a doctor seriously who could take *him* so seriously, but he enjoyed this gushing modern youth and felt with an acute pang that there would still be work to do in a world in which such odd combinations were presented. It wasn't true, what he had tried for renunciation's sake to believe, that all the combinations were exhausted. They weren't by any means— they were infinite: the exhaustion was in the miserable artist.

Doctor Hugh, an ardent physiologist, was saturated with the spirit of the age—in other words he had just taken his degree; but he was independent and various, he talked like a man who would have preferred to love literature best. He would fain have made fine phrases, but nature had denied him the trick. Some of the finest in "The Middle Years" had struck him inordinately, and he took the liberty of reading them to Dencombe in support of his plea. He grew vivid, in the balmy air, to his companion, for whose deep refreshment he seemed to have been sent; and was particularly ingenuous in describing how recently he had become acquainted, and how instantly infatuated, with the only man who had put flesh between the ribs of an art that was starving on superstitions. He hadn't yet written to him—he was deterred by a strain of respect. Dencombe at this moment rejoiced more inwardly than ever that he had never answered the photographers. His vistor's attitude promised him a luxury of intercourse, though he was sure a due freedom for Doctor Hugh would depend not a little on the Countess. He learned without delay what type of Countess was involved, mastering as well the nature of the tie that united the curious trio.

The large lady, an Englishwoman by birth and the daughter of a celebrated baritone, whose taste *minus* his talent she had inherited, was the widow of a French nobleman and mistress of all that remained of the handsome fortune, the fruit of her father's earnings, that had constituted her dower. Miss Vernham, an odd creature but an accomplished pianist, was attached to her person at a salary. The Countess was generous, independent, eccentric, she traveled with her minstrel and her medical man. Ignorant and passionate she had nevertheless moments in which she was almost irresistible. Dencombe saw her sit for her portrait in Doctor Hugh's free sketch, and felt the picture of his young friend's relation to her frame itself in his mind. This young friend, for a representative of the new psychology, was himself easily hypnotized, and if he became abnormally communicative it was only a sign of his real subjection. Dencombe did accordingly what he wanted with him, even without being known as Dencombe.

Taken ill on a journey in Switzerland the Countess had picked him up at an hotel, and the accident of his happening to please her had made her offer him, with her imperious liberality, terms that couldn't fail to dazzle a practitioner without patients and whose resources had been drained dry by his studies. It wasn't the way he would have proposed to spend his time, but it was time that would pass quickly, and meanwhile she was wonderfully kind. She exacted perpetual attention, but it was impossible not to like her. He gave details about his queer patient, a "type" if there ever was one, who had in connection with her flushed obesity, and in addition to the morbid strain of a violent and aimless will, a grave organic disorder; but he came back to his loved novelist, whom he was so good as to pronounce more essentially a poet than many of those who went in for verse, with a zeal excited, as all his indiscretion had been excited, by the happy chance of Dencombe's sympathy and the coincidence of their occupation. Dencombe had confessed to a slight personal acquaintance with the author of "The Middle Years," but had not felt himself as ready as he could have wished when his companion, who had never yet encountered a being so privileged, began to be eager for particulars. He even divined in Doctor Hugh's eye at that moment a glimmer of suspicion. But the young man was too inflamed to be shrewd and repeatedly caught up the book to exclaim: "Did you notice this?" or "Weren't you immensely struck with that?" "There's a beautiful passage toward the end," he broke out; and again he laid his hand on the volume. As he turned the pages he came upon something else, while Dencombe saw him suddenly change color. He had taken up as it lay on the bench Dencombe's copy instead of his own, and his neighbor at once guessed the reason of his start. Doctor Hugh looked grave an instant; then he said: "I see you've been altering the text!" Dencombe was a passionate corrector, a fingerer of style; the last thing he ever arrived at was a form final for himself. His ideal would have been to publish secretly, and then, on the published text, treat himself to the terrified revise, sacrificing always a first edition and beginning for posterity and even for the collectors, poor dears, with a second. This morning, in "The Middle Years," his pencil had pricked a dozen lights. He was amused at the effect of the young man's reproach; for an instant it made him change color. He stammered at any

rate ambiguously, then through a blur of ebbing consciousness saw Doctor
Hugh's mystified eyes. He only had time to feel he was about to be ill again—
that emotion, excitement, fatigue, the heat of the sun, the solicitation of the air,
had combined to play him a trick, before, stretching out a hand to his visitor with
a plaintive cry, he lost his senses altogether.

Later he knew he had fainted and that Doctor Hugh had got him home in a
Bath-chair, the conductor of which, prowling within hail for custom, had
happened to remember seeing him in the garden of the hotel. He had recovered
his perception on the way, and had, in bed that afternoon, a vague recollection
of Doctor Hugh's young face, as they went together, bent over him in a
comforting laugh and expressive of something more than a suspicion of his
identity. That identity was ineffaceable now, and all the more that he was rueful
and sore. He had been rash, been stupid, had gone out too soon, stayed out too
long. He oughtn't to have exposed himself to strangers, he ought to have taken
his servant. He felt as if he had fallen into a hole too deep to descry any little
patch of heaven. He was confused about the time that had passed—he pieced
the fragments together. He had seen his doctor, the real one, the one who had
treated him from the first and who had again been very kind. His servant was in
and out on tiptoe, looking very wise after the fact. He said more than once
something about the sharp young gentleman. The rest was vagueness in so far as
it wasn't despair. The vagueness, however, justified itself by dreams, dozing
anxieties from which he finally emerged to the consciousness of a dark room and
a shaded candle.

"You'll be all right again—I know all about you now," said a voice near
him that he felt to be young. Then his meeting with Doctor Hugh came back.
He was too discouraged to joke about it yet, but made out after a little that the
interest was intense for his visitor. "Of course I can't attend you professionally—
you've got your own man with whom I've talked and who's excellent," Doctor
Hugh went on. "But you must let me come to see you as a good friend. I've just
looked in before going to bed. You're doing beautifully, but it's a good job I was
with you on the cliff. I shall come in early to-morrow. I want to do something for
you. I want to do everything. You've done a tremendous lot for me." The young
man held his hand, hanging over him, and poor Dencombe, weakly aware of his
living pressure, simply lay there and accepted his devotion. He couldn't do
anything less—he needed help too much.

The idea of the help he needed was very present to him that night, which
he spent in a lucid stillness, an intensity of thought that constituted a reaction
from his hours of stupor. He was lost, he was lost—he was lost if he couldn't be
saved. He wasn't afraid of suffering, of death, wasn't even in love with life; but
he had had a deep demonstration of desire. It came over him in the long quiet
hours that only with "The Middle Years" had he taken his flight; only on that
day, visited by soundless processions, had he recognized his kingdom. He had
had a revelation of his range. What he dreaded was the idea that his reputation
should stand on the unfinished. It wasn't with his past but with his future that it
should properly be concerned. Illness and age rose before him like specters with

pitiless eyes: how was he to bribe such fates to give him the second chance? He had had the one chance that all men have—he had had the chance of life. He went to sleep again very late, and when he awoke Doctor Hugh was sitting at hand. There was already by this time something beautifully familiar in him.

"Don't think I've turned out your physician," he said: "I'm acting with his consent. He has been here and seen you. Somehow he seems to trust me. I told him how we happened to come together yesterday, and he recognizes that I've a peculiar right."

Dencombe felt his own face pressing. "How have you squared the Countess?"

The young man blushed a little, but turned it off. "Oh never mind the Countess!"

"You told me she was very exacting."

Doctor Hugh had a wait. "So she is."

"And Miss Vernham's an *intrigante.*"

"How do you know that?"

"I know everything. One *has* to, to write decently!"

"I think she's mad," said limpid Doctor Hugh.

"Well, don't quarrel with the Countess—she's a present help to you."

"I don't quarrel," Doctor Hugh returned. "But I don't get on with silly women." Presently he added: "You seem very much alone."

"That often happens at my age. I've outlived, I've lost by the way."

Doctor Hugh faltered; then surmounting a soft scruple: "Whom have you lost?"

"Every one."

"Ah no," the young man breathed, laying a hand on his arm.

"I once had a wife—I once had a son. My wife died when my child was born, and my boy, at school, was carried off by typhoid."

"I wish I'd been there!" cried Doctor Hugh.

"Well—if you're here!" Dencombe answered with a smile that, in spite of dimness, showed how he valued being sure of his companion's whereabouts.

"You talk strangely of your age. You're not old."

"Hypocrite—so early!"

"I speak physiologically."

"That's the way I've been speaking for the last five years, and it's exactly what I've been saying to myself. It isn't till we *are* old that we begin to tell ourselves we're not."

"Yet I know I myself am young," Doctor Hugh returned.

"Not so well as I!" laughed his patient, whose visitor indeed would have established the truth in question by the honesty with which he changed the point of view, remarking that it must be one of the charms of age—at any rate in the case of high distinction—to feel that one has labored and achieved. Doctor Hugh employed the common phrase about earning one's rest, and it made poor Dencombe for an instant almost angry. He recovered himself, however, to explain, lucidly enough, that if, ungraciously, he knew nothing of such a balm, it was doubtless because he had wasted inestimable years. He had followed literature from the first, but he had taken a lifetime to get abreast of her. Only to-day at last had he begun to *see,* so that all he had hitherto shown was a movement without a direction. He had ripened too late and was so clumsily constituted that he had had to teach himself by mistakes.

"I prefer your flowers then to other people's fruit, and your mistakes to other people's successes," said gallant Doctor Hugh. "It's for your mistakes I admire you."

"You're happy—you don't know," Dencombe answered.

Looking at his watch the young man had got up; he named the hour of the afternoon at which he would return. Dencombe warned him against committing himself too deeply, and expressed again all his dread of making him neglect the Countess—perhaps incur her displeasure.

"I want to be like you—I want to learn by mistakes!" Doctor Hugh laughed.

"Take care you don't make too grave a one! But do come back," Dencombe added with the glimmer of a new idea.

"You should have had more vanity!" His friend spoke as if he knew the exact amount required to make a man of letters normal.

"No, no—I only should have had more time. I want another go."

"Another go?"

"I want an extension."

"An extension?" Again Doctor Hugh repeated Dencombe's words, with which he seemed to have been struck.

"Don't you know?—I want to what they call 'live.'"

The young man, for good-bye, had taken his hand, which closed with a certain force. They looked at each other hard. "You *will* live," said Doctor Hugh.

"Don't be superficial. It's too serious!"

"You *shall* live!" Dencombe's visitor declared, turning pale.

"Ah that's better!" And as he retired the invalid, with a troubled laugh, sank gratefully back.

All that day and all the following night he wondered if it mightn't be arranged. His doctor came again, his servant was attentive, but it was to his confident young friend that he felt himself mentally appeal. His collapse on the cliff was plausibly explained and his liberation, on a better basis, promised for the morrow; meanwhile, however, the intensity of his meditations kept him tranquil and made him indifferent. The idea that occupied him was none the less absorbing because it was a morbid fancy. Here was a clever son of the age, ingenious and ardent, who happened to have set him up for connoisseurs to worship. This servant of his altar had all the new learning in science and all the old reverence in faith; wouldn't he therefore put his knowledge at the disposal of his sympathy, his craft at the disposal of his love? Couldn't he be trusted to invent a remedy for a poor artist to whose art he had paid a tribute? If he couldn't the alternative was hard: Dencombe would have to surrender to silence unvindicated and undivined. The rest of the day and all the next he toyed in secret with this sweet futility. Who would work the miracle for him but the young man who could combine such lucidity with such passion? He thought of the fairy-tales of science and charmed himself into forgetting that he looked for a magic that was not of this world. Doctor Hugh was an apparition, and that placed him above the law. He came and went while his patient, who now sat up, followed him with supplicating eyes. The interest of knowing the great author had made the young man begin "The Middle Years" afresh and would help him to find a richer sense between its covers. Dencombe had told him what he "tried for"; with all his intelligence, on a first perusal, Doctor Hugh had failed to guess it. The baffled celebrity wondered then who in the world *would* guess it: he was amused once more at the diffused massive weight that could be thrown into the missing of an intention. Yet he wouldn't rail at the general mind today—consoling as that ever had been: the revelation of his own slowness had seemed to make all stupidity sacred.

Doctor Hugh, after a little, was visibly worried, confessing, on inquiry, to a source of embarrassment at home. "Stick to the Countess—don't mind me," Dencombe said repeatedly; for his companion was frank enough about the large lady's attitude. She was so jealous that she had fallen ill—she resented such a breach of allegiance. She paid so much for his fidelity that she must have it all: she refused him the right to other sympathies, charged him with scheming to make her die alone, for it was needless to point out how little Miss Vernham was a resource in trouble. When Doctor Hugh mentioned that the Countess would already have left Bournemouth if he hadn't kept her in bed, poor Dencombe held his arm tighter and said with decision: "Take her straight away." They had gone out together, walking back to the sheltered nook in which, the other day, they had met. The young man, who had given his companion a personal support, declared with emphasis that his conscience was clear—he could ride two horses at once. Didn't he dream for his future of a time when he should have to ride five hundred? Longing equally for virtue, Dencombe replied that in that golden age no patient would pretend to have contracted with him for his whole attention. On the part of the Countess wasn't such an avidity lawful? Doctor Hugh denied it, said there was no contract, but only a free understanding, and that a sordid servitude was impossible to a generous spirit; he liked moreover to talk about art, and that was the subject on which, this time, as they sat together on the sunny bench, he tried most to engage the author of "The Middle Years." Dencombe, soaring again a little on the weak wings of convalescence and still haunted by that happy notion of an organized rescue, found another strain of eloquence to plead the cause of a certain splendid "last manner," the very citadel, as it would prove, of his reputation, the stronghold into which his real treasure would be gathered. While his listener gave up the morning and the great still sea ostensibly waited he had a wondrous explanatory hour. Even for himself he was inspired as he told what his treasure would consist of; the precious metals he would dig from the mine, the jewels rare, strings of pearls, he would hang between the columns of his temple. He was wondrous for himself, so thick his convictions crowded, but still more wondrous for Doctor Hugh, who assured him none the less that the very pages he had just published were already encrusted with gems. This admirer, however, panted for the combinations to come and, before the face of the beautiful day, renewed to Dencombe his guarantee that his profession would hold itself responsible for such a life. Then he suddenly clapped his hand upon his watch-pocket and asked leave to absent himself for half an hour. Dencombe waited there for his return, but was at last recalled to the actual by the fall of a shadow across the ground. The shadow darkened into that of Miss Vernham, the young lady in attendance on the Countess; whom Dencombe, recognizing her, perceived so clearly to have come to speak to him that he rose from his bench to acknowledge the civility. Miss Vernham indeed proved not particularly civil; she looked strangely agitated, and her type was now unmistakable.

"Excuse me if I do ask," she said, "whether it's too much to hope that you may be induced to leave Doctor Hugh alone." Then before our poor friend, greatly disconcerted, could protest: "You ought to be informed that you stand in his light—that you may do him a terrible injury."

"Do you mean by causing the Countess to dispense with his services?"

"By causing her to disinherit him." Dencombe stared at this, and Miss Vernham pursued, in the gratification of seeing she could produce an impression: "It has depended on himself to come into something very handsome. He has had a grand prospect, but I think you've succeeded in spoiling it."

"Not intentionally, I assure you. Is there no hope the accident may be repaired?" Dencombe asked.

"She was ready to do anything for him. She takes great fancies, she lets herself go—it's her way. She has no relations, she's free to dispose of her money, and she's very ill," said Miss Vernham for a climax.

"I'm very sorry to hear it," Dencombe stammered.

"Wouldn't it be possible for you to leave Bournemouth? That's what I've come to see about."

He sank to his bench. "I'm very ill myself, but I'll try!"

Miss Vernham still stood there with her colorless eyes and the brutality of her good conscience. "Before it's too late, please!" she said; and with this she turned her back, in order, quickly, as if it had been a business to which she could spare but a precious moment, to pass out of his sight.

Oh yes, after this Dencombe was certainly very ill. Miss Vernham had upset him with her rough fierce news; it was the sharpest shock to him to discover what was at stake for a penniless young man of fine parts. He sat trembling on his bench, staring at the waste of waters, feeling sick with the directness of the blow. He was indeed too weak, too unsteady, too alarmed; but he would make the effort to get away, for he couldn't accept the guilt of interference and his honor was really involved. He would hobble home, at any rate, and then think what was to be done. He made his way back to the hotel and, as he went, had a characteristic vision of Miss Vernham's great motive. The Countess hated women of course—Dencombe was lucid about that; so the hungry pianist had no personal hopes and could only console herself with the bold conception of helping Doctor Hugh in order to marry him after he should get his money or else induce him to recognize her claim for compensation and buy her off. If she had befriended him at a fruitful crisis he would really, as a man of delicacy—and she knew what to think of that point—have to reckon with her.

At the hotel Dencombe's servant insisted on his going back to bed. The invalid had talked about catching a train and had begun with orders to pack; after which his racked nerves had yielded to a sense of sickness. He consented to see his physician, who immediately was sent for, but he wished it to be understood that his door was irrevocably closed to Doctor Hugh. He had his plan, which was so fine that he rejoiced in it after getting back to bed. Doctor Hugh, suddenly finding himself snubbed without mercy, would, in natural disgust and to the joy of Miss Vernham, renew his allegiance to the Countess. When his physician arrived Dencombe learned that he was feverish and that this was very wrong; he was to cultivate calmness and try, if possible, not to think. For the rest of the day he wooed stupidity; but there was an ache that kept him sentient, the probable sacrifice of his "extension," the limit of his course. His medical adviser was anything but pleased; his successive relapses were ominous. He charged this personage to put out a strong hand and take Doctor Hugh off his mind—it would contribute so much to his being quiet. The agitating name, in his room, was not mentioned again, but his security was a smothered fear, and it was not confirmed by the receipt, at ten o'clock that evening, of a telegram which his servant opened and read him and to which, with an address in London, the signature of Miss Vernham was attached. "Beseech you to use all influence to make our friend join us here in the morning. Countess much the worse for dreadful journey, but everything may still be saved." The two ladies had gathered themselves up and had been capable in the afternoon of a spiteful revolution. They had started for the capital, and if the elder one, as Miss Vernham had announced, was very ill, she had wished to make it clear that she was proportionately reckless. Poor Dencombe, who was not reckless and who only desired that everything should indeed be "saved," sent this missive straight off to the young man's lodging and had on the morrow the pleasure of knowing that he had quitted Bournemouth by an early train.

Two days later he pressed in with a copy of a literary journal in his hand. He had returned because he was anxious and for the pleasure of flourishing the great review of "The Middle Years." Here at least was something adequate—it rose to the occasion; it was an acclamation, a reparation, a critical attempt to place the author in the niche he had fairly won. Dencombe accepted and submitted; he made neither objection nor inquiry, for old complications had returned and he had had two dismal days. He was convinced not only that he should never again leave his bed, so that his young friend might pardonably remain, but that the demand he should make on the patience of beholders would be of the most moderate. Doctor Hugh had been to town, and he tried to find in his eyes some confession that the Countess was pacified and his legacy clinched; but all he could see there was the light of his juvenile joy in two or three of the phrases of the newspaper. Dencombe couldn't read them, but when his visitor had insisted on repeating them more than once he was able to shake an unintoxicated head. "Ah no—but they would have been true of what I *could* have done!"

"What people 'could have done' is mainly what they've in fact done," Doctor Hugh contended.

"Mainly, yes; but I've been an idiot!" Dencombe said.

Doctor Hugh did remain; the end was coming fast. Two days later his patient observed to him, by way of the feeblest of jokes, that there would now be no question whatever of a second chance. At this the young man stared; then he exclaimed: "Why it has come to pass—it has come to pass! The second chance has been the public's—the chance to find the point of view, to pick up the pearl!"

"Oh the pearl!" poor Dencombe uneasily sighed. A smile as cold as a winter sunset flickered on his drawn lips as he added: "The pearl is the unwritten—the pearl is the unalloyed, the *rest*, the lost!"

From that hour he was less and less present, heedless to all appearance of what went on round him. His disease was definitely mortal, of an action as relentless, after the short arrest that had enabled him to fall in with Doctor Hugh, as a leak in a great ship. Sinking steadily, though this visitor, a man of rare resources, now cordially approved by his physician, showed endless art in guarding him from pain, poor Dencombe kept no reckoning of favor or neglect, betrayed no symptom of regret or speculation. Yet toward the last he gave a sign of having noticed how for two days Doctor Hugh hadn't been in his room, a sign that consisted of his suddenly opening his eyes to put a question. Had he spent those days with the Countess?

"The Countess is dead," said Doctor Hugh. "I knew that in a particular contingency she wouldn't resist. I went to her grave."

Dencombe's eyes opened wider. "She left you 'something handsome'?"

The young man gave a laugh almost too light for a chamber of woe. "Never a penny. She roundly cursed me."

"Cursed you?" Dencombe wailed.

"For giving her up. I gave her up for *you*. I had to choose," his companion explained.

"You chose to let a fortune go?"

"I chose to accept, whatever they might be, the consequences of my infatuation," smiled Doctor Hugh. Then as a larger pleasantry: "The fortune be hanged! It's your own fault if I can't get your things out of my head."

The immediate tribute to his humor was a long bewildered moan; after which, for many hours, many days, Dencombe lay motionless and absent. A response so absolute, such a glimpse of a definite result and such a sense of credit, worked together in his mind and, producing a strange commotion, slowly altered and transfigured his despair. The sense of cold submersion left him—he seemed to float without an effort. The incident was extraordinary as evidence, and it shed an intenser light. At last he signed to Doctor Hugh to listen and, when he was down on his knees by the pillow, brought him very near. "You've made me think it all a delusion."

"Not your glory, my dear friend," stammered the young man.

"Not my glory—what there is of it! It *is* glory—to have been tested, to have had our little quality and cast our little spell. The thing is to have made somebody care. You happen to be crazy of course, but that doesn't affect the law."

"You're a great success!" said Doctor Hugh, putting into his young voice the ring of a marriage-bell.

Dencombe lay taking this in; then he gathered strength to speak once more. "A second chance—*that's* the delusion. There never was to be but one. We work in the dark—we do what we can—we give what we have. Our doubt is our passion and our passion is our task. The rest is the madness of art."

"If you've doubted, if you've despaired, you've always 'done' it," his visitor subtly argued.

"We've done something or other," Dencombe conceded.

"Something or other is everything. It's the feasible. It's *you!*"

"Comforter!" poor Dencombe ironically sighed.

"But it's true," insisted his friend.

"It's true. It's frustration that doesn't count."

"Frustration's only life," said Doctor Hugh.

"Yes, it's what passes." Poor Dencombe was barely audible, but he had marked with the words the virtual end of his first and only chance.

Q U E S T I O N S

1. In the second paragraph, Dencombe uses his novelistic imagination to create a fiction involving Doctor Hugh and the two women. Is the relationship Dencombe imagines true to the facts as revealed later in the story? In what ways does Dencombe's imagined drama help characterize him?

2. Fictional characters interested James "in proportion as they feel their respective situations." Discuss this statement as it applies to Doctor Hugh. In what way does Doctor Hugh's obsession with Dencombe's book and his neglect of both the ocean and his companions foreshadow his subsequent actions?

3. Examine the role of chance and coincidence in this story. Do you feel that James relies too heavily on coincidence and is guilty of contrivance? Or is coincidence justified and acceptable?

4. What reason does Miss Vernham give when she asks Dencombe to renounce Doctor Hugh's companionship? Later Dencombe has a "characteristic vision of Miss Vernham's great motive." What is Dencombe's insight? Do you think his assessment is correct? Explain.

5. Do you agree with Doctor Hugh's statement, "'What people could have done is mainly what they've in fact done'"? Does this observation apply to Dencombe? to Doctor Hugh?

6. Early in the story, Dencombe laments: "He had done all he should ever do, and yet hadn't done what he wanted." He longs for "an extension"—for another and better chance. At the conclusion of the story, does he still want a second chance?

7. Examine James's use of imagery—in particular, descriptions of the sea and of light. How are these images used to characterize Dencombe? Doctor Hugh? How do they relate to the theme?

8. In addition to being about art, this story is about life. Does the story support the observation that life is art, and art is life? Why does James imply that being a good reader is as important as being an artist?

Characters

THEOPHRASTUS

The Oligarchical Man

Translations by Warren Anderson

As it would appear, the tendency toward oligarchy is an appetite for high office accompanied by power and financial gain. The oligarchical man is the kind who comes forward to state his opinion as the assembly is deliberating about the election of men to help arrange for the procession. He claims they should have full powers of independent action; and if somebody else proposes ten he answers, "One will be enough, provided he's a real man." The only line of Homer he remembers, moreover, is the one that says "The rule of many is not good; let one be ruler"—he doesn't know another word.

Also, he is apt to use this sort of language: "We must meet by ourselves to discuss these matters and get clear of the democratic rabble and the market place; likewise we must stop trying for elected office, putting ourselves at the mercy of these fellows in the assembly for praise or blame." Or he will say, "Either *we* take charge of things in Athens, or *they* do." And at high noon he ventures out, coat slung over his shoulder, hair neatly trimmed, and nails manicured to perfection, so that he can parade around town making remarks like "What with the informers, Athens isn't a fit place to live in," or "We're suffering terribly from bought juries in our court system," or "I can't think what makes people want to go into public life," or "The common man doesn't know what gratitude is: he'll sell himself every time to anybody at all for a present or a bribe." And he tells you how ashamed he feels when some unwashed pauper comes and sits down next to him in the assembly.

"When are they going to stop ruining us," he asks, "with special assessments against the rich?" Or he swears, "How I hate all rabble-rousers!" According to him it was Theseus, the first democrat, who originally got Athens into trouble, and when the citizens threw him out ahead of everybody else it was just what he deserved. [He goes on like this to strangers or to fellow-citizens who have the same politics, or the same tastes, that he does.]

The Offensive Man

Offensiveness can be defined with no difficulty: it is amusing yourself in an obtrusive, objectionable way. The offensive man is the kind who exposes himself when he passes respectable married women on the street. At the theater he goes on clapping after everyone else has stopped and hisses the actors who are public favorites; should there be general silence for a moment, he cocks his head and lets out a belch to make the audience turn round in their seats.

What's more, during the busiest part of the day downtown he strolls over where nuts and berries are on sale, and stands there munching them without paying while he talks to the poor merchant. He shouts a greeting to someone he hardly knows, too, and uses the man's name in a familiar way; or he calls, "Stop a minute!" to people who are obviously in a hurry; or if you have just lost an important case, he stops you outside the courtroom and jokes about what happened. He also goes shopping personally for fancy items—and lays out money for a party-girl. Then he shows off his purchase to everybody he meets, with an invitation to stop by and sample this specialty. And he lounges around outside the barber shop explaining in full detail his intention to get drunk.

He damns fortune-tellers up and down, too, with his mother just back from seeing one, and during the service of prayer and libation he lets the cup drop and laughs as if he had done something clever. Or while the others are all quietly listening to the playing of a girl entertainer, he makes himself conspicuous by clapping time and whistling along with the music and then criticizing her for stopping so soon. At a formal dinner he goes to spit across the table and hits the waiter.

QUESTIONS

1. The Characters of Theophrastus are noted for their objectivity; in fact, their impartiality has been said to approach that of the natural sciences. Support or refute this statement with examples from the sketches.

2. References to everyday objects and activities abound in the Characters. Give some examples from the sketches and discuss the strong sense of realism these details provide.

3. After an initial definition of the type to be described, the sketches proceed in a seemingly random order—that is, behavior is depicted without building in intensity or moving toward a definite conclusion. Find evidence to support or refute this statement.

4. In our own society, can you think of a counterpart to the Oligarchical Man? Discuss.

JOSEPH ADDISON

Sketch of Will Wimble

Gratìs anbelans, multa agendo nibil agens.[1]

Phaed.

As I was Yesterday Morning walking with Sir ROGER before his House, a Country-Fellow brought him a huge Fish, which, he told him, Mr. *William Wimble*[2] had caught that very Morning; and that he presented it, with his Service, to him, and intended to come and dine with him. At the same Time he delivered a Letter, which my Friend read to me as soon as the Messenger left him.

Sir Roger,
'I DESIRE you to accept of a Jack, which is the best I have caught this Season. I intend to come and stay with you a Week, and see how

---

[1] *Motto.* Phaedrus, *Fables,* 2. 5. 3: Puffing hard, and making much to do about nothing.

[2] The supposed 'original' of this character was a certain Thomas Morecraft, who died at Dublin on 2 July 1741 and was at that time described in the *Gentleman's Magazine* as 'the Person mentioned by the Spectator in the Character of *Will. Wimble'* (xi. 387). There seems to be no evidence for Nichols's statement (in a note to No. 269 (vol. ii)) that 'Steele, who knew him very early in life, introduced him to Addison, by whose bounty he was for some years supported'. Like 'the Hon. Thomas Gules' of *Tatler* 256, Will Wimble embodies in himself all the traits of the idle younger son in an ancient family, 'bred to no Business and born to no Estate'. In *The Midwife, or the Old Woman's Magazine,* published by Newbery 1750–3 and edited mainly by Christopher Smart, is a sketch of Will Wimble, amplifying the account in the *Spectator (The Midwife,* no. vi, pp. 264–9).

the Perch bite in the *Black River.* I observed, with some Concern, the last Time I saw you upon the Bowling-Green, that your Whip wanted a Lash to it: I will bring half a Dozen with me that I twisted last Week, which I hope will serve you all the Time you are in the Country. I have not been out of the Saddle for six Days last past, having been at *Eaton* with Sir *John's* eldest Son. He takes to his Learning hugely.

> *I am,*
> SIR,
>
> > *Your humble Servant,*
> > Will. Wimble.'

This extraordinary Letter, and Message that accompanied it, made me very curious to know the Character and Quality of the Gentleman who sent them; which I found to be as follows: *Will. Wimble* is younger Brother to a Baronet, and descended of the ancient Family of the *Wimbles.* He is now between Forty and Fifty; but being bred to no Business and born to no Estate, he generally lives with his elder Brother as Superintendant of his Game. He hunts a Pack of Dogs better than any Man in the Country, and is very famous for finding out a Hare. He is extremely well versed in all the little Handicrafts of an idle Man: He makes a *May*-fly to a Miracle; and furnishes the whole Country with Angle-Rods. As he is a good-natur'd officious[1] Fellow, and very much esteemed upon Account of his Family, he is a welcome Guest at every House, and keeps up a good Correspondence among all the Gentlemen about him. He carries a Tulip-Root[2] in his Pocket from one to another, or exchanges a Puppy between a couple of Friends that live perhaps in the opposite Sides of the County. *Will.* is a particular Favourite of all the young Heirs, whom he frequently obliges with a Net that he has weaved, or a Setting-dog that he has *made*[3] himself: He now and then presents a Pair of Garters of his own knitting to their Mothers or Sisters, and raises a great deal of Mirth among them, by enquiring as often as he meets them *how they wear?* These Gentleman-like Manufactures and obliging little Humours, make *Will.* the Darling of the Country.

Sir ROGER was proceeding in the Character of him, when we saw him make up to us, with two or three Hazle-twigs in his Hand that he had cut in Sir ROGER's Woods, as he came through them, in his Way to the House. I was very much pleased to observe on one Side the hearty and sincere Welcome with

---

[1]'Doing or ready to do kind offices; eager to serve or please; attentive, obliging, kind' (OED). The word is frequently used in this sense in the *Spectator,* now obsolete; the last quotation in OED is dated 1827.

[2]The tulip-mania of the late seventeenth century was still a subject of satire. In *Tatler* 218 Addison had described an enthusiast: 'He seemed a very plain honest Man, and a Person of good Sense, had not his Head been touched with that Distemper which *Hippocrates* calls the *Tulippo-Mania,* τυλιππομανια, insomuch that he would talk very rationally on any Subject in the World but a Tulip.'

[3]Used here in the specialized sense of *training.*

which Sir ROGER received him, and on the other the secret Joy which his Guest discovered at Sight of the good old Knight. After the first Salutes were over, *Will.* desired Sir ROGER to lend him one of his Servants to carry a Set of Shuttle-cocks he had with him in a little Box to a Lady that liv'd about a Mile off, to whom it seems he had promised such a Present for above this half Year. Sir ROGER's Back was no sooner turn'd, but honest *Will.* begun to tell me of a large Cock-Pheasant that he had sprung in one of the neighbouring Woods, with two or three other Adventures of the same Nature. Odd and uncommon Characters are the Game that I look for, and most delight in; for which Reason I was as much pleased with the Novelty of the Person that talked to me, as he could be for his Life with the springing of a Pheasant, and therefore listned to him with more than ordinary Attention.

In the Midst of his Discourse the Bell rung to Dinner, where the Gentleman I have been speaking of had the Pleasure of seeing the huge Jack, he had caught, served up for the first Dish in a most sumptuous Manner. Upon our sitting down to it he gave us a long Account how he had hooked it, played with it, foiled it, and at length drew it out upon the Bank, with several other Particulars that lasted all the first Course. A Dish of Wild-fowl that came afterwards furnished Conversation for the rest of the Dinner, which concluded with a late Invention of *Will's* for improving the Quail Pipe.

Upon withdrawing into my Room after Dinner, I was secretly touched with Compassion towards the honest Gentleman that had dined with us; and could not but consider with a great deal of Concern, how so good an Heart and such busy Hands were wholly employed in Trifles; that so much Humanity should be so little beneficial to others, and so much Industry so little advantageous to himself. The same Temper of Mind and Application to Affairs might have recommended him to the publick Esteem, and have raised his Fortune in another Station of Life. What Good to his Country or himself might not a Trader or Merchant have done with such useful tho' ordinary Qualifications?

Will. Wimble's is the Case of many a younger Brother of a great Family, who had rather see their Children starve like Gentlemen, than thrive in a Trade or Profession that is beneath their Quality. This Humour fills several Parts of *Europe* with Pride and Beggary. It is the Happiness of a trading Nation, like ours, that the younger Sons, tho' uncapable of any liberal Art or Profession, may be placed in such a Way of Life, as may perhaps enable them to vie with the best of their Family: Accordingly we find several Citizens that were launched into the World with narrow Fortunes, rising by an honest Industry to greater Estates than those of their elder Brothers. It is not improbable but *Will.* was formerly tried at Divinity, Law, or Physick; and that finding his Genius did not lie that Way, his Parents gave him up at length to his own Inventions: But certainly, however improper he might have been for Studies of a higher Nature, he was perfectly well turned for the Occupations of Trade and Commerce. As I think this is a Point which cannot be too much inculcated, I shall desire my Reader to compare what I have here written with what I have said in my Twenty first Speculation.

Ned Softly the Poet

Idem inficeto est inficetior rure,
Simul poemata attigit; neque idem unquam
Aeque est beatus, ac poema cum scribit:
Tam gaudet in se, tamque se ipse miratur.
Nimirum idem omnes fallimur; neque est quisquam,
Quem non in aliqua re videre Suffenum
Possis. *

Catullus, xxii. 14.

Will's Coffee-house, April 24.

I yesterday came hither about two hours before the company generally make their appearance, with a design to read over all the newspapers; but upon my sitting down, I was accosted by Ned Softly, who saw me from a corner in the other end of the room, where I found he had been writing something. "Mr. Bickerstaff," says he, "I observe by a late paper of yours, that you and I are just of a humour; for you must know, of all impertinences, there is nothing which I so much hate as news. I never read a Gazette in my life; and never trouble my head about our armies, whether they win or lose, or in what part of the world they lie encamped." Without giving me time to reply, he drew a paper of verses out of his pocket, telling me, that he had something which would entertain me more agreeably, and that he would desire my judgment upon every line, for that we had time enough before us till the company came in.

Ned Softly is a very pretty poet, and a great admirer of easy lines. Waller is his favourite: and as that admirable writer has the best and worst verses of any among our great English poets, Ned Softly has got all the bad ones without book, which he repeats upon occasion, to show his reading, and garnish his conversation. Ned is indeed a true English reader, incapable of relishing the great and masterly strokes of this art; but wonderfully pleased with the little Gothic ornaments of epigrammatical conceits, turns, points, and quibbles, which are so frequent in the most admired of our English poets, and practised by those who want genius and strength to represent, after the manner of the ancients, simplicity in its natural beauty and perfection.

Finding myself unavoidably engaged in such a conversation, I was resolved

---

*Suffenus has no more wit than a mere clown, when he attempts to write verses; and yet he is never happier than when he is scribbling; so much does he admire himself and his compositions. And, indeed, this is the foible of every one of us; for there is no man living who is not a Suffenus in one thing or other.

to turn my pain into a pleasure, and to divert myself as well as I could with so very odd a fellow. "You must understand," says Ned, "that the sonnet I am going to read to you was written upon a lady, who showed me some verses of her own making, and is perhaps the best poet of our age. But you shall hear it." Upon which he began to read as follows:

"*To Mira on her Incomparable Poems.*

I.

"When dressed in laurel wreaths you shine,
    And tune your soft melodious notes,
    You seem a sister of the Nine,
    Or Phoebus' self in petticoats.

II.

"I fancy, when your song you sing
    (Your song you sing with so much art),
    Your pen was plucked from Cupid's wing;
    For ah! it wounds me like his dart."

"Why," says I, "this is a little nosegay of conceits, a very lump of salt: every verse has something in it that piques; and then the dart in the last line is certainly as pretty a sting in the tail of an epigram (for so I think your critics call it) as ever entered into the thought of a poet." "Dear Mr. Bickerstaff," says he, shaking me by the hand, "everybody knows you to be a judge of these things; and to tell you truly, I read over Roscommon's translation of Horace's 'Art of Poetry' three several times, before I sat down to write the sonnet which I have shown you. But you shall hear it again, and pray observe every line of it, for not one of them shall pass without your approbation.

"When dressed in laurel wreaths you shine.

"That is," says he, "when you have your garland on; when you are writing verses." To which I replied, "I know your meaning: a metaphor!" "The same," said he, and went on:

"And tune your soft melodious notes.

"Pray observe the gliding of that verse; there is scarce a consonant in it: I took care to make it run upon liquids. Give me your opinion of it." "Truly," said I, "I think it as good as the former." "I am very glad to hear you say so," says he; "but mind the next:

"You seem a sister of the Nine.

"That is," says he, "you seem a sister of the Muses; for if you look into ancient authors, you will find it was their opinion, that there were nine of them." "I remember it very well," said I; "but pray proceed."

"Or Phoebus' self in petticoats.

"Phoebus," says he, "was the God of Poetry. These little instances, Mr. Bickerstaff, show a gentleman's reading. Then to take off from the air of learning, which Phoebus and the Muses have given to this first stanza, you may observe how it falls all of a sudden into the familiar; 'in petticoats!'

"Or Phoebus' self in petticoats."

"Let us now," says I, "enter upon the second stanza. I find the first line is still a continuation of the metaphor:

"I fancy, when your song you sing."

"'It is very right," says he; "but pray observe the turn of words in those two lines. I was a whole hour in adjusting of them, and have still a doubt upon me, whether in the second line it should be, 'Your song you sing'; or, 'You sing your song'? You shall hear them both:

"I fancy, when your song you sing
    (Your song you sing with so much art).

Or,

"I fancy, when your song you sing
    (You sing your song with so much art)."

"Truly," said I, "the turn is so natural either way, that you have made me almost giddy with it." "Dear sir," said he, grasping me by the hand, "you have a great deal of patience; but pray what do you think of the next verse:

"Your pen was plucked from Cupid's wing?"

"Think!" says I; "I think you have made Cupid look like a little goose." "That was my meaning," says he; "I think the ridicule is well enough hit off. But we now come to the last, which sums up the whole matter:

"For ah! it wounds me like his dart.

"Pray, how do you like that 'Ah!' Does it not make a pretty figure in that place? 'Ah!' It looks as if I felt the dart, and cried out at being pricked with it:

"For ah! it wounds me like his dart.

"My friend Dick Easy," continued he, "assured me he would rather have written that 'Ah!' than to have been the author of the 'Aeneid.' He indeed objected that I made Mira's pen like a quill in one of the lines, and like a dart in the other. But as to that——" "Oh! as to that," says I, "it is but supposing Cupid to be like a porcupine, and his quills and darts will be the same thing." He was going to embrace me for the hint; but half a dozen critics coming into the room, whose faces he did not like, he conveyed the sonnet into his pocket, and whispered me in the ear, he would show it me again as soon as his man had written it over fair.

QUESTIONS

1. Find passages showing that the Character as written by Addison has a more narrative quality than the Character of Theophrastus.

2. Addison's Characters are more subjective than the Characters of Theophrastus. Explain, using Will Wimble as an example.

3. Like Theophrastus, Addison uses details of everyday life to give his sketches a strong sense of realism. Find some details in "Ned Softly" that contribute to this sense of realism.

4. The narrator of "Will Wimble" tells us, "I was secretly touched with Compassion towards the honest Gentleman that had dined with us. . . ." Why is he compassionate toward Will? Does he feel the same compassion for Ned Softly?

5. In "The Oligarchical Man," Theophrastus is interested in the workings of democracy. Addison's interest in Will Wimble also has a nationalistic motive. Explain.

7. The dialogue in "Ned Softly" not only contributes to the fictional quality of the sketch but is responsible for much of the satire. Discuss, choosing several examples of dialogue as illustrations.

8. Addison's sketches are noted for their urbane wit, the Characters of Theophrastus for their absence of wit. Discuss.

THE BROTHERS GRIMM

Cinderella

Adapted from the Margaret Hunt translation

The wife of a rich man fell sick, and as she felt that her end was drawing near, she called her only daughter to her bedside and said, "Dear child, be good and pious, and then the good God will always protect you and I will look down on you from heaven and be near you." Thereupon she closed her eyes and departed. Every day the maiden went out to her mother's grave and wept, and she remained pious and good. When winter came the snow spread a white sheet over the grave, and when the spring sun had drawn it off again, the man had taken another wife.

The woman had brought two daughters into the house with her, who were beautiful and fair of face, but vile and black of heart. Now began a bad time for the poor step-child. "Is the stupid goose to sit in the parlor with us?" said they. "He who wants to eat bread must earn it; out with the kitchen-wench." They took her pretty clothes away from her, put an old grey bedgown on her, and gave her wooden shoes. "Just look at the proud princess, how decked out she is!" they cried, and laughed, and led her into the kitchen. There she had to do hard work from morning till night, get up before daybreak, carry water, light fires, cook and wash. Besides this, the sisters did her every imaginable injury— they mocked her and emptied her peas and lentils into the ashes, so that she was forced to sit and pick them out again. In the evening when she had worked till she was weary she had no bed to go to, but had to sleep by the fireside in the ashes. And as on that account she always looked dusty and dirty, they called her Cinderella. It happened that the father was once going to the fair, and he asked his two step-daughters what he should bring back for them. "Beautiful dresses," said one, "Pearls and jewels," said the second. "And you, Cinderella," said he, "what will you have?" "Father, break off for me the first branch which knocks against your hat on your way home." So he bought beautiful dresses, pearls and jewels for his two step-daughters, and on his way home as he was riding through a green thicket, a hazel twig brushed against him and knocked off his hat. Then he broke off the branch and took it with him. When he reached home he gave his step-daughters the things which they had wished for, and to Cinderella he gave the branch from the hazel-bush. Cinderella thanked him, went to her mother's grave and planted the branch on it, and wept so much that the tears fell down on it and watered it. It grew and became a handsome tree. Three times a day Cinderella went and sat beneath it, and wept and prayed, and a little white bird always came on the tree, and if Cinderella expressed a wish, the bird threw down to her what she had wished for.

It happened, however, that the King appointed a festival which was to last three days, and to which all the beautiful young girls in the country were invited, in order that his son might choose himself a bride. When the two step-sisters heard that they too were to appear among the number, they were delighted, called Cinderella and said, "Comb our hair for us, brush our shoes and fasten our buckles, for we are going to the festival at the King's palace." Cinderella obeyed, but wept, because she too would have liked to go with them to the dance, and begged her step-mother to allow her to do so. "You go, Cinderella!" said she; "you are dusty and dirty, and would go to the festival? You have no clothes and shoes, and yet would dance!" As, however, Cinderella went on asking, the step-mother at last said, "I have emptied a dish of lentils into the ashes for you; if you have picked them out again in two hours, you shall go with us." The maiden went through the back-door into the garden, and called, "You tame pigeons, you turtledoves, and all you birds beneath the sky, come and help me to pick

"The good into the pot
The bad into the crop."

Then two white pigeons came in by the kitchen-window, and afterwards the turtle-doves, and at last all the birds beneath the sky, came whirring and crowding in, and alighted among the ashes. And the pigeons nodded with their heads and began pick, pick, pick, pick, and the rest began also pick, pick, pick, pick, and gathered all the good grains into the dish. Hardly had one hour passed before they had finished, and all flew out again. Then the girl took the dish to her step-mother, and was glad, and believed that now she would be allowed to go with them to the festival. But the step-mother said, "No, Cinderella, you have no clothes and you cannot dance; you would only be laughed at." And as Cinderella wept at this, the step-mother said, "If you can pick two dishes of lentils out of the ashes for me in one hour, you shall go with us." And she thought to herself, "That she most certainly cannot do." When the step-mother had emptied the two dishes of lentils amongst the ashes, the maiden went through the back-door into the garden and cried, "You tame pigeons, you turtle-doves, and all you birds under heaven, come and help me to pick

"The good into the pot,
The bad into the crop."

Then two white pigeons came in by the kitchen-window, and afterwards the turtle-doves, and at length all the birds beneath the sky, came whirring and crowding in, and alit among the ashes. And the doves nodded with their heads and began pick, pick, pick, pick, and the others began also pick, pick, pick, pick, and gathered all the good seeds into the dishes, and before half an hour was over they had already finished, and all flew out again. Then the maiden carried the dishes to the step-mother and was delighted, and believed that she might now go with them to the festival. But the step-mother said, "All this will not help you; you cannot go with us, for you have no clothes and cannot dance; we should be ashamed of you!" On this she turned her back on Cinderella, and hurried away with her two proud daughters.

As no one was now at home, Cinderella went to her mother's grave beneath the hazel-tree, and cried,

"Shiver and quiver, little tree,
Silver and gold throw over me."

Then the bird threw a gold and silver dress down to her, and slippers embroidered with silk and silver. She put on the dress with all speed, and went to the festival. Her step-sisters and the step-mother however did not know her, and thought she must be a foreign princess, for she looked so beautiful in the golden dress. They never once thought of Cinderella, and believed that she was sitting at home in the dirt, picking lentils out of the ashes. The prince went to meet her, took her by the hand and danced with her. He would dance with no other maiden, and never let go of her hand, and if any one else came to invite her, he said, "This is my partner."

She danced till it was evening, and then she wanted to go home. But the King's son said, "I will go with you and keep you company," for he wished to see to whom the beautiful maiden belonged. She escaped from him, however, and sprang into the pigeon-house. The King's son waited until her father came, and then he told him that the stranger maiden had leapt into the pigeon-house. The old man thought, "Can it be Cinderella?" and they had to bring him an axe and a pickaxe that he might hew the pigeon-house to pieces, but no one was inside it. And when they got home Cinderella lay in her dirty clothes among the ashes, and a dim little oil-lamp was burning on the mantle-piece, for Cinderella had jumped quickly down from the back of the pigeon-house and had run to the little hazel-tree, and there she had taken off her beautiful clothes and laid them on the grave, and the bird had taken them away again, and then she had placed herself in the kitchen among the ashes in her grey gown.

Next day when the festival began afresh, and her parents and the step-sisters had gone once more, Cinderella went to the hazel-tree and said—

> "Shiver and quiver, my little tree,
> Silver and gold throw over me."

Then the bird threw down a much more beautiful dress than on the preceding day. And when Cinderella appeared at the festival in this dress, every one was astonished at her beauty. The King's son had waited until she came, and instantly took her by the hand and danced with no one but her. When others came and invited her, he said, "She is my partner." When evening came she wished to leave, and the King's son followed her and wanted to see into which house she went. But she sprang away from him, and into the garden behind the house. Therein stood a beautiful tall tree on which hung the most magnificent pears. She clambered so nimbly between the branches like a squirrel, that the King's son did not know where she had gone. He waited until her father came, and said to him, "The stranger-maiden has escaped from me, and I believe she has climbed up the pear-tree." The father thought, "Can it be Cinderella?" and had an axe brought and cut the tree down, but no one was in it. And when they got into the kitchen, Cinderella lay there among the ashes, as usual, for she had jumped down on the other side of the tree, had taken the beautiful dress to the bird on the little hazel-tree, and put on her grey gown.

On the third day, when the parents and sisters had gone away, Cinderella once more went to her mother's grave and said to the little tree—

> "Shiver and quiver, my little tree,
> Silver and gold throw over me."

And now the bird threw down to her a dress which was more splendid and magnificent than any she had yet had, and the slippers were golden. And when she went to the festival in the dress, no one knew how to speak for astonishment. The King's son danced with her only, and if any one invited her to dance, he said, "She is my partner."

When evening came, Cinderella wished to leave, and the King's son was anxious to go with her, but she escaped from him so quickly that he could not follow her. The King's son had, however, used a stratagem, and had caused the whole staircase to be smeared with pitch, and there, when she ran down, had the maiden's left slipper remained sticking. The King's son picked it up, and it was small and dainty, and all golden. Next morning, he went with it to the father, and said to him, "No one shall be my wife but she whose foot this golden slipper fits." Then were the two sisters glad, for they had pretty feet. The eldest went with the shoe into her room and wanted to try it on, and her mother stood by. But she could not get her big toe into it, and the shoe was too small for her. Then her mother gave her a knife and said, "Cut the toe off; when you are Queen you will have no more need to go on foot." The maiden cut the toe off, forced the foot into the shoe, swallowed the pain, and went out to the King's son. Then he took her on his horse as his bride and rode away with her. They were, however, obliged to pass the grave, and there, on the hazel-tree, sat the two pigeons and cried,

> "Turn and peep, turn and peep,
> There's blood within the shoe,
> The shoe it is too small for her,
> The true bride waits for you."

Then he looked at her foot and saw how the blood was streaming from it. He turned his horse round and took the false bride home again, and said she was not the true one, and that the other sister was to put the shoe on. Then this one went into her chamber and got her toes safely into the shoe, but her heel was too large. So her mother gave her a knife and said, "Cut a bit off your heel; when you are Queen you will have no more need to go on foot." The maiden cut a bit off her heel, forced her foot into the shoe, swallowed the pain, and went out to the King's son. He took her on his horse as his bride, and rode away with her, but when they passed by the hazel-tree, two little pigeons sat on it and cried,

> "Turn and peep, turn and peep,
> There's blood within the shoe,
> The shoe it is too small for her,
> The true bride waits for you."

He looked down at her foot and saw how the blood was running out of her shoe, and how it had stained her white stocking. Then he turned his horse and took the false bride home again. "This also is not the right one," said he, "have you no other daughter?" "No," said the man. "There is still a little stunted kitchen-wench which my late wife left behind her, but she cannot possibly be the bride." The King's son said he was to send her up to him; but the mother answered, "Oh no, she is much too dirty, she cannot show herself!" He absolutely insisted on it, and Cinderella had to be called. She first washed her hands and face clean, and then went and bowed down before the King's son, who gave her the golden shoe. Then she seated herself on a stool, drew her foot out of the heavy wooden shoe, and put it into the slipper, which fitted like a glove. And when she rose up and the King's son looked at her face he recognized the beautiful maiden who had danced with him and cried, "That is the true bride!" The step-mother and the two sisters were terrified and became pale with rage; he, however, took Cinderella on his horse and rode away with her. As they passed by the hazel-tree, the two white doves cried,

> "Turn and peep, turn and peep,
> No blood is in the shoe,

> The shoe is not too small for her,
> The true bride rides with you,"

and when they had cried that, the two came flying down and placed themselves on Cinderella's shoulders, one on the right, the other on the left, and remained sitting there.

When the wedding with the King's son was celebrated, the two false sisters came and wanted to get into favor with Cinderella and share her good fortune. When the betrothed couple went to church, the elder was at the right side and the younger at the left, and the pigeons pecked out one eye of each of them. Afterwards as they came back, the elder was at the left, and the younger at the right, and then the pigeons pecked out the other eye of each. And thus, for their wickedness and falsehood, they were punished with blindness as long as they lived.

QUESTIONS

1. What stereotype does each of the principal characters represent?

2. Examine the use of repetition. What function does repetition serve?

3. The scenes in which the stepsisters cut off portions of their feet in order to fit into the golden slipper have been deleted from the version read by most American children. Does all this blood and gore bother you? Do you think it would trouble young children?

4. In the tamer, less gory version, Cinderella forgives her stepsisters and marries them to rich gentlemen of the court. Do you prefer this ending or the more violent ending printed here? Why? Discuss the function of poetic justic in each version.

5. In the version printed here, magical birds replace Cinderella's fairy godmother. These creatures play a more active role than the godmother, who appears in the story only once when she turns a pumpkin into a coach, mice into horses, a rat into a coachman, and so forth. Which version of the magical happenings do you prefer? Why?

6. The "Cinderella myth" has been criticized for putting false notions about love and marriage in young readers' heads. Examine the underlying assumptions about love and marriage in this story. Do you find them false? Is the "Cinderella myth" pervasive in our culture today? Is it damaging?

RICHARD WRIGHT

The Man Who Was Almost a Man

Dave struck out across the fields, looking homeward through paling light. Whut's the use talkin wid em niggers in the field? Anyhow, his mother was putting supper on the table. Them niggers can't understan nothing. One of these days he was going to get a gun and practice shooting, then they couldn't talk to him as though he were a little boy. He slowed, looking at the ground. Shucks, Ah ain scareda them even ef they are biggern me! Aw, Ah know whut Ahma do. Ahm going by ol Joe's sto n git that Sears Roebuck catlog n look at them guns. Mebbe Ma will lemme buy one when she gits mah pay from ol man Hawkins. Ahma beg her t gimme some money. Ahm ol ernough to hava gun. Ahm seventeen. Almost a man. He strode, feeling his long loose-jointed limbs. Shucks, a man oughta hava little gun aftah he done worked hard all day.

He came in sight of Joe's store. A yellow lantern glowed on the front porch. He mounted steps and went through the screen door, hearing it bang behind him. There was a strong smell of coal oil and mackerel fish. He felt very confident until he saw fat Joe walk in through the rear door, then his courage began to ooze.

"Howdy, Dave! Whutcha want?"

"How yuh, Mistah Joe? Aw, Ah don wanna buy nothing. Ah jus wanted t see ef yuhd lemme look at tha catlog erwhile."

"Sure! You wanna see it here?"

"Nawsuh, Ah wans t take it home wid me. Ah'll bring it back termorrow when Ah come in from the fiels."

188

"You plannin on buying something?"

"Yessuh."

"Your ma lettin you have your own money now?"

"Shucks. Mistah Joe, Ahm gittin t be a man like anybody else!"

Joe laughed and wiped his greasy white face with a red bandanna.

"Whut you plannin on buyin?"

Dave looked at the floor, scratched his head, scratched his thigh, and smiled. Then he looked up shyly.

"Ah'll tell yuh, Mistah Joe, ef yuh promise yuh won't tell."

"I promise."

"Waal, Ahma buy a gun."

"A gun? Whut you want with a gun?"

"Ah wanna keep it."

"You ain't nothing but a boy. You don't need a gun."

"Aw, lemme have the catlog, Mistah Joe. Ah'll bring it back."

Joe walked through the rear door. Dave was elated. He looked around at barrels of sugar and flour. He heard Joe coming back. He craned his neck to see if he was bringing the book. Yeah, he's got it. Gawddog, he's got it!

"Here, but be sure you bring it back. It's the only one I got."

"Sho, Mistah Joe."

"Say, if you wanna buy a gun, why don't you buy one from me? I gotta gun to sell."

"Will it shoot?"

"Sure it'll shoot."

"Whut kind is it?"

"Oh, it's kinda old . . . a left-hand Wheeler. A pistol. A big one."

"Is it got bullets in it?"

"It's loaded."

"Kin Ah see it?"

"Where's your money?"

"Whut yuh wan fer it?"

"I'll let you have it for two dollars."

"Just two dollahs? Shucks, Ah could buy tha when Ah git mah pay."

"I'll have it here when you want it."

"Awright, suh. Ah be in fer it."

He went through the door, hearing it slam again behind him. Ahma git some money from Ma n buy me a gun! Only two dollahs! He tucked the thick catalogue under his arm and hurried.

"Where yuh been, boy?" His mother held a steaming dish of black-eyed peas.

"Aw, Ma, Ah jus stopped down the road t talk wid the boys."

"Yuh know bettah t keep suppah waitin."

He sat down, resting the catalogue on the edge of the table.

"Yuh git up from there and git to the well n wash yosef! Ah ain feedin no hogs in mah house!"

She grabbed his shoulder and pushed him. He stumbled out of the room, then came back to get the catalogue.

"Whut this?"

"Aw, Ma, it's jusa catlog."

"Who yuh git it from?"

"From Joe, down at the sto."

"Waal, thas good. We kin use it in the outhouse."

"Naw, Ma." He grabbed for it. "Gimme ma catlog, Ma."

She held onto it and glared at him.

"Quit hollerin at me! Whut's wrong wid yuh? Yuh crazy?"

"But Ma, please. It ain mine! It's Joe's! He tol me t bring it back t im termorrow."

She gave up the book. He stumbled down the back steps, hugging the thick book under his arm. When he had splashed water on his face and hands, he groped back to the kitchen and fumbled in a corner for the towel. He bumped into a chair; it clattered to the floor. The catalogue sprawled at his feet. When he had dried his eyes he snatched up the book and held it again under his arm. His mother stood watching him.

"Now, ef yuh gonna act a fool over that ol book, Ah'll take it n burn it up."

"Naw, Ma, please."

"Waal, set down n be still!"

He sat down and drew the oil lamp close. He thumbed page after page, unaware of the food his mother set on the table. His father came in. Then his small brother.

"Whutcha got there, Dave?" his father asked.

"Jusa catlog," he answered, not looking up.

"Yeah, here they is!" His eyes glowed at blue-and-black revolvers. He glanced up, feeling sudden guilt. His father was watching him. He eased the book under the table and rested it on his knees. After the blessing was asked, he ate. He scooped up peas and swallowed fat meat without chewing. Buttermilk helped to wash it down. He did not want to mention money before his father. He would do much better by cornering his mother when she was alone. He looked at his father uneasily out of the edge of his eye.

"Boy, how come yuh don quit foolin wid tha book n eat yo suppah?"

"Yessuh."

"How you n old man Hawkins gitten erlong?"

"Suh?"

"Can't yuh hear? Why don yuh lissen? Ah ast yu how wuz yuh n ol man Hawkins gittin erlong?"

"Oh, swell, Pa. Ah plows mo lan than anybody over there."

"Waal, yuh oughta keep yo mind on whut yuh doin."

"Yessuh."

He poured his plate full of molasses and sopped it up slowly with a chunk of cornbread. When his father and brother had left the kitchen, he still sat and looked again at the guns in the catalogue, longing to muster courage enough to present his case to his mother. Lawd, ef Ah only had tha pretty one! He could almost feel the slickness of the weapon with his fingers. If he had a gun like that he would polish it and keep it shining so it would never rust. N Ah'd keep it loaded, by Gawd!

"Ma?" His voice was hesitant.

"Hunh?"

"Ol man Hawkins give yuh mah money yit?"

"Yeah, but ain no usa yuh thinking bout throwin nona it erway. Ahme keepin tha money sos yuh kin have cloes t go to school this winter."

He rose and went to her side with the open catalogue in his palms. She was washing dishes, her head bent low over a pan. Shyly he raised the book. When he spoke, his voice was husky, faint.

"Ma, Gawd knows Ah wans one of these."

"One of whut?" she asked, not raising her eyes.

"One of these," he said again, not daring even to point. She glanced up at the page, then at him with wide eyes.

"Nigger, is yuh gone plumb crazy?"

"Aw, Ma—"

"Git outta here! Don yuh talk t me bout no gun! Yuh a fool!"

"Ma, Ah kin buy one fer two dollahs."

"Not ef Ah knows it, yuh ain!"

"But yuh promised me one—"

"Ah don care whut Ah promised! Yuh ain nothing but a boy yit!"

"Ma, ef yuh lemme buy one Ah'll *never* ast yuh fer nothing no mo."

"Ah tol yuh t git outta here! Yuh ain gonna toucha penny of tha money fer no gun! Thas how come Ah has Mistah Hawkins t pay yo wages t me, cause Ah knows yuh ain got no sense."

"But, Ma, we needa gun. Pa ain got no gun. We needa gun in the house. Yuh kin never tell whut might happen."

"Now don yuh try to maka fool outta me, boy! Ef we did hava gun, yuh wouldn't have it!"

He laid the catalogue down and slipped his arm around her waist.

"Aw, Ma, Ah done worked hard alla summer n ain ast yuh fer nothin, is Ah, now?"

"Thas whut yuh spose t do!"

"But Ma, Ah wans a gun. Yuh kin lemme have two dollahs outta mah money. Please, Ma. I kin give it to Pa . . . Please, Ma! Ah loves yuh, Ma."

When she spoke her voice came soft and low.

"Whut yu wan wida gun, Dave? Yuh don need no gun. Yuh'll git in trouble. N ef yo pa jus thought Ah let yuh have money t buy a gun he'd hava fit."

"Ah'll hide it, Ma. It ain but two dollahs."

"Lawd, chil, whut's wrong wid yuh?"

"Ain nothin wrong, Ma. Ahm almos a man now. Ah wans a gun."

"Who gonna sell yuh a gun?"

"Ol Joe at the sto."

"'N it don cos but two dollahs?"

"Thas all, Ma. Jus two dollahs. Please, Ma."

She was stacking the plates away; her hands moved slowly, reflectively. Dave kept an anxious silence. Finally, she turned to him.

"Ah'll let yuh git tha gun ef yuh promise me one thing."

"Whut's tha, Ma?"

"Yuh bring it straight back t me, yuh hear? It be fer Pa."

"Yessum! Lemme go now, Ma."

She stooped, turned slightly to one side, raised the hem of her dress, rolled down the top of her stocking, and came up with a slender wad of bills.

"Here," she said. "Lawd knows yuh don need no gun. But yer pa does. Yuh bring it right back t me, yuh hear? Ahma put it up. Now ef yuh don, Ahma have yuh pa lick yuh so hard yuh won fergit it."

"Yessum."

He took the money, ran down the steps, and across the yard.

"Dave! Yuuuuuh Daaaaave!"

He heard, but he was not going to stop now. "Naw, Lawd!"

The first movement he made the following morning was to reach under his pillow for the gun. In the gray light of dawn he held it loosely, feeling a sense of power. Could kill a man with a gun like this. Kill anybody, black or white. And if he were holding his gun in his hand, nobody could run over him; they would have to respect him. It was a big gun, with a long barrel and a heavy handle. He raised and lowered it in his hand, marveling at its weight.

He had not come straight home with it as his mother had asked; instead he had stayed out in the fields, holding the weapon in his hand, aiming it now and then at some imaginary foe. But he had not fired it; he had been afraid that his father might hear. Also he was not sure he knew how to fire it.

To avoid surrendering the pistol he had not come into the house until he knew that they were all asleep. When his mother had tiptoed to his bedside late that night and demanded the gun, he had first played possum; then he had told her that the gun was hidden outdoors, that he would bring it to her in the morning. Now he lay turning it slowly in his hands. He broke it, took out the cartridges, felt them, and then put them back.

He slid out of bed, got a long strip of old flannel from a trunk, wrapped the gun in it, and tied it to his naked thigh while it was still loaded. He did not go in to breakfast. Even though it was not yet daylight, he started for Jim Hawkins' plantation. Just as the sun was rising he reached the barns where the mules and plows were kept.

"Hey! That you, Dave?"

He turned. Jim Hawkins stood eying him suspiciously.

"What're yuh doing here so early?"

"Ah didn't know Ah wuz gittin up so early, Mistah Hawkins. Ah wuz fixin t hitch up ol Jenny n take her t the fiels."

"Good. Since you're so early, how about plowing that stretch down by the woods?"

"Suits me, Mistah Hawkins."

"O.K. Go to it!"

He hitched Jenny to a plow and started across the fields. Hot dog! This was just what he wanted. If he could get down by the woods, he could shoot his gun and nobody would hear. He walked behind the plow, hearing the traces creaking, feeling the gun tied tight to his thigh.

When he reached the woods, he plowed two whole rows before he decided to take out the gun. Finally, he stopped, looked in all directions, then untied the gun and held it in his hand. He turned to the mule and smiled.

"Know whut this is , Jenny? Naw, yuh wouldn know! Yuhs jusa ol mule! Anyhow, this is a gun, n it kin shoot, by Gawd!"

He held the gun at arm's length. Whut t hell, Ahma shoot this thing! He looked at Jenny again.

"Lissen here, Jenny! When Ah pull this ol trigger, Ah don wan yuh t run n acka fool now!"

Jenny stood with head down, her short ears pricked straight. Dave walked off about twenty feet, held the gun far out from him at arm's length, and turned his head. Hell, he told himself, Ah ain afraid. The gun felt loose in his fingers; he waved it wildly for a moment. Then he shut his eyes and tightened his forefinger. Bloom! A report half deafened him and he thought his right hand was torn from his arm. He heard Jenny whinnying and galloping over the field, and he found himself on his knees, squeezing his fingers hard between his legs. His hand was numb; he jammed it into his mouth, trying to warm it, trying to stop the pain. The gun lay at his feet. He did not quite know what had happened. He stood up and stared at the gun as though it were a living thing. He gritted his teeth and kicked the gun. Yuh almos broke mah arm! He turned to look for Jenny; she was far over the fields, tossing her head and kicking wildly.

"Hol on there, ol mule!"

When he caught up with her she stood trembling, walling her big white eyes at him. The plow was far away; the traces had broken. Then Dave stopped short, looking, not believing. Jenny was bleeding. Her left side was red and wet with blood. He went closer. Lawd, have mercy! Wondah did Ah shoot this mule? He grabbed for Jenny's mane. She flinched, snorted, whirled, tossing her head.

"Hol on now! Hol on."

Then he saw the hole in Jenny's side, right between the ribs. It was round, wet, red. A crimson stream streaked down the front leg, flowing fast, Good Gawd! Ah wuzn't shootin at tha mule. He felt panic. He knew he had to stop that blood, or Jenny would bleed to death. He had never seen so much blood in all his life. He chased the mule for half a mile, trying to catch her. Finally she stopped, breathing hard, stumpy tail half arched. He caught her mane and led her back to where the plow and gun lay. Then he stooped and grabbed handfuls of damp black earth and tried to plug the bullet hole. Jenny shuddered, whinnied, and broke from him.

"Hol on! Hol on now!"

He tried to plug it again, but blood came anyhow. His fingers were hot and sticky. He rubbed dirt into his palms, trying to dry them. Then again he attempted to plug the bullet hole, but Jenny shied away, kicking her heels high. He stood helpless. He had to do something. He ran at Jenny; she dodged him. He watched a red stream of blood flow down Jenny's leg and from a bright pool at her feet.

"Jenny . . . Jenny," he called weakly.

His lips trembled. She's beeding t death! He looked in the direction of home, wanting to go back, wanting to get help. But he saw the pistol lying in the damp black clay. He had a queer feeling that if he only did something, this would not be; Jenny would not be there bleeding to death.

When he went to her this time, she did not move. She stood with sleepy, dreamy eyes; and when he touched her she gave a low-pitched whinny and knelt to the ground, her front knees slopping in blood.

"Jenny . . . Jenny . . ." he whispered.

For a long time she held her neck erect; then her head sank, slowly. Her ribs swelled with a mighty heave and she went over.

Dave's stomach felt empty, very empty. He picked up the gun and held it gingerly between his thumb and forefinger. He buried it at the foot of a tree. He took a stick and tried to cover the pool of blood with dirt—but what was the use? There was Jenny lying with her mouth open and her eyes walled and glassy. He could not tell Jim Hawkins he had shot his mule. But he had to tell something. Yeah, Ah'll tell em Jenny started gittin wil n fell on the joint of the plow. . . . But that would hardly happen to a mule. He walked across the field slowly, head down.

It was sunset. Two of Jim Hawkins' men were over near the edge of the woods digging a hole in which to bury Jenny. Dave was surrounded by a knot of people, all of whom were looking down at the dead mule.

"I don't see how in the world it happened," said Jim Hawkins for the tenth time.

The crowd parted and Dave's mother, father, and small brother pushed into the center.

"Where Dave?" his mother called.

"There he is," said Jim Hawkins.

His mother grabbed him.

"What happened, Dave? Whut yuh done?"

"Nothin."

"C mon, boy, talk," his father said.

Dave took a deep breath and told the story he knew nobody believed.

"Waal," he drawled. "Ah brung ol Jenny down here sos Ah could do mah plowin. Ah plowed bout two rows, just like yuh see." He stopped and pointed at the long rows of upturned earth. "Then somethin musta been wrong wid ol Jenny. She wouldn ack right a-tall. She started snortin n kickin her heels. Ah tried t hol her, but she pulled erway, rearin n goin in. Then when the point of the plow was stickin up in the air, she swung erroun n twisted herself back on it . . . She stuck herself n started t bleed. N fo Ah could do anything, she wuz dead."

"Did you ever hear of anything like that in all your life?" asked Jim Hawkins.

There were white and black standing in the crowd. They murmured. Dave's mother came close to him and looked hard into his face. "Tell the truth, Dave," she said.

"Looks like a bullet hole to me," said one man.

"Dave, whut yuh do wid the gun?" his mother asked.

The crowd surged in, looking at him. He jammed his hands into his pockets, shook his head slowly from left to right, and backed away. His eyes were wide and painful.

"Did he hava gun?" asked Jim Hawkins.

"By Gawd, Ah tol yuh that wuz a gun wound," said a man, slapping his thigh.

His father caught his shoulders and shook him till his teeth rattled.

"Tell whut happened, yuh rascal! Tell whut . . ."

Dave looked at Jenny's stiff legs and began to cry.

"Whut yuh do wid tha gun?" his mother asked.

"Whut wuz he doin wida gun?" his father asked.

"Come on and tell the truth," said Hawkins. "Ain't nobody going to hurt you . . ."

His mother crowded close to him.

"Did yuh shoot tha mule, Dave?"

Dave cried, seeing blurred white and black faces.

"Ahh ddinn gggo tt sshooot hher . . . Ah ssswear ffo Gawd Ahh ddin. . . . Ah wuz a-tryin t sssee ef the old gggun would sshoot—"

"Where yuh git the gun from?" his father asked.

"Ah got it from Joe, at the sto."

"Where yuh git the money?"

"Ma give it t me."

"He kept worryin me, Bob. Ah had t. Ah tol im t bring the gun right back t me . . . It was fer yuh, the gun."

"But how yuh happen to shoot that mule?" asked Jim Hawkins.

"Ah wuzn shootin at the mule, Mistah Hawkins. The gun jumped when Ah pulled the trigger . . . N fo Ah knowed anythin Jenny was there a-bleedin."

Somebody in the crowd laughed. Jim Hawkins walked close to Dave and looked into his face.

"Well, looks like you have bought you a mule, Dave."

"Ah swear fo Gawd, Ah didn go t kill the mule, Mistah Hawkins!"

"But you killed her!"

All the crowd was laughing now. They stood on tiptoe and poked heads over one another's shoulders.

"Well, boy, look like yuh done bought a dead mule! Hahaha!"

"Ain tha ershame."

"Hohohohoho."

Dave stood, head down, twisting his feet in the dirt.

"Well, you needn't worry about it, Bob," said Jim Hawkins to Dave's father. "Just let the boy keep on working and pay me two dollars a month."

"Whut yuh wan fer yo mule, Mistah Hawkins?"

Jim Hawkins screwed up his eyes.

"Fifty dollars."

"Whut yuh do wid tha gun?" Dave's father demanded.

Dave said nothing.

"Yuh wan me t take a tree n beat yuh till yuh talk!"

"Nawsuh!"

"Whut yuh do wid it?"

"Ah throwed it erway."

"Where?"

"Ah . . . Ah throwed it in the creek."

"Waal, c mon home. N firs thing in the mawnin git to tha creek n fin tha gun."

"Yessuh."

"What yuh pay fer it?"

"Two dollahs."

"Take tha gun n git yo money back n carry it t Mistah Hawkins, yuh hear? N don fergit Ahma lam you black bottom good fer this! Now march yosef on home, suh!"

Dave turned and walked slowly. He heard people laughing. Dave glared, his eyes welling with tears. Hot anger bubbled in him. Then he swallowed and stumbled on.

That night Dave did not sleep. He was glad that he had gotten out of killing the mule so easily, but he was hurt. Something hot seemed to turn over inside him each time he remembered how they had laughed. He tossed on his bed, feeling his hard pillow. N Pa says he's gonna beat me . . . He remembered other beatings, and his back quivered. Naw, naw, Ah sho don wan im t beat me tha way no mo. Dam em all! Nobody ever gave him anything. All he did was work. They treat me like a mule, n then they beat me. He gritted his teeth. N Ma had t tell on me.

Well, if he had to, he would take old man Hawkins that two dollars. But that meant selling the gun. And he wanted to keep that gun. Fifty dollars for a dead mule.

He turned over, thinking how he had fired the gun. He had an itch to fire it again. Ef other men kin shoota gun, by Gawd, Ah kin! He was still, listening. Mebbe they all sleepin now. The house was still. He heard the soft breathing of his brother. Yes, now! He would go down and get that gun and see if he could fire it! He eased out of bed and slipped into overalls.

The moon was bright. He ran almost all the way to the edge of the woods. He stumbled over the ground, looking for the spot where he had buried the gun. Yeah, here it is. Like a hungry dog scratching for a bone, he pawed it up. He puffed his black cheeks and blew dirt from the trigger and barrel. He broke it and found four cartridges unshot. He looked around; the fields were filled with silence and moonlight. He clutched the gun stiff and hard in his fingers. But, as soon as he wanted to pull the trigger, he shut his eyes and turned his head. Naw, Ah can't shoot wid mah eyes closed n mah head turned. With effort he held his eyes open; then he squeezed. *Blooooom!* He was stiff, not breathing. The gun was still in his hands. Dammit, he'd done it. He fired again. *Blooooom!* He smiled. *Bloooom! Blooooom! Click, click.* There! It was empty. If anybody could shoot a gun, he could. He put the gun into his hip pocket and started across the fields.

When he reached the top of a ridge he stood straight and proud in the moonlight, looking at Jim Hawkins' big white house, feeling the gun sagging in his pocket. Lawd, ef Ah had just one mo bullet Ah'd taka shot at tha house. Ah'd like t scare ol man Hawkins jusa little . . . Jusa enough t let im know Dave Saunders is a man.

To his left the road curved, running to the tracks of the Illinois Central. He jerked his head, listening. From far off came a faint *hoooof-hoooof; hoooof-hoooof; hoooof-hoooof.* . . . He stood rigid. Two dollahs a mont. Les see now . . . Tha means it'll take bout two years. Shucks! Ah'll be dam!

He started down the road, toward the tracks. Yeah, here she comes! He stood beside the track and held himself stiffly. Here she comes, erroun the ben . . . C mon, yuh slow poke! C mon! He had his hand on his gun; something quivered in his stomach. Then the train thundered past, the gray and brown box cars rumbling and clinking. He gripped the gun tightly; then he jerked his hand out of his pocket. Ah betcha Bill wouldn't do it! Ah betcha . . . The cars slid past, steel grinding upon steel. Ahm ridin yuh ternight, so hep me Gawd! He was hot all over. He hesitated just a moment; then he grabbed, pulled atop of a car, and lay flat. He felt his pocket; the gun was still there. Ahead the long rails were glinting in the moonlight, stretching away, away to somewhere, somewhere where he could be a man . . .

QUESTIONS

1. Is Dave a sympathetic character? Given his situation, is it reasonable or unreasonable for him to equate manhood with a gun? Assess the importance of point of view in engaging—or not engaging—your sympathy.

2. The speech of the characters and Dave's unvoiced thoughts and feelings are expressed in dialect. Is the use of dialect effective? Find places where the

subjective third-person narrator uses standard English. Do you find this mixture of styles acceptable?

3. His mother gives Dave money to buy the pistol on the condition that the gun will belong to his father. Is this the real reason that she relents? Discuss the relationship between Dave and his mother, between Dave and his father.

4. How much money does Mr. Hawkins ask for the dead mule? Does Mr. Hawkins treat Dave fairly?

5. Near the end of the story, Dave equates himself with a mule. Is this a valid assessment?

6. At the end of the story, with the gun in his pocket, Dave hops a train to go someplace where he can "be a man." Do you think this will happen?

VIRGINIA WOOLF

Lappin and Lapinova

They were married. The wedding march pealed out. The pigeons fluttered. Small boys in Eton jackets threw rice; a fox terrier sauntered across the path; and Ernest Thorburn led his bride to the car through that small inquisitive crowd of complete strangers which always collects in London to enjoy other people's happiness or unhappiness. Certainly he looked handsome and she looked shy. More rice was thrown, and the car moved off.

That was on Tuesday. Now it was Saturday. Rosalind had still to get used to the fact that she was Mrs. Ernest Thorburn. Perhaps she never would get used to the fact that she was Mrs. Ernest Anybody, she thought, as she sat in the bow window of the hotel looking over the lake to the mountains, and waited for her husband to come down to breakfast. Ernest was a difficult name to get used to. It was not the name she would have chosen. She would have preferred Timothy, Antony, or Peter. He did not look like Ernest either. The name suggested the Albert Memorial, mahogany sideboards, steel engravings of the Prince Consort with his family—her mother-in-law's dining-room in Porchester Terrace in short.

But here he was. Thank goodness he did not look like Ernest—no. But what did he look like? She glanced at him sideways. Well, when he was eating toast he looked like a rabbit. Not that anyone else would have seen a likeness to a creature so diminutive and timid in this spruce, muscular young man with the straight nose, the blue eyes, and the very firm mouth. But that made it all the more amusing. His nose twitched very slightly when he ate. So did her pet rabbit's. She kept watching his nose twitch; and then she had to explain, when he caught her looking at him, why she laughed.

"It's because you're like a rabbit, Ernest," she said. "Like a wild rabbit," she added, looking at him. "A hunting rabbit; a King Rabbit; a rabbit that makes laws for all the other rabbits."

Ernest had no objection to being that kind of rabbit, and since it amused her to see him twitch his nose—he had never known that his nose twitched—he twitched it on purpose. And she laughed and laughed; and he laughed too, so that the maiden ladies and the fishing man and the Swiss waiter in his greasy black jacket all guessed right; they were very happy. But how long does such happiness last? they asked themselves; and each answered according to his own circumstances.

At lunch time, seated on a clump of heather beside the lake, "Lettuce, rabbit?" said Rosalind, holding out the lettuce that had been provided to eat with the hard-boiled eggs. "Come and take it out of my hand," she added, and he stretched out and nibbled the lettuce and twitched his nose.

"Good rabbit, nice rabbit," she said, patting him, as she used to pat her tame rabbit at home. But that was absurd. He was not a tame rabbit, whatever he was. She turned it into French. "Lapin," she called him. But whatever he was, he was not a French rabbit. He was simply and solely English—born at Porchester Terrace, educated at Rugby; now a clerk in His Majesty's Civil Service. So she tried "Bunny" next; but that was worse. "Bunny" was someone plump and soft and comic; he was thin and hard and serious. Still, his nose twitched. "Lappin," she exclaimed suddenly; and gave a little cry as if she had found the very word she looked for.

"Lappin, Lappin, King Lappin," she repeated. It seemed to suit him exactly; he was not Ernest, he was King Lappin. Why? She did not know.

When there was nothing new to talk about on their long solitary walks— and it rained, as everyone had warned them that it would rain; or when they were sitting over the fire in the evening, for it was cold, and the maiden ladies had gone and the fishing man, and the waiter only came if you rang the bell for him, she let her fancy play with the story of the Lappin tribe. Under her hands— she was sewing; he was reading—they became very real, very vivid, very amusing. Ernest put down the paper and helped her. There were the black rabbits and the red; there were the enemy rabbits and the friendly. There were the wood in which they lived and the outlying prairies and the swamp. Above all there was King Lappin, who, far from having only the one trick—that he twitched his nose—became as the days passed an animal of the greatest character; Rosalind was always finding new qualities in him. But above all he was a great hunter.

"And what," said Rosalind, on the last day of the honeymoon, "did the King do to-day?"

In fact they had been climbing all day; and she had worn a blister on her heel; but she did not mean that.

"To-day," said Ernest, twitching his nose as he bit the end off his cigar, "he chased a hare." He paused; struck a match, and twitched again.

"A woman hare," he added.

"A white hare!" Rosalind exlaimed, as if she had been expecting this. "Rather a small hare; silver grey; with big bright eyes?"

"Yes," said Ernest, looking at her as she had looked at him, "a smallish animal; with eyes popping out of her head, and two little front paws dangling." It was exactly how she sat, with her sewing dangling in her hands; and her eyes, that were so big and bright, were certainly a little prominent.

"Ah, Lapinova," Rosalind murmured.

"Is that what she's called?" said Ernest—"the real Rosalind?" He looked at her. He felt very much in love with her.

"Yes; that's what she's called," said Rosalind. "Lapinova." And before they went to bed that night it was all settled. He was King Lappin; she was Queen Lapinova. They were the opposite of each other; he was bold and determined; she wary and undependable. He ruled over the busy world of rabbits; her world was a desolate, mysterious place, which she ranged mostly by moonlight. All the same, their territories touched; they were King and Queen.

Thus when they came back from their honeymoon they possessed a private world, inhabited, save for the one white hare, entirely by rabbits. No one guessed that there was such a place, and that of course made it all the more amusing. It made them feel, more even than most young married couples, in league together against the rest of the world. Often they looked slyly at each other when people talked about rabbits and woods and traps and shooting. Or they winked furtively across the table when Aunt Mary said that she could never bear to see a hare in a dish—it looked so like a baby: or when John, Ernest's sporting brother, told them what price rabbits were fetching that autumn in Wiltshire, skins and all. Sometimes when they wanted a gamekeeper, or a poacher or a Lord of the Manor, they amused themselves by distributing the parts among their friends. Ernest's mother, Mrs. Reginald Thorburn, for example, fitted the part of the Squire to perfection. But it was all secret—that was the point of it; nobody save themselves knew that such a world existed.

Without that world, how, Rosalind wondered, that winter could she have lived at all? For instance, there was the golden-wedding party, when all the Thorburns assembled at Porchester Terrace to celebrate the fiftieth anniversary of that union which had been so blessed—had it not produced Ernest Thorburn? and so fruitful—had it not produced nine other sons and daughters into the bargain, many themselves married and also fruitful? She dreaded that party. But it was inevitable. As she walked upstairs she felt bitterly that she was an only child and an orphan at that; a mere drop among all those Thorburns assembled in the great drawing-room with the shiny satin wallpaper and the lustrous family portraits. The living Thorburns much resembled the painted; save that instead of painted lips they had real lips; out of which came jokes; jokes about schoolrooms, and how they had pulled the chair from under the governess; jokes about frogs and how they had put them between the virgin sheets of maiden ladies. As for herself, she had never even made an apple-pie bed. Holding her present in her hand she advanced toward her mother-in-law sumptuous in yellow satin; and toward her father-in-law decorated with a rich yellow carnation. All round them on tables and chairs there were golden tributes, some nestling in cotton wool; others branching resplendent—candlesticks; cigar boxes; chains; each stamped with the goldsmith's proof that it was solid gold, hall-marked, authentic. But her present was only a little pinchbeck box pierced with holes; an old sand caster, an eighteenth-century relic, once used to sprinkle sand over wet ink. Rather a senseless present she felt—in an age of blotting paper; and as she proffered it, she saw in front of her the stubby black handwriting in which her mother-in-law when they were engaged had expressed the hope that "My son will make you happy." No, she was not happy. Not at all happy. She looked at Ernest, straight as a ramrod with a nose like all the noses in the family portraits; a nose that never twitched at all.

Then they went down to dinner. She was half hidden by the great chrysanthemums that curled their red and gold petals into large tight balls. Everything was gold. A gold-edged card with gold initials intertwined recited the list of all the dishes that would be set one after another before them. She dipped her spoon in a plate of clear golden fluid. The raw white fog outside had been turned by the lamps into a golden mesh that blurred the edges of the plates and gave the pineapples a rough golden skin. Only she herself in her white wedding dress peering ahead of her with her prominent eyes seemed insoluble as an icicle.

As the dinner wore on, however, the room grew steamy with heat. Beads of perspiration stood out on the men's foreheads. She felt that her icicle was being turned to water. She was being melted; dispersed; dissolved into nothingness; and would soon faint. Then through the surge in her head and the din in her ears she heard a woman's voice exclaim, "But they breed so!"

The Thorburns—yes; they breed so, she echoed; looking at all the round red faces that seemed doubled in the giddiness that overcame her; and magnified in the gold mist that enhaloed them. "They breed so." Then John bawled:

"Little devils! . . . Shoot'em! Jump on'em with big boots! That's the only way to deal with 'em . . . rabbits!"

At that word, that magic word, she revived. Peeping between the chrysanthemums she saw Ernest's nose twitch. It rippled, it ran with successive twitches. And at that a mysterious catastrophe befell the Thorburns. The golden table became a moor with the gorse in full bloom; the din of voices turned to one peal of lark's laughter ringing down from the sky. It was a blue sky—clouds passed slowly. And they had all been changed—the Thorburns. She looked at her father-in-law, a furtive little man with dyed moustaches. His foible was collecting things—seals, enamel boxes, trifles from eighteenth-century dressing tables which he hid in the drawers of his study from his wife. Now she saw him as he was—a poacher, stealing off with his coat bulging with pheasants and partridges to drop them stealthily into a three-legged pot in his smoky little cottage. That was her real father-in-law—a poacher. And Celia, the unmarried daughter, who always nosed out other people's secrets, the little things they wished to hide— she was a white ferret with pink eyes, and a nose clotted with earth from her horrid underground nosings and pokings. Slung round men's shoulders, in a net, and thrust down a hole—it was a pitiable life—Celia's; it was none of her fault. So she saw Celia. And then she looked at her mother-in-law—whom they dubbed The Squire. Flushed, coarse, a bully—she was all that, as she stood returning thanks, but now that Rosalind—that is Lapinova—saw her, she saw behind her the decayed family mansion, the plaster peeling off the walls, and heard her, with a sob in her voice, giving thanks to her children (who hated her) for a world that had ceased to exist. There was a sudden silence. They all stood with their glasses raised; they all drank; then it was over.

"Oh, King Lappin!" she cried as they went home together in the fog, "if your nose hadn't twitched just at that moment, I should have been trapped!"

"But you're safe," said King Lappin, pressing her paw.

"Quite safe," she answered.

And they drove back through the Park, King and Queen of the marsh, of the mist, and of the gorse-scented moor.

Thus time passed; one year; two years of time. And on a winter's night, which happened by a coincidence to be the anniversary of the golden-wedding party—but Mrs. Reginald Thorburn was dead; the house was to let; and there was only a caretaker in residence—Ernest came home from the office. They had a nice little home; half a house above a saddler's shop in South Kensington, not far from the tube station. It was cold, with fog in the air, and Rosalind was sitting over the fire, sewing.

"What d'you think happened to me to-day?" she began as soon as he had settled himself down with his legs stretched to the blaze. "I was crossing the stream when——"

"What stream?" Ernest interrupted her.

"The stream at the bottom, where our wood meets the black wood," she explained.

Ernest looked completely blank for a moment.

"What the deuce are you talking about?" he asked.

"My dear Ernest!" she cried in dismay, "King Lappin," she added, dangling her little front paws in the firelight. But his nose did not twitch. Her hands— they turned to hands—clutched the stuff she was holding; her eyes popped half out of her head. It took him five minutes at least to change from Ernest Thorburn to King Lappin; and while she waited she felt a load on the back of her neck, as if somebody were about to wring it. At last he changed to King Lappin; his nose twitched; and they spent the evening roaming the woods much as usual.

But she slept badly. In the middle of the night she woke, feeling as if something strange had happened to her. She was stiff and cold. At last she turned on the light and looked at Ernest lying beside her. He was sound asleep. He snored. But even though he snored, his nose remained perfectly still. It looked as if it had never twitched at all. Was it possible that he was really Ernest;

and that she was really married to Ernest? A vision of her mother-in-law's dining-room came before her; and there they sat, she and Ernest, grown old, under the engravings, in front of the sideboard. . . . It was their golden-wedding day. She could not bear it.

"Lappin, King Lappin!" she whispered, and for a moment his nose seemed to twitch of its own accord. But he still slept. "Wake up, Lappin, wake up!" she cried.

Ernest woke; and seeing her sitting bolt upright beside him he asked: "What's the matter?"

"I thought my rabbit was dead!" she whimpered. Ernest was angry.

"Don't talk such rubbish, Rosalind," he said. "Lie down and go to sleep."

He turned over. In another moment he was sound asleep and snoring.

But she could not sleep. She lay curled up on her side of the bed, like a hare in its form. She had turned out the light, but the street lamp lit the ceiling faintly, and the trees outside made a lacy network over it as if there were a shadowy grove on the ceiling in which she wandered, turning, twisting, in and out, round and round, hunting, being hunted, hearing the bay of hounds and horns; flying, escaping . . . until the maid drew the blinds and brought their early tea.

Next day she could settle to nothing. She seemed to have lost something. She felt as if her body had shrunk; it had grown small, and black and hard. Her joints seemed stiff too, and when she looked in the glass, which she did several times as she wandered about the flat, her eyes seemed to burst out of her head, like currants in a bun. The rooms also seemed to have shrunk. Large pieces of furniture jutted out at odd angles and she found herself knocking against them. At last she put on her hat and went out. She walked along the Cromwell Road; and every room she passed and peered into seemed to be a dining-room where people sat eating under steel engravings, with thick yellow lace curtains, and mahogany sideboards. At last she reached the Natural History Museum; she used to like it when she was a child. But the first thing she saw when she went in was a stuffed hare standing on sham snow with pink glass eyes. Somehow it made her shiver all over. Perhaps it would be better when dusk fell. She went home and sat over the fire, without a light, and tried to imagine that she was out alone on a moor; and there was a stream rushing; and beyond the stream a dark wood. But she could get no further than the stream. At last she squatted down on the bank on the wet grass, and sat crouched in her chair, with her hands dangling empty, and her eyes glazed, like glass eyes, in the firelight. Then there was the crack of a gun. . . . She started as if she had been shot. It was only Ernest, turning his key in the door. She waited, trembling. He came in and switched on the light. There he stood, tall, handsome, rubbing his hands that were red with cold.

"Sitting in the dark?" he said.

"Oh, Ernest, Ernest!" she cried, starting up in her chair.

"Well, what's up now?" he asked briskly, warming his hands at the fire.

"It's Lapinova . . ." she faltered, glancing wildly at him out of her great started eyes. "She's gone, Ernest. I've lost her!"

Ernest frowned. He pressed his lips tight together.

"Oh, that's what's up, is it?" he said, smiling rather grimly at his wife. For ten seconds he stood there, silent; and she waited, feeling hands tightening at the back of her neck.

"Yes," he said at length. "Poor Lapinova . . ." He straightened his tie at the looking-glass over the mantelpiece.

"Caught in a trap," he said, "killed," and sat down and read the newspaper.

So that was the end of that marriage.

QUESTIONS

1. Examine the presentation of facts in the first paragraph. Find an example of a periodic sentence, of a balanced sentence. Discuss the effect of sentence variety.

2. Why does Rosalind consider Ernest "a difficult name to get used to?" How does this opinion aid in revealing Rosalind's character?

3. What circumstances prompt Rosalind's fantasy? Why does Ernest participate in the fantasy? Is the fantasy beneficial or injurious to the marriage?

4. What characteristics do King Lappin and Queen Lapinova share with their real-life counterparts? The choice of rabbits is an ironic commentary on the marriage. Why?

5. At the Thorburns' golden-wedding party, Rosalind indulges in a private fantasy about the Thorburns. Describe this fantasy. What does it reveal about Rosalind's feelings toward her husband's family? toward Ernest?

6. Why does Ernest end the fantasy? When the fantasy ends, what else ends? Is the conclusion happy, unhappy, inconclusive? Can the fantasy be examined as an extended metaphor of the marriage?

7. What point of view is used? How does the point of view help establish tone? Discuss your concept of the implied author.

ROBERT HEMENWAY

The Girl Who Sang with the Beatles

Of course their tastes turned out to be different. Cynthia was twenty-eight when they married, and looked younger, in the way small, very pretty women can—so much younger sometimes that bartenders would ask for her I.D. Larry was close to forty and gray, a heavy man who, when he moved, moved slowly. He had been an English instructor once, though now he wrote market-research reports, and there was still something bookish about him. Cynthia, who was working as an interviewer for Larry's company when he met her, had been a vocalist with several dance bands for a while in the fifties before she quit to marry her first husband. She had left high school when she was a junior to take her first singing job. She and Larry were from different generations, practically, and from different cultures, and yet when they were married they both liked the same things. That was what brought them together. Thirties movies. Old bars— not the instant-tradition places but what was left of the old ones, what Cynthia called the bar bars. Double features in the loge of the Orpheum, eating hot dogs and drinking smuggled beer. Gibsons before dinner and Scotch after. Their TV nights, eating delicatessen while they watched. "Mr. Lucky" or "Route 66" or "Ben Casey," laughing at the same places, choking up at the same places, howling together when something was just too *much*. And then the eleven-o'clock news and the Late and Late Late Shows, while they drank and necked and sometimes made love. And listening to Cynthia's records—old Sinatras and Judys, and Steve and Eydie, or "The Fantasticks" or "Candide." They even agreed on redecorating Cynthia's apartment, which was full of leftovers from her first marriage. They agreed on all of it—the worn (but genuine) Oriental rugs; the low carved Spanish tables; the dusky colors, grays and mauve and rose; the damask sofa with its down pillows; and, in the bedroom, the twin beds, nearly joined but held separate by an ornate brass bedstead. Cynthia's old double bed had been impractical; Larry was too big, and Cynthia kicked. When they came back from their Nassau honeymoon and saw the apartment for the first time in ten days, Cynthia said, "God, Larry, I *love* it. It's pure *Sunset Boulevard* now."

The place made Larry think of Hyde Park Boulevard in Chicago, where he had grown up in a mock-Tudor house filled with the wrought iron and walnut of an earlier Spanish fad. Entering the apartment was like entering his childhood. "Valencia!" sang in his head. "Valencia! In my dreams it always seems I hear you softly call to me. Valencia!"

They were married in the summer of 1962 and by the spring of 1963 the things they had bought no longer looked quite right. Everyone was buying Spanish now, and there was too much around in the cheap stores. Larry and Cynthia found themselves in a dowdy apartment full of things that looked as if they had been there since the twenties. It was depressing. They began to ask each other what they had done. Not that either of them wanted out, exactly, but what had they done? Why had they married? Why couldn't they have gone on with their affair? Neither had married the other for money, that was certain. Larry had made Cynthia quit work (not that she minded) and now they had only his salary, which was barely enough.

"We still love each other, don't we? I mean, I know I love you." Cynthia was in Larry's bed and Larry was talking. It was three in the morning, and they had come back from their usual Saturday-night tour of the neighborhood bars. "I love you," Larry said.

"You don't like me."

"I *love* you, Cynthia."

"You don't like me." Propped up by pillows, she stared red-eyed at a great paper daisy on the wall.

"I love you, Cindy."

"So? Big deal. Men have been telling me they loved me since I was fourteen. I thought you were different."

Larry lay flat on his back. "Don't be tough. It's not like you," he said.

"I *am* tough. That's what you won't understand. You didn't marry *me*. You married some nutty idea of your own. I was your secret fantasy. You told me so." Cynthia was shivering.

"Lie down," Larry said. "I'll rub your back."

"You won't get around me that way," Cynthia said, lying down. "You tricked me. I thought you liked the things I liked. You won't even watch TV with me anymore."

Larry began to rub the back of Cynthia's neck and play with the soft hairs behind one ear.

"Why don't you ever watch with me?" Cynthia said.

"You know. I get impatient."

"You don't like me." Cynthia was teasing him by now. "If you really liked me, you'd watch," she said. "You'd *like* being bored."

Larry sat up. "That isn't it," he said. "You know what it is? It's the noise. All the things you like make *noise*."

"I read."

"Sure. With the radio or the stereo or the TV on. I can't. I have to do one thing at a time," Larry said. "What if I want to sit home at night and read a book?"

"So read."

"When you have these programs you quote have to watch unquote?"

"Get me headphones. That's what my first husband did when he stopped talking to me. Or go in the bedroom and shut the door. I don't mind."

"We'll do something," Larry said, lying down again. "Now let's make love."

"Oh, it's no use, Larry," Cynthia said. "Not when we're like this. I'll only sweat."

And so it went on many nights, and everything seemed tainted by their disagreements, especially their times in bed. After they had made love, they would slip again into these exchanges, on and on. What Cynthia seemed to resent most was that Larry had not been straightforward with her. Why had he let her think he cared for her world of song and dance? She knew it was trivial. She had never tried to make him think she was deep. Why had he pretended he was something he wasn't?

How was Larry to tell her the truth without making her think he was either a snob or a fool? There was no way. The thing was, he said, that when they met he *did* like what she liked, period. Just because she liked it. What was wrong with that? He wanted to see her enjoying herself, so they did what she wanted to do—went to Radio City to see the new Doris Day, or to Basin Street East to hear Peggy Lee, or to revivals of those fifties musicals Cynthia liked so much. Forget the things he liked if she didn't—foreign movies and chamber music and walks in Central Park, all that. She must have known what he liked, after all. She had been in his apartment often enough before they were married, God knows. She had seen his books and records. She knew his tastes.

"I thought you gave all that up," Cynthia said. "I thought you'd changed."

"I thought you *would* change," Larry said. "I thought you wanted to. I thought if you wanted to marry me you must want to change."

"Be an *intellectual?*" Cynthia said. "You must be kidding."

No, he was serious. Why didn't she get bored with the stuff she watched and the junk she read? *He* did. When you had seen three Perry Masons, you had seen them all, and that went for Doris Day movies, the eleven-o'clock news, and "What's My Line?"

"I know all that," Cynthia said. She *liked* to be bored. God, you couldn't keep thinking about *reality* all the time. You'd go out of your mind. She liked stories and actors that she knew, liked movies she had seen a dozen times and books she could read over and over again. Larry took his reading so seriously. As if reading were *life*.

Larry tried to persuade himself that Cynthia was teasing him, but it was no use. She meant what she said. She *liked East of Eden, Marjorie Morningstar, Gone with the Wind.* She liked Elizabeth Taylor movies. She found nourishment in that Styrofoam. He could see it in her childlike face, which sometimes shone as if she were regarding the beatific vision when she was under the spell of the sorriest trash. What repelled him brought her to life. He could feel it in her when they touched and when, after seeing one of her favorite movies, they made love. How odd that he should have married her! And yet he loved her, he thought, and he thought she loved him—needed him, anyway.

Sometimes they talked of having a child, or of Cynthia's going back to work or of attending night classes together at Columbia or the New School, but nothing came of it. They were both drinking too much, perhaps, and getting too little exercise, yet it was easier to let things go on as they were. Larry did set out to read Camus, the first serious reading he had done since their marriage, and in the evenings after dinner he would go into the bedroom, shut the door, turn on WNCN to muffle the sounds from the living room, put Flents in his ears, and read. Although the meaningless noises from the TV set—the not quite comprehensible voices, the sudden surges of music—still reached him, he was reluctant to buy Cynthia the headphones she had suggested. They would be too clear a symbol of their defeat.

Cynthia often stayed up until three or four watching the late movies or playing her records, and Larry, who usually fell asleep around midnight, would sometimes wake after two or three hours and come out of the bedroom shouting "Do you know what *time* it is?" and frighten her. Sometimes, though, he would make a drink for himself and watch her movie, too, necking with her the way they used to do, without saying much. They were still drawn to each other.

Sometimes, very late at night when she was quite drunk, Cynthia would stand before the full-length mirror in their bedroom and admire herself. "I'm beautiful," she would say. "Right now, I'm really beautiful, and who can see me?" Larry would watch her from the bed. Something slack in her would grow taut as she looked in the mirror. She would draw her underpants down low on her hips, then place her hands on her shoulders, her crossed arms covering her bare breasts, and smile at her reflection, a one-sided smile. "I'm a narcissist," she would say, looking at Larry in the mirror. "I'm a sexual narcissist. How can you stand me?" Then she would join Larry in his bed.

Larry couldn't deny Cynthia anything for long. If he insisted on it, she would turn off the set, but then she would sulk until he felt he had imposed upon her, and he would turn the set back on or take her out for a drink. How could he blame her? They had so little money. What else was there for her to do?

One Saturday night after their tour of the bars, Cynthia changed clothes and came out of the bedroom wearing a twenties black dress and black net stockings and pumps. The dress was banded with several rows of fringe and stopped just at the knee. She had had to add the last row of fringe, she told

Larry. Her first husband had made her, just before they went to a costume party, because the dress showed too much of her thighs. Larry knelt before her and tore off the last row. Cynthia danced for him (a Charleston, a shimmy, a Watusi) and after that she sang. She had sung to him now and then late at night before they were married—just a few bars in a soft, almost inaudible voice. Tonight the voice seemed full and touching to Larry, and with a timbre and sadness different from any voice he had ever heard. "*Like* me. Please like me," the voice seemed to say. "Just like me. That's all I need. I'll be nice then." She might have been the star she wanted to be, Larry thought. She had the charm and the need for love, but perhaps the voice was too small and her need to great. She had told him that twice while she was singing with a band in Las Vegas she had been "discovered" by assistant directors and offered a movie audition, and that each time she had been sick in the studio—literally sick to her stomach—and unable to go on. She had been too scared. Yet she still might have a career somehow, Larry thought. He could encourage her to practice. It would be an interest for her—something to do. She was barely past thirty and looked less. There was time.

Larry decided to read Camus in French and to translate some of the untranslated essays, just for practice, into English. One night he came home with the headphones Cynthia wanted, the old-fashioned kind made of black Bakelite, and hooked them up to the TV set through a control box that had an off-on switch for the speaker. Now that he could blank out the commercials, Larry would watch with Cynthia now and then—some of the news specials, and the Wide World of Sports, and the late-night reruns of President Kennedy's press conferences, one of the few things they both enjoyed. They could both acknowledge his power, pulsing in him and out toward them—that sure, quick intelligence and that charm.

Cynthia was happier now, because with the headphones on and the speakers off she could watch as late as she wanted without being afraid of Larry. When the phone rang, she would not hear it. Larry would answer, finally, and if it was for her he would stand in front of the set gesturing until she took the headphones off. She would sit on the sofa for hours, dressed as if for company, her eyes made up to look even larger than they were, wearing one of the at-home hostessy things from Jax or Robert Leader she had bought before they were married, which hardly anyone but she and Larry had ever seen. Looking so pretty, and with those radio operator's black headphones on her ears.

The sight made Larry melancholy, and he continued to work lying on his bed, propped up with a writing board on his lap. He would hear Cynthia laughing sometimes in the silent living room, and now and then, hearing thin sounds from her headphones, he would come out to find her crying, the phones on her lap and the final credits of a movie on the screen. "I always cry at this one," she would say. With the headphones, Cynthia was spending more time before the set than ever. Larry encouraged her to sing—to take lessons again if she wanted. But she did sing, she said, in the afternoons. She sang with her records, usually. There were a few songs of Eydie's and Peggy's and Judy's she liked. She sang along with those.

In spite of everything, when Larry compared his life now with his first marriage or with the bitter years after that, he could not say that this was worse. Cynthia seemed almost content. She made no demands upon him and left him free to think or read what he pleased. But there were nights when he would put his book aside and lie on his bed, hearing Cynthia laugh now and then or get up to make herself another drink, and ask himself why he was there. Little, in his job or in his life, seemed reasonable or real.

Why had he fallen in love with Cynthia? It was just because she was so *American,* he decided one night. She *liked* canned chili and corned-beef hash, the Academy Awards, cole slaw, barbecued chicken, the Miss America contest, head lettuce with Russian dressing, astrology columns, *Modern Screen,* take-out pizza pies. She liked them and made faces at them at the same time, looking up or over at him and saying, "Oh God, isn't this awful? Isn't this vile?" Everything he had turned his back on in the name of the Bauhaus and the Institute of Design, of Elizabeth David and James Beard, of Lewis Mumford, Paul Goodman, D. H. Lawrence, Henry Miller, Frank Lloyd Wright—here it all was dished up before him in Cynthia. All the things that (to tell the truth) he had never had enough of. He had lost out on them in high school, when he had really wanted them, because he was studious and shy. He had rejected them in college, where it was a matter of political principle among his friends to reject them, before he had the chance to find out what they were like. At thirty-eight, when he met Cynthia, what did he know? Weren't there vast areas of the American experience that he had missed? Why, until Cynthia he had never shacked up in a motel. Nor had he ever been in a barroom fight, or smoked pot, or been ticketed for speeding, or blacked out from booze.

What had he fallen in love with, then, but pop America! One more intellectual seduced by kitsch! He could almost see the humor in it. It was the first solid discovery about himself he had made for years, and he lay back in his bed, smiling. How glittering Cynthia's world had seemed, he thought. The sixties—this is what they *were!* Thruways, motels, Point Pleasant on a Saturday night twisting to the juke! That trip to Atlantic City in winter where, at the Club Hialeah, the girls from South Jersey danced on the bar, and in the Hotel Marlborough-Blenheim he and Cynthia wandered through the cold deserted corridors and public rooms like actors in a shabby *Marienbad.* And the music! Miles, Monk, Chico, Mingus, the M.J.Q., Sinatra and Nelson Riddle, Belafonte, Elvis, Ray Charles, Dion, Lena Horne—all new to him. He had stopped listening to music before bop, and with Cynthia he listened to everything. Progressive or pop or rhythm and blues, whatever. Did he like it all—how was it possible to like it *all?* — because Cynthia did, or did he fall in love with Cynthia because she liked it all? What difference did it make? It was all new—a gorgeous blur of enthusiasms. For the first time in his life he had given himself away. How wonderful it had been, at thirty-eight, on the edge of middle age—*in* middle age—to play the fool! This was experience, this was *life,* this was the sixties—*his* generation, with his peers in charge, the Kennedys and the rest. Wasn't that coming alive, when you were free enough to play the fool and not care? And if there had been enough money, he and Cynthia might have kept it up. . . . They might.

Yet hardly a moment had passed during the first months with Cynthia when he did not know what he was doing. He had got into a discussion of pop culture one night in the Cedar Street Tavern not long after he and Cynthia were married. "You don't know what you're talking about," he had said to the others while Cynthia was on a trip to the head. "You only dip into it. Listen. You don't know. I've *married* it. I've married the whole great American *schmier.*"

But how nearly he had been taken in! Cynthia never had. She knew show business from the inside, after all. She dug it, and liked it, and laughed at herself for liking it. She knew how shabby it was. Yet it did something for her—that trumpery, that fake emotion, that sincere corn. Once he found out something was bad, how could he care for it any longer? It was impossible. If he had gone overboard at first for Cynthia's world, wasn't that because it was new to him and he saw fresh energy there? And how spurious that energy had turned out to be—how slick, how manufactured, how dead! And how dull. Yet something in it rubbed off on Cynthia, mesmerized her, and made her glamorous, made her attractive to him still. That was the trouble. He still wanted her. He was as mesmerized as she. Wasn't it the fakery he despised that shone in Cynthia and drew him to her? Then what in their marriage was real? He felt as detached from his life as a dreamer at times feels detached from his dream.

Quiet and sedentary as it had become, Larry's life continued to be charged with a forced excitement. The pop love songs, the photographs of beautiful men and women in the magazines Cynthia read, the romantic movies on TV, Cynthia herself—changing her clothes three or four times a day as if she were the star in a play and Larry the audience—all stimulated him in what he considered an unnatural way. He recognized in himself an extravagant lust that was quickly expended but never spent when he and Cynthia made love, as if she were one of the idealized photographs of which she was so fond and he were returning within her to the fantasies of his adolescence, their intercourse no more than the solitary motions of two bodies accidentally joined.

"We shouldn't have got married," Cynthia said one hot Saturday night in the summer of 1963 as they were lying in their beds trying to fall asleep.

"Maybe not," Larry said.

"Marriage turns me off. Something happens. I told you."

"I didn't believe you," Larry said. "And anyway we're married."

"We sure are."

"I picked a lemon in the garden of love," Larry said. Cynthia laughed and moved into Larry's bed.

Late that night, though, he said something else. "We're like Catholics and their sacrament," he said. "When you're married for the second time, you're practically stuck with each other. You've almost got to work it out."

"You may think you're stuck, but *I'm* not," Cynthia said, and moved back to her own bed. The next Saturday night she brought up what Larry had said about being "stuck." Why had he said it? Didn't he know her at all? Whenever she felt bound she had to break free—right out the door, sooner or later. That was what had always happened. Was he trying to drive her away? He knew how independent she'd been. That's what he liked about her, he'd said once. All that talk about protecting each other's freedom! What a lot of crap. Look at them now. Two birds in a cage, a filthy cage.

Cynthia's anger frightened Larry, and, to his surprise, the thought of her leaving frightened him, too. But nothing changed. There wasn't much chance of her breaking away, after all. They didn't have enough money to separate, and neither of them really wanted to—not *that* routine, not again.

More and more often now Larry would sit in the living room reading while Cynthia watched her programs, headphones on her ears. He would look over at her, knowing that at that moment she was content, and feel some satisfaction, even a sense of domestic peace. At times he would lie with his head on Cynthia's lap while she watched, and she would stroke his hair.

One payday Larry came home with a second pair of headphones, made of green plastic and padded with foam rubber, the sort disc jockeys and astronauts wear, and plugged them into the stereo through a box that permitted turning off the speakers. Now he, like Cynthia, could listen in silence. He stacked some of his records on the turntable—the Mozart horn concertos, a Bach cantata, Gluck. It was eerie, Larry thought, for them both to be so completely absorbed, sitting twenty feet apart in that silent living room, and on the first night he found himself watching Cynthia's picture on the TV screen as the music in his ears seemed to fade away. Finally, he took off his earphones, joined Cynthia on the sofa, and asked her to turn on the sound. After a few nights, however, the sense of eeriness wore off, and Larry was as caught up in his music as Cynthia was in her shows. The stereo sound was so rich and pure; unmixed with other noises, the music carried directly into his brain, surrounding and penetrating him. It was so intense, so mindless. Listening was not a strong enough word for what was happening. The music flowed through him and swallowed him up. He felt endowed with a superior sense, as if he were a god. Yet there was something illicit about their both finding so intense a pleasure in isolation. He was troubled, off and on, by what they were falling into, but their life was tranquil and that was almost enough.

One night when Larry was reading (something he rarely did now) and there was nothing on TV she cared for, Cynthia put some of her records on the turntable and Larry's headphones on her ears and listened to Eydie and Judy and Frank, dancing a few steps now and then and singing the words softly. "Why didn't you tell me!" she said. It was *fantastic.* She could hear all the bass, and the color of the voices, and things in some of the arrangements she had never known were there. More and more often as the summer wore on, Cynthia would listen to her music instead of watching the tube, and Larry, thinking this a step in the right direction—toward her singing, perhaps—turned the stereo over to her several evenings a week and tried to concentrate again on his reading. But music now held him in a way books no longer could, and after a few weeks he bought a second stereo phonograph and a second set of headphones. By the fall of 1963, he and Cynthia had begun to listen, each to his own music, together. "This is really a kick," Cynthia would say. The intensity of it excited them both.

On the day President Kennedy was assassinated, Larry and Cynthia were having one of their rare lunches in midtown at an Italian place near Blooming-dale's, where Cynthia planned to go shopping afterward. There was a small television set above the restaurant bar, and people stood there waiting for definite news after the first word of the shooting. When it was clear that the President was dead, Larry and Cynthia went back to their apartment. Larry didn't go back to work. They watched television together that afternoon and evening, and then they went to bed and began to weep. When Larry stopped, Cynthia would sob, and then Larry would start again. So it went until after four in the morning, when they fell asleep. Until the funeral was over, Cynthia sat before the set most of the day and night. Much of the time she was crying, and every night when she came to bed the tears would start. Larry, dry-eyed sooner than she was, was at first sympathetic, then impatient, then annoyed.

"He was such a *good* man," Cynthia would say, or "He was *ours*. He was all we had," and after the burial she said, half smiling, "He was a wonderful star." Nothing in her actual life could ever move her so deeply, Larry thought. How strange, to feel real sorrow and weep real tears for an unreal loss! But she was suffering, no question of that, and she could not stop crying. The Christmas season came and went, and she still wept. She had begun to drink heavily, and often Larry would put her to bed. On the edge of unconsciousness, she would continue to cry.

What was she, he thought, but a transmitter of electronic sensations? First she had conveyed the nation's erotic fantasies to him, and now it was the national sorrow, and one was as unreal as the other. But there was more to it than that. John Kennedy had been a figure in her own erotic fantasies. She had told Larry so. She wept for him as a woman would for her dead lover. She was like a woman betrayed by Death, Larry thought, when what had betrayed her was the television set she had counted upon to shield her from the real. It had always told her stories of terror and passion that, because they were fictitious, might be endured, and now it had shown her actual death and actual sorrow. There was no way to console her, because her loss was not an actual loss, and Larry began to think her suffering more than he could endure. He began to wonder if she might not have lost her mind.

Cynthia read nothing for weeks after the assassination but articles on it, and so she did not hear of the Beatles until Larry, hoping to distract her, brought home their first album. She thought little of it at first, but after the Beatles appeared on the Ed Sullivan Show in February she became an admirer and then a devotee. Larry brought her the new Beatles 45's as they came out, and he stood in line with teen-age girls at the newsstands on Forty-second Street to buy the Beatles fan magazines. "I guess the period of mourning is over," Cynthia said one Saturday night. She still saved articles about the assassination, though, and photographs of Jacqueline in black.

When Cynthia began to sing as she listened to the Beatles late at night, Larry, listening from the bedroom, was pleased. She would play their records over and over, accompanying them in a voice that seemed flat and unresonant, perhaps because with the headphones on she could not hear the sounds she made. She no longer wept, or Larry was asleep when she did.

One night, Larry woke around three to the tinny noise of "I Want to Hold Your Hand" spilling from Cynthia's phones and found he was hungry. On his way to the kitchen, he stopped in the dark hall to watch Cynthia, who stood in the center of the living room with the astronaut headphones on, singing what sounded like a harmonizing part, a little off-key, holding an imaginary guitar, swaying jerkily, and smiling as if she were before an audience. Her performance, empty as it was, seemed oddly polished and professional. Afraid of startling her, he stood watching until the end of the song before he entered the room.

"How much did you see?" Cynthia said.

"Nothing," Larry said. "I was going to get a glass of milk, that's all." The look on Cynthia's face as she stood before him with those enormous headphones clamped to her ears troubled him, as if he had discovered her in some indecency better forgotten. "After this I'll flick out the lights and warn you," he said.

And he said no more about it, though often now he awoke during the night to the faint sounds from Cynthia's headphones and wondered what she was doing that held her so fast. He was jealous of it in a way. She was rarely in bed before four, and always in bed when he left for work in the morning. In the evening, though, as she watched television, she seemed happy enough, and much as she had been before Kennedy's death.

For some time after the assassination, they gave up their Saturday nights in the bars, but by April they were again making their rounds. Once, when they came home higher and happier than usual, Cynthia danced and sang for Larry as she had before, and for a while Larry danced with her, something he did not do often. They were having such a pleasant time that when Larry put on a Beatles album and Cynthia began her performance for him, she explained. "We're at the Palladium in London, you see," she said. "The place is mobbed. . . . The Beatles are onstage. . . . I'm singing with them, and naturally everybody loves us. I work through the whole show . . . playing second guitar. I back up George." And then she sang, a third or so below the melody, "'She was just seventeen if you know what I mean. . . .'"

"I never sing lead," Cynthia said when the number was over. "I play a minor role."

"Is this what you do at night?" Larry asked her.

Cynthia was breathing heavily. "Sure," she said. "It sounds silly, but it's not. Besides, it's possible, isn't it? It *could* happen. I can sing." She looked at Larry, her eyes candid and kind. "Don't worry," she said. "I'm not losing my grip."

"It's a nice game," Larry said later when they were in bed.

"Oh, it's more than a game," Cynthia said. "When I'm with them in the Palladium, I'm really *there*. It's more real than here. I know it's a fantasy, though."

"How did you meet the Beatles?" Larry asked her.

"D'you really want to hear?" Cynthia said. She seemed pleased at his interest, Larry thought, but then she was drunk. They both were.

"It's not much of a story," she said. "The details vary, but basically I am standing on Fifth Avenue there near the Plaza in the snow waiting for a cab at three in the afternoon, dressed in my black flared coat and black pants and the black boots you gave me, and I have a guitar. No taxis, or they're whipping right by, and I'm *cold*. You know how cold I can get. And then this Bentley stops with a couple of guys in front and in back is George Harrison all alone, though sometimes it's Paul. He gives me a lift and we talk. He's completely polite and sincere, and I can see he likes me. It seems the Beatles are rehearsing for a television special at Central Plaza and they'll be there the next day, so he asks me to come up and bring my guitar. I go, naturally, and it turns out they are auditioning girls, and I'm the winner. What would be the point if I wasn't? They want a girl for just one number, but when they see how terrific I am, of course they love me, and when they find out I've already worked up all their songs I'm in."

"You join them."

"Sure. They insist. I have to leave you, but you don't mind, not anymore. In one year, we're The Beatles and Cynthia and we're playing the Palladium, and Princess Margaret and Tony are there, and Frank, and Peter O'Toole, and David McCallum, and Steve McQueen, and Bobby Kennedy. And all those men *want* me, I can feel it, and I'm going to meet them afterward at the Savoy in our suite."

"'Our'?"

"I'm married to a rich diamond merchant who lets me do whatever I want. Played by George Sanders."

"I thought you were married to me," Larry said.

"Oh, no. You divorced me, alleging I was mentally cruel. Maybe I was once, but I'm not anymore, because the Beatles love me. They're my brothers. They're not jealous of me at all."

"Are you putting me on?" Larry said.

"No. Why should I? I made it all up, if that's what you mean, but I *really* made it up."

"Do you believe any of it?" Larry said.

Cynthia smiled at him. "Don't you? You used to say I had a good voice and you used to say I was pretty. Anyway, I don't have fantasies about things that couldn't possibly happen. I could get a job tomorrow if you'd let me."

Cynthia's voice had the lilt Larry remembered from the days before they were married. The whole thing was so convincing and so insane. He began to indulge her in it. "I'm going to Beatle now," Cynthia would say nearly every night after dinner, and Larry would go into the bedroom. Whenever he came out, he would flick the hall lights and she would stop. She was shy and did not let him watch often at first. She seemed embarrassed that she had told him as much as she had—if, indeed, she remembered telling him anything at all.

Larry liked the Beatles more and more as the nights went by, and often he would listen to their records with the speakers on before Cynthia began her performance. "Listen, Cynthia," he said one Saturday night. "The Beatles are filled with the Holy Ghost." He was really quite drunk. "Do you know that? They came to bring us back to life! Out of the old nightmare. Dallas, Oswald, Ruby, all of it, cops, reporters, thruways, lies, crises, missiles, heroes, cameras, fear—all that mishmash, and all of it dead. All of us dead watching the burial of the dead. Look at *you*. They've brought you back to life. I couldn't—not after November. Nothing could."

"You're right," Cynthia said. "I didn't want to tell you. I thought you'd be jealous."

"Jealous? Of the Beatles?"

"They're very real to me, you know."

"I'm not jealous," Larry said.

"Then will you read to me the way you used to? Read me to sleep?"

"Sure."

"Can I get in your bed?"

"Sure."

Before Larry had finished a page, he was asleep, and Cynthia was asleep before him.

For her birthday in September, Larry gave Cynthia an electric guitar. Though she could not really play it and rarely even plugged it in, she used the guitar now in her performances, pretending to pluck the strings. She began to dress more elaborately for her Beatling, too, making up as if for the stage.

She was a little mad, no question of it, Larry thought, but it did no harm. He no longer loved her, nor could he find much to like in her, and yet he cared for her, he felt, and he saw that she was too fragile to be left alone. She was prettier now than he had ever seen her. She *should* have been a performer. She needed applause and admirers and whatever it was she gave herself in her fantasies—something he alone could not provide. Their life together asked little of him at any rate, and cost little. By now he and Cynthia rarely touched or embraced; they were like old friends—fellow-conspirators even, for who knew of Cynthia's Beatle world but him?

Cynthia discussed her performances with Larry now, telling him of the additions to her repertoire and of the new places she and the Beatles played— Kezar Stadium, the Hollywood Bowl, Philharmonic Hall. She began to permit him in the living room with her, and he would lie on the sofa listening to his music while her Beatling went on. He felt sometimes that by sharing her fantasies he might be sharing her madness, but it seemed better for them both to be innocently deranged than to be as separate as they had been before. All of it tired Larry, though. He was past forty. He felt himself growing old, and his tastes changing. Now he listened to the things he had liked in college—the familiar Beethoven and Mozart symphonies, and Schubert, and Brahms, in new stereophonic recordings. Often as he listened he would fall asleep and be awakened by the silence when the last of the records stacked on the turntable had been played. Usually Cynthia's performance would still be going on, and he would rise, take off his headphones and go to bed.

One night Larry fell asleep toward the end of the "Messiah," with the bass singing "The trumpet shall sound . . ." and the trumpet responding, and woke as usual in silence, the headphones still on his ears. This time, he lay on the sofa looking at Cynthia, his eyes barely open. She had changed clothes again, he saw, and was wearing the silver lamé pants suit, left over from her singing days, that she had worn the first night he had come to her apartment. He saw her bow, prettily and lightly in spite of the headphones on her ears, and extend her arms to her imaginary audience. Then he watched her begin a slow, confined dance, moving no more than a step to the side or forward and then back. She seemed to be singing, but with his headphones on Larry could not hear. She raised her arms again, this time in a gesture of invitation, and although she could not know he was awake it seemed to Larry that she was beckoning to him and not to an imaginary partner—that this dance, one he had never seen, was for him, and Cynthia was asking him to join her in that slow and self-contained step.

Larry rose and sat looking at her, his head by now nearly clear. "Come," she beckoned. "Come." He saw her lips form the word. Was it he to whom she spoke or one of her fantasies? What did it matter? She stood waiting for her partner—for him—and Larry got up, unplugged his headphones, and walked across the room to her. The movement seemed to him a movement of love. He plugged his headphones in next to Cynthia's and stood before her, almost smiling. She smiled, and then, in silence, not quite touching her in that silent room, with the sound of the Beatles loud in his ears, Larry entered into her dance.

QUESTIONS

1. Characterization is developed by references to the general culture. For example, Larry values the Bauhaus, Camus, James Beard, chamber music, Lewis Mumford, Paul Goodman, D. H. Lawrence, Henry Miller, Frank Lloyd Wright. Identify and discuss each allusion and explain how these references provide a sense of Larry as a person.

2. Cynthia prefers *East of Eden, Marjorie Morningstar, Gone With the Wind,* Perry Mason, Doris Day movies, Peggy Lee at Basin Street East, head lettuce with

Russian dressing, the Miss America contest, *Modern Screen,* take-out pizza pies. Identify and discuss each allusion and explain how these references provide a sense of Cynthia as a person.

3. Explain how the headphones act as a natural symbol in this story.

4. At one point, Larry sees Cynthia as a "transmitter of electronic sensations." What does he mean by this metaphor? Do you agree?

5. Although the story is told from the omniscient point of view, Hemenway has, in Henry James' words, "placed a mind of some sort—in the sense of a reflecting and coloring medium—in possession of the general adventure." Why is Larry a more appropriate reflector (in the Jamesian sense) than Cynthia?

6. Are Larry and Cynthia sympathetic characters? Discuss, in terms of the relationship between point of view and esthetic distance.

7. Throughout the story, arguments between Larry and Cynthia alternate between dialogue and paraphrase. Do you find this technique effective or ineffective?

8. On two occasions, Cynthia was scheduled to audition for the movies. What happened on each occasion? How do these events make you understand why Cynthia's "Beatling" is "more than a game"? What other traits make Cynthia's obsessive fantasy plausible? Is her fantasy destructive?

9. Why does Larry begin to share her fantasy? Discuss the implications of the last paragraph. Is the ending happy, unhappy, or inconclusive?

10. How is the tone shaped by the point of view?

Plot, Form, and Time

STEPHEN CRANE

The Bride Comes to Yellow Sky

I

The great Pullman was whirling onward with such dignity of motion that a glance from the window seemed simply to prove that the plains of Texas were pouring eastward. Vast flats of green grass, dull-hued spaces of mesquite and cactus, little groups of frame houses, woods of light and tender trees, all were sweeping into the east, sweeping over the horizon, a precipice.

A newly married pair had boarded this coach at San Antonio. The man's face was reddened from many days in the wind and sun, and a direct result of his new black clothes was that his brick-colored hands were constantly performing in a most conscious fashion. From time to time he looked down respectfully at his attire. He sat with a hand on each knee, like a man waiting in a barber's shop. The glances he devoted to other passengers were furtive and shy.

The bride was not pretty, nor was she very young. She wore a dress of blue cashmere, with small reservations of velvet here and there, and with steel buttons abounding. She continually twisted her head to regard her puff sleeves, very stiff, straight, and high. They embarrassed her. It was quite apparent that she had cooked, and that she expected to cook, dutifully. The blushes caused by the careless scrutiny of some passengers as she had entered the car were strange to see upon this plain, underclass countenance, which was drawn in placid, almost emotionless lines.

They were evidently very happy. "Ever been in a parlor car before?" he asked, smiling with delight.

"No," she answered, "I never was. It's fine, ain't it?"

"Great! And then after a while we'll go forward to the diner, and get a big layout. Finest meal in the world. Charge a dollar."

"Oh, do they?" cried the bride. "Charge a dollar? Why, that's too much—for us—ain't it, Jack?"

"Not this trip, anyhow," he answered bravely. "We're going to go the whole thing."

Later he explained to her about the trains. "You see, it's a thousand miles from one end of Texas to the other; and this train runs right across it, and never stops but four times." He had the pride of an owner. He pointed out to her the dazzling fittings of the coach; and in truth her eyes opened wider as she contemplated the sea-green figured velvet, the shining brass, silver, and glass, the wood that gleamed as darkly brilliant as the surface of a pool of oil. At one end, a bronze figure sturdily held a support for a separated chamber, and at convenient places on the ceiling were frescos in olive and silver.

To the minds of the pair, their surroundings reflected the glory of their marriage that morning in San Antonio; this was the environment of their new estate; and the man's face in particular beamed with an elation that made him appear ridiculous to the Negro porter. This individual at times surveyed them from afar with an amused and superior grin. On other occasions, he bullied them with skill in ways that did not make it exactly plain to them that they were being bullied. He subtly used all the manners of the most unconquerable kind of snobbery. He oppressed them; but of this oppression they had small knowledge, and they speedily forgot that infrequently a number of travelers covered them with stares of derisive enjoyment. Historically there was supposed to be something infinitely humorous in their situation.

"We are due in Yellow Sky at three forty-two," he said, looking tenderly into her eyes.

"Oh, are we?" she said, as if she had not been aware of it. To evince surprise at her husband's statement was part of her wifely amiability. She took from a pocket a little silver watch; and as she held it before her, and stared at it with a frown of attention, the new husband's face shone.

"I bought it in San Anton' from a friend of mine," he told her gleefully.

"It's seventeen minutes past twelve," she said, looking up at him with a kind of shy and clumsy coquetry. A passenger, noting this play, grew excessively sardonic, and winked at himself in one of the numerous mirrors.

At last they went to the dining car. Two rows of Negro waiters, in glowing white suits, surveyed their entrance with the interest, and also the equanimity, of men who had been forewarned. The pair fell to the lot of a waiter who happened to feel pleasure in steering them through their meal. He viewed them with the manner of a fatherly pilot, his countenance radiant with benevolence. The patronage, entwined with the ordinary deference, was not plain to them. And yet, as they returned to their coach, they showed in their faces a sense of escape.

To the left, miles down a long, purple slope, was a little ribbon of mist where moved the keening Rio Grande. The train was approaching it at an angle, and the apex was Yellow Sky. Presently it was apparent that, as the distance from Yellow Sky grew shorter, the husband became commensurately restless. His brick-red hands were more insistent in their prominence. Occasionally he was even rather absentminded and faraway when the bride leaned forward and addressed him.

As a matter of truth, Jack Potter was beginning to find the shadow of a deed weigh upon him like a leaden slab. He, the town marshal of Yellow Sky, a man known, liked, and feared in his corner, a prominent person, had gone to San Antonio to meet a girl he believed he loved, and there, after the usual prayers, had actually induced her to marry him, without consulting Yellow Sky for any part of the transaction. He was now bringing his bride before an innocent and unsuspecting community.

Of course, people in Yellow Sky married as it pleased them, in accordance with a general custom; but such was Potter's thought of his duty to his friends, or of their idea of his duty, or of an unspoken form which does not control men in these matters, that he felt he was heinous. He had committed an extraordinary crime. Face to face with this girl in San Antonio, and spurred by his sharp impulse, he had gone headlong over all the social hedges. At San Antonio he was like a man hidden in the dark. A knife to sever any friendly duty, any form, was easy to his hand in that remote city. But the hour of Yellow Sky—the hour of daylight—was approaching.

He knew full well that his marriage was an important thing to his town. It could only be exceeded by the burning of the new hotel. His friends could not forgive him. Frequently he had reflected on the advisability of telling them by telegraph, but a new cowardice had been upon him. He feared to do it. And now the train was hurrying him toward a scene of amazement, glee, and reproach. He glanced out of the window at the line of haze swinging slowly in toward the train.

Yellow Sky had a kind of brass band, which played painfully, to the delight of the populace. He laughed without heart as he thought of it. If the citizens could dream of his prospective arrival with his bride, they would parade the band at the station and escort them, amid cheers and laughing congratulations, to his adobe home.

He resolved that he would use all the devices of speed and plainscraft in making the journey from the station to his house. Once within that safe citadel, he could issue some sort of vocal bulletin, and then not go among the citizens until they had time to wear off a little of their enthusiasm.

The bride looked anxiously at him. "What's worrying you, Jack?"

He laughed again. "I'm not worrying, girl; I'm only thinking of Yellow Sky."

She flushed in comprehension.

A sense of mutual guilt invaded their minds and developed a finer tenderness. They looked at each other with eyes softly aglow. But Potter often laughed the same nervous laugh; the flush upon the bride's face seemed quite permanent.

The traitor to the feelings of Yellow Sky narrowly watched the speeding landscape. "We're nearly there," he said.

Presently the porter came and announced the proximity of Potter's home. He held a brush in his hand, and with all his airy superiority gone, he brushed Potter's new clothes as the latter slowly turned this way and that way. Potter fumbled out a coin and gave it to the porter, as he had seen others do. It was a heavy and muscle-bound business, as that of a man shoeing his first horse.

The porter took their bag, and as the train began to slow, they moved forward to the hooded platform of the car. Presently the two engines and their long string of coaches rushed into the station of Yellow Sky.

"They have to take water here," said Potter, from a constricted throat and in mournful cadence, as one announcing death. Before the train stopped, his eye had swept the length of the platform, and he was glad and astonished to see there was none upon it but the station agent, who, with a slightly hurried and anxious air was walking toward the water tanks. When the train had halted, the porter alighted first, and placed in position a little temporary step.

"Come on, girl," said Potter hoarsely. As he helped her down, they each laughed on a false note. He took the bag from the Negro, and bade his wife cling to his arm. As they slunk rapidly away, his hangdog glance perceived that they were unloading the two trunks, and also that the station agent, far ahead near the baggage car, had turned and was running toward him, making gestures. He laughed, and groaned as he laughed, when he noted the first effect of his marital bliss upon Yellow Sky. He gripped his wife's arm firmly to his side, and they fled. Behind them the porter stood, chuckling fatuously.

II

The California express on the Southern Railway was due at Yellow Sky in twenty-one minutes. There were six men at the bar of the Weary Gentleman saloon. One was a drummer who talked a great deal and rapidly; three were Texans who did not care to talk at that time; and two were Mexican sheepherders, who did not talk as a general practice in the Weary Gentleman saloon. The barkeeper's dog lay on the boardwalk that crossed in front of the door. His head was on his paws, and he glanced drowsily here and there with the constant vigilance of a dog that is kicked on occasion. Across the sandy street were some vivid green glass plots, so wonderful in appearance, amid the sands that burned near them in a blazing sun, that they caused a doubt in the mind. They exactly resembled the grass mats used to represent lawns on the stage. At the cooler end of the railway station, a man without a coat sat in a tilted chair and smoked his pipe. The fresh-cut bank of the Rio Grande circled near the town, and there could be seen beyond it a great, plum-colored plain of mesquite.

Save for the busy drummer and his companions in the saloon, Yellow Sky was dozing. The newcomer leaned gracefully upon the bar, and recited many tales with the confidence of a bard who has come upon a new field.

"—and at the moment that the old man fell downstairs with the bureau in his arms, the old woman was coming up with two scuttles of coal, and of course—"

The drummer's tale was interrupted by a young man who suddenly appeared in the open door. He cried, "Scratchy Wilson's drunk, and has turned loose with both hands." The two Mexicans at once set down their glasses and faded out of the rear entrance of the saloon.

The drummer, innocent and jocular, answered, "All right, old man. S'pose he had? Come in and have a drink, anyhow."

But the information had made such an obvious cleft in every skull in the room that the drummer was obliged to see its importance. All had become instantly solemn. "Say," said he, mystified, "what is this?" His three companions made the introductory gesture of eloquent speech; but the young man at the door forestalled them.

"It means, my friend," he answered, as he came into the saloon, "that for the next two hours this town won't be a health resort."

The barkeeper went to the door, and locked and barred it; reaching out of the window, he pulled in heavy wooden shutters, and barred them. Immediately a solemn, chapel-like gloom was upon the place. The drummer was looking from one to another.

"But say," he cried, "what is this, anyhow? You don't mean there is going to be a gun fight?"

"Don't know whether there'll be a fight or not," answered one man grimly, "but there'll be some shootin'—some good shootin'."

The young man who had warned them waved his hand. "Oh, there'll be a fight fast enough, if anyone wants it. Anybody can get a fight out there in the street. There's a fight just waiting."

The drummer seemed to be swayed between the interest of a foreigner and a perception of personal danger.

"What did you say his name was?" he asked.

"Scratchy Wilson," they answered in chorus.

"And will he kill anybody? What are you going to do? Does this happen often? Does he rampage around like this once a week or so? Can he break in that door?"

"No; he can't break down that door," replied the barkeeper. "He's tried it three times. But when he comes, you'd better lay down on the floor, stranger. He's dead sure to shoot at it, and a bullet may come through."

Thereafter the drummer kept a strict eye upon the door. The time had not yet been called for him to hug the floor, but as a minor precaution, he sidled near to the wall. "Will he kill anybody?" he said again.

The men laughed low and scornfully at the question.

"He's out to shoot, and he's out for trouble. Don't see any good in experimentin' with him."

"But what do you do in a case like this? What do you do?"

A man responded, "Why, he and Jack Potter—"

"But," in chorus the other men interrupted, "Jack Potter's in San Anton'."

"Well, who is he? What's he got to do with it?"

"Oh, he's the town marshal. He goes out and fights Scratchy when he gets on one of these tears."

"Wow!" said the drummer, mopping his brow. "Nice job he's got."

The voices had toned away to mere whisperings. The drummer wished to ask further questions, which were born of an increasing anxiety and bewilderment; but when he attempted them, the men merely looked at him in irritation and motioned him to remain silent. A tense, waiting hush was upon them. In the deep shadows of the room, their eyes shone as they listened for sounds from the street. One man made three gestures at the barkeeper; and the latter, moving like a ghost, handed him a glass and a bottle. The man poured a full glass of whisky, and set down the bottle noiselessly. He gulped the whisky in a swallow, and turned again toward the door in immovable silence. The drummer saw that the barkeeper, without a sound, had taken a Winchester from beneath the bar. Later he saw this individual beckoning to him, so he tiptoed across the room.

"You better come with me back of the bar."

"No, thanks," said the drummer, perspiring. "I'd rather be where I can make a break for the back door."

Whereupon the man of bottles made a kindly but peremptory gesture. The drummer obeyed it, and finding himself seated on a box with his head below the level of the bar, balm was laid upon his soul at sight of various zinc and copper fittings that bore a resemblance to armor plate. The barkeeper took a seat comfortably upon an adjacent box.

"You see," he whispered, "this here Scratchy Wilson is a wonder with a gun—a perfect wonder; and when he goes on the war trail, we hunt our holes— naturally. He's about the last one of the old gang that used to hang out along the river here. He's a terror when he's drunk. When he's sober he's all right—kind of simple—wouldn't hurt a fly—nicest fellow in town. But when he's drunk— whoo!"

There were periods of stillness. "I wish Jack Potter was back from San Anton'," said the barkeeper. "He shot Wilson up once—in the leg—and he would sail in and pull out the kinks in this thing."

Presently they heard from a distance the sound of a shot, followed by three wild yowls. It instantly removed a bond from the men in the darkened saloon. There was a shuffling of feet. They looked at each other. "Here he comes," they said.

III

A man in a maroon-colored flannel shirt, which had been purchased for purposes of decoration, and made principally by some Jewish women on the East Side of New York, rounded a corner and walked into the middle of the main street of Yellow Sky. In either hand the man held a long, heavy, blue-black revolver. Often he yelled, and these cries rang through a semblance of a deserted village, shrilly flying over the roofs in a volume that seemed to have no relation to the ordinary vocal strength of a man. It was as if the surrounding stillness formed the arch of a tomb over him. These cries of ferocious challenge rang against walls of silence. And his boots had red tops with gilded imprints, of the kind beloved in winter by little sledding boys on the hillsides of New England.

The man's face flamed in a rage begot of whisky. His eyes, rolling, and yet keen for ambush, hunted the still doorways and windows. He walked with the creeping movement of the midnight cat. As it occurred to him, he roared menacing information. The long revolvers in his hands were as easy as straws; they were moved with an electric swiftness. The little fingers of each hand played sometimes in a musician's way. Plain from the low collar of the shirt, the cords of his neck straightened and sank, straightened and sank, as passion moved him. The only sounds were his terrible invitations. The calm adobes preserved their demeanor at the passing of this small thing in the middle of the street.

There was no offer of fight—no offer of fight. The man called to the sky. There were no attractions. He bellowed and fumed and swayed his revolvers here and everywhere.

The dog of the barkeeper of the Weary Gentleman saloon had not appreciated the advance of events. He yet lay dozing in front of his master's door. At sight of the dog, the man paused and raised his revolver humorously. At sight of the man, the dog sprang up and walked diagonally away, with a sullen head, and growling. The man yelled, and the dog broke into a gallop. As it was about to enter an alley, there was a loud noise, a whistling, and something spat the ground directly before it. The dog screamed, and wheeling in terror, galloped headlong in a new direction. Again there was a noise, a whistling, and sand was kicked viciously before it. Fearstricken, the dog turned and flurried like an animal in a pen. The man stood laughing, his weapons at his hips.

Ultimately the man was attracted by the closed door of the Weary Gentleman saloon. He went to it, and hammering with a revolver, demanded drink.

The door remaining imperturbable, he picked a bit of paper from the walk, and nailed it to the framework with a knife. He then turned his back contemptuously upon this popular resort, and walking to the opposite side of the street and spinning there on his heel quickly and lithely, fired at the bit of paper. He missed it by a half inch. He swore at himself, and went away. Later he comfortably fusilladed the windows of his most intimate friend. The man was playing with this town; it was a toy for him.

But still there was no offer of fight. The name of Jack Potter, his ancient antagonist, entered his mind, and he concluded that it would be a glad thing if he should go to Potter's house, and by bombardment induce him to come out and fight. He moved in the direction of his desire, chanting Apache scalp music.

When he arrived at it, Potter's house presented the same still front as had the other adobes. Taking up a strategic position, the man howled a challenge. But this house regarded him as might a great stone god. It gave no sign. After a decent wait, the man howled further challenges, mingling with them wonderful epithets.

Presently there came the spectacle of a man churning himself into deepest rage over the immobility of a house. He fumed at it as the winter wind attacks a prairie cabin in the North. To the distance there should have gone the sound of a tumult like the fighting of two hundred Mexicans. As necessity bade him, he paused for breath or to reload his revolvers.

IV

Potter and his bride walked sheepishly and with speed. Sometimes they laughed together shamefacedly and low.

"Next corner, dear," he said finally.

They put forth the efforts of a pair walking bowed against a strong wind. Potter was about to raise a finger to point the first appearance of the new home when, as they circled the corner, they came face to face with a man in a maroon-colored shirt, who was feverishly pushing cartridges into a large revolver. Upon the instant the man dropped his revolver to the ground and, like lightning, whipped another from its holster. The second weapon was aimed at the bride-groom's chest.

There was a silence. Potter's mouth seemed to be merely a grave for his tongue. He exhibited an instinct to at once loosen his arm from the woman's grip, and he dropped the bag to the sand. As for the bride, her face had gone as yellow as old cloth. She was a slave to hideous rites, gazing at the apparitional snake.

The two men faced each other at a distance of three paces. He of the revolver smiled with a new and quiet ferocity.

"Tried to sneak up on me," he said. "Tried to sneak up on me!" His eyes grew more baleful. As Potter made a slight movement, the man thrust his revolver venomously forward. "No; don't you do it, Jack Potter. Don't you move a finger toward a gun just yet. Don't you move an eyelash. The time has come for me to settle with you, and I'm goin' to do it my own way, and loaf along with no interferin'. So if you don't want a gun bent on you, just mind what I tell you."

Potter looked at his enemy. "I ain't got a gun on me, Scratchy," he said. "Honest, I ain't." He was stiffening and steadying, but yet somewhere at the back of his mind a vision of the Pullman floated: the sea-green figured velvet, the shining brass, silver, and glass, the wood that gleamed as darkly brilliant as the surface of a pool of oil—all the glory of the marriage, the environment of the new estate. "You know I fight when it comes to fighting, Scratchy Wilson; but I ain't got a gun on me. You'll have to do all the shootin' yourself."

His enemy's face went livid. He stepped forward, and lashed his weapon to and fro before Potter's chest. "Don't you tell me you ain't got no gun on you, you whelp. Don't tell me no lie like that. There ain't a man in Texas ever seen you without no gun. Don't take me for no kid." His eyes blazed with light, and his throat worked like a pump.

"I ain't takin' you for no kid," answered Potter. His heels had not moved an inch backward. "I'm takin' you for a damn fool. I tell you I ain't got a gun, and I ain't. If you're goin' to shoot me up, you better begin now; you'll never get a chance like this again."

So much enforced reasoning had told on Wilson's rage; he was calmer. "If you ain't got a gun, why ain't you got a gun?" he sneered. "Been to Sunday school?"

"I ain't got a gun because I've just come from San Anton' with my wife. I'm married," said Potter. "And if I'd thought there was going to be any galoots like you prowling around when I brought my wife home, I'd had a gun, and don't you forget it."

"Married!" said Scratchy, not at all comprehending.

"Yes, married. I'm married," said Potter distinctly.

"Married?" said Scratchy. Seemingly for the first time, he saw the drooping, drowning woman at the other man's side. "No!" he said. He was like a creature allowed a glimpse of another world. He moved a pace backward, and his arm, with the revolver, dropped to his side. "Is this the lady?" he asked.

"Yes; this is the lady," answered Potter.

There was another period of silence.

"Well," said Wilson at last, slowly, "I s'pose it's all off now."

"It's all off if you say so, Scratchy. You know I didn't make the trouble." Potter lifted his valise.

"Well, I 'low it's off, Jack," said Wilson. He was looking at the ground. "Married!" He was not a student of chivalry; it was merely that in the presence of this foreign condition he was a simple child of the earlier plains. He picked up his starboard revolver, and placing both weapons in their holsters, he went away. His feet made funnel-shaped tracks in the heavy sand.

QUESTIONS

1. Explain how the reaction of the porter, waiter, and the other passengers help to characterize Jack Potter and his bride.

2. Why is it important to the plot that Jack Potter did not tell anyone in Yellow Sky of his impending marriage? Is his secrecy believable, or has Crane created an artificial situation purely to suit plot and theme?

3. Show how Crane's descriptions manage to convey a feeling of the train's speed and direction.

4. Discuss the role of chance and coincidence. Does the plot depend too heavily on coincidence?

5. Parallel action occurs when two lines of activities going on simultaneously but in different places converge and interact. Discuss parallel action and convergence as a plot strategem in this story.

6. What function does the drummer in the Weary Gentleman saloon serve?

7. Is there enough evidence to support the interpretation that this story is about the end of the frontier? If so, what does Scratchy Wilson represent? Jack Potter? his bride? the train?

EDGAR ALLAN POE

The Purloined Letter

Nil sapientiae odiosius acumine nimio.*

—Seneca

At Paris, just after dark one gusty evening in the autumn of 18—, I was enjoying the twofold luxury of meditation and a meerschaum, in company with my friend, C. Auguste Dupin, in his little back library, or bookcloset, *au troisiême,* No. 33 *Rue Dunôt, Faubourg St. Germain.* For one hour at least we had maintained a profound silence; while each, to any casual observer, might have seemed intently and exclusively occupied with the curling eddies of smoke that oppressed the atmosphere of the chamber. For myself, however, I was mentally discussing certain topics which had formed matter for conversation between us at an earlier period of the evening; I mean the affair of the Rue Morgue, and the mystery attending the murder of Marie Rogêt. I looked upon it, therefore, as something of a coincidence, when the door of our apartment was thrown open and admitted our old acquaintance, Monsieur G——, the Prefect of the Parisian police.

We have him a hearty welcome; for there was nearly half as much of the entertaining as of the contemptible about the man, and we had not seen him for

*("Nothing is more offensive to wisdom than too much smartness.")

231

several years. We had been sitting in the dark, and Dupin now arose for the purpose of lighting a lamp, but sat down again, without doing so, upon G.'s saying that he had called to consult us, or rather to ask the opinion of my friend, about some official business which had occasioned a great deal of trouble.

"If it is any point requiring reflection," observed Dupin, as he forebore to enkindle the wick, "we shall examine it to better purpose in the dark."

"That is another of your odd notions," said the Prefect, who had the fashion of calling every thing "odd" that was beyond his comprehension, and thus lived amid an absolute legion of "oddities."

"Very true," said Dupin, as he supplied his visiter with a pipe, and rolled toward him a comfortable chair.

"And what is the difficulty now?" I asked. "Nothing more in the assassination way I hope?"

"Oh, no; nothing of that nature. The fact is, the business is *very* simple indeed, and I make no doubt that we can manage it sufficiently well ourselves; but then I thought Dupin would like to hear the details of it, because it is so excessively *odd.*"

"Simple and odd," said Dupin.

"Why, yes; and not exactly that either. The fact is, we have all been a good deal puzzled because the affair *is* so simple, and yet baffles us altogether."

"Perhaps it is the very simplicity of the thing which puts you at fault," said my friend.

"What nonsense you *do* talk!" replied the Prefect, laughing heartily.

"Perhaps the mystery is a little *too* plain," said Dupin.

"Oh, good heavens! who ever heard of such an idea?"

"A little *too* self-evident."

"Ha! ha! ha!—ha! ha! ha!—ho! ho! ho!" roared our visitor, profoundly amused, "oh, Dupin, you will be the death of me yet!"

"And what, after all, *is* the matter on hand?" I asked.

"Why, I will tell you," replied the Prefect, as he gave a long, steady, and contemplative puff, and settled himself in his chair. "I will tell you in a few words; but, before I begin, let me caution you that this is an affair demanding the greatest secrecy, and that I should most probably lose the position I now hold, were it known that I confided it to any one."

"Proceed," said I.

"Or not," said Dupin.

"Well, then; I have received personal information, from a very high quarter, that a certain document of the last importance has been purloined from the royal apartments. The individual who purloined it is known; this beyond a doubt; he was seen to take it. It is known, also, that it still remains in his possession."

"How is this known?" asked Dupin.

"It is clearly inferred," replied the Prefect, "from the nature of the document, and from the non-appearance of certain results which would at once arise from its passing *out* of the robber's possession;—that is to say, from his employing it as he must design in the end to employ it."

"Be a little more explicit," I said.

"Well, I may venture so far as to say that the paper gives its holder a certain power in a certain quarter where such power is immensely valuable." The Prefect was fond of the cant of diplomacy.

"Still I do not quite understand," said Dupin.

"No? Well; the disclosure of the document to a third person, who shall be nameless, would bring in question the honor of a personage of most exalted station; and this fact gives the holder of the document an ascendancy over the illustrious personage whose honor and peace are so jeopardized."

"But this ascendancy," I interposed, "would depend upon the robber's knowledge of the loser's knowledge of the robber. Who would dare—"

"The thief," said G——, "is the Minister D——, who dares all things, those unbecoming as well as those becoming a man. The method of the theft was not less ingenious than bold. The document in question—a letter, to be frank—had been received by the personage robbed while alone in the royal *boudoir*. During its perusal she was suddenly interrupted by the entrance of the other exalted personage from whom especially it was her wish to conceal it. After a hurried and vain endeavor to thrust it in a drawer, she was forced to place it, open as it was, upon a table. The address, however, was uppermost, and, the contents thus unexposed, the letter escaped notice. At this juncture enters the Minister D——. His lynx eye immediately perceives the paper, recognizes the handwriting of the address, observes the confusion of the personage addressed, and fathoms her secret. After some business transactions, hurried through in his ordinary manner, he produces a letter somewhat similar to the one in question, opens it, pretends to read it, and then places it in close juxtaposition to the other. Again he converses, for some fifteen minutes, upon the public affairs. At length, in taking leave, he takes also from the table the letter to which he had no claim. Its rightful owner saw, but, of course, dared not call attention to the act, in the presence of the third personage who stood at her elbow. The minister decamped; leaving his own letter—one of no importance—upon the table."

"Here, then," said Dupin to me, "you have precisely what you demand to make the ascendancy complete—the robber's knowledge of the loser's knowledge of the robber."

"Yes," replied the Prefect; "and the power thus attained has, for some months past, been wielded, for political purposes, to a very dangerous extent. The personage robbed is more thoroughly convinced, every day, of the necessity of reclaiming her letter. But this, of course, cannot be done openly. In fine, driven to despair, she had committed the matter to me."

"Than whom," said Dupin, amid a perfect whirlwind of smoke, "no more sagacious agent could, I suppose, be desired, or even imagined."

"You flatter me," replied the Prefect; "but it is possible that some such opinion may have been entertained."

"It is clear," said I, "as you observe, that the letter is still in the possession of the minister; since it is this possession, and not any employment of the letter, which bestows the power. With the employment the power departs."

"True," said G.; "and upon this conviction I proceeded. My first care was to make thorough search of the minister's hotel; and here my chief embarrassment lay in the necessity of searching without his knowledge. Beyond all things, I have been warned of the danger which would result from giving him reason to suspect our design."

"But," said I, "you are quite *au fait* in these investigations. The Parisian police have done this thing often before."

"Oh, yes; and for this reason I did not despair. The habits of the minister gave me, too, a great advantage. He is frequently absent from home all night. His servants are by no means numerous. They sleep at a distance from their master's apartment, and, being chiefly Neapolitans, are readily made drunk. I have keys, as you know, with which I can open any chamber or cabinet in Paris. For three months a night has not passed, during the greater part of which I have not been engaged, personally, in ransacking the D—— Hotel. My honor is interested, and, to mention a great secret, the reward is enormous. So I did not abandon the search until I had become fully satisfied that the thief is a more astute man than myself. I fancy that I have investigated every nook and corner of the premises in which it is possible that the paper can be concealed."

"But is it not possible," I suggested, "that although the letter may be in possession of the minister, as it unquestionably is, he may have concealed it elsewhere than upon his own premises?"

"This is barely possible," said Dupin. "The present peculiar condition of affairs at court, and especially of those intrigues in which D—— is known to be involved, would render the instant availability of the document—its susceptibility of being produced at a moment's notice—a point of nearly equal importance with its possession."

"Its susceptibility of being produced?" said I.

"That is to say, of being *destroyed*," said Dupin.

"True," I observed; "the paper is clearly then upon the premises. As for its being upon the person of the minister, we may consider that as out of the question."

"Entirely," said the Prefect. "He has been twice waylaid, as if by footpads, and his person rigorously searched under my own inspection."

"You might have spared yourself this trouble," said Dupin. "D——, I presume, is not altogether a fool, and, if not, must have anticipated these waylayings, as a matter of course."

"Not *altogether* a fool," said G., "but then he is a poet, which I take to be only one remove from a fool."

"True," said Dupin, after a long and thoughtful whiff from his meerschaum, "although I have been guilty of certain doggerel myself."

"Suppose you detail," said I, "the particulars of your search."

"Why, the fact is, we took our time, and we searched *everywhere.* I have had long experience in these affairs. I took the entire building, room by room; devoting the nights of a whole week to each. We examined, first, the furniture of each apartment. We opened every possible drawer; and I presume you know that, to a properly trained police agent, such a thing as a *'secret'* drawer is impossible. Any man is a dolt who permits a 'secret' drawer to escape him in a search of this kind. The thing is *so* plain. There is a certain amount of bulk—of space—to be accounted for in every cabinet. Then we have accurate rules. The fiftieth part of a line could not escape us. After the cabinets we took the chairs. The cushions we probed with the fine long needles you have seen me employ. From the tables we removed the tops."

"Why so?"

"Sometimes the top of a table, or other similarly arranged piece of furniture, is removed by the person wishing to conceal an article; then the leg is excavated, the article deposited within the cavity, and the top replaced. The bottoms and tops of bedposts are employed in the same way."

"But could not the cavity be detected by sounding?" I asked.

"By no means, if, when the article is deposited, a sufficient wadding of cotton be placed around it. Besides, in our case, we were obliged to proceed without noise."

"But you could not have removed—you could not have taken to pieces *all* articles of furniture in which it would have been possible to make a deposit in the manner you mention. A letter may be compressed into a thin spiral roll, not differing much in shape or bulk from a large knitting-needle, and in this form it might be inserted into the rung of a chair, for example. You did not take to pieces all the chairs?"

"Certainly not; but we did better—we examined the rungs of every chair in the hotel, and, indeed, the jointings of every description of furniture, by the aid of a most powerful microscope. Had there been any traces of recent disturbance we should not have failed to detect it instantly. A single grain of gimlet-dust, for example, would have been as obvious as an apple. Any disorder in the gluing—any unusual gaping in the joints—would have sufficed to insure detection."

"I presume you looked to the mirrors, between the boards and the plates, and you probed the beds and the bedclothes, as well as the curtains and carpets."

"That of course; and when we had absolutely completed every particle of the furniture in this way, then we examined the house itself. We divided its entire surface into compartments, which we numbered, so that none might be missed; then we scrutinized each individual square inch throughout the premises, including the two houses immediately adjoining, with the microscope, as before."

"The two houses adjoining!" I exclaimed; "you must have had a great deal of trouble."

"We had; but the reward offered is prodigious."

"You include the *grounds* about the houses?"

"All the grounds are paved with brick. They gave us comparatively little trouble. We examined the moss between the bricks, and found it undisturbed."

"You looked among D——'s papers, of course, and into the books of the library?"

"Certainly; we opened every package and parcel; we not only opened every book, but we turned over every leaf in each volume, not contenting ourselves with a mere shake, according to the fashion of some of our police officers. We also measured the thickness of every book-*cover,* with the most accurate admeasurement, and applied to each the most jealous scrutiny of the microscope. Had any of the bindings been recently meddled with, it would have been utterly impossible that the fact should have escaped observation. Some five or six volumes, just from the hands of the binder, we carefully probed, longitudinally, with the needles."

"You explored the floors beneath the carpets?"

"Beyond doubt. We removed every carpet, and examined the boards with the microscope."

"And the paper on the walls?"

"Yes."

"You looked into the cellars?"

"We did."

"Then," I said, "you have been making a miscalculation, and the letter is *not* upon the premises, as you suppose."

"I fear you are right there," said the Prefect. "And now, Dupin, what would you advise me to do?"

"To make a thorough research of the premises."

"That is absolutely needless," replied G——. "I am not more sure that I breathe than I am that the letter is not at the hotel."

"I have no better advice to give you," said Dupin. "You have, of course, an accurate description of the letter?"

"Oh, yes!"—And here the Prefect, producing a memorandum-book, proceeded to read aloud a minute account of the internal, and especially of the external appearance of the missing document. Soon after finishing the perusal of this description, he took his departure, more entirely depressed in spirits than I had ever known the good gentleman before.

In about a month afterward he paid us another visit, and found us occupied very nearly as before. He took a pipe and a chair and entered into some ordinary conversation. At length I said:

"Well, but G——, what of the purloined letter? I presume you have at last made up your mind that there is no such thing as overreaching the Minister?"

"Confound him, say I—yes; I made the re-examination, however, as Dupin suggested—but it was all labor lost, as I knew it would be."

"How much was the reward offered, did you say?" asked Dupin.

"Why, a very great deal—a *very* liberal reward—I don't like to say how much, precisely; but one thing I *will* say, that I wouldn't mind giving my individual check for fifty thousand francs to any one who could obtain me that letter. The fact is, it is becoming of more and more importance every day; and the reward has been lately doubled. If it were trebled, however, I could do no more than I have done."

"Why, yes," said Dupin, drawlingly between the whiffs of his meerschaum. "I really—think, G——, you have not exerted yourself—to the utmost in this matter. You might—do a little more, I think, eh?"

"How?—in what way?"

"Why—puff, puff—you might—puff, puff—employ counsel in the matter, eh?—puff, puff, puff. Do you remember the story they tell of Abernethy?"

"No; hang Abernethy!"

"To be sure! hang him and welcome. But, once upon a time, a certain rich miser conceived the design of sponging upon this Abernethy for a medical opinion. Getting up, for this purpose, an ordinary conversation in a private company, he insinuated his case to the physician, as that of an imaginary individual.

"'We will suppose,' said the miser, 'that his symptoms are such and such; now, doctor, what would *you* have directed him to take?'

"'Take!' said Abernethy, 'why, take *advice,* to be sure.'"

"But," said the Prefect, a little discomposed, "I am *perfectly* willing to take advice, and to pay for it. I would *really* give fifty thousand francs to any one who would aid me in the matter."

"In that case," replied Dupin, opening a drawer, and producing a check-book, "you may as well fill me up a check for the amount mentioned. When you have signed it, I will hand you the letter."

I was astounded. The Prefect appeared absolutely thunder-stricken. For some minutes he remained speechless and motionless, looking incredulously at my friend with open mouth, and eyes that seemed starting from their sockets; then apparently recovering himself in some measure, he seized a pen, and after several pauses and vacant stares, finally filled up and signed a check for fifty thousand francs, and handed it across the table to Dupin. The latter examined it carefully and deposited it in his pocket-book; then, unlocking an *escritoire,* took thence a letter and gave it to the Prefect. This functionary grasped it in a perfect agony of joy, opened it with a trembling hand, cast a rapid glance at its contents, and then scrambling and struggling to the door, rushed at length unceremoniously from the room and from the house, without having uttered a syllable since Dupin had requested him to fill up the check.

When he had gone, my friend entered into some explanations.

"The Parisian police," he said, "are exceedingly able in their way. They are persevering, ingenious, cunning, and thoroughly versed in the knowledge which their duties seem chiefly to demand. Thus, when G—— detailed to us his mode of searching the premises at the Hotel D——, I felt entire confidence in his having made a satisfactory investigation—so far as his labors extended."

"So far as his labors extended?" said I.

"Yes," said Dupin. "The measures adopted were not only the best of their kind, but carried out to absolute perfection. Had the letter been deposited within the range of their search, these fellows would, beyond a question, have found it."

I merely laughed—but he seemed quite serious in all that he said.

"The measures then," he continued, "were good in their kind, and well executed; their defect lay in their being inapplicable to the case and to the man. A certain set of highly ingenious resources are, with the Prefect, a sort of Procrustean bed, to which he forcibly adapts his designs. But he perpetually errs by being too deep or too shallow for the matter in hand; and many a schoolboy is a better reasoner than he. I knew one about eight years of age, whose success at guessing in the game of 'even and odd' attracted universal admiration. This game is simple, and is played with marbles. One player holds in his hand a number of these toys, and demands of another whether that number is even or odd. If the guess is right, the guesser wins one; if wrong, he loses one. The boy to whom I allude won all the marbles of the school. Of course he had some principle of guessing; and this lay in mere observation and admeasurement of the astuteness of his opponents. For example, an arrant simpleton is his opponent, and, holding up his closed hand, asks, 'Are they even or odd?' Our schoolboy replies, 'Odd,' and loses; but upon the second trial he wins, for he then says to himself: 'The simpleton had them even upon the first trial, and his amount of cunning is just sufficient to make him have them odd upon the second; I will therefore guess odd';—he guesses odd, and wins. Now, with a simpleton a degree above the first, he would have reasoned thus: 'This fellow finds that in the first instance I guessed odd, and, in the second, he will propose to himself, upon the first impulse, a simple variation from even to odd, as did the first simpleton; but then a second thought will suggest that this is too simple a variation, and finally he will decide upon putting it even as before. I will therefore guess even';—he guesses even, and wins. Now this mode of reasoning in the schoolboy, whom his fellows termed 'lucky,'—what, in its last analysis, is it?"

"It is merely," I said, "an identification of the reasoner's intellect with that of his opponent."

"It is," said Dupin; "and, upon inquiring of the boy by what means he effected the *thorough* identification in which his success consisted, I received answer as follows: 'When I wish to find out how wise, or how stupid, or how good, or how wicked is any one, or what are his thoughts at the moment, I fashion the expression of my face, as accurately as possible, in accordance with the expression of his, and then wait to see what thoughts or sentiments arise in my mind or heart, as if to match or correspond with the expression.' This response of the schoolboy lies at the bottom of all the spurious profundity which has been attributed to Rochefoucault, to La Bougive, to Machiavelli, and to Campanella."

"And the identification," I said, "of the reasoner's intellect with that of his opponent, depends, if I understand you aright, upon the accuracy with which the opponent's intellect is admeasured."

"For its practical value it depends upon this," replied Dupin: "and the

Prefect and his cohort fail so frequently, first by default of his identification, and, secondly, by ill-admeasurement, or rather through nonadmeasurement, of the intellect with which they are engaged. They consider only their *own* ideas of ingenuity; and, in searching for anything hidden advert only to the modes in which *they* would have hidden it. They are right in this much—that their own ingenuity is a faithful representative of that of the *mass;* but when the cunning of the individual felon is diverse in character from their own, the felon foils them, of course. This always happens when it is above their own, and very usually when it is below. They have no variation of principle in their investigations; at best, when urged by some unusual emergency—by some extraordinary reward—they extend or exaggerate their old modes of *practice,* without touching their principles. What, for example, in this case of D——, has been done to vary the principle of action? What is all this boring, and probing, and sounding, and scrutinizing with the microscope, and dividing the surface of the building into registered square inches—what is it all but an exaggeration *of the application* of the one principle or set of principles of search, which are based upon the one set of notions regarding human ingenuity, to which the Prefect, in the long routine of his duty, has been accustomed? Do you not see he has taken it for granted that *all* men proceed to conceal a letter—not exactly in a gimlet-hole bored in a chair-leg, but, at least, in *some* out-of-the-way hole or corner suggested by the same tenor of thought which would urge a man to secrete a letter in a gimlet-hole bored in a chair-leg? And do you not see also that such *recherchés* nooks for concealment are adapted only for ordinary occasions, and would be adopted only by ordinary intellects; for, in all cases of concealment, a disposal of the article concealed—a disposal of it in this *recherché* manner,—is in the very first instance, presumable and presumed; and thus its discovery depends, not at all upon the acumen, but altogether upon the mere care, patience, and determination of the seekers; and where the case is of importance—or, what amounts to the same thing in the political eyes, when the reward is of magnitude,—the qualities in question have *never* been known to fail. You will now understand what I meant in suggesting that, had the purloined letter been hidden anywhere within the limits of the Prefect's examination—in other words, had the principle of its concealment been comprehended within the principles of the Prefect—its discovery would have been a matter altogether beyond question. This functionary, however, has been thoroughly mystified; and the remote source of his defeat lies in the supposition that the Minister is a fool, because he has acquired renown as a poet. All fools are poets; this the Prefect feels; and he is merely guilty of a *non distributio medii* in thence inferring that all poets are fools."

"But is this really the poet?" I asked. "There are two brothers, I know; and both have attained reputation in letters. The minister I believe has written learnedly on the Differential Calculus. He is a mathematician, and no poet."

"You are mistaken; I know him well; he is both. As poet *and* mathematician, he would reason well; as mere mathematician, he could not have reasoned at all, and thus would have been at the mercy of the Prefect."

"You surprise me," I said, "by these opinions, which have been contradicted by the voice of the world. You do not mean to set at naught the well-digested idea of centuries. The mathematical reason has long been regarded as *the* reason *par excellence.*"

"*Il y à parièr,'*" replied Dupin, quoting from Chamfort, '*que toute idée publique, toute convention reçue, est une sottise, car elle a convenue au plus grand nombre.*' The mathematicians, I grant you, have done their best to promulgate the popular error to which you allude, and which is none the less an error for its promulgation as truth. With an art worthy a better cause, for example, they have insinuated the term 'analysis' into application to algebra. The French are the originators of this particular deception; but if a term is of any importance—if words derive any value from applicability—then 'analysis' conveys 'algebra' about as much as, in Latin, '*ambitus*' implies 'ambition,' '*religio*' 'religion,' or '*homines honesti*' a set of *honorable* men."

"You have a quarrel on hand, I see," said I, "with some of the algebraists of Paris; but proceed."

"I dispute the availability, and thus the value, of that reason which is cultivated in any especial form other than the abstractly logical. I dispute, in particular, the reason educed by mathematical study. The mathematics are the science of form and quantity; mathematical reasoning is merely logic applied to observation upon form and quantity. The great error lies in supposing that even the truths of what is called *pure* algebra are abstract or general truths. And this error is so egregious that I am confounded at the universality with which it has been received. Mathematical axioms are *not* axiom; of general truth. What is true of *relation*—of form and quantity—is often grossly false in regard to morals, for example. In this latter science it is very usually *un*true that the aggregated parts are equal to the whole. In chemistry also the axiom fails. In the consideration of motive it fails; for two motives, each of a given value, have not necessarily, a value when united, equal to the sum of their values apart. There are numerous other mathematical truths which are only truths within the limits of *relation.* But the mathematician argues from his *finite truths,* through habit, as if they were of an absolutely general applicability—as the world indeed imagines them to be. Bryant, in his very learned 'Mythology,' mentions an analogous source of error, when he says that 'although the Pagan fables are not believed, yet we forget ourselves continually, and make inferences from them as existing realities.' With the algebraists, however, who are Pagans themselves, the 'Pagan fables' *are* believed, and the inferences are made, not so much through lapse of memory as through an unaccountable addling of the brains. In short, I never yet encountered the mere mathematician who could be trusted out of equal roots, or one who did not clandestinely hold it as a point of his faith that $x^2 + px$ was absolutely and unconditionally equal to q. Say to one of these gentlemen, by way of experiment, if you please, that you believe occasions may occur where $x^2 + px$ is not altogether equal to q, and, having made him understand what you mean, get out of his reach as speedily as convenient, for, beyond doubt, he will endeavor to knock you down.

"I mean to say," continued Dupin, while I merely laughed at his last observations, "that if the Minister had been no more than a mathematician, the Prefect would have been under no necessity of giving me this check. I knew him, however, as both mathematician and poet, and my measures were adapted to his capacity, with reference to the circumstances by which he was surrounded. I knew him as a courtier, too, and as a bold *intriguant.* Such a man, I considered, could not fail to be aware of the ordinary political modes of action. He could not have failed to anticipate—and events have proved that he did not fail to anticipate—the waylayings to which he was subjected. He must have forseen, I reflected, the secret investigations of his premises. His frequent absences from home at night, which were hailed by the Prefect as certain aids to his success, I regarded only as *ruses,* to afford opportunity for thorough search to the police, and thus the sooner to impress them with the conviction to which G——, in fact, did finally arrive—the conviction that the letter was not upon the premises. I felt, also, that the whole train of thought, which I was at some pains in detailing to you just now, concerning the invariable principle of political action in searches for articles concealed—I felt that this whole train of thought would necessarily pass through the mind of the Minister. It would imperatively lead him to despise all the ordinary *nooks* of concealment. *He* could not, I reflected, be so weak as not to see that the most intricate and remote recess of his hotel would be as open as his commonest closets to the eyes, to the probes, to the gimlets, and to the microscopes of the Prefect. I saw, in fine, that he would be driven, as a matter of course, to *simplicity,* if not deliberately induced to it as a matter of choice. You will remember, perhaps, how desperately the Prefect laughed when I suggested, upon our first interview, that it was just possible this mystery troubled him so much on account of its being so *very* self-evident."

"Yes," said I, "I remember his merriment well. I really thought he would have fallen into convulsions."

"The material world," continued Dupin, "abounds with very strict analogies to the immaterial; and thus some color of truth has been given to the rhetorical dogma, that metaphor, or simile, may be made to strengthen an argument as well as to embellish a description. The principle of the *vis inertiae,* for example, seems to be identical in physics and metaphysics. It is not more true in the former, that a large body is with more difficulty set in motion than a smaller one, and that its subsequent *momentum* is commensurate with this difficulty, than it is, in the latter, that intellects of the vaster capacity, while more forcible, more constant, and more eventful in their movements than those of inferior grade, are yet the less readily moved, and more embarrassed, and full of hesitation in the first few steps of their progress. Again: have you ever noticed which of the street signs, over the shop doors, are the most attractive of attention?"

"I have never given the matter a thought," I said.

"There is a game of puzzles," he resumed, "which is played upon a map. One party playing requires another to find a given word—the name of town, river, state, or empire—any word, in short, upon the motley and perplexed surface of the chart. A novice in the game generally seeks to embarrass his opponents by giving them the most minutely lettered names; but the adept selects such words as stretch, in large characters, from one end of the chart to the other. These, like the over-largely lettered signs and placards of the street, escape observation by dint of being excessively obvious; and here the physical oversight is precisely analogous with the moral inapprehension by which the intellect suffers to pass unnoticed those considerations which are too obtrusively and too palpably self-evident. But this is a point, it appears, somewhat above or beneath the understanding of the Prefect. He never once thought it probable, or possible, that the Minister had deposited the letter immediately beneath the nose of the whole world by way of best preventing any portion of that world from perceiving it.

"But the more I reflected upon the daring, dashing, and discriminating ingenuity of D——; upon the fact that the document must always have been *at hand,* if he intended to use it to good purpose; and upon the decisive evidence, obtained by the Prefect, that it was not hidden within the limits of that dignitary's ordinary search—the more satisfied I became that, to conceal this letter, the Minister had resorted to the comprehensive and sagacious expedient of not attempting to conceal it at all.

"Full of these ideas, I prepared myself with a pair of green spectacles, and called one fine morning quite by accident, at the Ministerial hotel. I found D—— at home, yawning, lounging, and dawdling, as usual, and pretending to be in the last extremity of *ennui.* He is, perhaps, the most really energetic human being now alive—but that is only when nobody sees him.

"To be even with him, I complained of my weak eyes, and lamented the necessity of the spectacles, under cover of which I cautiously and thoroughly surveyed the whole apartment, while seemingly intent only upon the conversation of my host.

"I paid especial attention to a large writing-table near which he sat, and upon which lay confusedly, some miscellaneous letters and other papers, with one or two musical instruments and a few books. Here, however, after a long and very deliberate scrutiny, I saw nothing to excite particular suspicion.

"At length my eyes, in going the circuit of the room, fell upon a trumpery filigree card-rack of pasteboard, that hung dangling by a dirty blue ribbon, from a little brass knob just beneath the middle of the mantel-piece. In this rack, which had three or four compartments, were five or six visiting cards and a solitary letter. This last was much soiled and crumpled. It was torn nearly in two, across the middle—as if a design, in the first instance, to tear it entirely up as worthless, had been altered or stayed in the second. It had a large black seal, bearing the D—— cipher *very* conspicuously, and was addressed, in a diminutive female hand, to D——, the minister, himself. It was thrust carelessly, and even, as it seemed, contemptuously, into one of the uppermost divisions of the rack.

"No sooner had I glanced at this letter than I concluded it to be that of which I was in search. To be sure, it was, to all appearance, radically different from the one of which the Prefect had read us so minutely a description. Here the seal was large and black, with the D—— cipher; there it was small and red, with the ducal arms of the S—— family. Here, the address, to the Minister, was diminutive and feminine; there the superscription, to a certain royal personage, was markedly bold and decided; the size alone formed a point of correspondence. But, then, the *radicalness* of these differences, which was excessive; the dirt; the soiled and torn condition of the paper, so inconsistent with the *true* methodical habits of D——, and so suggestive of a design to delude the beholder into an idea of the worthlessness of the document;—these things, together with the hyperobtrusive situation of this document, full in the view of every visiter, and thus exactly in accordance with the conclusions to which I had previously arrived; these things, I say, were strongly corroborative of suspicion, in one who came with the intention to suspect.

"I protracted my visit as long as possible, and, while I maintained a most animated discussion with the Minister, upon a topic which I knew well had never failed to interest and excite him, I kept my attention really riveted upon the letter. In this examination, I committed to memory its external appearance and arrangement in the rack; and also fell, at length, upon a discovery which set at rest whatever trivial doubt I might have entertained. In scrutinizing the edges of the paper, I observed them to be more *chafed* than seemed necessary. They presented the *broken* appearance which is manifested when a stiff paper, having been once folded and pressed with a folder, is refolded in a reversed direction, in the same creases or edges which had formed the original fold. This discovery was sufficient. It was clear to me that the letter had been turned as a glove, inside out, re-directed and re-sealed. I bade the Minister good-morning, and took my departure at once, leaving a gold snuff-box upon the table.

"The next morning I called for the snuff-box, when we resumed, quite eagerly, the conversation of the preceding day. While thus engaged, however, a loud report, as if of a pistol, was heard immediately beneath the windows of the hotel, and was succeeded by a series of fearful screams, and the shoutings of a terrified mob. D—— rushed to a casement, threw it open, and looked out. In the meantime I stepped to the card-rack, took the letter, put it in my pocket, and replaced it by a *fac-simile,* (so far as regards externals) which I had carefully prepared at my lodgings—imitating the D—— cipher, very readily, by means of a seal formed of bread.

"The disturbance in the street had been occasioned by the frantic behavior of a man with a musket. He had fired it among a crowd of women and children. It proved, however, to have been without ball, and the fellow was suffered to go his way as a lunatic or a drunkard. When he had gone, D —— came from the window, whither I had followed him immediately upon securing the object in view. Soon afterward I bade him farewell. The pretended lunatic was a man in my own pay."

"But what purpose had you," I asked, "in replacing the letter by a *fac-simile?* Would it not have been better at the first visit, to have seized it openly, and departed?"

"D——," replied Dupin, "is a desperate man, and a man of nerve. His hotel, too, is not without attendants devoted to his interests. Had I made the wild attempt you suggest, I might never have left the Ministerial presence alive. The good people of Paris might have heard of me no more. But I had an object apart from these considerations. You know my political prepossessions. In this matter, I act as a partisan of the lady concerned. For eighteen months the Minister has had her in his power. She has now him in hers—since, being unaware that the letter is not in his possession, he will proceed with his exactions as if it was. Thus will he inevitably commit himself, at once, to his political destruction. His downfall, too, will not be more precipitate than awkward. It is all very well to talk about the *facilis descensus Averni;* but in all kinds of climbing, as Catalani said of singing, it is far more easy to get up than to come down. In the present instance I have no sympathy—at least no pity—for him who descends. He is that *monstrum horrendum,* an unprincipled man of genius. I confess, however, that I should like very well to know the precise character of his thoughts, when, being defied by her whom the Prefect terms 'a certain person-age,' he is reduced to opening the letter which I left for him in the card-rack."

"How? did you put any thing particular in it?"

"Why—it did not seem altogether right to leave the interior blank—that would have been insulting. D——, at Vienna once, did me an evil turn, which I told him, quite good-humoredly, that I should remember. So, as I knew he would feel some curiosity in regard to the identity of the person who had outwitted him, I thought it a pity not to give him a clew. He is well acquainted with my MS., and I just copied into the middle of the blank sheet the words—

"'Un dessein si funeste,
S'il n'est digne d' Atrée, est digne de Thyeste.'

They are to be found in Crébillon's 'Atrée.'"

QUESTIONS

1. Is the first-person narrator also the story's protagonist? Which character serves as the antagonist? Are protagonist and antagonist well matched?

2. How is point of view related to suspense and surprise? Discuss point of view and its usefulness in allowing Poe to conceal information.

3. Why does Dupin consider himself smarter than Monsieur G——, the Prefect of the Parisian police? Is the story of the game of "even and odd" an appropriate and revealing illustration?

4. Explain the relationship between Dupin's story of a "game of puzzles. . . played upon a map" and his solution of the crime.

5. Discuss the significance of the ironic epigraph.

6. Is the conflict physical, intellectual, moral, or emotional?

7. Although this story is famous as a detective tale, it contains elements of a vengeance story. What are these elements?

8. The crime is solved halfway through the story when Dupin gives Monsieur G—— the missing letter and receives payment for his services. Do you find the explanation in the second half interesting? boring? appropriate? informative?

9. The narrator views the initial arrival of Monsieur G—— as "something of a coincidence." But the story concerns the possibility of projecting oneself imaginatively into someone else's personality. Explain why the arrival of Monsieur G—— may not be a coincidence.

ARTHUR CONAN DOYLE

A Scandal in Bohemia

I

To Sherlock Holmes she is always *the* woman. I have seldom heard him mention her under any other name. In his eyes she eclipses and predominates the whole of her sex. It was not that he felt any emotion akin to love for Irene Adler. All emotions, and that one particularly, were abhorrent to his cold, precise, but admirably balanced mind. He was, I take it, the most perfect reasoning and observing machine that the world has seen; but, as a lover, he would have placed himself in a false position. He never spoke of the softer passions, save with a gibe and a sneer. They were admirable things for the observer—excellent for drawing the veil from men's motives and actions. But for the trained reasoner to admit such intrusions into his own delicate and finely adjusted temperament was to introduce a distracting factor which might throw a doubt upon all his mental results. Grit in a sensitive instrument, or a crack in one of his own high-power lenses, would not be more disturbing than a strong emotion in a nature such as his. And yet there was but one woman to him, and that woman was the late Irene Adler, of dubious and questionable memory.

I had seen little of Holmes lately. My marriage had drifted us away from each other. My own complete happiness, and the home-centered interests which rise up around the man who first finds himself master of his own establishment, were sufficient to absorb all my attention; while Holmes, who loathed every form of society with his whole Bohemian soul, remained in our lodgings in

246

Baker Street, buried among his old books, and alternating from week to week between cocaine and ambition, the drowsiness of the drug, and the fierce energy of his own keen nature. He was still, as ever, deeply attracted by the study of crime, and occupied his immense faculties and extraordinary powers of observation in following out those clues, and clearing up those mysteries, which had been abandoned as hopeless by the official police. From time to time I heard some vague account of his doings: of his summons to Odessa in the case of the Trepoff murder, of his clearing up of the singular tragedy of the Atkinson brothers at Trincomalee, and finally of the mission which he had accomplished so delicately and successfully for the reigning family of Holland. Beyond these signs of his activity, however, which I merely shared with all the readers of the daily press, I knew little of my former friend and companion.

One night—it was on the 20th of March, 1888—I was returning from a journey to a patient (for I had now returned to civil practice), when my way led me through Baker Street. As I passed the well-remembered door, which must always be associated in my mind with my wooing, and with the dark incidents of the Study in Scarlet, I was seized with a keen desire to see Holmes again, and to know how he was employing his extraordinary powers. His rooms were brilliantly lit, and, even as I looked up, I saw his tall, spare figure pass twice in a dark silhouette against the blind. He was pacing the room swiftly, eagerly, with his head sunk upon his chest and his hands clasped behind him. To me, who knew his every mood and habit, his attitude and manner told their own story. He was at work again. He had arisen out of his drug-created dreams, and was hot upon the scent of some new problem. I rang the bell, and was shown up to the chamber which had formerly been in part my own.

His manner was not effusive. It seldom was; but he was glad, I think, to see me. With hardly a word spoken, but with a kindly eye, he waved me to an armchair, threw across his case of cigars, and indicated a spirit case and a gasogene in the corner. Then he stood before the fire, and looked me over in his singular introspective fashion.

"Wedlock suits you," he remarked. "I think, Watson, that you have put on seven and a half pounds since I saw you."

"Seven!" I answered.

"Indeed, I should have thought a little more. Just a trifle more, I fancy, Watson. And in practice again, I observe. You did not tell me that you intended to go into harness."

"Then, how do you know?"

"I see it, I deduce it. How do I know that you have been getting yourself very wet lately, and that you have a most clumsy and careless servant girl?"

"My dear Holmes," said I, "this is too much. You would certainly have been burned, had you lived a few centuries ago. It is true that I had a country walk on Thursday and came home in a dreadful mess; but, as I have changed my clothes, I can't imagine how you deduce it. As to Mary Jane, she is incorrigible, and my wife has given her notice; but there, again, I fail to see how you work it out."

He chuckled to himself and rubbed his long, nervous hands together.

"It is simplicity itself," said he; "my eyes tell me that on the inside of your left shoe, just where the firelight strikes it, the leather is scored by six almost parallel cuts. Obviously they have been caused by some one who has very carelessly scraped round the edges of the sole in order to remove crusted mud from it. Hence, you see, my double deduction that you had been out in vile weather, and that you had a particularly malignant boot-slitting specimen of the London slavey. As to your practice, if a gentleman walks into my rooms smelling of iodoform, with a black mark of nitrate of silver upon his right forefinger, and a bulge on the side of his top-hat to show where he has secreted his stethoscope, I must be dull, indeed, if I do not pronounce him to be an active member of the medical profession."

I could not help laughing at the ease with which he explained his process of deduction. "When I hear you give your reasons," I remarked, "The thing always appears to me to be so ridiculously simple that I could easily do it myself, though at each successive instance of your reasoning I am baffled, until you explain your process. And yet I believe that my eyes are as good as yours."

"Quite so," he answered, lighting a cigarette, and throwing himself down into an arm-chair. "You see, but you do not observe. The distinction is clear. For example, you have frequently seen the steps which lead up from the hall to this room."

"Frequently."

"How often?"

"Well, some hundreds of times."

"Then how many are there?"

"How many? I don't know."

"Quite so! You have not observed. And yet you have seen. That is just my point. Now, I know that there are seventeen steps, because I have both seen and observed. By the way, since you are interested in these little problems, and since you are good enough to chronicle one or two of my trifling experiences, you may be interested in this." He threw over a sheet of thick, pink-tinted note-paper which had been lying open upon the table. "It came by the last post," said he. "Read it aloud."

The note was undated, and without either signature or address.

"There will call upon you to-night, at a quarter to eight o'clock," it said, "a gentleman who desires to consult you upon a matter of the very deepest moment. Your recent services to one of the royal houses of Europe have shown that you are one who may safely be trusted with matters which are of an importance which can hardly be exaggerated. This account of you we have from all quarters received. Be in your chamber then at that hour, and do not take it amiss if your visitor wear a mask."

"This is indeed a mystery," I remarked, "What do you imagine that it means?"

"I have no data yet. It is a capital mistake to theorize before one has data. Insensibly one begins to twist facts to suit theories, instead of theories to suit facts. But the note itself. What do you deduce from it?"

I carefully examined the writing, and the paper upon which it was written.

"The man who wrote it was presumably well to do," I remarked, endeavoring to imitate my companion's processes. "Such paper could not be bought under half a crown a packet. It is peculiarly strong and stiff."

"Peculiar—that is the very word," said Holmes. "It is not an English paper at all. Hold it up to the light."

I did so, and saw a large *E* with a small *g,* a *P,* and a large *G* with a small *t* woven into the texture of the paper.

"What do you make of that?" asked Holmes.

"The name of the maker, no doubt; or his monogram, rather."

"Not at all. The *G* with the small *t* stands for 'Gesellschaft,' which is the German for 'Company.' It is a customary contraction like our 'Co.' *P,* of course, stands for 'Papier.' now for the *Eg.* Let us glance at our Continental Gazetteer." He took down a heavy brown volume from his shelves. "Eglow, Eglonitz—here we are, Egria. It is in a German-speaking country—in Bohemia, not far from Carlsbad. 'Remarkable as being the scene of the death of Wallenstein, and for its numerous glass-factories and paper-mills.' Ha, ha, my boy, what do you make of that?" His eyes sparkled, and he sent up a great blue triumphant cloud from his cigarette.

"The paper was made in Bohemia," I said.

"Precisely. And the man who wrote is a German. Do you note the peculiar construction of the sentence—'This account of you we have from all quarters received.' A Frenchman or Russian could not have written that. It is the German who is so uncourteous to his verbs. It only remains, therefore, to discover what is wanted by this German who writes upon Bohemian paper, and prefers wearing a mask to showing his face. And here he comes, if I am not mistaken, to resolve all our doubts."

As he spoke there was the sharp sound of horses' hoofs and grating wheels against the curb, followed by a sharp pull at the bell. Holmes whistled.

"A pair, by the sound," said he. "Yes," he continued, glancing out of the window. "A nice little brougham and a pair of beauties. A hundred and fifty guineas apiece. There's money in this case, Watson, if there is nothing else."

"I think that I had better go, Holmes."

"Not a bit, doctor. Stay where you are. I am lost without my Boswell. And this promises to be interesting. It would be a pity to miss it."

"But your client—"

"Never mind him. I may want your help, and so may he. Here he comes. Sit down in that arm-chair, doctor, and give us your best attention."

A slow and heavy step, which had been heard upon the stairs and in the passage, paused immediately outside the door. Then there was a loud and authoritative tap.

"Come in!" said Holmes.

A man entered who could hardly have been less than six feet six inches in height, with the chest and limbs of a Hercules. His dress was rich with a richness which would, in England, be looked upon as akin to bad taste. Heavy bands of Astrakhan were slashed across the sleeves and fronts of his double-breasted coat, while the deep blue cloak which was thrown over his shoulders was lined with flame-colored silk, and secured at the neck with a brooch which consisted of a single flaming beryl. Boots which extended half-way up his calves, and which were trimmed at the tops with rich brown fur, completed the impression of barbaric opulence which was suggested by his whole appearance. He carried a broad-brimmed hat in his hand, while he wore across the upper part of his face, extending down past the cheekbones, a black vizard mask, which he had apparently adjusted that very moment, for his hand was still raised to it as he entered. From the lower part of the face he appeared to be a man of strong character, with a thick, hanging lip, and a long, straight chin, suggestive of resolution pushed to the length of obstinacy.

"You had my note?" he asked, with a deep harsh voice and a strongly marked German accent. "I told you that I would call." He looked from one to the other of us, as if uncertain which to address.

"Pray take a seat," said Holmes. "This is my friend and colleague, Dr. Watson, who is occasionally good enough to help me in my cases. Whom have I the honor to address?"

"You may address me as the Count Von Kramm, a Bohemian nobleman. I understand that this gentleman, your friend, is a man of honor and discretion, whom I may trust with a matter of the most extreme importance. If not, I should much prefer to communicate with you alone."

I rose to go, but Holmes caught me by the wrist and pushed me back into my chair. "It is both, or none," said he. "You may say before this gentleman anything which you may say to me."

The count shrugged his broad shoulders. "Then I must begin," said he, "by binding you both to absolute secrecy for two years, at the end of that time the matter will be of no importance. At present it is not too much to say that it is of such weight it may have an influence upon European history ."

"I promise," said Holmes.

"And I."

"You will excuse this mask," continued our strange visitor. "The august person who employs me wishes his agent to be unknown to you, and I may confess at once that the title by which I have just called myself is not exactly my own."

"I was aware of it," said Holmes, dryly.

"The circumstances are of great delicacy, and every precaution has to be taken to quench what might grow to be an immense scandal and seriously compromise one of the reigning families of Europe. To speak plainly, the matter implicates the great House of Ormstein, hereditary kings of Bohemia."

"I was also aware of that," murmured Holmes, settling himself down in his arm-chair and closing his eyes.

Our visitor glanced with some apparent surprise at the languid, lounging figure of the man who had been no doubt depicted to him as the most incisive reasoner and most energetic agent in Europe. Holmes slowly reopened his eyes and looked impatiently at his gigantic client.

"If your Majesty would condescend to state your case," he remarked, "I should be better able to advise you."

The man sprang from his chair and paced up and down the room in uncontrollable agitation. Then, with a gesture of desperation, he tore the mask from his face and hurled it upon the ground. "You are right," he cried; "I am the King. Why should I attempt to conceal it?"

"Why indeed?" murmured Holmes. "Your Majesty had not spoken before I was aware that I was addressing Wilhelm Gottsreich Sigismond von Ormstein, Grand Duke of Cassel-Felstein, and hereditary King of Bohemia."

"But you can understand," said our strange visitor, sitting down once more and passing his hand over his high, white forehead, "you can understand that I am not accustomed to doing such business in my own person. Yet the matter was so delicate that I could not confide it to an agent without putting myself in his power. I have come *incognito* from Prague for the purpose of consulting you."

"Then, pray consult," said Holmes, shutting his eyes once more.

"The facts are briefly these: Some five years ago, during a lengthy visit to Warsaw, I made the acquaintance of the well-known adventuress, Irene Adler. The name is no doubt familiar to you."

"Kindly look her up in my index, doctor," murmured Holmes, without opening his eyes. For many years he had adopted a system of docketing all paragraphs concerning men and things, so that it was difficult to name a subject or a person on which he could not at once furnish information. In this case I found her biography sandwiched in between that of a Hebrew Rabbi and that of a staff-commander who had written a monograph upon the deep-sea fishes.

"Let me see!" said Holmes. "Hum! Born in New Jersey in the year 1858. Contralto—hum! La Scala, hum! Prima donna Imperial Opera of Warsaw—Yes! Retired from operatic stage—ha! Living in London—quite so! Your Majesty, as I understand, became entangled with this young person, wrote her some compromising letters, and is now desirous of getting those letters back."

"Precisely so. But how—"

"Was there a secret marriage?"

"None."

"No legal papers or certificates?"

"None."

"Then I fail to follow your Majesty. If this young person should produce her letters for blackmailing or other purposes, how is she to prove their authenticity?"

"There is the writing."

"Pooh, pooh! Forgery."

"My private note-paper."

"Stolen."

"My own seal."

"Imitated."

"My photograph."

"Bought."

"We were both in the photograph."

"Oh dear! That is very bad! Your Majesty has indeed committed an indiscretion."

"I was mad—insane."

"You have compromised yourself seriously."

"I was only Crown Prince then. I was young. I am but thirty now."

"It must be recovered."

"We have tried and failed."

"Your Majesty must pay. It must be bought."

"She will not sell."

"Stolen, then."

"Five attempts have been made. Twice burglars in my pay ransacked her house. Once we diverted her luggage when she traveled. Twice she has been waylaid. There has been no result."

"No sign of it?"

"Absolutely none."

Holmes laughed. "It is quite a pretty little problem," said he.

"But a very serious one to me," returned the King, reproachfully.

"Very, indeed. And what does she propose to do with the photograph?"

"To ruin me."

"But how?"

"I am about to be married."

"So I have heard."

"To Clotilde Lothman von Saxe-Meningen, second daughter of the King of Scandinavia. You may know the strict principles of her family. She is herself the very soul of delicacy. A shadow of a doubt as to my conduct would bring the matter to an end."

"And Irene Adler?"

"Threatens to send them the photograph. And she will do it. I know that she will do it. You do not know her, but she has a soul of steel. She has the face of the most beautiful of women, and the mind of the most resolute of men. Rather than I should marry another woman, there are no lengths to which she would not go—none."

"You are sure that she has not sent it yet?"

"I am sure."

"And why?"

"Because she has said that she would send it on the day when the betrothal was publicly proclaimed. That will be next Monday."

"Oh, then, we have three days yet," said Holmes, with a yawn. "That is very fortunate, as I have one or two matters of importance to look into just at present. Your Majesty will, of course, stay in London for the present?"

"Certainly. You will find me at the Langham, under the name of the Count Von Kramm."

"Then I shall drop you a line to let you know how we progress."

"Pray do so. I shall be all anxiety."

"Then, as to money?"

"You have *carte blanche*."

"Absolutely?"

"I tell you that I would give one of the provinces of my kingdom to have that photograph."

"And for present expenses?"

The king took a heavy chamois leather bag from under his cloak and laid it on the table.

"There are three hundred pounds in gold and seven hundred in notes," he said.

Holmes scribbled a receipt upon a sheet of his note-book and handed it to him.

"And mademoiselle's address?" he asked.

"Is Briony Lodge, Serpentine Avenue, St. John's Wood."

Holmes took a note of it. "One other question," said he. "Was the photograph a cabinet?"

"It was."

"Then, good-night, your Majesty, and I trust that we shall soon have some good news for you. And good-night, Watson," he added, as the wheels of the royal brougham rolled down the street. "If you will be good enough to call to-morrow afternoon, at three o'clock, I should like to chat this little matter over with you."

II

At three o'clock precisely I was at Baker Street, but Holmes had not yet returned. The landlady informed me that he had left the house shortly after eight o'clock in the morning. I sat down beside the fire, however, with the intention of awaiting him, however long he might be. I was already deeply interested in his inquiry, for, though it was surrounded by none of the grim and strange features which were associated with the two crimes which I have already recorded, still, the nature of the case and the exalted station of his client gave it a character of its own. Indeed, apart from the nature of the investigation which my friend had on hand, there was something in his masterly grasp of a situation, and his keen, incisive reasoning, which made it a pleasure to me to study his system of work, and to follow the quick, subtle methods by which he disentangled the most inextricable mysteries. So accustomed was I to his invariable success that the very possibility of his failing had ceased to enter into my head.

It was close upon four before the door opened, and a drunken-looking groom, ill-kempt and side-whiskered, with an inflamed face and disreputable clothes, walked into the room. Accustomed as I was to my friend's amazing powers in the use of disguises, I had to look three times before I was certain that it was indeed he. With a nod he vanished into the bedroom, whence he emerged in five minutes tweed-suited and respectable as of old. Putting his hands into his pockets, he stretched out his legs in front of the fire, and laughed heartily for some minutes.

"Well, really!" he cried, and then he choked; and laughed again until he was obliged to lie back, limp and helpless, in the chair.

"What is it?"

"It's quite too funny. I am sure you could never guess how I employed my morning, or what I ended by doing."

"I can't imagine. I suppose that you have been watching the habits, and perhaps the house, of Miss Irene Adler."

"Quite so; but the sequel was rather unusual. I will tell you, however. I left the house a little after eight o'clock this morning, in the character of a groom out of work. There is a wonderful sympathy and freemasonry among horsey men. Be one of them, and you will know all that there is to know. I soon found Briony Lodge. It is a *bijou* villa, with a garden at the back, but built out in front right up to the road, two stories. Chubb lock to the door. Large sitting-room on the right side, well furnished, with long windows almost to the floor, and those preposterous English window fasteners which a child could open. Behind there was nothing remarkable, save that the passage window could be reached from the top of the coach-house. I walked round it and examined it closely from every point of view, but without noting anything else of interest.

"I then lounged down the street, and found, as I expected, that there was a mews in a lane which runs down by one wall of the garden. I lent the ostlers a hand in rubbing down their horses, and I received in exchange twopence, a glass of half-and-half, two fills of shag tobacco, and as much information as I could desire about Miss Adler, to say nothing of half a dozen other people in the neighborhood in whom I was not in the least interested, but whose biographies I was compelled to listen to."

"And what of Irene Adler?" I asked.

"Oh, she has turned all the men's heads down in that part. She is the daintiest thing under a bonnet on this planet. So say the Serpentine-mews, to a man. She lives quietly, sings at concerts, drives out at five every day, and returns at seven sharp for dinner. Seldom goes out at other times, except when she sings. Has only one male visitor, but a good deal of him. He is dark, handsome, and dashing, never calls less than once a day, and often twice. He is a Mr. Godfrey Norton, of the Inner Temple. See the advantages of a cabman as a confidant. They had driven him home a dozen times from Serpentine-mews, and knew all about him. When I had listened to all that they had to tell, I began to walk up and down near Briony Lodge once more, and to think over my plan of campaign.

"This Godfrey Norton was evidently an important factor in the matter. He was a lawyer. That sounded ominous. What was the relation between them, and what the object of his repeated visits? Was she his client, his friend, or his mistress? If the former, she had probably transferred the photograph to his keeping. If the latter, it was less likely. On the issue of this question depended whether I should continue my work at Briony Lodge, or turn my attention to the gentleman's chambers in the Temple. It was a delicate point, and it widened the field of my inquiry. I fear that I bore you with these details, but I have to let you see my little difficulties, if you are to understand the situation."

"I am following you closely," I answered.

"I was still balancing the matter in my mind, when a hansom cab drove up to Briony Lodge, and a gentleman sprang out. He was a remarkably handsome man, dark, aquiline, and mustached—evidently the man of whom I had heard. He appeared to be in a great hurry, shouted to the cabman to wait, and brushed past the maid who opened the door with the air of a man who was thoroughly at home.

"He was in the house about half an hour, and I could catch glimpses of him in the windows of the sitting-room, pacing up and down, talking excitedly, and waving his arms. Of her I could see nothing. Presently he emerged, looking even more flurried than before. As he stepped up to the cab, he pulled a gold watch from his pocket and looked at it earnestly. 'Drive like the devil,' he shouted, 'first to Gross & Hankey's in Regent Street, and then to the church of St. Monica in the Edgware Road. Half a guinea if you do it in twenty minutes!'

"Away they went, and I was just wondering whether I should not do well to follow them, when up the lane came a neat little landau, the coachman with his coat only half-buttoned, and his tie under his ear, while all the tags of his harness were sticking out of the buckles. It hadn't pulled up before she shot out of the hall door and into it. I only caught a glimpse of her at the moment, but she was a lovely woman, with a face that a man might die for.

"'The Church of St. Monica, John,' she cried, 'and half a sovereign if you reach it in twenty minutes.'

"This was quite too good to lose, Watson. I was just balancing whether I should run for it, or whether I should perch behind her landau, when a cab came through the street. The driver looked twice at such a shabby fare; but I jumped in before he could object. 'The Church of St. Monica,' said I, 'and half a sovereign if you reach it in twenty minutes.' It was twenty-five minutes to twelve, and of course it was clear enough what was in the wind.

"My cabby drove fast. I don't think I ever drove faster, but the others were there before us. The cab and the landau with their steaming horses were in front of the door when I arrived. I paid the man and hurried into the church. There was not a soul there save the two whom I had followed and a surpliced clergyman, who seemed to be expostulating with them. They were all three standing in a knot in front of the altar. I lounged up the side aisle like any other idler who has dropped into a church. Suddenly, to my surprise, the three at the altar faced round to me, and Godfrey Norton came running as hard as he could towards me."

"Thank God!" he cried. "You'll do. Come! Come!"

"What then?" I asked.

"Come, man, come, only three minutes, or it won't be legal."

I was half-dragged up to the altar, and, before I knew where I was, I found myself mumbling responses which were whispered in my ear, and vouching for things of which I knew nothing, and generally assisting in the secure tying up of Irene Adler, spinster, to Godfrey Norton, bachelor. It was all done in an instant, and there was the gentleman thanking me on the one side and the lady on the other, while the clergyman beamed on me in front. It was the most preposterous position in which I ever found myself in my life, and it was the thought of it that started me laughing just now. It seems that there had been some informality about their license, that the clergyman absolutely refused to marry them without a witness of some sort, and that my lucky appearance saved the bridegroom from having to sally out into the streets in search of a best man. The bride gave me a sovereign, and I mean to wear it on my watch-chain in memory of the occasion."

"This is a very unexpected turn of affairs," said I; "and what then?"

"Well, I found my plans very seriously menaced. It looked as if the pair might take an immediate departure, and so necessitate very prompt and energetic measures on my part. At the church door, however, they separated, he driving back to the Temple, and she to her own house. 'I shall drive out in the park at five as usual,' she said, as she left him. I heard no more. They drove away in different directions, and I went off to make my own arrangements."

"Which are?"

"Some cold beef and a glass of beer," he answered, ringing the bell. "I have been too busy to think of food, and I am likely to be busier still this evening. By the way, doctor, I shall want your co-operation."

"I shall be delighted."

"You don't mind breaking the law?"

"Not in the least."

"Nor running a chance of arrest?"

"Not in a good cause."

"Oh, the cause is excellent!"

"Then I am your man."

"I was sure that I might rely on you."

"But what is it you wish?"

"When Mrs. Turner has brought in the tray I will make it clear to you. Now," he said, as he turned hungrily on the simple fare that our landlady had provided, "I must discuss it while I eat, for I have not much time. It is nearly five now. In two hours we must be on the scene of action. Miss Irene, or Madame, rather, returns from her drive at seven. We must be at Briony Lodge to meet her."

"And what then?"

"You must leave that to me. I have already arranged what is to occur. There is only one point on which I must insist. You must not interfere, come what may. You understand?"

"I am to be neutral?"

"To do nothing whatever. There will probably be some small unpleasantness. Do not join in it. It will end in my being conveyed into the house. Four or five minutes afterwards the sitting-room window will open. You are to station yourself close to that open window."

"Yes."

"You are to watch me, for I will be visible to you."

"Yes."

"And when I raise my hand—so—you will throw into the room what I give you to throw, and will, at the same time, raise the cry of fire. You quite follow me?"

"Entirely."

"It is nothing very formidable," he said, taking a long cigar-shaped roll from his pocket. "It is an ordinary plumber's smoke-rocket, fitted with a cap at either end to make it self-lighting. Your task is confined to that. When you raise your cry of fire, it will be taken up by quite a number of people. You may then walk to the end of the street, and I will rejoin you in ten minutes. I hope that I have made myself clear?"

"I am to remain neutral, to get near the window, to watch you, and, at the signal, to throw in this object, then to raise the cry of fire, and to wait you at the corner of the street."

"Precisely."

"Then you may entirely rely on me."

"That is excellent. I think, perhaps, it is almost time that I prepare for the new role I have to play."

He disappeared into his bedroom, and returned in a few minutes in the character of an amiable and simple-minded Nonconformist clergyman. His broad black hat, his baggy trousers, his white tie, his sympathetic smile, and general look of peering and benevolent curiosity were such as Mr. John Hare alone could have equalled. It was not merely that Holmes changed his costume. His expression, his manner, his very soul seemed to vary with every fresh part that he assumed. The stage lost a fine actor, even as science lost an acute reasoner, when he became a specialist in crime.

It was a quarter past six when we left Baker Street, and it still wanted ten minutes to the hour when we found ourselves in Serpentine Avenue. It was already dusk, and the lamps were just being lighted as we paced up and down in front of Briony Lodge, waiting for the coming of its occupant. The house was just such as I had pictured it from Sherlock Holmes' succinct description, but the locality appeared to be less private than I expected. On the contrary, for a small street in a quiet neighborhood, it was remarkably animated. There was a group of shabbily-dressed men smoking and laughing in a corner, a scissors-grinder with his wheel, two guardsmen who were flirting with a nurse-girl, and several well-dressed young men who were lounging up and down with cigars in their mouths.

"You see," remarked Holmes, as we paced to and fro in front of the house, "This marriage rather simplifies matters. The photograph becomes a double-edged weapon now. The chances are that she would be as averse to its being seen by Mr. Godfrey Norton, as our client is to its coming to the eyes of his princess. Now the question is, Where are we to find the photograph?"

"Where, indeed?"

"It is most unlikely that she carries it about with her. It is cabinet size. Too large for easy concealment about a woman's dress. She knows that the King is capable of having her waylaid and searched. Two attempts of the sort have already been made. We may take it, then, that she does not carry it about with her."

"Where, then?"

"Her banker or her lawyer. There is that double possibility. But I am inclined to think neither. Women are naturally secretive, and they like to do their own secreting. Why should she hand it over to any one else? She could trust her own guardianship, but she could not tell what indirect or political influence might be brought to bear upon a business man. Besides, remember that she had resolved to use it within a few days. It must be where she can lay her hands upon it. It must be in her own house."

"But it was twice been burgled."

"Pshaw! They did not know how to look."

"But how will you look?"

"I will not look."

"What then?"

"I will get her to show me."

"But she will refuse."

"She will not be able to. But I hear the rumble of wheels. It is her carriage. Now carry out my orders to the letter."

As he spoke the gleam of the side-lights of a carriage came round the curve of the avenue. It was a smart little landau which rattled up to the door of Briony Lodge. As it pulled up, one of the loafing men at the corner dashed forward to open the door in the hope of earning a copper, but was elbowed away by another loafer, who had rushed up with the same intention. A fierce quarrel broke out, which was increased by the two guardsmen, who took sides with one of the loungers, and by the scissors-grinder, who was equally hot upon the other side. A blow was struck, and in an instant the lady, who had stepped from her carriage, was the centre of a little knot of flushed and struggling men, who struck savagely at each other with their fists and sticks. Holmes dashed into the crowd to protect the lady; but just as he reached her he gave a cry and dropped to the ground, with the blood running freely down his face. At his fall the guardsmen took to their heels in one direction and the loungers in the other, while a number of better dressed people, who had watched the scuffle without taking part in it, crowded in to help the lady and to attend to the injured man. Irene Adler, as I will still call her, had hurried up the steps; but she stood at the top with her superb figure outlined against the lights of the hall, looking back into the street.

"Is the poor gentleman much hurt?" she asked.

"He is dead," cried several voices.

"No, no, there's life in him!" shouted another. "But he'll be gone before you can get him to hospital."

"He's a brave fellow," said a woman. "They would have had the lady's purse and watch if it hadn't been for him. They were a gang, and a rough one, too. Ah, he's breathing now."

"He can't lie in the street. May we bring him in marm?"

"Surely. Bring him into the sitting-room. There is a comfortable sofa. This way, please!"

Slowly and solemnly he was borne into Briony Lodge and laid out in the principal room, while I still observed the proceedings from my post by the window. The lamps had been lit, but the blinds had not been drawn, so that I could see Holmes as he lay upon the couch. I do not know whether he was seized with compunction at that moment for the part he was playing, but I know that I never felt more heartily ashamed of myself in my life than when I saw the beautiful creature against whom I was conspiring, or the grace and kindliness with which she waited upon the injured man. And yet it would be the blackest treachery to Holmes to draw back now from the part which he had intrusted to me. I hardened my heart, and took the smoke-rocket from under my ulster. After all, I thought, we are not injuring her. We are but preventing her from injuring another.

Holmes had sat up upon the couch, and I saw him motion like a man who is in need of air. A maid rushed across and threw open the window. At the same instant I saw him raise his hand, and at the signal I tossed my rocket into the room with a cry of "Fire!" The word was no sooner out of my mouth than the whole crowd of spectators, well dressed and ill—gentlemen, ostlers, and servant-maids—joined in a general shriek of "Fire!" Thick clouds of smoke curled through the room and out at the open window. I caught a glimpse of rushing figures, and a moment later the voice of Holmes from within assuring them that it was a false alarm. Slipping through the shouting crowd I made my way to the corner of the street, and in ten minutes was rejoiced to find my friend's arm in mine, and to get away from the scene of uproar. He walked swiftly and in silence for some few minutes, until we had turned down one of the quiet streets which lead towards the Edgware Road.

"You did it very nicely, doctor," he remarked. "Nothing could have been better. It is all right."

"You have the photograph?"

"I know where it is."

"And how did you find out?"

"She showed me, as I told you that she would."

"I am still in the dark."

"I do not wish to make a mystery," said he, laughing. "The matter was perfectly simple. You, of course, saw that every one in the street was an accomplice. They were all engaged for the evening."

"I guessed as much."

"Then, when the row broke out, I had a little moist red paint in the palm of my hand. I rushed forward, fell down, clapped my hand to my face, and became a piteous spectacle. It is an old trick."

"That also I could fathom."

"Then they carried me in. She was bound to have me in. What else could she do? And into her sitting-room, which was the very room which I suspected. It lay between that and her bedroom, and I was determined to see which. They laid me on a couch, I motioned for air, they were compelled to open the window, and you had your chance."

"How did that help you?"

"It was all-important. When a woman thinks that her house is on fire, her instinct is at once to rush to the thing which she values most. It is a perfectly overpowering impulse, and I have more than once taken advantage of it. In the case of the Darlington Substitution Scandal it was of use to me, and also in the Arnsworth Castle business. A married woman grabs at her baby; an unmarried one reaches for her jewel-box. Now it was clear to me that our lady of to-day had nothing in the house more precious to her than what we are in quest of. She would rush to secure it. The alarm of fire was admirably done. The smoke and shouting were enough to shake nerves of steel. She responded beautifully. The photograph is in a recess behind a sliding panel just above the right bell-pull. She was there in an instant, and I caught glimpse of it as she half-drew it out. When I cried out that it was a false alarm, she replaced it, glanced at the rocket, rushed from the room, and I have not seen her since. I rose, and, making my excuses, escaped from the house. I hesitated whether to attempt to secure the photograph at once; but the coachman had come in, and as he was watching me narrowly, it seemed safer to wait. A little over-precipitance may ruin all."

"And now?" I asked.

"Our quest is practically finished. I shall call with the King to-morrow, and with you, if you care to come with us. We will be shown into the sitting-room to wait for the lady, but it is probable that when she comes she may find neither us nor the photograph. It might be a satisfaction to His Majesty to regain it with his own hands."

"And when will you call?"

"At eight in the morning. She will not be up, so that we shall have a clear field. Besides, we must be prompt, for this marriage may mean a complete change in her life and habits. I must wire to the King without delay."

We had reached Baker Street, and had stopped at the door. He was searching his pockets for the key, when some one passing said:

"Good-night, Mister Sherlock Holmes."

There were several people on the pavement at the time, but the greeting appeared to come from a slim youth in an ulster who had hurried by.

"I've heard that voice before," said Holmes, staring down the dimly-lit street. "Now, I wonder who the deuce that could have been."

III

I slept at Baker Street that night, and we were engaged upon our toast and coffee in the morning when the King of Bohemia rushed into the room.

"You have really got it!" he cried, grasping Sherlock Holmes by either shoulder, and looking eagerly into his face.

"Not yet."

"But you have hopes?"

"I have hopes."

"Then, come. I am all impatience to be gone."

"We must have a cab."

"No, my brougham is waiting."

"Then that will simplify matters." We descended, and started off once more for Briony Lodge.

"Irene Adler is married," remarked Holmes.

"Married! When?"

"Yesterday."

"But to whom?"

"To an English lawyer named Norton."

"But she could not love him?"

"I am in hopes that she does."

"And why in hopes?"

"Because it would spare your Majesty all fear of future annoyance. If the lady loves her husband, she does not love your Majesty. If she does not love your Majesty, there is no reason why she should interfere with your Majesty's plan."

"It is true. And yet— Well! I wish she had been of my own station! What a queen she would have made!" He relapsed into a moody silence, which was not broken until we drew up to Serpentine Avenue.

The door of Briony Lodge was open, and an elderly woman stood upon the steps. She watched us with a sardonic eye as we stepped from the brougham.

"Mr. Sherlock Holmes, I believe?" said she.

"I am Mr. Holmes," answered my companion, looking at her with a questioning and rather startled gaze.

"Indeed! My mistress told me that you were likely to call. She left this morning with her husband by the 5:15 train from Charing Cross for the Continent."

"What!" Sherlock Holmes staggered back, white with chagrin and surprise. "Do you mean that she has left England?"

"Never to return."

"And the papers?" asked the King, hoarsely. "All is lost."

"We shall see." He pushed past the servant and rushed into the drawing-room, followed by the King and myself. The furniture was scattered about in every direction, with dismantled shelves and open drawers, as if the lady had hurriedly ransacked them before her flight. Holmes rushed at the bell-pull, tore back a small sliding shutter, and, plunging in his hand, pulled out a photograph and a letter. The photograph was of Irene Adler herself in evening dress, the letter was superscribed to "Sherlock Holmes, Esq. To be left till called for." My friend tore it open, and we all three read it together. It was dated at midnight of the preceding night, and ran in this way:

"My dear Mr. Sherlock Holmes,
    You really did it very well. You took me in completely. Until after

the alarm of fire, I had not a suspicion. But then, when I found how I had betrayed myself, I began to think. I had been warned against you months ago. I had been told that, if the King employed an agent, it would certainly be you. And your address had been given me. Yet, with all this, you made me reveal what you wanted to know. Even after I became suspicious, I found it hard to think evil of such a dear, kind old clergyman. But, you know, I have been trained as an actress myself. Male costume is nothing new to me. I often take advantage of the freedom which it gives. I sent John, the coachman, to watch you, ran up-stairs, got into my walking-clothes, as I call them, and came down just as you departed.

"Well, I followed you to your door, and so made sure that I was really an object of interest to the celebrated Mr. Sherlock Holmes. Then I, rather imprudently, wished you good-night, and started for the Temple to see my husband.

"We both thought the best resource was flight, when pursued by so formidable an antagonist; so you will find the nest empty when you call to-morrow. As to the photograph, your client may rest in peace. I love and am loved by a better man than he. The King may do what he will without hinderance from one whom he has cruelly wronged. I keep it only to safeguard myself, and to preserve a weapon which will always secure me from any steps which he might take in the future. I leave a photograph which he might care to possess; and I remain, dear Mr. Sherlock Holmes, very truly yours,

Irene Norton, née Adler."

"What a woman—oh, what a woman!" cried the King of Bohemia, when we had all three read this epistle. "Did I not tell you how quick and resolute she was? Would she not have made an admirable queen? Is it not a pity that she was not on my level?"

"From what I have seen of the lady she seems indeed to be on a very different level to your Majesty," said Holmes, coldly. "I am sorry that I have not been able to bring your Majesty's business to a more successful conclusion."

"On the contrary, my dear sir," cried the King; "nothing could be more successful. I know that her word is inviolate. The photograph is now as safe as if it were in the fire."

"I am glad to hear your Majesty say so."

"I am immensely indebted to you. Pray tell me in what way I can reward you. This ring—" He slipped an emerald snake ring from his finger and held it out upon the palm of his hand.

"Your Majesty has something which I should value even more highly," said Holmes.

"You have but to name it."

"This photograph!"

The King stared at him in amazement.

"Irene's photograph!" he cried. "Certainly, if you wish it."

"I thank your Majesty. Then there is no more to be done in the matter. I have the honor to wish you a very good-morning." He bowed, and, turning away without observing the hand which the King had stretched out to him, he set off in my company for his chambers.

And that was how a great scandal threatened to affect the kingdom of Bohemia, and how the best plans of Mr. Sherlock Holmes were beaten by a woman's wit. He used to make merry over the cleverness of women, but I have not heard him do it of late. And when he speaks of Irene Adler, or when he refers to her photograph, it is always under the honorable title of *the* woman.

QUESTIONS

1. The first paragraph provides a set piece. Explain. Based on what follows, is Watson's description accurate?

2. When Holmes greets Watson after a lengthy absence, he makes several deductions based on Watson's appearance. What are they? Are they accurate? What do they reveal about Holmes? about Watson? about Arthur Conan Doyle as a storyteller?

3. How does the anonymous note serve to advance the plot and reveal the differences between Holmes and Watson?

4. Holmes says to Watson, "Stay where you are. I am lost without my Boswell." What is the meaning of this remark?

5. Are any of the characters evil? criminals? Does the solution fit the crime?

6. How does point of view serve the purpose of mystery?

7. Describing Holmes, Watson says, "The stage lost a fine actor, even as science lost an acute reasoner, when he became a specialist in crime." Is Holmes the only character in the story with acting ability?

8. Preparatory to throwing the smoke bomb, Watson rationalizes his role as Holmes' accomplice. Do you agree with his justification?

9. As further payment for his service, Holmes asks for Irene Adler's photograph. Is this request consistent with his views on women and with his personality as revealed in this story?

FRANZ KAFKA

A Hunger Artist

Translation by Willa and Edwin Muir

During these last decades the interest in professional fasting has markedly diminished. It used to pay very well to stage such great performances under one's own management, but today that is quite impossible. We live in a different world now. At one time the whole town took a lively interest in the hunger artist; from day to day of his fast the excitement mounted; everybody wanted to see him at least once a day; there were people who bought season tickets for the last few days and sat from morning till night in front of his small barred cage; even in the nighttime there were visiting hours, when the whole effect was heightened by torch flares; on fine days the cage was set out in the open air, and then it was the children's special treat to see the hunger artist; for their elders he was often just a joke that happened to be in fashion, but the children stood open-mouthed, holding each other's hands for greater security, marveling at him as he sat there pallid in black tights, with his ribs sticking out so prominently, not even on a seat but down among straw on the ground, sometimes giving a courteous nod, answering questions with a constrained smile, or perhaps stretching an arm through the bars so that one might feel how thin it was, and then again withdrawing deep into himself, paying no attention to anyone or anything, not even to the all-important striking of the clock that was the only piece of furniture in his cage, but merely staring into vacancy with half-shut eyes, now and then taking a sip from a tiny glass of water to moisten his lips.

Besides casual onlookers there were also relays of permanent watchers selected by the public, usually butchers, strangely enough, and it was their task to watch the hunger artist day and night, three of them at a time, in case he should have some secret recourse to nourishment. This was nothing but a formality, instituted to reassure the masses, for the initiates knew well enough that during his fast the artist would never in any circumstances, not even under forcible compulsion, swallow the smallest morsel of food; the honor of his profession forbade it. Not every watcher, of course, was capable of understanding this, there were often groups of night watchers who were very lax in carrying out their duties and deliberately huddled together in a retired corner to play cards with great absorption, obviously intending to give the hunger artist the chance of a little refreshment, which they supposed he could draw from some private hoard. Nothing annoyed the artist more than such watchers; they made him miserable; they made his fast seem unendurable; sometimes he mastered his feebleness sufficiently to sing during their watch for as long as he could keep going, to show them how unjust their suspicions were. But that was of little use; they only wondered at his cleverness in being able to fill his mouth even while singing. Much more to his taste were the watchers who sat close up to the bars, who were not content with the dim night lighting of the hall but focused him in the full glare of the electric pocket torch given them by the impresario. The harsh light did not trouble him at all, in any case he could never sleep properly, and he could always drowse a little, whatever the light, at any hour, even when the hall was thronged with noisy onlookers. He was quite happy at the prospect of spending a sleepless night with such watchers; he was ready to exchange jokes with them, to tell them stories out of his nomadic life, anything at all to keep them awake and demonstrate to them again that he had no eatables in his cage and that he was fasting as not one of them could fast. But his happiest moment was when the morning came and an enormous breakfast was brought them, at his expense, on which they flung themselves with the keen appetite of healthy men after a weary night of wakefulness. Of course there were people who argued that this breakfast was an unfair attempt to bribe the watchers, but that was going rather too far, and when they were invited to take on a night's vigil without a breakfast, merely for the sake of the cause, they made themselves scarce, although they stuck stubbornly to their suspicions.

Such suspicions, anyhow, were a necessary accompaniment to the profession of fasting. No one could possibly watch the hunger artist continuously, day and night, and so no one could produce first-hand evidence that the fast had really been rigorous and continuous; only the artist himself could know that, he was therefore bound to be the sole completely satisfied spectator of his own fast. Yet for other reasons he was never satisfied; it was not perhaps mere fasting that has brought him to such skeleton thinness that many people had regretfully to keep away from his exhibitions, because the sight of him was too much for them, perhaps it was dissatisfaction with himself that had worn him down. For he alone knew, what no other initiate knew, how easy it was to fast. It was the easiest thing in the world. He made no secret of this, yet people did not believe him, at the best they set him down as modest, most of them, however, thought he was out for publicity or else was some kind of cheat who found it easy to fast because he had discovered a way of making it easy, and then had the impudence to admit the fact, more or less. He had to put up with all that, and in the course of time had got used to it, but his inner dissatisfaction always rankled, and never yet, after any term of fasting—this must be granted to his credit—had he left the cage of his own free will. The longest period of fasting was fixed by his impresario at forty days, beyond that term he was not allowed to go, not even in great cities, and there was good reason for it, too. Experience had proved that for about forty days the interest of the public could be stimulated by a steadily increasing pressure of advertisement, but after that the town began to lose interest, sympathetic support began notably to fall off; there were of course local variations as between one town and another or one country and another, but as a general rule forty days marked the limit. So on the fortieth day the flower-bedecked cage was opened, enthusiastic spectators filled the hall, a military band played, two doctors entered the cage to measure the results of the fast, which were announced through a megaphone, and finally two young ladies appeared, blissful at having been selected for the honor, to help the hunger artist down the few steps leading to a small table on which was spread a carefully chosen invalid repast. And at this very moment the artist always turned stubborn. True, he would entrust his bony arms to the outstretched helping hands of the ladies bending over him, but stand up he would not. Why stop fasting at this particular moment, after forty days of it? He had held out for a long time, an illimitably long time; why stop now, when he was in his best fasting form, or rather, not yet quite in his best fasting form? Why should he be cheated of the fame he would get for fasting longer, for being not only the record hunger artist of all time, which presumably he was already, but for beating his own record by a performance beyond human imagination, since he felt that there were no limits to his capacity for fasting? His public pretended to admire him so much, why should it have so little patience with him; if he could endure fasting longer, why shouldn't the public endure it? Besides, he was tired, he was comfortable sitting in the straw, and now he was supposed to lift himself to his full height and go down to a meal the very thought of which gave him a nausea that only the presence of the ladies kept him from betraying, and even that with an effort. And he looked up into the eyes of the ladies who were apparently so friendly and in reality so cruel, and shook his head, which felt too heavy on its strengthless neck. But then there happened yet again what always happened. The impresario came forward, without a word—for the band made speech impossible—lifted his arms in the air above the artist, as if inviting Heaven to look down upon its creature here in the straw, this suffering martyr, which indeed he was, although in quite another sense; grasped him round the emaciated waist, with exaggerated caution, so that the frail condition he was in might be appreciated; and committed him to the care of the blenching ladies, not without secretly giving him a shaking so that his legs and body tottered and swayed. The artist now submitted completely; his head lolled on his breast as if it had landed there by chance; his body was hollowed out; his legs in a spasm of self-preservation clung close to each other at the knees, yet scraped on the ground as if it were not really solid ground, as if they were only trying to find solid ground; and the whole weight of his body, a featherweight after all, relapsed onto one of the ladies, who, looking round for help and panting a little—this post of honor was not at all what she had expected it to be—first stretched her neck as far as she could to keep her face at least free from contact with the artist, then finding this impossible, and her more fortunate companion not coming to her aid but merely holding extended on her own trembling hand the little bunch of knucklebones that was the artist's, to the great delight of the spectators burst into tears and had to be replaced by an attendant who had long been stationed in readiness. Then came the food, a little of which the impresario managed to get between the artist's lips, while he sat in a kind of half-fainting trance, to the accompaniment of cheerful patter designed to distract the public's attention from the artist's condition; after that, a toast was drunk to the public, supposedly prompted by a whisper from the artist in the impresario's ear; the band confirmed it with a mighty flourish, the spectators melted away, and no one had any cause to be dissatisfied with the proceedings, no one except the hunger artist himself, he only, as always.

So he lived for many years, with small regular intervals of recuperation, in visible glory, honored by the world, yet in spite of that troubled in spirit, and all the more troubled because no one would take his trouble seriously. What comfort could he possibly need? What more could he possibly wish for? And if some good-natured person, feeling sorry for him, tried to console him by pointing out that his melancholy was probably caused by fasting, it could happen, especially when he had been fasting for some time, that he reacted with an outburst of fury and to the general alarm began to shake the bars of his cage like a wild animal. Yet the impresario had a way of punishing these outbreaks which he rather enjoyed putting into operation. He would apologize publicly for the artist's behavior, which was only to be excused, he admitted, because of the irritability caused by fasting; a condition hardly to be understood by well-fed people; then by natural transition he went on to mention the artist's equally incomprehensible boast that he could fast for much longer than he was doing; he praised the high ambition, the good will, the great self-denial undoubtedly implicit in such a statement; and then quite simply countered it by bringing out photographs, which were also on sale to the public, showing the artist on the fortieth day of a fast lying in bed almost dead from exhaustion. This perversion of the truth, familiar to the artist though it was, always unnerved him afresh and proved too much for him. What was a consequence of the premature ending of his fast was here presented as the cause of it! To fight against this lack of understanding, against a whole world of non-understanding, was impossible. Time and again in good faith he stood by the bars listening to the impresario, but as soon as the photographs appeared he always let go and sank with a groan back on to his straw, and the reassured public could once more come close and gaze at him.

A few years later when the witnesses of such scenes called them to mind, they often failed to understand themselves at all. For meanwhile the aforementioned change in public interest had set in; it seemed to happen almost overnight; there may have been profound causes for it, but who was going to bother about that; at any rate the pampered hunger artist suddenly found himself deserted one fine day by the amusement seekers, who went streaming past him to other more favored attractions. For the last time the impresario hurried him over half Europe to discover whether the old interest might still survive here and there; all in vain; everywhere, as if by secret agreement, a positive revulsion from professional fasting was in evidence. Of course it could not really have sprung up so suddenly as all that, and many premonitory symptoms which had not been sufficiently remarked or suppressed during the rush and glitter of success now came retrospectively to mind, but it was now too late to take any countermeasures. Fasting would surely come into fashion again at some future date, yet that was no comfort for those living in the present. What, then, was the hunger artist to do? He had been applauded by thousands in his time and could hardly come down to showing himself in a street booth at village fairs, and as for adopting another profession, he was not only too old for that but too fanatically devoted to fasting. So he took leave of the impresario, his partner in an unparalleled career, and hired himself to a large circus; in order to spare his own feelings he avoided reading the conditions of his contract.

A large circus with its enormous traffic in replacing and recruiting men, animals and apparatus can always find a use for people at any time, even for a hunger artist, provided of course that he does not ask too much, and in this particular case anyhow it was not only the artist who was taken on but his famous and long-known name as well, indeed considering the peculiar nature of his performance, which was not impaired by advancing age, it could not be objected that here was an artist past his prime, no longer at the height of his professional skill, seeking a refuge in some quiet corner of a circus; on the contrary, the hunger artist averred that he could fast as well as ever, which was entirely credible, he even alleged that if he were allowed to fast as he liked, and this was at once promised him without more ado, he could astound the world by establishing a record never yet achieved, a statement which certainly provoked a smile among the other professionals, since it left out of account the change in public opinion, which the hunger artist in his zeal conveniently forgot.

He had not, however, actually lost his sense of the real situation and took it as a matter of course that he and his cage should be stationed, not in the middle of the ring as a main attraction, but outside, near the animal cages, on a site that was after all easily accessible. Large and gaily painted placards made a frame for the cage and announced what was to be seen inside it. When the public came thronging out in the intervals to see the animals, they could hardly avoid passing the hunger artist's cage and stopping there for a moment, perhaps they might even have stayed longer had not those pressing behind them in the narrow gangway, who did not understand why they should be held up on their way toward the excitements of the menagerie, made it impossible for anyone to stand gazing quietly for any length of time. And that was the reason why the hunger artist, who had of course been looking forward to these visiting hours as the main achievement of his life, began instead to shrink from them. At first he could hardly wait for the intervals; it was exhilarating to watch the crowds come streaming his way, until only too soon—not even the most obstinate self-deception, clung to almost consciously, could hold out against the fact—the conviction was borne in upon him that these people, most of them, to judge from their actions, again and again, without exception, were all on their way to the menagerie. And the first sight of them from the distance remained the best. For when they reached his cage he was at once deafened by the storm of shouting and abuse that arose from the two contending factions, which renewed themselves continuously, of those who wanted to stop and stare at him—he soon began to dislike them more than the others—not out of real interest but only out of obstinate self-assertiveness, and those who wanted to go straight on to the animals. When the first great rush was past, the stragglers came along, and these, whom nothing could have prevented from stopping to look at him as long as they had breath, raced past with long strides, hardly even glancing at him, in their haste to get to the menagerie in time. And all too rarely did it happen that he had a stroke of luck, when some father of a family fetched up before him with his children, pointed a finger at the hunger artist and explained at length what the phenomenon meant, telling stories of earlier years when he himself had watched similar but much more thrilling performances, and the children, still rather uncomprehending, since neither inside nor outside school had they been sufficiently prepared for this lesson—what did they care about fasting?—yet showed by the brightness of their intent eyes that new and better times might be coming. Perhaps, said the hunger artist to himself many a time, things would be a little better if his cage were set not quite so near the menagerie. That made it too easy for people to make their choice, to say nothing of what he suffered from the stench of the menagerie, the animals' restlessness of night, the carrying past of raw lumps of flesh for the beasts of prey, the roaring at feeding times, which depressed him continually. But he did not dare to lodge a complaint with the management; after all, he had the animals to thank for the troops of people who passed his cage, among whom there might always be one here and there to take an interest in him, and who could tell where they might seclude him if he called attention to his existence and thereby to the fact that, strictly speaking, he was only an impediment on the way to the menagerie.

A small impediment, to be sure, one that grew steadily less. People grew familiar with the strange idea that they could be expected, in times like these, to take an interest in a hunger artist, and with this familiarity the verdict went out against him. He might fast as much as he could, and he did so; but nothing could save him now, people passed him by. Just try to explain to anyone the art of fasting! Anyone who has no feeling for it cannot be made to understand it. The fine placards grew dirty and illegible, they were torn down; the little notice board telling the number of fast days achieved, which at first was changed carefully every day, had long stayed at the same figure, for after the first few weeks even this small task seemed pointless to the staff; and so the artist simply fasted on and on, as he had once dreamed of doing, and it was no trouble to him, just as he had always foretold, but no one counted the days, no one, not even the artist himself, knew what records he was already breaking, and his heart grew heavy. And when once in a time some leisurely passer-by stopped, made merry over the old figure on the board and spoke of swindling, that was in its way the stupidest lie ever invented by indifference and inborn malice, since it was not the hunger artist who was cheating; he was working honestly, but the world was cheating him of his reward.

Many more days went by, however, and that too came to an end. An overseer's eye fell on the cage one day and he asked the attendants why this perfectly good cage should be left standing there unused with dirty straw inside it; nobody knew, until one man, helped out by the notice board, remembered about the hunger artist. They poked into the straw with sticks and found him in it. "Are you still fasting?" asked the overseer. "When on earth do you mean to stop?" "Forgive me, everybody," whispered the hunger artist; only the overseer, who had his ear to the bars, understood him. "Of course," said the overseer, and tapped his forehead with a finger to let the attendants know what state the man was in, "we forgive you." "I always wanted you to admire my fasting," said the hunger artist. "We do admire it," said the overseer, affably. "But you shouldn't admire it," said the hunger artist. "Well, then we don't admire it," said the overseer, "but why shouldn't we admire it?" "Because I have to fast, I can't help it," said the hunger artist. "What a fellow you are," said the overseer, "and why can't you help it?" "Because," said the hunger artist, lifting his head a little and speaking, with his lips pursed, as if for a kiss, right into the overseer's ear, so that no syllable might be lost, "because I couldn't find the food I liked. If I had found it, believe me, I should have made no fuss and stuffed myself like you or anyone else." These were his last words, but in his dimming eyes remained the firm though no longer proud persuasion that he was still continuing to fast.

"Well, clear this out now!" said the overseer, and they buried the hunger artist, straw and all. Into the cage they put a young panther. Even the most insensitive felt it refreshing to see this wild creature leaping around the cage that had so long been dreary. The panther was all right. The food he liked was brought him without hesitation by the attendants; he seemed not even to miss his freedom; his noble body, furnished almost to the bursting point with all that it needed, seemed to carry freedom around with it too; somewhere in his jaws it seemed to lurk; and the joy of life streamed with such ardent passion from his throat that for the onlookers it was not easy to stand the shock of it. But they braced themselves crowded round the cage, and did not want ever to move away.

QUESTIONS

1. How does the first sentence foreshadow the action that follows?
2. The omniscient narrator relies heavily on narrative summary to depict action rather than on dramatization through dialogue. At the conclusion of the story,

however, the hunger artist speaks to the overseer. What is the effect of using dialogue at this time?

3. The meaning of this story lies at the level of symbolism. What does the hunger artist symbolize?

4. Even when public fasting was fashionable and attracted large crowds, the hunger artist had detracters. Expalin the symbolic significance of the "watchers" described in the second paragraph.

5. At times, the story seems to demand that it be read as religious allegory. Find evidence to support this statement.

6. Explain why the hunger artist was the only "completely satisfied spectator of his own fast" and yet was never satisfied with his performance. Discuss the symbolic meaning of this paradox.

7. Discuss the differences between the impresario's treatment of the hunger artist and the overseer's. Which treatment is more honest? What do the impresario and the overseer represent?

8. What does the hunger artist's cage symbolize? Does he like or dislike being caged?

9. The hunger artist dies without knowing the length of his final fast and therefore does not know the records he has broken. Discuss the significance of this statement.

10. Is the hunger artist a sympathetic character? unsympathetic? pathetic? admirable? How does your reaction to the hunger artist affect your interpretation of the story's theme.

11. Is the panther a suitable substitute for the hunger artist? unsuitable? different but acceptable? Explain.

PHILIP ROTH

"I Always Wanted You to Admire My Fasting"; or, Looking at Kafka

*To the students of English 275,
University of Pennsylvania,
Fall 1972*

"I always wanted you to admire my fasting," said the hunger artist. "We do admire it," said the overseer, affably. "But you shouldn't admire it," said the hunger artist. "Well then we don't admire it," said the overseer, "but why shouldn't we admire it?" "Because I have to fast, I can't help it," said the hunger artist. "What a fellow you are," said the overseer, "and why can't you help it?" "Because," said the hunger artist, lifting his head a little and speaking, with his lips pursed, as if for a kiss, right into the overseer's ear, so that no syllable might be lost, "because I couldn't find the food I liked. If I had found it, believe me, I should have made no fuss and stuffed myself like you or anyone else." These were his last words, but in his dimming eyes remained the firm though no longer proud persuasion that he was still continuing to fast.

—*"A Hunger Artist,"* Franz Kafka

1

I am looking, as I write of Kafka, at the photograph taken of him at the age of forty (my age)—it is 1924, as sweet and hopeful a year as he may ever have known as a man, and the year of his death. His face is sharp and skeletal, a burrower's face: pronounced cheekbones made even more conspicuous by the absence of sideburns; the ears shaped and angled on his head like angel wings; an intense, creaturely gaze of startled composure—enormous fears, enormous control; a black towel of Levantine hair pulled close around the skull the only sensuous feature; there is a familiar Jewish flare in the bridge of the nose, the nose itself is long and weighted slightly at the tip—the nose of half the Jewish boys who were my friends in high school. Skulls chiseled like this one were shoveled by the thousands from the ovens; had he lived, his would have been among them, along with the skulls of his three younger sisters. Of course it is no more horrifying to think of Franz Kafka in Auschwitz than to think of anyone in Auschwitz—to paraphrase Tolstoy, it is just horrifying in its own way. But he died too soon for the holocaust. Had he lived, perhaps he would have escaped with his good friend and great advocate Max Brod, who eventually found refuge in Palestine, a citizen of Israel until his death there in 1970. But *Kafka* escaping? It seems unlikely for one so fascinated by entrapment and careers that culminate in anguished death. Still, there is Karl Rossman, his American greenhorn. Having imagined Karl's escape to America and his mixed luck here, could not Kafka have found a way to execute an escape for himself. The New School for Social Research in New York becoming *his* Great Nature Theater of Oklahoma? Or perhaps through the influence of Thomas Mann, a position in the German department at Princeton . . . But then had Kakfa lived it is not at all certain that the books of his which Mann celebrated from *his* refuge in New Jersey would ever have been published; eventually Kafka might either have destroyed those manuscripts that he had once bid Max Brod to dispose of at his death, or, at the least, continued to keep them his secret. The Jewish refugee arriving in America in 1938 would not then have been Mann's "religious humorist," but a frail and bookish fifty-five-year-old bachelor, formerly a lawyer for a government insurance firm in Prague, retired on a pension in Berlin at the time of Hitler's rise to power—an author, yes, but of a few eccentric stories, mostly about animals, stories no one in America had ever heard of and only a handful in Europe had read; a homeless K., but without K.'s willfulness and purpose, a homeless Karl, but without Karl's youthful spirit and resilience; just a Jew lucky enough to have escaped with his life, in his possession a suitcase containing some clothes, some family photos, some Prague mementos, and the manuscripts, still unpublished and in pieces, of *Amerika, The Trial, The Castle,* and (stranger things happen) three more fragmented novels, no less remarkable than the bizarre masterworks that he keeps to himself out of Oedipal timidity, perfectionist madness, and insatiable longings for solitude and spiritual purity.

July, 1923: Eleven months before he will die in a Vienna sanatorium, Kafka somehow finds the resolve to leave Prague and his father's home for good. Never before has he even remotely succeeded in living apart, independent of his mother, his sisters and his father, nor has he been a writer other than in those few hours when he is not working in the legal department of the Workers' Accident Insurance Office in Prague; since taking his law degree at the university, he has been by all reports the most dutiful and scrupulous of employees, though he finds the work tedious and enervating. But in June of 1923—having some months earlier been pensioned from his job because of his illness—he meets a young Jewish girl of nineteen at a seaside resort in Germany, Dora Dymant, an employee at the vacation camp of the Jewish People's Home of Berlin. Dora has left her Orthodox Polish family to make a life of her own (at half Kafka's age); she and Kafka—who has just turned forty—fall in love . . . Kafka has by now been engaged to two somewhat more conventional Jewish girls—twice to one of them—hectic, anguished engagements wrecked largely by his fears. "I am mentally incapable of marrying," he writes his father in the forty-five-page letter he gave to his mother to deliver, " . . . the moment I make up my mind to marry I can no longer sleep, my head burns day and night, life can no longer be called life." He explains why. "Marrying is barred to me," he tells his father, "because it is your domain. Sometimes I imagine the map of the world spread out and you stretched diagonally across it. And I feel as if I could consider living in only those regions that either are not covered by you or are not within your reach. And in keeping with the conception I have of your magnitude, these are not many and not very comforting regions—and marriage is not among them." The letter explaining what is wrong between this father and this son is dated November, 1919; the mother thought it best not even to deliver it, perhaps for lack of courage, probably, like the son, for lack of hope.

During the following two years Kafka attempts to wage an affair with Milena Jesenská-Pollak, an intense young woman of twenty-four who has translated a few of his stories into Czech and is most unhappily married in Vienna; his affair with Milena, conducted feverishly, but by and large through the mails, is even more demoralizing to Kafka than the fearsome engagements to the nice Jewish girls. They aroused only the paterfamilias longings that he dared not indulge, longings inhibited by his exaggerated awe of his father—"spellbound," says Brod, "in the family circle"—and the hypnotic spell of his own solitude; but the Czech Milena, impetuous, frenetic, indifferent to conventional restraints, a woman of appetite and anger, arouses more elemental yearnings and more elemental fears. According to a Prague critic, Rio Preisner, Milena was "psychopathic"; according to Margaret Buber-Neumann, who lived two years beside her in the German concentration camp where Milena died following a kidney operation in 1944, she was powerfully sane, extraordinarily humane and courageous. Milena's obituary for Kafka was the only one of consequence to appear in the Prague press; the prose is strong, so are the claims she makes for Kafka's accomplishment. She is still only in her twenties, the dead man is hardly known as a writer beyond his small circle of friends—yet Milena writes, "His knowledge of the world was exceptional and deep, and he was a deep and exceptional world in himself . . . [He had] a delicacy of feeling bordering on the miraculous and a mental clarity that was terrifyingly uncompromising, and in turn he loaded on to his illness the whole burden of his mental fear of life . . . He wrote the most important books in recent German literature." One can imagine this vibrant young woman stretched diagonally across the bed, as awesome to

Kafka as his own father spread out across the map of the world. His letters to her are disjointed, unlike anything else of his in print; the word fear, frequently emphasized, appears on page after page. "We are both married, you in Vienna, I to my Fear in Prague." He yearns to lay his head upon her breast; he calls her "Mother Milena"; during at least one of their two brief rendezvous, he is hopelessly impotent. At last he has to tell her to leave him be, an edict that Milena honors though it leaves her hollow with grief. "Do not write," Kafka tells her, "and let us not see each other; I ask you only to quietly fulfill this request of mine; only on those conditions is survival possible for me; everything else continues the process of destruction."

Then in the early summer of 1923, during a visit to his sister who is vacationing with her children by the Baltic Sea, he finds young Dora Dymant, and within a month Franz Kafka has gone off to live with her in two rooms in a suburb of Berlin, out of reach at last of the "claws" of Prague and home. How can it be? How can he, in his illness, have accomplished so swiftly and decisively the leave-taking that was so beyond him in his healthiest days? The impassioned letter-writer who could equivocate interminably about which train to catch to Vienna to meet with Milena (if he should meet with her for the weekend at all); the bourgeois suitor in the high collar, who, during his drawn-out agony of an engagement with the proper Fräulein Bauer, secretly draws up a memorandum for himself, countering the arguments "for" marriage with the arguments "against"; the poet of the ungraspable and the unresolved, whose belief in the immovable barrier separating the wish from its realization is at the heart of his excruciating visions of defeat, the Kafka whose fictions refute every easy, touching, humanish daydream of salvation and justice and fulfillment with densely imagined counter-dreams that mock all solutions and escapes—this Kafka, escapes! Overnight! K. penetrates the Castle walls—Joseph K. evades his indictment—"a breaking away from it altogether, a mode of living completely outside the jurisdiction of the court." Yes, the possibility of which Joseph K. has just a glimmering in the Cathedral but can neither fathom nor effectuate—"not . . . some influential manipulation of the case, but . . . a circumvention of it"— Kafka realizes in the last year of his life.

Was it Dora Dymant or was it death that pointed the new way? Perhaps it could not have been one without the other. We know that the "illusory emptiness" at which K. gazed upon first entering the village and looking up through the mist and the darkness to the Castle was no more vast and incomprehensible than was the idea of himself as a husband and father to the young Kafka; but now it seems the prospect of a Dora forever, of a wife, home, and children everlasting, is no longer the terrifying, bewildering prospect it would once have been, for now "everlasting" is undoubtedly not much more than a matter of months. Yes, the dying Kafka is determined to marry, and writes to Dora's Orthodox father for his daughter's hand. But the imminent death that has resolved all contradictions and uncertainties in Kafka is the very obstacle placed in his path by the young girl's father. The request of Franz Kafka, a dying man, to bind to him in his invalidism Dora Dymant, a healthy young girl is—denied!

If there is not one father standing in Kafka's way, there is another—and, to be sure, another beyond him. Dora's father, writes Max Brod in his biography of Kafka, "set off with [Kafka's] letter to consult the man he honored most, whose authority counted more than anything else for him, the 'Gerer Rebbe.' The rabbi read the letter, put it to one side, and said nothing more than the single syllable, 'No.'" *No.* Klamm himself could have been no more abrupt—or any more removed from the petitioner. *No.* In its harsh finality, as telling and inescapable as the curselike threat delivered by his father to Georg Bendemann, that thwarted fiancé: "Just take your bride on your arm and try getting in my way. I'll sweep her from your very side, you don't know how!" *No.* Thou shalt not have, say the fathers, and Kafka agrees that he shall not. The habit of obedience and renunciation; also his own distaste for the diseased and reverence for strength, appetite, and health. "Well, clear this out now!' said the overseer, and they buried the hunger artist, straw and all. Into the cage they put a young panther. Even the most insensitive felt it refreshing to see this wild creature leaping around the cage that had so long been dreary. The panther was all right. The food he liked was brought him without hesitation by the attendants; he seemed not even to miss his freedom; his noble body, furnished almost to the bursting point with all that it needed, seemed to carry freedom around with it too; somewhere in his jaws it seemed to lurk; and the joy of life streamed with such ardent passion from his throat that for the onlookers it was not easy to stand the shock of it. But they braced themselves, crowded around the cage, and did not want ever to move away." So no is no; he knew as much himself. A healthy young girl of nineteen cannot, *should* not, be given in matrimony to a sickly man twice her age, who spits up blood ("I sentence you," cries Georg Bendemann's father, "to death by drowning!") and shakes in his bed with fevers and chills. What sort of un-Kafka-like dream had Kafka been dreaming?

And those nine months spent with Dora have still other "Kafka-esque" elements: a fierce winter in quarters inadequately heated; the inflation that makes a pittance of his own meager pension, and sends into the streets of Berlin the hungry and needy whose sufferings, says Dora, turn Kafka "ash-gray"; and his tubercular lungs, flesh transformed and punished. Dora cares as devotedly and tenderly for the diseased writer as does Gregor Samsa's sister for her brother, the bug. Gregor's sister plays the violin so beautifully that Gregor "felt as if the way were opening before him to the unknown nourishment he craved"; he dreams, in his condition, of sending his gifted sister to the Conservatory! Dora's music is Hebrew, which she reads aloud to Kafka, and with such skill that, according to Brod, "Franz recognized her dramatic talent; on his advice and under his direction she later educated herself in the art . . ."

Only Kafka is hardly vermin to Dora Dymant, *or to himself.* Away from Prague and his father's home, Kafka, in his fortieth year, seems at last to have been delivered from the self-loathing, the self-doubt, and those guilt-ridden impulses to dependence and self-effacement that had nearly driven him mad throughout his twenties and thirties; all at once he seems to have shed the pervasive sense of hopeless despair that informs the great punitive fantasies of *The Trial,* "The Penal Colony," and "The Metamorphosis." Years earlier, in Prague, he had directed Max Brod to destroy all his papers, including three unpublished novels, upon his death; now, in Berlin, when Brod introduces him to a German publisher interested in his work, Kafka consents to the publication of a volume of four stories, and consents, says Brod, "without much need of long arguments to persuade him." With Dora to help, he diligently resumes his study of Hebrew; despite his illness and the harsh winter, he travels to the Berlin Academy for Jewish Studies to attend a series of lectures on the Talmud—a very different Kafka from the estranged melancholic who once wrote in his diary, "What have I in common with the Jews? I have hardly anything in common with myself and should stand very quietly in a corner, content that I can breathe." And to further mark the change, there is ease and happiness with a woman: with this young and adoring companion, he is playful, he is pedagogical, and one would guess, in light of his illness (*and* his happiness), he is chaste. If not a husband (such as he had striven to be to the conventional Frälein Bauer), if not a lover (as he struggled hopelessly to be with Milena), he would seem to have become something no less miraculous in his scheme of things: a father, a kind of father to this sisterly, mothering daughter. *As Franz Kafka awoke one morning from uneasy dreams he found himself tranformed in his bed into a father, a writer and a Jew.*

"I have completed the construction of my burrow," begins the long, exquisite, and tedious story that he wrote that winter in Berlin, "and it seems to be successful. . . . Just the place where, according to my calculations, the Castle Keep should be, the soil was very loose and sandy and had literally to be hammered and pounded into a firm state to serve as a wall for the beautifully vaulted chamber. But for such tasks the only tool I possess is my forehead. So I had to run with my forehead thousands and thousands of times, for whole days and nights, against the ground, and I was glad when the blood came, for that was proof that the walls were beginning to harden; in that way, as everybody must admit, I richly paid for my Castle Keep." "The Burrow" is the story of an animal with a keen sense of peril whose life is organized around the principle of defense, and whose deepest longings are for security and serenity; with teeth and claws—*and* forehead—the burrower constructs an elaborate and ingeniously intricate system of underground chambers and corridors that are designed to afford it some peace of mind; however, while this burrow does succeed in reducing the sense of danger from without, its maintenance and protection are equally fraught with anxiety: "these anxieties are different from ordinary ones, prouder, richer in content, often long repressed, but in their destructive effects they are perhaps much the same as the anxieties that existence in the outer world gives rise to." The story (whose ending is lost) terminates with the burrower fixated upon distant subterranean noises that cause it "to assume the existence of a great beast," itself burrowing in the direction of the Castle Keep.

Another grim tale of entrapment, and of obsession so absolute that no distinction is possible between character and predicament. Yet this fiction imagined in the last "happy" months of his life is touched with a spirit of personal reconciliation and sardonic self-acceptance, with a tolerance for one's own brand of madness, that is not apparent in "The Metamorphosis"; the piercing masochistic irony of the early animal story—as of "The Judgment" and *The Trial*—has given way here to a critique of the self and its preoccupations that, though bordering on mockery, no longer seeks to resolve itself in images of the uttermost humiliation and defeat . . . But there is more here than a metaphor for the insanely defended ego, whose striving for invulnerability produces a defensive system that must in its turn become the object of perpetual concern— that is also a very unromantic and hard-headed fable about how and why art is made, a portrait of the artist in all his ingenuity, anxiety, isolation, dissatisfaction, relentlessness, obsessiveness, secretiveness, paranoia, and self-addiction, a portrait of the magical thinker at the end of his tether, Kafka's Prospero . . . It is an infinitely suggestive story, this story of life in a hole. For, finally, remember the proximity of Dora Dymant during the months that Kafka was at work on "The Burrow" in the two underheated rooms that was their illicit home. Certainly a dreamer like Kafka need never have entered the young girl's body for her tender presence to kindle in him a fantasy of a hidden orifice that promises "satisfied desire," "achieved ambition," and "profound slumber," but that once penetrated and in one's possession, arouses the most terrifying and heartbreaking fears of retribution and loss. "For the rest I try to unriddle the beast's plans. Is it on its wanderings, or is it working on its own burrow? If it is on its wanderings then perhaps an understanding with it might be possible. If it should really break through to the burrow I shall give it some of my stores and it will go on its way again. It will go on its way again, a fine story! Lying in my heap of earth I can naturally dream of all sorts of things, even of an understanding with the beast, though I know well enough that no such thing can happen, and that at the instant when we see each other, more, at the moment when we merely guess at each other's presence, we shall blindly bare our claws and teeth . . ."

He died of tuberculosis of the lungs and the larynx a month short of his forty-first birthday, June 3, 1924. Dora, inconsolable, whispers for days afterward, "My love, my love, my good one . . ."

2

1942. I am nine; my Hebrew school teacher, Dr. Kafka, is fifty-nine. To the little boys who must attend his "four to five" class each afternoon, he is known— in part because of his remote and melancholy foreignness, but largely because we vent on him our resentment at having to learn an ancient calligraphy at the very hour we should be out screaming our heads off on the ballfield—he is known as Dr. Kishka. Named, I confess, by me. His sour breath, spiced with intestinal juices by five in the afternoon, makes the Yiddish word for "insides" particularly telling. I think. Cruel, yes, but in truth I would have cut out my tongue had I ever imagined the name would become legend. A coddled child, I do not yet think of myself as persuasive, nor, quite yet, as a literary force in the world. My jokes don't hurt, how could they, I'm so adorable. And if you don't believe me, just ask my family and the teachers in school. Already at nine, one foot in Harvard, the other in the Catskills. Little Borscht Belt comic that I am outside the classroom, I amuse my friends Schlossman and Ratner on the dark walk home from Hebrew school with an imitation of Kishka, his precise and finicky professorial manner, his German accent, his cough, his gloom. "Doctor *Kishka!*" cries Schlossman, and hurls himself savagely against the newsstand that belongs to the candy store owner whom Schlossman drives just a little crazier each night. "Doctor Franz—Doctor Franz—Doctor Franz—*Kishka!*" screams Ratner, and my chubby little friend who lives upstairs from me on nothing but chocolate milk and Mallomars does not stop laughing until, as is his wont (his mother has asked me "to keep an eye on him" for just this reason), he wets his pants. Schlossman takes the occasion of Ratner's humiliation to pull the little boy's paper out of his notebook and wave it in the air—it is the assignment Dr. Kafka has just returned to us, graded; we were told to make up an alphabet of our own, out of straight lines and curved lines and dots. "That is all an alphabet is," he had explained. "That is all Hebrew is. That is all English is. Straight lines and curved lines and dots." Ratner's alphabet, for which he received a C, looks like twenty-six skulls strung in a row. I received my A for a curlicued alphabet inspired largely (as Dr. Kafka would seem to have surmised from his comment at the top of the page) by the number eight. Schlossman received an F for forgetting even to do it—and a lot he seems to care, too. He is content—he is *overjoyed*—with things as they are. Just waving a piece of paper in the air, and screaming, *"Kishka! Kishka!"* makes him deliriously happy. We should all be so lucky.

At home, alone in the glow of my goose-necked "desk" lamp (plugged after dinner into an outlet in the kitchen, my study) the vision of our refugee teacher, sticklike in a fraying three-piece blue suit, is no longer very funny— particularly after the entire beginner's Hebrew class, of which I am the most studious member, takes the name "Kishka" to its heart. My guilt awakens redemptive fantasies of heroism. I have them often about "the Jews in Europe." I must save him. If not me, who? The demonic Schlossman? The babyish Ratner? And if not now, when? For I have learned in the ensuing weeks that Dr. Kafka lives in "a room" in the house of an elderly Jewish lady on the shabby lower stretch of Avon Avenue, where the trolley still runs, and the poorest of Newark's Negroes shuffle meekly up and down the street, for all they seem to know still back in Mississippi. A *room*. And *there!* My family's apartment is no palace, but it is ours at least, so long as we pay the thirty-eight-fifty a month in rent; and though our neighbors are not rich, they refuse to be poor and they refuse to be meek. Tears of shame and sorrow in my eyes, I rush into the living room to tell my parents what I have heard (though not that I heard it during a quick game of "aces up" played a minute before class against the synagogue's rear wall—worse, played directly beneath a stained glass window embossed with the names of the dead): "My Hebrew teacher lives in a *room*."

My parents go much further than I could imagine anybody going in the real world. Invite him to dinner, my mother says. *Here?* Of course here—Friday night; I'm sure he can stand a home-cooked meal and a little pleasant company. Meanwhile my father gets on the phone to call my Aunt Rhoda, who lives with my grandmother and tends her and her potted plants in the apartment house at the corner of our street. For nearly two decades now my father has been introducing my mother's forty-year-old "baby" sister to the Jewish bachelors and widowers of New Jersey. No luck so far. Aunt Rhoda, an "interior decorator" in the dry goods department of "The Big Bear," a mammoth merchandise and produce market in industrial Elizabeth, wears falsies (this information by way of my older brother) and sheer frilly blouses, and family lore has it that she spends hours in the bathroom every day applying powders and sweeping her stiffish hair up into a dramatic pile on her head; but despite all this dash and display, she is, in my father's words, "still afraid of the facts of life." He, however, is undaunted, and administers therapy regularly and gratis: "Let 'em squeeze ya, Rhoda—it *feels* good!" I am his flesh and blood, I can reconcile myself to such scandalous talk in our kitchen—*but what will Dr. Kafka think?* Oh, but it's too late to do anything now. The massive machinery of matchmaking has been set in motion by my undiscourageable father, and the smooth engines of my proud homemaking mother's hospitality are already purring away. To throw my body into the works in an attempt to bring it all to a halt—well, I might as well try to bring down the New Jersey Bell Telephone Company by leaving our receiver off the hook. Only Dr. Kafka can save me now. But to my muttered invitation, he replies, with a formal bow that turns me scarlet—who has ever seen a person do such a thing outside of a movie house?—he replies that he would be *honored* to be my family's dinner guest. "My aunt," I rush to tell him, "will be there too." It appears that I have just said something mildly humorous; odd to see Dr. Kafka smile. Sighing, he says, "I will be delighted to meet her." Meet her? He's supposed to *marry* her. How do I warn him? And how do I warn Aunt Rhoda (a very great admirer of me and my marks) about his sour breath, his roomer's pallor, his Old World ways, so at odds with her up-to-dateness? My face feels as if it will ignite of its own—and spark the fire that will engulf the synagogue, Torah and all—when I see Dr. Kafka scrawl our address in his notebook, and beneath it, some words *in German.* "Good night, Dr. Kafka!" "Good night, and thank you, thank you." I turn to run, I go, but not fast enough: out on the street I hear Schlossman—that fiend!—announcing to my classmates who are punching one another under the lamplight down from the synagogue steps (where a card game is also in progress, organized by the Bar Mitzvah boys): "Roth invited Kishka to his *house!* To *eat!*"

Does my father do a job on Kafka! Does he make a sales pitch for familial bliss! What it means to a man to have two fine boys and a wonderful wife! Can Dr. Kafka imagine what that's like? The thrill? The satisfaction? The pride? He tells our visitor of the network of relatives on his mother's side that are joined in a "family association" of over two hundred and fifty people located in seven states, including the state of Washington! Yes, relatives even in the Far West: here are their photographs, Dr. Kafka; this is a beautiful book we published entirely on our own for five dollars a copy, pictures of every member of the family, including infants, and a family history by "Uncle" Lichtblau, the eighty-five-year-old patriarch of the clan. This is our family newsletter that is published twice a year and distributed nationwide to all the relatives. This, in the frame, is the menu from the banquet of the family association, held last year in a ballroom of the "Y" in Newark, in honor of my father's mother on her seventy-fifth birthday. My mother, Dr. Kafka learns, has served *six consecutive years* as the secretary-treasurer of the family association. My father has served a two-year term as president, as have each of his three brothers. We now have fourteen boys in the family in uniform. Philip writes a letter on V-mail stationery to five of his cousins in the Army every single month. "Religiously," my mother puts in, smoothing my hair. "I firmly believe," says my father, "that the family is the cornerstone of everything." Dr. Kafka, who has listened with close attention to my father's *spiel,* handling the various documents that have been passed to him with great delicacy and poring over them with a kind of rapt absorption that reminds me of myself over the watermarks of my stamps, now for the first time expresses himself on the subject of family; softly he says, "I agree," and inspects again the pages of our family book. "Alone," says my father, in conclusion, "alone, Dr. Kafka, is a stone." Dr. Kafka, setting the book gently upon my mother's gleaming coffee table, allows with a nod how that is so. My mother's fingers are now turning in the curls behind my ears; not that I even know it at the time, or that she does. Being stroked is my life, stroking me, my father, and my brother is hers.

My brother goes off to a Boy Scout "council" meeting, but only after my father has him stand in his neckerchief before Dr. Kafka and describe to him the skills he has mastered to earn each of his badges. I am invited to bring my stamp album into the living room and show Dr. Kafka my set of triangular stamps from Zanzibar. "Zanzibar!" says my father rapturously, as though I, not even ten, have already been there and back. My father accompanies Dr. Kafka and myself into the "sun parlor," where my tropical fish swim in the aerated, heated, and hygienic paradise I have made for them with my weekly allowance and my Hanukah *gelt.* I am encouraged to tell Dr. Kafka what I know about the temperament of the angelfish, the function of the catfish, and the family life of the black molly. I know quite a bit. "All on his own he does that," my father says to Kafka. "He gives me a lecture on one of those fish, it's seventh heaven, Dr. Kafka." "I can imagine," Kafka replies.

Back in the living room my Aunt Rhoda suddenly launches into a rather recondite monologue on "scotch plaids," designed, it would appear, only for the edification of my mother. At least she looks fixedly at my mother while she delivers it. I have not yet seen her look directly at Dr. Kafka; she did not even turn his way at dinner when he asked how many employees there were at "The Big Bear." "How would I know?" she replies, and continues conversing with my mother, something about a grocer or a butcher who would take care of her "under the counter" if she could find him nylons for his wife. It never occurs to me that she will not look at Dr. Kafka because she is shy—nobody that dolled up could, in my estimation, be shy—I can only think that she is outraged. *It's his breath. It's his accent. It's his age.* I'm wrong—it turns out to be what Aunt Rhoda calls his "superiority complex." "Sitting there, sneering at us like that," says my aunt, somewhat superior now herself:: "Sneering?" repeats my father, incredulous. "Sneering and laughing, yes!" says Aunt Rhoda. My mother shrugs: "*I* didn't think he was laughing." "Oh, don't worry, by himself there he was having a very good time—*at our expense.* I know the European-type man. Underneath they think they're all lords of the manor," Rhoda says. "You know something, Rhoda?" says my father, tilting his head and pointing a finger, "I think you fell in love." "With *him?* Are your *crazy?*" "He's too quiet for Rhoda," my mother says, "I think maybe he's a little bit of a wallflower. Rhoda is a lively person, she needs lively people around her." "Wallflower? He's not a wallflower! He's a gentleman, that's all. And he's lonely," my father says assertively, glaring at my mother for coming in over his head like this *against* Kafka. My Aunt Rhoda is forty years old—it is not exactly a shipment of brand-new goods that he is trying to move. "He's a gentleman, he's an educated man, and I'll tell you something, he'd give his eye teeth to have a nice home and a wife." "Well," says my Aunt Rhoda, "let him find one then, if he's so educated. Somebody who's his equal, who he doesn't have to look down his nose at with his big sad refugee eyes!" "Yep, she's in love." my father announces, squeezing Rhoda's knee in triumph. "With him?" she cries, jumping to her feet, taffeta crackling around her like a bonfire. "With *Kafka?*" she snorts, "I wouldn't given an old man like him the time of day!"

Dr. Kafka calls and takes my Aunt Rhoda to a movie. I am astonished, both that he calls and that she goes; it seems there is more desperation in life than I have come across yet in my fish tank. Dr. Kafka takes my Aunt Rhoda to a play performed at the "Y." Dr. Kafka eats Sunday dinner with my grandmother and my Aunt Rhoda, and at the end of the afternoon, accepts with that formal bow of his the Mason jar of barley soup that my grandmother presses him to carry back to his room with him on the No. 8 bus. Apparently he was very taken with my grandmother's jungle of potted plants—and she, as a result, with him. Together they spoke in Yiddish about gardening. One Wednesday morning, only an hour after the store has opened for the day, Dr. Kafka shows up at the dry goods department of "The Big Bear"; he tells Aunt Rhoda that he just wanted to see where she worked. That night he writes in his diary, "With the customers she is forthright and cheery, and so managerial about 'taste' that when I hear her explain to a chubby young bride why green and blue do not 'go,' I am myself ready to believe that Nature is in error and R. is correct."

One night, at ten, Dr. Kafka and Aunt Rhoda come by unexpectedly, and a small impromptu party is held in the kitchen—coffee and cake, even a thimbleful of whiskey all around, to celebrate the resumption of Aunt Rhoda's career on the stage. I have only heard tell of my aunt's theatrical ambitions. My brother says that when I was small she used to come to entertain the two of us on Sundays with her puppets—she was at that time employed by the W.P.A. to travel around New Jersey and put on puppet shows in schools and even in churches. Aunt Rhoda did all the voices, male and female, and with the help of another young girl, manipulated the manikins on their strings. Simultaneously she had been a member of the "Newark Collective Theater," a troupe organized primarily to go around to strike groups to perform *Waiting for Lefty;* everybody in Newark (as I understood it) had had high hopes that Rhoda Pilchik would go on to Broadway—everybody except my grandmother. To me this period of history is as difficult to believe in as the era of the lake-dwellers that I am studying in school; of course, people say it was once so, so I believe them, but nonetheless it is hard to grant such stories the status of the real, given the life I see around me.

Yet my father, a very avid realist, is in the kitchen, *schnapps* glass in hand, toasting Aunt Rhoda's success. She has been awarded one of the starring roles in the Russian masterpiece, *The Three Sisters,* to be performed six weeks hence by the amateur group at the Newark "Y." Everything, announces Aunt Rhoda, everything she owes to Franz, and his encouragement. One conversation— "One!" she cries gaily—and Dr. Kafka had apparently talked my grandmother out of her lifelong belief that actors are not serious human beings. And what an actor *he* is, in his own right, says Aunt Rhoda. How he had opened her eyes to the meaning of things, by reading her the famous Chekhov play—yes, read it to her from the opening line to the final curtain, all the parts, and actually left her in tears. Here Aunt Rhoda says, "Listen, listen—this is the first line of the play— it's the key to everything. Listen—I just think about what it was like that night Pop passed away, how I thought and thought what would happen, what would we all do—and, and, listen—"

"We're listening," laughs my father.

Pause; she must have walked to the center of the kitchen linoleum. She says, sounding a little surprised, "'It's just a year ago today that father died.'"

"Shhh," warns my mother, "you'll give the little one nightmares."

I am not alone in finding my aunt "a changed person" during the ensuing weeks of rehearsal. My mother says this is just what she was like as a little girl. "Red cheeks, always those hot, red cheeks—and everything exciting, even taking a bath." "She'll calm down, don't worry," says my father, "and then he'll pop the question." "Knock on wood," says my mother. "Come on," says my father, "he knows what side his bread is buttered on—he sets foot in this house, he sees what a family is all about, and believe me, he's licking his chops. Just look at him when he sits in that club chair. This is his dream come true." "Rhoda says that in Berlin, before Hitler, he had a young girlfriend, years and years it went on, and then she left him. For somebody else. She got tired of waiting." "Don't worry," says my father, "when the time comes I'll give him a little nudge. He ain't going to live forever, either, and he knows it."

Then one weekend, as a respite from the "strain" of nightly rehearsals—which Dr. Kafka regularly visits, watching in his hat and coat from a seat at the back of the auditorium until it is time to accompany Aunt Rhoda home—they take a trip to Atlantic City. Ever since he arrived on these shores Dr. Kafka has wanted to see the famous boardwalk and the horse that dives from the high board. But in Atlantic City something happens that I am not allowed to know about; any discussion of the subject conducted in my presence is in Yiddish. Dr. Kafka sends Aunt Rhoda four letters in three days. She comes to us for dinner and sits till midnight crying in our kitchen; she calls the "Y" on our phone to tell them (weeping) that her mother is still ill and she cannot come to rehearsal again—she may even have to drop out of the play—no, she can't, she can't; her mother is too ill, she herself is too upset! Good-bye! Then back to the kitchen table to cry; she wears no pink powder and no red lipstick, and her stiff brown hair, down, is thick and spiky as a new broom.

My brother and I listen from our bedroom through the door that silently he has pushed ajar.

"Have you ever?" says Aunt Rhoda, weeping. "Have you *ever?*"

"Poor soul," says my mother.

"*Who?*" I whisper to my brother. "Aunt Rhoda or—"

"Shhh!" he says, "Shut *up!*"

In the kitchen my father grunts. "Hmm. Hmm." I hear him getting up and walking around and sitting down again—and then grunting. I am listening so hard that I can hear the letters being folded and unfolded, stuck back into their envelopes and then removed to be puzzled over one more time.

"Well?" demands Aunt Rhoda. "*Well?*"

"Well what?" answers my father.

"Well what do you want to say now?"

"He's *meshugeh,*" admits my father. "Something is wrong with him all right."

"But," sobs Aunt Rhoda, "no one would believe me when *I* said it!"

"Rhody, Rhody," croons my mother in that voice I know from those times that I have had to have stitches taken, or when I awaken in tears, somehow on the floor beside my bed, "Rhody, don't be hysterical, darling. It's over, kitten, it's all over."

I reach across to my brother's "twin" bed and tug on the blanket. I don't think I've ever been so confused in my life, not even by death. The speed of things! Everything good undone in a moment! By what? "*What?*" I whisper. "*What is it?*"

My brother, the Boy Scout, smiles leeringly and with a fierce hiss that is no answer and enough answer, addresses my bewilderment: "Sex!"

Years later, a junior at college, I receive an envelope from home containing Dr. Kafka's obituary, clipped from the *Jewish News,* the tabloid of Jewish affairs that is mailed each week to the homes of the Jews of Essex County. It is summer, the semester is over, but I have stayed on at school, alone in my room in the town, trying to write short stores; I am fed by a young English professor and his wife in exchange for babysitting; I tell the sympathetic couple, who are also loaning me the money for my rent, why it is I can't go home. My tearful fights with my father are all I can talk about at their dinner table. "Keep him away from me!" I scream at my mother. "But, darling," she asks me, "what is going on? What is this all about?"—the very same question with which I used to plague my older brother, asked of me now out of the same bewilderment and innocence. "He *loves* you," she explains. But that, of all things, seems to me to be precisely what is blocking my way. Others are crushed by paternal criticism—I find myself oppressed by his high opinion of me! Can it possibly be true (and can I possibly admit) that I am coming to hate him for loving me so? praising me so? But that makes no sense—the ingratitude! the stupidity! the contrariness! Being loved is so obviously a blessing, *the* blessing, praise such a rare bequest; only listen late at night to my closest friends on the literary magazine and in the drama society— they tell horror stories of family life to rival *The Way of All Flesh,* they return shell-shocked from vacations, drift back to school as though from the wars. What they would give to be in my golden slippers! "What's going on?" my mother begs me to tell her; but how can I, when I can neither fully believe that this is happening to us, nor that I am the one who is making it happen. That they, who together cleared all obstructions from my path, should seem now to be my final obstruction! No wonder my rage must filter through a child's tears of shame, confusion, and loss. All that we have constructed together over the course of two century-long decades, and look how I must bring it down—in the name of this tyrannical need that I call my "independence"! Born, I am told, with the umbilical cord around my neck, it seems I will always come close to strangulation trying to deliver myself from my past into my future. . . . My mother, keeping the lines of communication open, sends a note to me at school: "We miss you"— and encloses the very brief obituary notice. Across the margin at the bottom of the clipping, she has written (in the same hand that she wrote notes to my teachers and signed my report cards, in the very same handwriting that once eased my way in the world), "Remember poor Kafka, Aunt Rhoda's beau?"

"Dr. Franz Kafka," the notice reads, "a Hebrew teacher at the Talmud Torah of the Schley Street Synagogue from 1939 to 1948, died on June 3 in the Deborah Tuberculosis Sanitorium in Browns Mills, New Jersey. Dr. Kafka had been a patient there since 1950. He was 70 years old. Dr. Kafka was born in Prague, Czechoslovakia, and was a refugee from the Nazis. He leaves no survivors."

He also leaves no books: no *Trial,* no *Castle,* no "Diaries." The dead man's papers are claimed by no one, and disappear—all except those four "*meshuge-neh*" letters that are, to this day as far as I know, still somewhere in amongst the memorabilia accumulated in her dresser drawers by my spinster aunt, along with a collection of Broadway "Playbills," sales citations from "The Big Bear," and transatlantic steamship stickers.

Thus all trace of Dr. Kafka disappears. Destiny being destiny, how could it be otherwise? Does the Land Surveyor reach the Castle? Does K. escape the judgment of the Court, or Georg Bendemann the judgment of his father? "'Well, clear this out now!' said the overseer, and they buried the hunger artist, straw and all." No, it simply is not in the cards for Kafka ever to become *the*

Kafka—why, that would be stranger even than a man turning into an insect. No one would believe it, Kafka least of all.

QUESTIONS

1. Roth wrote this story because he admires Kafka's writing and because he wanted his students at the University of Pennsylvania "to read Kafka's fiction without becoming Biblical exegesists in the process. Sometimes serious students of literature tend to read Kafka as though he had written his stories on Mars, or in graduate school, instead of in Prague." Accordingly, in the first half of the story, Roth wrote an intimate portrait of Franz Kafka, drawing parallels between Kafka's life and the fiction he created. Does Franz Kafka, the historical author, emerge as a round character? a flat character? a static character? a dynamic character?

2. Examine the parallels between the fictional Dr. Kafka and Franz Kafka, the writer. In what ways are the two men different? Is Dr. Kafka round, flat, static, or dynamic?

3. The title of the story comes from the hunger artist's conversation with the overseer. Explain how this conversation provides a key to understanding both fictions—Kafka's and Roth's.

4. At the conclusion of the story, the narrator, now a college student, describes his fitful relationship with his family. How is it similar or dissimilar to Franz Kafka's relationship to his family? By introducing the narrator as a young writer, explain how Roth is trying to universalize the predicament of the writer—therefore giving additional meaning to Franz Kafka's life and to "A Hunger Artist."

5. Discuss the ways in which the story creates a dense, realistic picture of Jewish family life in Newark of the 1930s.

6. Discuss the implications of the final paragraph. Is Roth separating the two Kafkas? What statement is he making about the relationship between life and art?

7. Examine how the story shifts from the narrative present, to half a century earlier, to the 1930s, and then to the early 1950s. Were you able to follow those shifts in time and locate the action properly? If you had any difficulty, discuss the reason for it.

8. Considered separately, does the story of Franz Kafka have a plot? Does the story of Dr. Kafka have a plot? Considered as a whole, does the story have a plot? Or is it unified by formalistic considerations?

JOHN CHEEVER

The Jewels of the Cabots

Funeral services for the murdered man were held in the Unitarian church in the little village of St. Botolphs. The architecture of the church was Bullfinch with columns and one of those ethereal spires that must have dominated the landscape a century ago. The service was a random collection of Biblical quotations closing with a verse. "Amos Cabot, rest in peace/Now your mortal trials have ceased. . . ." The church was full. Mr. Cabot had been an outstanding member of the community. He had once run for governor. For a month or so, during his campaign, one saw his picture on barns, walls, buildings, and telephone poles. I don't suppose the sense of walking through a shifting mirror—he found himself at every turn—unsettled him as it would have unsettled me. (Once, for example, when I was in an elevator in Paris I noticed a woman carrying a book of mine. There was a photograph on the jacket and one image of me looked over her arm at another. I wanted the picture, wanted I suppose to destroy it. That she should walk away with my face under her arm seemed to threaten my self-esteem. She left the elevator at the fourth floor and the parting of these two images was confusing. I wanted to follow her, but how could I explain in French—or in any other language—what I felt.) Amos Cabot was not at all like this. He seemed to enjoy seeing himself, and when he lost the election and his face vanished (excepting for a few barns in the back country where it peeled for a month or so) he seemed not perturbed.

There are, of course, the wrong Lowells, the wrong Hallowells, the wrong Eliots, Cheevers, Codmans, and Englishes but today we will deal with the wrong Cabots. Amos came from the South Shore and may never have heard of the

287

North Shore branch of the family. His father had been an auctioneer, which meant in those days an entertainer, horse trader, and sometime crook. Amos owned real state, the hardware store, the public utilities, and was a director of the bank. He had an office in the Cartwright Block, opposite the green. His wife came from Connecticut, which was, for us at that time, a distant wilderness on whose eastern borders stood the City of New York. New York was populated by harried, nervous, avaricious foreigners who lacked the character to bathe in cold water at six in the morning and to live, with composure, lives of grueling boredom. Mrs. Cabot, when I knew her, was probably in her early forties. She was a short woman with the bright red face of an alcoholic although she was a vigorous temperance worker. Her hair was as white as snow. Her back and her front were prominent and there was a memorable curve to her spine that could have been a cruel corset or the beginnings of lordosis. No one quite knew why Mr. Cabot had married this eccentric from faraway Connecticut—it was, after all, no one's business—but she did own most of the frame tenements on the East Bank of the river where the workers in the table silver factory lived. Her tenements were profitable but it would have been unwarranted simplification to conclude that he had married for real estate. She collected the rents herself. I expect that she did her own housework, and she dressed simply, but she wore on her right hand seven large diamond rings. She had evidently read somewhere that diamonds were a sound investment and the blazing stones were about as glamorous as a passbook. There were round diamonds, square diamonds, rectangular diamonds, and some of those diamonds that are set in prongs. On Thursday morning she would wash her diamonds in some jewelers' solution and hang them out to dry in the clothes yard. She never explained this, but the incidence of eccentricity in the village ran so high that her conduct was not thought unusual.

Mrs. Cabot spoke once or twice a year at the St. Botolphs Academy, where many of us went to school. She had three subjeccts: My Trip to Alaska (slides), The Evils of Drink, and The Evils of Tobacco. Drink was for her so unthinkable a vice that she could not attack it with much vehemence, but the thought of tobacco made her choleric. Could one imagine Christ on the Cross, smoking a cigarette, she would ask us. Could one imagine the Virgin Mary *smoking?* A drop of nicotine fed to a pig by trained laboratory technicians had killed the beast. Etc. She made smoking irresistible, and if I die of lung cancer I shall blame Mrs. Cabot. These performances took place in what we called the Great Study Hall. This was a large room on the second floor that could hold us all. The academy had been built in the 1850s and had the lofty, spacious, and beautiful windows of that period in American architecture. In the spring and in the autumn the building seemed gracefully suspended in its grounds but in the winter a glacial cold fell off the large window lights. In the Great Study Hall we were allowed to wear coats, hats, and gloves. This situation was heightened by the fact that my Great-aunt Anna had bought in Athens a large collection of plaster casts so that we shivered and memorized the donative verbs in the company of at least a dozen buck-naked gods and goddesses. So it was to

Hermes and Venus as well as to us that Mrs. Cabot railed against the poisons of tobacco. She was a woman of vehement and ugly prejudice, and I suppose she would have been happy to include the blacks and the Jews but there was only one black and one Jewish family in the village and they were exemplary. The possibility of intolerance in the village did not occur to me until much later, when my mother came to our house in Westchester for Thanksgiving.

This was some years ago, when the New England highways had not been completed and the trip from New York or Westchester took over four hours. I left quite early in the morning and drove first to Haverhill, where I stopped at Miss Peacock's School and picked up my niece. I then went on to St. Botolphs, where I found Mother sitting in the hallway in an acolyte's chair. The chair had a steepled back, topped with a wooden fleur-de-lis. From what rain-damp church had this object been stolen? She wore a coat and her bag was at her feet. "I'm ready," she said. She must have been ready for a week. She seemed terribly lonely. "Would you like a drink?" she asked. I knew enough not to take this bait. Had I said yes she would have gone into the pantry and returned, smiling sadly, to say: "Your brother has drunk all the whiskey." So we started back for Westchester. It was a cold, overcast day and I found the drive tiring, although I think fatigue had nothing to do with what followed. I left my niece at my brother's house in Connecticut and drove on to my place. It was after dark when the trip ended. My wife had made all the preparations that were customary for Mother's arrival. There was an open fire, a vase of roses on the piano, and tea with anchovy-paste sandwiches. "How lovely to have flowers," said Mother. "I so love flowers. I can't live without them. Should I suffer some financial reverses and have to choose between flowers and groceries I believe I would choose flowers. . . ."

I do not want to give the impression of an elegant old lady because there were lapses in her performance. I bring up, with powerful unwillingness, a fact that was told to me by her sister after Mother's death. It seems that at one time she applied for a position with the Boston Police Force. She had plenty of money at the time and I have no idea of why she did this. I suppose that she wanted to be a policewoman. I don't know what branch of the force she planned to join, but I've always imagined her in a dark-blue uniform with a ring of keys at her waist and a billy club in her right hand. My grandmother dissuaded her from this course, but the image of a policewoman was some part of the figure she cut, sipping tea by our fire. She meant this evening to be what she called Aristocratic. In this connection she often said: "There must be at least a drop of plebeian blood in the family. How else can one account for your taste in torn and shabby clothing. You've always had plenty of clothes but you've always chosen rags."

I mixed a drink and said how much I had enjoyed seeing my niece.

"Miss Peacock's has changed," Mother said sadly.

"I didn't know," I said. "What do you mean?"

"They've let down the bars."

"I don't understand."

"They're letting in Jews," she said. She fired out the last word.

"Can we change the subject?" I asked.

"I don't see why," she said. "You brought it up."

"My wife is Jewish, Mother," I said. My wife was in the kitchen.

"That is not possible," my mother said. "Her father is Italian."

"Her father," I said, "is a Polish Jew."

"Well," Mother said, "I come from old Massachusetts stock and I'm not ashamed of it although I don't like being called a Yankee."

"There's a difference."

"Your father said that the only good Jew was a dead Jew although I did think Justice Brandeis charming."

"I think it's going to rain." I said. It was one of our staple conversational switch-offs, used to express anger, hunger, love, and the fear of death. My wife joined us and Mother picked up the routine. "It's nearly cold enough for snow," she said. "When you were a boy you used to pray for snow or ice. It depended upon whether you wanted to skate or ski. You were very particular. You would kneel by your bed and loudly ask God to manipulate the elements. You never prayed for anything else. I never once heard you ask for a blessing on your parents. In the summer you didn't pray at all."

The Cabots had two daughters—Geneva, and Molly. Geneva was the older and thought to be the more beautiful. Molly was my girl for a year or so. She was a lovely young woman with a sleepy look that was quickly dispelled by a brilliant smile. Her hair was pale brown and held the light. When she was tired or excited sweat formed on her upper lip. In the evenings I would walk to their house and sit with her in the parlor under the most intense surveillance. Mrs. Cabot, of course, regarded sex with utter panic. She watched us from the dining room. From upstairs there were loud and regular thumping sounds. This was Amos Cabot's rowing machine. We were sometimes allowed to take walks together if we kept to the main streets, and when I was old enough to drive I took her to the dances at the club. I was intensely—morbidly—jealous and when she seemed to be enjoying herself with someone else I would stand in the corner, thinking of suicide. I remember driving her back one night to the house on Shore Road.

At the turn of the century someone decided that St. Botolphs might have a future as a resort, and five mansions, or follies, were built at the end of Shore Road. The Cabots lived in one of these. All mansions had towers. These were round with conical roofs, rising a story or so above the rest of the frame buildings. The towers were strikingly unmilitary, and so I suppose they were meant to express romance. What did they contain? Dens, I guess, maids' rooms, broken furniture, trunks, and they must have been the favorite of hornets. I parked my car in front of the Cabots' and turned off the lights. The house above us was dark.

It was long ago, so long ago that the foliage of elm trees was part of the summer night. (It was so long ago that when you wanted to make a left turn you cranked down the car window and *pointed* in that direction. Otherwise you were not allowed to point. Don't point, you were told. I can't imagine why, unless the gesture was thought to be erotic.) The dances—the Assemblies—were formal and I would be wearing a tuxedo handed down from my father to my brother and from my brother to me like some escutcheon or sumptuary torch. I took Molly in my arms. She was completely responsive. I am not a tall man (I am sometimes inclined to stoop), but the conviction that I am loved and loving affects me like a military bracing. Up goes my head. My back is straight. I am six foot seven and sustained by some clamorous emotional uproar. Sometimes my ears ring. It can happen anywhere—in a ginseng house in Seoul, for example— but it happened that night in front of the Cabots' house on Shore Road. Molly said then that she had to go. Her mother would be watching from a window. She asked me not to come up to the house. I mustn't have heard. I went with her up the walk and the stairs to the porch, where she tried the door and found it locked. She asked me again to go, but I couldn't abandon her there, could I? Then a light went on and the door was opened by a dwarf. He was exhaustively misshapen. The head was hydrocephalic, the features were swollen, the legs were thick and cruelly bowed. I thought of the circus. The lovely young woman began to cry. She stepped into the house and closed the door and I was left with the summer night, the elms, the taste of an east wind. After this she avoided me for a week or so and I was told the facts by Maggie, our old cook.

But more facts first. It was in the summer, and in the summer most of us went to a camp on the Cape run by the headmaster of the St. Botolphs Academy. The months were so feckless, so blue, that I can't remember them at all. I slept next to a boy named DeVarrenes whom I had known all my life. We were together most of the time. We played marbles together, slept together, played together on the same backfield, and once together took a ten-day canoe trip during which we nearly drowned together. My brother claimed that we had begun to look alike. It was the most gratifying and unself-conscious relationship I had known. (He still calls me once or twice a year from San Francisco, where he lives unhappily with his wife and three unmarried daughters. He sounds drunk. "We were happy, weren't we," he asks.) One day another boy, a stranger named Wallace, asked if I wanted to swim across the lake. I might claim that I knew nothing about Wallace, and I knew very little, but I did know or sense that he was lonely. It was as conspicuous as—or more conspicuous than—any of his features. He did what was expected of him. He played ball, made his bed, took sailing lessons, and got his life-saving certificate, but this seemed more like a careful imposture than any sort of participation. He was miserable, he was lonely, and sooner or later, rain or shine, he would say so and, in the act of confession, make an impossible claim on one's loyalty. One knew all of this but one pretended not to. We got a permission from the swimming instructor and swam across the lake. We used a clumsy sidestroke that still seems to me more serviceable than the overhand that is obligatory these days in those swimming pools where I spend most of my time. The sidestroke is Lower Class. I've seen it once in a swimming pool, and when I asked who the swimmer was I was told he was the butler. When the ship sinks, when the plane ditches I will try to reach the life raft with an overhand and drown stylishly, whereas if I had used a Lower-Class sidestroke I would have lived forever.

We swam the lake, rested in the sun—no confidences—and swam home. When I came up to our cabin DeVarennes took me aside. "Don't ever let me see you with Wallace again," he said. I asked why. He told me. "Wallace is Amos Cabot's bastard. His mother is a whore. They live in one of the tenements across the river."

The next day was hot and brilliant and Wallace asked if I wanted to swim the lake again. I said sure, sure and we did. When we came back to camp DeVarennes wouldn't speak to me. That night a northeaster blew up and it rained for three days. DeVarennes seems to have forgiven me and I don't recall having crossed the lake with Wallace again. As for the dwarf, Maggie told me he was a son of Mrs. Cabot from an earlier marriage. He worked at the table silver factory but he went to work early in the morning and didn't return until after dark. His existence was meant to be kept a secret. This was unusual but not—at the time of which I'm writing—unprecedented. The Trumbulls kept Mrs. Trumbull's crazy sister hidden in the attic and Uncle Peepee Marshmallow—an exhibitionist—was often hidden for months.

It was a winter afternoon, an early winter afternoon, Mrs. Cabot washed her diamonds and hung them out to dry. She then went upstairs to take a nap. She claimed that she had never taken a nap in her life, and the sounder she slept the more vehement were her claims that she didn't sleep. This was not so much an eccentricity on her part as it was a crabwise way of presenting the facts that was prevalent in that part of the world. She woke at four and went down to gather her stones. They were gone. She called Geneva, but there was no answer. She got a rake and scored the stubble under the clothesline. There was nothing. She called the police.

As I say, it was a winter afternoon and the winters there were very cold. We counted for heat—sometimes for survival—on wood fires and large coal-burning furnaces that sometimes got out of hand. A winter night was a threatening fact, and this may have partly accounted for the sentiment with which we watched—in late November and December—the light burn out in the west. (My father's journals, for example, were full of descriptions of winter twilights, not because he was at all crepuscular but because the coming of the night might mean danger and pain.) Geneva had packed a bag, gathered the diamonds, and taken the last train out of town: the 4:37. How thrilling it must have been. The diamonds were meant to be stolen. They were a flagrant snare and she did what she was meant to do. She took a train to New York that night and sailed three days later for Alexandria on a Cunarder—the S.S. *Serapis*. She took a boat from Alexandria to Luxor, where, in the space of two months, she joined the Moslem faith and married an Egyptian noble.

I read about the theft next day in the evening paper. I delivered papers. I had begun my route on foot, moved on to a bicycle, and was assigned, when I was sixteen, to an old Ford truck. I was a truck driver! I hung around the linotype room until the papers were printed and then drove around to the four

neighboring villages, tossing out bundles at the doors of the candy and stationery stores. During the World Series a second edition with box scores was
brought out, and after dark I would make the trip again to Travertine and the
other places along the shore. The roads were dark, there was very little traffic,
and leaf-burning had not been forbidden so that the air was tannic, melancholy,
and exciting. One can attach a mysterious and inordinate amount of importance
to some simple journey, and this second trip with the box scores made me very
happy. I dreaded the end of the World Series as one dreads the end of any
pleasure, and had I been younger I would have prayed. CABOT JEWELS STOLEN
was the headline and the incident was never again mentioned in the paper. It was
not mentioned at all in our house, but this was not unusual. When Mr. Abbott
hung himself from the pear tree next door this was never mentioned.

Molly and I took a walk on the beach at Travertine that Sunday afternoon.
I was troubled, but Molly's troubles were much graver. It did not disturb her
that Geneva had stolen the diamonds. She only wanted to know what had
become of her sister, and she was not to find out for another six weeks.
However, something had happened at the house that night. There had been a
scene between her parents and her father had left. She described this to me. We
were walking barefoot. She was crying. I would like to have forgotten the scene
as soon as she finished her description.

Children drown, beautiful women are mangled in automobile accidents,
cruise ships founder, and men die lingering deaths in mines and submarines, but
you will find none of this in my accounts. In the last chapter the ship comes
home to port, the children are saved, the miners will be rescued. Is this an
infirmity of the genteel or a conviction that there are discernible moral truths?
Mr. X defecated in his wife's top drawer. This is a fact, but I claim that it is not a
truth. In describing St. Botolphs I would sooner stay on the West Bank of the
river where the houses were white and where the church bells rang, but over the
bridge there was the table silver factory, the tenements (owned by Mrs. Cabot),
and the Commercial Hotel. At low tide one could smell the sea gas from the
inlets at Travertine. The headlines in the afternoon paper dealt with a trunk
murder. The women on the streets were ugly. Even the dummies in the one
store window seemed stooped, depressed, and dressed in clothing that neither
fitted nor became them. Even the bride in her splendor seemed to have got
some bad news. The politics were neofacist, the factory was nonunion, the food
was unpalatable, and the night wind was bitter. This was a provincial and a
traditional world enjoying few of the rewards of smallness and traditionalism,
and when I speak of the blessedness of all small places I speak of the West Bank.
On the East Bank was the Commercial Hotel, the demesne of Doris, a male
prostitute who worked as a supervisor in the factory during the day and hustled
the bar at night, exploiting the extraordinary moral lassitude of the place.
Everybody knew Doris, and many of the customers had used him at one time or
another. There was no scandal and no delight involved. Doris would charge a
traveling salesman whatever he could get but he did it with the regulars for
nothing. This seemed less like tolerance than hapless indifference, the absence

of vision, moral stamina, the splendid Ambitiousness of romantic love. On fight night Doris drifts down the bar. Buy him a drink and he'll put his hand on your arm, your shoulder, your waist, and move a fraction of an inch in his direction and he'll reach for the cake. The steam fitter buys him a drink, the high school dropout, the watch repairman. (Once a stranger shouted to the bartender: "Tell that sonofabitch to take his tongue out of my ear"—but he was a stranger.) This is not a transient world, these are not drifters, more than half of these men will never live in any other place, and yet this seems to be the essence of spiritual nomadism. The telephone rings and the bartender beckons to Doris. There's a customer in room eight. Why would I sooner be on the West Shore where my parents are playing bridge with Mr. and Mrs. Eliot Pinkham in the golden light of a great gas chandelier?

I'll blame it on the roast, the roast, the Sunday roast bought from a butcher who wore a straw boater with a pheasant wing in the hat band. I suppose the roast entered our house, wrapped in bloody paper on Thursday or Friday, traveling on the back of a bicycle. It would be a gross exaggeration to say that the meat had the detonative force of a land mine that could savage your eyes and your genitals but its powers were disproportionate. We sat down to dinner after church. (My brother was living in Omaha so we were only three.) My father would hone the carving knife and make a cut in the meat. My father was very adroit with an ax and a crosscut saw and could bring down a large tree with dispatch, but the Sunday roast was something else. After he had made the first cut my mother would sigh. This was an extraordinary performance so loud, so profound, that it seemed as if her life were in danger. It seemed as if her very soul might come unhinged and drift out of her open mouth. "Will you never learn, Leander, that lamb must be carved against the grain?" she would ask. Once the battle of the roast had begun the exchanges were so swift, predictable, and tedious that there would be no point in reporting them. After five or six wounding remarks my father would wave the carving knife in the air and shout: "Will you kindly mind your own business, will you kindly shut up?" She would sigh once more and put her hand to her heart. Surely this was her last breath. Then, studying the air above the table she would say: "Feel that refreshing breeze."

There was, of course, seldom a breeze. It could be airless, midwinter, rainy, anything. The remark was one for all season. Was it a commendable metaphor for hope, for the serenity of love (which I think she had never experienced), was it nostalgia for some summer evening when, loving and understanding, we sat contentedly on the lawn above the river? Was it no better or no worse than the sort of smile thrown at the evening star by a man who is in utter despair? Was it a prophecy of that generation to come who would be so drilled in evasiveness that they would be denied forever the splendors of a passionate confrontation?

The scene changes to Rome. It is spring when the canny swallows flock into the city to avoid the wingshots in Ostia. The noise the birds make seems like light as the light of day loses its brilliance. Then one hears, across the courtyard, the voice of an American woman. She is screaming. "You're a goddamned fucked-up no-good insane piece of shit. You can't make a nickel, you don't have a friend in the world, and in bed you stink. . . ." There is no reply, and one wonders if she is railing at the dark. Then you hear a man cough. That's all you will hear from him. "Oh, I know I've lived with you for eight years, but if you ever thought I liked it, any of it, it's only because you're such a chump you wouldn't know the real thing if you had it. When I really come the pictures *fall* off the walls. With you it's always an act. . . ." The highlow bells that ring in Rome at that time of day have begun to chime. I smile at this sound although it has no bearing on my life, my faith, no true harmony, nothing like the revelations in the voice across the court. Why would I sooner describe church bells and flocks of swallows? Is this puerile, a sort of greeting-card mentality, a whimsical and effeminate refusal to look at facts? On and on she goes but I will follow her no longer. She attacks his hair, his brain, and his spirit while I observe that a light rain has begun to fall and that the effect of this is to louden the noise of traffic on the Corso. Now she is hysterical—her voice is breaking—and I think perhaps that at the height of her malediction she will begin to cry and ask his forgiveness. She will not, of course. She will go after him with a carving knife and he will end up in the emergency ward of the Policlinico, claiming to have wounded himself, but as I go out for dinner, smiling at beggars, fountains, children, and the first stars of evening, I assure myself that everything will work out for the best. Feel that refreshing breeze.

My recollections of the Cabots are only a footnote to my principal work and I go to work early these winter mornings. It is still dark. Here and there, standing on street corners, waiting for buses, are women dressed in white. They wear white shoes, white stockings, and white uniforms can be seen below their winter coats. Are they nurses, beauty parlor operators, dentists' helpers? I'll never know. They usually carry a brown paper bag holding, I guess, a ham on rye and a Thermos of buttermilk. Traffic is light at this time of day. A laundry truck delivers uniforms to the Fried Chicken Shack and in Asburn Place there is a milk truck—the last of that generation. It will be half an hour before the yellow school buses start their rounds.

I work in an apartment house called the Prestwick. It is seven stories high and dates, I guess, from the late twenties. It is of a Tudor persuasion. The bricks are irregular, there is a parapet on the roof, and the sign advertising vacancies is literally a shingle that hangs from iron chains and creaks romantically in the wind. On the right of the door there is a list of perhaps twenty-five doctors' names, but these are not gentle healers with stethoscopes and rubber hammers, these are psychiatrists, and this is the country of the plastic chair and the full ashtray. I don't know why they should have chosen this place, but they outnumber the other tenants. Now and then you see, waiting for the elevator, a woman with a grocery wagon and a child, but you mostly see the sometimes harried faces of men and women with trouble. They sometimes smile; they sometimes talk to themselves. Business seems slow these days, and the doctor whose office is next to mine often stands in the hallway, staring out of the window. What does a psychiatrist think? Does he wonder what has become of those patients who gave up, who refused Group Therapy, who disregarded his warnings and admonitions? He will know their secrets. I tried to murder my husband. I tried to murder my wife. Three years ago I took an overdose of sleeping pills. The year before that I cut my wrists. My mother wanted me to be a girl. My mother wanted me to be a boy. My mother wanted me to be a homosexual. Where had they gone, what were they doing? Were they still married, quarreling at the dinner table, decorating the Christmas tree? Had they divorced, remarried, jumped off bridges, taken Seconal, struck some kind of truce, turned homosexual, or moved to a farm in Vermont where they planned to raise strawberries and lead a simple life? The doctor sometimes stands by the window for an hour.

My real work these days is to write an edition of *The New York Times* that will bring gladness to the hearts of men. How better could I occupy myself? The *Times* is a critical if rusty link in my ties to reality, but in these last years its tidings have been monotonous. The prophets of doom are out of work. All one can do is to pick up the pieces. The lead story is this: PRESIDENT'S HEART TRANSPLANT DEEMED SUCCESSFUL. There is this box on the lower left: COST OF J. EDGAR HOOVER MEMORIAL CHALLENGED. "The subcommittee on memorials threatened today to halve the seven million dollars appropriated to commemorate the late J. Edgar Hoover with a Temple of Justice. . . ." Column three: CONTROVERSIAL LEGISLATION REPEALED BY SENATE. "The recently enacted bill, making it a felony to have wicked thoughts about the administration, was repealed this afternoon by a standup vote of forty-three to seven." On and on it goes. There are robust and heartening editorials, thrilling sports news, and the weather of course is always sunny and warm unless we need rain. Then we have rain. The air pollutant gradient is zero, and even in Tokyo fewer and fewer people are wearing surgical masks. All highways, throughways, and expressways will be closed for the holiday weekend. Joy to the World!

But to get back to the Cabots. The scene that I would like to overlook or forget took place the night after Geneva had stolen the diamonds. It involves plumbing. Most of the houses in the village had relatively little plumbing. There was usually a water closet in the basement for the cook and the ash man and a single bathroom on the second floor for the rest of the household. Some of these rooms were quite large, and the Endicotts had a fireplace in their bathroom. Somewhere along the line Mrs. Cabot decided that the bathroom was her demesne. She had a locksmith come and secure the door. Mr. Cabot was allowed to take his sponge bath every morning, but after this the bathroom door was locked and Mrs. Cabot kept the key in her pocket. Mr. Cabot was obliged to use a chamber pot, but since he came from the South Shore I don't suppose this was much of a hardship. It may even have been nostalgic. He was using the chamber pot late that night when Mrs. Cabot came to the door of his room. (They slept in separate rooms.) "Will you close the door?" she screamed. "Will you close the door? Do I have to listen to that horrible noise for the rest of my life?" They would both be in nightgowns, her snow-white hair in braids. She picked up the chamber pot and threw its contents at him. He kicked down the door of the locked bathroom, washed, dressed, packed a bag, and walked over the bridge to Mrs. Wallace's place on the East Bank.

He stayed there for three days and then returned. He was worried about Molly, and in such a small place there were appearances to be considered—Mrs. Wallace's as well as his own. He divided his time between the East and the West banks of the river until a week or so later, when he was taken ill. He felt languid. He stayed in bed until noon. When he dressed and went to his office he returned after an hour or so. The doctor examined him and found nothing wrong.

One evening Mrs. Wallace saw Mrs. Cabot coming out of the drugstore on the East Bank. She watched her rival cross the bridge and then went into the drugstore and asked the clerk if Mrs. Cabot was a regular customer. "I've been wondering about that myself," the clerk said. "Of course she comes over here to collect her rents, but I always thought she used the other drugstore. She comes in here to buy ant poison—arsenic, that is. She says they have these terrible ants in the house on Shore Road and arsenic is the only way of getting rid of them. From the way she buys arsenic the ants must be terrible." Mrs. Wallace might have warned Mr. Cabot but she never saw him again.

She went after the funeral to Judge Simmons and said that she wanted to charge Mrs. Cabot with murder. The drug clerk would have a record of her purchase of arsenic that would be incriminating. "He may have them," the judge said, "but he won't give them to you. What you are asking for is an exhumation of the body and a long trial in Barnstable, and you have neither the money nor the reputation to support this. You were his friend, I know, for sixteen years. He was a splendid man and why don't you console yourself with the thought of how many years it was that you knew him? And another thing. He's left you and Wallace a substantial legacy. If Mrs. Cabot were provoked to contest the will you could lose this."

I went out to Luxor to see Geneva. I flew to London in a 747. There were only three passengers; but as I say the prophets of doom are out of work. I went from Cairo up the Nile in a low-flying two-motor prop. The sameness of wind erosion and water erosion makes the Sahara there seem to have been gutted by floods, rivers, courses, streams, and brooks, the thrust of a natural search. The scorings are watery and arboreal, and as a false stream bed spreads out it takes the shape of a tree, striving for light. It was freezing in Cairo when we left before dawn. Luxor, where Geneva met me at the airport, was hot.

I was very happy to see her, so happy I was unobservant, but I did notice that she had gotten fat. I don't mean that she was heavy; I mean that she weighed about three hundred pounds. She was a fat woman. Her hair, once a coarse yellow, was now golden but her Massachusetts accent was as strong as ever. It sounded like music to me on the Upper Nile. Her husband—now a colonel— was a slender, middle-aged man, a relative of the last king. He owned a restaurant at the edge of the city and they lived in a pleasant apartment over the dining room. The colonel was humorous, intelligent—a rake, I guess—and a heavy drinker. When we went to the temple at Karnak our dragoman carried ice, tonic, and gin. I spent a week with them, mostly in temples and graves. We spent the evenings in his bar. War was threatening—the air was full of Russian planes—and the only other tourist was an Englishman who sat at the bar, reading his passport. On the last day I swam in the Nile—overhand—and they drove me to the airport, where I kissed Geneva—and the Cabots—good-bye.

QUESTIONS

1. Explain the meaning of the following statement: "There are, of course, the wrong Lowells, the wrong Hallowells, the wrong Eliots, Cheevers, Codmans, and Englishes but today we will deal with the wrong Cabots." How does this statement help identify the region in which the story is set?

2. Outline the major shifts in time and show how Cheever handles these transitions.

3. Explain how dialogue characterizes the narrator's mother and establishes the narrator as a very different person from his mother. What effect is achieved by this separation?

4. Does the first-person narrator emerge as a likable person? sensitive? superior? cold? hypocritical? Evaluate the kinds of information the reader receives from him. Explain how his relationship to the Cabots allows him to sustain suspense and surprise in legitimate ways.

5. In the paragraph that begins. "Children drown, beautiful women are mangled in automobile accidents, cruise ships founder, and men die lingering deaths in mines and submarines, but you will find none of this in my accounts," the narrator makes a statement about fiction writing. Discuss. Can you find additional statements that describe the narrator's esthetic as a writer? Do the narrator's statements about writing constitute John Cheever's beliefs and practices as a writer?

6. Is the description of the psychiatrists a digression? Or does this description fit into the formal design of the story?

7. Does the narrator ever get around to relating the story Molly tells of the "scene between her parents"? What is the effect of this delay?

8. Is the narrator's visit with Geneva in Luxor an appropriate or inappropriate ending? Is it integral to the formal design of the story?

Setting

NATHANIEL HAWTHORNE

My Kinsman,
Major Molineux

After the kings of Great Britain had assumed the right of appointing the colonial governors, the measures of the latter seldom met with the ready and general approbation which had been paid to those of their predecessors, under the original charters. The people looked with most jealous scrutiny to the exercise of power which did not emanate from themselves, and they usually rewarded their rulers with slender gratitude for the compliances by which, in softening their instructions from beyond the sea, they had incurred the reprehension of those who gave them. The annals of Massachusetts Bay will inform us, that of six governors in the space of about forty years from the surrender of the old charter, under James II, two were imprisoned by a popular insurrection; a third, as Hutchinson inclines to believe, was driven from the province by the whizzing of a musket-ball; a fourth, in the opinion of the same historian, was hastened to his grave by continual bickerings with the House of Representatives; and the remaining two, as well as their successors, till the Revolution, were favored with few and brief intervals of peaceful sway. The inferior members of the court party, in times of high political excitement, led scarcely a more desirable life. These remarks may serve as a preface to the following adventures, which chanced upon a summer night, not far from a hundred years ago. The reader, in order to avoid a long and dry detail of colonial affairs, is requested to dispense with an account of the train of circumstances that had caused much temporary inflammation of the popular mind.

It was near nine o'clock of a moonlight evening, when a boat crossed the ferry with a single passenger, who had obtained his conveyance at that unusual hour by the promise of an extra fare. While he stood on the landing-place, searching in either pocket for the means of fulfilling his agreement, the ferryman lifted a lantern, by the aid of which, and the newly risen moon, he took a very accurate survey of the stranger's figure. He was a youth of barely eighteen years, evidently country-bred, and now, as it should seem, upon his first visit to town. He was clad in a coarse gray coat, well worn, but in excellent repair; his under garments were durably constructed of leather, and fitted tight to a pair of serviceable and well-shaped limbs; his stockings of blue yarn were the incontrovertible work of a mother or a sister; and on his head was a three-cornered hat, which in its better days had perhaps sheltered the graver brow of the lad's father. Under his left arm was a heavy cudgel formed of an oak sapling, and retaining a part of the hardened root; and his equipment was completed by a wallet, not so abundantly stocked as to incommode the vigorous shoulders on which it hung. Brown, curly hair, well-shaped features, and bright, cheerful eyes were nature's gifts, and worth all that art could have done for his adornment.

The youth, one of whose names was Robin, finally drew from his pocket the half of a little province bill of five shillings, which, in the depreciation in that sort of currency, did but satisfy the ferryman's demand, with the surplus of a sexangular piece of parchment, valued at three pence. He then walked forward into the town, with as light a step as if his day's journey had not already exceeded thirty miles, and with as eager an eye as if he were entering London City, instead of the little metropolis of a New England colony. Before Robin had proceeded far, however, it occurred to him that he knew not whither to direct his steps; so he paused, and looked up and down the narrow street, scrutinizing the small and mean wooden buildings that were scattered on either side.

"This low hovel cannot be my kinsman's dwelling," thought he, "nor yonder old house, where the moonlight enters at the broken casement; and truly I see none hereabouts that might be worthy of him. It would have been wise to inquire my way of the ferryman, and doubtless he would have gone with me, and earned a shilling from the Major for his pains. But the next man I meet will do as well."

He resumed his walk, and was glad to perceive that the street now became wider, and the houses more respectable in their appearance. He soon discerned a figure moving on moderately in advance, and hastened his steps to overtake it. As Robin drew nigh, he saw that the passenger was a man in years, with a full periwig of gray hair, a wide-skirted coat of dark cloth, and silk stockings rolled above his knees. He carried a long and polished cane, which he struck down perpendicularly before him at every step; and at regular intervals he uttered two successive hems, of a peculiarly solemn and sepulchral intonation. Having made these observations, Robin laid hold of the skirt of the old man's coat, just when the light from the open door and windows of a barber's shop fell upon both their figures.

"Good evening to you, honored sir," said he, making a low bow, and still retaining his hold of the skirt. "I pray you tell me whereabouts is the dwelling of my kinsman, Major Molineux."

The youth's question was uttered very loudly; and one of the barbers, whose razor was descending on a well-soaped chin, and another who was dressing a Ramillies wig, left their occupations, and came to the door. The citizen, in the mean time, turned a long-favored countenance upon Robin, and answered him in a tone of excessive anger and annoyance. His two sepulchral hems, however, broke into the very centre of his rebuke, with most singular effect, like a thought of the cold grave obtruding among wrathful passions.

"Let go my garment, fellow! I tell you, I know not the man you speak of. What! I have authority, I have—hem, hem—authority; and if this be the respect you show for your betters, your feet shall be brought acquainted with the stocks by daylight, tomorrow morning!"

Robin released the old man's skirt, and hastened away, pursued by an ill-mannered roar of laughter from the barber's shop. He was at first considerably surprised by the result of his question, but, being a shrewd youth, soon thought himself able to account for the mystery.

"This is some country representative," was his conclusion, "who has never seen the inside of my kinsman's door, and lacks the breeding to answer a stranger civilly. The man is old, or verily—I might be tempted to turn back and smite him on the nose. Ah, Robin, Robin! even the barber's boys laugh at you for choosing such a guide! You will be wiser in time, friend Robin!"

He now became entangled in a succession of crooked and narrow streets, which crossed each other, and meandered at no great distance from the water-side. The smell of tar was obvious to his nostrils, the masts of vessels pierced the moonlight above the tops of the buildings, and the numerous signs, which Robin paused to read, informed him that he was near the center of business. But the streets were empty, the shops were closed, and lights were visible only in the second stories of a few dwelling-houses. At length, on the corner of a narrow lane, through which he was passing, he beheld the broad countenance of a British hero swinging before the door of an inn, whence proceeded the voices of many guests. The casement of one of the lower windows was thrown back, and a very thin curtain permitted Robin to distinguish a party at supper, round a well-furnished table. The fragrance of the good cheer steamed forth into the outer air, and the youth could not fail to recollect that the last remnant of his travelling stock of provision had yielded to his morning appetite, and that noon had found and left him dinnerless.

"Oh, that a parchment three-penny might get me a right to sit down at yonder table!" said Robin, with a sigh. "But the Major will make me welcome to the best of his victuals; so I will even step boldly in, and inquire my way to his dwelling."

He entered the tavern, and was guided by the murmur of voices and the fumes of tobacco to the public-room. It was a long and low apartment, with oaken walls, grown dark in the continual smoke, and a floor which was thickly sanded, but of no immaculate purity. A number of persons—the larger part of whom appeared to be mariners, or in some way connected with the sea— occupied the wooden benches, or leather-bottomed chairs, conversing on various matters, and occasionally lending their attention to some topic of general interest. Three of four little groups were draining as many bowls of punch, which the West India trade had long since made a familiar drink in the colony. Others, who had the appearance of men who lived by regular and laborious handicraft, preferred the insulated bliss of an unshared potation, and became more taciturn under its influence. Nearly all, in short, evinced a predilection for the Good Creature in some of its various shapes, for this is a vice to which, as Fast Day sermons of a hundred years ago will testify, we have a long hereditary claim. The only guests to whom Robin's sympathies inclined him were two or three sheepish countrymen, who were using the inn somewhat after the fashion of a Turkish caravansary; they had gotten themselves into the darkest corner of the room, and heedless of the Nicotian atmosphere, were supping on the bread of their own ovens, and the bacon cured in their own chimney-smoke. But though Robin felt a sort of brotherhood with these strangers, his eyes were attracted from them to a person who stood near the door, holding whispered conversation with a group of ill-dressed associates. His features were separately striking almost to grotesqueness, and the whole face left a deep impression on the memory. The forehead bulged out into a double prominence, with a vale between; the nose came boldly forth in an irregular curve, and its bridge was of more than a finger's breadth; the eyebrows were deep and shaggy, and the eyes glowed beneath them like fire in a cave.

While Robin deliberated of whom to inquire respecting his kinsman's dwelling, he was accosted by the innkeeper, a little man in a stained white apron, who had come to pay his professional welcome to the stranger. Being in the second generation from a French Protestant, he seemed to have inherited the courtesy of his parent nation; but no variety of circumstances was ever known to change his voice from the one shrill note in which he now addressed Robin.

"From the country, I presume, sir?" said he, with a profound bow. "Beg leave to congratulate you on your arrival, and trust you intend a long stay with us. Fine town here, sir, beautiful buildings, and much that may interest a stranger. May I hope for the honor of your commands in respect to supper?"

"The man sees a family likeness! the rogue has guesses that I am related to the Major!" thought Robin, who had hitherto experienced little superfluous civility.

All eyes were now turned on the country lad, standing at the door, in his worn three-cornered hat, gray coat, leather breeches, and blue yarn stockings, leaning on an oaken cudgel, and bearing a wallet on his back.

Robin replied to the courteous innkeeper, with such an assumption of confidence as befitted the Major's relative. "My honest friend," he said, "I shall make it a point to patronize your house on some occasion, when"—here he could not help lowering his voice—"when I may have more than a parchment three-pence in my pocket. My present business," continued he, speaking with lofty confidence, "is merely to inquire my way to the dwelling of my kinsman, Major Molineux."

There was a sudden and general movement in the room, which Robin interpreted as expressing the eagerness of each individual to become his guide. But the innkeeper turned his eyes to a written paper on the wall, which he read, or seemed to read, with occasional recurrences to the young man's figure.

"What have we here?" said he, breaking his speech into little dry fragments. "'Left the house of the subscriber, bounden servant, Hezekiah Mudge—had on, when he went away, gray coat, leather breeches, master's third-best hat. One pound currency reward to whosoever shall lodge him in any jail of the province.' Better trudge, boy; better trudge!"

Robin had begun to draw his hand towards the lighter end of the oak cudgel, but a strange hostility in every countenance induced him to relinquish his purpose of breaking the courteous innkeeper's head. As he turned to leave the room, he encountered a sneering glance from the bold-featured personage whom he had before noticed; and no sooner was he beyond the door, than he heard a general laugh, in which the innkeeper's voice might be distinguished, like the dropping of small stones into a kettle.

"Now, is it not strange," thought Robin, with his usual shrewdness, "is it not strange that the confession of an empty pocket should outweigh the name of my kinsman, Major Molineux? Oh, if I had one of those grinning rascals in the woods, where I and my oak sapling grew up together, I would teach him that my arm is heavy though my purse be light!"

On turning the corner of the narrow lane, Robin found himself in a spacious street, with an unbroken line of lofty houses on each side, and a steepled building at the upper end, whence the ringing of a bell announced the hour of nine. The light of the moon, and the lamps from the numerous shop-windows, discovered people promenading on the pavement, and amongst them Robin hoped to recognize his hitherto inscrutable relative. The result of his former inquiries made him unwilling to hazard another, in a scene of such publicity, and he determined to walk slowly and silently up the street, thrusting his face close to that of every elderly gentleman, in search of the Major's lineaments. In his progress, Robin encountered many gay and gallant figures. Embroidered garments of showy colors, enormous periwigs, gold-laced hats, and silver-hilted swords glided past him and dazzled his optics. Travelled youths, imitators of the European fine gentlemen of the period, trod jauntily along, half dancing to the fashionable tunes which they hummed, and making poor Robin ashamed of his quiet and natural gait. At length, after many pauses to examine the gorgeous display of goods in the shop-windows, and after suffering some rebukes for the impertinence of his scrutiny into people's faces, the Major's kinsman found himself near the steepled building, still unsuccessful in his search. As yet, however, he had seen only one side of the thronged street; so Robin crossed, and continued the same sort of inquisition down the opposite pavement, with stronger hopes than the philosopher seeking an honest man, but with no better fortune. He had arrived about midway towards the lower end, from which his course began, when he overheard the approach of some one who struck down a cane on the flag-stones at every step, uttering, at regular intervals, two sepulchral hems.

"Mercy on us!" quoth Robin, recognizing the sound.

Turning a corner, which chanced to be close at his right hand, he hastened to pursue his researches in some other part of the town. His patience now was wearing low, and he seemed to feel more fatigue from his rambles since he crossed the ferry, than from his journey of several days on the other side. Hunger also pleaded loudly within him, and Robin began to balance the propriety of demanding, violently, and with lifted cudgel, the necessary guidance from the first solitary passenger whom he should meet. While a resolution to this effect was gaining strength, he entered a street of mean appearance, on either side of which a row of ill-built houses was straggling towards the harbor. The moonlight fell upon no passenger along the whole extent, but in the third domicile which Robin passed there was a half-opened door, and his keen glance detected a woman's garment within.

"My luck may be better here," said he to himself.

Accordingly, he approached the door, and beheld it shut closer as he did so; yet an open space remained, sufficing for the fair occupant to observe the stranger, without a corresponding display on her part. All that Robin could discern was a strip of scarlet petticoat, and the occasional sparkle of an eye, as if the moonbeams were trembling on some bright thing.

"Pretty mistress," for I may call her so with a good conscience, thought the shrewd youth, since I know nothing to the contrary, "my sweet pretty mistress, will you be kind enough to tell me whereabouts I must seek the dwelling of my kinsman, Major Molineux?"

Robin's voice was plaintive and winning, and the female, seeing nothing to be shunned in the handsome country youth, thrust open the door, and came forth into the moonlight. She was a dainty little figure, with a white neck, round arms, and a slender waist, at the extremity of which her scarlet petticoat jutted over a hoop, as if she were standing in a balloon. Moreover, her face was oval and pretty, her hair dark beneath the little cap, and her bright eyes possessed a sly freedom, which triumphed over those of Robin.

"Major Molineux dwells here," said this fair woman.

Now, her voice was the sweetest Robin had heard that night, the airy counterpart of a stream of melted silver; yet he could not help doubting whether that sweet voice spoke Gospel truth. He looked up and down the mean street, and then surveyed the house before which they stood. It was a small, dark edifice of two stories, the second of which projected over the lower floor, and the front apartment had the aspect of a shop for petty commodities.

"Now, truly, I am in luck," replied Robin, cunningly, "and so indeed is my kinsman, the Major, in having so pretty a housekeeper. But I prithee trouble him to step to the door; I will deliver him a message from his friends in the country, and then go back to my lodgings at the inn."

"Nay, the Major has been abed this hour or more," said the lady of the scarlet petticoat; "and it would be to little purpose to disturb him to-night, seeing his evening draught was of the strongest. But he is a kind-hearted man, and it would be as much as my life's worth to let a kinsman of his turn away from the door. You are the good old gentleman's very picture, and I could swear that was his rainy-weather hat. Also he has garments very much resembling those leather small-clothes. But come in, I pray, for I bid you hearty welcome in his name."

So, saying, the fair and hospitable dame took our hero by the hand; and the touch was light, and the force was gentleness, and though Robin read in her eyes what he did not hear in her words, yet the slender-waisted woman in the scarlet petticoat proved stronger than the athletic country youth. She had drawn his half-willing footsteps nearly to the threshold, when the opening of a door in the neighborhood startled the Major's housekeeper, and, leaving the Major's kinsman, she vanished speedily into her own domicile. A heavy yawn preceded the appearance of a man, who, like the Moonshine of Pyramus and Thisbe, carried a lantern, needlessly aiding his sister luminary in the heavens. As he walked sleepily up the street, he turned his broad, dull face on Robin, and displayed a long staff, spiked at the end.

"Home, vagabond, home!" said the watchman, in accents that seemed to fall asleep as soon as they were uttered. "Home, or we'll set you in the stocks by peep of day!"

"This is the second hint of the kind," thought Robin. "I wish they would end my difficulties, by setting me there to-night."

Nevertheless, the youth felt an instinctive antipathy towards the guardian of midnight order, which at first prevented him from asking his usual question. But just when the man was about to vanish behind the corner, Robin resolved not to lose the opportunity, and shouted lustily after him—

"I say, friend! will you guide me to the house of my kinsman, Major Molineux?"

The watchman made no reply, but turned the corner and was gone; yet Robin seemed to hear the sound of drowsy laughter stealing along the solitary street. At that moment, also, a pleasant titter saluted him from the open window above his head; he looked up, and caught the sparkle of a saucy eye; a round arm beckoned to him, and next he heard light footsteps descending the staircase within. But Robin, being of the household of a New England clergyman, was a good youth, as well as a shrewd one; so he resisted temptation, and fled away.

He now roamed desperately, and at random, through the town, almost ready to believe that a spell was on him, like that by which a wizard of his country had once kept three pursuers wandering, a whole winter night, within twenty paces of the cottage which they sought. The streets lay before him, strange and desolate, and the lights were extinguished in almost every house. Twice, however, little parties of men, among whom Robin distinguished individuals in outlandish attire, came hurrying along; but, though on both occasions they paused to address him, such intercourse did not at all enlighten his perplexity. They did but utter a few words in some language of which Robin knew nothing, and perceiving his inability to answer, bestowed a curse upon him in plain English and hastened away. Finally, the lad determined to knock at the door of every mansion that might appear worthy to be occupied by his kinsman, trusting that perseverance would overcome the fatality that had hitherto thwarted him. Firm in this resolve, he was passing beneath the walls of a church, which formed the corner of two streets, when, as he turned into the shade of its steeple, he encountered a bulky stranger, muffled in a cloak. The man was proceeding with the speed of earnest business, but Robin planted himself full before him, holding the oak cudgel with both hands across his body as a bar to further passage.

"Halt, honest man, and answer me a question," said he, very resolutely, "Tell me, this instant, whereabouts is the dwelling of my kinsman, Major Molineux!"

"Keep your tongue between your teeth, fool, and let me pass!" said a deep, gruff voice, which Robin partly remembered. "Let me pass, I say, or I'll strike you to the earth!"

"No, no, neighbor!" cried Robin, flourishing his cudgel, and then thrusting its larger end close to the man's muffled face. "No, no, I'm not the fool you take me for, nor do you pass till I have an answer to my question. Whereabout is the dwelling of my kinsman, Major Molineux?"

The stranger, instead of attempting to force his passage, stepped back into the moonlight, unmuffled his face, and stared full into that of Robin.

"Watch here an hour, and Major Molineux will pass by," said he.

Robin gazed with dismay and astonishment on the unprecedented physiognomy of the speaker. The forehead with its double prominence, the broad hooked nose, the shaggy eyebrows, and fiery eyes were those which he had noticed at the inn, but the man's complexion had undergone a singular, or, more properly, a twofold change. One side of the face blazed an intense red, while the other was black as midnight, the division line being in the broad bridge of the nose; and a mouth which seemed to extend from ear to ear was black or red, in contrast to the color of the cheek. The effect was as if two individual devils, a fiend of fire and a fiend of darkness, had united themselves to form this infernal visage. The stranger grinned in Robin's face, muffled his party-colored features, and was out of sight in a moment.

"Strange things we travellers see!" ejaculated Robin.

He seated himself, however, upon the steps of the church-door, resolving to wait the appointed time for his kinsman. A few moments were consumed in philosophical speculations upon the species of man who had just left him; but having settled this point shrewdly, rationally, and satisfactorily, he was compelled to look elsewhere for his amusement. And first he threw his eyes along the street. It was of more respectable appearance than most of those into which he had wandered; and the moon, creating, like the imaginative power, a beautiful strangeness in familiar objects, gave something of romance to a scene that might not have possessed it in the light of day. The irregular and often quaint architecture of the houses, some of whose roofs were broken into numerous little peaks, while others ascended, steep and narrow, into a single point, and others again were square; the pure snow-white of some of their complexions, the aged darkness of others, and the thousand sparklings, reflected from bright substances in the walls of many; these matters engaged Robin's attention for a while, and then began to grow wearisome. Next he endeavored to define the forms of distant objects, starting away, with almost ghostly indistinctness, just as his eye appeared to grasp them; and finally he took a minute survey of an edifice which stood on the opposite side of the street, directly in front of the churchdoor, where he was stationed. It was a large, square mansion, distinguished from its neighbors by a balcony, which rested on tall pillars, and by an elaborate Gothic window, communicating therewith.

"Perhaps this is the very house I have been seeking," thought Robin.

Then he strove to speed away the time, by listening to a murmur which swept continually along the street, yet was scarcely audible, except to an unaccustomed ear like his; it was a low, dull, dreamy sound, compounded of many noises, each of which was at too great a distance to be separately heard. Robin marvelled at this snore of a sleeping town, and marvelled more whenever its continuity was broken by now and then a distant shout, apparently loud where it originated. But altogether it was a sleep-inspiring sound, and, to shake off its drowsy influence, Robin arose, and climbed a window-frame, that he might view the interior of the church. There the moonbeams came trembling in, and fell down upon the deserted pews, and extended along the quiet aisles. A fainter yet more awful radiance was hovering around the pulpit, and one solitary ray had dared to rest upon the open page of the great Bible. Had nature, in that deep hour, become a worshipper in the house which man had builded? Or was that heavenly light the visible sanctity of the place—visible because no earthly and impure feet were within the walls? The scene made Robin's heart shiver with a sensation of loneliness stronger than he had ever felt in the remotest depths of his native woods; so he turned away and sat down again before the door. There were graves around the church, and now an uneasy thought obtruded into Robin's breast. What if the object of his search, which had been so often and so strangely thwarted, were all the time mouldering in his shroud? What if his kinsman should glide through yonder gate, and nod and smile to him in dimly passing by?

"Oh that any breathing thing were here with me!" said Robin.

Recalling his thoughts from this uncomfortable track, he sent them over forest, hill, and stream, and attempted to imagine how that evening of ambiguity and weariness had been spent by his father's household. He pictured them assembled at the door, beneath the tree, the great old tree, which had been spared for its huge twisted trunk and venerable shade, when a thousand leafy brethren fell. There, at the going down of the summer sun, it was his father's custom to perform domestic worship, that the neighbors might come and join with him like brothers of the family, and that the wayfaring man might pause to drink at the fountain, and keep his heart pure by freshening the memory of home. Robin distinguished the seat of every individual of the little audience; he saw the good man in the midst, holding the Scriptures in the golden light that fell from the western clouds; he beheld him close the book and all rise up to pray. He heard the old thanksgivings for daily mercies, the old supplications for their continuance, to which he had so often listened in weariness, but which were now among his dear remembrances. He perceived the slight inequality of his father's voice when he came to speak of the absent one; he noted how his mother turned her face to the broad and knotted trunk; how his elder brother scorned, because the beard was rough upon his upper lip, to permit his features to be moved; how the younger sister drew down a low hanging branch before her eyes; and how the littlest one of all, whose sports had hitherto broken the decorum of the scene, understood the prayer for her playmate, and burst into clamorous grief. Then he saw them go in at the door; and when Robin would have entered also, the latch tinkled into its place, and he was excluded from his home.

"Am I here, or there?" cried Robin, starting; for all at once, when his thoughts had become visible and audible in a dream, the long, wide, solitary street shone out before him.

He aroused himself, and endeavored to fix his attention steadily upon the large edifice which he had surveyed before. But still his mind kept vibrating between fancy and reality; by turns, the pillars of the balcony lengthened into the tall, bare stems of pines, dwindled down to human figures, settled again into their true shape and size, and then commenced a new succession of changes. For a single moment, when he deemed himself awake, he could have sworn that a visage—one which he seemed to remember, yet could not absolutely name as his kinsman's—was looking towards him from the Gothic window. A deeper sleep wrestled with and nearly overcame him, but fled at the sound of footsteps along the opposite pavement. Robin rubbed his eyes, discerned a man passing at the foot of the balcony, and addressed him in a loud, peevish, and lamentable cry.

"Hallo, friend! must I wait here all night for my kinsman, Major Molineux?"

The sleeping echoes awoke, and answered the voice; and the passenger, barely able to discern a figure sitting in the oblique shade of the steeple, traversed the street to obtain a nearer view. He was himself a gentleman in his prime, of open, intelligent, cheerful, and altogether prepossessing countenance. Perceiving a country youth, apparently homeless and without friends, he accosted him in a tone of real kindness, which had become strange to Robin's ears.

"Well, my good lad, who are you sitting here?" inquired he. "Can I be of service to you in any way?"

"I am afraid not, sir," replied Robin, despondingly; "yet I shall take it kindly, if you'll answer me a single question. I've been searching, half the night, for one Major Molineux; now, sir, is there really such a person in these parts, or am I dreaming?"

"Major Molineux! The name is not altogether strange to me," said the gentleman, smiling. "Have you any objection to telling me the nature of your business with him?"

Then Robin briefly related that his father was a clergyman, settled on a small salary, at a long distance back in the country, and that he and Major Molineux were brothers' children. The Major, having inherited riches, and acquired civil and military rank, had visited his cousin, in great pomp, a year or two before; had manifested much interest in Robin and an elder brother, and, being childless himself, had thrown out hints respecting the future establishment of one of them in life. The elder brother was destined to succeed to the farm which his father cultivated in the interval of sacred duties; it was therefore determined that Robin should profit by his kinsman's generous intentions, especially as he seemed to be rather the favorite, and was thought to possess other necessary endowments.

"For I have the name of being a shrewd youth," observed Robin, in this part of his story.

"I doubt not you deserve it," replied his new friend, good-naturedly; "but pray proceed."

"Well, sir, being nearly eighteen years old, and well grown, as you see," continued Robin, drawing himself up to his full height, "I thought it high time to begin the world. So my mother and sister put me in handsome trim, and my father gave me half the remnant of his last year's salary, and five days ago I started for this place, to pay the Major a visit. But, would you believe it, sir! I crossed the ferry a little after dark, and have yet found nobody that would show me the way to his dwelling; only, an hour or two since, I was told to wait here, and Major Molineux would pass by."

"Can you describe the man who told you this?" inquired the gentleman.

"Oh, he was a very ill-favored fellow, sir," replied Robin, "with two great bumps on his forehead, a hook nose, fiery eyes; and, what struck me as the strangest, his face was of two different colors. Do you happen to know such a man, sir?"

"Not intimately," answered the stranger, "but I chanced to meet him a little time previous to your stopping me. I believe you may trust his word, and that the Major will very shortly pass through this street. In the mean time, as I have a singular curiosity to witness your meeting, I will sit down here upon the steps and bear you company."

He seated himself accordingly, and soon engaged his companion in animated discourse. It was but of brief continuance, however, for a noise of shouting, which had long been remotely audible, drew so much nearer that Robin inquired its cause.

"What may be the meaning of this uproar?" asked he. "Truly, if your town be always as noisy, I shall find little sleep while I am an inhabitant."

"Why, indeed, friend Robin, there do appear to be three or four riotous fellows abroad to-night," replied the gentleman. "You must not expect all the stillness of your native woods here in our streets. But the watch will shortly be at the heels of these lads and—"

"Ay, and set them in the stocks by peep of day," interrupted Robin, recollecting his own encounter with the drowsy lantern-bearer. "But, dear sir, if I may trust my ears, an army of watchmen would never make head against such a multitude of rioters. There were at least a thousand voices went up to make that one shout."

"May not a man have several voices, Robin, as well as two complexions?" said his friend.

"Perhaps a man may; but Heaven forbid that a woman should!" responded the shrewd youth, thinking of the seductive tones of the Major's housekeeper.

The sounds of a trumpet in some neighboring street now became so evident and continual, that Robin's curiosity was strongly excited. In addition to the shouts, he heard frequent bursts from many instruments of discord, and a wild and confused laughter filled up the intervals. Robin rose from the steps, and looked wistfully towards a point whither people seemed to be hastening.

"Surely some prodigious merry-making is going on," exclaimed he. "I have laughed very little since I left home, sir, and should be sorry to lose an opportunity. Shall we step round the corner by that darkish house, and take our share of the fun?"

"Sit down again, sit down, good Robin," replied the gentleman, laying his hand on the skirt of the gray coat. "You forget that we must wait here for your kinsman; and there is reason to believe that he will pass by, in the course of a very few moments."

The near approach of the uproar had now disturbed the neighborhood; windows flew open on all sides; and many heads, in the attire of the pillow, and confused by sleep suddenly broken, were protruded to the gaze of whoever had leisure to observe them. Eager voices hailed each other from house to house, all demanding the explanation, which not a soul could give. Half-dressed men hurried towards the unknown commotion, stumbling as they went over the stone steps that thrust themselves into the narrow foot-walk. The shouts, the laughter, and the tuneless bray, the antipodes of music, came onwards with increasing din, till scattered individuals, and then denser bodies, began to appear round a corner at the distance of a hundred yards.

"Will your recognize your kinsman, if he passes in this crowd?" inquired the gentleman.

"Indeed, I can't warrant it, sir; but I'll take my stand here, and keep a bright lookout," answered Robin, descending to the outer edge of the pavement.

A mighty stream of people now emptied into the street, and came rolling slowly towards the church. A single horseman wheeled the corner in the midst of them, and close behind him came a band of fearful wind-instruments, sending forth a fresher discord now that no intervening buildings kept it from the ear. Then a redder light disturbed the moonbeams, and a dense multitude of torches shone along the street, concealing, by their glare, whatever object they illuminated. The single horseman, clad in a military dress, and bearing a drawn sword, rode onward as the leader, and, by his fierce and variegated countenance, appeared like war personified; the red of one cheek was an emblem of fire and sword; the blackness of the other betokened the mourning that attends them. In his train were wild figures in the Indian dress, and many fantastic shapes without a model, giving the whole march a visionary air, as if a dream had broken forth from some feverish brain, and were sweeping visibly through the midnight streets. A mass of people, inactive, except as applauding spectators, hemmed the procession in; and several women ran along the sidewalk, piercing the confusion of heavier sounds with their shrill voices of mirth or terror.

"The double-faced fellow has his eye upon me," muttered Robin, with an indefinite but an uncomfortable idea that he was himself to bear a part in the pageantry.

The leader turned himself in the saddle, and fixed his glance full upon the country youth, as the steed went slowly by. When Robin had freed his eyes from those fiery ones, the musicians were passing before him, and the torches were close at hand; but the unsteady brightness of the latter formed a veil which he could not penetrate. The rattling of wheels over the stones sometimes found its way to his ear, and confused traces of a human form appeared at intervals, and then melted into the vivid light. A moment more, and the leader thundered a command to halt: the trumpets vomited a horrid breath, and then held their peace; the shouts and laughter of the people died away, and there remained only a universal hum, allied to silence. Right before Robin's eyes was an uncovered cart. There the torches blazed the brightest, there the moon shone out like day, and there, in tar-and-feathery dignity, sat his kinsman, Major Molineux!

He was an elderly man, of large and majestic person, and strong, square features, betokening a steady sould; but steady as it was, his enemies had found means to shake it. His face was pale as death, and far more ghastly; the broad forehead was contracted in his agony, so that his eyebrows formed one grizzled line; his eyes were red and wild, and the foam hung white upon his quivering lip. His whole frame was agitated by a quick and continual tremor, which his pride strove to quell, even in those circumstances of overwhelming humiliation. But perhaps the bitterest pang of all was when his eyes met those of Robin; for he evidently knew him on the instant, as the youth stood witnessing the foul disgrace of a head grown gray in honor. They stared at each other in silence, and Robin's knees shook, and his hair bristled, with a mixture of pity and terror. Soon, however, a bewildering excitement began to seize upon his mind; the preceding adventures of the night, the unexpected appearance of the crowd, the torches, the confused din and the hush that followed, the spectre of his kinsman reviled by that great multitude—all this, and, more than all, a perception of tremendous ridicule in the whole scene, affected him with a sort of mental inebrity. At that moment a voice of sluggish merriment saluted Robin's ears; he turned instinctively, and just behind the corner of the church stood the lantern-bearer, rubbing his eyes, and drowsily enjoying the lad's amazement. Then he heard a peal of laughter like the ringing of silvery bells; a woman twitched his arm, a saucy eye met his, and he saw the lady of the scarlet petticoat. A sharp, dry cachinnation appealed to his memory, and, standing on tiptoe in the crowd, with his white apron over his head, he beheld the courteous little innkeeper. And lastly, there sailed over the heads of the multitude a great, broad laugh, broken in the midst by two sepulchral hems; thus, "Haw, haw, haw—hem, hem—haw, haw, haw, haw!"

The sound proceeded from the balcony of the opposite edifice, and thither Robin turned his eyes. In front of the Gothic window stood the old citizen, wrapped in a wide gown, his gray periwig exchanged for a nightcap, which was thrust back from his forehead, and his silk stockings hanging about his legs. He supported himself on his polished cane in a fit of convulsive merriment, which manifested itself on his solemn old features like a funny inscription on a tombstone. Then Robin seemed to hear the voices of the barbers, of the guests of the inn, and of all who had made sport of him that night. The contagion was spreading among the multitude, when all at once, it seized upon Robin, and he sent forth a shout of laughter that echoed through the street—every man shook his sides, every man emptied his lungs, but Robin's shout was the loudest there. The cloud-spirits peeped from their silvery islands, as the congregated mirth went roaring up the sky! The Man in the Moon heard the far bellow. "Oho," quoth he, "the old earth is frolicsome to-night!"

When there was a momentary calm in that tempestuous sea of sound, the leader gave the sign, the procession resumed its march. On they went, like fiends that throng in mockery around some dead potentate, mighty no more, but majestic still in his agony. On they went, in counterfeited pomp, in senseless uproar, in frenzied merriment, trampling all on an old man's heart. On swept the tumult, and left a silent street behind.

"Well, Robin, are you dreaming?" inquired the gentleman, laying his hand on the youth's shoulder.

Robin started, and withdrew his arm from the stone post to which he had instinctively clung, as the living stream rolled by him. His cheek was somewhat pale, and his eye not quite as lively as in the earlier part of the evening.

"Will you be kind enough to show me the way to the ferry?" said he, after a moment's pause.

"You have, then, adopted a new subject of inquiry?" observed his companion, with a smile.

"Why, yes, sir," replied Robin, rather dryly. "Thanks to you, and to my other friends, I have at last met my kinsman, and he will scarce desire to see my face again. I begin to grow weary of a town life, sir. Will you show me the way to the ferry?"

"No, my good friend Robin—not to-night at least," said the gentleman. "Some few days hence, if you wish it, I will speed you on your journey. Or, if you prefer to remain with us, perhaps, as you are a shrewd youth, you may rise in the world without the help of your kinsman, Major Molineux."

QUESTIONS

1. The first paragraph provides a frame. Discuss the effect of the narrator's remarks on your perception of the story that follows.

2. Through what character's eyes do we first view Robin? Discuss the effect achieved by this perspective.

3. The city is seen through Robin's eyes. How effective is this perspective in making the city seem both hostile and alluring?

4. The darkened city is illuminated by moonlight, by torches and lanterns, and by light spilling from doors and windows, producing a sharp contrast of light and dark. Discuss, relating lighting to mood.

5. What is Robin's reaction to the interior of the church? Why does the church turn his thoughts toward his home and family? How does "his father's household" contrast with his experiences in the city?

6. Describe the use of aural imagery as a way of creating suspense and building to a climax. Examine in particular laughter as a unifying motif. Robin's laughter is described as the "loudest there." Explain the significance of this statement.

7. Robin's experiences in the city can be interpreted as an initiation into adulthood. Is his newly acquired maturity unequivocally good? Explain.

8. Robin comes to the city in hopes that his kinsman will help him. Find at least three references to Major Molineux that indicate Robin's dependence on the man. After the events of the night reverse the boy's expectations, what advice does the kindly gentleman give him? Discuss the significance of the gentleman as Robin's new mentor.

9. Another interpretation views the story as political allegory, with the insurrection standing for the American Revolution and Robin representing the apolitical but "shrewd" pioneer who must come to terms with the Revolutionary spirit. If so, what does Major Molineux represent? the kindly gentleman? the leader of the mob? What is the implication of the conclusion?

10. Examine the attitude of the implied author to the city, to its inhabitants, to the mob's leader, to Major Molineux. Discuss the relationship of tone to meaning.

F. SCOTT FITZGERALD

Babylon Revisited

"And where's Mr. Campbell?" Charlie asked.

"Gone to Switzerland. Mr. Campbell's a pretty sick man, Mr. Wales."

"I'm sorry to hear that. And George Hardt?" Charlie inquired.

"Back in America, gone to work."

"And where is the Snow Bird?"

"He was in here last week. Anyway, his friend, Mr. Schaeffer, is in Paris."

Two familiar names from the long list of a year and a half ago. Charlie scribbled an address in his notebook and tore out the page.

"If you see Mr. Schaeffer, give him this," he said. "It's my brother-in-law's address. I haven't settled on a hotel yet."

He was not really disappointed to find Paris was so empty. But the stillness in the Ritz bar was strange and portentous. It was not an American bar any more—he felt polite in it, and not as if he owned it. It had gone back into France. He felt the stillness from the moment he got out of the taxi and saw the doorman, usually in a frenzy of activity at this hour, gossiping with a *chasseur* by the servants' entrance.

Passing through the corridor, he heard only a single, bored voice in the once-clamorous women's room. When he turned into the bar he traveled the twenty feet of green carpet with his eyes fixed straight ahead by old habit; and then, with his foot firmly on the rail, he turned and surveyed the room, encountering only a single pair of eyes that fluttered up from a newspaper in the corner. Charlie asked for the head barman, Paul, who in the latter days of the bull market had come to work in his own custom-built car—disembarking,

315

however, with due nicety at the nearest corner. But Paul was at his country
house today and Alix giving him information.

"No, no more," Charlie said, "I'm going slow these days."

Alix congratulated him: "You were going pretty strong a couple of years
ago."

"I'll stick to it all right," Charlie assured him. "I've stuck to it for over a
year and a half now."

"How do you find conditions in America?"

"I haven't been to America for months, I'm in business in Prague, representing a couple of concerns there. They don't know about me down there."

Alix smiled.

"Remember the night of George Hardt's bachelor dinner here?" said
Charlie. "By the way, what's become of Claude Fessenden?"

Alix lowered his voice confidentially: "He's in Paris, but he doesn't come
here any more. Paul doesn't allow it. He ran up a bill of thirty thousand francs,
charging all his drinks and his lunches, and usually his dinner, for more than a
year. And when Paul finally told him he had to pay, he gave him a bad check."

Alix shook his head sadly.

"I don't understand it, such a dandy fellow. Now he's all bloated up—" He
made a plump apple of his hands.

Charlie watched a group of strident queens installing themselves in a
corner.

"Nothing affects them," he thought. "Stocks rise and fall, people loaf or
work, but they go on forever." The place oppressed him. He called for the dice
and shook with Alix for the drink.

"Here for long, Mr. Wales?"

"I'm here for four or five days to see my little girl."

"Oh-h! You have a little girl?"

Outside, the fire-red, gas-blue, ghost-green signs shone smokily through
the tranquil rain. It was late afternoon and the streets were in movement; the
bistros gleamed. At the corner of the Boulevard des Capucines he took a taxi.
The Place de la Concorde moved by in pink majesty; they crossed the logical
Seine, and Charlie felt the sudden provincial quality of the left bank.

Charlie directed his taxi to the Avenue de l'Opera, which was out of his
way. But he wanted to see the blue hour spread over the magnificent façade, and
imagine that the cab horns, playing endlessly the first few bars of *Le Plus que
Lent,* were the trumpets of the Second Empire. They were closing the iron grill
in front of Brentano's Book-store, and people were already at dinner behind the
trim little bourgeois hedge of Duval's. He had never eaten at a really cheap
restaurant in Paris. Five-course dinner, four francs fifty, eighteen cents, wine
included. For some odd reason he wished that he had.

As they rolled on to the Left Bank and he felt its sudden provincialism, he
thought, "I spoiled this city for myself. I didn't realize it, but the days came along
one after another, and then two years were gone, and everything was gone, and I
was gone."

He was thirty-five, and good to look at. The Irish mobility of his face was sobered by a deep wrinkle between his eyes. As he rang his brother-in-law's bell in the Rue Palatine, the wrinkle deepened till it pulled down his brows; he felt a cramping sensation in his belly. From behind the maid who opened the door darted a lovely little girl of nine who shrieked "Daddy!" and flew up, struggling like a fish, into his arms. She pulled his head around by one ear and set her cheek against his.

"My old pie," he said.

"Oh, daddy, daddy, daddy, daddy, dads, dads, dads!"

She drew him into the salon, where the family waited, a boy and a girl his daughter's age, his sister-in-law and her husband. He greeted Marion with his voice pitched carefully to avoid either feigned enthusiasm or dislike, but her response was more frankly tepid, though she minimized her expression of unalterable distrust by directing her regard toward his child. The two men clasped hands in a friendly way and Lincoln Peters rested his for a moment on Charlie's shoulder.

The room was warm and comfortably American. The three children moved intimately about, playing through the yellow oblongs that led to other rooms; the cheer of six o'clock spoke in the eager smacks of the fire and the sounds of French activity in the kitchen. But Charlie did not relax; his heart sat up rigidly in his body and he drew confidence from his daughter, who from time to time came close to him, holding in her arms the doll he had brought.

"Really extremely well," he declared in answer to Lincoln's question. "There's a lot of business there that isn't moving at all, but we're doing even better than ever. In fact, damn well. I'm bringing my sister over from America next month to keep house for me. My income last year was bigger than it was when I had money. You see, the Czechs——"

His boasting was for a specific purpose; but after a moment, seeing a faint restiveness in Lincoln's eye, he changed the subject:

"Those are fine children of yours, well brought up, good manners."

"We think Honoria's a great little girl too."

Marion Peters came back from the kitchen. She was a tall woman with worried eyes, who had once possessed a fresh American loveliness. Charlie had never been sensitive to it and was always surprised when people spoke of how pretty she had been. From the first there had been an instinctive antipathy between them.

"Well, how do you find Honoria?" she asked.

"Wonderful. I was astonished how much she's grown in ten months. All the children are looking well."

"We haven't had a doctor for a year. How do you like being back in Paris?"

"It seems very funny to see so few Americans around."

"I'm delighted," Marion said vehemently. "Now at least you can go into a store without their assuming you're a millionaire. We've suffered like everybody, but on the whole it's a good deal pleasanter."

"But it was nice while it lasted," Charlie said. "We were a sort of royalty, almost infallible, with a sort of magic around us. In the bar this afternoon"—he stumbled, seeing his mistake—"there wasn't a man I knew."

She looked at him keenly. "I should think you'd have had enough of bars."

"I only stayed a minute. I take one drink every afternoon, and no more."

"Don't you want a cocktail before dinner?" Lincoln asked.

"I take only one drink every afternoon, and I've had that."

"I hope you keep to it," said Marion.

Her dislike was evident in the coldness with which she spoke, but Charlie only smiled; he had larger plans. Her very aggressiveness gave him an advantage, and he knew enough to wait. He wanted them to initiate the discussion of what they knew had brought him to Paris.

At dinner he couldn't decide whether Honoria was most like him or her mother. Fortunate if she didn't combine the traits of both that had brought them to disaster. A great wave of protectiveness went over him. He thought he knew what to do for her. He believed in character; he wanted to jump back a whole generation and trust in character again as the eternally valuable element. Everything else wore out.

He left soon after dinner, but not to go home. He was curious to see Paris by night with clearer and more judicious eyes than those of other days. He bought a *strapontin* for the Casino and watched Josephine Baker go through her chocolate arabesques.

After an hour he left and strolled toward Montmartre, up the Rue Pigalle into the Place Blanche. The rain had stopped and there were a few people in evening clothes disembarking from taxis in front of cabarets, and *cocottes* prowling singly or in pairs, and many Negroes. He passed a lighted door from which issued music, and stopped with the sense of familiarity; it was Bricktop's, where he had parted with so many hours and so much money. A few doors farther on he found another ancient rendezvous and incautiously put his head inside. Immediately an eager orchestra burst into sound, a pair of professional dancers leaped to their feet and a maître d'hôtel swooped toward him, crying, "Crowd just arriving, sir!" But he withdrew quickly.

"You have to be damn drunk," he thought.

Zelli's was closed, the bleak and sinister cheap hotels surrounding it were dark; up in the Rue Blanche there was more light and a local, colloquial French crowd. The Poet's Cave had disappeared, but the two great mouths of the Café of Heaven and the Café of Hell still yawned—even devoured, as he watched, the meager contents of a tourist bus—a German, a Japanese, and an American couple who glanced at him with frightened eyes.

So much for the effort and ingenuity of Montmartre. All the catering to vice and waste was on an utterly childish scale, and he suddenly realized the meaning of the word "dissipate"—to dissipate into thin air; to make nothing out of something. In the little hours of the night every move from place to place was an enormous human jump, an increase of paying for the privilege of slower and slower motion.

He remembered thousand-franc notes given to an orchestra for playing a single number, hundred-franc notes tossed to a doorman for calling a cab.

But it hadn't been given for nothing.

It had been given, even the most wildly squandered sum, as an offering to destiny that he might not remember the things most worth remembering, the things that now he would always remember—his child taken from his control, his wife escaped to a grave in Vermont.

In the glare of a *brasserie* a woman spoke to him. He bought her some eggs and coffee, and then, eluding her encouraging stare, gave her a twenty-franc note and took a taxi to his hotel.

II

He woke upon a fine fall day—football weather. The depression of yesterday was gone and he liked the people on the streets. At noon he sat opposite Honoria at Le Grand Vatel, the only restaurant he could think of not reminiscent of champagne dinners and long luncheons that began at two and ended in a blurred and vague twilight.

"Now, how about vegetables? Oughtn't you to have some vegetables?"

"Well, yes."

"Here's *épinards* and *chou-fleur* and carrots and *haricots*."

"I'd like *chou-fleur*."

"Wouldn't you like to have two vegetables?"

"I usually only have one at lunch."

The waiter was pretending to be inordinately fond of children. "*Qu'elle est mignonne la petite! Elle parle exactement comme une Française.*"

"How about dessert? Shall we wait and see?"

The waiter disappeared. Honoria looked at her father expectantly.

"What are we going to do?"

"First, we're going to that toy store in the Rue Saint-Honoré and buy you anything you like. And then we're going to the vaudeville at the Empire."

She hesitated. "I like it about the vaudeville, but not the toy store."

"Why not?"

"Well, you brought me this doll." She had it with her. "And I've got lots of things. And we're not rich any more, are we?"

"We never were. But today you are to have anything you want."

"All right," she agreed resignedly.

When there had been her mother and a French nurse he had been inclined to be strict; now he extended himself, reached out for a new tolerance; he must be both parents to her and not shut any of her out of communication.

"I want to get to know you," he said gravely. "First let me introduce myself. My name is Charles J. Wales, of Prague."

"Oh, daddy!" her voice cracked with laughter.

"And who are you, please?" he persisted, and she accepted a rôle immediately: "Honoria Wales, Rue Palatine, Paris."

"Married or single?"

"No, not married. Single."

He indicated the doll. "But I see you have a child, madame."

Unwilling to disinherit it, she took it to here heart and thought quickly: "Yes, I've been married, but I'm not married now. My husband is dead."

He went on quickly, "And the child's name?"

"Simone. That's after my best friend at school."

"I'm very pleased that you're doing so well at school."

"I'm third this month," she boasted. "Elsie"—that was her cousin—"is only about eighteenth, and Richard is about at the bottom."

"You like Richard and Elsie, don't you?"

"Oh, yes. I like Richard quite well and I like her all right."

Cautiously and casually he asked: "And Aunt Marion and Uncle Lincoln—which do you like best?"

"Oh, Uncle Lincoln, I guess."

He was increasingly aware of her presence. As they came in, a murmur of " . . . adorable" followed them, and now the people at the next table bent all their silences upon her, staring as if she were something no more conscious than a flower.

"Why don't I live with you?" she asked suddenly. "Because mamma's dead?"

"You must stay here and learn more French. It would have been hard for daddy to take care of you so well."

"I don't really need much taking care of any more. I do everything for myself."

Going out of the restaurant, a man and a woman unexpectedly hailed him.

"Well, the old Wales!"

"Hello there, Lorraine. . . . Dunc."

Sudden ghosts out of the past: Duncan Schaeffer, a friend from college. Lorraine Quarrles, a lovely, pale blonde of thirty; one of a crowd who had helped them make months into days in the lavish times of three years ago.

"My husband couldn't come this year," she said, in answer to his question. "We're poor as hell. So he gave me two hundred a month and told me I could do my worst on that. . . . This your little girl?"

"What about coming back and sitting down?" Duncan asked.

"Can't do it." He was glad for an excuse. As always, he felt Lorraine's passionate, provocative attraction, but his own rhythm was different now.

"Well, how about dinner?" she asked.

"I'm not free. Give me your address and let me call you."

"Charlie, I believe you're sober," she said judicially. "I honestly believe he's sober, Dunc. Pinch him and see if he's sober."

Charlie indicated Honoria with his head. They both laughed.

"What's your address?" said Duncan skeptically.

He hesitated, unwilling to give the name of his hotel.

"I'm not settled yet. I'd better call you. We're going to see the vaudeville at the Empire."

"There! That's what I want to do," Lorraine said. "I want to see some clowns and acrobats and jugglers. That's just what we'll do, Dunc."

"We've got to do an errand first," said Charlie. "Perhaps we'll see you there."

"All right, you snob. . . . Good-by, beautiful little girl."

"Good-by."

Honoria bobbed politely.

Somehow, an unwelcome encounter. They liked him because he was functioning, because he was serious; they wanted to see him, because he was stronger than they were now, because they wanted to draw a certain sustenance from his strength.

At the Empire, Honoria proudly refused to sit upon her father's folded coat. She was already an individual with a code of her own, and Charlie was more and more absorbed by the desire of putting a little of himself into her before she crystallized utterly. It was hopeless to try to know her in so short a time.

Between the acts they came upon Duncan and Lorraine in the lobby where the band was playing.

"Have a drink?"

"All right, but not up at the bar. We'll take a table."

"The perfect father."

Listening abstractedly to Lorraine, Charlie watched Honoria's eyes leave their table, and he followed them wistfully about the room, wondering what they saw. He met her glance and she smiled.

"I liked that lemonade," she said.

What had she said? What had he expected? Going home in a taxi afterward, he pulled her over until her head rested against his chest.

"Darling, do you ever think about your mother?"

"Yes, sometimes," she answered vaguely.

"I don't want you to forget her. Have you got a picture of her?"

"Yes, I think so. Anyhow, Aunt Marion has. Why don't you want me to forget her?"

"She loved you very much."

"I loved her too."

They were silent for a moment.

"Daddy, I want to come and live with you," she said suddenly.

His heart leaped; he had wanted it to come like this.

"Aren't you perfectly happy?"

"Yes, but I love you better than anybody. And you love me better than anybody, don't you, now that mummy's dead?"

"Of course I do. But you won't always like me best, honey. You'll grow up and meet somebody your own age and go marry him and forget you ever had a daddy."

"Yes, that's true," she agreed tranquilly.

He didn't go in. He was coming back at nine o'clock and he wanted to keep himself fresh and new for the thing he must say then.

"When you're safe inside, just show yourself in that window."

"All right. Good-by, dads, dads, dads, dads."

He waited in the dark street until she appeared, all warm and glowing, in the window above and kissed her fingers out into the night.

III

They were waiting, Marion sat behind the coffee service in a dignified black dinner dress that just faintly suggested mourning. Lincoln was walking up and down with the animation of one who had already been talking. They were as anxious as he was to get into the question. He opened it almost immediately:

"I suppose you know what I want to see you about—why I really came to Paris."

Marion played with the black stars on her necklace and frowned.

"I'm awfully anxious to have a home," he continued. "And I'm awfully anxious to have Honoria in it. I appreciate your taking in Honoria for her mother's sake, but things have changed now"—he hesitated and then continued more forcibly—"changed radically with me, and I want to ask you to reconsider the matter. It would be silly for me to deny that about three years ago I was acting badly——"

Marion looked up at him with hard eyes.

"—but all that's over. As I told you, I haven't had more than a drink a day for over a year, and I take that drink deliberately, so that the idea of alcohol won't get too big in my imagination. You see the idea?"

"No," said Marion succinctly.

"It's a sort of stunt I set myself. It keeps the matter in proportion."

"I get you," said Lincoln. "You don't want to admit it's got any attraction for you."

"Something like that. Sometimes I forget and don't take it. But I try to take it. Anyhow, I couldn't afford to drink in my position. The people I represent are more than satisfied with what I've done, and I'm bringing my sister over from Burlington to keep house for me, and I want awfully to have Honoria too. You know that even when her mother and I weren't getting along well we never let anything that happened touch Honoria. I know she's fond of me and I know I'm able to take care of her and—well, there you are. How do you feel about it?"

He knew that now he would have to take a beating. It would last an hour or two hours, and it would be difficult, but if he modulated his inevitable resentment to the chastened attitude of the reformed sinner, he might win his point in the end.

Keep your temper, he told himself. You don't want to be justified. You want Honoria.

Lincoln spoke first: "We've been talking it over ever since we got your letter last month. We're happy to have Honoria here. She's a dear little thing, and we're glad to be able to help her, but of course that isn't the question——"

Marion interrupted suddenly. "How long are you going to stay sober, Charlie?" she asked.

"Permanently, I hope."

"How can anybody count on that?"

"You know I never did drink heavily until I gave up business and came over here with nothing to do. Then Helen and I began to run around with——"

"Please leave Helen out of it. I can't bear to hear you talk about her like that."

He stared at her grimly; he had never been certain how fond of each other the sisters were in life.

"My drinking only lasted about a year and a half—from the time we came over until I—collapsed."

"It was time enough."

"It was time enough," he agreed.

"My duty is entirely to Helen," she said. "I try to think what she would have wanted me to do. Frankly, from the night you did that terrible thing you haven't really existed for me. I can't help that. She was my sister."

"Yes."

"When she was dying she asked me to look out for Honoria. If you hadn't been in a sanitarium then, it might have helped matters."

He had no answer.

"I'll never in my life be able to forget the morning when Helen knocked at my door, soaked to the skin and shivering and said you'd locked her out."

Charlie gripped the sides of the chair. This was more difficult than he expected; he wanted to launch out into a long expostulation and explanation, but he only said: "The night I locked her out—" and she interrupted, "I don't feel up to going over that again."

After a moment's silence Lincoln said: "We're getting off the subject. You want Marion to set aside her legal guardianship and give you Honoria. I think the main point for her is whether she has confidence in you or not."

"I don't blame Marion," Charlie said slowly, "but I think she can have entire confidence in me. I had a good record up to three years ago. Of course, it's within human possibilities I might go wrong any time. But if we wait much longer I'll lose Honoria's childhood and my chance for a home." He shook his head, "I'll simply lose her, don't you see?"

"Yes, I see," said Lincoln.

"Why didn't you think of all this before?" Marion asked.

"I suppose I did, from time to time, but Helen and I were getting along badly. When I consented to the guardianship, I was flat on my back in a sanitarium and the market had cleaned me out. I knew I'd acted badly, and I thought if it would bring any peace to Helen, I'd agree to anything. But now it's different. I'm functioning, I'm behaving damn well, so far as——"

"Please don't swear at me," Marion said.

He looked at her, startled. With each remark the force of her dislike became more and more apparent. She had built up all her fear of life into one wall and faced it toward him. This trivial reproof was possibly the result of some trouble with the cook several hours before. Charlie became increasingly alarmed at leaving Honoria in this atmosphere of hostility against himself; sooner or later it would come out, in a word here, a shake of the head there, and some of that distrust would be irrevocably implanted in Honoria. But he pulled his temper down out of his face and shut it up inside him; he had won a point, for Lincoln realized the absurdity of Marion's remark and asked her lightly since when she had objected to the word "damn."

"Another thing," Charlie said: "I'm able to give her certain advantages now. I'm going to take a French governess to Prague with me. I've got a lease on a new apartment——"

He stopped, realizing that he was blundering. They couldn't be expected to accept with equanimity the fact that his income was again twice as large as their own.

"I suppose you can give her more luxuries than we can," said Marion. "When you were throwing away money we were living along watching every ten francs. . . . I suppose you'll start doing it again."

"Oh, no," he said. "I've learned. I worked hard for ten years, you know— until I got lucky in the market, like so many people. Terribly lucky. It won't happen again."

There was a long silence. All of them felt their nerves straining, and for the first time in a year Charlie wanted a drink. He was sure now that Lincoln Peters wanted him to have his child.

Marion shuddered suddenly; part of her saw that Charlie's feet were planted on the earth now, and her own maternal feeling recognized the natural-ness of his desire; but she had lived for a long time with a prejudice—a prejudice founded on a curious disbelief in her sister's happiness, and which, in the shock of one terrible night, had turned to hatred for him. It had all happened at a point in her life where the discouragement of ill health and adverse circumstances made it necessary for her to belive in tangible villainy and a tangible villain.

"I can't help what I think!" she cried out suddenly. "How much you were responsible for Helen's death, I don't know. It's something you'll have to square with your own conscience."

An electric current of agony surged through him; for a moment he was almost on his feet, an unuttered sound echoing in his throat. He hung on to himself for a moment, another moment.

"Hold on there," said Lincoln uncomfortably. "I never thought you were responsible for that."

"Helen died of heart trouble," Charlie said dully.

"Yes, heart trouble," Marion spoke as if the phrase had another meaning for her.

Then, in the flatness that followed her outburst, she saw him plainly and she knew he had somehow arrived at control over the situation. Glancing at her husband, she found no help from him, and as abruptly as if it were a matter of no importance, she threw up the sponge.

"Do what you like!" she cried, springing up from her chair. "She's your child. I'm not the person to stand in your way. I think if it were my child I'd rather see her—" She managed to check herself. "You two decide it. I can't stand this. I'm sick. I'm going to bed."

She hurried from the room; after a moment Lincoln said:

"This has been a hard day for her. You know how strongly she feels—" His voice was almost apologetic: "When a woman gets an idea in her head."

"Of course."

"It's going to be all right. I think she sees now that you—can provide for the child, and so we can't very well stand in your way or Honoria's way."

"Thank you, Lincoln."

"I'd better go along and see how she is."

"I'm going."

He was still trembling when he reached the street, but a walk down the Rue Bonaparte to the *quais* set him up, and as he crossed the Seine, fresh and new by the *quai* lamps, he felt exultant. But back in his room he couldn't sleep. The image of Helen haunted him. Helen whom he had loved so until they had senselessly begun to abuse each other's love, tear it into shreds. On that terrible February night that Marion remembered so vividly, a slow quarrel had gone on for hours. There was a scene at the Florida, and then he attempted to take her home, and then she kissed young Webb at a table; after that there was what she had hysterically said. When he arrived home alone he turned the key in the lock in wild anger. How could he know she would arrive an hour later alone, that there would be a snowstorm in which she wandered about in slippers, too confused to find a taxi? Then the aftermath, her escaping pneumonia by a miracle, and all the attendant horror. They were "reconciled," but that was the beginning of the end, and Marion, who had seen with her own eyes and who imagined it to be one of many scenes from her sister's martyrdom, never forgot.

Going over it again brought Helen nearer, and in the white, soft light that steals upon half sleep near morning he found himself talking to her again. She said that he was perfectly right about Honoria and that she wanted Honoria to be with him. She said she was glad he was being good and doing better. She said a lot of other things—very friendly things—but she was in a swing in a white dress, and swinging faster and faster all the time, so that at the end he could not hear clearly all that she said.

IV

He woke up feeling happy. The door of the world was open again. He made plans, vistas, futures for Honoria and himself, but suddenly he grew sad, remembering all the plans he and Helen had made. She had not planned to die. The present was the thing—work to do and someone to love. But not to love too much, for he knew the injury that a father can do to a daughter or a mother to a son by attaching them too closely; afterward, out in the world, the child would seek in the marriage partner the same blind tenderness and, failing probably to find it, turn against love and life.

It was another bright, crisp day. He called Lincoln Peters at the bank where he worked and asked if he could count on taking Honoria when he left for Prague. Lincoln agreed that there was no reason for delay. One thing—the legal guardianship. Marion wanted to retain that a while longer. She was upset by the whole matter, and it would oil things if she felt that the situation was still in her control for another year. Charlie agreed, wanting only the tangible, visible child.

Then the question of a governess. Charles sat in a gloomy agency and talked to a cross Béarnaise and to a buxom Breton peasant, neither of whom he could have endured. There were others whom he would see tomorrow.

He lunched with Lincoln Peters at Griffons, trying to keep down his exultation.

"There's nothing quite like your own child," Lincoln said. "But you understand how Marion feels too."

"She's forgotten how hard I worked for seven years there," Charlie said. "She just remembers one night."

"There's another thing." Lincoln hesitated. "While you and Helen were tearing around Europe throwing money away, we were just getting along. I didn't touch any of the prosperity because I never got ahead enough to carry anything but my insurance. I think Marion felt there was some kind of injustice in it—you not even working toward the end, and getting richer and richer."

"It went just as quick as it came," said Charlie.

"Yes, a lot of it stayed in the hands of *chasseurs* and saxophone players and maîtres d'hôtel—well, the big party's over now. I just said that to explain Marion's feeling about those crazy years. If you drop in about six o'clock tonight before Marion's too tired, we'll settle the details on the spot."

Back at his hotel, Charlie found a *pneumatique* that had been redirected from the Ritz bar where Charlie had left his address for the purpose of finding a certain man.

"Dear Charlie:

You were so strange when we saw you the other day that I wondered if I did something to offend you. If so, I'm not conscious of it. In fact, I have thought about you too much for the last year, and it's always been in the back of my mind that I might see you if I came over here. We *did* have such good times that crazy spring, like the night you and I stole the butcher's tricycle, and the time we tried to call on the president and you had the old derby rim and the wire cane. Everybody seems so old lately, but I don't feel old a bit. Couldn't we get together some time today for old time's sake? I've got a vile hang-over for the moment, but will be feeling better this afternoon and will look for you about five in the sweatshop at the Ritz.

"Always devotedly,
"Lorraine."

His first feeling was one of awe that he had actually, in his mature years, stolen a tricycle and pedaled Lorraine all over the Étoile between the small hours and dawn. In retrospect it was a nightmare. Locking out Helen didn't fit in with any other act of his life, but the tricycle incident did—it was one of many. How many weeks or months of dissipation to arrive at that condition of utter irresponsibility?

He tried to picture how Lorraine had appeared to him then—very attractive; Helen was unhappy about it, though she said nothing. Yesterday, in the restaurant, Lorraine had seemed trite, blurred, worn away. He emphatically did not want to see her, and he was glad Alix had not given away his hotel address. It was a relief to think, instead, of Honoria, to think of Sundays spent with her and of saying good morning to her and of knowing she was there in his house at night, drawing her breath in the darkness.

At five he took a taxi and bought presents for all the Peters—a piquant cloth doll, a box of Roman soldiers, flowers for Marion, big linen handkerchiefs for Lincoln.

He saw, when he arrived in the apartment, that Marion had accepted the inevitable. She greeted him now as though he were a recalcitrant member of the family, rather than a menacing outsider. Honoria had been told she was going; Charlie was glad to see that her tact made her conceal her excessive happiness. Only on his lap did she whisper her delight and the question "When?" before she slipped away with the other children.

He and Marion were alone for a minute in the room, and on an impulse he spoke out boldly:

"Family quarrels are bitter things. They don't go according to any rules. They're not like aches or wounds; they're more like splits in the skin that won't heal because there's not enough material. I wish you and I could be on better terms."

"Some things are hard to forget," she answered. "It's a question of confidence." There was no answer to this and presently she asked, "When do you propose to take her?"

"As soon as I can get a governess. I hoped the day after tomorrow."

"That's impossible. I've got to get her things in shape. Not before Saturday."

He yielded. Coming back into the room, Lincoln offered him a drink. "I'll take my daily whisky," he said.

It was warm here, it was a home, people together by a fire. The children felt very safe and important; the mother and father were serious, watchful. They had things to do for the children more important than his visit here. A spoonful of medicine was, after all, more important than the strained relations between Marion and himself. They were not dull people, but they were very much in the grip of life and circumstances. He wondered if he couldn't do something to get Lincoln out of his rut at the bank.

A long peal at the door-bell; the *bonne à tout faire* passed through and went down the corridor. The door opened upon another long ring, and then voices, and the three in the salon looked up expectantly; Richard moved to bring the corridor within his range of vision, and Marion rose. Then the maid came back along the corridor, closely followed by the voices, which developed under the light into Duncan Schaeffer and Lorraine Quarrles.

They were gay, they were hilarious, they were roaring with laughter. For a moment Charlie was astounded; unable to understand how they ferreted out the Peters' address.

"Ah-h-h!" Duncan wagged his finger roguishly at Charlie. "Ah-h-h!"

They both slid down another cascade of laughter. Anxious and at a loss, Charlie shook hands with them quickly and presented them to Lincoln and Marion. Marion nodded, scarcely speaking. She had drawn back a step toward the fire; her little girl stood beside her, and Marion put an arm about her shoulder.

With growing annoyance at the intrusion, Charlie waited for them to explain themselves. After some concentration Duncan said: "We came to invite you out to dinner. Lorraine and I insist that all this shishi, cagy business 'bout your address got to stop."

Charlie came closer to them, as if to force them backward down the corridor.

"Sorry, but I can't. Tell me where you'll be and I'll phone you in half an hour."

This made no impression. Lorraine sat down suddenly on the side of a chair, and focusing her eyes on Richard, cried, "Oh, what a nice little boy! Come here, little boy," Richard glanced at his mother, but did not move. With a perceptible shrug of her shoulders, Lorraine turned back to Charlie:

"Come and dine. Sure your cousins won' mine. See you so sel'om. Or solemn."

"I can't," said Charlie sharply. "You two have dinner and I'll phone you."

Her voice became suddenly unpleasant. "All right, we'll go. But I remember once when you hammered on my door at four A.M. I was enough of a good sport to give you a drink. Come on, Dunc."

Still in slow motion, with blurred, angry faces, with uncertain feet, they retired along the corridor.

"Good night," Charlie said.

"Good night!" responded Lorraine emphatically.

When he went back into the salon Marion had not moved, only now her son was standing in the circle of her other arm. Lincoln was still swinging Honoria back and forth like a pendulum from side to side.

"What an outrage!" Charlie broke out. "What an absolute outrage!"

Neither of them answered, Charlie dropped into an armchair, picked up his drink, set it down again and said:

"People I haven't seen for two years having the colossal nerve——"

He broke off. Marion had made the sound "Oh!" in one swift, furious breath, turned her body from him with a jerk and left the room.

Lincoln set down Honoria carefully.

"You children go in and start your soup," he said, and when they obeyed, he said to Charlie:

"Marion's not well and she can't stand shocks. That kind of people make her really physically sick."

"I didn't tell them to come here. They wormed your name out of somebody. They deliberately——"

"Well, it's too bad. It doesn't help matters. Excuse me a minute."

Left alone, Charlie sat tense in his chair. In the next room he could hear the children eating, talking in monosyllables, already oblivious to the scene between their elders. He heard a murmur of conversation from a farther room and then the ticking bell of a telephone receiver picked up, and in a panic he moved to the other side of the room and out of earshot.

In a minute Lincoln came back. "Look here, Charlie. I think we'd better call off dinner for tonight. Marion's in bad shape."

"Is she angry with me?"

"Sort of," he said, almost roughly. "She's not strong and——"

"You mean she's changed her mind about Honoria?"

"She's pretty bitter right now. I don't know. You phone me at the bank tomorrow."

"I wish you'd explain to her I never dreamed these people would come here. I'm just as sore as you are."

"I couldn't explain anything to her now."

Charlie got up. He took his coat and hat and started down the corridor. Then he opened the door of the dining room and said in a strange voice, "Good night, children."

Honoria rose and ran around the table to hug him.

"Good night, sweetheart," he said vaguely, and then trying to make his voice more tender, trying to conciliate something, "Good night, dear children."

V

Charlie went directly to the Ritz bar with the furious idea of finding Lorraine and Duncan, but they were not there, and he realized that in any case there was nothing he could do. He had not touched his drink at the Peters, and now he ordered a whisky-and-soda. Paul came over to say hello.

"It's a great change," he said sadly. "We do about half the business we did. So many fellows I hear about back in the States lost everything, maybe not in the first crash, but then in the second. Your friend George Hardt lost every cent, I hear. Are you back in the States?"

"No, I'm in business in Prague."

"I heard that you lost a lot in the crash."

"I did," and he added grimly, "but I lost everything I wanted in the boom."
"Selling short."

"Something like that."

Again the memory of those days swept over him like a nightmare—the people they had met travelling; then people who couldn't add a row of figures or speak a coherent sentence. The little man Helen had consented to dance with at the ship's party, who had insulted her ten feet from the table; the women and girls carried screaming with drink or drugs out of public places——

—The men who locked their wives out in the snow, because the snow of twenty-nine wasn't real snow. If you didn't want it to be snow, you just paid some money.

He went to the phone and called the Peters' apartment; Lincoln answered.

"I called up because this thing is on my mind. Has Marion said anything definite?"

"Marion's sick," Lincoln answered shortly. "I know this thing isn't altogether your fault, but I can't have her go to pieces about it. I'm afraid we'll have to let it slide for six months; I can't take the chance of working her up to this state again."

"I see."

"I'm sorry, Charlie."

He went back to his table. His whisky glass was empty, but he shook his head when Alix looked at it questioningly. There wasn't much he could do now except send Honoria some things; he would send her a lot of things tomorrow. He thought rather angrily that this was just money—he had given so many people money. . . .

"No, no more," he said to another waiter. "What do I owe you?"

He would come back some day; they couldn't make him pay forever. But he wanted his child, and nothing was much good now, beside that fact. He wasn't young any more, with a lot of nice thoughts and dreams to have by himself. He was absolutely sure Helen wouldn't have wanted him to be so alone.

QUESTIONS

1. Discuss the significance of the title, making specific references to descriptions of the Paris Charles Wales remembers and the Paris he visits almost two years later.

2. Although the setting is Paris, the story contains numerous references to America. Examine the sense of America and being an American revealed in Charlie's conversations and thoughts.

3. The first and last scenes take place in a bar. Discuss the appropriateness of this setting to the meaning of the story.

4. Discuss Charles Wales' relation to Honoria. Is fatherly love the only reason for his wanting custody of his daughter?

5. Identify the point of view and discuss its effect on characterization. Is Charlie a sympathetic character? Marion Peters? Lorraine Quarrles?

6. Discuss the turning point in the action. Does Fitzgerald rely too heavily on coincidence here, or is the coincidence justified?

7. Is Charlie's defeat permanent or temporary? Would you call the ending happy, unhappy, or inconclusive?

8. Time and memory assume an almost tangible presence, so that they almost become part of the setting. Discuss time and memory as thematic concerns.

9. Find as many references to money as you can. Discuss money as a means of establishing and developing character, setting, plot, and theme.

RICHARD DOKEY

Sanchez

That summer the son of Juan Sanchez went to work for the Flotill Cannery in Stockton. Juan drove with him to the valley in the old Ford.

While they drove, the boy, whose name was Jesus, told him of the greatness of the cannery, of the great aluminum buildings, the marvelous machines, and the belts of cans that never stopped running. He told him of the building on one side of the road where the cans were made and how the cans ran in a metal tube across the road to the cannery. He described the food machines, the sanitary precautions. He laughed when he spoke of the labeling. His voice was serious about the money.

When they got to Stockton, Jesus directed him to the central district of town, the skidrow where the boy was to live while he worked for the Flotill. It was a cheap hotel on Center Street. The room smelled. There was a table with one chair. The floor was stained like the floor of a public urinal and the bed was soiled, as were the walls. There were no drapes on the windows. A pall spread out from the single light bulb overhead that was worked with a length of grimy string.

"I will not stay much in the room," Jesus said, seeing his father's face. "It is only for sleep. I will be working overtime too. There is also the entertainment."

Jesus led him from the room and they went out into the street. Next to the hotel there was a vacant lot where a building had stood. The hole which was left had that recent, peculiar look of uprootedness. There were the remains of the foundation, the broken flooring, and the cracked bricks of tired red to which the gray blotches of mortar clung like dried phlegm. But the ground had not yet taken on the opaqueness of wear that the air and sun give it. It gleamed dully in the light and held to itself where it had been torn, as earth does behind a plow. Juan studied the hole for a time; then they walked up Center Street to Main, passing other empty lots, and then moved east toward Hunter Street. At the corner of Hunter and Main a wrecking crew was at work. An iron ball was suspended from the end of a cable and tall machine swung the ball up and back and then whipped it forward against the building. The ball was very thick-looking, and when it struck the wall the building trembled, spurted dust, and seemed to cringe inward. The vertical lines of the building had gone awry. Juan shook each time the iron struck the wall.

"They are tearing down the old buildings," Jesus explained. "Redevelopment," he pronounced. "Even my building is to go someday."

Juan looked at his son. "And what of the men?" he asked. "Where do the men go when there are no buildings?"

Jesus, who was a head taller than his father, looked down at him and then shrugged in that Mexican way, the head descending and cocking while the shoulders rise as though on puppet strings. "*Quien sabe?*"

"And the large building there?" Juan said, looking across the rows of parked cars in Hunter Square. "The one whose roof rubs the sky. Of what significance?"

"That is the new courthouse," Jesus said.

"There are no curtains on the windows."

"They do not put curtains on such windows," Jesus explained.

"No," Juan sighed, "that is true."

They walked north on Hunter past the new Bank of America and entered an old building. They stood to one side of the entrance. Jesus smiled proudly and inhaled the stale air.

"This is the entertainment," he said.

Juan looked about. A bar was at his immediate left and a bald man in a soiled apron stood behind it. Beyond the bar there were many thick-wooded tables covered with green material. Men crouched over them and cone-shaped lights hung low from the ceiling casting broadening cones of light downward upon the men and tables. Smoke drifted and rolled in the light and pursued the men when they moved quickly. There was the breaking noise of balls striking together, the hard wooden rattle of the cues in the racks upon the wall, the hum slither of the scoring disks along the loose wires overhead, the explosive cursing of the men. The room was warm and dirty. Juan shook his head.

"I have become proficient at the game," Jesus said.

"This is the entertainment," Juan said still moving his head.

Jesus turned and walked outside. Juan followed. The boy pointed across the parked cars past the courthouse to a marquee on Main Street.

"There are also motion pictures," Jesus said.

Juan had seen one movie as a young man working in the fields near Fresno. He had understood no English then. He sat with his friends in the leather seats that had gum under the arms and watched the images move upon the white canvas. The images were dressed in expensive clothes. There was laughing and dancing. One of the men did kissing with two very beautiful women, taking turns with each when the other was absent. This had embarrassed Juan, the embracing and unhesitating submission of the women with so many unfamiliar people to watch. Juan loved his wife, was very tender and gentle with her before she died. He never went to another motion picture, even after he had learned English, and this kept him from the Spanish films as well.

"We will go to the cannery now," Jesus said, taking his father's arm. "I will show you the machines."

Juan permitted himself to be led away, and they moved back past the bank to where the men were destroying the building. A ragged hole, like a wound, had been opened in the wall. Juan stopped and watched. The iron ball came forward tearing at the hole, enlarging it, exposing the empty interior space that had once been a room. The floor of the room teetered at a precarious angle. The wood was splintered and very dry in the noon light.

"I do not think I will go to the cannery," Juan said.

The boy looked at his father like a child who has made a toy out of string and bottle caps only to have it ignored.

"But it is honorable work," Jesus said, suspecting his father. "And it pays well."

"Honor," Juan said. "Honor is a serious matter. It is not a question of honor. You are a man now. All that is needed is a room and a job at the Flotill. Your father is tired, that is all."

"You are disappointed," Jesus said, hanging his head.

"No," Juan said, "I am beyond disappointment. You are my son. Now you have a place in the world. You have the Flotill."

Nothing more was said, and they walked to the car. Juan got in behind the wheel. Jesus stood beside the door, his arms at his sides, the fingers spread. Juan looked up at him. The boy's eyes were big.

"You are my son," Juan said, "and I love you. Do not have disappointment. I am not of the Flotill. Seeing the machines would make it worse. You understand, *niño?*"

"Si, Papa," Jesus said. He put a hand on his father's shoulder.

"It is a strange world, *niñito,*" Juan said.

"I will earn money. I will buy a red car and visit you. All in Twin Pines will be envious of the son of Sanchez, and they will say that Juan Sanchez has a son of purpose."

"Of course, Jesus *mio,*" Juan said. He bent and placed his lips against the boy's hand. "I will look for the bright car. I will write regardless." He smiled, showing yellowed teeth. "Goodbye, *querido,*" he said. He started the car, raced the engine once too high, and drove off up the street.

When Juan Sanchez returned to Twin Pines, he drove the old Ford to the top of Bear Mountain and pushed it over. He then proceeded systematically to burn all that was of importance to him, all that was of nostalgic value, and all else that meant nothing in itself, like the extra chest of drawers he had kept after his wife's death, the small table in the bedroom, and the faded mohogany stand in which he kept his pipe and tobacco and which sat next to the stuffed chair in the front room. He broke all the dishes, cups, plates, discarded all the cooking and eating utensils in the same way. The fire rose in the blue wind carrying dust wafers of ash in quick, breathless spirals and then released them in a panoply of diluted smoke, from which they drifted and spun and fell like burnt snow. The forks, knives, and spoons became very black with a flaky crust of oxidized metal. Then Juan burned his clothing, all that was unnecessary, and the smoke dampened and took on a thick smell. Finally he threw his wife's rosary into the flames. It was a cheap one, made of wood, and disappeared immediately. He went into his house then and lay down on the bed. He went to sleep.

When he awoke, it was dark and cool. He stepped outside, urinated, and then returned, shutting the door. The darkness was like a mammoth held breath, and he felt very awake listening to the beating of his heart. He knew he would not be able to sleep any more now, and so he lay awake thinking.

He thought of his village in Mexico, the baked clay of the small houses spread like little forts against the stillness of the bare mountains, the men with their great wide hats, their wide, white pants, and their naked brown-skinned feet, splayed against the fine dust of the road. He saw the village cistern and the women all so big and slow, always with child, enervated by the earth and the unbearable sun, the enervation passing into their very wombs like the heat from the yellow sun so that the wombs themselves bred quiet acceptance, slow, silent blood. The men walked bent as though carrying the air or sky, slept against the buildings in the shade like old dogs, ate dry, hot food that dried them inside and seemed to bake the moisture from the flesh, so that the men and women while still young had faces like eroded fields and fingers like stringy, empty stream beds. It was a hard land. It took the life of his father and mother before he was twelve and the life of his aunt, with whom he then lived, before he was sixteen.

When he was seventeen he went to Mexicali because he had heard much of America and the money to be obtained there. They took him in a truck with other men to work in the fields around Bakersfield, then in the fields near Fresno. On his return to Mexicali he met La Belleza, as he came to call her: loveliness. He married her when he was nineteen and she only fifteen. The following year she had a baby girl. It was stillborn and the birth almost killed her, for the doctor said the passage was oversmall. The doctor cautioned him (warned him, really) La Belleza could not have children and live, and he went outside into the moonlight and wept.

He had heard much of the loveliness of the Sierra Nevada above what was called the Mother Lode, and because he feared the land, believed almost that it possessed the power to kill him—as it had killed his mother and father, his aunt, was in fact, slow killing so many of his people—he wanted to run away from it to the high white cold of the California mountains, where he believed his heart would grow, his blood run and, perhaps, the passage of La Belleza might open. Two years later he was taken in the trucks to Stockton in the San Joaquin Valley to pick tomatoes and he saw the Sierra Nevada above the Mother Lode.

It was from a distance, of course, and in the summer, so that there was no snow. But when he returned he told La Belleza about the blueness of the mountains in the warm, still dawn, the extension of them, the aristocracy of their unmoving height, and that they were only fifty miles away from where he had stood.

He worked very hard now and saved his money. He took La Belleza back to his village, where he owned the white clay house of his father. It was cheaper to live there while he waited, fearing the sun, the dust, and the dry, airless silence, for the money to accumulate. That fall La Belleza became pregnant again by an accident of passion and the pregnancy was very difficult. In the fifth month the doctor—who was an atheist—said that the baby would have to be taken or else the mother would die. The village priest, a very loud dramatic man—an educated man who took pleasure in striking a pose—proclaimed the wrath of God in the face of such sacrilege. It was the child who must live, the priest cried. The pregnancy must go on. There was the immortal soul of the child to consider. But Juan decided for the atheist doctor, who did take the child. La Belleza lost much blood. At one point her heart had stopped beating. When the child was torn from its mother and Juan saw that it was a boy, he ran out of the clay house of his father and up the dusty road straight into a hideous red moon. He cursed the earth, the sky. He cursed his village, himself, the soulless indifference of the burnt mountains. He cursed God.

Juan was very afraid now, and though it cost more money he had himself tied by the atheist doctor so that he could never again put the life of La Belleza in danger, for the next time, he knew with certainty, would kill her.

The following summer he went again on the trucks to the San Joaquin Valley. The mountains were still there, high and blue in the quiet dawn, turned to a milky pastel by the heat swirls and haze of midday. Sometimes at night he stepped outside the shacks in which the men were housed and faced the darkness. It was tragic to be so close to what you wanted, he would think, and be unable to possess it. So strong was the feeling in him, particularly during the hot, windless evenings, that he sometimes went with the other men into Stockton, where he stood on the street corners of skidrow and talked, though he did not get drunk on cheap wine or go to the whores, as did the other men. Nor did he fight.

They rode in old tilted trucks covered with canvas and sat on rude benches staring out over the slats of the tail gate. The white glare of headlights crawled up and lay upon them, waiting to pass. They stared over the whiteness. When the lights swept out and by, the glass of the side windows shone. Behind the windows sometimes there would be the ghost of an upturned face, before the darkness clamped shut. Also, if one of the men had a relative who lived in the area, there was the opportunity to ride in a car.

He had done so once. He had watched the headlights of the car pale then whiten outward and the looks on the faces that seemed to float upon the whiteness of the light. The men sat forward, arms on knees, and looked over the glare into the darkness. After that he always rode in the trucks.

When he returned to his village after that season's harvest, he knew they could wait no longer. He purchased a dress of silk for La Belleza and in a secondhand store bought an American suit for himself. He had worked hard, sold his father's house, saved all his money, and on a bright day in early September they crossed the border at Mexicali and caught the Greyhound for Fresno.

Juan got up from his bed to go outside. He stood looking up at the stars. The stars were pinned to the darkness, uttering little flickering cries of light, and as always he was moved by the nearness and profusion of their agony. His mother had told him the stars were a kind of purgatory in which souls burned in cold, silent repentance. He had wondered after her death if the earth too were not a star burning in loneliness, and he could never look at them later without thinking this and believing that the earth must be the brightest of all stars. He walked over to the remains of the fire. A dull heat came from the ashes and a column of limp smoke rose and then bent against the night wind. He studied the ashes for a time and then looked over the tall pine shapes of the southern sky. It was there all right. He could feel the dry char of its heat, that deeper, dryer burning. He imagined it, of course. But it was there nevertheless. He went back into the cabin and lay down, but now his thoughts were only of La Belleza and the beautiful Sierra Nevada.

From Fresno all the way up the long valley to Stockton they had been full with pride and expectation. They had purchased oranges and chocolate bars and they ate them laughing. The other people on the bus looked at them, shook their heads and slept or read magazines. He and La Belleza gazed out the window at the land.

In Stockton they were helped by a man named Eugenio Mendez. Juan had met him while picking tomatoes in the delta. Eugenio had eight children and a very fat but very kind and tolerant wife named Anilla. He helped them find a cheap room off Center Street, where they stayed while determining their next course of action. Eugenio had access to a car, and it was he who drove them finally to the mountains.

It was a day like no other day in his life: to be sitting in the car with La Belleza, to be in this moving car with his Belleza heading straight toward the high, lovely mountains. The car was traveling from the flatness of the valley into the rolling brown swells of the foothills, where hundreds of deciduous and evergreen oaks grew, their puffball shapes still pictures of exploding holiday rockets, only green, but spreading up and out and then around and down in nearly perfect canopies. At Jackson the road turned and began an immediate, constant climb upward.

It was as though his dream about it had materialized. He had never seen so many trees, great with dignity: pines that had bark gray twisted and stringy like hemp; others whose bark resembled dry, flat ginger cookies fastened with black glue about a drum, and others whose bark pulled easily away; and those called redwoods, standing stiff and tall, amber-hued with straight rolls of bark as thick as his fist, flinging out high above great arms of green. And the earth, rich red, as though the blood of scores of Indians had just flowed there and dried. Dark patches of shadow stunned with light, blue flowers, orange flowers, birds, even deer. They saw them all on that first day.

"*A donde vamos?*" Eugenio had asked. "Where are we going?"

"*Bellisima,*" Juan replied. "Into much loveliness."

They did not reach Twin Pines that day. But on their return a week later they inquired in Jackson about the opportunity of buying land or a house in the mountains. The man, though surprised, told them of the sawmill town of Twin Pines, where there were houses for sale.

Their continued luck on that day precipitated the feeling in Juan that it was indeed the materialization of a dream. He had been able in all those years to save two thousand dollars and a man had a small shack for sale at the far edge of town. He looked carefully at Juan, at La Belleza and said, "One thousand dollars," believing they could never begin to possess such a sum. When Juan handed him the money, the man was so struck that he made out a bill of sale. Juan Sanchez and his wife had their home in the Sierra.

When Juan saw the cabin close up, he knew the man had stolen their money. It was small, the roof slanted to one side, the door would not close evenly. The cabin was gradually falling downhill. But it was theirs and he could, with work, repair it. Hurriedly they drove back to Jackson, rented a truck, bought some cheap furniture and hauled it back to the cabin. When they had moved in, Juan brought forth a bottle of whiskey and for the first time in his life proceeded to get truly drunk.

Juan was very happy with La Belleza. She accepted his philosophy completely, understood his need, made it her own. In spite of the people of the town, they created a peculiar kind of joy. And anyway Juan had knowledge about the people.

Twin Pines had been founded, he learned, by one Benjamin Carter, who lived with his daughter in a magnificent house on the hill overlooking town. This Benjamin Carter was a very wealthy man. He had come to the mountains thirty years before to save his marriage, for he had been poor once and loved when he was poor, but then he grew very rich because of oil discovered on his father's Ohio farm and he went away to the city and became incapable of love in the pursuit of money and power. When he at last married the woman whom he had loved, a barrier had grown between them, for Ben Carter had changed but the woman had not. Then the woman became ill and Ben Carter promised her he would take her West, all the way West away from the city so that it could be as it had been in the beginning of their love. But the woman was with child. And so Ben Carter rushed to the California mountains, bought a thousand acres of land, and hurried to build his house before the rain and snows came. He hired many men and the house was completed, except for the interior work and the furnishings. All that winter men he had hired worked in the snow to finish the house while Ben Carter waited with his wife in the city. When it was early spring they set out for California, Ben Carter, his wife, and the doctor, who strongly advised against the rough train trip and the still rougher climb by horse and wagon from Jackson to the house. But the woman wanted the child born properly, so they went. The baby came the evening of their arrival at the house, and the woman died all night having it. It was this Ben Carter who lived with that daughter now in the great house on the hill, possessing her to the point, it was said about his madness, that he had murdered a young man who had shown interest in her.

Juan learned all this from a Mexican servant who had worked at the great house from the beginning, and when he told the story to La Belleza she wept because of its sadness. It was a tragedy of love, she explained, and Juan—soaring to the heights of his imagination—believed that the town, all one hundred souls, had somehow been infected with the tragedy, as they were touched by the shadow of the house itself, which crept directly up the highway each night when the sun set. This was why they left dead chickens and fish on the porch of the cabin or dumped garbage into the yard. He believed he understood something profound and so did nothing about these incidents, which, after all, might have been the pranks of boys. He did not want the infection to touch him, nor the deeper infection of their prejudice because he was Mexican. He was not indifferent. He was simply too much in love with La Belleza and the Sierra Nevada. Finally the incidents stopped.

Now the life of Juan Sanchez entered its most beautiful time. When the first snows fell he became delirious, running through the pines, shouting, rolling on the ground, catching the flakes in his open mouth, bringing them in his cupped hands to rub in the hair of La Belleza, who stood in the doorway of their cabin laughing at him. He danced, made up a song about snowflakes falling on a desert and then a prayer which he addressed to the Virgin of Snowflakes. That night while the snow fluttered like wings against the bedroom window, he celebrated the coming of the whiteness with La Belleza.

He understood that first year in the mountains that love was an enlargement of himself, that it enabled him to be somehow more than he had ever been before, as though certain pores of his senses had only just been opened. Whereas before he had desired the Sierra Nevada for its beauty and contrast to his harsh fatherland, now he came to acquire a love for it, and he loved it as he loved La Belleza; he loved it as a woman. Also in that year he came to realize that there was a fear or dread about such love. It was more a feeling than anything else, something which reached thought now and then, particularly in those last moments before sleep. It was an absolutely minor thing. The primary knowledge was of the manner in which this love seemed to assimilate everything, rejecting all that would not yield. This love was a kind of blindness.

That summer Juan left La Belleza at times to pick the crops of the San Joaquin Valley. He had become good friends with the servant of the big house and this man had access to the owner's car, which he always drove down the mountain in a reckless but confident manner. After that summer Juan planned also to buy a car, not out of material desire, but simply because he believed this man would one day kill himself, and also because he did not wish to be dependent.

He worked in the walnuts near the town of Linden and again in the tomatoes of the rich delta. He wanted very much to have La Belleza with him, but that would have meant more money and a hotel room in the skidrow, and that was impossible because of the pimps and whores, the drunks and criminals and the general despair, which the police always tapped at periodic intervals, as one does a vat of fermenting wine. The skidrow was a place his love could not assimilate, but he could not ignore it because so many of his people were lost there. He stayed in the labor camps, which were also bad because of what the men did with themselves, but they were tolerable. He worked hard and as often as he could and gazed at the mountains, which he could always see clearly in the morning light. When tomato season was over he returned to La Belleza.

Though the town would never accept them as equals, it came that summer to tolerate their presence. La Belleza made straw baskets which she sold to the townspeople and which were desired for their beauty and intricacy of design. Juan carved animals, a skill he had acquired from his father, and these were also sold. The activity succeeded so well that Juan took a box of their things to Jackson, where they were readily purchased. The following spring he was able to buy the Ford.

Juan acquired another understanding that second year in the mountains. It was, he believed, that love, his love, was the single greatness of which he was capable, the thing which ennobled him and gave him honor. Love, he became convinced, was his only ability, the one success he had accomplished in a world of insignificance. It was a simple thing, after all, made so painfully simple each time he went to the valley to work with face toward the ground, every time he saw the men in the fields and listened to their talk and watched them drive off to the skidrow at night. After he had acquired this knowledge, the nights he had to spend away from La Belleza were occupied by a new kind of loneliness, as though a part of his body had been separated from the whole. He began also to understand something more of the fear or dread that seemed to trail behind love.

It happened late in the sixth year of their marriage. It was impossible, of course, and he spent many hours at the fire in their cabin telling La Belleza of the impossibility, for the doctor had assured him that all had been well tied. He had conducted himself on the basis of that assumption. But doctors can be wrong. Doctors can make mistakes. La Belleza was with child.

For the first five months the pregnancy was not difficult, and he came almost to believe that indeed the passage of La Belleza would open. He prayed to God. He prayed to the earth and sky. He prayed to the soul of his mother. But after the fifth month the true sickness began and he discarded prayer completely in favor of blasphemy. There was no God and never could be God in the face of such sickness, such unbelievable human sickness. Even when he had her removed to the hospital in Stockton, the doctors could not stop it, but it continued so terribly that he believed that La Belleza carried sickness itself in her womb.

After seven months the doctors decided to take the child. They brought La Belleza into a room with lights and instruments. They worked on her for a long time and she died there under the lights with the doctors cursing and perspiring above the large wound of her pain. They did not tell him of the child, which they had cleaned and placed in an incubator, until the next day. That night he sat in the Ford and tried to see it all, but he could only remember the eyes of La Belleza in the vortex of pain. They were of an almost eerie calmness. They had possessed calmness, as one possesses the truth. Toward morning he slumped sideways on the seat and went to sleep.

So he put her body away in the red earth of the town cemetery beyond the cabin. The pines came together overhead and in the heat of midday a shadow sprinkled with spires of light lay upon the ground so that the earth was cool and clean to smell. He did not even think of taking her back to Mexico, since, from the very beginning, she had always been part of that dream he had dreamed. Now she would always be in the Sierra Nevada, with the orange and blue flowers, the quiet deep whiteness of winter, and all that he ever was or could be was with her.

But he did not think these last thoughts then, as he did now. He had simply performed them out of instinct for their necessity, as he had performed the years of labor while waiting for the infant Jesus to grow to manhood. Jesus. Why had he named the boy Jesus? That, perhaps, had been instinct too. He had stayed after La Belleza's death for the boy, to be with him until manhood, to show him the loveliness of the Sierra Nevada, to instruct him toward true manhood. But Jesus. Ah, Jesus. Jesus the American. Jesus of the Flotill. Jesus understood nothing. Jesus, he believed, was forever lost to knowledge. That day with Jesus had been his own liberation.

For a truth had come upon him after the years of waiting, the ultimate truth that he understood only because La Belleza had passed through his life. Love was beauty, La Belleza and the Sierra Nevada, a kind of created or made thing. But there was another kind of love, a very profound, embracing love that he had felt of late blowing across the mountains from the south and that, he knew now, had always been there from the beginning of his life, disguised in the sun and wind. In this love there was blood and earth and, yes, even God, some kind of god, at least the power of a god. This love wanted him for its own. He understood it, that it had permitted him to have La Belleza and that without it there could have been no Belleza.

Juan placed an arm over his eyes and turned to face the wall. The old bed sighed. An image went off in his head and he remembered vividly the lovely body of La Belleza. In that instant the sound that loving had produced with the bed was alive in him like a forgotten melody, and his body seemed to swell and press against the ceiling. It was particularly cruel because it was so sudden, so intense, and came from so deep within him that he knew it must all still be alive somewhere, and that was the cruelest part of all. He wept softly and held the arm across his eyes.

In the dark morning the people of the town were awakened by the blaze of fire that was the house of Juan Sanchez. Believing that he had perished in the flames, several of the townspeople placed a marker next to the grave of his wife with his name on it. But, of course, on that score they were mistaken. Juan Sanchez had simply gone home.

QUESTIONS

1. Discuss how Jesus's opinion of Stockton is very different from his father's. How do their disparate views characterize father and son?

2. Examine the similes and metaphors used to describe the town when Juan views it. Can you find examples of personification? Discuss how figurative language heightens your sense of the revulsion Juan feels for Stockton.

3. What does Juan mean when he says to Jesus, "Honor is a serious matter. It is not a question of honor"?

4. Why does Juan fear the land of his native Mexico? Is his fear justified?

5. Why does Juan revere the mountains? Examine the metaphors and similes used to describe the mountains. Can you find examples of personification? Discuss how figurative language heightens your sense of Juan's exalted view of the Sierra Nevada.

6. In some ways, the story of Ben Carter parallels the story of Juan and La Belleza. Explain.

7. Discuss Juan's concept of love. Why does he come "to realize that there was a fear or dread about such love"?

8. Review how time shifts from present to past. Discuss the use of transitional devices to effect these shifts.

9. Why were the townspeople mistaken when they "placed a marker next to the grave of his wife with his name on it"?

ALEXANDER SOLZHENITSYN

Zakhar-the-Pouch

Translation by Michael Glenny

You asked me to tell you something about my cycling holiday last summer. Well, if it's not too boring, listen to this one about Kulikovo Field.

We had been meaning to go there for a long time, but it was somehow a difficult place to reach. There are no brightly painted notices or signposts to show you the way, and you won't find it on a single map, even though this battle cost more Russian lives in the fourteenth century than Borodino did in the nineteenth. There has been only one such encounter for fifteen hundred years, not only in Russia but in all Europe. It was a battle not merely between principalities or nation-states, but between continents.

Perhaps we chose a rather roundabout way to get there: from Epiphania through Kazanovka and Monastirshchina. It was only because there had been no rain till then that we were able to ride instead of pushing our bikes; to cross the Don, which was not yet in full spate, and its tributary, the Nepriadva, we wheeled them over narrow, two-plank footbridges.

After a long trek, we stood on a hill and caught sight of what looked like a needle pointing into the sky from a distant flat-topped rise. We went downhill and lost sight of it. Then we started to climb again, and the grey needle reappeared, this time more distinct, and next to it we saw what looked like a church. There seemed to be something uniquely strange about its design, something never seen except in fairy tales: its domes looked transparent and fluid; they shimmered deceptively in the cascading sunlight of the hot August day—one minute they were there and the next they were gone.

We guessed rightly that we would be able to quench our thirst and fill our

343

water bottles at the well in the valley, which proved to be invaluable later on. But the peasant who handed us the bucket, in reply to our question: "Where's Kulikovo Field?" just stared at us as if we were idiots.

"You don't say Kulikóvo, you say Kulíkovo. The village of Kulíkovka is right next to the battlefield, but Kulikóvka's over there, on the other side of the Don."

After our meeting with this man, we traveled along deserted country lanes, and until we reached the monument several kilometers away, we did not come across a single person. It must have been because no one happened to be around on that particular day, for we could see the wheel of a combine harvester flailing somewhere in the distance. People obviously frequented this place and would do so again, because all the land had been planted with crops as far as the eye could see, and the harvest was almost ready—buckwheat, clover, sugar beet, rye, and peas (we had shelled some of those young peas); yet we saw no one that day and we passed through what seemed like the blessed calm of a reservation. Nothing disturbed us from musing on the fate of those fair-haired warriors, nine out of every ten of whom lay seven feet beneath the present topsoil, and whose bones had now dissolved into the earth, in order that Holy Russia might rid herself of the heathen Mussulman.

The features of the land—this wide slope gradually ascending to Mamai Hill—could not have greatly changed over six centuries, except that the forest had disappeared. Spread out before us was the very place where they had crossed the Don in the evening and the night of September 7, 1380, then settled down to feed their horses (though the majority were foot soldiers), sharpen their swords, restore their morale, pray, and hope—almost a quarter of a million Russians, certainly more than two hundred thousand. The population of Russia then was barely a seventh of what it is now, so that an army of that size staggers the imagination.

And for nine out of every ten warriors, that was to be their last morning on earth.

On that occasion our men had not crossed the Don from choice, for what army would want to stand and fight with its retreat blocked by a river? The truth of history is bitter but it is better to admit it: Mamai had as allies not only Circassians, Genoese, and Lithuanians but also Prince Oleg of Ryazan. (One must understand Oleg's motives also: he had no other way of protecting his territory from the Tartars, as it lay right across their path. His land had been ravaged by fire three times in the preceding seven years.) That is why the Russians had crossed the Don—to protect their rear from their own people, the men of Ryazan: in any other circumstances, Orthodox Christians would not have attacked them.

The needle loomed up in front of us, though it was no longer a needle but an imposing tower, unlike anything I had ever seen. We could not reach it directly: the tracks had come to an end and we were confronted by standing crops. We wheeled our bicycles round the edges of the fields and, finally, starting nowhere in particular, there emerged from the ground an old, neglected, abandoned road, overgrown with weeds, which grew more distinct as it drew nearer to the monument and even had ditches on either side of it.

Suddenly the crops came to an end and the hillside became even more like a reservation, a piece of fallow land overgrown with tough rye-grass instead of the usual feather-grass. We paid homage to this ancient place in the best way possible—just by breathing the pure air. One look around, and behold!—there in the light of sunrise the Mongol chief Telebei is engaged in single combat with Prince Peresvet, the two leaning against each other like two sheaves of wheat; the Mongolian cavalry are shooting their arrows and brandishing their spears; with faces contorted with blood lust, they trample on the Russian infantry, breaking through the core of their formation and driving them back to where a milky cloud of mist has risen from the Nepriadva and the Don.

Our men were mown down like wheat, and we were trampled to death beneath their hoofs.

Here, at the very axis of the bloody carnage, provided that the person who guessed the spot did so correctly, are the monument and the church with the unearthly domes which had so amazed us from afar. There turned out to be a simple solution to the puzzle: the local inhabitants have ripped off the metal from all five domes for their own requirements, so the domes have become transparent; their delicate structure is still intact, except that it now consists of nothing but the framework, and from a distance it looks like a mirage.

The monument, too, is remarkable at close quarters. Unless you go right up to it and touch it, you will not understand how it was made. Although it was built in the last century, in fact well over a hundred years ago, the idea—of piecing the monument together from sections of cast iron—is entirely modern, except that nowadays it would not be cast in iron. It is made up of two square platforms, one on top of another, then a twelve-sided structure which gradually becomes round; the lower part is decorated in relief with iron shields, swords, helmets, and Slavonic inscriptions. Farther up, it rises in the shape of a fourfold cylinder cast so that it looks like four massive organ pipes welded together. Then comes a capping piece with an incised pattern, and above it all a gilded cross triumphing over a crescent. The whole tower—fully thirty metres high—is made up of figured slabs so tightly bolted together that not a single rivet or seam is visible, just as if the monument had been cast in a single piece—at least until time, or more likely the sons and grandsons of the men who put it up, had begun to knock holes in it.

After the long route to the monument through empty fields, we had assumed that the place would be deserted. As we walked along, we were wondering why it was in this state. This was, after all, a historic spot. What happened here was a turning point in the fate of Russia. For our invaders have not always come from the West . . . Yet this place is spurned, forgotten.

How glad we were to be mistaken! At once, not far from the monument, we caught sight of a grey-haired old man and two young boys. They had thrown down their rucksacks and were lying in the grass, writing something in a large book the size of a class register. When we approached, we found that he was a literature teacher who had met the boys somewhere nearby, and that the book was not a school exercise book, but none other than the Visitor' Comments Book. But there was no museum here; where, then, in all this wild field was the book kept?

Suddenly a massive shadow blotted out the sun. We turned. It was the Keeper of Kulikovo Field—the man whose duty it was to guard our glorious heritage.

We did not have time to focus the camera, and in any case it was impossible to take a snapshot into the sun. What is more, the Keeper would have refused to be photographed (he knew what he was worth and refused to let himself be photographed all day). How shall I set about describing him? Should I begin with the man himself? Or start with his sack? (He was carrying an ordinary peasant's sack, only half full and evidently not very heavy since he was holding it without effort.)

The Keeper was a hot-tempered muzhik who looked something of a ruffian. His arms and legs were hefty, and his shirt was dashingly unbuttoned. Red hair stuck out from under the cap planted sideways on his head, and although it was obviously a week since he had shaved, a fresh reddish scratch ran right across his cheek.

"Ah!" he greeted us in a disapproving voice as he loomed over us. "You've just arrived, have you? How did you get here?"

He seemed puzzled, as if the place were completely fenced in and we had found a hole to crawl through. We nodded towards the bicycles, which we had propped up in the bushes. Although he was holding the sack as though about to board a train, he looked as if he would demand to see our passports. His face was haggard, with a pointed chin and a determined expression.

"I'm warning you! Don't damage the grass with your bicycles!"

With this, he let us know immediately that here, on Kulikovo Field, you were not free to do as you liked.

The Keeper's unbuttoned coat was long-skirted and enveloped him like a parka; it was patched in a few places and was the color you read about in folk tales—somewhere between grey, brown, red, and purple. A star glinted in the lapel of his jacket; at first we thought it was a medal, but then we realized it was just the ordinary little badge, with Lenin's head in a circle, that everyone buys on Revolution Day. A long blue-and-white-striped linen shirt, obviously home-made, was hanging out from underneath his jacket and was gathered at the waist by an army belt with a five-pointed star on the buckle. His second-hand officer's breeches were tucked into the frayed tops of his canvas boots.

"Well?" he asked the teacher, in a much gentler tone of voice. "How's the writing going?"

"Fine, Zakhar Dmitrich," he replied, calling him by name. "We've nearly finished."

"Will *you*"—more sternly again—"be writing too?"

"Later on." We tried to escape from his insistent questions by cutting in: "Do you know when this monument was built?"

"Of course I do!" he snapped, offended, coughing and spluttering at the insult. "What do you think I'm here for?"

And carefully lowering his sack (which clinked with what sounded like bottles), the Keeper pulled a document out of his pocket and unfolded it; it was a page of an exercise book on which was written, in capital letters and in complete disregard of the ruled lines, a copy of the monument's dedication to Dmitry Donskoi and the year—1848.

"What is that?"

"Well, comrades," sighed Zakhar Dmitrich, revealing by his frankness that he was not quite the tyrant that he had at first pretended to be, "it's like this. I copied it myself from the plaque because everyone asks when it was built. I'll show you where the plaque was, if you like."

"What became of it?"

"Some rogue from our village pinched it—and we can't do anything about it."

"Do you know who it was?"

"Of course I know. I scared off some of his gang of louts, I dealt with them all right, but he and the rest got away. I'd like to lay my hands on all those vandals, I'd show 'em."

"But why did he steal the plaque?"

"For his house."

"Can't you take it back?"

"Ha, ha!" Zakhar threw back his head in reply to our foolish question. "That's the problem! I don't have any authority. They won't give me a gun. I need a machine gun in a job like this."

Looking at the scratch across his cheek, we thought to ourselves it was just as well they didn't give him a gun.

Then the teacher finished what he was writing and handed back the Comments Book. We thought that Zakhar Dmitrich would put it under his arm or into his sack, but we were wrong. He opened the flap of his dirty jacket and revealed, sewn inside, a sort of pocket or bag made of sacking (in fact, it was more like a pouch than anything else), the exact size of the Comments Book, which fitted neatly into it. Also attached to the pouch was a slot for the blunt indelible pencil which he lent to visitors.

Convinced that we were now suitably intimidated, Zakhar-the-Pouch picked up his sack (the clinking *was* glass) and went off with his long, loping stride into the bushes. Here the brusque forcefulness with which he had first met us vanished. Hunching himself miserably, he sat down, lit a cigarette, and smoked with such unalleviated grief, with such despair, that one might have thought all those who had perished on this battlefield had died only yesterday and had been his closest relatives, and that now he did not know how to go on living.

We decided to spend the whole day and night here: to see whether nighttime at Kulikovo really was as Blok described it in his poem. Without hurrying, we walked over to the monument, inspected the abandoned church, and wandered over the field, trying to imagine the dispositions of the battlefield on that eighth of September; then we clambered up onto the iron surface of the monument.

Plenty of people had been here before us. It would be quite wrong to say that the monument had been forgotten. People had been busy carving the iron surface of the monument with chisels and scratching it with nails, while those with less energy had written more faintly on the church walls with charcoal: "Maria Polyneyeva and Nikolai Lazarev were here from 8/5/50 to 24/5 . . . " "Delegates of the regional conference were here . . . " "Workers from the Kimovskaya Postal Administration were here 23/6/52 . . . " And so on and so on.

Then three young working lads from Novomoskovsk drove up on motor-bikes. Jumping off lightly onto the iron surface, they started to examine the warm grey-black body of the monument and slapped it affectionately; they were surprised at how well made it was and explained to us how it had been done. In return, from the top platform we pointed out everything we knew about the battle.

But who can know nowadays exactly where and how it took place? According to the manuscripts, the Mongol-Tartar cavalry cut into our infantry regiments, decimated them, and drove them back towards the crossings over the Don, thus turning the Don from a protective moat against Oleg into a possible death trap. If the worst had happened, Dmitry would have been called "Don-skoi" for the opposite reason. But he had taken everything into careful account and stood his ground, something of which not every grand duke was capable. He left a boyar dressed in his, Dmitry's, attire, fighting beneath his flag, while he himself fought as an ordinary foot soldier, and he was once seen taking on four Tartars at once. But the grand-ducal standard was chopped down and Dmitry, his armour severely battered, barely managed to crawl to the wood, when the Mongols broke through the Russian lines and drove them back. But then another Dmitry, Volinsky-Bobrok, the governor of Moscow, who had been lying in ambush with his army, attacked the ferocious Tartars from the rear. He drove them back, harrying them as they galloped away. Then he wheeled sharply and forced them into the river Nepriadva. From that moment the Russians took heart: they re-formed and turned on the Tartars, rose from the ground and drove all the khans, the enemy commanders, even Mamai himself, forty versts away across the river Ptan as far as Krasivaya Mech. (But here one legend contradicts another. An old man from the neighboring village of Iva-novka had his own version: the mist, he said, had not lifted, and in the mist Mamai, thinking a broad oak tree beside him was a Russian warrior, took fright—"Ah, mighty is the Christian God!"—and so fled.)

Afterwards the Russians cleared the field of battle and buried the dead: it took them eight days.

"There's one they didn't pick up—they left him behind!" the cheerful fitter from Novomoskovsk said accusingly.

We turned around and could not help but burst out laughing. Yes!—one fallen warrior was lying there this very day, not far from the monument, face down on mother earth—his native land. His bold head had dropped to the ground and his valiant limbs were spread-eagled; he was without his shield or sword and, in place of his helmet, wore a threadbare cap, and near his hand lay a sack. (All the same, he was careful not to crush the edge of his jacket with the pouch in it, where he kept the Comments Book; he had pulled it out from underneath his stomach and it lay on the grass beside him.) Perhaps he was just lying there in a drunken stupor, but if he was sleeping or thinking, then the way he was sprawled across the ground was very touching. He went perfectly with the field. They should cast an iron figure like that and place it here.

However, for all his height, Zakhar was too skinny to be a warrior.

"He doesn't want to work on the kolkhoz, so he found himself a soft government job where he can get a suntan," one of the lads growled.

What we disliked most of all was the way Zakhar flew at all the new arrivals, especially those who looked as if they might cause him trouble. During the day a few more people arrived; when he heard their cars he would get up, shake himself, and pounce on them with threats, as if they, not he, were responsible for the monument. Before they had time to be annoyed, Zakhar himself would give vent to violent indignation about the desolation of the place. It seemed incredible that he could harbor such passion.

"Don't you think it's a disgrace?" he said, waving his arms aggressively, to four people who got out of a Zaporozhetz car. "I'll bide my time, then I'll walk right through the regional department of culture." (With those long legs he could easily have done it.) "I'll take leave and I'll go to Moscow, right to Furtseva, the Minister of Culture herself. I'll tell her everything."

Then, as soon as he noticed that the visitors were intimidated and were not standing up to him, he picked up his sack with an air of importance, as an official picks up his briefcase, and went off to have a smoke and a nap.

Wandering here and there, we met Zakhar several times during the day. We noticed that when he walked he limped in one leg, and we asked him what had caused this.

He replied proudly: "It's a souvenir from the war!"

Again we did not believe him: he was just a practised liar.

We had drunk our water bottles dry, so we wnt up to Zakhar and asked him where we could get some water. Wa-ater? The whole trouble was, he explained, that there was no well here and they wouldn't allocate any money to dig one. The only source of drinking water in the whole field was the puddles. The well was in the village.

After that, he no longer bothered to get up to talk to us, as if we were old friends.

When we complained about the inscriptions having been hacked away or scratched over, Zakhar retorted: "Have a look and see if you can read any of the dates. If you find any new damage, then you can blame me. All this vandalism was done before my time; they don't dare try it when I'm around! Well, perhaps some scoundrel hid in the church and then scribbled on the walls—I've only got one pair of legs, you know!"

The church, dedicated to St. Sergei of Radonezh, who united the Russian forces and brought them to battle and soon afterwards effected the reconciliation between Dmitry Donskoi and Oleg of Ryazan, was a sturdy fortresslike building with tightly interlocking limbs: the truncated pyramid of the nave, a cloister surmounted by a watchtower, and two round castellated towers. There were a few windows like loopholes.

Inside it, everything had been stripped and there wasn't even a floor—you walked over sand. We asked Zakhar about it.

"Ha, ha, ha! It was all pinched!" He gloated over us. "It was during the war. Our people in Kulikovo tore up all the slabs from the floors and paved their yards, so they wouldn't have to walk in the muck. I made a list of who took the slabs . . . Then the war ended, but they still went on pinching the stuff. Even before that, our troops had used all the ikon screens to put round the edges of dugouts and for heating their stoves."

As the hours passed and he got used to us, Zakhar was no longer embarrassed to delve into his sack in front of us, and we gradually found out exactly what was inside it. It contained empty bottles (twelve kopecks) and jam jars (five kopecks) left behind by visitors—he picked them up in the bushes after their picnics—and also a full bottle of water, because he had no other access to drinking water during the day. He carried two loaves of rye bread, which he broke bits off of now and again and chewed for his frugal meals.

"People come here in crowds all day long. I don't have any time to go off to the village for a meal."

On some days he probably carried a precious half bottle of vodka in there or some canned fish; then he would clutch the sack tightly, afraid to leave it anywhere. That day, when the sun had already begun to set, a friend on a motorbike came to see him; they sat in the bushes for an hour and a half. Then the friend went away and Zakhar came back without his sack. He talked rather more loudly, waved his arms more vigorously, and, noticing that I was writing something, warned us: "I'm in charge here, let me tell you! In '57 they decided to put a building up here. See those posts over there, planted round the monument? They've been here since then. They were cast in Tula. They were supposed to join up the posts with chains, but the chains never came. So they gave me this job and they pay me for it. Without me, the whole place would be in ruins!"

"How much do you get paid, Zakhar Dmitrich?"

After a sigh like a blacksmith's bellows, he was speechless for a moment. He mumbled something, then said quietly: "Twenty-seven roubles."

"What? The minimum's thirty."

"Well, maybe it is . . . And I don't get any days off, either. Morning to dusk I'm on the job without a break, and I even have to come back late at night too."

What an incorrigible old liar he is, we thought.

"Why do you have to be here at night?"

"Why d'you think?" he said in an offended voice. "How can I leave the place at night? Someone's got to watch it all the time. If a car comes, I have to make a note of its number."

"Why the number?"

"Well, they won't let me have a gun. They say I might shoot the visitors. The only authority I've got is to take their number. And supposing they do some damage?"

"What do you do with the number afterwards?"

"Nothing. I just keep it . . . Now they've built a house for tourists, have you seen it? I have to guard that too."

We had, of course, seen the house. Single-story, with several rooms, it was near completion but was still kept locked. The windows had been put in, and several were already broken; the floors were laid, but the plastering was not yet finished.

"Will you let us stay the night there?" (Towards sunset, it had begun to get cold; it was going to be a bitter night.)

"In the tourist house? No, it's impossible."

"Then who's it for?"

"No, it can't be done. Anyway, I haven't got the keys. So you needn't bother to ask. You can sleep in my shed."

His low shed with its sloping roof was designed for a half a dozen sheep. Bending down, we peered inside. Broken, trampled straw was scattered around; on the floor there was a cooking pot with some leftovers in it, a few more empty bottles, and a desiccated piece of bread. However, there was room for our bikes, and we could lie down and still leave enough space for Zakhar to stretch out.

He made use of our stay to take some time off.

"I'm off to Kulikovo to have supper at home. Grab a bite of something hot. Leave the door on the hook."

"Knock when you want to come in," we said, laughingly.

"O.K."

Zakhar-the-Pouch turned back the other flap of his miraculous jacket, to reveal two loops sewn into it. Out of his inexhaustible sack he drew an axe with a shortened handle and placed it firmly in the loops.

"Well," he said gloomily, "that's all I have for protection. They won't allow me anything else."

He said this in a tone of the deepest doom, as if he were expecting a horde of infidels to gallop up one of these nights and overthrow the monument, and he would have to face them alone with his little hatchet. We even shuddered at his voice as we sat there in the half light. Perhaps he wasn't a buffoon at all? Perhaps he really believed that if he didn't stand guard every night the battlefield and the monument were doomed?

Weakened by drink and a day of noisy activity, stooping and barely managing to hobble, Zakhar went off to his village and we laughed at him once more.

As had been our wish, we were left alone on Kulikovo Field. Night set in, with a full moon. The tower of the monument and the fortress-like church were silhouetted against it like great black screens. The distant lights of Kulikovka and Ivanovka competed faintly with the light of the moon. Not one aeroplane flew overhead; no motorcar rumbled by, no train rattled past in the distance. By moonlight the pattern of the nearby fields was no longer visible. Earth, grass, and moonlit solitude were as they had been in 1380. The centuries stood still, and as we wandered over the field we could evoke the whole scene—the campfires and the troops of dark horses. From the river Nepriadva came the sound of swans, just as Blok had described.

We wanted to understand the battle of Kulikovo in its entirety, grasp its inevitability, ignore the infuriating ambiguities of the chronicles: nothing had been as simple or as straightforward as it seemed; history had repeated itself after a long time-lag, and when it did, the result was disastrous. After the victory, the warriors of Russia faded away. Tokhtamysh immediately replaced Mamai, and two years after Kulikovo, he crushed the power of Muscovy; Dmitry Donskoi fled to Kostroma, while Tokhtamysh again destroyed both Ryazan and Moscow, took the Kremlin by ruse, plundered it, set it afire, chopped off heads, and dragged his prisoners back in chains to the Golden Horde, the Tartar capital.

Centuries pass and the devious path of history is simplified for the distant spectator until it looks as straight as a road drawn by a cartographer.

The night turned bitterly cold, but we shut ourselves in the shed and slept soundly right through it. We had decided to leave early in the morning. It was hardly light when we pushed our bicycles out and, with chattering teeth, started to load up.

The grass was white with hoarfrost; wisps of fog stretched from the hollow in which Kulikovka village lay and across the fields, dotted with haycocks. Just as we emerged from the shed to mount our bicycles and leave, we heard a loud, ferocious bark coming from one of the haycocks, and a shaggy grey dog ran out and made straight for us. As it bounded out, the haycock collapsed behind it; wakened by the barking, a tall figure arose from beneath it, called for the dog, and began to shake off the straw. It was already light enough for us to recognise him as our Zakhar-the-Pouch, still wearing his curious short-sleeved overcoat.

He had spent the night in the haycock, in the bone-chilling cold. Why? Was it anxiety or was it devotion to the place that had made him do it?

Immediately our previous attitude of amused condescension vanished. Rising out of the haycock on that frosty morning, he was no longer the ridiculous Keeper but rather the Spirit of the Field, a kind of guardian angel who never left the place.

He came towards us, still shaking himself and rubbing his hands together, and with his cap pushed back on his head, he seemed like a dear old friend.

"Why didn't you knock, Zakhar Dmitrich?" "I didn't want to disturb you." He shrugged his shoulders and yawned. He was covered all over in straw and fluff. As he unbuttoned his coat to shake himself, we caught sight of both the

Comments Book and his sole legal weapon, the hatchet, in their respective places.

The grey dog by his side was baring its teeth.

We said goodbye warmly and were already pedalling off as he stood there with his long arm raised, calling out: "Don't worry! I'll see to it! I'll go right to Furtseva! To Furtseva herself!"

That was two years ago. Perhaps the place is tidier now and better cared for. I have been a bit slow about writing this, but I haven't forgotten the Field of Kulikovo, or its Keeper, its red-haired tutelary spirit.

And let it be said that we Russians would be very foolish to neglect that place.

QUESTIONS

1. The story makes use of a frame. Do you find this technique effective?

2. Is Zakhar a round or flat character? Is his behavior plausible? Discuss.

3. What is the narrator's initial reaction to Zakhar? Why does he change his opinion? What does he mean when he describes Zakhar as the field's "red-haired tutelary spirit"?

4. Does the story have a plot? If so, what is the conflict? What use does the story make of suspense? of surprise?

5. To the narrator, the mutilated monument and desecrated church and even Kulikovo Field itself have symbolic functions. Explain.

6. In places, the narrator seems to be making a plea to the Russian people. What is this plea? Do you find the story overly didactic?

ROSELLEN BROWN

The Only Way to Make It in New York

She had caught him going through her jewelry. She stood on the threshold in her slick raincoat, balancing on her toes, looking casual, almost, as though she were coming in to tell him, "Dinner is served." It was faintly amusing—he would pick up a necklace, hold it toward the ceiling light critically, then fling it down. She was embarrassed, it was like being in an accident and worrying in the ambulance about your dirty underwear. There was so little there, only a ring or two of sentimental value, if that. (Grandma gave her a sapphire at graduation, but Grandma was a shrew in Palm Beach who had chewed her mouth away—or so it had always looked—and had sharpened her voice till it was a pointed stick to skewer the world with. When she'd been eighteen and stayed out late, Grandma had taken to calling her "Chippie," so what was her ring supposed to be worth?) Oh—Martin's watch with the good expanding band. Into his lumpy pocket it went. Her good pearls were hanging out like a dirty hanky.

She was waiting to be frightened. But she wouldn't be. He had no gun that she could see. He was not the man she was expecting, anyway, so she was not about to be intimidated. In fact he was pathetic by comparison. That was funny enough to make her smile and she was sure he would turn around at that; the mock-bitter movement of her lips had sent a million hairline cracks through the air as though it were ice.

She'd been sure, after the first robbery, that it was Tony Aguilar's brother-in-law. Together he and Tony had been building closets and a room divider

354

between the front bedroom and Wendy's little L. The lousy apartment with its painted-over marble fireplaces (styles change but then, dammit, they change back again and you're left with a gallon of paint stripper. She tended to think of it as a fifty-buck-a-month place. Too bad the landlord didn't). Tony was a wide, brown, rough, sweet man with miles of kinky hair, raised around the corner and making good, good enough, with his carpentry. He was a daddy, and respected. His wife's brother was a junkie. Willie came to work and took off his shirt first thing, showing muscles that made her stomach sink. It was a disgusting reaction, adolescent, but she couldn't help it. He had a clean face, sharply cut, Aztec, with a distant vulnerability in the eyes which could only have been the drugs. Something about him was like cream, maple cream, incredibly inviting to touch, where it dipped and flowed over his shoulder blades as he hammered boards inexpertly. She got out fast, later to work each day: she saw his back all the way to the subway. She'd have thought a junkie would look unhealthy. Martin, seamy and mustard-yellow under his tee shirt, looked unhealthy.

Well, the junkie didn't look good when he came around at dinnertime, worse at two in the morning, banging angrily as though they ought to have been expecting him. Money, money, just an advance against more nailing, more sawing so they would have closets for their nice nice clothes. Lady listen. My grandmother, I need it. Near tears, those eyes racing all around ready for escape, his knuckles white, fingertips biting palms cruelly. Martin has asked why Tony couldn't help, or his sister. There was a muttered reply. From where she lay, Martin looked like the heavy. He breathed hard in his maroon robe, laboring at saying no, making it a whole moral business, who cared, who wanted speeches, explanations, truth? Martin was always giving quarters to beggars on the street after he'd extracted the name of the wine they were going to spend it on. A quarter was cheap for that song and dance. He came back to bed shaking his head.

"Don't you think he wanted a fix?" She had lit a cigarette and pushed the smoke out with the force of her irritation.

"Well, I wasn't going to let him have it."

"What will he do?"

"Do you really want to concern yourself with that? What do you care what a dope addict does? He must have friends in some alley somewhere. Let him get his assistance elsewhere."

He took off his robe and sat on the edge of the bed, looking perplexed, his pale flesh gathering in dewlaps around his middle. They were so deep there was true shadow under them, she thought idly. Can you hold a pencil under your breasts? Under your flaps of fat, my dear, can you hold a candle.

Tony's brother came back the next two nights, banging and threatening, but apologetic when they opened the door, as though passion had unmanned him, then let him go. He was a small animal, a ferret, in the mouth of a predator, and one of these days it wasn't going to spit him out alive. Then he stopped coming. But at the end of the week they let themselves in after a party and found all their electrical appliances gone. Wendy had been staying with a friend that night or she'd have been home alone; this was her first season baby-sitting herself.

She had walked around picking things up and dropping them. She felt strangely like a mother cat—no, what animal was it? A mouse?—that loses interest in its babies once they've been handled by someone else. Her underwear, Martin's, lying in a twisted heap, was dishonored, as if by a voyeur. Books lay in a blasted mountain where they'd been tipped off the mantel. Her one poor fur was gone, an antique muskrat that would get the thief a dollar on a good day. The silver was still there—she opened and closed the drawer with astonishing indifference; none of the details mattered much. All the cupboard doors were open in the kitchen and there was one mug, soiled at the lip, in the middle of the floor, a rootbeer bottle tipped over beside it. She picked it up gingerly as if by the tail and dropped it in the wastebasket. The mail drawer was rifled, letters perhaps read. She felt incredibly dirty, but that was all. It came as a shock to realize that she cared not one little bit about what had been taken.

The question then was, reporting to the police, should they implicate Aguilar's wife's brother? Willie—whatever his name was. He could have made a key so easily, both of them out all day. Wendy in school. How much trust it took to get through a single day in the world. . . . But she felt queasy about that, on what she called "moral grounds." Martin, angry, dismissed morality.

"Your grandiloquence could find a better cause. I don't want to get sued for false arrest. Accusation. Whatever the hell it is."

"Oh, he'd never *sue* you."

"Who knows what he'd do, a desperate man?" Martin had been going around making an inventory of their losses for his tax return. He seemed mildly elated by the coincidence that would bring them next year's models of solid-state this and automatic-refraction-tuning that, with a tax write-off at current resale values.

"The hundred dollars deductible is deplorable," he was saying—he said it three times—while she picked up a pair of pantyhose that was twined around the bodice of a slip, saw a greasy fingerprint on the daisy embroidery, and dropped it again.

"Who are you?" was all she could think to say now, stupid as it sounded. He was compact, dark, dirty, and concentrating hard on the pathetic cache of jewelry like a competent workman puzzling over shoddy goods.

She was still in the doorway. She could run, she had calculated, if he turned on her. But she didn't think he would.

He looked at her levelly.

"Who are you?"

"Why do you want to know my name? I just took a couple of your rings, that's all you got to know, right?"

He was wearing a red-checked shirt too heavy for late spring, and he was sweating. "You got a lot of junk, you know?"

She smiled her coolest smile. "Am I supposed to apologize?"

"Do what you want." He was deciding whether to get out the same way he got in, his eyes were traveling over the walls, the moldings, the ceiling.

"Take it easy," she said, almost maternally, "I'm not calling the police. I just—I wish you'd wash your hands before you go around fingering everything." She was relieved he wasn't Willie, who would have terrified her.

He nodded gravely, then laughed. "Oh, lady. Clean your fence out there—" He gestured to the back window with his head. The curtains in Wendy's room were gusting out lazily and she could see the inky handprints on the jamb all the way to the front. The cops said they couldn't lift them off that kind of paint; he must know that.

She approached a step. "Well, I wasn't expecting you."

Who did he look like—Yogi Berra? Some baseball player, PeeWee Reese? She had rooted for the Yankees when she was little; California didn't have a single major league team of its own back then. Now she could vaguely see their faces, the swarthy ones with five-o'clock shadow explaining how they had met the ball on the 3–2 pitch. Hank Bauer with her pearls in his pocket.

He sat down on the couch gingerly; suddenly his clothes must have felt very dirty to him, she saw him hunch as though to make himself lighter. She handed him a beer.

"So—you always entertain guys who come in the back window and swipe your stuff?"

She shrugged. "Doesn't happen so often. We probably haven't been here long enough."

"You don't look so mad."

She looked at him with what she knew was an inscrutable face. She felt very good; a funny kind of power it gave you to catch someone right in the middle of a compromising act. Martin did nothing compromising. In all things he did the equivalent of undressing in the closet.

"You look like you have a family, you could have a regular job, if you wanted." His dirty hands made him look as though he was on his way home from work with a lunch box and thermos. Maybe he was. Certainly he didn't have the knife-eyed desperation of an addict.

"Lady—" He spread those hands wide. She was asking him what kind of wine he liked.

She shook her head at herself impatiently. "Well, I suppose you're what we had to have next."

He raised one eyebrow politely. How much should a caught burgular talk? A problem for Amy Vanderbilt.

She looked off. Surviving—the cost of it was going up like the price of milk. She began, patiently. "We moved here from Los Angeles because we were in the earthquake."

In it? Like being in the war? In a play? Yes, in. Among the objects tossed and plummeted. Or within range. Yes, like in the war. The Blitz. Whatever.

"San Fernando, actually. Our house—the back of it, you know—the garage and sun porch and my kitchen, I was in my kitchen—were hanging over a cliff. In about a second—" She snapped her fingers. "My daughter, she's nine? She was playing out back and she came in to get something, a glass of milk, I don't remember, and before she could go back out again there was no back yard."

He was looking at her with steady eyes, keeping quiet.

"Every other thing broke—glass and pictures and a stone vase I had? And things kept tumbling, falling downhill. I close my eyes and everything turns over like—I don't know." She laughed to disparage it. "You know those rides in the amusement park?"

"Yeah, that turn all the way over? You sit on them?"

"It's like that, I get dizzy when I close my eyes so I don't sleep any more. A little, it's getting a little better."

He blinked. "You ought to go to a doctor or something, get some pills, they'll put you out."

"Did you ever go without a lot of sleep?"

He looked up from his beer, considering the question slowly, like a taste. "During the war I did, yeah, in the foxholes. You figured you went to sleep you'd never wake up."

"That's true," she said distantly; she didn't really want to share it, it couldn't have been the same, the suddenness. He probably enlisted, went looking for trouble. She could see him in khakis, his dark hair clipped, his obedient small-dog face snapping to attention, saluting. "That's true. A soldier would . . ."

She had slipped so far, so deep in her dreaming, she had become part of the landslide forever, she held one of the timbers of the porch like someone thrown clear of a wrecked ship and she fell over and over, neat as a hoop, she must have been curled in a ball, a baby, knees up, bumping over stones and boulders, into the center where the earth was hot. Everyone was there, her neighbors were being stirred, heads bobbed out of the stew, popped up like bubbles all around, boiling, then sank back and it closed over. It was all silent, silence seemed right, it went with the suddenness; faster than sound, all of it. What was the broth made of? Molten bones and rock and blood and the earth's own spring water. Top soil, bottom soil, granite shoulders, sand and grass. A dog bone flew past and vanished. Men and women and animals and the roots of trees were thrown up embracing and fell back in slow motion; still tangled they made an opening in the soup and vanished, leaving circles in circles in circles. She skimmed across the surface—a rock skimming, once, three times, seven times, good!—feeling her scraped side, raw, and sank into darkness, and breathed one time only and her lungs were black, charred, gone. She had to scream and felt them try to inflate. But they were full of holes, burst balloons, blood balloons gone lacy and dark. Each time it ended there, like a movie. Nothing more till she started it up again. It made her infinitely weary.

"So my husband said we'd better leave. I was very upset. Coming apart, kind of." She laughed, pulling hard on the fingers of one hand with the other, tugging at herself as though she were a scarf. "You don't have earthquakes here," she said simply.

He had listened very carefully, his hands in his lap looking cut loose, nothing to do with them, company posture. His beer was finished.

"No earthquakes, no tornadoes I don't think. Hurricanes once in a while. Snowstorms . . . " It was a tone he would use on his children, if he had children: full of tact and the distance of years, of small wisdom out of which even a two-bit second-story man could fashion small assurances.

"Robberies" she said, smiling bitterly. "Muggings." Rapes.

She would not tell him how she was closed up by it, cauterized. Here and there her skin puckered with memory. She got through the day. She got through the night. Martin asked her one night, turning from her, taking his hand off her shoulder, "Where the hell are you anyway?"

So she played it out, denial, reassurance, careful kisses applied to his neck where he liked them, put in place just so, like a salve. But she was gone off by herself, going nowhere she couldn't keep an eye on everything she owned. And yet she let it go so easily, her rings, her radio . . . The earth wasn't solid. "We could all do with a little less passion," she said once, sharply, just as he was moving into her, and Martin—proud of what he called his "regularity" in bed as though it had something to do with prunes—had gone slack, furiously, and rolled her away roughly like a stone in the garden. It was like being closed tight, sewn by the heat at the center of the earth. Isn't plastic sewn up that way? Then she was plastic, flesh-colored, clean, and everything stayed either outside or inside. Martin had suggested "Getting Help." But she was not guilty and God knows there was nothing to analyze because she was not to blame. Even his damn insurance policies exempted acts of God.

She looked at her caught man coolly. He was shaking his head. Pitying her?

"Don't you believe me?"

"Sure I do. Why not? I saw all that on the news, the six-o'clock news. All them bodies, listen. You're damn lucky."

She sipped her beer. Wendy would be coming home soon. She had to get dinner. "So now you come along."

"Listen, nobody ever said I was a earthquake. You don't watch out I'm gonna be flattered." He laughed, still looking at her strangely, as though from behind something. "I mean, I crowbar your window, I take a couple things out, most of it ain't much good to me anyway—"

"You sell it? Take it to somebody?"

He picked up his empty beer can looked under it. "You got your friendly neighborhood fence right down there, don't you know Anthony's?" The dark little store where everything lay sunk under years of dust. She had wondered what moved through those bleak aisles, since it clearly wasn't groceries. "Come on, everybody knows Anthony," he said firmly. She bought milk there, expecting it to be sour.

"You shouldn't have told me that."

"Oh lady you couldn't of been here long, like you say. No secret! Tony does a good business, the cops deal down there too so, you know—no sweat."

No, she didn't want to know. Strike it from the record.

Now, how do you get rid of a burglar nicely, she wondered, and felt like a schoolteacher. Something about her dispassionate slightly disapproving face; she felt thin-lipped, as though she were someone she'd known once and hadn't especially liked. That and her indifference at the core: Only till three, then I go home. She was very tired; breathing was hard under this damn dirty sky.

So she stood, feeling strong in her indifference. "Well, what do I do with you now? What you took was worth a lot."

"You don't look too stung."

She felt scolded. "That doesn't matter. That stuff is expensive to replace." He had probably looked in their bankbook.

He smiled. "So don't replace it."

"Is that what we have to expect from now on? Strangers walking through our house putting their dirty hands on everything?"

"Jesus, that dirt really gets you, don't it? You ought to meet my mother, you'd get along."

She stood up and paced like some woman on a soap opera, distraught on a small stage. "God, every place I turn. I feel like the apocalypse is coming, bit by bit dribbling away . . . "

"Take it easy, I ain't no earthquake, I ain't a member of the acopalypse. I live in Red Hook, I'm a little hard up, O.K.? I don't even do this regular, so relax."

She gave him a sour look. "Why don't you just go? Only give me what you've taken today. I want that back."

He looked at her, head to foot, as he stood up. "Thanks for the beer," he said quietly in an ordinary voice, a bank teller asking if she'd take singles. "Hey, try to relax a little. You'll make it better. There ain't gonna be no earthquake, you better believe it. Mayor don't allow it." He turned and walked to the front door, unhurried, leaving the footprints of his heavy work shoes on the rug. The cops couldn't get those either. He turned both locks casually, without the usual scrutiny that distracted her visitors from their good-bys. "I'll wash my hands next time." He closed the door exactly as Martin did, sturdily, with one quick push from outside to make sure the lock had clicked.

She sat down on the couch where he'd been sitting. It was so warm it was almost damp. Evisceration, she said to herself, turning the word over, thinking of chickens. Some women get their insides plucked out at around her age anyway. Same difference only cheaper, no Blue Cross. Her womb, her guts, all that dark eternally dangerous stuff stolen. Before it explodes. Dried up; out of business; kaput. Even if Willie came in that window with its curtains dancing up and out, and wanted what was left of her, right here and now before dinner. he'd jimmy her open and find her gone. The only way to make it in New York, she said to herself, and stood up wearily to get the chops out of the freezer. Spread the word.

QUESTIONS

1. The similes in the first paragraph reveal the woman's concern with dirt. Find additional references that show her obsession with cleanliness. Explain how the figures of speech make clear that the dirt she abhors is both physical and symbolic.

2. The woman seems to accept the burglar as an inevitable consequence of living in New York. Discuss.

3. The woman and her husband react differently to their apartment being burglarized. What do their differing reactions reveal about their personalities?

4. Is the dialogue between the woman and the burglar comic? believable? moving?

5. The woman does not want to admit that the burglar's experiences in the war are as significant as her experiences in the California earthquake. Why not?

6. The woman says that she had slipped "so deep in her dreaming" that "she had become part of the landslide forever." Explain.

7. What is the antecedent of the pronoun *it* in the following sentence: "She would not tell him how she was closed up by it, cauterized."

8. Does the burglar return the jewelry before leaving? The narrator likens his exit to the husband's leave-taking rather than to the good-bys of visitors. Why? Do the jewels have a symbolic meaning?

9. What is the woman's "solution" to making it in New York? Why does she refer to Willie in the last paragraph? Do you think she will put her solution into effect or does it symbolize an attitude?

RAY BRADBURY

August 2026:
There Will Come Soft Rains

In the living room the voice-clock sang, *Tick-tock, seven o'clock, time to get up, time to get up, seven o'clock!* as if it were afraid that nobody would. The morning house lay empty. The clock ticked on, repeating and repeating its sounds into the emptiness. *Seven-nine, breakfast time, seven-nine!*

In the kitchen the breakfast stove gave a hissing sigh and ejected from its warm interior eight pieces of perfectly browned toast, eight eggs sunnyside up, sixteen slices of bacon, two coffees, and two cool glasses of milk.

"Today is August 4, 2026," said a second voice from the kitchen ceiling, "in the city of Allendale, California." It repeated the date three times for memory's sake. "Today is Mr. Featherstone's birthday. Today is the anniversary of Tilita's marriage. Insurance is payable, as are the water, gas, and light bills."

Somewhere in the walls, relays clicked, memory tapes glided under electric eyes.

Eight-on, tick-tock, eight-one o'clock, off to school, off to work, run, run, eight-one! But no doors slammed, no carpets took the soft tread of rubber heels. It was raining outside. The weather box on the front door sang quietly: "Rain, rain, go away; rubbers, raincoats for today . . ." And the rain tapped on the empty house, echoing.

Outside, the garage chimed and lifted its door to reveal the waiting car. After a long wait the door swung down again.

At eight-thirty the eggs were shriveled and the toast was like stone. An aluminum wedge scraped them into the sink, where hot water whirled them down a metal throat which digested and flushed them away to the distant sea. The dirty dishes were dropped into a hot washer and emerged twinkling dry.

Nine-fifteen, sang the clock, *time to clean.*

Out of warrens in the wall, tiny robot mice darted. The rooms were acrawl with the small cleaning animals, all rubber and metal. They thudded against chairs, whirling their mustached runners, kneading the rug nap, sucking gently at hidden dust. Then, like mysterious invaders, they popped into their burrows. Their pink electric eyes faded. The house was clean.

Ten o'clock. The sun came out from behind the rain. The house stood alone in a city of rubble and ashes. This was the one house left standing. At night the ruined city gave off a radioactive glow which could be seen for miles.

Ten-fifteen. The garden sprinklers whirled up in golden founts, filling the soft morning air with scatterings of brightness. The water pelted windowpanes, running down the charred west side where the house had been burned evenly free of its white paint. The entire west face of the house was black, save for five places. Here the silhouette in paint of a man mowing a lawn. Here, as in a photograph, a woman bent to pick flowers. Still farther over, their images burned on wood in one titanic instant, a small boy, hands flung into the air; higher up, the image of a thrown ball, and opposite him a girl, hands raised to catch a ball which never came down.

The five spots of paint—the man, the woman, the children, the ball—remained. The rest was a thin charcoaled layer.

The gentle sprinkler rain filled the garden with falling light.

Until this day, how well the house had kept its peace. How carefully it had inquired, "Who goes there? What's the password?" and, getting no answer from lonely foxes and whining cats, it had shut up its windows and drawn shades in an old-maidenly preoccupation with self-protection which bordered on a mechanical paranoia.

It quivered at each sound, the house did. If a sparrow brushed a window, the shade snapped up. The bird, startled, flew off! No, not even a bird must touch the house!

The house was an altar with ten thousand attendants, big, small, servicing, attending, in choirs. But the gods had gone away, and the ritual of the religion continued senselessly, uselessly.

Twelve noon.

A dog whined, shivering, on the front porch.

The front door recognized the dog voice and opened. The dog, once huge and fleshy, but now gone to bone and covered with sores, moved in and through the house, tracking mud. Behind it whirred angry mice, angry at having to pick up mud, angry at inconvenience.

For not a leaf fragment blew under the door but what the wall panels flipped open and the copper scrap rats flashed swiftly out. The offending dust, hair, or paper, seized in miniature steel jaws, was raced back to the burrows.

There, down tubes which fed into the cellar, it was dropped into the sighing vent of an incinerator which sat like evil Baal in a dark corner.

The dog ran upstairs, hysterically yelping to each door, at last realizing, as the house realized, that only silence was here.

It sniffed the air and scratched the kitchen door. Behind the door, the stove was making pancakes which filled the house with a rich baked odor and the scent of maple syrup.

The dog frothed at the mouth, lying at the door, sniffing, its eyes turned to fire. It ran wildly in circles, biting at its tail, spun in a frenzy, and died. It lay in the parlor for an hour.

Two o'clock, sang a voice.

Delicately sensing decay at last, the regiments of mice hummed out as softly as blown gray leaves in an electrical wind.

Two-fifteen.

The dog was gone.

In the cellar, the incinerator glowed suddenly and a whirl of sparks leaped up the chimney.

Two thirty-five.

Bridge tables sprouted from patio walls. Playing cards fluttered onto pads in a shower of pips. Martinis manifested on an oaken bench with egg-salad sandwiches. Music played.

But the tables were silent and the cards untouched.

At four o'clock the tables folded like great butterflies back through the paneled walls.

Four-thirty.

The nursery walls glowed.

Animals took shape: yellow giraffes, blue lions, pink antelopes, lilac panthers cavorting in crystal substance. The walls were glass. They looked out upon color and fantasy. Hidden films clocked through well-oiled sprockets, and the walls lived. The nursery floor was woven to resemble a crisp, cereal meadow. Over this ran aluminum roaches and iron crickets, and in the hot still air butterflies of delicate red tissue wavered among the sharp aroma of animal spoors! There was the sound like a great matted yellow hive of bees within a dark bellows, the lazy bumble of a purring lion. And there was the patter of okapi feet and the murmur of a fresh jungle rain, like other hoofs, falling upon the summer-starched grass. Now the walls dissolved into distances of parched weed, mile on mile, and warm endless sky. The animals drew away into thorn brakes and water holes.

It was the children's hour.

Five o'clock. The bath filled with clear hot water.

Six, seven, eight o'clock. The dinner dishes manipulated like magic tricks, and in the study a *click.* In the metal stand opposite the hearth where a fire now blazed up warmly, a cigar popped out, half an inch of soft gray ash on it, smoking, waiting.

Nine o'clock. The beds warmed their hidden circuits, for nights were cool here.

Nine-five. A voice spoke from the study ceiling:

"Mrs. McClellan, which poem would you like this evening?"

The house was silent.

The voice said at last, "Since you express no preference, I shall select a poem at random." Quiet music rose to back the voice. "Sara Teasdale. As I recall, your favorite. . . .

> There will come soft rains and the smell of the ground,
> And swallows circling with their shimmering sound;
>
> And frogs in the pools singing at night,
> And wild plum trees in tremulous white;
>
> Robins will wear their feathery fire,
> Whistling their whims on a low fence-wire;
>
> And not one will know of the war, not one
> Will care at last when it is done.
>
> Not one would mind, neither bird nor tree,
> If mankind perished utterly;
>
> And Spring herself, when she woke at dawn
> Would scarcely know that we were gone."

The fire burned on the stone hearth and the cigar fell away into a mound of quiet ash on its tray. The empty chairs faced each other between the silent walls, and the music played.

At ten o'clock the house began to die.

The wind blew. A falling tree bough crashed through the kitchen window. Cleaning solvent, bottled, shattered over the stove. The room was ablaze in an instant!

"Fire!" screamed a voice. The house lights flashed, water pumps shot water from the ceilings. But the solvent spread on the linoleum, licking, eating, under the kitchen door, while the voices took it up in chorus: "Fire, fire, fire!"

The house tried to save itself. Doors sprang tightly shut, but the windows were broken by the heat and the wind blew and sucked upon the fire.

The house gave ground as the fire in ten billion angry sparks moved with flaming ease from room to room and then up the stairs. While scurrying water rats squeaked from the walls, pistoled their water, and ran for more. And the wall sprays let down showers of mechanical rain.

But too late. Somewhere, sighing, a pump shrugged to a stop. The quenching rain ceased. The reserve water supply which had filled baths and washed dishes for many quiet days was gone.

The fire crackled up the stairs. It fed upon Picassos and Matisses in the upper halls, like delicacies, baking off the oily flesh, tenderly crisping the canvases into black shavings.

Now the fire lay in beds, stood in windows, changed the colors of drapes! And then, reinforcements.

From attic trapdoors, blind robot faces peered down with faucet mouths gushing green chemical.

The fire backed off, as even an elephant must at the sight of a dead snake. Now there were twenty snakes whipping over the floor, killing the fire with a clear cold venom of green froth.

But the fire was clever. It had sent flames outside the house, up through the attic to the pumps there. An explosion! The attic brain which directed the pumps was shattered into bronze shrapnel on the beams.

The fire rushed back into every closet and felt of the clothes hung there.

The house shuddered, oak bone on bone, its bared skeleton cringing from the heat, its wire, its nerves revealed as if a surgeon had torn the skin off to let the red veins and capillaries quiver in the scalded air. Help, help! Fire! Run, run! Heat snapped mirrors like the brittle winter ice. And the voices wailed Fire, fire, run, run, like a tragic nursery rhyme, a dozen voices, high, low, like children dying in a forest, alone, alone. And the voices fading as the wires popped their sheathings like hot chestnuts. One, two, three, four, five voices died.

In the nursery the jungle burned. Blue lions roared, purple giraffes bounded off. The panthers ran in circles changing color, and ten million animals, running before the fire, vanished off toward a distant steaming river. . . .

Ten more voices died. In the last instant under the fire avalanche, other choruses, oblivious, could be heard announcing the time, playing music, cutting the lawn by remote-control mower, or setting an umbrella frantically out and in the slamming and opening front door, a thousand things happening, like a clock shop when each clock strikes the hour insanely before or after the other, a scene of maniac confusion, yet unity; singing, screaming, a few last cleaning mice darting bravely out to carry the horrid ashes away! And one voice, with sublime disregard for the situation, read poetry aloud in the fiery study, until all the film spools burned, until all the wires withered and the circuits cracked.

The fire burst the house and let it slam flat down, puffing out skirts of spark and smoke.

In the kitchen, an instant before the rain of fire and timber, the stove could be seen making breakfasts at a psychopathic rate, ten dozen eggs, six loaves of toast, twenty dozen bacon strips, which, eaten by fire, started the stove working again, hysterically hissing!

The crash. The attic smashing into kitchen and parlor. The parlor into cellar, cellar into sub-cellar. Deep freeze, armchair, film tapes, circuits, beds, and all like skeletons thrown in a cluttered mound deep under.

Smoke and silence. A great quantity of smoke.

Dawn showed faintly in the east. Among the ruins, one wall stood alone. Within the wall, a last voice said, over and over again and again, even as the sun rose to shine upon the heaped rubble and steam:

"Today is August 5, 2026, today is August 5, 2026, today is . . ."

QUESTIONS

1. The objects, the mechanized appliances, and the recorded messages give a sense of everyday life in the year 2026. In what ways is the life suggested in the story similar to American life today? dissimilar?

2. Discuss the use of personification. Can the setting be considered a character in this story?

3. Explain how setting can be viewed as plot.

4. Who is the last living occupant? How does his death advance the plot and the theme? How does the fire start? Is the fire plausible given the setting?

5. Discuss the use of irony. Explain why the Sara Teasdale poem is ironically appropriate.

6. State the story's theme, showing the inappropriateness or appropriateness of point of view to setting, plot, and theme.

Style

SAMUEL L. CLEMENS (MARK TWAIN)

Journalism in Tennessee

> *The editor of the Memphis* Avalanche *swoops thus mildly down upon a correspondent who posted him as a Radical:—"While he was writing the first word, the middle, dotting his i's, crossing his t's, and punching his period, he knew he was concocting a sentence that was saturated with infamy and reeking with falsehood."*
>
> —Exchange.

I was told by the physician that a Southern climate would improve my health, and so I went down to Tennessee, and got a berth on the *Morning Glory and Johnson County War-Whoop* as associate editor. When I went on duty I found the chief editor sitting tilted back in a three-legged chair with his feet on a pine table. There was another pine table in the room and another afflicted chair, and both were half buried under newspapers and scraps and sheets of manuscript. There was a wooden box of sand, sprinkled with cigar stubs and "old soldiers," and a stove with a door hanging by its upper hinge. The chief editor had a long-tailed black cloth frock-coat on, and white linen pants. His boots were small and neatly blacked. He wore a ruffled shirt, a large seal-ring, a standing collar of obsolete pattern, and a checkered neckerchief with the ends hanging down. Date of costume about 1848. He was smoking a cigar, and trying to think of a word, and in pawing his hair he had rumpled his locks a good deal. He was scowling fearfully, and I judged that he was concocting a particularly knotty editorial. He told me to take the exchanges and skim through them and write up the "Spirit of the Tennessee Press," condensing into the article all of their contents that seemed of interest.

I wrote as follows:

SPIRIT OF THE TENNESSEE PRESS

The editors of the *Semi-Weekly Earthquake* evidently labor under a misapprehension with regard to the Ballyhack railroad. It is not the object of the company to leave Buzzardville off to one side. On the contrary, they consider it one of the most important points along the line, and consequently can have no desire to slight it. The gentlemen of the *Earthquake* will, of course, take pleasure in making the correction.

John W. Blossom, Esq., the able editor of the Higginsville *Thunderbolt and Battle Cry of Freedom,* arrived in the city yesterday. He is stopping at the Van Buren House.

We observe that our contemporary of the Mud Springs *Morning Howl* has fallen into the error of supposing that the election of Van Werter is not an established fact, but he will have discovered his mistake before this reminder reaches him, no doubt. He was doubtless misled by incomplete election returns.

It is pleasant to note that the city of Blathersville is endeavoring to contract with some New York gentlemen to pave its well-nigh impassable streets with the Nicholson pavement. The *Daily Hurrah* urges the measure with ability, and seems confident of ultimate success.

I passed my manuscript over to the chief editor for acceptance, alteration, or destruction. He glanced at it and his face clouded. He ran his eye down the pages, and his countenance grew portentous. It was easy to see that something was wrong. Presently he sprang up and said:

"Thunder and lightning! Do you suppose I am going to speak of those cattle that way? Do you suppose my subscribers are going to stand such gruel as that? Give me the pen!"

I never saw a pen scrape and scratch its way so viciously, or plow through another man's verbs and adjectives so relentlessly. While he was in the midst of his work, somebody shot at him through the open window, and marred the symmetry of my ear.

"Ah," said he, "that is that scoundrel Smith, of the *Moral Volcano*—he was due yesterday." And he snatched a navy revolver from his belt and fired. Smith dropped, shot in the thigh. The shot spoiled Smith's aim, who was just taking a second chance, and he crippled a stranger. It was me. Merely a finger shot off.

Then the chief editor went on with his erasures and interlineations. Just as he finished them a hand-grenade came down the stove-pipe, and the explosion shivered the stove into a thousand fragments. However, it did no further damage, except that a vagrant piece knocked a couple of my teeth out.

"That stove is utterly ruined," said the chief editor.

I said I believed it was.

"Well, no matter—don't want it this kind of weather. I know the man that did it. I'll get him. Now, *here* is the way this stuff ought to be written."

I took the manuscript. It was scarred with erasures and interlineations till its mother wouldn't have known it if it had had one. It now read as follows:

SPIRIT OF THE TENNESSEE PRESS

The inveterate liars of the *Semi-Weekly Earthquake* are evidently endeavoring to palm off upon a noble and chivalrous people another of their vile and brutal falsehoods with regard to that most glorious conception of the nineteenth century, the Ballyhack railroad. The idea that Buzzardville was to be left off at one side originated in their own fulsome brains—or rather in the settlings which *they* regard as brains. They had better swallow this lie if they want to save their abandoned reptile carcasses the cowhiding they so richly deserve.

That ass, Blossom, of the Higginsville *Thunderbolt and Battle Cry of Freedom,* is down here again sponging at the Van Buren.

We observe that the besotted blackguard of the Mud Springs *Morning Howl* is giving out, with his usual propensity for lying, that Van Werter is not elected. The heaven-born mission of journalism is to disseminate truth; to eradicate error; to educate, refine, and elevate the tone of public morals and manners, and make all men more gentle, more virtuous, more charitable, and in all ways better, and holier, and happier; and yet this black-hearted scoundrel degrades his great office persistently to the dissemination of falsehood, calumny, vituperation, and vulgarity.

Blathersville wants a Nicholson pavement—it wants a jail and a poorhouse more. The idea of a pavement in a one-horse town composed of two gin-mills, a blacksmith shop, and that mustard-plaster of a newspaper, the *Daily Hurrah!* The crawling insect, Buckner, who edits the *Hurrah,* is braying about his business with his customary imbecility, and imagining that he is talking sense.

"Now *that* is the way to write—peppery and to the point. Mush-and-milk journalism gives me the fan-tods."

About this time a brick came through the window with a splintering crash, and gave me a considerable of a jolt in the back. I moved out of range—I began to feel in the way.

The chief said, "That was the Colonel, likely. I've been expecting him for two days. He will be up now right away."

He was correct. The Colonel appeared in the door a moment afterward with a dragoon revolver in his hand.

He said, "Sir, have I the honor of addressing the poltroon who edits this mangy sheet?"

"You have. Be seated, sir. Be careful of the chair, one of its legs is gone. I believe I have the honor of addressing the putrid liar, Colonel Blatherskite Tecumseh?"

"Right, sir. I have a little account to settle with you. If you are at leisure we will begin."

"I have an article on the 'Encouraging Progress of Moral and Intellectual Development in America' to finish, but there is no hurry. Begin."

Both pistols rang out their fierce clamor at the same instant. The chief lost a lock of his hair, and the Colonel's bullet ended its career in the fleshy part of my thigh. The Colonel's left shoulder was clipped a little. They fired again. Both missed their men this time, but I got my share, a shot in the arm. At the third fire both gentlemen were wounded slightly, and I had a knuckle chipped. I then said, I believed I would go out and take a walk, as this was a private matter, and I had a delicacy about participating in it further. But both gentlemen begged me to keep my seat, and assured me that I was not in the way.

They then talked about the elections and the crops while they reloaded, and I fell to tying up my wounds. But presently they opened fire again with animation, and every shot took effect—but it is proper to remark that five out of the six fell to my share. The sixth one mortally wounded the Colonel, who remarked, with fine humor, that he would have to say good morning now, as he had business uptown. He then inquired the way to the undertaker's and left.

The chief turned to me and said, "I am expecting company to dinner, and shall have to get ready. It will be a favor to me if you will read proof and attend to the customers."

I winced a little at the idea of attending to the customers, but I was too bewildered by the fusillade that was still ringing in my ears to think of anything to say.

He continued, "Jones will be here at three—cowhide him. Gillespie will call earlier, perhaps—throw him out of the window. Ferguson will be along about four—kill him. That is all for to-day, I believe. If you have any odd time, you may write a blistering article on the police—give the chief inspector rats. The cowhides are under the table; weapons in the drawer—ammunition there in the corner—lint and bandages up there in the pigeon-holes. In case of accident, go to Lancet, the surgeon, down-stairs. He advertises—we take it out in trade."

He was gone. I shuddered. At the end of the next three hours I had been through perils so awful that all peace of mind and all cheerfulness were gone from me. Gillespie had called and thrown *me* out of the window. Jones arrived promptly, and when I got ready to do the cowhiding he took the job off my hands. In an encounter with a stranger, not in the bill of fare, I had lost my scalp. Another stranger, by the name of Thompson, left me a mere wreck and ruin of chaotic rags. And at last, at bay in the corner, and beset by an infuriated mob of editors, blacklegs, politicians, and desperadoes, who raved and swore and flourished their weapons about my head till the air shimmered with glancing flashes of steel, I was in the act of resigning my berth on the paper when the chief arrived, and with him a rabble of charmed and enthusiastic friends. Then ensued a scene of riot and carnage such as no human pen, or steel one either, could describe. People were shot, probed, dismembered, blown up, thrown out of the window. There was a brief tornado of murky blasphemy, with a confused and frantic war-dance glimmering through it, and then all was over. In five minutes there was silence, and the gory chief and I sat alone and surveyed the sanguinary ruin that strewed the floor around us.

He said, "You'll like this place when you get used to it."

I said, "I'll have to get you to excuse me; I think maybe I might write to suit you after a while; as soon as I had had some practice and learned the language I am confident I could. But, to speak the plain truth, that sort of energy of expression has its inconveniences, and a man is liable to interruption. You see that yourself. Vigorous writing is calculated to elevate the public, no doubt, but then I do not like to attract so much attention as it calls forth. I can't write with comfort when I am interrupted so much as I have been to-day. I like this berth well enough, but I don't like to be left here to wait on the customers. The experiences are novel, I grant you, and entertaining, too, after a fashion, but they are not judiciously distributed. A gentleman shoots at you through the window and cripples *me;* a bombshell comes down the stove-pipe for your gratification and sends the stove door down *my* throat; a friend drops in to swap compliments with you, and freckles *me* with bullet-holes till my skin won't hold my principles; you go to dinner, and Jones comes with his cowhide, Gillespie throws me out of the window, Thompson tears all my clothes off, and an entire stranger takes my scalp with the easy freedom of an old acquaintance; and in less than five minutes all the blackguards in the country arrive in their war-paint, and proceed to scare the rest of me to death with their tomahawks. Take it altogether, I never had such a spirited time in all my life as I have had to-day. No; I like you, and I like your calm unruffled way of explaining things to the customers, but you see I am not used to it. The Southern heart is too impulsive; Southern hospitality is too lavish with the stranger. The paragraphs which I have written to-day, and into whose cold sentences your masterly hand has infused the fervent spirit of Tennesseean journalism, will wake up another nest of hornets. All that mob of editors will come—and they will come hungry, too, and want somebody for breakfast. I shall have to bid you adieu. I decline to be present at these festivities. I came South for my health, I will go back on the same errand, and suddenly. Tennesseean journalism is too stirring for me."

After which we parted with mutual regret, and I took apartments at the hospital.

QUESTIONS

1. Discuss understatement and hyperbole as sources of verbal humor.

2. Are the characters round? flat? static? dynamic? sympathetic? unsympathetic? Why does the narrator pay so much attention to the editor's clothing?

3. Examine the differences between the narrator's article and the editor's rewritten

version. What do his revisions tell you about the "spirit of the Tennessee Press"?

4. What is ironical about the editor's description of the "mission of journalism"? What is the target of satire in this story? Is the story effective as satire?

5. Discuss the story as an example of a tall tale.

ERNEST HEMINGWAY

Hills Like White Elephants

The hills across the valley of the Ebro were long and white. On this side there was no shade and no trees and the station was between two lines of rails in the sun. Close against the side of the station there was the warm shadow of the building and a curtain, made of strings of bamboo beads, hung across the open door into the bar, to keep out flies. The American and the girl with him sat at a table in the shade, outside the building. It was very hot and the express from Barcelona would come in forty minutes. It stopped at this junction for two minutes and went on to Madrid.

"What should we drink?" the girl asked. She had taken off her hat and put it on the table.

"It's pretty hot," the man said.

"Let's drink beer."

"Dos cervezas," the man said into the curtain.

"Big ones?" a woman asked from the doorway.

"Yes. Two big ones."

The woman brought two glasses of beer and two felt pads. She put the felt pads and the beer glasses on the table and looked at the man and the girl. The girl was looking off at the line of hills. They were white in the sun and the country was brown and dry.

"They look like white elephants," she said.

"I've never seen one," the man drank his beer.

"No, you wouldn't have."

"I might have," the man said. "Just because you say I wouldn't have doesn't prove anything."

The girl looked at the bead curtain. "They've painted something on it," she said. "What does it say?"

"Anis del Toro. It's a drink."

"Could we try it?"

The man called "Listen" through the curtain. The woman came out from the bar.

"Four reales."

"We want two Anis del Toro."

"With water?"

"Do you want it with water?"

"I don't know," the girl said. "Is it good with water?"

"It's all right."

"You want them with water?" asked the woman.

"Yes, with water."

"It tastes like licorice," the girl said and put the glass down.

"That's the way with everything."

"Yes," said the girl. "Everything tastes of licorice. Especially all the things you've waited so long for, like absinthe."

"Oh, cut it out."

"You started it," the girl said. "I was being amused. I was having a fine time."

"Well, let's try and have a fine time."

"All right. I was trying. I said the mountains looked like white elephants. Wasn't that bright?"

"That was bright."

"I wanted to try this new drink. That's all we do, isn't it—look at things and try new drinks?"

"I guess so."

The girl looked across at the hills.

"They're lovely hills," she said. "They don't really look like white elephants. I just meant the coloring of their skin through the trees."

"Should we have another drink?"

"All right."

The warm wind blew the bead curtain against the table.

"The beer's nice and cool," the man said.

"It's lovely," the girl said.

"It's really an awfully simple operation, Jig," the man said. "It's not really an operation at all."

The girl looked at the ground the table legs rested on.

"I know you wouldn't mind it, Jig. It's really not anything. It's just to let the air in."

The girl did not say anything.

"I'll go with you and I'll stay with you all the time. They just let the air in and then it's all perfectly natural."

"Then what will we do afterward?"

"We'll be fine afterward. Just like we were before."

"What makes you think so?"

"That's the only thing that bothers us. It's the only thing that's made us unhappy."

The girl looked at the bead curtain, put her hand out and took hold of two of the strings of beads.

"And you think then we'll be all right and be happy."

"I know we will. You don't have to be afraid. I've known lots of people that have done it."

"So have I," said the girl. "And afterward they were all so happy."

"Well," the man said, "if you don't want to you don't have to. I wouldn't have you do it if you didn't want to. But I know it's perfectly simple."

"And you really want to?"

"I think it's the best thing to do. But I don't want you to do it if you don't really want to."

"And if I do it you'll be happy and things will be like they were and you'll love me?"

"I love you now. You know I love you."

"I know. But if I do it, then it will be nice again if I say things are like white elephants, and you'll like it?"

"I'll love it. I love it now but I just can't think about it. You know how I get when I worry."

"If I do it you won't ever worry?"

"I won't worry about that because it's perfectly simple."

"Then I'll do it. Because I don't care about me."

"What do you mean?"

"I don't care about me."

"Well, I care about you."

"Oh, yes. But I don't care about me. And I'll do it and then everything will be fine."

"I don't want you to do it if you feel that way."

The girl stood up and walked to the end of the station. Across, on the other side, were fields of grain and trees along the banks of the Ebro. Far away, beyond the river, were mountains. The shadow of a cloud moved across the field of grain and she saw the river through the trees.

"And we could have all this," she said. "And we could have everything and every day we make it more impossible."

"What did you say?"

"I said we could have everything."

"We can have everything."

"No, we can't."

"We can have the whole world."

"No, we can't."

"We can go everywhere."

"No, we can't. It isn't ours any more."

"It's ours."

"No, it isn't. And once they take it away, you never get it back."

"But they haven't taken it away."

"We'll wait and see."

"Come on back in the shade," he said. "You mustn't feel that way."

"I don't feel any way," the girl said. "I just know things."

"I don't want you to do anything that you don't want to do——"

"Nor that isn't good for me," she said. "I know. Could we have another beer?"

"All right. But you've got to realize——"

"I realize," the girl said. "Can't we maybe stop talking?"

They sat down at the table and the girl looked across at the hills on the dry side of the valley and the man looked at her and at the table.

"You've got to realize," he said, "that I don't want you to do it if you don't want to. I'm perfectly willing to go through with it if it means anything to you."

"Doesn't it mean anything to you? We could get along."

"Of course it does. But I don't want anybody but you. I don't want any one else. And I know it's perfectly simple."

"Yes, you know its perfectly simple."

"It's all right for you to say that, but I do know it."

"Would you do something for me now?"

"I'd do anything for you."

"Would you please please please please please please please stop talking?"

He did not say anything but looked at the bags against the wall of the station. There were labels on them from all the hotels where they had spent nights.

"But I don't want you to," he said, "I don't care anything about it."

"I'll scream," the girl said.

The woman came out through the curtains with two glasses of beer and put them down on the damp felt pads. "The train comes in five minutes," she said.

"What did she say?" asked the girl.

"That the train is coming in five minutes."

The girl smiled brightly at the woman, to thank her.

"I'd better take the bags over to the other side of the station," the man said. She smiled at him.

"All right. Then come back and we'll finish the beer."

He picked up the two heavy bags and carried them around the station to the other tracks. He looked up the tracks but could not see the train. Coming back, he walked through the barroom, where people waiting for the train were drinking. He drank an Anis at the bar and looked at the people. They were all waiting reasonably for the train. He went out through the bead curtain. She was sitting at the table and smiled at him.

"Do you feel better?" he asked.

"I feel fine," she said. "There's nothing wrong with me. I feel fine."

QUESTIONS

1. Examine the function of objective description in creating a sense of place. How else is setting depicted?

2. Give a thumbnail sketch of the woman. Discuss the ways in which action and dialogue reveal her personality.

3. Give a thumbnail sketch of the man. Discuss the ways in which action and dialogue reveal his personality.

4. Are the characters sympathetic? unsympathetic? flat? round? static? dynamic? Are the man and the woman compatible? in love? Does the woman want to have an abortion? Why does the man want her to have an abortion?

5. Characterization is achieved with minimal biographical information. We are not told about the age, education, social class, past romantic relationships, aspirations, or means of financial support of the man and woman. Neither are we told if they are married. Is this omitted information necessary? Discuss the role of inference in your understanding of the characters.

6. Explain the significance of the title.

7. Discuss the meaning of the following passage:

   Across, on the other side, were fields of grain and trees along the banks of the Ebro. Far away, beyond the river, were mountains. The shadow of a cloud moved across the field of grain and she saw the river through the trees.
   "And we could have all this," she said. "And we could have everything and every day we make it more impossible."

8. What is the antecedent of the pronoun *they* in the following sentence: "And once they take it away, you never get it back"? How does this statement contribute to your understanding of the story's theme?

JAMES JOYCE

Araby

North Richmond Street, being blind, was a quiet street except at the hour when the Christian Brothers School set the boys free. An uninhabited house of two stories stood at the blind end, detached from its neighbors in a square ground. The other houses of the street, conscious of decent lives within them, gazed at one another with brown imperturbable faces.

The former tenant of our house, a priest, had died in the back drawing-room. Air, musty from having been long enclosed, hung in all the rooms, and the waste room behind the kitchen was littered with old useless papers. Among these I found a few paper-covered books, the pages of which were curled and damp: *The Abbott,* by Walter Scott, *The Devout Communicant* and *The Memoirs of Vidocq.* I liked the last best because its leaves were yellow. The wild garden behind the house contained a central apple-tree and a few straggling bushes under one of which I found the late tenant's rusty bicycle-pump. He had been a very charitable priest; in his will he had left all his money to institutions and the furniture of his house to his sister.

When the short days of winter came dusk fell before we had well eaten our dinners. When we met in the street the houses had grown somber. The space of sky above us was the color of ever-changing violet and towards it the lamps of the street lifted their feeble lanterns. The cold air stung us and we played till our bodies glowed. Our shouts echoed in the silent street. The career of our play brought us through the dark muddy lanes behind the houses where we ran the gauntlet of the rough tribes from the cottages, to the back doors of the dark dripping gardens where odors arose from the ashpits, to the dark odorous stables where a coachman smoothed and combed the horse or shook music from the buckled harness. When we returned to the street light from the kitchen windows had filled the areas. If my uncle was seen turning the corner we hid in the shadow until we had seen him safely housed. Or if Mangan's sister came out on the doorstep to call her brother in to his tea we watched her from our shadow peer up and down the street. We waited to see whether she would remain or go in and, if she remained, we left our shadow and walked up to Mangan's steps resignedly. She was waiting for us, her figure defined by the light from the half-opened door. Her brother always teased her before he obeyed and I stood by the railings looking at her. Her dress swung as she moved her body and the soft rope of her hair tossed from side to side.

Every morning I lay on the floor in the front parlor watching her door. The blind was pulled down to within an inch of the sash so that I could not be seen. When she came out on the doorstep my heart leaped. I ran to the hall, seized my books and followed her. I kept her brown figure always in my eye and, when we came near the point at which our ways diverged, I quickened my pace and passed her. This happened morning after morning. I had never spoken to her, except for a few casual words, and yet her name was like a summons to all my foolish blood.

Her image accompanied me even in places the most hostile to romance. On Saturday evenings when my aunt went marketing I had to go to carry some of the parcels. We walked through the flaring streets, jostled by drunken men and bargaining women, amid the curses of laborers, the shrill litanies of shop-boys who stood on guard by the barrels of pigs' cheeks, the nasal chanting of street-singers, who sang a *come-all-you* about O'Donovan Rossa, or a ballad about the troubles in our native land. These noises converged in a single sensation of life for me: I imagined that I bore my chalice safely through a throng of foes. Her name sprang to my lips at moments in strange prayers and praises which I myself did not understand. My eyes were often full of tears (I could not tell why) and at times a flood from my heart seemed to pour itself out into my bosom. I thought little of the future. I did not know whether I would ever speak to her or not or, if I spoke to her, how I could tell her of my confused adoration. But my body was like a harp and her words and gestures were like fingers running upon the wires.

One evening I went into the back drawing-room in which the priest had died. It was a dark rainy evening and there was no sound in the house. Through one of the broken panes I heard the rain impinge upon the earth, the fine incessant needles of water playing in the sodden beds. Some distant lamp or lighted window gleamed below me. I was thankful that I could see so little. All my senses seemed to desire to veil themselves and, feeling that I was about to slip from them, I pressed the palms of my hands together until they trembled, murmuring: *"O love! O love!"* many times.

At last she spoke to me. When she addressed the first words to me I was so confused that I did not know what to answer. She asked me was I going to

Araby. I forgot whether I answered yes or no. It would be a splendid bazaar, she said she would love to go.

"And why can't you?" I asked.

While she spoke she turned a silver bracelet round and round her wrist. She could not go, she said, because there would be a retreat that week in her convent. Her brother and two other boys were fighting for their caps and I was alone at the railings. She held one of the spikes, bowing her head towards me. The light from the lamp opposite our door caught the white curve of her neck, lit up her hair that rested there and, falling, lit up the hand upon the railing. It fell over one side of her dress and caught the white border of a petticoat, just visible as she stood at ease.

"It's well for you," she said.

"If I go," I said, "I will bring you something."

What innumerable follies laid waste my waking and sleeping thoughts after that evening! I wished to annihilate the tedious intervening days. I chafed against the work of school. At night in my bedroom and by day in the classroom her image came between me and the page I strove to read. The syllables of the word *Araby* were called to me through the silence in which my soul luxuriated and cast an Eastern enchantment over me. I asked for leave to go to the bazaar on Saturday night. My aunt was surprised and hoped it was not some Freemason affair. I answered few questions in class. I watched my master's face pass from amiability to sternness; he hoped I was not beginning to idle. I could not call my wandering thoughts together. I had hardly any patience with the serious work of life which, now that it stood between me and my desire, seemed to me child's play, ugly monotonous child's play.

On Saturday morning I reminded my uncle that I wished to go to the bazaar in the evening. He was fussing at the hallstand, looking for the hat-brush, and answered me curtly:

"Yes, boy, I know."

As he was in the hall I could not go into the front parlor and lie at the window. I left the house in bad humor and walked slowly towards the school. The air was pitilessly raw and already my heart misgave me.

When I came home to dinner my uncle had not yet been home. Still it was early. I sat staring at the clock for some time and, when its ticking began to irritate me, I left the room. I mounted the staircase and gained the upper part of the house. The high cold empty gloomy rooms liberated me and I went from room to room singing. From the front window I saw my companions playing below in the street. Their cries reached me weakened and indistinct and, leaning my forehead against the cool glass, I looked over at the dark house where she lived. I may have stood there for an hour, seeing nothing but the brown-clad figure cast by my imagination, touched discreetly by the lamplight at the curved neck, at the hand upon the railings and at the border below the dress.

When I came downstairs again I found Mrs. Mercer sitting at the fire. She was an old garrulous woman, a pawnbroker's widow, who collected used stamps for some pious purpose. I had to endure the gossip of the tea-table. The meal was prolonged beyond an hour and still my uncle did not come. Mrs. Mercer stood up to go: she was sorry she couldn't wait any longer, but it was after eight o'clock and she did not like to be out late, as the night air was bad for her. When she had gone I began to walk up and down the room, clenching my fists. My aunt said:

"I'm afraid you may put off your bazaar for this night of Our Lord."

At nine o'clock I heard my uncle's latchkey in the halldoor. I heard him talking to himself and heard the hallstand rocking when it had received the weight of his overcoat. I could interpret these signs. When he was midway through his dinner I asked him to give me the money to go to the bazaar. He had forgotten.

"The people are in bed and after their first sleep now," he said.

I did not smile. My aunt said to him energetically:

"Can't you give him the money and let him go? You've kept him late enough as it is."

My uncle said he was very sorry he had forgotten. He said he believed in the old saying: "All work and no play makes Jack a dull boy." He asked me where I was going and, when I had told him a second time he asked me did I know *The Arab's Farewell to his Steed.* When I left the kitchen he was about to recite the opening lines of the piece to my aunt.

I held a florin tightly in my hand as I strode down Buckingham Street towards the station. The sight of the streets thronged with buyers and glaring with gas recalled to me the purpose of my journey. I took my seat in a third-class carriage of a deserted train. After an intolerable delay the train moved out of the station slowly. It crept onward among ruinous houses and over the twinkling river. At Westland Row Station a crowd of people pressed to the carriage doors; but the porters moved them back, saying that it was a special train for the bazaar. I remained alone in the bare carriage. In a few minutes the train drew up beside an improvised wooden platform. I passed out on to the road and saw by the lighted dial of a clock that it was ten minutes to ten. In front of me was a large building which displayed the magical name.

I could not find any sixpenny entrance and, fearing that the bazaar would be closed, I passed in quickly through a turnstile, handing a shilling to a weary-looking man. I found myself in a big hall girdled at half its height by a gallery. Nearly all the stalls were closed and the greater part of the hall was in darkness. I recognized a silence like that which pervades a church after a service. I walked into the center of the bazaar timidly. A few people were gathered about the stalls which were still open. Before a curtain, over which the words *Café Chantant* were written in colored lamps, two men were counting money on a salver. I listened to the fall of the coins.

Remembering with difficulty why I had come I went over to one of the stalls and examined porcelain vases and flowered tea-sets. At the door of the stall a young lady was talking and laughing with two young gentlemen. I remarked their English accents and listened vaguely to their conversation.

"O, I never said such a thing!"

"O, but you did!"

"O, but I didn't!"

"Didn't she say that?"

"Yes. I heard her."

"O, there's a . . . fib!"

Observing me the young lady came over and asked me did I wish to buy anything. The tone of her voice was not encouraging; she seemed to have spoken to me out of a sense of duty. I looked humbly at the great jars that stood like eastern guards at either side of the dark entrance to the stall and murmured:

"No, thank you."

The young lady changed the position of one of the vases and went back to the two young men. They began to talk of the same subject. Once or twice the young lady glanced at me over her shoulder.

I lingered before her stall, though I knew my stay was useless, to make my interest in her wares seem the more real. Then I turned away slowly and walked down the middle of the bazaar. I allowed the two pennies to fall against the sixpence in my pocket. I heard a voice call from one end of the gallery that the light was out. The upper part of the hall was now completely dark.

Gazing up into the darkness I saw myself as a creature driven and derided by vanity; and my eyes burned with anguish and anger.

QUESTIONS

1. What is the meaning of the word *blind* in the following sentence: "North Richmond Street, being blind, was a quiet street except at the hour when the Christian Brothers School set the boys free"? Comment on the way the opening paragraph shifts from literalness to figurative language in the final sentence.

2. What, if any, necessary information does the second paragraph contain? Could this paragraph be deleted without loss to the story? How does the description of the boy's neighborhood in the third paragraph affect your understanding of the events that follow?

3. Find at least three examples of religious imagery. Discuss its effect on characterization and its use as a unifying motif. Explain how the boy's religiosity influences his perception of his experiences.

4. How does Mrs. Mercer help define the boy's family and his life within that family? Is the uncle a sympathetic character?

5. The impact and meaning of the story depend upon the reader's identifying with the boy's idealized love for Mangan's sister. How does Joyce dramatize the intensity of the boy's love? Is the story successful in conveying this emotion?

6. Although narrated in the first person, the narrator is separated by perception and diction from the youthful protagonist. Explain, discussing the role of this separation in establishing psychic distance.

7. Why does the boy want to go to the bazaar? What does Araby represent to him? Why does he judge himself so harshly at the conclusion of the story? Is his negative opinion justified?

8. Are the boy's emotions and experiences sufficiently universal so that they can be viewed as an archetype? Discuss this story as an embodiment of the rite of passage. Does the religious imagery enhance the story as archetype?

ANTON CHEKHOV

Daydreams

Translation by Avrahm Yarmolinsky

Two rural constables—one a black-bearded stocky fellow with such extraordinarily short legs that if you look at him from the rear it seems as though they begin much lower down than other people's; the other, tall, lean, and straight as a stick, with a skimpy reddish beard—are taking to the county seat a tramp who has refused to give his name. The first waddles along, glances about, chews now a straw, now his own sleeve, slaps himself on the thighs, hums, and generally has a carefree, lighthearted air about him; the other, in spite of his gaunt face and narrow shoulders, looks solid, serious, and substantial; his whole appearance and the way he carries himself suggest a priest of the Old Believers' sect or a warrior in an ancient icon. "Forasmuch as he is wise, God hath added unto his brow"—in other words, he is bald—which increases the resemblance just mentioned. The name of the first is Andrey Ptaha, that of the second Nikandr Sapozhnikov.

The man they are escorting does not at all fit the usual conception of a tramp. He is a puny little man, feeble and sickly, with small, colorless, extremely blurred features. His eyebrows are scanty, his expression gentle and submissive; he has hardly a trace of a mustache, although he is over thirty. He moves timidly, a hunched figure, his hands thrust into his sleeves. The collar of his threadbare cloth overcoat, which is not a peasant's, is turned up to the very edge of his cap, so that only his little red nose ventures to peep out into God's world. He speaks in a small, wheedling tenor and coughs continually. It is very, very hard to accept him as a tramp who is concealing his identity. He looks more like a priest's son, a poor devil of a fellow, reduced to beggary; a clerk sacked for drunkenness; a

387

merchant's son or nephew who has tested his feeble powers on the stage and is now going home to play the last act in the parable of the prodigal son. Perhaps, to judge from the dull patience with which he is struggling against the impassable autumn mud, he is a fanatic, a novice, wandering from one Russian monastery to another, continually seeking "a life of peace that knoweth no sin" and not finding it. . . .

The men have been walking for a long time but they seem to be unable to leave one small patch of land. Before them stretch some thirty feet of road, black-brown and muddy, behind them is an identical stretch of road, and beyond, wherever one looks, there is an impenetrable wall of white fog. They walk on and on, but the ground remains the same, the wall is no nearer, and the patch is the same. Sometimes there floats past them a white, angular boulder, a gulley, or an armful of hay fallen from a passing cart; or a large, muddy puddle will gleam briefly, or, suddenly, a shadow with vague outlines will come into view ahead of them, growing smaller and darker as they approach, and finally there will loom before the wayfarers a slanting milestone with a half-effaced number on it, or a pitiful birch tree, drenched and bare as a wayside beggar. The little birch whispers something with what remains of its yellow leaves, one leaf breaks off and floats lazily to the ground. . . . And then once more, fog, mud, brown grass at the edges of the road. Dull, unkind tears hang on the grass. They are not the tears of quiet joy that the earth sheds on greeting the summer sun and on parting from it, not the tears that she gives the quails, corncrakes, and graceful, long-beaked curlews to drink at dawn. The wayfarers' feet stick in the heavy, clinging mud. Every step costs an effort.

Andrey Ptaha is somewhat agitated. He keeps starting at the tramp and trying to understand how a living, sober human being can fail to recall his own name.

"You are an Orthodox Christian, no?" he asks.

"I am that," the tramp answers meekly.

"Hm—then you were christened?"

"Why, sure! I'm no Turk. I go to church and take the sacrament and don't eat forbidden food on fast days. I don't neglect my religious duties none—"

"Well, what name do they call you by, then?"

"Call me what you please, mate."

Ptaha shrugs his shoulders and slaps himself on the thighs in extreme perplexity. The other constable, Nikandr Sapozhnikov, maintains a dignified silence. He is not so naive as Ptaha, and knows very well the reasons why an Orthodox Christian may wish to conceal his name from people. His expressive face is cold and stern. He walks apart and does not condescend to chatter idly with his companions, but tries to show everyone, as it were, even the fog, that he is staid and sensible.

"God knows what to make of you," Ptaha persists in pestering the tramp. "Peasant you ain't and gentleman you ain't, but something betwixt and between. The other day I was washing the sieves in the pond and I caught a viper—see, as long as a finger, with gills and a tail. At first I thought it was a fish, and then I looked—and damn the creature, if it hadn't paws! Maybe it was a fish, maybe it was a viper, the devil only knows what it was. Same with you. What are your folks?"

"I am a peasant, of peasant stock," the tramp sighs. "My dear mother was a house serf. True, I don't look like a peasant, but that was the way of it, my friend. My dear mother was a nurse to the master's children, and she had it very well, and I was her flesh and blood, so I lived with her in the big house. She took care of me and spoiled me and did all she could to raise me above my class and make something of me. I slept in a bed, I ate a regular dinner every day, I wore breeches and shoes like any gentleman's child. My dear mother fed me just what she ate; if they gave her material for a present, she made clothes for me out of it. What a life we had of it! I ate so much candy and cake when I was a child that if it could be sold now it would bring the price of a good horse. My dear mother taught me how to read and write, she put the fear of God in me when I was little, and she brought me up so that now I can't get myself to say an indelicate peasant word. And I don't drink vodka, mate, and I'm neat about my person, and I know how to behave properly in good society. If my dear mother is still living, God give her health; and if she has departed this life, then God rest her soul, and may she know peace in Thy kingdom, Lord, where the righteous are at rest."

The tramp bares his head with its scanty bristles, turns his eyes upward, and crosses himself twice.

"Grant her, O Lord, a green and peaceful resting-place," he says in a drawling voice, rather like an old woman's than a man's. "Instruct Thy servant, Xenia, in Thy ways, O Lord! If it had not been for my dear, darling mother I should have been a plain peasant with no understanding of anything! Now, mate, ask me what you like and I understand it all: the Holy Scriptures and profane writings, and every prayer and catechism. And I live according to the Scriptures, too. I don't harm anybody, I keep my body pure and chaste, I observe the fasts, I eat when it is proper. Another man takes no pleasure in anything but vodka and beastliness, but I, when I have time, I sit in a corner and read a book. I read and I cry and cry—"

"What do you cry about?"

"They write so pitifully! For some little book you pay no more than a five-kopeck piece, but how you weep and groan over it!"

"Is your father dead?" asks Ptaha.

"I don't know, mate. I don't know my father; it's no use hiding the sin. I judge that I was my dear mother's illegitimate child. My dear mother lived with the gentry all her life and she didn't want to marry a plain peasant—"

"And so she lit upon a master," Ptaha grins.

"She did not preserve her honor, that's true. She was pious and God-fearing, but she did not keep her maiden purity. Of course, it is a sin, a great sin, there's no doubt about it, but then, maybe there is noble blood in my veins. Maybe I am only a peasant by rank, but by nature I am a noble gentleman."

The "noble gentleman" says all this in a low, mawkish tenor voice, wrinkling up his narrow forehead and making creaking sounds with his red, frozen little nose. Ptaha listens and looks askance at him in wonder, and does not stop shrugging his shoulders.

After walking nearly four miles the constables and the tramp sit down on a hillock to rest.

"Even a dog knows his own name," mutters Ptaha. "My name is Andryushka, his is Nikandr; every man has his holy name, and it can't be forgotten. Nohow!"

"Who has any need to know my name?" sighs the tramp, resting his cheek on his fist. "And what good would it do me if they did know it? If they let me go where I liked—but this way, it would be worse for me than it is now. I know the law, friends. Now I am one of those tramps who don't tell who they are, and the most they can do is exile me to Eastern Siberia and give me thirty or forty lashes; but if I told them my real name and rank they would send me back to hard labor, I know!"

"Why, were you a convict?"

"I was, dear friend. For four years I went about with my head shaved and irons on my legs."

"What for?"

"For murder, my good friend! When I was still a lad of about eighteen, my dear mother accidentally poured arsenic instead of soda and acid into the master's glass. There were powders of all sorts in the storeroom; it was easy to make a mistake."

The tramp sighs, shakes his head, and says:

"My mother was a pious woman, but who knows? The soul of another is a dark forest! Maybe it was an accident, and maybe she couldn't bear the humiliation of seeing the master make a favorite of another servant. Maybe she put it in on purpose, God alone knows! I was young then, and didn't understand everything. Now I remember that as a matter of fact our master did take another paramour and my dear mother was greatly distressed. Our trial lasted nearly two years. My dear mother was sentenced to twenty years of hard labor, and I, because of my youth, only to seven."

"And where did you come in?"

"As an accomplice. It was me handed the glass to the master. That was how it always was. My dear mother prepared the soda and I handed it to him. Only I'm telling you this, brothers, as Christian to Christian, as I would say it before God. And don't you go telling anybody—"

"Oh, nobody's going to ask us," says Ptaha. "So you've run away from hard labor, have you?"

"Yes, dear friend. Some fourteen of us ran away. They ran away, God bless them, and took me with them. Now answer me, on your conscience, mate, what reason have I to tell who I am? They'll send me back to hard labor, you know! And what sort of a convict am I! I'm a refined man, and not in the best of health. I like it clean where I sleep and eat. When I pray to God I like to light a little lamp or a candle, and not have a racket around me. When I bow down and touch the ground with my forehead, I don't like the floor to be dirty or covered with spittle. And for my dear mother's sake I bow down forty times morning and evening."

The tramp takes off his cap and crosses himself.

"Let them exile me to Eastern Siberia," he says. "I'm not afraid of that."

"Is that any better?"

"It's a different thing altogether. Doing hard labor you're like a lobster in a basket: there's crowding, crushing, jostling, no room to breathe; it's plain hell— may the Queen of Heaven deliver us from such hell! You're a criminal and treated like a criminal—worse than any dog. You can't eat, you can't sleep, or even say your prayers. But it's not like that in a colony of exiles. In such a settlement, first thing I do is join the community like the others. The authorities are bound by law to give me my allotment. Ye-es! They say the land is free there, like snow; take as much as you please! They'll give me plow land, and land for a kitchen garden, and a building lot. . . . I'll plow my fields like other people, I'll sow. I'll have cattle and all sorts of things, bees, sheep, dogs—a Siberian cat, so that rats and mice don't eat up my stores. I'll build a house, brother, I'll buy icons—Please God, I'll get married, and have children. . . ."

The tramp mumbles and looks away from his listeners. Naive as his daydreams are, they are uttered in such a sincere, heartfelt manner that it is hard not to credit them. The tramp's little mouth is distorted by a smile. His eyes, his little nose, his whole face, are set and dazed with blissful anticipation of distant happiness. The constables listen and look at him gravely, not without sympathy. They share his faith.

"I am not afraid of Siberia," the tramp goes on mumbling. "Siberia is Russia too, and has the same God and Czar as here. They talk the language of Orthodox Christians, just like you and me. Only there's more free space there and people are better off. Everything's better there. The rivers there, for instance, are way better than those we have here. And there's fish, and game, no end of it all. And there's nothing in the world, brothers, that I'd rather do than fish. Don't give me bread, just let me sit with a hook and line, by God! I use a line and I set creels and when the ice breaks then I take a casting-net. If I'm not strong enough to handle the net, I hire a man for five kopecks. And, Lord, what a pleasure it is! You catch an eel-pout or a chub of some sort and are as pleased as if you'd found your own brother. And let me tell you, there's a special trick with every fish: you catch one with a minnow, you catch another with a worm, the third with a frog or a grasshopper. You have to understand all that, of course! Take the eel-pout, for instance. An eel-pout is a coarse fish—it will grab even a perch; a pike loves a gudgeon, the bullhead likes a butterfly. There's no greater pleasure than to fish for chub where the current is strong. You cast a seventy-foot line without a sinker, using a butterfly or a beetle, so that the bait floats on the surface; you stand in the water with your pants off and let it go with the current, and smack! the chub jerks it! Only you've got to be on the lookout that it doesn't snatch your bait away, the damned creature. As soon as it tugs at your line, you must give it a pull: don't wait. What a lot of fish I've caught in my time! When we ran away, the other convicts used to sleep in the forest; but I couldn't sleep, I made for the river. The rivers there are wide and rapid, the banks are steep—fearfully! And all along the banks there are dense forests. The trees are so tall that you get dizzy looking up to the top of them. At the prices timber brings here, every pine would fetch ten rubles."

Overwhelmed by the disorderly onrush of reveries, idealized images of the past, and sweet anticipations of happiness, the wretched fellow sinks into silence, merely moving his lips as though whispering to himself. A dazed, blissful smile never leaves his face. The constables are silent. They are sunk in thought, their heads bowed. In the autumn stillness, when the chill, sullen mist that hangs over the earth weighs upon the heart, when it looms like a prison wall before the eyes, and bears witness to the limited scope of man's will, it is sweet to think of broad, swift rivers, with steep banks open to the sky, of impenetrable forests, of boundless plains. Slowly and tranquilly imagination conjures up the picture of a man, early in the morning, before the flush of dawn has left the sky, making his way along the steep, lonely bank, looking like a tiny speck: age-old pines, fit for ships' masts, rise up in terraces on both sides of the torrent, gaze sternly at the free man and murmur menacingly; roots, huge boulders, and thorny bushes bar his way, but he is strong in body and bold in spirit, and fears neither the pine trees nor the boulders, nor his solitude, nor the reverberant echo that repeats the sound of his every footstep.

The constables picture to themselves a free life such as they have never lived; whether they vaguely remember scenes from stories heard long ago or whether they have inherited notions of a free life from remote free ancestors with their flesh and blood, God alone knows!

The first to break the silence is Nikandr Sapozhnikov, who until now has not uttered a single word. Whether he envies the tramp's illusory happiness, or whether he feels in his heart that dreams of happiness are out of keeping with the gray fog and the dirty brown mud—at all events, he looks grimly at the tramp and says:

"That's all right, to be sure, but you won't never get to them free lands, brother. How can you? You'd walk two hundred miles and you'd give up the ghost. Look, you're half dead already! You've hardly gone five miles and you can't get your breath."

The tramp turns slowly toward Nikandr, and his blissful smile vanishes. He looks with a scared and guilty air at the constable's sedate face, apparently remembers something, and lets his head drop. Silence falls again. All three are pensive. The constables are struggling to grasp with their imagination what can perhaps be grasped by none but God—that is, the vast expanse which separates them from the land of freedom. But the tramp's mind is filled with clear, distinct images more terrible than that expanse. He envisages vividly legal red tape and procrastinations, jails used as distributing centers and regular penal institutions, prison barracks, exhausting delays en route, cold winters, illnesses, deaths of comrades. . . .

The tramp blinks guiltily, passes his sleeve across his forehead that is beaded with tiny drops of sweat, and puffs hard as though he had just emerged from a steaming bathhouse, then wipes his forehead with his other sleeve and looks round timorously.

"That's a fact; you won't get there!" Ptaha agrees. "What kind of a walker are you, anyway? Look at you—nothing but skin and bone! You'll die, brother!"

"Sure he'll die. How can he help it?" says Nikandr. "They'll put him in the hospital straight off. Sure!"

The man who will not reveal his identity looks with horror at the stern, dispassionate faces of his sinister companions, and without removing his cap, hurriedly crosses himself, his eyes bulging. He trembles all over, shakes his head, and begins writhing, like a caterpillar that has been stepped on.

"Well, it's time to go," says Nikandr, getting to his feet; "we've had a rest."

A minute later the wayfarers are stepping along the muddy road. The tramp is more hunched than before, and his hands are thrust deeper into his sleeves. Ptaha is silent.

QUESTIONS

1. In what ways are the two constables dissimilar? similar?

2. How does Ptaha's story of the viper prefigure the story the prisoner tells?

3. Why does the prisoner refuse to reveal his name?

4. The prisoner describes his mother as "pious and God-fearing." Based on the story he tells, would you judge her as kindly?

5. How is the setting a visible refutation of the prisoner's daydreams?

6. Find several examples of personification. Do you find assigning animate qualities to inanimate objects offensive? useful? appropriate? Discuss.

7. How does the omniscient narrator not only reveal but conceal information? What is the effect of his concealment?

8. A central item in the tramp's fantasies is the pleasures of fishing. How does this rhapsodic monologue help characterize the tramp?

9. The constables' prediction causes the prisoner to tremble and to writhe "like a caterpillar that has been stepped on." Why?

10. The last line of the story reads, "Ptaha is silent." Why do you suppose Chekhov chose to end his story with a description of the constable?

JOHN UPDIKE

The Day of the Dying Rabbit

The shutter clicks, and what is captured is mostly accident—that happy foreground diagonal, the telling expression forever pinned in mid-flight between two plateaus of vacuity. Margaret and I didn't exactly intend to have six children. At first, we were trying until we got a boy. Then, after Jimmy arrived, it was half our trying to give him a brother so he wouldn't turn queer under all those sisters, and half our missing, the both of us, the way new babies are. You know how they are—delicate as film, wrapped in bunting instead of lead foil, but coiled with that same miraculous brimming whatever-it-is: *susceptibility,* let's say. That wobbly hot head. Those navy-blue eyes with the pupils set at f/2. The wrists hinged on silk and the soles of the feet as tender as the eyelids: film that fine-grained would show a doghouse roof from five miles up.

Also, I'm a photographer by trade and one trick of the trade is a lot of takes. In fact, all six kids have turned out pretty well, now that we've got the baby's feet to stop looking at each other and Deirdre fitted out with glasses. Having so many works smoothly enough in the city, where I go off to the studio and they go off to school, but on vacations things tend to jam. We rent the same four-room shack every August. When the cat dragged in as a love present this mauled rabbit it had caught, it was minutes before I could get close enough even to *see.*

Henrietta—she's the second youngest, the last girl—screamed. There are screams like flashbulbs—just that cold. This one brought Linda out from her murder mystery and Cora up from her Beatles magazine, and they crowded into the corridor that goes with the bedrooms the landlord added to the shack to

394

make it more rentable and that isn't wide enough for two pairs of shoulders. Off this corridor into the outdoors is a salt-pimpled aluminum screen door with a misadjusted pneumatic attachment that snaps like lightning the first two-thirds of its arc and then closes the last third slow as a clock, ticking. That's how the cat got in. It wasn't our cat exactly, just a tattered calico stray the children had been feeding salami scraps to out in the field between our yard and the freshwater pond. Deirdre had been helping Margaret with the dishes, and they piled into the corridor just ahead of me, in time to hear Linda let crash with a collection of those four-letter words that come out of her face more and more. The more pop out, the more angelic her face grows. She is thirteen, and in a few years I suppose it will be liquor and drugs, going in. I don't know where she gets the words, or how to stop them coming. Her cheeks are trimming down, her nose bones edging up, her mouth getting witty in the corners, and her eyes gathering depth; and I don't know how to stop that coming, either. Faces, when you look at them through a lens, are passageways for angels, sometimes whole clouds of them. Jimmy told me the other day—he's been reading books of records, mostly sports—about a man so fat he had been buried in a piano case for a casket, and he asked me what a casket was, and I told him, and a dozen angels overlapped in his face as he mentally matched up casket with fatness, and piano, and earth; and got the picture. Click.

After Linda's swearing, there was the sound of a slap and a second's silence while it developed who had been hit: Henrietta. Her crying clawed the corridor walls, and down among our legs the cat reconsidered its offer to negotiate and streaked back out the screen door, those last ticking inches, leaving the rabbit with us. Now I could see it: a half-grown rabbit huddled like a fur doorstop in the doorway to the bigger girls' room. No one dared touch it. We froze around it in a circle. Henrietta was still sobbing, and Cora's transistor was keeping the beat with static, like a heart stuffed with steel wool. Then God came down the hall from the smaller children's room.

Godfrey is the baby, the second boy. We were getting harder up for names, which was one reason we stopped. Another was, the club feet seemed a warning. He was slow to walk after they took the casts off, and at age four he marches along with an unstoppable sort of deliberate dignity, on these unde-formed but somehow distinctly rectangular big feet. He pushed his way through our legs and without hesitation squatted and picked up the rabbit. Cora, the most squeamish of the children—the others are always putting worms down her back—squealed, and God twitched and flipped the bunny back to the floor; it hit neck first, and lay there looking bent. Linda punched Cora, and Henrietta jabbed God, but still none of the rest of us was willing to touch the rabbit, which might be dead this time, so we let God try again. We needed Jimmy. He and Deirdre have the natural touch—middle children tend to. But all month he's been out of the shack, out of our way, playing catch with himself, rowing in the pond, brooding on what it means to be a boy. He's ten. I've missed him. A father is like a dog—he needs a boy for a friend.

This time in God's arms, the rabbit made a sudden motion that felt ticklish, and got dropped again, but the sign of life was reassuring, and Deirdre pushed through at last, and all evening there we were, paying sick calls on this shoebox, whispering, while Deirdre and Henrietta alternately dribbled milk in a dropper, and God kept trying to turn it into a Steiff stuffed animal, and Cora kept screwing up her nerve to look the bunny in its left eye, which had been a little chewed, so it looked like isinglass. Jimmy came in from the pond after dark and stood at the foot of Deirdre's bed, watching her try to nurse the rabbit back to health with a dropper of stale milk. She was crooning and crying. No fuss; just the tears. The rabbit was lying panting on its right side, the bad eye up. Linda was on the next bed, reading her mystery, above it all. God was asleep. Jimmy's nostrils pinched in, and he turned his back on the whole business. He had got the picture. The rabbit was going to die. At the back of my brain I felt tired, damp, and cold.

What was it in the next twenty-four hours that slowly flooded me, that makes me want to get the day on some kind of film? I don't know exactly, so I must put everything in, however underexposed.

Linda and Cora were still awake when headlights boomed in the drive-way—we're a city block from the nearest house and a half mile from the road—and the Pingrees came by. Ian works for an ad agency I've photographed some nudes shampooing in the shower for, and on vacation he lives in boatneck shirts and cherry-red Bermudas and blue sunglasses, and grows a salt-and-pepper beard—a Verichrome fathead, and nearsighted at that. But his wife, Jenny, is nifty: low forehead, like a fox. Freckles. Thick red sun-dulled hair ironed flat down her back. Hips. And an angle about her legs, the way they're put together, slightly bowed but with the something big and bland and smooth and unimpeachable about the thighs that you usually find only in the fenders of new cars. Though she's very serious and liberal and agitated these days, I could look at her forever, she's such fun for the eyes. Which isn't the same as being photogenic. The few shots I've taken of her show a staring woman with baby fat, whereas some skinny snit who isn't even a name to me comes over in the magazines as my personal version of Eros. The camera does lie, all the time. It has to.

Margaret doesn't mind the Pingrees, which isn't the same as liking them, but in recent years she doesn't much admit to liking anybody; so it was midnight when they left, all of us giddy with drink and talk under the stars, that seem so presiding and reproachful when you're drunk, shouting goodbye in the drive-way, and agreeing on tennis tomorrow. I remembered the rabbit. Deirdre, Linda, and Cora were asleep, Linda with the light still on and the mystery rising and falling on her chest, Cora floating above her, in the upper bunk bed. The rabbit was in the shoebox under a protective lean-to of cookout grilles, in case the cat came back. We moved a grille aside and lit a match, expecting the rabbit to be dead. Photograph by sulphur-glow: undertakers at work. But though the rabbit wasn't hopping, the whiskers were moving, back and forth no more than a millimeter or two at the tips, but enough to signify breathing, life, hope, what else? Eternal solicitude brooding above us, also holding a match, and burning Its fingers. Our detection of life, magnified by liquor, emboldened us to make love for the first time in, oh, days beyond counting. She's always tired, and says the Pill depresses her, and a kind of arms race of avoidance has grown up around her complaints. Moonlight muted by window screens. Great eyesockets beneath me, looking up. To the shack smells of mist and cedar and salt we added musk. Margaret slipped into sleep quick as a fish afterward, but for an uncertain length of time—the hours after midnight lose their numbers, if you don't remind them with a luminous dial—I lay there, the rabbit swollen huge and oppressive, blanketing all of us, a clenching of the nerves snatching me back from sleep by a whisker, the breathing and rustling all around me precarious, the rumbling and swaying of a ship that at any moment, the next or then the next, might hit an iceberg.

Morning. The rabbit took some milk, and his isinglass eye slightly widened. The children triumphantly crowed. Jubilant sun-sparkle on the sea beyond the sand beyond the pond. We rowed across, six in the rowboat and two in the kayak. The tides had been high in the night, delivering debris dropped between here and Portugal. Jimmy walked far down the beach, collecting light bulbs jettisoned from ships—they are vacuums and will float forever, if you let them. I had put the 135mm. telephoto on the Nikon and loaded in a roll of Plus-X and took some shots of the children (Cora's face, horrified and ecstatic, caught in the translucent wall of a breaker about to submerge her; Godfrey, his close-cut blond hair shiny as a helmet, a Tritonesque strand of kelp slung across his shoulders) but most of grass and sand and shadows, close-up, using the ultraviolet filter, trying to get, what may be ungettable, the way the shadow edges stagger from grain to grain on the sand, and the way some bent-over grass blades draw circles around themselves, to keep time away.

Jimmy brought the bulbs back and arranged them in order of size, and before I could get to him had methodically smashed two. All I could see was bleeding feet but I didn't mean to grab him so hard. The marks of my hand were still red on his arm a half hour later. Our fight depressed Henrietta; like a seismograph, she feels all violence as hers. God said he was hungry and Deirdre began to worry about the rabbit: there is this puffy look children's faces get that I associate with guilt but that can also signal grief. Deirdre and Jimmy took the kayak, to be there first, and Linda, who maybe thinks the exercise will improve her bosom, rowed the rest of us to our dock. We walked to the house, heads down. Our path is full of poison ivy, our scorched lawn full of flat thistles. In our absence, the rabbit, still lying on its side, had created a tidy little heap of pellet-like feces. The children were ecstatic; they had a dirty joke and a miracle all in one. The rabbit's recovery was assured. But the eye looked cloudier to me, and the arc of the whisker tips even more fractional.

Lunch: soup and sandwiches. In the sky, the clouding over from the west that often arrives around noon. The level of light moved down, and the hands of the year swept forward a month. It was autumn, every blade of grass shining. August has this tinny, shifty quality, the only month without a holiday to pin it down. Our tennis date was at two. You can picture for yourself Jenny Pingree in tennis whites: those rounded guileless thighs, and the bobbing, flying hair tied behind with a kerkchief of blue gauze, and that humorless, utterly intent clumsiness—especially when catching the balls tossed to her as server—that we love in children, trained animals, and women who are normally graceful. She and I, thanks to my predatory net play, took Ian and Margaret, 6–3, and the next set was called at 4–4, when our hour on the court ran out. A moral triumph for Margaret, who played like the swinger of fifteen years ago, and passed me in the alley half a dozen times. Dazzling with sweat, she took the car and went shopping with the four children who had come along to the courts; Linda had stayed in the shack with another book, and Jimmy had walked to a neighboring house, where there was a boy his age. The Pingrees dropped me off at our mailbox. Since they were going back to the city Sunday, we had agreed on a beach picnic tonight. The mail consisted of forwarded bills, pencil-printed letters to the children from their friends on other islands or beside lakes, and *Life*. While walking down our dirt road I flicked through an overgorgeous photographic essay on Afghanistan. Hurrying blurred women in peacock-colored saris, mud palaces, rose dust, silver rivers high in the Hindu Kush. An entire valley—misted, forested earth—filled the center page spread. The *lenses* those people have! Nothing beautiful on earth is as selfless as a beautiful lens.

Entering the shack, I shouted out to Linda, "It's just me," thinking she would be afraid of rapists. I went into her room and looked in the shoebox. The eye was lustreless and the whiskers had stopped moving, even infinitesimally.

"I think the bunny's had it," I said.

"Don't make me look," she said, propped up in the lower bunk, keeping her eyes deep in a paperback titled *A Stitch in Time Kills Nine*. The cover showed a dressmaker's dummy pierced by a stiletto, and bleeding. "I couldn't *stand it*," she said.

"What should I do?" I asked her.

"Bury it." She might have been reading from the book. Her profile, I noticed, was becoming a cameo, with a lovely gentle bulge to the forehead, high like Margaret's. I hoped being intelligent wouldn't cramp her life.

"Deirdre will want to see it," I argued. "It's her baby."

"It will only make her *sad*," Linda said. "And dis*gust* me. Already it must be *full* of *ver*min."

Nothing goads me to courage like some woman's taking a high tone. Afraid to touch the rabbit's body while life was haunting it, I touched it now, and found it tepid, and lifted it from the box. The body, far from stiff, felt unhinged; its back or neck must have been broken since the moment the cat pounced. Blood had dried in the ear—an intricate tunnel leading brainwards, velvety at the tip, oddly muscular at the root. The eye not of isinglass was an opaque black bead. Linda was right; there was no need for Deirdre to see. I took the rabbit out beyond the prickly yard, into the field, and laid it below the least stunted swamp oak, where any child who wanted to be sure that I hadn't buried it alive could come and find it. I put a marsh marigold by its nose, in case it was resurrected and needed to eat, and paused above the composition—fur, flower, the arty shape of fallen oak leaves—with a self-congratulatory sensation that must have carried on my face back to the shack, for Margaret, in the kitchen loading the refrigerator, looked up at me and said, "Say. I don't mind your being partners with Jenny, but you don't have to toss the balls to her in that cute confiding way."

"The poor bitch can't catch them otherwise. You saw that."

"I saw more than I wanted to. I nearly threw up."

"That second set," I said, "your backhand was terrific. The Maggie-O of old."

Deirdre came down the hall from the bedrooms. Her eyes seemed enormous; I went to her and kneeled to hold her around the waist, and began, "Sweetie, I have some sad news."

"Linda told me," she said, and walked by me into the kitchen. "Mommy, can I make the cocoa?"

"You did everything you could," I called after her. "You were a wonderful nurse and made the bunny's last day very happy."

"I know," she called in answer. "Mommy, I *promise* I won't let the milk boil over this time."

Of the children, only Henrietta and Godfrey let me lead them to where the rabbit rested. Henrietta skittishly hung back, and never came closer than ten yards. God marched close, gazed down sternly, and said, "Get up." Nothing happened, except the ordinary motions of the day: the gulls and stately geese beating home above the pond, the traffic roaring invisible along the highway. He squatted down, and I prevented him from picking up the rabbit, before I saw it was the flower he was after.

Jimmy, then, was the only one who cried. He came home a half hour after we had meant to set out rowing across the pond to the beach picnic, and rushed into the field toward the tree with the tallest silhouette and came back carrying on his cheeks stains he tried to hide by thumping God. "If *you* hadn't dropped him," he said. "You *ba*by."

"It was nobody's fault," Margaret told him, impatiently cradling her basket of hot dogs and raw hamburger.

"I'm going to kill that cat," Jimmy said. He added, cleverly, an old grievance: "Other kids my age have BB guns."

"Oh, our big man," Cora said. He flew at her in a flurry of fists and sobs, and ran away and hid. At the dock I let Linda and Cora take the kayak, and the rest of us waited a good ten minutes with the rowboat before Jimmy ran down the path in the dusk, himself a silhouette, like the stunted trees and the dark bar of dunes between two sheets of reflected sunset. Ever notice how sunsets upside down look like stairs?

"Somehow," Margaret said to me, as we waited, "You've deliberately dramatized this." But nothing could fleck the happiness widening within me, to capture the dying light.

The Pingrees had brought swordfish and another, older couple—the man was perhaps an advertising client. Though he was tanned like a tobacco leaf and wore the smartest summer playclothes, a pleading uncertainty in his manner seemed to crave the support of advertisement. His wife had once been beautiful and held herself lightly, lithely at attention—a soldier in the war of self-preservation. With them came two teen-age boys clad in jeans and buttonless vests and hair so long their summer complexions had remained sallow. One was their son, the other his friend. We all collected driftwood—a wandering, lonely, prehistoric task that frightens me. Darkness descended too soon, as it does in the tropics, where the warmth leads us to expect an endless June evening from childhood. We made a game of popping champagne corks, the kids trying to catch them on the fly. Startling, how high they soared, in the open air. The two boys gathered around Linda, and I protectively eavesdropped, and was shamed by the innocence and long childish pauses of what I overheard: "Philadelphia . . . just been in the airport, on our way to my uncle's, he lives in Virginia . . . wonderful horses, super . . . it's not actually blue, just bluey-green, blue only I guess by comparison . . . was in France once, and went to the races . . . never been . . . I want to go." Margaret and Jenny, kneeling in the sand to cook, setting out paper plates on tables that were merely wide pieces of driftwood, seemed sisters. The woman of the strange couple tried to flirt with me, talking of foreign places: "Paris is so dead, suddenly . . . the girls fly over to London to buy their clothes, and then their mothers won't let them wear them . . . Malta . . . Istanbul . . . life . . . sincerity . . . the *people* . . . the poor Greeks . . . a friend absolutely assures me, the C.I.A. engineered . . . apparently used the NATO contingency plan." Another champagne cork sailed in the air, hesitated, and drifted down, Jimmy diving but missing, having misjudged. A remote light, a lightship, or the promontory of a continent hidden in daylight, materialized on the horizon, beyond the shushing of the surf. Margaret and Jenny served us. Hamburgers and swordfish full of woodsmoke. Celery and sand. God, sticky with things he had spilled upon himself, sucked his thumb and rubbed against Margaret's legs. Jimmy came to me, furious because the big boys wouldn't Indian-wrestle with him, only with Linda and Cora: "Showing off for their boyfriends . . . whacked me for no reason . . . just because I said 'sex bomb.'"

We sat in a ring, survivors, around the fire, the heart of a collapsing star, fed anew by paper plates. The man of the older couple, in whose breath the champagne had undergone an acrid chemical transformation, told me about his money—how as a youth just out of business school, in the depth so the Depression, he had made a million dollars in some deal involving Stalin and surplus wheat. He had liked Stalin, and Stalin had liked him. "The thing we must realize about your Communist is that he's just another kind of businessman." Across the fire I watched his wife, spurned by me, ardently gesturing with the teen-age boy who was not her son, and wondered how I would take their picture. Tri-X, wide-open, at 1/60; but the shadows would be lost, the subtle events within them, and the highlights would be vapid blobs. There is no adjustment, no darkroom trickery, equivalent to the elastic tolerance of our eyes as they travel.

As my new friend murmured on and on about his money, and the champagne warming in my head released carbon dioxide to the air, exposures flickered in and out around the fire: glances, inklings, angels. Margaret gazing, the nick of a frown erect between her brows. Henrietta's face vertically compressing above an ear of corn she was devouring. The well-preserved woman's face a mask of bronze with cunningly welded seams, but her hand an exclamatory white as it touched her son's friend's arm in some conversational urgency lost in the crackle of driftwood. The halo of hair around Ian's knees, innocent as babies' pates. Jenny's hair an elongated flurry as she turned to speak to the older couple's son; his bearded face was a blur in the shadows, melancholy, the eyes seeming closed, like the Jesus on a faded, drooping veronica. I heard Jenny say, " . . . *must* destroy the system! We've forgotten how to *love!*" Deirdre's glasses, catching the light, leaped like moth wings toward the fire, escaping perspective. Beside me, the old man's face went silent, and suffered a deflation wherein nothing held firm but the reflected glitter of firelight on a tooth his grimace had absentmindedly left exposed. Beyond him, on the edge of the light, Cora and Linda were revealed sitting together, their legs stretched out long before them, warming, their faces in shadow, sexless and solemn, as if attentive to the sensations of the revolution of the earth beneath them. Godfrey was asleep, his head pillowed on Margaret's thigh, his body suddenly wrenched by a dream sob, and a heavy succeeding sigh.

It was strange, after these fragmentary illuminations, to stumble through the unseen sand and grass, with our blankets and belongings, to the boats on the shore of the pond. Margaret and five children took the rowboat; I nominated Jimmy to come with me in the kayak. The night was starless. The pond, between the retreating campfire and the slowly nearing lights of our neighbors' houses, was black. I could scarcely see his silhouette as it struggled for the rhythm of the stroke: left, a little turn with the wrists, right, the little turn reversed, left. Our paddles occasionally clashed, or snagged on the weeds that clog this pond. But the kayak sits lightly, and soon we put the confused conversation of the rowers, and their wildly careening flashlight beam, behind. Silence widened around us. Steering the rudder with the foot pedals, I let Jimmy paddle alone, and stared upward until I had produced, in the hazed sky overhead, a single, unsteady star. It winked out. I returned to paddling and received an astonishing impression of phosphorescence: every stroke, right and left, called into visibility a rich arc of sparks, animalcula hailing our passage with bright shouts. The pond was more populous than China. My son and I were afloat on a firmament warmer than the heavens.

"Hey, Dad."

His voice broke the silence carefully; my benevolence engulfed him, my fellow-wanderer, my leader, my gentle, secretive future. "What, Jimmy?"

"I think we're about to hit something."

We stopped paddling, and a mass, gray etched on gray, higher than a man, glided swiftly toward us and struck the prow of the kayak. With this bump, and my awakening laugh, the day of the dying rabbit ended. Exulting in homogenous glory, I had steered us into the bank. We pushed off, and by the lights of our neighbors' houses navigated to the dock, and waited for the rowboat with its

tangle of voices and impatience and things that would snag. The days since have
been merely happy days. This day was singular in its, let's say, *gallantry:* between
the cat's gallant intentions and my son's gallantly calm warning, the dying rabbit
sank like film in the developing pan, and preserved us all.

Q U E S T I O N S

1. Photography is used as metaphor and simile throughout this story. Find at least
   ten passages in which photography is used figuratively. Do you find this
   extended metaphor contrived? appropriate? a fresh way of imbuing ordinary
   events with meaning?

2. Find at least five examples of the narrator's colloquial diction. Do you find that
   his informal language mixes awkwardly with the poetic metaphors?

3. The differing attitudes of the children toward the dying rabbit succinctly reveal
   their different personalities. Discuss.

4. Examine the narrator's descriptions of people. Are they effective in revealing
   character? Explain the meaning of the narrator's statement: "Faces, when you
   look at them through a lens, are passageways for angels, sometimes whole
   clouds of them."

5. Why does the narrator find the day of the dying rabbit "singular in its . . .
   gallantry"? Do you agree? Explain, discussing the rabbit as a created symbol in
   this story.

6. The events are commonplace—almost trivial—yet the day is meaningful to the
   narrator. Do you find the story meaningful? instructive? boring? uplifting?
   much ado about nothing?

7. Discuss tone as it is shaped by narrative point of view, plot, and imagery.

URSULA K. LE GUIN

Nine Lives

She was alive inside, but dead outside, her face a black and dun net of wrinkles, tumors, cracks. She was bald and blind. The tremors that crossed Libra's face were mere quiverings of corruption: underneath, in the black corridors, the halls beneath the skin, there were crepitations in darkness, ferments, chemical nightmares that went on for centuries. "Oh the damned flatulent planet," Pugh murmured as the dome shook and a boil burst a kilometer to the southwest, spraying silver pus across the sunset. The sun had been setting for the last two days. "I'll be glad to see a human face."

"Thanks," said Martin.

"Yours is human to be sure," said Pugh, "but I've seen it so long I can't see it."

Radvid signals cluttered the communicator which Martin was operating, faded, returned as face and voice. The face filled the screen, the nose of an Assyrian king, the eyes of a samurai, skin bronze, eyes the color of iron: young, magnificent. "Is that what human beings look like?" said Pugh with awe. "I'd forgotten."

"Shut up, Owen, we're on."

"Libra Exploratory Mission Base, come in please, this is *Passerine* launch."

"Libra here. Beam fixed. Come on down, launch."

"Expulsion in seven E-seconds. Hold on." The screen blanked and sparkled.

"Do they all look like that? Martin, you and I are uglier men than I thought."

"Shut up, Owen. . . ."

For twenty-two minutes Martin followed the landing-craft down by signal and then through the cleared dome they saw it, small star in the blood-colored east, sinking. It came down neat and quiet, Libra's thin atmosphere carrying little sound. Pugh and Martin closed the headpieces of their imsuits, zipped out of the dome airlocks, and ran with soaring strides, Nijinsky and Nureyev, toward the boat. Three equipment modules came floating down at four-minute intervals from each other and hundred-meter intervals east of the boat. "Come on out," Martin said on his suit radio, "we're waiting at the door."

"Come on in, the methane's fine," said Pugh.

The hatch opened. The young man they had seen on the screen came out with one athletic twist and leaped down onto the shaky dust and clinkers of Libra. Martin shook his hand, but Pugh was staring at the hatch, from which another young man emerged with the same neat twist and jump, followed by a young woman who emerged with the same neat twist, ornamented with a wriggle, and a jump. They were all tall, with bronze skin, black hair, high-bridged noses, epicanthic fold, the same face. They all had the same face. The fourth was emerging from the hatch with a neat twist and jump. "Martin bach," said Pugh, "we've got a clone."

"Right," said one of them, "we're a tenclone. John Chow's the name. You're Lieutenant Martin?"

"I'm Owen Pugh."

"Alvaro Guillen Martin," said Martin, formal, bowing slightly. Another girl was out, the same beautiful face; Martin stared at her and his eye rolled like a nervous pony's. Evidently he had never given any thought to cloning, and was suffering technological shock. "Steady," Pugh said in the Argentine dialect, "it's only excess twins." He stood close by Martin's elbow. He was glad himself of the contact.

It is hard to meet a stranger. Even the greatest extrovert meeting even the meekest stranger knows a certain dread, though he may not know he knows it. Will he make a fool of me wreck my image of myself invade me destroy me change me? Will he be different from me? Yes, that he will. There's the terrible thing: the strangeness of the stranger.

After two years on a dead planet, and the last half year isolated as a team of two, oneself and one other, after that it's even harder to meet a stranger, however welcome he may be. You're out of the habit of difference, you've lost the touch; and so the fear revives, the primitive anxiety, the old dread.

The clone, five males and five females, had got done in a couple of minutes what a man might have got done in twenty: greeted Pugh and Martin, had a glance at Libra, unloaded the boat, made ready to go. They went, and the dome filled with them, a hive of golden bees. They hummed and buzzed quietly, filled up all silences, all spaces with a honey-brown swarm of human presence. Martin looked bewilderedly at the long-limbed girls, and they smiled at him, three at once. Their smile was gentler than that of the boys, but no less radiantly self-possessed.

"Self-possessed," Owen Pugh murmured to his friend, "that's it. Think of it, to be oneself ten times over. Nine seconds for every motion, nine ayes on every vote. It would be glorious!" But Martin was asleep. And the John Chows had all gone to sleep at once. The dome was filled with their quiet breathing. They were young, they didn't snore. Martin sighed and snored, his Hershey-bar-colored face relaxed in the dim afterglow of Libra's primary, set at last. Pugh had cleared the dome and stars looked in, Sol among them, a great company of lights, a clone of splendors. Pugh slept and dreamed of a one-eyed giant who chased him through the shaking halls of Hell.

From his sleeping-bag Pugh watched the clone's awakening. They all got up within one minute except for one pair, a boy and a girl, who lay snugly tangled and still sleeping in one bag. As Pugh saw this there was a shock like one of Libra's earthquakes inside him, a very deep tremor. He was not aware of this, and in fact thought he was pleased at the sight; there was no other such comfort on this dead hollow world; more power to them, who made love. One of the others stepped on the pair. They woke and the girl sat up flushed and sleepy, with bare golden breasts. One of her sisters murmured something to her; she shot a glance at Pugh and disappeared in the sleeping-bag, followed by a giant giggle, from another direction a fierce stare, from still another direction a voice: "Christ, we're used to having a room to ourselves. Hope you don't mind, Captain Pugh."

"It's a pleasure," Pugh said half-truthfully. He had to stand up then, wearing only the shorts he slept in, and he felt like a plucked rooster, all white scrawn and pimples. He had seldom envied Martin's compact brownness so much. The United Kingdom had come through the Great Famines well, losing less than half its population: a record achieved by rigorous food-control. Black-marketeers and hoarders had been executed. Crumbs had been shared. Where in richer lands most had died and a few had thrived, in Britain fewer died and none throve. They all got lean. Their sons were lean, their grandsons lean, small, brittle-boned, easily infected. When civilization became a matter of standing in lines, the British had kept queue, and so had replaced the survival of the fittest with the survival of the fair-minded. Owen Pugh was a scrawny little man. All the same, he was there.

At the moment he wished he wasn't.

At breakfast a John said, "Now if you'll brief us, Captain Pugh—"

"Owen, then."

"Owen, we can work out our schedule. Anything new on the mine since your last report to your Mission? We saw your reports when *Passerine* was orbiting Planet V, where they are now."

Martin did not answer, though the mine was his discovery and project, and Pugh had to do his best. It was hard to talk to them. The same faces, each with the same expression of intelligent interest, all leaned toward him across the table at almost the same angle. They all nodded together.

Over the Exploitation Corps insignia on their tunics each had a nameband, first name John and last name Chow of course, but the middle names different.

The men were Aleph, Kaph, Yod, Gimel, and Samedh; the women Sadhe, Daleth, Zayin, Beth, and Resh. Pugh tried to use the names but gave it up at once; he could not even tell sometimes which one had spoken, for the voices were all alike.

Martin buttered and chewed his toast, and finally interrupted: "You're a team. Is that it?"

"Right," said two Johns.

"God, what a team! I hadn't seen the point. How much do you each know what the others are thinking?"

"Not at all, properly speaking," replied one of the girls, Zayin. The others watched her with the proprietary, approving look they had. "No ESP, nothing fancy. But we think alike. We have exactly the same equipment. Given the same stimulus, the same problem, we're likely to be coming up with the same reactions and solutions at the same time. Explanations are easy—don't even have to make them, usually. We seldom misunderstand each other. It does facilitate our working as a team."

"Christ yes," said Martin. "Pugh and I have spent seven hours out of ten for six months misunderstanding each other. Like most people. What about emergencies, are you as good at meeting the unexpected problem as a nor . . . an unrelated team?"

"Statistics so far indicate that we are," Zayin answered readily. Clones must be trained, Pugh thought, to meet questions, to reassure and reason. All they said had the slightly bland and stilted quality of answers furnished to the Public. "We can't brainstorm as singletons can, we as a team don't profit from the interplay of varied minds; but we have a compensatory advantage. Clones are drawn from the best human material, individuals of IIQ 99th percentile, Genetic Constitution alpha double A, and so on. We have more to draw on than most individuals do."

"And it's multiplied by a factor of ten. Who is—who was John Chow?"

"A genius surely," Pugh said politely. His interest in cloning was not so new and avid as Martin's.

"Leonardo Complex type," said Yod. "Biomath, also a cellist, and an undersea hunter, and interested in structural engineering problems, and so on. Died before he'd worked out his major theories."

"Then you each represent a different facet of his mind, his talents?"

"No," said Zayin, shaking her head in time with several others. "We share the basic equipment and tendencies, of course, but we're all engineers in Planetary Exploitation. A later clone can be trained to develop other aspects of the basic equipment. It's all training; the genetic substance is identical. We *are* John Chow. But we were differently trained."

Martin looked shell-shocked. "How old are you?"

"Twenty-three."

"You say he died young— Had they taken germ cells from him beforehand or something?"

Gimel took over: "He died at twenty-four in an aircar crash. They couldn't save the brain, so they took some intestinal cells and cultured them for cloning. Reproductive cells aren't used for cloning since they have only half the chromosomes. Intestinal cells happen to be easy to despecialize and reprogram for total growth."

"All chips off the old block," Martin said valiantly. "But how can . . . some of you be women . . .?"

Beth took over: "It's easy to program half the clonal mass back to the female. Just delete the male gene from half the cells and they revert to the basic, that is, the female. It's trickier to go the other way, have to hook in artificial Y chromosomes. So they mostly clone from males, since clones function best bisexually."

Gimel again: "They've worked these matters of technique and function out carefully. The taxpayer wants the best for his money, and of course clones are expensive. With the cell-manipulations, and the incubation in Ngama Placentae, and the maintenance and training of the foster-parent groups, we end up costing about three million apiece."

"For your next generation," Martin said, still struggling, "I suppose you . . . you breed?"

"We females are sterile," said Beth with perfect equanimity; "you remember that the Y chromosome was deleted from our original cell. The males can interbreed with approved singletons, if they want to. But to get John Chow again as often as they want, they just reclone a cell from this clone."

Martin gave up the struggle. He nodded and chewed cold toast. "Well," said one of the Johns, and all changed mood, like a flock of starlings that change course in one wingflick, following a leader so fast that no eye can see which leads. They were ready to go. "How about a look at the mine? Then we'll unload the equipment. Some nice new models in the roboats; you'll want to see them. Right?" Had Pugh or Martin not agreed they might have found it hard to say so. The Johns were polite but unanimous; their decisions carried. Pugh, Commander of Libra Base 2 felt a qualm. Could he boss around this supermanwoman-entity-of-ten? and a genius at that? He stuck close to Martin as they suited for outside. Neither said anything.

Four apiece in the three large jetsleds, they slipped off north from the dome, over Libra's dun rugose skin, in starlight.

"Desolate," one said.

It was a boy and girl with Pugh and Martin. Pugh wondered if these were the two that had shared a sleeping-bag last night. No doubt they wouldn't mind if he asked them. Sex must be as handy as breathing, to them. Did you two breathe last night?

"Yes," he said, "It is desolate."

"This is our first time Off, except training on Luna." The girl's voice was definitely a bit higher and softer.

"How did you take the big hop?"

"They doped us. I wanted to experience it." That was the boy; he sounded wistful. They seemed to have more personality, only two at a time. Did repetition of the individual negate individuality?

"Don't worry," said Martin, steering the sled, "you can't experience no-time because it isn't there."

"I'd just like to once," one of them said. "So we'd know."

The Mountains of Merioneth showed leprotic in starlight to the east, a plume of freezing gas trailed silvery from a vent-hole to the west, and the sled tilted groundward. The twins braced for the stop at one moment, each with a slight protective gesture to the other. Your skin is my skin, Pugh thought, but literally, no metaphor. What would it be like, then, to have someone as close to you as that? Always to be aswered when you spoke, never to be in pain alone. Love your neighbor as you love yourself. . . . That hard old problem was solved. The neighbor was the self: the love was perfect.

And here was Hellmouth, the mine.

Pugh was the Exploratory Mission's ET geologist, and Martin his technician and cartographer; but when in the course of a local survey Martin had discovered the U-mine, Pugh had given him full credit, as well as the onus of prospecting the lode and planning the Exploitation Team's job. These kids had been sent out from Earth years before Martin's reports got there, and had not known what their job would be until they got here. The Exploitation Corps simply sent out teams regularly and blindly as a dandelion sends out its seeds, knowing there would be a job for them on Libra or the next planet out or one they hadn't even heard about yet. The Government wanted uranium too urgently to wait while reports drifted home across the light-years. The stuff was like gold, old-fashioned but essential, worth mining extraterrestrially and shipping interstellar. Worth its weight in people, Pugh thought sourly, watching the tall young men and women go one by one, glimmering in starlight, into the black hole Martin had named Hellmouth.

As they went in their homeostatic forehead-lamps brightened. Twelve nodding gleams ran along the moist, wrinkled walls. Pugh heard Martin's radiation counter peeping twenty to the dozen up ahead. "Here's the drop-off," said Martin's voice in the suit intercom, drowning out the peeping and the dead silence that was around them. "We're in a side-fissure; this is the main vertical vent in front of us." The black void gaped, its far side not visible in the headlamp beams. "Last vulcanism seems to have been a couple of thousand years ago. Nearest fault is twenty-eight kilos east, in the Trench. This region seems to be as safe seismically as anything in the area. The big basalt-flow overhead stabilizes all these substructures, so long as it remains stable itself. Your central lode is thirty-six meters down and runs in a series of five bubble-caverns northeast. It is a lode, a pipe of very high-grade ore. You saw the percentage figures, right? Extraction's going to be no problem. All you've got to do is get the bubbles topside."

"Take off the lid and let 'em float up." A chuckle. Voices began to talk, but they were all the same voice and the suit radio gave them no location in space. "Open the thing right up. —Safer that way. —But it's a solid basalt roof, how thick, ten meters here? —Three to twenty, the report said. —Blow good ore all over the lot. —Use this access we're in, straighten it a bit and run slider-rails for the robos. —Import burros. —Have we got enough propping material? —What's your estimate of total payload mass, Martin?"

"Say over five million kilos and under eight."

"Transport will be here in ten E-months. —It'll have to go pure. —No, they'll have the mass problem in NAFAL shipping licked by now; remember it's been sixteen years since we left Earth last Tuesday. —Right, they'll send the whole lot back and purify it in Earth orbit. —Shall we go down, Martin?"

"Go on. I've been down."

The first one—Aleph? (Heb., the ox, the leader)—swung onto the ladder and down; the rest followed. Pugh and Martin stood at the chasm's edge. Pugh set his intercom to exchange only with Martin's suit, and noticed Martin doing the same. It was a bit wearing, this listening to one person think aloud in ten voices, or was it one voice speaking the thoughts of ten minds?

"A great gut," Pugh said, looking down into the black pit, its veined and warted walls catching stray gleams of headlamps far below. "A cow's bowel. A bloody great constipated intestine."

Martin's counter peeped like a lost chicken. They stood inside the epileptic planet, breathing oxygen from tanks, wearing suits impermeable to corrosives and harmful radiations, resistant to a two-hundred-degree range of temperatures, tear-proof, and as shock-resistant as possible given the soft vulnerable stuff inside.

"Next hop," Martin said, "I'd like to find a planet that has nothing whatever to exploit."

"You found this."

"Keep me home next time."

Pugh was pleased. He had hoped Martin would want to go on working with him, but neither of them was used to talking much about their feelings, and he had hesitated to ask. "I'll try that," he said.

"I hate this place. I like caves, you know. It's why I came in here. Just spelunking. But this one's a bitch. Mean. You can't ever let down in here. I guess this lot can handle it, though. They know their stuff."

"Wave of the future, whatever," said Pugh.

The wave of the future came swarming up the ladder, swept Martin to the entrance, gabbled at and around him: "Have we got enough material for supports? —If we convert one of the extractor-servos to anneal, yes. —Sufficient if we miniblast? —Kaph can calculate stress."

Pugh had switched his intercom back to receive them; he looked at them, so many thoughts jabbering in an eager mind, and at Martin standing silent among them, and at Hellmouth, and the wrinkled plain. "Settled! How does that strike you as a preliminary schedule, Martin?"

"It's your baby," Martin said.

Within five E-days, the Johns had all their material and equipment unloaded and operating, and were starting to open up the mine. They worked with total efficiency. Pugh was fascinated and frightened by their effectiveness, their confidence, their independence. He was no use to them at all. A clone, he thought, might indeed be the first truly stable, self-reliant human being. Once adult it would need nobody's help. It would be sufficient to itself physically, sexually, emotionally, intellectually. Whatever he did, any member of it would always receive the support and approval of his peers, his other selves. Nobody else was needed.

Two of the clone stayed in the dome doing calculations and paperwork, with frequent sled-trips to the mine for measurements and tests. They were the mathematicians of the clone, Zayin and Kaph. That is, as Zayin explained, all ten had had thorough mathematical training from age three to twenty-one, but from twenty-one to twenty-three she and Kaph had gone on with math while the others intensified other specialities, geology, mining engineering, electronic engineering, equipment robotics, applied atomics, and so on. "Kaph and I feel," she said, "that we're the element of the clone closest to what John Chow was in his singleton lifetime. But of course he was principally in biomath, and they didn't take us far in that."

"They needed us most in this field," Kaph said, with the patriotic priggishness they sometimes evinced.

Pugh and Martin soon could distinguish this pair from the others, Zayin by gestalt, Kaph only by a discolored left fourth fingernail, got from an ill-aimed hammer at the age of six. No doubt there were many such differences, physical and psychological, among them; nature might be identical, nurture could not be. But the differences were hard to find. And part of the difficulty was that they really never talked to Pugh and Martin. They joked with them, were polite, got along fine. They gave nothing. It was nothing one could complain about; they were very pleasant, they had the standardized American friendliness. "Do you come from Ireland, Owen?"

"Nobody comes from Ireland, Zayin."

"There are lots of Irish-Americans."

"To be sure, but no more Irish. A couple of thousand in all the island, the last I knew. They didn't go in for birth-control, you know, so the food ran out. By the Third Famine there were no Irish left at all but the priesthood, and they were all celibate, or nearly all."

Zayin and Kaph smiled stiffly. They had no experience of either bigotry or irony. "What are you then, ethnically?" Kaph asked, and Pugh replied, "A Welshman."

"Is it Welsh that you and Martin speak together?"

None of your business, Pugh thought, but said, "No, it's his dialect, not mine: Argentinean. A descendent of Spanish."

"You learned it for private communication?"

"Whom had we here to be private from? It's just that sometimes a man likes to speak his native language."

"Ours is English," Kaph said unsympathetically. Why should they have sympathy? That's one of the things you give because you need it back.

"Is Wells quaint?" asked Zayin.

"Wells? Oh, Wales, it's called. Yes. Wales is quaint." Pugh switched on his rock-cutter, which prevented further conversation by a synapse-destroying whine, and while it whined he turned his back and said a profane word in Welsh.

That night he used the Argentine dialect for private communication. "Do they pair off in the same couples, or change every night?"

Martin looked surprised. A prudish expression, unsuited to his features, appeared for a moment. It faded. He too was curious. "I think it's random."

"Don't whisper, man, it sounds dirty. I think they rotate."

"On a schedule?"

"So nobody gets omitted."

Martin gave a vulgar laugh and smothered it. "What about us? Aren't we omitted?"

"That doesn't occur to them."

"What if I proposition one of the girls?"

"She'd tell the others and they'd decide as a group."

"I am not a bull," Martin said, his dark, heavy face heating up. "I will not be judged—"

"Down, down, *machismo*," said Pugh. "Do you mean to proposition one?"

Martin shrugged, sullen. "Let 'em have their incest."

"Incest is it, or masturbation?"

"I don't care, if they'd do it out of earshot!"

The clone's early attempts at modesty had soon worn off, unmotivated by any deep defensiveness of self or awareness of others. Pugh and Martin were daily deeper swamped under the intimacies of its constant emotional-sexual-mental interchange: swamped yet excluded.

"Two months to go," Martin said one evening.

"To what?" snapped Pugh. He was edgy lately and Martin's sullenness got on his nerves.

"To relief."

In sixty days the full crew of their Exploratory Mission were due back from their survey of the other planets of the system. Pugh was aware of this.

"Crossing off the days on your calendar?" he jeered.

"Pull yourself together, Owen."

"What do you mean?"

"What I say."

They parted in contempt and resentment.

Pugh came in after a day alone on the Pampas, a vast lava-plain the nearest edge of which was two hours south by jet. He was tired, but refreshed by solitude. They were not supposed to take long trips alone, but lately had often done so. Martin stooped under bright lights, drawing one of his elegant, masterly charts: this one was of the whole face of Libra, the cancerous face. The dome was otherwise empty, seeming dim and large as it had before the clone came. "Where's the golden horde?"

Martin grunted ignorance, crosshatching. He straightened his back to glance around at the sun, which squatted feebly like a great red toad on the eastern plain, and at the clock, which said 18:45. "Some big quakes today," he said, returning to his map. "Feel them down there? Lots of crates were falling around. Take a look at the seismo."

The needle jigged and wavered on the roll. It never stopped dancing here. The roll had recorded five quakes of major intensity back in mid-afternoon; twice the needle had hopped off the roll. The attached computer had been activated to emit a slip reading, "Epicenter 61' N by 4'24" E."

"Not in the Trench this time."

"I thought it felt a bit different from usual. Sharper."

"In Base One I used to lie awake all night feeling the ground jump. Queer how you get used to things."

"Go spla if you didn't. What's for dinner?"

"I thought you'd have cooked it."

"Waiting for the clone."

Feeling put upon, Pugh got out a dozen dinnerboxes, stuck two in the Instobake, pulled them out. "All right, here's dinner."

"Been thinking," Martin said, coming to the table. "What if some clone cloned itself? Illegally. Made a thousand duplicates—ten thousand. Whole army. They could make a tidy power-grab, couldn't they?"

"But how many millions did this lot cost to rear? Artificial placentae and all that. It would be hard to keep secret, unless they had a planet to themselves. . . . Back before the Famines when Earth had national governments, they talked about that: clone your best soldiers, have whole regiments of them. But the food ran out before they could play that game."

They talked amicably, as they used to do.

"Funny," Martin said, chewing. "They left early this morning, didn't they?"

"All but Kaph and Zayin. They thought they'd get the first payload aboveground today. What's up?"

"They weren't back for lunch."

"They won't starve, to be sure."

"They left at seven."

"So they did." Then Pugh saw it. The air-tanks held eight hours' supply.

"Kaph and Zayin carried out spare cans when they left. Or they've got a heap out there."

"They did, but they brought the whole lot in to recharge." Martin stood up, pointing to one of the stacks of stuff that cut the dome into rooms and alleys.

"There's an alarm signal on every imsuit."

"It's not automatic."

Pugh was tired and still hungry. "Sit down and eat, man. That lot can look after themselves."

Martin sat down, but did not eat. "There was a big quake, Owen. The first one. Big enough, it scared me."

After a pause Pugh sighed and said, "All right."

Unenthusiastically, they got out the two-man sled that was always left for them, and headed it north. The long sunrise covered everything in poisonous red Jell-O. The horizontal light and shadow made it hard to see, raised walls of fake iron ahead of them through which they slid, turned the convex plain beyond Hellmouth into a great dimple full of bloody water. Around the tunnel entrance a wilderness of machinery stood, cranes and cables and servos and wheels and diggers and robocarts and sliders and control-huts, all slanting and bulking incoherently in the red light. Martin jumped from the sled, ran into the mine. He came out again, to Pugh. "Oh God, Owen, it's down," he said. Pugh went in and saw, five meters from the entrance, the shiny, moist, black wall that ended the tunnel. Newly exposed to air, it looked organic, like visceral tissue. The tunnel entrance, enlarged by blasting and double-tracked for robocarts, seemed unchanged until he noticed thousands of tiny spiderweb cracks in the walls. The floor was wet with some sluggish fluid.

"They were inside," Martin said.

"They may be still. They surely had extra air-cans—"

"Look, Owen, look at the basalt flow, at the roof; don't you see what the quake did, look at it."

The low hump of land that roofed the caves still had the unreal look of an optical illusion. It had reversed itself, sunk down, leaving a vast dimple or pit. When Pugh walked on it he saw that it too was cracked with many tiny fissures. From some a whitish gas was seeping, so that the sunlight on the surface of the gas-pool was shafted as if by the waters of a dim red lake.

"The mine's not on the fault. There's no fault here!"

Pugh came back to him quickly. "No, there's no fault, Martin. Look, they surely weren't all inside together."

Martin followed him and searched among the wrecked machines dully, then actively. He spotted the airsled. It had come down heading south, and struck at an angle in a pothole of colloidal dust. It had carried two riders. One was half sunk in the dust, but his suit-meters registered normal functioning; the other hung strapped onto the tilted sled. Her imsuit had burst open on the broken legs, and the body was frozen hard as any rock. That was all they found. As both regulation and custom demanded, they cremated the dead at once with the laser-guns they carried by regulation and had never used before. Pugh, knowing he was going to be sick, wrestled the survivor onto the two-man sled and sent Martin off to the dome with him. Then he vomited, and flushed the waste out of his suit, and finding one four-man sled undamaged followed after Martin, shaking as if the cold of Libra had got through to him.

The survivor was Kaph. He was in deep shock. They found a swelling on the occiput that might mean concussion, but no fracture was visible.

Pugh brought two glasses of food-concentrate and two chasers of aquavit. "Come on," he said. Martin obeyed, drinking off the tonic. They sat down on crates near the cot and sipped the aquavit.

Kaph lay immobile, face like beeswax, hair bright black to the shoulders, lips stiffly parted for faintly gasping breaths.

"It must have been the first shock, the big one," Martin said. "It must have slid the whole structure sideways. Till it fell in on itself. There must be gas layers in the lateral rocks, like those formations in the Thirty-first Quadrant. But there wasn't any sign—" As he spoke the world slid out from under them. Things leaped and clattered, hopped and jigged, shouted Ha! Ha! Ha! "It was like this at fourteen hours," said Reason shakily in Martin's voice, amidst the unfastening and ruin of the world. But Unreason sat up, as the tumult lessened and things ceased dancing, and screamed aloud.

Pugh leaped across his spilled aquavit and held Kaph down. The muscular body flailed him off. Martin pinned the shoulders down. Kaph screamed, struggled, choked; his face blackened. "Oxy," Pugh said, and his hand found the right needle in the medical kit as if by homing instinct; while Martin held the mask he stuck the needle home to the vagus nerve, restoring Kaph to life.

"Didn't know you knew that stunt," Martin said, breathing hard.

"The Lazarus Jab; my father was a doctor. It doesn't often work," Pugh said. "I want that drink I spilled. Is the quake over? I can't tell."

"Aftershocks. It's not just you shivering."

"Why did he suffocate?"

"I don't know, Owen. Look in the book."

Kaph was breathing normally and his color was restored, only his lips were still darkened. They poured a new shot of courage and sat down by him again with their medical guide. "Nothing about cyanosis or asphyxiation under 'shock' or 'concussion.' He can't have breathed in anything with his suit on. I don't know. We'd get as much good out of *Mother Mog's Home Herbalist.* . . . 'Anal Hemorrhoids,' fy!" Pugh pitched the book to a crate-table. It fell short, because either Pugh or the table was still unsteady.

"Why didn't he signal?"

"Sorry?"

"The eight inside the mine never had time. But he and the girl must have been outside. Maybe she was in the entrance, and got hit by the first slide. He must have been outside, in the control-hut maybe. He ran in, pulled her out, strapped her onto the sled, started for the dome. And all that time never pushed the panic button in his imsuit. Why not?"

"Well, he'd had that whack on his head. I doubt he ever realized the girl was dead. He wasn't in his senses. But if he had been I don't know if he'd have thought to signal us. They looked to one another for help."

Martin's face was like an Indian mask, grooves at the mouth-corners, eyes of dull coal. "That's so. What must he have felt, then, when the quake came and he was outside, alone—"

In answer Kaph screamed.

He came up off the cot in the heaving convulsions of one suffocating, knocked Pugh right down with his flailing arm, staggered into a stack of crates and fell to the floor, lips blue, eyes white. Martin dragged him back onto the cot and gave him a whiff of oxygen, then knelt by Pugh, who was just sitting up, and wiped at his cut cheekbone. "Owen, are you all right, are you going to be all right, Owen?"

"I think I am," Pugh said. "Why are you rubbing that on my face?"

It was a short length of computer-tape, now spotted with Pugh's blood. Martin dropped it. "Thought it was a towel. You clipped your cheek on that box there."

"Is he out of it?"

"Seems to be."

They stared down at Kaph lying stiff, his teeth a white line inside dark parted lips.

"Like epilepsy. Brain damage maybe?"

"What about shooting him full of meprobamate?"

Pugh shook his head. "I don't know what's in that shot I already gave him for shock. Don't want to overdose him."

"Maybe he'll sleep it off now."

"I'd like to myself. Between him and the earthquake I can't seem to keep on my feet."

"You got a nasty crack there. Go on, I'll sit up a while."

Pugh cleaned his cut cheek and pulled off his shirt, then paused.

"Is there anything we ought to have done—have tried to do—"

"They're all dead," Martin said heavily, gently.

Pugh lay down on top of his sleeping-bag, and one instant later was wakened by a hideous, sucking, struggling noise. He staggered up, found the needle, tried three times to jab it in correctly and failed, began to massage over Kaph's heart. "Mouth-to-mouth," he said, and Martin obeyed. Presently Kaph drew a harsh breath, his hearbeat steadied, his rigid muscles began to relax.

"How long did I sleep?"

"Half an hour."

They stood up sweating. The ground shuddered, the fabric of the dome sagged and swayed. Libra was dancing her awful polka gain, her Totentanz. The sun, though rising, seemed to have grown larger and redder; gas and dust must have been stirred up in the feeble atmosphere.

"What's wrong with him, Owen?"

"I think he's dying with them."

"Them —But they're dead, I tell you."

"Nine of them. They're all dead, they were crushed or suffocated. They were all him, he is all of them. They died, and now he's dying their deaths one by one."

"Oh pity of God," said Martin.

The next time was much the same. The fifth time was worse, for Kaph fought and raved, trying to speak but getting no words out, as if his mouth were stopped with rocks or clay. After that the attacks grew weaker, but so did he. The eighth seizure came at about four-thirty; Pugh and Martin worked till five-thirty doing all they could to keep life in the body that slid without protest into death. They kept him, but Martin said, "The next will finish him." And it did; but Pugh breathed his own breath into the inert lungs, until he himself passed out.

He woke. The dome was opaqued and no light on. He listened and heard the breathing of two sleeping men. He slept, and nothing woke him till hunger did.

The sun was well up over the dark plains, and the planet had stopped dancing. Kaph lay asleep. Pugh and Martin drank tea and looked at him with proprietary triumph.

When he woke Martin went to him: "How do you feel, old man?" There was no answer. Pugh took Martin's place and looked into the brown, dull eyes that gazed toward but not into his own. Like Martin he quickly turned away. He heated food-concentrate and brought it to Kaph. "Come on, drink."

He could see the muscles in Kaph's throat tighten. "Let me die," the young man said.

"You're not dying."

Kaph spoke with clarity and precision: "I am nine-tenths dead. There is not enough of me left alive."

That precision convinced Pugh, and he fought the conviction. "No," he said, peremptorily. "They are dead. The others. Your brothers and sisters. You're not them, you're alive. You are John Chow. Your life is in your own hands."

The young man lay still, looking into a darkness that was not there.

Martin and Pugh took turns taking the Exploitation hauler and a spare set of robos over to Hellmouth to salvage equipment and protect it from Libra's sinister atmosphere, for the value of the stuff was, literally, astronomical. It was slow work for one man at a time, but they were unwilling to leave Kaph by himself. The one left in the dome did paperwork, while Kaph sat or lay and stared into his darkness, and never spoke, The days went by silently.

The radio spat and spoke: the Mission calling from ship. "We'll be down on Libra in five weeks, Owen. Thirty-four E-days nine hours I make it as of now. How's tricks in the old dome?"

"Not good, chief. The Exploit team were killed, all but one of them in the mine. Earthquake. Six days ago."

The radio crackled and sang starsong. Sixteen seconds lag each way; the ship was out around Planet 11 now. "Killed, all but one? You and Martin were unhurt?"

"We're all right, chief."

Thirty-two seconds.

"*Passerine* left an Exploit team out here with us. I may put them on the Hellmouth project then, instead of the Quadrant Seven project. We'll settle that when we come down. In any case you and Martin will be relieved at Dome Two. Hold tight. Anything else?"

"Nothing else."

Thirty-two seconds.

"Right then. So long, Owen."

Kaph had heard all this, and later on Pugh said to him, "The chief may ask you to stay here with the other Exploit team. You know the ropes here." Knowing the exigencies of Far Out Life, he wanted to warn the young man. Kaph made no answer. Since he had said, "There is not enough of me left alive," he had not spoken a word.

"Owen," Martin said on suit intercom, "he's spla. Insane. Psycho."

"He's doing very well for a man who's died nine times."

"Well? Like a turned-off android is well? The only emotion he has left is hate. Look at his eyes."

"That's not hate, Martin. Listen, it's true that he has, in a sense, been dead. I cannot imagine what he feels. But it's not hatred. He can't even see us. It's too dark."

"Throats have been cut in the dark. He hates us because we're not Aleph and Yod and Zayin."

"Maybe. But I think he's alone. He doesn't see us or hear us, that's the truth. He never had to see anyone else before. He never was alone before. He had himself to see, talk with, live with, nine other selves all his life. He doesn't know how you go it alone. He must learn. Give him time."

Martin shook his heavy head. "Spla," he said. "Just remember when you're alone with him that he could break your neck one-handed."

"He could do that," said Pugh, a short, soft-voiced man with a scarred cheekbone; he smiled. They were just outside the dome airlock, programming one of the servos to repair a damaged hauler. They could see Kaph sitting inside the great half-egg of the dome like a fly in amber.

"Hand me the insert pack there. What makes you think he'll get any better?"

"He has a strong personality, to be sure."

"Strong? Crippled. Nine-tenths dead, as he put it."

"But he's not dead. He's a live man: John Kaph Chow. He had a jolly queer upbringing, but after all every boy has got to break free of his family. He will do it."

"I can't see it."

"Think a bit, Martin bach. What's this cloning for? To repair the human race. We're in a bad way. Look at me. My IIQ and GC are half this John Chow's. Yet they wanted me so badly for the Far Out Service that when I volunteered they took me and fitted me out with an artificial lung and corrected my myopia. Now if there were enough good sound lads about would they be taking one-lunged shortsighted Welshmen?"

"Didn't know you had an artificial lung."

"I do then. Not tin, you know. Human, grown in a tank from a bit of somebody; cloned, if you like. That's how they make replacement-organs, the same general idea as cloning, but bits and pieces instead of whole people. It's my own lung now, whatever. But what I am saying is this: there are too many like me these days and not enough like John Chow. They're trying to raise the level of the human genetic pool, which is a mucky little puddle since the population crash. So then if a man is cloned, he's a strong and clever man. It's only logic, to be sure."

Martin grunted; the servo began to hum.

Kaph had been eating little; he had trouble swallowing his food, choking on it, so that he would give up trying after a few bites. He had lost eight or ten kilos. After three weeks or so, however, his appetite began to pick up, and one day he began to look through the clone's possessions, the sleeping-bags, kits, papers which Pugh had stacked neatly in a far angle of a packing-crate alley. He sorted, destroyed a heap of papers and oddments, made a small packet of what remained, then relapsed into his walking coma.

Two days later he spoke. Pugh was trying to correct a flutter in the tape-player, and failing; Martin had the jet out, checking their maps of the Pampas. "Hell and damnation!" Pugh said, and Kaph said in a toneless voice, "Do you want me to do that?"

Pugh jumped, controlled himself, and gave the machine to Kaph. The young man took it apart, put it back together, and left it on the table.

"Put on a tape," Pugh said with careful casualness, busy at another table.

Kaph put on the topmost tape, a chorale. He lay down on his cot. The sound of a hundred human voices singing together filled the dome. He lay still, his face blank.

In the next days he took over several routine jobs, unasked. He undertook nothing that wanted initiative, and if asked to do anything he made no response at all.

"He's doing well," Pugh said in the dialect of Argentina.

"He's not. He's turning himself into a machine. Does what he's programmed to do, no reaction to anything else. He's worse off than when he didn't function at all. He's not human any more."

Pugh sighed. "Well, good night," he said in English. "Good night, Kaph."

"Good night," Martin said; Kaph did not.

Next morning at breakfast Kaph reached across Martin's plate for the toast. "Why don't you ask for it?" Martin said with the geniality of repressed exasperation. "I can pass it."

"I can reach it." Kaph said in his flat voice.

"Yes, but look. Asking to pass things, saying good night or hello, they're not important, but all the same when somebody says something a person ought to answer. . . ."

The young man looked indifferently in Martin's direction; his eyes still did not seem to see clear through to the person he looked toward. "Why should I answer?"

"Because somebody has said something to you."

"Why?"

Martin shrugged and laughed. Pugh jumped up and turned on the rock-cutter.

Later on he said, "Lay off that, please, Martin."

"Manners are essential in small isolated crews, some kind of manners, whatever you work out together. He's been taught that, everybody in Far Out knows it. Why does he deliberately flout it?"

"Do you tell yourself good night?"

"So?"

"Don't you see Kaph's never known anyone but himself?"

Martin brooded and then broke out, "Then by God this cloning business is all wrong. It won't do. What are a lot of duplicate geniuses going to do for us when they don't even know we exist?"

Pugh nodded. "It might be wiser to separate the clones and bring them up with others. But they make such a grand team this way."

"Do they? I don't know. If this lot had been ten average inefficient ET engineers, would they all have been in the same place at the same time: Would they all have got killed? What if, when the quake came and things started caving in, what if all those kids ran the same way, farther into the mine, maybe, to save the one that was farthest in? Even Kaph was outside and went in. . . . It's hypothetical. But I keep thinking, out of ten ordinary confused guys, more might have got out."

"I don't know. It's true that identical twins tend to die at about the same time, even when they have never seen each other. Identity and death, it is very strange. . . ."

The days went on, the red sun crawled across the dark sky, Kaph did not speak when spoken to, Pugh and Martin snapped at each other more frequently each day. Pugh complained of Martin's snoring. Offended, Martin moved his cot clear across the dome and also ceased speaking to Pugh for some while. Pugh whistled Welsh dirges until Martin complained, and then Pugh stopped speaking for a while.

The day before the Mission ship was due Martin announced he was going over to Merioneth.

"I thought at least you'd be giving me a hand with the computer to finish the rock-analyses," Pugh said, aggrieved.

"Kaph can do that. I want one more look at the Trench. Have fun," Martin added in dialect, and laughed, and left.

"What is that language?"

"Argentinean. I told you that once, didn't I?"

"I don't know." After a while the young man added, "I have forgotten a lot of things, I think."

"It wasn't important, to be sure," Pugh said gently, realizing all at once how important this conversation was. "Will you give me a hand running the computer, Kaph?"

He nodded.

Pugh had left a lot of loose ends, and the job took them all day. Kaph was a good co-worker, quick and systematic, much more so than Pugh himself. His flat voice, now that he was talking again, got on the nerves; but it didn't matter, there was only this one day left to get through and then the ship would come, the old crew, comrades and friends.

During tea-break Kaph said, "What will happen if the Explorer ship crashes?"

"They'd be killed."

"To you, I mean."

"To us? We'd radio SOS all signals, and live on half rations till the rescue cruiser from Area Three Base came. Four and half E-years away it is. We have life-support here for three men for, let's see, maybe between four and five years. A bit tight, it would be."

"Would they send a cruiser for three men?"

"They would."

Kaph said no more.

"Enough cheerful speculations," Pugh said cheerfully, rising to get back to work. He slipped sideways and the chair avoided his hand; he did a sort of half-pirouette and fetched up hard against the dome-hide. My goodness," he said, reverting to his native idiom, "what is it?"

"Quake," said Kaph.

The teacups bounced on the table with a plastic cackle, a litter of papers slid off a box, the skin of the dome swelled and sagged. Underfoot there was a huge noise, half sound half shaking, a subsonic boom.

Kaph sat unmoved. An earthquake does not frighten a man who died in an earthquake.

Pugh, white-faced, wiry black hair sticking out, a frightened man, said, "Martin is in the Trench."

"What trench?"

"The big fault line. The epicenter for the local quakes. Look at the seismograph." Pugh struggled with the stuck door of a still-jittering locker.

"Where are you going?"

"After him."

"Martin took the jet. Sleds aren't safe to use during quakes. They go out of control."

"For God's sake, man, shut up."

Kaph stood up, speaking in a flat voice as usual. "It's unnecessary to go out after him now. It's taking an unnecessary risk."

"If his alarm goes off, radio me," Pugh said, shut the headpiece of his suit, and ran to the lock. As he went out Libra picked up her ragged skirts and danced a bellydance from under his feet clear to the red horizon.

Inside the dome, Kaph saw the sled go up, tremble like a meteor in the dull red daylight, and vanish to the northeast. The hide of the dome quivered; the earth coughed. A vent south of the dome belched up a slow-flowing bile of black gas.

A bell shrilled and a red light flashed on the central control board. The sign under the light read Suit Two and scribbled under that, A.G.M. Kaph did not turn the signal off. He tried to radio Martin, then Pugh, but got no reply from either.

When the aftershocks decreased he went back to work, and finished up Pugh's job. It took him about two hours. Every half hour he tried to contact Suit One, and got no reply, then Suit Two and got no reply. The red light had stopped flashing after an hour.

It was dinnertime. Kaph cooked dinner for one, and ate it. He lay down on his cot.

The aftershocks had ceased except for faint rolling tremors at long intervals. The sun hung in the west, oblate, pale-red, immense. It did not sink visibly. There was no sound at all.

Kaph got up and began to walk about the messy, half-packed-up, over-crowded, empty dome. The silence continued. He went to the player and put on the first tape that came to hand. It was pure music, electronic, without harmonies, without voices. It ended. The silence continued.

Pugh's uniform tunic, one button missing, hung over a stack of rock-samples. Kaph stared at it awhile.

The silence continued.

The child's dream: There is no one else alive in the world but me. In all the world.

Low, north of the dome, a meteor flickered.

Kaph's mouth opened as if he were trying to say something, but no sound came. He went hastily to the north wall and peered out into the gelatinous red light.

The little star came in and sank. Two figures blurred the airlock. Kaph stood close beside the lock as they came in. Martin's imsuit was covered with some kind of dust so that he looked raddled and warty like the surface of Libra. Pugh had him by the arm.

"Is he hurt?"

Pugh shucked his suit, helped Martin peel off his. "Shaken up," he said, curt.

"A piece of cliff fell onto the jet," Martin said, sitting down at the table and waving his arms. "Not while I was in it, though. I was parked, see, and poking about that carbon-dust area when I felt things humping. So I went out onto a nice bit of early igneous I'd noticed from above, good footing and out from under the cliffs. Then I saw this bit of the planet fall off onto the flyer, quite a sight it was, and after a while it occurred to me the spare air-cans were in the flyer, so I leaned on the panic button. But I didn't get any radio reception, that's always happening here during quakes, so I didn't know if the signal was getting through either. And things went on jumping around and pieces of the cliff coming off. Little rocks flying around, and so dusty you couldn't see a meter ahead. I was really beginning to wonder what I'd do for breathing in the small hours, you know, when I saw old Owen buzzing up the Trench in all that dust and junk like a big ugly bat—"

"Want to eat?" said Pugh.

"Of course I want to eat. How'd you come through the quake here, Kaph? No damage? It wasn't a big one actually, was it, what's the seismo say? My trouble was I was in the middle of it. Old Epicenter Alvaro. Felt like Richter Fifteen there—total destruction of planet—"

"Sit down," Pugh said. "Eat."

After Martin had eaten a little his spate of talk ran dry. He very soon went off to his cot, still in the remote angle where he had removed it when Pugh complained of his snoring. "Good night, you one-lunged Welshman," he said across the dome.

"Good night."

There was no more out of Martin. Pugh opaqued the dome, turned the lamp down to a yellow glow less than a candle's light, and sat doing nothing, saying nothing, withdrawn.

The silence continued.

"I finished the computations."

Pugh nodded thanks.

"The signal from Martin came through, but I couldn't contact you or him."

Pugh said with effort, "I should not have gone. He had two hours of air left even with only one can. He might have been heading home when I left. This way we were all out of touch with one another. I was scared."

The silence came back, punctuated now by Martin's long, soft snores.

"Do you love Martin?"

Pugh looked up with angry eyes: "Martin is my friend. We've worked together, he's a good man." He stopped. After a while he said, "Yes, I love him. Why did you ask that?"

Kaph said nothing, but he looked at the other man. His face was changed, as if he were glimpsing something he had not seen before; his voice too was changed. "How can you . . .? How do you . . .?"

But Pugh could not tell him. "I don't know," he said, "it's practice, partly. I don't know, We're each of us alone, to be sure. What can you do but hold your hand out in the dark?"

Kaph's strange gaze dropped, burned out by its own intensity.

"I'm tired," Pugh said. "that was ugly, looking for him in all that black dust and muck, and mouths opening and shutting in the ground. . . . I'm going to bed. The ship will be transmitting to us by six or so." He stood up and stretched.

"It's a clone," Kaph said. "The other Exploit team they're bringing with them."

"Is it, then?"

"A twelveclone. They came out with us on the *Passerine*."

Kaph sat in the small yellow aura of the lamp seeming to look past it at what he feared: the new clone, the multiple self of which he was not part. A lost piece of a broken set, a fragment, inexpert at solitude, not knowing even how you go about giving love to another individual, now he must face the absolute, closed self-sufficiency of the clone of twelve; that was a lot to ask of the poor fellow, to be sure. Pugh put a hand on his shoulder in passing. "The chief won't ask you to stay here with a clone. You can go home. Or since you're Far Out maybe you'll come on farther out with us. We could use you. No hurry deciding. You'll make out all right."

Pugh's quiet voice trailed off. He stood unbuttoning his coat, stooped a little with fatigue. Kaph looked at him and saw the thing he had never seen before: saw him: Owen Pugh, the other, the stranger who held his hand out in the dark.

"Good night," Pugh mumbled, crawling into his sleeping-bag and half-asleep already, so that he did not hear Kaph reply after a pause, repeating across darkness, benediction.

QUESTIONS

1. Do you find the personification of Libra effective? ineffective? overly artificial? lyrical?

2. Find examples of sci-fi jargon. Are these technical terms intelligible? necessary? intrusive? overdone? Are they functional or merely ornamental?

3. Identify the point of view. Which character, if any, is "in possession of the general adventure" and functions, therefore, as a mirroring consciousness? As a result, do you feel more or less sympathy for this character?

4. Explain the relationship of the title to the events of the story.

5. Although the story is set on a distant planet in a distant future, the meaning lies in its exploration of humanness. Discuss.

6. It is not at all unlikely that cloning will play a role in human reproduction in future societies. Accordingly, the meaning of this story is relevant and profound in its implications. Martin asks an important question when he speculates: " . . . This cloning business is all wrong. It won't do. What are a lot of duplicate geniuses going to do for us when they don't even know we exist?" Do you agree with Martin, or do you consider his point of view short-sighted?

Tone

AESOP

Translations by Lloyd W. Daly

The Old Lion and the Fox

A lion who was growing old and couldn't get his food by force decided he would have to get it by wit. So he went into a cave where he lay down and played sick. When the other animals came in to visit him, he would eat them. After many animals had been done away with, a fox, who had seen through his trick, came along and, standing at a distance from the cave, asked him how he was. When the lion said he was not well and asked why he didn't come in, the fox said, "Why, I would if I didn't see so many tracks going in but none coming out."

So it is that intelligent men sense danger from signs in advance and avoid it.

The Crow and the Fox

A crow who had stolen some meat perched in a tree. A fox caught sight of him and, wishing to get the meat, stood there and began to praise him for his size and beauty, telling him that of all the birds he might most appropriately be king and that he certainly would be if he had any kind of a voice. The crow wanted to show the fox that he did have a voice and so dropped the meat and raised a great croaking. The fox ran up, seized the meat, and said, "Friend Crow, if you had any kind of sense, you would be completely equipped to be king of all."

The fable is appropriate for a senseless person.

QUESTIONS

1. Scholars have noted that some of Aesop's fables are more instructive than moralistic. Is the story of the lion and the fox moralistic or instructive? If moralistic, discuss its ethical dimension. If instructive, discuss what lesson it teaches.

2. Which of the characters deserves the label "cynic"? Why?

3. This translation reproduces the direct and simple language of the fables. Discuss, using "The Old Lion and the Fox" as an example.

4. Aristotle commented in his *Rhetoric* that fables are useful to the orator because, unlike historical parallels which are often difficult to find, fables can be invented—that is, they are products of the imagination. Explain. Then invent a contemporary analogy to "The Old Lion and the Fox" using human beings as characters.

5. In "The Crow and the Fox," what strategem does the fox employ to get the stolen meat from the crow?

6. The fox not only gets the meat but he gets the last word. Are you satisfied with his retort, or do you find it anticlimactic or inappropriate to the situation?

7. The Greeks used fables in argumentation. Why are they useful for this purpose?

8. In *Education of the Orator,* Quintilian advocated that Roman school children "learn to paraphrase Aesop's fables, the natural successors of the fairy stories of the nursery, in simple language, and subsequently to set down this paraphrase in writing with the same simplicity of style." After this faithful paraphrase, the children were encouraged to write a freer version in which they were permitted to abridge and to embellish "so far as this may be done without losing the poet's meaning." Do you think this is good or bad advice? Would it be better for children to copy the fairy tale rather than the fable?

JAMES THURBER

The Fox and the Crow

A crow, perched in a tree with a piece of cheese in his beak, attracted the eye and nose of a fox. "If you can sing as prettily as you sit," said the fox, "then you are the prettiest singer within my scent and sight." The fox had read somewhere, and somewhere, and somewhere else, that praising the voice of a crow with a cheese in his beak would make him drop the cheese and sing. But this is not what happened to this particular crow in this particular case.

"They say you are sly and they say you are crazy," said the crow, having carefully removed the cheese from his beak with the claws of one foot, "but you must be nearsighted as well. Warblers wear gay hats and colored jackets and bright vests, and they are a dollar a hundred. I wear black and I am unique." He began nibbling the cheese, dropping not a single crumb.

"I am sure you are," said the fox, who was neither crazy nor nearsighted, but sly. "I recognize you, now that I look more closely, as the most famed and talented of all birds, and I fain would hear you tell about yourself, but I am hungry and must go."

"Tarry awhile," said the crow quickly, "and share my lunch with me." Whereupon he tossed the cunning fox the lion's share of the cheese, and began to tell about himself. "A ship that sails without a crow's nest sails to doom," he said. "Bars may come and bars may go, but crow bars last forever. I am the pioneer of flight, I am the map maker. Last, but never least, my flight is known to scientists and engineers, geometrists and scholars, as the shortest distance between two points. Any two points," he concluded arrogantly.

"Oh, every two points, I am sure," said the fox. "And thank you for the lion's share of what I know you could not spare." And with this he trotted away into the woods, his appetite appeased, leaving the hungry crow perched forlornly in the tree.

MORAL: *'Twas true in Aesop's time, and La Fontaine's, and now, no one else can praise thee quite so well as thou.*

The Lover and His Lass

An arrogant gray parrot and his arrogant mate listened, one African afternoon, in disdain and derision, to the lovemaking of a lover and his lass, who happened to be hippopotamuses.

"He calls her snooky-ookums," said Mrs. Gray. "Can you believe that?"

"No," said Gray. "I don't see how any male in his right mind could entertain affection for a female that has no more charm than a capsized bathtub."

"Capsized bathtub, indeed!" exclaimed Mrs. Gray. "Both of them have the appeal of a coastwise fruit steamer with a cargo of waterlogged basketballs."

But it was spring, and the lover and his lass were young, and they were oblivious of the scornful comments of their sharp-tongued neighbors, and they continued to bump each other around in the water, happily pushing and pulling, backing and filling, and snorting and snaffling. The tender things they said to each other during the monolithic give-and-take of their courtship sounded as lyric to them as flowers in bud or green things opening. To the Grays, however, the bumbling romp of the lover and his lass was hard to comprehend and even harder to tolerate, and for a time they thought of calling the A.B.I., or African Bureau of Investigation, on the ground that monolithic lovemaking by enormous creatures who should have become decent fossils long ago was probably a threat to the security of the jungle. But they decided instead to phone their friends and neighbors and gossip about the shameless pair, and describe them in mocking and monstrous metaphors involving skidding busses on icy streets and overturned moving vans.

Late that evening, the hippopotamus and the hippopotama were surprised and shocked to hear the Grays exchanging terms of endearment. "Listen to those squawks," wuffled the male hippopotamus.

"What in the world can they see in each other?" gurbled the female hippopotamus.

"I would as soon live with a pair of unoiled garden shears," said her inamoratus.

They called up their friends and neighbors and discussed the incredible fact that a male gray parrot and a female gray parrot could possibly have any sex appeal. It was long after midnight before the hippopotamuses stopped criticizing the Grays and fell asleep, and the Grays stopped maligning the hippopotamuses and retired to their beds.

MORAL: *Laugh and the world laughs with you, love and you love alone.*

Q U E S T I O N S

1. Discuss how Thurber has drawn from and enlarged on Aesop's "The Crow and the Fox."

2. What makes Thurber's fable more humorous than Aesop's? Is either version moralistic?

3. Explain the allusions in the following sentences:
    1. "I am the pioneer of flight, I am the map maker."
    2. "My flight is known to scientists and engineers, geometrists and scholars, as the shortest distance between two points."
   What is the crow saying in these two remarks—the same thing or two different things?

4. As in Aesop's fables, Thurber's diction is direct and simple. Yet the tone of Thurber's version is less harsh than that of Aesop's. Discuss.

5. Is "The Lover and His Lass" either moralistic or instructive? If moralistic, discuss its ethical dimension. If instructive, discuss what lesson it teaches. If neither instructive nor moralistic, explain why.

6. Thurber's fables, like Aesop's, are paradigmatic, in that they act as examples of human behavior. Does "The Lover and His Lass" provide an accurate reflection of human nature?

7. Discuss the ways in which dialogue heightens the comedy of "The Lover and His Lass," and discuss this fable as satire.

MAX APPLE

The Oranging of America

I

From the outside it looked like any ordinary 1964 Cadillac limousine. In the expensive space between the driver and passengers, where some installed bars or even bathrooms, Mr. Howard Johnson kept a tidy ice cream freezer in which there were always at least eighteen flavors on hand, though Mr. Johnson ate only vanilla. The freezer's power came from the battery with an independent auxiliary generator as a backup system. Although now Howard Johnson means primarily motels, Millie, Mr. HJ, and Otis Brighton, the chauffeur, had not forgotten that ice cream was the cornerstone of their empire. Some of the important tasting was still done in the car. Mr. HJ might have reports in his pocket from sales executives and marketing analysts, from home economists and chemists, but not until Mr. Johnson reached over the lowered plexiglass to spoon a taste or two into the expert waiting mouth of Otis Brighton did he make any final flavor decisions. He might go ahead with butterfly shrimp, with candy kisses, and with packaged chocolate chip cookies on the opinion of the specialists, but in ice cream he trusted only Otis. From the back seat Howard Johnson would keep his eye on the rearview mirror where the reflection of pleasure or disgust showed itself in the dark eyes of Otis Brighton no matter what the driving conditions. He could be stalled in a commuter rush with the engine overheating and a dripping oil pan, and still a taste of the right kind never went unappreciated.

When Otis finally said, "Mr. Howard, that shore is sumpin, that one is um-hum. That is it, my man, that is it." Then and not until then did Mr. HJ finally decide to go ahead with something like banana fudge ripple royale.

Mildred rarely tasted and Mr. HJ was addicted to one scoop of vanilla every afternoon at three, eaten from his aluminum dish with a disposable plastic spoon. The duties of Otis, Millie, and Mr. Johnson were so divided that they rarely infringed upon one another in the car, which was their office. Neither Mr. HJ nor Millie knew how to drive, Millie and Otis understood little of financing and leasing, and Mr. HJ left the compiling of the "Traveling Reports" and "The Howard Johnson Newsletter" strictly to the literary style of his longtime associate, Miss Mildred Bryce. It was an ideal division of labor, which, in one form or another, had been in continuous operation for well over a quarter of a century.

While Otis listened to the radio behind his soundproof plexiglass, while Millie in her small, neat hand compiled data for the newsletter, Mr. HJ liked to lean back into the spongy leather seat looking through his specially tinted windshield at the fleeting land. Occasionally, lulled by the hum of the freezer, he might doze off, his large pink head lolling toward the shoulder of his blue suit, but there was not too much that Mr. Johnson missed, even in advanced age.

Along with Millie, he planned their continuous itinerary as they traveled. Mildred would tape a large green relief map of the United States to the plexiglass separating them from Otis. The mountains on the map were light brown and seemed to melt toward the valleys like the crust of a fresh apple pie settling into cinnamon surroundings. The existing HJ houses (Millie called the restaurants and motels houses) were marked by orange dots, while projected future sites bore white dots. The deep green map with its brown mountains and colorful dots seemed much more alive than the miles that twinkled past Mr. Johnson's gaze, and nothing gave the ice cream king greater pleasure than watching Mildred with her fine touch, and using the original crayon, turn an empty white dot into an orange fulfillment.

"It's like a seed grown into a tree, Millie," Mr. HJ liked to say at such moments when he contemplated the map and saw that it was good.

They had started traveling together in 1925. Mildred then a secretary to Mr. Johnson, a young man with two restaurants and a dream of hospitality, and Otis, a 20-year-old busboy and former driver of a Louisiana mule. When Mildred graduated from college, her father, a Michigan doctor who kept his money in a blue steel box under the examining table, encouraged her to try the big city. He sent her a monthly allowance. In those early days, she always had more than Mr. Johnson, who paid her $16.50 a week and meals. In the first decade they traveled only on weekends, but every year since 1936, they had spent at least six months on the road, and it might have gone on much longer if Mildred's pain and the trouble in New York with Howard Jr. had not come so close together.

There were all stoical at the Los Angeles International Airport. Otis waited at the car for what might be his last job while Miss Bryce and Mr. Johnson traveled toward the New York plane along a silent moving floor. Millie stood beside Howard while they passed a mural of a Mexican landscape and some Christmas drawings by fourth graders from Watts. For 40 years they had been together in spite of Howard Jr. and the others, but at this most recent appeal from New York, Millie urged him to go back. Howard Jr. had cabled "My God, Dad, you're 69 years old, haven't you been a gypsy long enough? Board meeting December 3 with or without you. Policy changes imminent."

Normally, they ignored Howard Jr.'s cables but this time Millie wanted him to go, wanted to be alone with the pain that had recently come to her. She had left Howard holding the new canvas suitcase in which she had packed her three notebooks of regional reports along with his aluminum dish, and in a moment of real despair, she had even packed the orange crayon. When Howard boarded Flight 965 he looked old to Millie. His feet dragged in the wing-tipped shoes, the hand she shook was moist, the lip felt dry, and as he passed from her sight down the entry ramp Mildred Bryce felt a fresh new ache that sent her hobbling toward the car. Otis had unplugged the freezer and the silence caused by the missing hum was as intense to Millie as her abdominal pain.

It had come quite suddenly in Albuquerque, New Mexico, at the grand opening of a 210-unit house. She did not make a fuss. Mildred Bryce had never caused trouble to anyone, except perhaps to Mrs. HJ. Millie's quick precise actions, angular face, and thin body made her seem birdlike, especially next to Mr. HJ, six-three with splendid white hair accenting his dark blue gabardine suits. Howard was slow and sure. He could sit in the same position for hours while Millie fidgeted on the seat, wrote memos, and filed reports in the small gray cabinet that sat in front of her and parallel to the ice cream freezer. Her health had always been good, so at first she tried to ignore the pain. It was gas: it was perhaps the New Mexico water or the cooking oil in the fish dinner. But she could not convince away the pain. It stayed like a match burning around her belly, etching itself into her as the round HJ emblem was so symmetrically embroidered into the bedspread, which she had kicked off in the flush that accompanied the pain. She felt as if her sweat would engulf the foam mattress and crisp percale sheet. Finally, Millie brought up her knees and made a ball of herself as if being as small as possible might make her misery disappear. It worked for everything except the pain. The little circle of hot torment was all that remained of her, and when finally at sometime in the early morning it left, it occurred to her that perhaps she had struggled with a demon and been suddenly relieved by the coming of daylight. She stepped lightly into the bathroom and before a full-length mirror (new in HJ motels exclusively) saw herself whole and unmarked, but sign enough to Mildred was her smell, damp and musty, sign enough that something had begun and that something else would therefore necessarily end.

II

Before she had the report from her doctor, Howard Jr.'s message had given her the excuse she needed. There was no reason why Millie could not tell Howard she was sick, but telling him would be admitting too much to herself.

Along with Howard Johnson, Millie had grown rich beyond dreams. Her inheritance, the $100,000 from her father's steel box in 1939, went directly to Mr. Johnson who desperately needed it, and the results of that investment brought Millie enough capital to employ two people at the Chase Manhattan with the management of her finances. With money beyond the hope of use, she had vacationed all over the world and spent some time in the company of celebrities, but the reality of her life, like his, was in the back seat of the limousine waiting for that point at which the needs of the automobile and the human body met the undeviating purpose of the highway and momentarily conquered it.

Her life was measured in rest stops. She, Howard, and Otis had found them out before they existed. They knew the places to stop between Buffalo and Albany, Chicago and Milwaukee, Toledo and Columbus, Des Moines and Minneapolis, they knew through their own bodies, measured in hunger and discomfort in the '30s and '40s when they would stop at remote places to buy land and borrow money, sensing in themselves the hunger that would one day be upon the place. People were wary and Howard had trouble borrowing (her $100,000 had perhaps been the key) but invariably he was right. Howard knew the land, Mildred thought, the way the Indians must have known it. There were even spots along the way where the earth itself seemed to make men stop. Howard had a sixth sense that would sometimes lead them from the main roads to, say, a dark green field in Iowa or Kansas. Howard, who might have seemed asleep, would rap with his knuckles on the plexiglass, causing the knowing Otis to bring the car to such a quick stop that Millie almost flew into her filing cabinet. And before the emergency brake had settled into its final prong, Howard Johnson was into the field and after the scent. While Millie and Otis waited, he would walk it out slowly. Sometimes he would sit down, disappearing in a field of long and tangled weeds, or he might find a large smooth rock to sit on while he felt some secret vibration from the place. Turning his back to Millie, he would mark the spot with his urine or break some of the clayey earth in his strong pink hands, sifting it like flour for a delicate recipe. She had actually seen him chew the grass, getting down on all fours like an animal and biting the tops without pulling the entire blade from the soil. At times he ran in a slow jog as far as his aging legs would carry him. Whenever he slipped out of sight behind the uneven terrain, Millie felt him in danger, felt that something alien might be there to resist the civilizing instinct of Howard Johnson. Once when Howard had been out of sight for more than an hour and did not respond to their frantic calls, Millie sent Otis into the field and in desperation flagged a passing car.

"Howard Johnson is lost in that field," she told the surprised driver. "He went in to look for a new location and we can't find him now."

"The restaurant Howard Johnson?" the man asked.

"Yes. Help us please."

The man drove off leaving Millie to taste in his exhaust fumes the barbarism of an ungrateful public. Otis found Howard asleep in a field of light blue wild flowers. He had collapsed from the exertion of his run. Millie brought water to him, and when he felt better, right there in the field, he ate his scoop of vanilla on the very spot where three years later they opened the first fully air-conditioned motel in the world. When she stopped to think about it, Millie knew they were more than businessmen, they were pioneers.

And once, while on her own, she had the feeling too. In 1951 when she visited the Holy Land there was an inkling of what Howard must have felt all the time. It happened without any warning on a bus crowded with tourists and resident Arabs on their way to the Dead Sea. Past ancient Sodom the bus creaked and bumped, down, down, toward the lowest point on earth, when suddenly in the midst of the crowd and her stomach queasy with the motion of the bus, Mildred Bryce experienced an overwhelming calm. A light brown patch of earth surrounded by a few pale desert rocks overwhelmed her perception, seemed closer to her than the Arab lady in the black flowered dress pushing her basket against Millie at that very moment. She wanted to stop the bus. Had she been near the door she might have actually jumped, so strong was her sensitivity to that barren spot in the endless desert. Her whole body ached for it as if in unison, bone by bone. Her limbs tingled, her breath came in short gasps, the sky rolled out of the bus windows and obliterated her view. The Arab lady spat on the floor, and moved a suspicious eye over a squirming Mildred.

When the bus stopped at the Dead Sea, the Arabs and tourists rushed to the soupy brine clutching damaged limbs, while Millie pressed $20 American into the dirty palm of a cabdriver who took her back to the very place where the music of her body began once more as sweetly as the first time. While the incredulous driver waited, Millie walked about the place wishing Howard were there to understand her new understanding of his kind of process. There was nothing there, absolutely nothing but pure bliss. The sun beat her like a wish, the air was hot and stale as a Viennese bathhouse, and yet Mildred felt peace and rest there, and as her cab bill mounted she actually did rest in the miserable barren desert of an altogether unsatisfactory land. When the driver, wiping the sweat from his neck asked, "Meesez . . . pleeze. Why American woman wants Old Jericho in such kind of heat?" when he said "Jericho" she understood that this was a place where men had always stopped. In dim antiquity Jacob had perhaps watered a flock here and not far away Lot's wife paused to scan for the last time the city of her youth. Perhaps Mildred now stood where Abraham had been visited by a vision and making a rock his pillow had first put the ease into the earth. Whatever it was, Millie knew from her own experience that rest was created here by historical precedent. She tried to buy that piece of land, going as far as King Hussein's secretary of the interior. She imagined a Palestinian HJ with an orange roof angling toward Sodom, a seafood restaurant, and an oasis of fresh fruit. But the land was in dispute between Israel and Jordan and even King Hussein, who expressed admiration for Howard Johnson, could not sell to Millie the place of her comfort.

That was her single visionary moment, but sharing them with Howard was almost as good. And to end all this, to finally stay in her 18th-floor Santa Monica penthouse, where the Pacific dived into California, this seemed to Mildred a paltry conclusion to an adventurous life. Her doctor said it was not so serious, she had a bleeding ulcer and must watch her diet. The prognosis was, in fact, excellent. But Mildred, 56 and alone in California, found the doctor less comforting than most of the rest stops she had experienced.

III

California, right after the Second War, was hardly a civilized place for travelers. Millie, HJ, and Otis had a 12-cylinder '47 Lincoln and snaked along five days between Sacramento and Los Angeles. "Comfort, comfort," said HJ as he surveyed the redwood forest and the bubbly surf while it slipped away from Otis who had rolled his trousers to chase the ocean away during a stop near San Francisco. Howard Johnson was contemplative in California. They had never been in the West before. Their route, always slightly new, was yet bound by Canada where a person couldn't get a tax break and roughly by the Mississippi as a western frontier. Their journeys took them up the eastern seaboard and through New England to the early reaches of the Midwest, stopping at the plains of Wisconsin and the cool crisp edge of Chicago where two HJ lodges twinkled at the lake.

One day in 1947 while on the way from Chicago to Cairo, Ill., HJ looked long at the green relief maps. While Millie kept busy with her filing, HJ loosened the tape and placed the map across his soft round knees. The map jiggled and sagged, the Mid- and Southwest hanging between his legs. When Mildred finally noticed that look, he had been staring at the map for perhaps 15 minutes, brooding over it, and Millie knew something was in the air.

HJ looked at that map the way some people looked down from an airplane trying to pick out the familiar from the colorful mass receding beneath them. Howard Johnson's eye flew over the land—over the Tetons, over the Sierra Nevada, over the long thin gouge of the Canyon flew his gaze—charting his course by rest stops the way an antique mariner might have gazed at the stars.

"Millie," he said just north of Carbondale, "Millie . . ." He looked toward her, saw her fingers engaged and her thumbs circling each other in anticipation. He looked at Millie and saw that she saw what he saw. "Millie"—HJ raised his right arm and its shadow spread across the continent like a prophecy—"Millie, what if we turn right at Cairo and go that way?" California, already peeling on the green map, balanced on HJ's left knee like a happy child.

Twenty years later Mildred settled in her 18th-floor apartment in the building owned by Lawrence Welk. Howard was in New York, Otis and the car waited in Arizona. The pain did not return as powerfully as it had appeared that night in Albuquerque, but it hurt with dull regularity and an occasional streak of dark blood in her bowels kept her mind on it even on painless days.

Directly beneath her gaze were the organized activities of the golden age groups, tiny figures playing bridge or shuffleboard or looking out at the water from their benches as she sat on her sofa and looked out at them and the fluffy ocean. Mildred did not regret family life. The HJ houses were her offspring. She had watched them blossom from the rough youngsters of the '40s with steam heat and even occasional kitchenettes into cool mature adults with king-sized beds, color TVs, and room service. Her late years were spent comfortably in the modern houses just as one might enjoy in age the benefits of a child's prosperity. She regretted only that it was probably over.

But she did not give up completely until she received a personal letter one day telling her that she was eligible for burial insurance until age 80. A $1,000 policy would guarantee a complete and dignified service. Millie crumpled the advertisement, but a few hours later called her Los Angeles lawyer. As she suspected, there were no plans, but as the executor of the estate he would assume full responsibility, subject of course to her approval.

"I'll do it myself," Millie had said, but she could not bring herself to do it. The idea was too alien. In more than 40 years Mildred had not gone a day without a shower and change of underclothing. Everything about her suggested order and precision. Her fingernails were shaped so that the soft meat of the tips could stroke a typewriter without damaging the apex of a nail, her arch slid over a six B shoe like an egg in a shell, and never in her adult life did Mildred recall having vomited. It did not seem right to suddenly let all this sink into the dark earth of Forest Hills because some organ or other developed a hole as big as a nickel. It was not right and she wouldn't do it. Her first idea was to stay in the apartment, to write it into the lease if necessary. She had the lawyer make an appointment for her with Mr. Welk's management firm, but canceled it the day before. "They will just think I'm crazy," she said aloud to herself, "and they'll bury me anyway."

She thought of cryonics while reading a biography of William Chesebrough, the man who invented petroleum jelly. Howard had known him and often mentioned that his own daily ritual of the scoop of vanilla was like old Chesebrough's two teaspoons of Vaseline every day. Chesebrough lived to be 90. In the biography it said that after taking the daily dose of Vaseline he drank three cups of green tea to melt everything down, rested for 12 minutes, and then felt fit as a young man, even in his late 80s. When he died, they froze his body and Millie had her idea. The Vaseline people kept him in a secret laboratory somewhere near Cleveland and claimed he was in better condition than Lenin, whom the Russians kept hermetically sealed, but at room temperature.

In the phone book she found the Los Angeles Cryonic Society and asked it to send her information. It all seemed very clean. The cost was $200 a year for maintaining the cold. She sent the pamphlet to her lawyer to be sure that the society was legitimate. It wasn't much money, but still if they were charlatans, she didn't want them to take advantage of her even if she would never know about it. They were aboveboard, the lawyer said. "The interest on a ten thousand dollar trust fund would pay about five hundred a year," the lawyer said, "and they only charge two hundred dollars. Still who knows what the cost might be in say two hundred years?" To be extra safe, they put $25,000 in trust for eternal maintenance, to be eternally overseen by Longstreet, Williams, and their eternal heirs. When it was arranged, Mildred felt better than she had in weeks.

IV

Four months to the day after she had left Howard at the Los Angeles International Airport, he returned for Mildred without the slightest warning. She was in her housecoat and had not even washed the night cream from her cheeks when she saw through the viewing space in her door the familiar long pink jowls, even longer in the distorted glass.

"Howard," she gasped, fumbling with the door, and in an instant he was there picking her up as he might a child or an ice cream cone while her tears fell like dandruff on his blue suit. While Millie sobbed into his soft padded shoulder, HJ told her the good news. "I'm chairman emeritus of the board now. That means no more New York responsibilities. They still have to listen to me because we hold the majority of the stock, but Howard Junior and Keyes will take care of the business. Our main job is new home-owned franchises. And, Millie, guess where we're going first?"

So overcome was Mildred that she could not hold back her sobs even to guess. Howard Johnson put her down, beaming pleasure through his old bright eyes. "Florida," HJ said, then slowly repeated it, "Flor-idda, and guess what we're going to do?"

"Howard," Millie said, swiping at her tears with the filmy lace cuffs of her dressing gown, "I'm so surprised I don't know what to say. You could tell me we're going to the moon and I'd believe you. Just seeing you again has brought back all my hope." They came out of the hallway and sat on the sofa that looked out over the Pacific. HJ, all pink, kept his hands on his knees like paperweights.

"Millie, you're almost right. I can't fool you about anything and never could. We're going down near where they launch the rockets from. I've heard . . ." HJ leaned toward the kitchen as if to check for spies. He looked at the stainless steel and glass table, at the built-in avocado appliances, then leaned his large moist lips toward Mildred's ear. "Walt Disney is planning right this minute a new Disneyland down there. They're trying to keep it a secret, but his brother Roy bought options on thousands of acres. We're going down to buy as much as we can as close in as we can." Howard sparkled. "Millie, don't you see, it's a sure thing."

After her emotional outburst at seeing Howard again, a calmer Millie felt a slight twitch in her upper stomach and in the midst of her joy was reminded of another sure thing.

They would be a few weeks in Los Angeles anyway. Howard wanted to thoroughly scout out the existing Disneyland, so Millie had some time to think it out. She could go, as her heart directed her, with HJ to Florida and points beyond. She could take the future as it happened like a Disneyland ride or she could listen to the dismal eloquence of her ulcer and try to make the best arrangements she could. Howard and Otis would take care of her to the end, there were no doubts about that, and the end would be the end. But if she stayed in this apartment, sure of the arrangements for later, she would miss whatever might still be left before the end. Mildred wished there were some clergyman she could consult, but she had never attended a church and believed in no religious doctrine. Her father had been a firm atheist to the very moment of his office suicide, and she remained a passive nonbeliever. Her theology was the order of her own life. Millie had never deceived herself, in spite of her riches all she truly owned was her life, a pocket of habits in the burning universe. But the habits were careful and clean and they were best represented in the body that was she. Freezing her remains was the closest image she could conjure of eternal life. It might not be eternal and it surely would not be life, but that damp musty feel, that odor she smelled on herself after the pain, that could be avoided, and who knew what else might be saved from the void for a small initial investment and $200 a year. And if you did not believe in a soul, was there not every reason to preserve a body?

Mrs. Allen of the Cryonic Society welcomed Mildred to a tour of the premises. "See it while you can," she cheerfully told the group (Millie, two men, and a boy with notebook and Polaroid camera). Mrs. Allen, a big woman perhaps in her mid-60s, carried a face heavy in flesh. Perhaps once the skin had been tight around her long chin and pointed cheekbones, but having lost its spring, the skin merely hung at her neck like a patient animal waiting for the rest of her to join in the decline. From the way she took the concrete stairs down to the vault, it looked as if the wait would be long. "I'm not ready for the freezer yet. I tell every group I take down here, it's gonna be a long time until they get me." Millie believed her. "I may not be the world's smartest cookie"—Mrs. Allen looked directly at Millie—"but a bird in the hand is the only bird I know, huh? That's why when it does come . . . Mrs. A is going to be right here in this facility, and you better believe it. Now, Mr. King on your left"—she pointed to a capsule that looked like a large bullet to Millie—"Mr. King is the gentleman who took me on my first tour, cancer finally but had everything perfectly ready and I would say he was in prime cooling state within seconds and I believe that if they ever cure cancer, and you know they will the way they do most everything nowadays, old Mr. King may be back yet. If anyone got down to low enough temperature immediately it would be Mr. King." Mildred saw the boy write, "Return of the King" in his notebook. "Over here is Mr. and Mizz Winkleman, married sixty years, and went off within a month of each other, a lovely, lovely couple."

While Mrs. Allen continued her necrology and posed for a photo beside the Winklemans, Millie took careful note of the neon-lit room filled with bulletlike capsules. She watched the cool breaths of the group gather like flowers on the steel and vanish without dimming the bright surface. The capsules stood in straight lines with ample walking space between them. To Mrs. Allen, they were friends, to Millie it seemed as if she were in a furniture store of the Scandinavian type where elegance is suggested by the absence of material, where straight lines of steel, wood, and glass indicate that relaxation too requires some taste and is not an indifferent sprawl across any soft object that happens to be nearby.

Cemeteries always bothered Millie, but here she felt none of the dread she had expected. She averted her eyes from the cluttered graveyards they always used to pass at the tips of cities in the early days. Fortunately, the superhighways twisted traffic into the city and away from those desolate marking places where used-car lots and the names of famous hotels inscribed on barns often neighbored the dead. Howard had once commented that never in all his experience did he have an intuition of a good location near a cemetery. You could put a lot of things there, you could put up a bowling alley, or maybe even a theater, but never a motel, and Millie knew he was right. He knew where to put his houses but it was Millie who knew how. From that first orange roof angling toward the east, the HJ design and the idea had been Millie's. She had not invented the motel, she had changed it from a place where you had to be to a place where you wanted to be. Perhaps, she thought, the Cryonic Society was trying to do the same for cemeteries.

When she and Howard had started their travels, the old motel courts huddled like so many dark graves around the stone marking of the highway. And what traveler coming into one of those dingy cabins could watch the watery rust dripping from his faucet without thinking of everything he was missing by being a traveler . . . his two-stall garage, his wife small in the half-empty bed, his children with hair the color of that rust. Under the orange Howard Johnson roof all this changed. For about the same price you were redeemed from the road. Headlights did not dazzle you on the foam mattress and percale sheets, your sanitized glasses and toilet appliances sparkled like the mirror behind them. The room was not just there, it awaited you, courted your pleasure, sat like a young bride outside the walls of the city wanting only to please you, you only you on the smoothly pressed sheets, your friend, your one-night destiny.

As if it were yesterday, Millie recalled right there in the cryonic vault the moment when she had first thought the thought that made Howard Johnson Howard Johnson's. And when she told Howard her decision that evening after cooking a cheese soufflé and risking a taste of wine, it was that memory she invoked for both of them, the memory of a cool autumn day in the '30s when a break in their schedule found Millie with a free afternoon in New Hampshire, an afternoon she had spent at the farm of a man who had once been her teacher and remembered her after 10 years. Otis drove her out to Robert Frost's farm where the poet made for her a lunch of scrambled eggs and 7-Up. Millie and Robert Frost talked mostly about the farm, about the cold winter he was expecting and the autumn apples they picked from the trees. He was not so famous then, his hair was only streaked with gray as Howard's was, and she told the poet about what she and Howard were doing, about what she felt about being on the road in America, and Robert Frost said he hadn't been that much but she sounded like she knew and he believed she might be able to accomplish something. He did not remember the poem she wrote in his class but that didn't matter.

"Do you remember, Howard, how I introduced you to him? Mr. Frost, this is Mr. Johnson. I can still see the two of you shaking hands there beside the car. I've always been proud that I introduced you to one another." Howard Johnson nodded his head at the memory, seemed as nostalgic as Millie while he sat in her apartment learning why she would not go to Florida to help bring Howard Johnson's to the new Disneyland.

"And after we left his farm, Howard, remember? Otis took the car in for servicing and left us with some sandwiches on the top of a hill overlooking a town, I don't even remember which one, maybe we never knew the name of it. And we stayed on that hilltop while the sun began to set in New Hampshire. I felt so full of poetry and"—she looked at Howard—"of love, Howard, only about an hour's drive from Robert Frost's farmhouse. Maybe it was just the way we felt then, but I think the sun set differently that night, filtering through the clouds like a big paintbrush making the top of the town all orange. And suddenly I thought what if the tops of our houses were that kind of orange, what a world it would be, Howard, and my God, that orange stayed until the last drop of light was left in it. I didn't feel the cold up there even though it took Otis so long to get back to us. The feeling we had about that orange, Howard, that was ours and that's what I've tried to bring to every house, the way we felt that night. Oh, it makes me sick to think of Colonel Sanders, and Big Boy, and Holiday Inn, and Best Western . . ."

"It's all right, Millie, it's all right." Howard patted her heaving back. Now that he knew about her ulcer and why she wanted to stay behind, the mind that had conjured butterfly shrimp and 28 flavors set himself a new project. He contemplated Millie sobbing in his lap the way he contemplated prime acreage. There was so little of her, less than 100 pounds, yet without her Howard Johnson felt himself no match for the wily Disneys gathering near the moonport.

He left her in all her sad resignation that evening, left her thinking she had to give up what remained here to be sure of the proper freezing. But Howard Johnson had other ideas. He did not cancel the advance reservations made for Mildred Bryce along the route to Florida, nor did he remove her filing cabinet from the limousine. The man who hosted a nation and already kept one freezer in his car merely ordered another, this one designed according to cryonic specifications and presented to Mildred housed in a 12-foot orange U-Haul trailer connected to the rear bumper of the limousine.

"Everything's here," he told the astonished Millie, who thought Howard had left the week before, "everything is here and you'll never have to be more than seconds away from it. It's exactly like a refrigerated truck." Howard Johnson opened the rear door of the U-Haul as proudly as he had ever dedicated a motel. Millie's steel capsule shone within, surrounded by an array of chemicals stored on heavily padded rubber shelves. The California sun was on her back but her cold breath hovered visibly within the U-Haul. No tears came to Mildred now; she felt relief much as she had felt that afternoon near ancient Jericho. On Santa Monica Boulevard, in front of Lawrence Welk's apartment building, Mildred Bryce confronted her immortality, a gift from the ice cream king, another companion for the remainder of her travels. Howard Johnson had turned away looking toward the ocean. To his blue back and patriarchal white hairs, Mildred said, "Howard, you can do anything," and closing the doors of the U-Haul, she joined the host of the highways, a man with two portable freezers, ready now for the challenge of Disneyworld.

"The Oranging of America" is fiction and its content derives entirely from Max Apple's imagination. Any similarities between his story and the lives of any persons, living or dead, are unintended and coincidental. Mr. Apple wishes it to be known that he "has no personal knowledge of Howard Johnson or of his friends and relatives and only a snacking acquaintance with the establishments so named."

The Editors

QUESTIONS

1. Identify the point of view. Is one of the characters "in possession of the general adventure"? If so, do you feel more or less sympathy for this character?

2. Are the characters round or flat? Static or dynamic? The relationship between Otis, Millie, and HJ can be called symbiotic. Why? Is Millie correct when she observes that they were "more than businessmen, they were pioneers"? Is HJ's solution to the problem of Millie's terminal illness appropriate to his character?

3. In what ways is the limousine a microcosm of Millie and HJ's larger world?

4. Show how the rituals invented for HJ and Millie contribute to the satire.

5. Satire often seeks to blend discordant elements. In this story, poetry fuses with materialism in the scene following Millie's visit to Robert Frost. Discuss, showing how this fusion enriches the satire.

6. At times, HJ's mission takes on the exaltation of a religious quest and the intensity of a religious vision. Discuss, showing how the fusion of religion and materialism contributes to the satire.

7. Examine the narrator's language. How would you characterize the diction? Lean? lyrical? informal? formal? allusive? literal?

8. This story uses the popular culture as subject matter and invents a history for an American institution. Do you find this treatment humorous? clichéd? provocative? trivial? pointless? pointed?

9. Can you formulate a theme for this story? Or does its meaning lie only in the

freshness of its vision of a commercialized and banal part of American life? Will you ever eat at a Howard Johnson's or stay at an HJ motel without thinking of this invented history?

10. The American road has fascinated writers and filmmakers. Discuss this story as a road story.

JORGE LUIS BORGES

Theme of the Traitor and the Hero

Translation by James E. Irby

So the Platonic year
Whirls out new right and wrong,
Whirls in the old instead;
All men are dancers and their tread
Goes to the barbarous clangour of a gong.

W. B. Yeats: *The Tower*

Under the notable influence of Chesterton (contriver and embellisher of elegant mysteries) and the palace counselor Leibniz (inventor of the preestablished harmony), in my idle afternoons I have imagined this story plot which I shall perhaps write someday and which already justifies me somehow. Details, rectifications, adjustments are lacking; there are zones of the story not yet revealed to me; today, January 3rd, 1944, I seem to see it as follows:

The action takes place in an oppressed and tenacious country: Poland, Ireland, the Venetian Republic, some South American or Balkan state. . . Or rather it has taken place, since, though the narrator is contemporary, his story occurred towards the middle or the beginning of the nineteenth century. Let us say (for narrative convenience) Ireland; let us say in 1824. The narrator's name is Ryan; he is the great-grandson of the young, the heroic, the beautiful, the assassinated Fergus Kilpatrick, whose grave was mysteriously violated, whose name illustrated the verses of Browning and Hugo, whose statue presides over a gray hill amid red marshes.

Kilpatrick was a conspirator, a secret and glorious captain of conspirators; like Moses, who from the land of Moab glimpsed but could not reach the promised land, Kilpatrick perished on the eve of the victorious revolt which he had premeditated and dreamt of. The first centenary of his death draws near; the circumstances of the crime are enigmatic; Ryan, engaged in writing a biography of the hero, discovers that the enigma exceeds the confines of a simple police investigation. Kilpatrick was murdered in a theater; the British police never found the killer; the historians maintain that this scarcely soils their good reputation, since it was probably the police themselves who had him killed. Other facets of the enigma disturb Ryan. They are of a cyclic nature; they seem to repeat or combine events of remote regions, of remote ages. For example, no one is unaware that the officers who examined the hero's body found a sealed letter in which he was warned of the risk of attending the theater that evening; likewise Julius Caesar, on his way to the place where his friends' daggers awaited him, received a note he never read, in which the treachery was declared along with the traitors' names. Caesar's wife, Calpurnia, saw in a dream the destruction of a tower decreed him by the Senate; false and anonymous rumors on the eve of Kilpatrick's death publicized throughout the country that the circular tower of Kilgarvan had burned, which could be taken as a presage, for he had been born in Kilgarvan. These parallelisms (and others) between the story of Caesar and the story of an Irish conspirator lead Ryan to suppose the existence of a secret form of time, a pattern of repeated lines. He thinks of the decimal history conceived by Condorcet, of the morphologies proposed by Hegel, Spengler and Vico, of Hesiod's men, who degenerate from gold to iron. He thinks of the transmigration of souls, a doctrine that lends horror to Celtic literature and that Caesar himself attributed to the British druids; he thinks that, before having been Fergus Kilpatrick, Fergus Kilpatrick was Julius Caesar. He is rescued from these circular labyrinths by a curious finding, a finding which then sinks him into other, more inextricable and heterogeneous labyrinths: certain words uttered by a beggar who spoke with Fergus Kilpatrick the day of his death were prefigured by Shakespeare in the tragedy *Macbeth*. That history should have copied history was already sufficiently astonishing; that history should copy literature was inconceivable . . . Ryan finds that, in 1814, James Alexander Nolan, the oldest of the hero's companions, had translated the principal dramas of Shakespeare into Gaelic; among these was *Julius Caesar*. He also discovers in the archives the manuscript of an article by Nolan on the Swiss *Festspiele:* vast and errant theatrical representations which require thousands of actors and repeat historical episodes in the very cities and mountains where they took place. Another unpublished document reveals to him that, a few days before the end, Kilpatrick, presiding over the last meeting, had signed the order for the execution of a traitor whose name has been deleted from the records. This order does not accord with Kilpatrick's merciful nature. Ryan investigates the matter (this investigation is one of the gaps in my plot) and manages to decipher the enigma.

Kilpatrick was killed in a theater, but the entire city was a theater as well, and the actors were legion, and the drama crowned by his death extended over many days and many nights. This is what happened:

On the 2nd of August, 1824, the conspirators gathered. The country was ripe for revolt; something, however, always failed: there was a traitor in the group. Fergus Kilpatrick had charged James Nolan with the responsibility of discovering the traitor. Nolan carried out his assignment: he announced in the very midst of the meeting that the traitor was Kilpatrick himself. He demonstrated the truth of his accusation with irrefutable proof; the conspirators condemned their president to die. He signed his own sentence, but begged that his punishment not harm his country.

It was then that Nolan conceived his strange scheme. Ireland idolized Kilpatrick; the most tenuous suspicion of his infamy would have jeopardized the revolt; Nolan proposed a plan which made of the traitor's execution an instrument for the country's emancipation. He suggested that the condemned man die at the hands of an unknown assassin in deliberately dramatic circumstances which would remain engraved in the imagination of the people and would hasten the revolt. Kilpatrick swore he would take part in the scheme, which gave him the occasion to redeem himself and for which his death would provide the final flourish.

Nolan, urged on by time, was not able to invent all the circumstances of the multiple execution; he had to plagiarize another dramatist, the English enemy William Shakespeare. He repeated scenes from *Macbeth,* from *Julius Caesar.* The public and secret enactment comprised various days. The condemned man entered Dublin, discussed, acted, prayed, reproved, uttered words of pathos, and each of these gestures, to be reflected in his glory, had been pre-established by Nolan. Hundreds of actors collaborated with the protagonist; the role of some was complex; that of others momentary. The things they did and said endure in the history books, in the impassioned memory of Ireland. Kilpatrick, swept along by this minutely detailed destiny which both redeemed him and destroyed him, more than once enriched the test of his judge with improvised acts and words. Thus the populous drama unfolded in time, until on the 6th of August, 1824, in a theater box with funereal curtains prefiguring Lincoln's, a long-desired bullet entered the breast of the traitor and hero, who, amid two effusions of sudden blood, was scarcely able to articulate a few foreseen words.

In Nolan's work, the passages imitated from Shakespeare are the *least* dramatic; Ryan suspects that the author interpolated them so that in the future someone might hit upon the truth. He understands that he too forms part of Nolan's plot . . . After a series of tenacious hesitations, he resolves to keep his discovery silent. He publishes a book dedicated to the hero's glory; this too, perhaps, was foreseen.

QUESTIONS

1. Discuss this story as a literary puzzle. How is it similar to a mystery story? Which character plays the role of detective? villain? accomplice? informer?

2. How does the title hold the key to the principal irony?

3. What causes Ryan to think "of the decimal history conceived by Condorcet, of the morphologies proposed by Hegel, Spengler and Vico"? Discuss the appropriateness of these allusions.

4. In what way does Ryan fit into Nolan's plot? And why does Ryan decide "to keep his discovery silent"?

5. Discuss tone in relation to point of view.

6. Ryan finds it inconceivable that "history should copy literature." Do you agree?

LESLIE SILKO

Lullaby

The sun had gone down but the snow in the wind gave off its own light. It came in thick tufts like new wool—washed before the weaver spins it. Ayah reached out for it like her own babies had, and she smiled when she remembered how she had laughed at them. She was an old woman now, and her life had become memories. She sat down with her back against the wide cottonwood tree, feeling the rough bark on her back bones; she faced east and listened to the wind and snow sing a high-pitched Yeibechei song. Out of the wind she felt warmer, and she could watch the wide fluffy snow fill in her tracks, steadily, until the direction she had come from was gone. By the light of the snow she could see the dark outline of the big arroyo a few feet away. She was sitting on the edge of Cebolleta Creek, where in the springtime the thin cows would graze on grass already chewed flat to the ground. In the wide deep creek bed where only a trickle of water flowed in the summer, the skinny cows would wander, looking for new grass along winding paths splashed with manure.

Ayah pulled the old Army blanket over her head like a shawl. Jimmie's blanket—the one he had sent to her. That was a long time ago and the green wool was faded, and it was unraveling on the edges. She did not want to think about Jimmie. So she thought about the weaving and the way her mother had done it. On the tall wooden loom set into the sand under a tamarack tree for shade. She could see it clearly. She had been only a little girl when her grandma

448

gave her the wooden combs to pull the twigs and burrs from the raw, freshly washed wool. And while she combed the wool, her grandma sat beside her, spinning a silvery strand of yard around the smooth cedar spindle. Her mother worked at the loom with yarns dyed bright yellow and red and gold. She watched them dye the yarn in boiling black pots full of beeweed petals, juniper berries, and sage. The blankets her mother made were soft and woven so tight that rain rolled off them like birds' feathers. Ayah remembered sleeping warm on cold windy nights, wrapped in her mother's blankets on the hogan's sandy floor.

The snow drifted now, with the northwest wind hurling it in gusts. It drifted up around her black overshoes—old ones with little metal buckles. She smiled at the snow which was trying to cover her little by little. She could remember when they had no black rubber overshoes; only the high buckskin leggings that they wrapped over their elk-hide moccasins. If the snow was dry or frozen, a person could walk all day and not get wet; and in the evenings the beams of the ceiling would hang with lengths of pale buckskin leggings, drying out slowly.

She felt peaceful remembering. She didn't feel cold any more. Jimmie's blanket seemed warmer than it had ever been. And she could remember the morning he was born. She could remember whispering to her mother who was sleeping on the other side of the hogan, to tell her it was time now. She did not want to wake the others. The second time she called to her, her mother stood up and pulled on her shoes; she knew. They walked to the old stone hogan together, Ayah walking a step behind her mother. She waited alone, learning the rhythms of the pains while her mother went to call the old woman to help them. The morning was already warm even before dawn and Ayah smelled the bee flowers blooming and the young willow growing at the springs. She could remember that so clearly, but his birth merged into the births of the other children and to her it became all the same birth. They named him for the summer morning and in English they called him Jimmie.

It wasn't like Jimmie died. He just never came back, and one day a dark blue sedan with white writing on its doors pulled up in front of the boxcar shack where the rancher let the Indians live. A man in a khaki uniform trimmed in gold gave them a yellow piece of paper and told them that Jimmie was dead. He said the Army would try to get the body back and then it would be shipped to them; but it wasn't likely because the helicopter had burned after it crashed. All of this was told to Chato because he could understand English. She stood inside the doorway holding the baby while Chato listened. Chato spoke English like a white man and he spoke Spanish too. He was taller than the white man and he stood straighter too. Chato didn't explain why; he just told the military man they could keep the body if they found it. The white man looked bewildered; he nodded his head and he left. Then Chato looked at her and shook his head. "Goddamn," he said in English, and then he told her "Jimmie isn't coming home anymore," and when he spoke, he used the words to speak of the dead. She didn't cry then, but she hurt inside with anger. And she mourned him as the years passed, when a horse fell with Chato and broke his leg, and the white rancher told them he wouldn't pay Chato until he could work again. She mourned Jimmie because he would have worked for his father then; he would have saddled the big bay horse and ridden the fence lines each day, with wire cutters and heavy gloves, fixing the breaks in the barbed wire and putting the stray cattle back inside again.

She mourned him after the white doctors came to take Danny and Ella away. She was at the shack alone that day when they came. It was back in the days before they hired Navajo women to go with them as interpreters. She recognized one of the doctors. She had seen him at the children's clinic at Cañoncito about a month ago. They were wearing khaki uniforms and they waved papers at her and a black ball point pen, trying to make her understand their English words. She was frightened by the way they looked at the children, like the lizard watches the fly. Danny was swinging on the tire swing in the elm tree behind the rancher's house, and Ella was toddling around the front door, dragging the broomstick horse Chato made for her. Ayah could see they wanted her to sign the papers, and Chato had taught her to sign her name. It was something she was proud of. She only wanted them to go, and to take their eyes away from her children.

She took the pen from the man without looking at his face and she signed the papers in three different places he pointed to. She stared at the ground by their feet and waited for them to leave. But they stood there and began to point and gesture at the children. Danny stopped swinging. Ayah could see his fear. She moved suddenly and grabbed Ella into her arms; the child squirmed, trying to get back to her toys. Ayah ran with the baby toward Danny; she screamed for him to run and then she grabbed him around his chest and carried him too. She ran south into the foothills of juniper trees and black lava rock. Behind her she heard the doctors running, but they had been taken by surprise, and as the hills became steeper and the cholla cactus were thicker, they stopped. When she reached the top of the hill, she stopped too to listen in case they were circling around her. But in a few minutes she heard a car engine start and they drove away. The children had been too surprised to cry while she ran with them. Danny was shaking and Ella's little fingers were gripping Ayah's blouse.

She stayed up in the hills for the rest of the day, sitting on a black lava boulder in the sunshine where she could see for miles all around her. The sky was light blue and cloudless, and it was warm for late April. The sun warmth relaxed her and took the fear and anger away. She lay back on the rock and watched the sky. It seemed to her that she could walk into the sky, stepping through clouds endlessly. Danny played with little pebbles and stones, pretending they were birds, eggs and then little rabbits. Ella sat at her feet and dropped fistfuls of dirt into the breeze, watching the dust and particles of sand intently. Ayah watched a hawk soar high above them, dark wings gliding; hunting or only watching, she did not know. The hawk was patient and he circled all afternoon before he disappeared around the high volcanic peak the Mexicans call Guadalupe.

Late in the afternoon, Ayah looked down at the gray boxcar shack with the paint all peeled from the wood; the stove pipe on the roof was rusted and crooked. The fire she had built that morning in the oil drum stove had burned out. Ella was asleep in her lap now and Danny sat close to her, complaining that he was hungry; he asked when they would go to the house. "We will stay up here until your father comes," she told him, "because those white men were chasing us." The boy remembered then and he nodded at her silently.

If Jimmie had been there he could have read those papers and explained to her what they said. Ayah would have known, then, never to sign them. The doctors came back the next day and they brought a BIA policeman with them. They told Chato they had her signature and that was all they needed. Except for the kids. She listened to Chato sullenly; she hated him when he told her it was the old woman who died in the winter, spitting blood; it was her old grandma who had given the children this disease. "They don't spit blood," she said coldly, "The whites lie." She held Ella and Danny close to her, ready to run to the hills again. "I want a medicine man first," she said to Chato, not looking at him. He shook his head. "It's too late now. The policeman is with them. You signed the paper." His voice was gentle.

It was worse than if they had died: to lose the children and to know that somewhere, in a place called Colorado, in a place full of sick and dying strangers, her children were without her. There had been babies that died soon after they were born, and one that died before he could walk. She had carried them herself, up to the boulders and great pieces of the cliff that long ago crashed down from Long Mesa; she laid them in the crevices of sandstone and buried them in fine brown sand with round quartz pebbles that washed down from the hills in the rain. She had endured it because they had been with her. But she could not bear this pain. She did not sleep for a long time after they took her children. She stayed on the hill where they had fled the first time, and she slept rolled up in the blanket Jimmie had sent her. She carried the pain in her belly and it was fed by everything she saw: the blue sky of their last day together and the dust and pebbles they played with; the swing in the elm tree and broomstick horse chocked life from her. The pain filled her stomach and there was no room for food or for her lungs to fill with air. The air and the food would have been theirs.

She hated Chato, not because he let the policeman and doctors put the screaming children in the government car, but because he had taught her to sign her name. Because it was like the old ones always told her about learning their language or any of their ways: it endangered you. She slept alone on the hill until the middle of November when the first snows came. Then she made a bed for herself where the children had slept. She did not lay down beside Chato again until many years later, when he was sick and shivering and only her body could keep him warm. The illness came after the white rancher told Chato he was too old to work for him any more, and Chato and his old woman should be out of the shack by the next afternoon because the rancher had hired new people to work there. That had satisfied her. To see how the white man repaid Chato's years of loyalty and work. All of Chato's fine-sounding English talk didn't change things.

II

It snowed steadily and the luminous light from the snow gradually diminished into the darkness. Somewhere in Cebolleta a dog barked and other village dogs joined with it. Ayah looked in the direction she had come, from the bar where Chato was buying the wine. Sometimes he told her to go on ahead and wait; and then he never came. And when she finally went back looking for him, she would find him passed out at the bottom of the wooden steps to Azzie's Bar. All the wine would be gone and most of the money too, from the pale blue check that came to them once a month in a government envelope. It was then that she would look at his face and his hands, scarred by ropes and the barbed wire of all those years, and she would think 'this man is a stranger'; for forty years she had smiled at him and cooked his food, but he remained a stranger. She stood up again, with the snow almost to her knees, and she walked back to find Chato.

It was hard to walk in the deep snow and she felt the air burn in her lungs. She stopped a short distance from the bar to rest and readjust the blanket. But this time he wasn't waiting for her on the bottom step with his old Stetson hat pulled down and his shoulders hunched up in his long wool overcoat.

She was careful not to slip on the wooden steps. When she pushed the door open, warm air and cigarette smoke hit her face. She looked around slowly and deliberately, in every corner, in every dark place that the old man might find to sleep. The barowner didn't like Indians in there, especially Navajos, but he let Chato come in because he could talk Spanish like he was one of them. The men at the bar stared at her, and the bartender saw that she left the door open wide. Snow flakes were flying inside like moths and melting into a puddle on the oiled wood floor. He motioned at her to close the door, but she did not see him. She held herself straight and walked across the room slowly, searching the room with every step. The snow in her hair melted and she could feel it on her forehead. At the far corner of the room, she saw red flames at the mica window of the old stove door; she looked behind the stove just to make sure. The bar got quiet except for the Spanish polka music playing on the jukebox. She stood by the stove and shook the snow from her blanket and held it near the stove to dry. The wet wool smell reminded her of new-born goats in early March, brought inside to warm near the fire. She felt calm.

In past years they would have told her to get out. But her hair was white now and her face was wrinkled. They looked at her like she was a spider crawling slowly across the room. They were afraid; she could feel the fear. She looked at their faces steadily. They reminded her of the first time the white people brought her children back to her that winter. Danny had been shy and hid behind the thin white woman who brought them. And the baby had not known her until Ayah took her into her arms, and then Ella had nuzzled close to her as she had when she was nursing. The blonde woman was nervous and kept looking at a dainty gold watch on her wrist. She sat on the bench near the small window and watched the dark snow clouds gather around the mountains; she was worrying about the unpaved road. She was frightened by what she saw inside too: the strips of venison drying on a rope across the ceiling and the children jabbering excitedly in a language she did not know. So they stayed for only a few hours. Ayah watched the government car disappear down the road and she knew they were already being weaned from these lava hills and from this sky. The last time they came was in early June, and Ella stared at her the way the men in the bar were now staring. Ayah did not try to pick her up; she smiled at her instead and spoke cheerfully to Danny. When he tried to answer her, he could not seem to remember and he spoke English words with the Navajo. But he gave her a scrap of paper that he had found somewhere and carried in his pocket; it was folded in half, and he shyly looked up at her and said it was a bird. She asked Chato if they were home for good this time. He spoke to the white woman and she shook her head. "How much longer," he asked, and she said she didn't know; but Chato saw how she stared at the box car shack. Ayah turned away then. She did not say good-bye.

III

She felt satisfied that the men in the bar feared her. Maybe it was her face and the way she held her mouth with teeth clenched tight, like there was nothing anyone could do to her now. She walked north down the road, searching for the old man. She did this because she had the blanket, and there would be no place for him except with her and the blanket in the old adobe barn near the arroyo. They always slept there when they came to Cebolleta. If the money and the wine were gone, she would be relieved because then they could go home again; back to the old hogan with a dirt roof and rock walls where she herself had been born. And the next day the old man could go back to the few sheep they still had, to follow along behind them, guiding them into dry sandy arroyos where sparse grass grew. She knew he did not like walking behind old ewes when for so many years he rode big quarter horses and worked with cattle. But she wasn't sorry for him; he should have known all along what would happen.

There had not been enough rain for their garden in five years; and that was when Chato finally hitched a ride into the town and brought back brown boxes of rice and sugar and big tin cans of welfare peaches. After that, at the first of the month they went to Cebolleta to ask the postmaster for the check; and then Chato would go to the bar and cash it. They did this as they planted the garden every May, not because anything would survive the summer dust, but because it was time to do this. And the journey passed the days that smelled silent and dry like the caves above the canyon with yellow painted buffaloes on their walls.

IV

He was walking along the pavement when she found him. He did not stop or turn around when he heard her behind him. She walked beside him and she noticed how slowly he moved now. He smelled strong of woodsmoke and urine.

Lately he had been forgetting. Sometimes he called her by his sister's name and she had been gone for a long time. Once she had found him wandering on the road to the white man's ranch, and she asked him why he was going that way; he laughed at her and said "you know they can't run that ranch without me," and he walked on determined, limping on the leg that had been crushed many years before. Now he looked at her curiously, as if for the first time, but he kept shuffling along, moving slowly along the side of the highway. His gray hair had grown long and spread out on the shoulders of the long overcoat. He wore the old felt hat pulled down over his ears. His boots were worn out at the toes and he had stuffed pieces of an old red shirt in the holes. The rags made his feet look like little animals up to their ears in snow. She laughed at his feet; the snow muffled the sound of her laugh. He stopped and looked at her again. The wind had quit blowing and the snow was falling straight down; the southeast sky was beginning to clear and Ayah could see a star.

"Let's rest awhile," she said to him. They walked away from the road and up the slope to the giant boulders that had tumbled down from the red sandrock mesa throughout the centuries of rainstorms and earth tremors. In a place where the boulders shut out the wind, they sat down with their backs against the rock. She offered half of the blanket to him and they sat wrapped together.

The storm passed swiftly. The clouds moved east. They were massive and full, crowding together across the sky. She watched them with the feeling of horses—steely blue-gray horses startled across the sky. The powerful haunches pushed into the distances and the tail hairs streamed white mist behind them. The sky cleared. Ayah saw that there was nothing between her and the stars. The light was crystalline. There was no shimmer, no distortion through earth haze. She breathed the clarity of the night sky; she smelled the purity of the half moon and the stars. He was lying on his side with his knees pulled up near his belly for warmth. His eyes were closed now, and in the light from the stars and the moon, he looked young again.

She could see it descend out of the night sky: an icy stillness from the edge of the thin moon. She recognized the freezing. It came gradually, sinking snow flake by snow flake until the crust was heavy and deep. It had the strength of the stars in Orion, and its journey was endless. Ayah knew that with the wine he would sleep. He would not feel it. She tucked the blanket around him, remembering how it was when Ella had been with her; and she felt the rush so big inside her heart for the babies. And she sang the only song she knew to sing for babies. She could not remember if she had ever sung it to her children, but she knew that her grandmother had sung it and her mother had sung it:

> *The earth is your mother,*
> *she holds you.*
> *The sky is your father,*
> *he protects you.*
> *sleep,*
> *sleep,*

Rainbow is your sister,
*   she loves you.*
The winds are your brothers,
*   they sing to you.*
sleep,
sleep,
We are together always
We are together always
There never was a time
when this
was not so.

QUESTIONS

1. Identify the point of view. How different would the story be had it been told from Chato's point of view or from the rancher's? Discuss the relationship between point of view and tone.

2. Ayah's black rubber overshoes have a symbolic value similar to that of the Army blanket. Why?

3. Relate the following sentence to the story's theme: "They named him for the summer morning and in English they called him Jimmie."

4. Why were Danny and Ella taken away from Ayah?

5. Why do the men in the bar fear Ayah? Why does she feel "satisfied that the men in the bar feared her"?

6. Will Ayah and Chato survive the freezing night? Ayah reflects that with the wine Chato "would sleep. He would not feel it." Does "it" refer to the freezing night? to death? or to both?

7. Is Ayah's song an appropriate conclusion to the story? Discuss the effect of this song on tone.

WILLIAM EASTLAKE

The Death of Sun

The Bird Sun was named Sun by the Indians because each day their final eagle circled this part of the reservation like the clock of sun. Sun, a grave and golden eagle-stream of light, sailed without movement as though propelled by some eternity, to orbit, to circumnavigate this moon of earth, to alight upon his aerie from which he had risen, and so Sun would sit with the same God dignity and decorous finality with which he had emerged—then once more without seeming volition ride the crest of an updraft above Indian Country on six-foot wings to settle again on his throne aerie in awful splendor, admonitory, serene— regal and doomed. I have risen.

"Man, Feodor Dostoevski said," the white teacher Mary-Forge said, "without a sure idea of himself and the purpose of his life cannot live and would sooner destroy himself than remain on earth."

"Who was Dostoevski?" the Navajo Indian Jesus Saves said.

"An Indian."

"What kind?"

"With that comment he could have been a Navajo," Mary-Forge said.

"No way," Jesus Saves said.

"Why, no way could Dostoevski be an Indian?"

"I didn't say Dostoevski couldn't be an Indian; I said he couldn't be a Navajo."

"Why is a Navajo different?"

"We are, that's all," Jesus Saves said. "In the words of Sören Kierkegaard—"

"Who was Sören Kierkegaard?"

"Another Russian," Jesus Saves said.

"Kierkegaard was a Dane."

"No, that was Hamlet," Jesus Saves said. "Remember?"

"You're peeved, Jesus Saves."

"No, I'm bugged," Jesus Saves said, "by people who start sentences with
'man.'"

"Dostoevski was accounting for the high suicide rate among Navajos.
Since the white man invaded Navajo country the Navajo sees no hope or
purpose to life."

"Then why didn't Dostoevski say that?"

"Because he never heard of the Navajo."

"Then I never heard of Dostoevski," Bull Who Looks Up said. "Two can
play at this game."

"That's right," Jesus Saves said, sure of himself now and with purpose.

"What is the purpose of your life, Jesus Saves?"

"To get out of this school," Jesus Saves said.

Jesus Saves was named after a signboard erected by the Albuquerque First
National Savings & Loan.

All of Mary-Forge's students were Navajos. When Mary-Forge was not
ranching she was running this free school that taught the Indians about themselves and their country—Indian country.

"What has Dostoevski got to do with Indian country?"

"I'm getting to that," Mary-Forge said.

"Will you hurry up?"

"No," Mary-Forge said.

"Is that any way for a teacher to speak to a poor Indian?"

"Sigmund Freud," the Medicine Man said, "said—more in anguish I
believe than in criticism—'What does the Indian want? My God, what does the
Indian want?'"

"He said that about women."

"If he had lived longer, he would have said it about Indians."

"True."

"Why?"

"Because it sounds good, it sounds profound, it tends to make you take off
and beat the hell out of the Indians."

"After we have finished off the women."

"The women were finished off a long time ago," the Medicine Man said.

"But like the Indians they can make a comeback."

"Who knows," the Medicine Man said, "we both may be a dying race."

"Who knows?"

"We both may have reached the point of no return, who knows?"

"If we don't want to find out, what the hell are we doing in school?"

"Who knows?"

"I know," Mary-Forge said, "I know all about the eagle."

"Tell us, Mary-Forge, all about the eagle."

"The eagle is being killed off."

"We know that; what do we do?"

"We get out of this school and find the people who are killing the eagle."

"Then?"

"Who knows?" Mary-Forge said.

Mary-Forge was a young woman—she was the youngest white woman the Navajos had ever seen. She was not a young girl, there are millions of young girls in America. In America young white girls suddenly become defeated women. A young white woman sure of herself and with a purpose in life such as Mary-Forge was unknown to the American Indian.

Mary-Forge had large, wide-apart, almond-shaped eyes, high full cheekbones, cocky let-us-all-give-thanks tipsy breasts, and good brains. The white American man is frightened by her brain. The Indian found it nice. They loved it. They tried to help Mary-Forge. Mary-Forge tried to help the Indians. They were both cripples. Both surrounded by the white reservation.

High on her right cheekbone Mary-Forge had a jagged two-inch scar caused by a stomping she got from high-heeled cowboy boots belonging to a sheep rancher from the Twin Slash Heart Ranch on the floor of the High Point Bar in Gallup.

Mary-Forge did not abruptly think of eagles in the little red schoolhouse filled with Indians. A helicopter had just flown over. The helicopter came to kill eagles. The only time the Indians ever saw or felt a helicopter on the red reservation was when the white ranchers came to kill eagles. Eagles killed sheep, they said, and several cases have been known, they said, where white babies have been plucked from playpens and dropped in the ocean, they said.

You could hear plainly the *whack-whack-whack* of the huge rotor blades of the copter in the red schoolhouse. The yellow and blue copter was being flown by a flat-faced doctor-serious white rancher named Ira Osmun, who believed in conservation through predator control. Eagles were fine birds, but the sheep must be protected. Babies, too.

"Mr. Osmun," Wilson Drago, the shotgun-bearing sado-child-appearing copilot asked, "have the eagles got any white babies lately?"

"No."

"Then?"

"Because we are exercising predator control."

"When was the last white baby snatched by eagles and dropped into the ocean?"

"Not eagles, Drago, eagle; it only takes one. As long as there is one eagle there is always the possibility of your losing your child."

"I haven't any child."

"If you did."

"But I haven't."

"Someone does."

"No one in the area does."

"If they did, there would be the possibility of their losing them."

"No one can say nay to that," Wilson Drago said. "When was the last time a child was snatched?"

"It must have been a long time ago."

"Before living memory?"

"Yes, even then, Drago, I believe the stories to be apocryphal."

"What's that mean?"

"Lies."

"Then why are we shooting the eagles?"

"Because city people don't care about sheep. City people care about babies. You tell the people in Albuquerque that their babies have an outside chance, any chance that their baby will be snatched up and the possibility that it will be dropped in the ocean, kerplunk, and they will let you kill eagles."

"How far is the ocean?"

"People don't care how far the ocean is; they care about their babies."

"True."

"It's that simple."

"When was the last lamb that was snatched up?"

"Yesterday."

"That's serious."

"You better believe it, Drago."

"Why are we hovering over his red hogan?"

"Because before we kill an eagle we got to make sure what Mary-Forge is up to."

"What was she up to last time you heard?"

"Shooting down helicopters."

"All by herself?"

"It only takes one shot."

"You know, I bet that's right."

"You better believe it, Drago."

"Is this where she lives?"

"No—this is the little red schoolhouse she uses to get the Indians to attack the whites."

"What happened to your other copilots?"

"They got scared and quit."

"The last one?"

"Scared and quit."

"Just because of one woman?"

"Yes. You're not scared of a woman, are you, Drago?"

"No, I mean yes."

"Which is it, yes or no?"

"Yes," Wilson Drago said.

Below in the red hogan that was shaped like a beehive with a hole on top for the smoke to come out, the Indians and Mary-Forge were getting ready to die on the spot.

"I'm not getting ready to die on the spot," Bull Who Looks Up said.

"You want to save the eagles, don't you?" Mary-Forge said.

"Let me think about that," Jesus Saves said.

"Pass me the gun," Mary-Forge said.

Now, from above in the copter the hogan below looked like a gun turret, a small fort defending the perimeter of Indian Country.

"Mary-Forge is an interesting problem," Ira Osmun said—shouted— above the *whack-whack-whack* of the rotors.

"Every woman is."

"But every woman doesn't end up living with the Indians, with the eagles."

"What causes that?"

"We believe the Indians and the eagles become their surrogate children."

"That they become a substitute for life."

"Oh? Why do you hate me?"

"What?"

"Why do you use such big words?"

"I'm sorry, Drago. Do you see any eagles?"

"No, but I see a gun."

"Where?"

"Coming out of the top of the hogan."

"Let Mary-Forge fire first."

"Why?"

"To establish a point of law. Then it's not between her eagles and my sheep."

"It becomes your ass or hers."

"Yes."

"But it could be my life."

"I've considered that, Drago."

"Thank you. Thank you very much," Wilson Drago said.

Sun, the golden eagle that was very carefully watching the two white animals that lived in the giant bird that went *whack-whack-whack,* was ready.

Today would be the day of death for Sun. His mate had been killed two days before. Without her the eaglets in the woven of yucca high basket nest would die. Today would be the day of death for Sun because, without a sure idea of himself, without purpose in life, an eagle would sooner destroy himself than remain on earth. The last day of Sun.

"Because," Mary-Forge said, and taking the weapon and jerking in a shell, "because I know, even though the Indians and us and the eagle, even though we have no chance ever, we can go through the motions of courage, compassion, and concern. Because we are Sun and men, too. Hello, Sun."

"Stop talking and aim carefully."

"Did I say something?"

"You made a speech."

"I'm sorry," Mary-Forge said.

"Aim carefully."

Mary-Forge was standing on the wide shoulders of an Indian named When Someone Dies He Is Remembered. All the other Indians who belonged in the little red schoolhouse stood around and below her in the dim and alive dust watching Mary-Forge revolve like a gun turret with her lever-operated Marlin .30-30 pointing out of the smoke hatch high up on the slow-turning and hard shoulders of When Someone Dies He Is Remembered.

"Why don't you shoot?" More Turquoise said. He almost whispered it, as though the great noise of the copter did not exist.

"The thing keeps bobbling," Mary-Forge shouted down to the Indians.

Looking through the gunsights she had to go up and down up and down to try and get a shot. She did not want to hit the cowboys. It would be good enough to hit the engine or the rotor blades. Why not hit the cowboys? Because there are always more cowboys. There are not many eagles left on the planet earth, there are several million cowboys. There are more cowboys than there are Indians. That's for sure. But what is important now is that if we give one eagle for one cowboy soon all the eagles will have disappeared from the earth and cowboys will be standing in your bed. No, the helicopter is scarce. They will not give one helicopter for one eagle. A helicopter costs too much money. How much? A quarter-million dollars, I bet. Hit them where their heart is. Hit them right in their helicopter.

But it danced. Now Mary-Forge noticed that although it was dancing it was going up and down with a rhythm. The thing to do is to wait until it hits bottom and then follow it up. She did and fired off a shot.

"Good girl," the Medicine Man said.

"That was close," Ira Osmun said to his shotgun, Wilson Drago. "Now that we know where Mary-Forge is we can chase the eagle."

Ira Osmun allowed the chopper to spurt up and away to tilt off at a weird angle so that it clawed its way sideways like a crab that flew, a piece of junk, of tin and chrome and gaudy paint, alien and obscene in the perfect pure blue New Mexican sky, an intruder in the path of sun. Now the chopper clawed its way to the aerie of Sun.

The eagle had watched it all happen. Sun had watched it happen many times now. Two days ago when they killed his mate was the last time. Sun looked down at his golden eagle chicks. The eaglets were absolute white, they would remain white and vulnerable for several months until the new feathers. But there was no more time. Sun watched the huge man junk bird clawing its way down the long valley that led to Mount Taylor. His home, his home and above all the homes of the Indians.

Like the Indians, the ancestors of Sun had one time roamed a virgin continent abloom with the glory of life, alive with fresh flashing streams, a smogless sky, all the world a sweet poem of life where all was beginning. Nothing ever ended. Now it was all ending. The eagle, Sun, did not prepare to defend himself. He would not defend himself. There was nothing now to defend. The last hour of Sun.

"Catch me," Mary-Forge shouted from the top of the hogan, and jumped. When she was caught by More Turquoise, she continued to shout, as the noise of the chopper was still there. "They've taken off for Mount Taylor to kill Sun. We've got to get on our horses and get our ass over there."

"Why?"

"To save Sun," Mary-Forge shouted. "Sun is the last eagle left in the county."

"But this is not a movie," the Medicine Man said. "We don't have to get on horses and gallop across the prairie. We can get in my pickup and drive there— quietly."

"On the road it will take two hours," Mary-Forge said. "And we'll need horses when we get there to follow the chopper."

"What would Dostoevski say about this?" the Medicine Man said.

"To hell with Dostoevski," Mary-Forge said.

Outside they slammed the saddles on the amazed Indian ponies, then threw themselves on and fled down the canyon, a stream of dust and light, a commingling of vivid flash and twirl so when they disappeared into the cottonwoods you held your breath until the phantoms, the abrupt magic of motion, appeared again on the Cabbrillo draw.

"Come on now, baby," Mary-Forge whispered to her horse Poco Mas. "What I said about Dostoevski I didn't mean. Poor Dostoevski. I meant seconds count. We didn't have time for a philosophical discussion. Come on now, baby, move good. Be good to me, baby, move good. Move good, baby. Move good. You can take that fence, baby. Take him! Good boy, baby. Good boy, Poco. Good boy. I'm sure the Medicine Man understands that when there are so few left, so few left Poco that there is not time for niceties. You'd think an Indian would understand that, wouldn't you? Still the Medicine Man is a strange Indian. A Freudian Medicine Man. But Bull Who Looks Up understands, look at him go. He's pulling ahead of us are you going to let him get away with that Poco?" Poco did not let the horse of Bull Who Looks Up stay ahead but passed him quickly, with Mary-Forge swinging her gun high and Bull Who Looks Up gesturing with his gun at the tin bird that crabbed across the sky.

"You see, Drago," Ira Osmun shouted to Wilson Drago, "we are the villains of the piece."

"What?"

"The bad guys."

"It's pretty hard to think of yourself as the bad guy, Mr. Osmun."

"Well, we are."

"Who are the good guys?"

"Mary-Forge."

"Screw me."

"No, she wouldn't do that because you're a bad guy. Because you kill eagles. People who never saw an eagle, never will see an eagle, never want to see an eagle, want eagles all over the place. Except the poor. The poor want sheep to eat. Did you ever hear of a poor person complaining about the lack of eagles? They have got an outfit of rich gentlemen called the Sierra Club. They egg on Indian-lovers like Mary-Forge to kill ranchers."

"Why?"

"They have nothing else to do."

"You think Mary-Forge actually has sex with the Indians?"

"Why else would she be on the reservation?"

"I never thought about that."

"Think about it."

"I guess you're right."

"Drago, what do you think about?"

"I don't think about eagles."

"What do you think about?"

"Ordinarily?"

"Yes."

"Like when I'm drinking?"

"Yes."

"Religion."

"Good, Drago, I like to hear you say that. Good. What religion?"

"They are all good. I guess Billy Graham is the best."

"Yes, if you're stupid."

"What?"

"Nothing, Drago. Keep your eye peeled for the eagle."

"You said I was stupid."

"I may have said the Sierra Club was stupid."

"Did you?"

"No, how could you be stupid and be that rich?"

"Why are they queer for eagles then?"

"They are for anything that is getting scarce. Indians, eagles, anything. Mary-Forge is against natural evolution, too."

"What's natural evolution mean?"

"When something is finished it's finished, forget it. We got a new evolution, the machine, this copter, a new bird."

"That makes sense."

"Remember we don't want to kill eagles."

"We have to."

"That's right."

The eagle that had to be killed, Sun, perched like an eagle on his aerie throne. A king, a keeper of one hundred square miles of Indian Country, an arbiter, a jury and judge, a shadow clock that had measured time for two thousand years in slow shadow circle and so now the earth, the Indians, the place, would be without reckoning, certainly without the serene majesty of Sun, without, and this is what is our epitaph and harbinger, without the gold of silence the long lonely shadow beneath silent wing replaced now by the *whack-whack-whack* of tin, proceeding with crablike crippled crawl—the sweet song of man in awkward crazy metallic and cockeyed pounce, approached Sun.

Sun looked down on the eaglets in the nest. The thing to do would be to glide away from the whack-bird away from the nest. To fight it out somewhere else. If he could tangle himself in the wings of the whack-bird, that would be the end of whack-bird. The end of Sun. Sun jumped off his aerie without movement, not abrupt or even peremptory but as though the reel of film had cut, and then proceeded to a different scene. The bird Sun, the eagle, the great golden glider moving across the wilds of purple mesa in air-fed steady no-beat, in hushed deadly amaze, seemed in funeral stateliness, mounting upward on invisible winds toward the other sun.

"If he climbs, we will climb with him, Drago. He is bound to run out of updrafts."

Wilson Drago slid open the door on his side and shifted the Harrington & Richardson pump gun into the ready position.

"How high will this thing climb, sir?"

"Ten thousand feet."

"The bird can climb higher than that."

"Yet he has to come down, Drago."

"How much fuel we got?"

"Fifty gallons."

"What are we consuming?"

"A gallon a minute."

"Shall I try a shot?"

"Yes."

Sun was spiraling upward in tight circles on a good rising current of air when the pellets of lead hit him. They hit like a gentle rain that gave him a quick lift. Sun was out of range. Both the copter and Sun were spiraling upward. The copter was gaining.

"Shall I try another shot?"

"Yes."

This time the lead pellets slammed into Sun like a hard rain and shoved him upward and crazy tilted him as a great ship will yaw in a sudden gust. Sun was still out of range.

Now the upward current of air ceased, collapsed under Sun abruptly and the copter closed the distance until Ira Osmun and Wilson Drago were alongside and looking into small yellow eyes as the great sailing ship of Sun coasted downward into deep sky.

"Shall I try a shot?"

"Yes."

Wilson Drago raised the Harrington & Richardson shotgun and pumped in a shell with a solid slam. He could almost touch Sun with the muzzle. The swift vessel of Sun sailed on as though expecting to take the broadside from the 12-gauge gun that would send him to the bottom—to the floor of earth.

"Now, Drago."

But the gliding ship of bird had already disappeared—folded its huge wing of sail and shot downward, down down down downward until just before earth it unleashed its enormous sail of wing and glided over the surface of earth—Indian Country. Down came the copter in quick chase.

There stood the Indians all in a row.

"Don't fire, men," Mary-Forge shouted, "until Sun has Passed."

As Sun sailed toward the Indians the shadow of Sun came first, shading each Indian separately. Now came the swifting Sun and each mounted Indian raised his gun in salute. Again separately and in the order which Sun arrived and passed, now the Indians leveled their guns to kill the whack-bird.

"Oh, this is great, Drago," Ira Osmun shouted, "the Indians want to fight."

"What's great about that?"

"It's natural to fight Indians."

"It is?"

"Yes."

"Well, I'll be."

"My grandfather would be proud of us now."

"Did he fight Indians?"

"He sure did. It's only a small part of the time the whites have been that they haven't fought Indians."

"Fighting has been hard on the Indians."

"That may well be, Drago, but it's natural."

"Why?"

"Because people naturally have a fear of strangers. It's called xenophobia. When you don't go along with nature you get into trouble. You suppress your natural instincts and that is dangerous. That's what's wrong with this country."

"It is? I wondered about that."

"There's nothing wrong with shooting Indians."

"I wondered about that."

"It's natural."

"No, Mr. Osmun there is something wrong."

"What's that?"

"Look. The Indians are shooting back."

Ira Osmun twisted the copter up and away. "Get out the rifle. We'll take care of the Indians."

"What about the eagle?"

"We've first got to take care of the Indians who are shooting at us and that girl who is shooting at us."

"Is she crazy?"

"Why else would she have intercourse with the Indians?"

"You mean screwing them?"

"Yes."

"She could have all sorts of reasons. We don't even know that she is screwing them. Maybe we are screwing the Indians."

"Drago, we discussed this before and decided that Mary-Forge was."

"What if she is?"

"Drago, you can't make up your mind about anything. You're being neurotic. When you don't understand why you do something you're being neurotic."

"I am?"

"Yes, get out the rifle."

"I still think it's her business if she is queer for Indians and eagles."

"But not if she shoots at us when she's doing it; that's neurotic."

"You're right there, Mr. Osmun."

"Get the rifle."

"O.K."

"You know, Drago, people, particularly people who love the Indians, are suppressing a need to kill them. It's called a love-hate relationship."

"It is? You can stop talking now, Mr. Osmun. I said I'd get the rifle."

Below the helicopter that circled in the brilliant, eye-hurting, New Mexican day, Mary-Forge told the Indians that the copter would be back, that the ranchers would not fight the eagle while being fired on by Indians. "The ranchers will not make the same mistake Custer did."

"What was that?"

"Fight on two fronts. Custer attacked the Sioux before he finished off Sitting Bull. We are the Sioux."

"We are? That's nice," the Navajo Bull Who Looks Up said. "When do we get out of this class?"

"We never do," Jesus Saves said.

"Get your ass behind the rocks!" the teacher Mary-Forge shouted. "Here they come!"

The copter flew over and sprayed the rocks with M-16 automatic rifle fire.

"That should teach the teacher that we outgun them, Drago," Ira Osmun said. "Now we can get the eagle!"

The golden eagle called Sun spiraled upward again, its wings steady, wild, sure, in the glorious and rapt quietude of the blue, blue, blue, New Mexico morning, a golden eagle against the blue, a kind of heliograph, and a flashing jewel in the perfect and New Mexico sea of sky. The gold eagle, recapitulent, lost then found as it twirled steady and upward in the shattered light, followed by the tin bird.

Sun knew that he must gain height. All the power of maneuver lay in getting above the tin bird. He knew, too, and from experience that the tin bird could only go a certain height. He knew, too, and from experience that the air current he rode up could collapse at once and without warning. He knew, too, and from the experience of several battles now with the bird of tin that the enemy was quick and could spit things out that could pain then kill. All this he knew from experience. But the tin bird was learning, too.

The tin bird jerked upward after the golden eagle. The golden eagle, Sun, wandered upward as though searching and lost. A last and final tryst in the list of Indian Country because now always until now, until now no one killed everything that moved. You always had a chance. Now there was no change. Soon there would be no Sun.

"Remember, Drago, I've got to stay away from him or above him—he can take us with him. The last time when we got his mate he almost took us with him; I just barely got away when he attacked the rotors—when the rotor goes we go, Drago—we fall like a rock, smash like a glass. They will pick you up with a dustpan."

"Who?"

"Those Indians down there."

"Mr. Osmun, I don't want to play this game."

"You want to save the sheep, don't you?"

"No."

"Why not?"

"I don't have any sheep to save."

"You don't have any sheep, you don't have any children. But you have pride."

"I don't know."

"Then fire when I tell you to and you'll get some."

"I don't know."

"Do you want eagles to take over the country?"

"I don't know."

"Eagles and Indians at one time controlled this whole country, Drago; you couldn't put out a baby or a lamb in my grandfather's time without an Indian or an eagle would grab it. Now we got progress. Civilization. That means a man is free to go about his business."

"It does?"

"Yes, now that we got them on those ropes we can't let them go, Drago."

"We can't?"

"No, that would be letting civilized people down. It would be letting my grandfather down. What would I say to him?"

"Are you going to see your grandfather?"

"No, he's dead. We'll be dead, too, Drago, if you don't shoot. That eagle will put us down there so those Indians will pick us up with a dustpan. You don't want that, do you?"

"I don't know."

"You better find out right smart or I'll throw you out of this whack-bird myself."

"Would you?"

"Someone's got to live, Drago. The eagle doesn't want to live."

"Why do you say that?"

"He knew we were after him. He knew we would get him; he could have left the country. He could have flown north to Canada. He would be protected there."

"Maybe he thinks this is his country."

"No, this is a civilized country. Will you shoot the eagle?"

"No."

"I like the eagle and the Indians as well as the next man, Drago, but we have to take sides. It's either my sheep or them. Whose side are you on, Drago?"

"I guess I'm on theirs."

The helicopter was much lighter now without Drago in it. The copter handled much better and was able to gain on the eagle.

Ira Osmun continued to talk to Wilson Drago as though he were still there. Wilson Drago was one of Ira Osmun's sheepherders and should have taken a more active interest in sheep.

"The way I see it, Drago, if you wouldn't defend me, the eagle would have brought us both down. It was only a small push I gave you, almost a touch as you were leaning out. By lightening the plane you made a small contribution to civilization.

"We all do what we can, Drago, and you have contributed your bit. If there is anything I can't stand, it's an enemy among my sheep."

The copter continued to follow the eagle up but now more lightsome and quick with more alacrity and interest in the chase.

The Indians on the ground were amazed to see the white man come down. Another dropout. "Poor old Wilson Drago. We knew him well. Another man who couldn't take progress—civilization. Many times has Drago shot at us while we were stealing his sheep. We thought anyone might be a dropout but not Wilson Drago. It shows you how tough it's getting on the white reservation. They're killing each other. Soon there will be nothing left but Indians."

"Good morning, Indian."

"Good morning, Indian."

"Isn't it a beautiful day. Do you notice there is nothing left but us Indians?"

"And one eagle."

The Indians were making all these strange observations over what remained of the body of the world's leading sheepherder, Wilson Drago.

"He created quite a splash."

"And I never thought he would make it."

"The last time I saw him drunk in Gallup I thought he was coming apart, but this is a surprise."

"I knew he had it in him, but I never expected it to come out all at once."

"I can't find his scalp. What do you suppose he did with it? Did he hide it?"

"The other white man got it."

"I bet he did."

"They don't care about Indians anymore."

"No, when they drop in on you they don't bring their scalp."

"Please, please," Mary-Forge said, "the man is dead."

"Man? Man? I don't see any man, just a lot of blood and shit."

"Well, there is a man, or was a man."

"Well, there's nothing now," Bull Who Looks Up said, "not even a goddamn scalp."

"Well, Drago's in the white man's heaven," More Turquoise said. "On streets of gold tending his flock."

"And shooting eagles."

"Drago's going higher and higher to white man's heaven, much higher than his what-do-you-call-it—"

"Helicopter."

"—can go," Jesus Saves said.

"I don't like all this sacrilege," Mary-Forge said. "Remember I am a Christian."

"What?"

"I was brought up in the Christian tradition."

"Now you're hedging," When Someone Dies He Is Remembered said.

Ah, these Indians, Mary-Forge thought, how did I get involved? And she said aloud, "Once upon a time I was young and innocent."

"Print that!" Bull Who Looks Up said.

"We better get higher up the mountain," Mary-Forge shouted at the Indians, "so when Osmun closes on the eagle we can get a better shot."

"O.K., Teacher."

"There's only one white guy left," she said.

"I find that encouraging if true," More Turquoise said.

"Load your rifles and pull your horses after you," Mary-Forge said.

"My Country 'Tis of Thee," Ira Osmun hummed as he swirled the copter in pursuit of the eagle. You didn't die in vain, Drago. That is, you were not vain, you were a very modest chap. We can climb much higher without you, Drago. I am going to get the last eagle this time, Drago. I think he's reached the top of his climb.

Sun watched the tin whack-bird come up. The tin bird came up *whack-whack-whack,* its wings never flapping just turning in a big circle. What did it eat? How did it mate? Where did it come from? From across the huge water on a strong wind. The evil wind. Sun circled seeing that he must get higher, the tin bird was coming up quicker today. Sun could see the people he always saw below. The people who lived in his country, filing up the mountain. They seemed to be wanting to get closer to him now.

Ira Osmun felt then saw all the Indians in the world firing at him from below. How are you going to knock down an eagle when all the Indians in the world are firing at you from Mount Taylor? It was Mary-Forge who put them up to it, for sure. An Indian would not have the nerve to shoot at a white man. You don't have to drop down and kill all the Indians. They—the people in the East—who have no sheep would call that a massacre. Indians are very popular at the moment. If you simply knock off Mary-Forge, that would do the trick. Women are not very popular at the moment. Why? Because they have a conspiracy against men. You didn't know that? It's true, Drago. The woman used to be happy to be on the bottom. Now she wants to be on the top.

No?

Did you say something, Drago?

I thought I heard someone say something. I must have been hit. My mind must be wandering. What was I saying? It's part of the conspiracy. What's that mean? Something. I must have been hit. What was I doing? Oh yes, I was going to get Mary-Forge—the girl who is queer for Indians and eagles. The eagle can wait.

And Ira Osmun put the copter in full throttle, then cradled the M-16 automatic rifle in his left arm with muzzle pointing out the door. With his right hand he placed the copter in a swift power glide down.

Sun saw the obscene tin bird go into its dive down. Now would be a chance to get it while the tin bird was busy hunting its prey on the ground. Sun took one more final look over the aerie nest to check the birds. The eaglets were doing fine. Drawing the enemy away from the nest had been successful. The eaglets craned their necks at the familiar shape before Sun folded his great span of wings and shot down on top of the tin bird.

Mary-Forge mounted on Poco Mas saw the tin bird coming, the M-16 quicking out nicks of flame. She could not get the Indians to take cover. The Indians had placed their horses behind the protection of the boulders and were all standing out in the open and were blasting away at the zooming-in copter. Mary-Forge was still shouting at the Indians, but they would not take cover. They have seen too many goddamn movies, Mary-Forge thought, they have read too many books. They are stupid, stupid, stupid, dumb, dumb, dumb Indians. How stupid and how dumb can you get? They want to save the eagle. Standing exposed naked to the machine gun. The stupid Indians. Mary-Forge raised her rifle at the zooming-in copter in a follow-me gesture, then took off in a straight line, the horse pounding, and the flame-nicking copter followed, so did Sun. So now there were three.

The tin bird was alive in flame all at once, something had hit the fuel tank and all of everything exploded in fire, the rotors of the tin bird were still turning and fanning the flame so that it was not only a streaking meteor across Indian Country but at once a boil of fire that shot downward from the terrific draft laying a torch of flame across the desert so that the mesquite and sagebrush became a steady line of flame ending where the tin whack-bird hit into the rocks and went silent in a grand tower of fire.

"It was Sun that did it," More Turquoise said.

The death of Sun.

All of the Indians and Mary-Forge were standing around the dying fire of the big whack-bird in the smoke that shrouded the death of Sun.

"When an eagle," the Medicine Man said, "—when a true bird has no hope—"

"Yes?"

"When the eagle is no more," the Medicine Man said.

"Yes?"

"Then we are no more."

"Yes," every person shrouded in smoke said.

Look up there. It was within three months when Someone Dies He Is Remembered remembered that an eagle named Star by the Medicine Man sailed in one beginning night to reclaim the country of Sun. Now Star's wide shadow passed over the dead tin whack-bird then he, the great eagle Star, settled on his throne aerie in awful and mimic splendor, and again admonitory, serene—regal and doomed?

QUESTIONS

1. How does the first paragraph foreshadow and parallel the final paragraph? Is the ending happy? unhappy? inconclusive?

2. Who is Feodor Dostoevski? Why does Mary-Forge call Dostoevski a Navaho? Is her explanation reasonable? Does this verbal exchange make sense or is it absurd?

3. Relate the conversation between Ira Osmun and Wilson Drago to esthetic distance, to meaning, to tone.

4. Identify the point of view. Discuss the relationship between point of view and tone.

5. Examine how rhythm is related to meaning in the following passage:
   Outside they slammed the saddles on the amazed Indian ponies, then threw themselves on and fled down the canyon, a stream of dust and light, a commingling of vivid flash and twirl so when they disappeared into the cottonwoods you held your breath until the phantoms, the abrupt magic of motion, appeared again on the Cabbrillo draw.

6. Explain how the sound of the following passage enhances its meaning:
   But the gliding ship of bird had already disappeared—folded its huge wing of sail and shot downward, down down down downward until just before earth it unleashed its enormous sail of wing and glided over the surface of earth—Indian Country. Down came the copter in quick chase.

7. Find descriptive passages in which the eagle Sun is assigned human characteristics. Is the anthropomorphism legitimate here, or is the author guilty of sentimentality? Is there a common denominator among Sun, the Navahos, women?

8. Examine the ways that popular myth shapes the story's meaning.

ISAAC BASHEVIS SINGER

Old Love

Translation by Joseph Singer

Harry Bendiner awoke at five with the feeling that as far as he was concerned the night was finished and he wouldn't get any more sleep. Actually, he woke up a dozen times every night. He had undergone an operation for his prostate years before, but this hadn't relieved the constant pressure on his bladder. He would sleep an hour or less, then wake up with the need to void. Even his dreams centered on this urge. He got out of bed and padded to the bathroom on shaky legs. On the way back he stepped out onto the balcony of his eleventh-story condominium. To the left he could see the skyscrapers of Miami, to the right the rumbling sea. The air had turned a bit cooler during the night, but it was still tropically tepid. It smelled of dead fish, oil, and perhaps of oranges as well. Harry stood there for a long while enjoying the breeze from the ocean on his moist forehead. Even though Miami Beach had become a big city, he imagined that he could feel the nearness of the Everglades, the smells and vapors of their vegetation and swamps. Sometimes a seagull would awake in the night screeching. It happened that the waves threw out onto the beach the carcass of a barracuda or even that of a small whale. Harry Bendiner looked off in the direction of Hollywood. How long was it since the whole area had been undeveloped? Within a few years a wasteland had been transformed into a settlement crowded with hotels, condominiums, restaurants, supermarkets, and banks. The street lights and neon signs dimmed the stars in the sky. Cars raced along even in the middle of the night. Where were all these people hurrying to before dawn? Didn't they ever sleep? What kind of force drove them on? "Well, it's no longer my world. Once you pass eighty, you're as good as a corpse."

He leaned his hand on the railing and tried to reconstruct the dream he had been having. He recalled only that all those who had appeared in the dream were now dead—the men and the women both. Dreams obviously didn't acknowledge death. In his dreams, his three wives were still alive, and so was his son, Bill, and his daughter, Sylvia. New York, his home town in Poland, and Miami Beach merged into one. He, Harry or Hershel, was both an adult and a cheder boy.

He closed his eyes for a moment. Why was it impossible to remember dreams? He could recall every detail of events that had happened seventy and even seventy-five years ago, but tonight's dreams dissolved like foam. Some force made sure that not a trace of them remained. A third of a person's life died before he went to his grave.

After a while Harry sat down on the plastic chaise on the balcony. He looked toward the sea, to the east, where day would soon be dawning. There was a time when he went swimming the first thing in the morning, particularly during the summer months, but he no longer had the desire to do such things. The newspapers occasionally printed accounts of sharks attacking swimmers, and there were other sea creatures whose bites caused serious complications. For him it now sufficed to take a warm bath.

His thoughts turned to matters of business. He knew full well that money couldn't help him; still, one couldn't constantly brood about the fact that everything was vanity of vanities. It was easier to think about practical matters. Stocks and bonds rose or fell. Dividends and other earnings had to be deposited in the bank and marked down in an account book for tax purposes. Telephone and electric bills and the maintenance of the apartment had to be paid. One day a week a woman came to do his cleaning and press his shirts and underwear. Occasionally he had to have a suit dry-cleaned and shoes repaired. He received letters that he had to answer. He wasn't involved with a synagogue all year, but on Rosh Hashanah and Yom Kippur he had to have a place to worship, and because of this he received appeals to help Israel, yeshivas, Talmud Torahs, old-age homes, and hospitals. Each day he got a pile of junk mail, and before he discarded it he had to open and glance at it at least.

Since he had resolved to live out his years without a wife or even a housekeeper, he had to arrange for his meals, and every other day he went shopping at the local supermarket. Pushing his cart through the aisles, he selected such items as milk, cottage cheese, fruit, canned vegetables, chopped meat, occasionally some mushrooms, a jar of borscht or gefilte fish. He certainly could have permitted himself the luxury of a maid, but some of the maids were thieves. And what would he do with himself if other people waited on him? He remembered a saying from the Gemara that slothfulness led to madness. Fussing over the electric stove in the kitchen, going to the bank, reading the newspaper—particularly the financial section—and spending an hour or two at the office of Merrill Lynch watching the quotations from the New York Exchange flash by on the board lifted his spirits. Recently he had had a television set installed, but he rarely watched it.

His neighbors in the condominium often inquired maliciously why he did things himself that others could do for him. It was known that he was rich. They offered him advice and asked him questions: Why didn't he settle in Israel? Why didn't he go to a hotel in the mountains during the summer? Why didn't he get married? Why didn't he hire a secretary? He had acquired the reputation of a miser. They constantly reminded him that "you can't take it with you"—as if this were some startling revelation. For this reason he stopped attending the tenants' meetings and their parties. Everyone tried in one way or another to get something out of him, but no one would have given him a penny if he needed it. A few years ago, he boarded a bus from Miami Beach to Miami and found he was two cents short of the fare. All he had with him was twenty-dollar bills. No one volunteered either to give him the two cents or to change one of his bills, and the driver made him get off.

The truth was, in no hotel could he feel as comfortable as he did in his own home. The meals served in hotels were too plentiful for him and not of the kind that he needed. He alone could see to it that his diet excluded salt, cholesterol, spices. Besides, plane and train rides were too taxing for a man of his delicate health. Nor did it make any sense to remarry at his age. Younger women demanded sex, and he hadn't the slightest interest in an old woman. Being what he was, he was condemned to live alone and to die alone.

A reddish glow had begun to tinge the eastern sky, and Harry went to the bathroom. He stood for a moment studying his image in the mirror—sunken cheeks, a bare skull with a few tufts of white hair, a pointed Adam's apple, a nose whose tip turned down like a parrot's beak. The pale-blue eyes were set somewhat off-center, one higher than the other, and expressed both weariness and traces of youthful ardor. He had once been a virile man. He had had wives and love affairs. He had a stack of love letters and photographs lying about somewhere.

Harry Bendiner hadn't come to America penniless and uneducated, like the other immigrants. He had attended the study house in his home town until the age of nineteen; he knew Hebrew and had secretly read newspapers and worldly books. He had taken lessons in Russian, Polish, and even German. Here in America he had attended Cooper Union for two years in the hope of becoming an engineer, but he had fallen in love with an American girl, Rosalie Stein, and married her, and her father, Sam Stein, had taken him into the construction business. Rosalie died of cancer at the age of thirty, leaving him with two small children. Even as the money came in to him so did death take from him. His son, Bill, a surgeon, died at forty-six, of a heart attack, leaving two children, neither of whom wanted to be Jewish. Their mother, a Christian, lived somewhere in Canada with another man. Harry's daughter, Sylvia, got the very same type of cancer as her mother, and at exactly the same age. Sylvia left no children. Harry refused to sire any more generations, even though his second wife, Edna, pleaded that he have a child or two with her.

Yes, the Angel of Death had taken everything from him. At first his grandchildren called him occasionally from Canada and sent him a card for the New Year. But now he never heard from them, and he had cut them out of his will.

Harry shaved and hummed a melody—where it had come from he didn't know. Was it something he had heard on television, or a tune revived in his memory from Poland? He had no ear for music and sang everything off-key, but he had retained the habit of singing in the bathroom. His toilet took a long time. For years the pills he took to relieve constipation had had no effect, and every other day he gave himself an enema—a long and arduous process for a man in his eighties. He tried to do calisthenics in the bathtub, raising his skinny legs and splashing his hands in the water as if they were paddles. These were all measures to lengthen life, but even as Harry performed them he asked himself, "Why go on living?" What flavor did his existence possess? No, his life made no sense whatever—but did that of his neighbors make more sense? The condominium was full of old people, all well off, many rich. Some of the men couldn't walk, or dragged their feet; some of the women leaned on crutches. A number suffered from arthritis and Parkinson's disease. This wasn't a building but a hospital. People died, and he didn't find out about it until weeks or months afterward. Although he had been among the first tenants in the condominium, he seldom recognized anybody. He didn't go to the pool and he didn't play cards. Men and women greeted him in the elevator and at the supermarket, but he didn't know who any of them were. From time to time someone asked him, "How are you, Mr. Bendiner?" And he usually replied, "How *can* you be at my age? Each day is a gift."

This summer day began like all the others. Harry prepared his breakfast in the kitchen—Rice Krispies with skimmed milk, and Sanka sweetened with saccharin. At about nine-thirty, he took the elevator down to get the mail. A day didn't go by that he didn't receive a number of checks, but this day brought a bounty. The stocks had fallen, but the companies kept paying the dividends as usual. Harry got money from buildings on which he held mortgages, from rents, bonds, and all kinds of business ventures that he barely remembered. An insurance company paid him an annuity. For years he had been getting a monthly check from Social Security. This morning's yield came to over eleven thousand dollars. True, he would have to withhold a great part of this for taxes, but it still left him with some five thousand dollars for himself. While he totalled up the figures, he deliberated: Should he go to the office of Merrill Lynch and see what was happening on the Exchange? No, there was no point to it. Even if the stocks rose early in the morning, the day would end in losses. "The market is completely crazy," he mumbled to himself. He had considered it an iron rule that inflation always went along with a bullish market, not with a bearish market. But now both the dollar *and* the stocks were collapsing. Well, you could never be sure about anything except death.

Around eleven o'clock, he went down to deposit the checks. The bank was a small one; all the employees knew him and said good morning. He had a safe-deposit box there, where he kept his valuables and jewelry. It so happened that all three of his wives had left him everything. He didn't know himself exactly how much he was worth, but it couldn't be less than five million dollars. Still, he walked down the street in a shirt and trousers that any pauper could afford and a cap and shoes he had worn for years. He poked with his cane and took tiny steps. Once in a while he cast a glance backward. Maybe someone was following him. Maybe some crook had found out how rich he was and was scheming to kidnap him. Although the day was bright and the street full of people, no one would interfere if he was grabbed, forced into a car, and dragged off to some ruin or cave. No one would pay ransom for him.

After he had concluded his business at the bank, he turned back toward home. The sun was high in the sky and poured down a blazing fire. Women stood in the shade of canopies looking at dresses, shoes, stockings, brassieres, and bathing suits in the store windows. Their faces expressed indecision—to buy or not to buy? Harry glanced at the windows. What could he buy there? There wasn't anything he could desire. From now until five, when he would prepare his dinner, he needed absolutely nothing. He knew precisely what he would do when he got home—take a nap on the sofa.

Thank God, no one kidnapped him, no one held him up, no one had broken into his apartment. The air-conditioner was working, and so was the plumbing in the bathroom. He took off his shoes and stretched out on the sofa.

Strange, he still daydreamed; he fantasized about unexpected successes, restored powers, masculine adventures. The brain wouldn't accept old age. It teemed with the same passions it had in his youth. Harry often said to his brain, "Don't be stupid. It's too late for everything. You have nothing to hope for anymore." But the brain was so constituted that it went on hoping nonetheless. Who was it who said it: A man takes his hopes into the grave.

He had dozed off and was awakened by a jangling at the door. He became alarmed. No one ever came to see him. It must be the exterminator, he decided. He opened the door the length of the chain and saw a small woman with reddish cheeks, yellow eyes, and a high pompadour of blond hair the color of straw. She wore a white blouse.

Harry opened the door, and the woman said in a foreign-accented English, "I hope I haven't wakened you. I'm your new neighbor on the left. I wanted to introduce myself to you. My name is Mrs. Ethel Brokeles. A funny name, eh? That was my late husband's name. My maiden name is Goldman."

Harry gazed at her in astonishment. His neighbor on the left had been an old woman living alone. He remembered her name—Mrs. Halpert. He asked, "What happened to Mrs. Halpert?"

"The same as happens to everybody," the woman replied smugly.

"When did it happen? I didn't know anything about it."

"It's more than five months already."

"Come in, come in. People die and you don't even know," Harry said.

"She was a nice woman . . . kept herself at a distance."

"I didn't know her. I bought the apartment from her daughter."

"Please have a seat. I don't even have anything to offer you. I have a bottle of liqueur somewhere, but—"

"I don't need any refreshments and I don't drink liqueur. Not in the middle of the day. May I smoke?"

"Certainly, certainly."

The woman sat down on the sofa. She snapped a fancy lighter expertly and lit her cigarette. She wore red nail polish, and Harry noticed a huge diamond on one of her fingers.

The woman asked, "You live here alone?"

"Yes, alone."

"I'm alone, too. What can you do? I lived with my husband some thirty years, and we didn't have one bad day. Our life together was all sunshine without a single cloud. Suddenly he passed away and left me alone and miserable. The New York climate is unhealthy for me. I suffer from rheumatism. I'll have to live out my years here."

"Did you buy the apartment furnished?" Harry asked in businesslike fasion.

"Everything. The daughter wanted nothing for herself besides the dresses and linen. She turned it all over to me for a song. I wouldn't have had the patience to go out and buy furniture and dishes. Do you live here a long time already?"

The woman posed one question after another, and Harry answered them willingly. She looked comparatively young—no more than fifty, or possibly even younger. He brought her an ashtray and put a glass of lemonade and a plate of cookies on the coffee table before her. Two hours went by, but he hardly noticed. Ethel Brokeles crossed her legs, and Harry cast glances at her round knees. She had switched to a Polish-accented Yiddish. She exuded the intimate air of a relative. Something within Harry exulted. It could be nothing else but that Heaven had acceded to his secret desires. Only now, as he listened to her, did he realize how lonely he had been all these years, how oppressed by the fact that he seldom exchanged a word with anyone. Even having her for a neighbor was better than nothing. He grew youthful in her presence, and loquacious. He told her about his three wives, the tragedies that had befallen his children. He even mentioned that, following the death of his first wife, he had had a sweetheart.

The woman said, "You don't have to make excuses. A man is a man."

"I've grown old."

"A man is never old. I had an uncle in Wloclawek who was eighty when he married a twenty-year-old girl, and she bore him three children."

"Wloclawek? That's near Kowal, my home town."

"I know. I've been to Kowal. I had an aunt there."

The woman glanced at her wristwatch. "It's one o'clock. Where are you having lunch?"

"Nowhere. I only eat breakfast and dinner."

"Are you on a diet?"

"No, but at my age—"

"Stop talking about your age!" the woman scolded him. "You know what? Come over to my place and we'll have lunch together. I don't like to eat by myself. For me, eating alone is even worse than sleeping alone."

"Really, I don't know what to say. What did I do to deserve this?"

"Come, come; don't talk nonsense. This is America, not Poland. My refrigerator is stuffed with goodies. I throw out more than I eat, may I be forgiven."

The woman used Yiddish expressions that Harry hadn't heard in at least sixty years. She took his arm and led him to the door. He didn't have to go more than a few steps. By the time he had locked his door she had opened hers. The apartment he went into was larger than his and brighter. There were pictures on the walls, fancy lamps, bric-a-brac. The windows looked out directly at the ocean. On the table stood a vase of flowers. The air in Harry's apartment smelled of dust, but here the air was fresh. "She wants something; she has some ulterior motive," Harry told himself. He recalled what he had read in the newspapers about female cheats who swindled fortunes out of men and out of other women, too. The main thing was to promise nothing, to sign nothing, not to hand over even a single penny.

She seated him at a table, and from the kitchen soon issued the bubbling sound of a percolator and the smell of fresh rolls, fruit, cheese, and coffee. For the first time in years Harry felt an appetite in the middle of the day. After a while they both sat down to lunch.

Between one bite and the next, the woman took a drag from a cigarette. She complained, "Men run after me, but when it comes down to brass tacks they're all only interested in how much money I have. As soon as they start talking about money I break up with them. I'm not poor; I'm even—knock wood—wealthy. But I don't want anyone to take me for my money."

"Thank God I don't need anyone's money," Harry said. "I've got enough even if I live a thousand years."

"That's good."

Gradually they began to discuss their finances, and the woman enumerated her possessions. She owned buildings in Brooklyn and on Staten Island; she had stocks and bonds. Based on what she said and the names she mentioned, Harry decided that she was telling the truth. She had, here in Miami, a checking account and a safe-deposit box in the very same bank as Harry's. Harry estimated that she was worth at least a million, or maybe more. She served him food with the devotion of a daughter or wife. She talked of what he should and shouldn't eat. Such miracles had occurred to him in his younger years. Women had met him, grown instantly intimate, and stuck with him, never to leave again. But that such a thing should happen to him at his age seemed like a dream. He asked abruptly, "Do you have children?"

"I have a daughter, Sylvia. She lives all alone in a tent in British Columbia."

"Why in a tent? My daughter's name was Sylvia, too. You yourself could be my daughter," he added, not knowing why he should have said such a thing.

"Nonsense. What are years? I always liked a man to be a lot older than me. My husband, may he rest in peace, was twenty years older, and the life we had together I would wish for every Jewish daughter."

"I've surely got forty years on you," Harry said.

The woman put down her spoon. "How old do you take me for?"

"Around forty-five," Harry said, knowing she was older.

"Add another twelve years and you've got it."

"You don't look it."

"I had a good life with my husband. I could get anything out of him—the moon, the stars, nothing was too good for his Ethel. That's why after he died I became melancholy. Also, my daughter was making me sick. I spent a fortune on psychiatrists, but they couldn't help me. Just as you see me now, I stayed seven months in an institution, a clinic for nervous disorders. I had a breakdown and I didn't want to live anymore. They had to watch me day and night. He was calling me from his grave. I want to tell you something, but don't misunderstand me."

"What is it?"

"You remind me of my husband. That's why—"

"I'm eighty-two," Harry said and instantly regretted it. He could have easily subtracted five years. He waited a moment, then added, "If I was ten years younger I'd make you a proposition."

Again he regretted his words. They had issued from his mouth as if of their own volition. He was still bothered by the fear of falling into the hands of a gold-digger.

The woman looked at him inquisitively and cocked an eyebrow. "Since I decided to live, I'll take you just as you are."

"How is this possible? How can it be?" Harry asked himself again and again. They spoke of getting married and of breaking through the wall that divided their apartments to make them into one. His bedroom was next to hers. She revealed the details of her financial situation to him. She was worth about a million and a half. Harry had already told her how much he had. He asked, "What will we do with so much money?"

"I wouldn't know what to do with money myself," the woman replied, "but together we'll take a trip around the world. We'll buy an apartment in Tel Aviv or Tiberias. The hot springs there are good for rheumatism. With me beside you, you'll live a long time. I guarantee you a hundred years, if not more."

"It's all in God's hands," Harry said, amazed at his own words. He wasn't religious. His doubts about God and His Providence had intensified over the years. He often said that, after what had happened to the Jews in Europe, one had to be a fool to believe in God.

Ethel stood up and so did he. They hugged and kissed. He pressed her close and youthful urges came throbbing back within him.

She said, "Wait till we've stood under the wedding canopy."

It struck Harry that he had heard these words before, spoken in the same voice. But when? And from whom? All three of his wives had been American-born and wouldn't have used this expression. Had he dreamed it? Could a person foresee the future in a dream? He bowed his head and pondered. When he looked up he was astounded. Within those few seconds the woman's appearance had undergone a startling transformation. She had moved away from him and he hadn't noticed it. Her face had grown pale, shrunken, and as if aged. Her hair seemed to him to have become suddenly dishevelled. She gazed at him sidelong with a dull, sad, even stern expression. Did I insult her or what, he wondered. He heard himself ask, "Is something wrong? Don't you feel well?"

"No, but you'd better go back to your own place now," she said in a voice that seemed alien, harsh, and impatient. He wanted to ask her the reason for the sudden change that had come over her, but a long-forgotten (or a never-forgotten) pride asserted itself. With women, you never knew where you stood anyhow. Still, he asked, "When will we see each other?"

"Not today anymore. Maybe tomorrow," she said after some hesitation.

"Goodbye. Thanks for the lunch."

She didn't even bother to escort him to the door. Inside his own apartment again, he thought, Well, she changed her mind. He was overcome with a feeling of shame—for himself and for her too. Had she been playing a game with him? Had malicious neighbors arranged to make a fool of him? His apartment struck him as half empty. I won't eat dinner, he decided. He felt a pressure in his stomach. "At my age one shouldn't make a fool of oneself," he murmured. He lay down on the sofa and dozed off, and when he opened his eyes again it was dark outside. Maybe she'll ring my doorbell again. Maybe I should call her? She had given him her phone number. Though he had slept, he woke up exhausted. He had letters to answer, but he put if off until morning. He went out onto the balcony. One side of his balcony faced a part of hers. They could see each other here and even converse, if she should still be interested in him. The sea splashed and foamed. There was a freighter far in the distance. A jet roared in the sky. A single star that no street lights or neon signs could dim appeared above. It's a good thing one can see at least one star. Otherwise one might forget that the sky exists altogether.

He sat on the balcony waiting for her to possibly show up. What could she be thinking? Why had her mood changed so abruptly? One minute she was as tender and talkative as a bride in love; a moment later she was a stranger.

Harry dozed off again, and when he awoke it was late in the evening. He wasn't sleepy, and he wanted to go downstairs for the evening edition of the morning paper, with the reports of the New York Exchange; instead he went to lie down on his bed. He had drunk a glass of tomato juice before and swallowed a pill. Only a thin wall separated him from Ethel, but walls possessed a power of their own. Perhaps this is the reason some people prefer to live in a tent, he thought. He assumed that his broodings would keep him from sleeping, but he quickly nodded off. He awoke with pressure on his chest. What time was it? The luminous dial on his wristwatch showed that he had slept two hours and a quarter. He had dreamed, but he couldn't remember what. He retained only the impression of nocturnal horrors. He raised his head. Was she asleep or awake? He couldn't hear even a rustle from her apartment.

He slept again and was awakened this time by the sound of many people talking, doors slamming, footsteps in the corridor, and running. He had always been afraid of fire. He read newspaper accounts of old people burning to death in old-age homes, hospitals, hotels. He got out of bed, put on his slippers and robe, and opened the door to the hall. There was no one there. Had he imagined it? He closed the door and went out onto the balcony. No, not a trace of firemen below. Only people coming home late, going out to night clubs, making drunken noise. Some of the condominium tenants sublet their apartments in the summer to South Americans. Harry went back to bed. It was quiet for a few minutes; then he again heard a din in the corridor and the sound of men's and women's voices. Something had happened, but what? He had an urge to get up and take another look, but he didn't. He lay there tense. Suddenly he heard a buzzing from the house phone in the kitchen. When he lifted the receiver, a man's voice said, "Wrong number." Harry had turned on the fluorescent light in the kitchen and the glare dazzled him. He opened the refrigerator, took out a jug of sweetened tea, and poured himself half a glass, not knowing whether he did this because he was thirsty or to buoy his spirits. Soon afterward, he had to urinate, and he went to the bathroom.

At that moment, his doorbell rang, and the sound curtailed his urge. Maybe robbers had broken into the building? The night watchman was an old man and hardly a match for intruders. Harry couldn't decide whether to go to the door or not. He stood over the toilet bowl trembling. *These might be my final moments on earth* flashed through his mind. "God Almighty, take pity on me," he murmured. Only now did he remember that he had a peephole in the door through which he could see the hall outside. How could I have forgotten about it, he wondered. I must be getting senile.

He walked silently to the door, raised the cover of the peephole, and looked out. He saw a white-haired woman in a robe. He recognized her; it was his neighbor on the right. In a second, everything became clear to him. She had a paralyzed husband, and something had happened to him. He opened the door. The old woman held out an unstamped envelope.

"Excuse me, Mr. Bendiner, the woman next door left this envelope by your door. Your name is on it."

"What woman?"

"On the left. She committed suicide."

Harry Bendiner felt his guts constrict and within seconds his belly grew as tight as a drum.

"The blond woman?"

"Yes."

"What did she do?"

"Threw herself out the window."

Harry held out his hand and the old woman gave him the envelope.

"Where is she?" he asked.

"They took her away."

"Dead?"

"Yes, dead."

"My God!"

"It's already the third such incident here. People lose their minds in America."

Harry's hand shook, and the envelope fluttered as if caught in a wind. He thanked the woman and closed the door. He went to look for his glasses, which his had put on his night table. "I dare not fall," he cautioned himself. "All I need now is a broken hip." He staggered over to his bed and lit the lamp. Yes, the eyeglasses were lying where he left them. He felt dizzy. The walls, the curtains, the dresser, the envelope all jerked and whirled like a blurry image on television. Am I going blind or what, he wondered. He sat and waited for the dizziness to pass. He barely had the strength to open the envelope. The note was written in pencil, in Yiddish. The lines were crooked, and the words badly spelled. It read:

Dear Harry, forgive me. I must go where my husband is. If it's not too much trouble, say Kaddish for me. I'll intercede for you where I'm going.

Ethel

He put the sheet of paper and his glasses down on the night table and switched off the lamp. He lay belching and hiccupping. His body twitched, and the bedsprings vibrated. Well, from now on I won't hope for anything, he decided with the solemnity of a man taking an oath. He felt cold, and he covered himself with the blanket.

It was ten past eight in the morning when he came out of his daze. A dream? No, the letter lay on the table. That day, Harry Bendiner did not go down for his mail. He did not prepare breakfast for himself, nor did he bother to bathe and dress. He kept on dozing in the plastic chaise on the balcony and thinking about that other Sylvia—Ethel's daughter—who was living in a tent in British Columbia. "Why had she run away so far?" he asked himself. Did her father's death drive her into despair? Could she not stand her mother? Or did she already at her age realize the futility of all human efforts and decide to become a hermit? Is she endeavoring to discover herself, or God? An adventurous idea came into the old man's mind: to fly to British Columbia, find the young woman in the wilderness, comfort her, be a father to her, and perhaps try to meditate together with her on why a man is born and why he must die.

QUESTIONS

1. Sometimes the third-person subjective narrator moves to a perspective outside Harry's consciousness and speaks to the reader directly, as in the italicized sentences in the following passage:

Harry often said to his brain, "Don't be stupid. It's too late for everything. You have nothing to hope for anymore." *But the brain was so constituted that it went on hoping nonetheless. Who was it who said it: A man takes his hopes into the grave.*

Find other examples where the narrator extends Harry's thoughts into a philosophical generalization. Discuss narrative voice in relation to character and tone.

2. Is Ethel Brokeles' suicide foreshadowed? Discuss point of view in relation to surprise.

3. What is Harry's initial reaction to the woman's suicide? What is his subsequent reaction? Is this plan in keeping with his temperament?

4. Is Harry a sympathetic character? unsympathetic? Discuss underdistancing and overdistancing in relationship to characterization and to tone.

5. Ethel Brokeles' suicide could have been treated sensationally, but the author chose to minimize this aspect. How does the suicide relate to the story's tone?

6. Would you classify the setting as flat or round? Explain, discussing how the sense of place is created less by physical description than by Harry's attitude toward the condominium. Is this particular setting essential, or could the story have taken place elsewhere?

7. Is the theme concerned with the loneliness of old age, or does the story have a larger meaning?

8. What is the significance of the title?

The Elements of
Fiction as Fiction

JOYCE CAROL OATES

The Girl

I *Background Material*

Came by with a truck, The Director and Roybay and a boy I didn't know. Roybay leaned out the window, very friendly. I got in and we drove around for a while. The Director telling us about his movie-vision, all speeded-up because his friend, his contact, had lent him the equipment from an educational film company in town, and it had to be back Sunday P.M.. The Director said: "It's all a matter of art and compromise." He was very excited. I knew him from before, a few days before; his name was DePinto or DeLino, something strange, but he was called The Director. He was in the third person most of the time.

Roybay, two hundred fifty pounds, very cheerful and easy and my closest friend of all of them, was The Motorcyclist. They used his motorcycle for an authentic detail. It didn't work; it was broken down. But they propped it up in the sand and it looked very real.

A boy with a scruffy face, like an explorer's face, was The Cop.

I was The Girl.

The Director said: "Oh Jesus honey your tan, your tanned legs, your feet, my God even your feet your toes, are tan, tanned, you're so lovely. . . ." And he stared at me, he stared. When we met before, he had not stared like this. His voice was hoarse, his eyebrows ragged. It was all music with him, his voice and his way of moving, the life inside him. "I mean, look at her! Isn't she—? Isn't it?"

486

"Perfect," Roybay said.

The boy with the scruffy face, wedged in between Roybay the driver and The Director, with me on The Director's lap and my legs sort of on his lap, stared at me and turned out to be a kid my age. I caught a look of his but rejected it. I never found out his name.

Later they said to me: "What were their names? Don't you know? Can't you remember? Can't you—?"

They were angry. They said: "Describe them."

But.

The Director. The Motorcyclist. The Cop. The Girl.

I thought there were more, more than that. If you eliminate The Girl. If you try to remember. More? More than two? Oh, I believe a dozen or two, fifty, any large reasonable number tramping down the sand. There was the motorcycle, broken. They hauled it out in the back of the truck with the film equipment and other stuff. I could describe the Santa Monica Freeway if I wanted to. But not them. I think there were more than three but I don't know. Where did they come from? Who were they? The reason I could describe the Freeway is that I knew it already, not memorized but in pieces, the way you know your environment.

I was The Girl. No need to describe. Anyone studying me, face to face, would be in my presence and would not need a description. I looked different. The costume didn't matter, the bright red and green shapes—cats and kittens—wouldn't show anyway. The film was black-and-white. It was a short-skirted dress, a top that tied in back, looped around and tied in back like a halter, the material just cotton or anything, bright shapes of red and green distortions in the material. It came from a Miss Chelsea shop in Van Nuys. I wasn't wearing anything else, anything underneath.

Someone real said to me later, a real policeman: " . . . need your cooperation. . . ."

The Director explained that he needed everyone's cooperation. He had assisted someone making a film once, or he had watched it happen, he said how crucial it is to cooperate; he wouldn't have the footage for re-takes and all the equipment had to be returned in eighteen hours. Had a sharkish skinny glamourish face, a wide-brimmed hat perched on his head. Wore sunglasses. We all did. The beach was very bright at three in the afternoon. I had yellow-lensed glasses with white plastic wrap-around frames, like goggles. It wasn't very warm. The wind came in from the ocean, chilly.

The way up, I got hypnotized by the expressway signs and all the names of the towns and beaches and the arrows pointing up off to the right, always up off to the right and off the highway and off the map.

"Which stretch of beach? Where? How far up the coast? Can't you identify it, can't you remember? We need your cooperation, can't you cooperate?"

On film, any stretch of beach resembles any stretch of beach. They called it The Beach.

II   *The Rehearsal*

The Director moved us around, walked with us; put his hands on me and turned me, stepped on my bare feet, scratched his head up beneath the straw-colored hat, made noises with his mouth, very excited, saying to himself little words: "Here—yeah—like this—this—this way—" The Motorcyclist, who was Roybay, straddled the motorcycle to wait. Had a sunny broad face with red-blond-brown hair frizzy all around it. Even his beard was frizzy. It wasn't hot but he looked hot. Was six foot three or four, taller than my father, who is or was six foot exactly. That is my way of telling if a man is tall: taller than my father, then he's *tall;* shorter than my father, *not tall*. The world could be divided that way.

No, I haven't seen my father for a while. But the world is still there.

The Director complained about the setting. The beach was beautiful but empty. "Got to imagine people crowding in, people in the place of boulders and rocks and scrubby damn flowers and sand dunes and eucalyptus and all this crap, it's hobbling to the eye," he said. He had wanted a city movie. He had wanted the movie to take place in the real world. "Really wanted Venice Beach on a Sunday, packed, but room for the motorcycle, and the whole world crowded in . . . a miscellaneous flood of people, souls, to represent the entire world . . . and the coming-together of the world in my story. In The Girl. Oh look at her," he said dreamily, looking at me, "couldn't the world come together in her? It could. But this place is so empty . . . it's wild here, a wild innocent natural setting, it's too beautiful, it could be a travelogue. . . ."

The Cop asked about splicing things together. Couldn't you—?

The Director waved him away. It was hard to concentrate.

The Cop giggled and whispered to me: "Jeeze, these guys are something, huh? How'd you meet them? I met them this morning. Where do you go to school? You go to school? Around here?"

I snubbed him, eye-to-eye.

He blushed. He was about sixteen, behind his bushy hair and sunglasses and policeman's hat. It had a tin badge on it. The Director had bought it at a costume store. The Cop had only a hat. The rest of him was a T-shirt and jeans. A club two feet long and maybe an inch and a half in diameter, but no gun. The Director had found the club in a garbage can, he said, months ago. He carried it everywhere with him. It had generated his need for a film, he said; he kept taking it from The Cop and using it to make lines in the sand.

The Director's mind was always going. It was white-hot. His body never stopped, his knees jerked as if keeping time to something. I felt the energy in him, even when he wasn't touching me. Only when he held the camera in his hands, between his hands, was he calmed down.

After a while, Roybay said, sounding nervous: "What do we do? What do I do? Somebody might come along here, huh?—we better hurry it up, huh?"

"This can't be hurried," The Director said.

The Motorcyclist was the only one of them I knew. His name was *Roybay*. Or *Robbie*. Or maybe it was *Roy Bean (?)* . . . sometimes just *Roy* or *Ray*. Said he came over from Trinidad, Colorado—I think. Or someone else his size said that, some other day. Had a big worried forehead tanned pink-red. You don't tan dark, with a complexion like that. He wore a crash helmet and goggles and a leather jacket, the sleeves a little short for his arms. The night I met him, he was explaining the fact that vegetables are not meek and passive, as people think, but exert great pressure in forcing themselves up through the soil . . . and think about vines, twisting tendrils, feelers that could choke large animals to death or pull them down into quicksand. . . . He was a vegetarian, but he scorned meekness. Believed in strength. Up at 7 A.M. for two hours of weight-lifting, very slow, Yoga-slow, and a careful diet of vegetables and vegetable juices. Said fruit was too acid, too sharp. Explained that an ox's muscles were extremely powerful and that the carnivores of the world could learn from the ox.

Or his name could have been something like *Roy baby, Roy, baby* if someone called out and slurred the words together.

The Director placed rocks on the sand. Kicked dents in the sand. He cleared debris out of the way, tossing things hand over hand, then he found a child's toy—a fire truck—and stood with it, spinning the little wheels, thinking, then he moved one of the rocks a few inches and said to me: "You walk to this point. Try it."

They watched.

The Director said that I was a sweet girl. He said that now I should practice running, from the rock out to the water. He followed alongside me. He told me when to stop. He kissed my forehead and said I was very sweet, this was part of the tragedy. He tossed the toy firetruck off to the side. Rubbed his hands together, excited, I could smell it on him, the excitement.

"I'm an orphan," he said suddenly. "I'm from a Methodist orphanage up in Seattle."

The Motorcyclist laughed. The Cop grinned stupidly; he was still standing where The Director had placed him.

"You don't get many chances in life," The Director said, "so I would hate to mess this up. It would make me very angry if something went wrong . . . if one of you went wrong. . . . But you're not going to, huh, are you? Not even you?" he said, looking at me. As if I was special. He had a sharkish look caused by one tooth, I think—a side tooth that was a little longer than the rest of his teeth. If you glanced at him you wouldn't notice that tooth, not really; but somehow you would start to think of a shark a few seconds later.

In a magical presence. I knew. I knew but I was outside, not on film. The Director walked with me along the beach, his feet in ankle-high boots and mine bare, talking to me, stroking my arm, saying . . . saying. . . . *What did he say? Don't remember?* No, the noise was too much. The waves. Gulls. Birds. Words come this way and that, I don't catch them all, try to ease with the feeling, the music behind them. I took music lessons once. Piano lessons with Miss Dorsey, three blocks from my grandmother's house; from ten until thirteen. Could memorize. Could count out a beat one two three, *one* two three, one *two* three, a habit to retain throughout life. When The Director told me what to do I listened to the beat of his voice. I knew I was in a magical presence, he was not an ordinary man, but I was outside him, outside waiting. I was not yet The Girl. I was The Girl later.

It was a movie, a movie-making! I screamed. When I woke for the half-dozenth time, snatching at someone's wrist. I clawed, had to make contact. I didn't want to sink back again. I said: It was real, it was a movie, there was film in the camera!

You mean someone filmed it? Filmed that? Someone had a camera?

The Director carried it in his hands. Had to adjust it, squinted down into it, made noises with his mouth; he took a long time. The Cop, licking his lips, said to me: "Hey, I thought the movie cameras were real big. Pushed around on wheels. With some moving parts, like a crane or something . . . ? Where are you from?"

"You couldn't push wheels in the sand," I told him.

The Director looked over at us. "What are you two talking about? Be quiet. You," he said to The Cop, "you, you're not in the script yet, you're off-camera, go stand on the other side of that hill. Don't clutter my mind."

He walked out to the surf, stood there, was very agitated. I looked at Roybay, who was looking at me. Our eyes didn't come together; he was looking at me like on film. The Girl. Over there, straddling the broken-down rusty-handle-barred motorcycle, was The Motorcyclist. He was not from Trinidad, Colorado, or from anywhere. I saw The Cop's cap disappear over a hill behind some spiky weeds and ridges of sand.

The Director came back. He said to The Motorcyclist, "What this is, maybe, it's a poem centered in the head of The Cop, but I had it off-center; I was imagining it in The Girl. But . . . but . . . it wasn't working. It's a test of The Cop. I don't know him. Do you? I don't know who the hell he is. It will be an experiment. He rushes in to the rescue . . . and sees the scene and . . . the test is upon him. The audience will see it too. I've been dreaming this for so long, this tiny eight-minute poem," he said, putting his arm around my shoulder now, excited, "I can't miss my chance. It's not just that it's crowding my head, but people are going to be very interested in this; I know certain people who are going to pay a lot to see it. Look, it's a poem, honey. The parts must cooperate. Nothing unripe or resisting. All parts in a poem . . . in a work of art. . . . Please, do you understand, do you?"

So sensitive. It was a sensitive moment. Staring eye-to-eye with me, dark green lenses and yellow lenses, shatter-proof.

I told him yes. I had to say yes. And it was almost true; some of his words caught in me, snagged, like the rough edge of a fingernail in your clothing.

The Director said softly: "What it is . . . is . . . it's a vision, it can't be resisted. Why resist? Resist? Resist anything? If a vision comes up from the inside of the earth, it must be sacred, or down out of the sky—even, equal—because the way up is the same as the way down, the sky is a mirror and vice versa. Right? I wanted The Girl to resist The Motorcyclist and I wanted The Cop to use the club like a Zen master's stick but now I see it differently, with the scene all set. It goes the way it must. You can't control a vision. It's like going down a stairway and you're cautious and frightened and then the stairway breaks, the last step gives way, and you fall and yet you're not afraid, you're not afraid after all, you're saved. You don't understand me, I know, but you'll feel it, you'll understand in a while. Don't resist," he said to me. "If you deny the way things must operate, you turn yourself and everyone else into a phantom. We'll all be here together. One thing. We'll be sacred. Don't doubt. Now I'll talk to The Cop, the Savior . . . he's the Savior. . . . I wonder can he bear the weight of the testing?"

III   *The Performance*

Space around me. Hair blowing, back toward shore an arrow out of sight. The air is cold. Nervous, but doing O.K.

The Director says in a whisper-shout: "Okay. Okay. No, slow down . . . slow . . . slow down. . . . Look over here. . . . The other way. . . ." It is very easy now that the camera is working. It is very easy. I am The Girl watching the film of The Girl walking on a beach watching the water. Now The Girl watching The Girl turning The Girl in black-and-white approached by a shape, a dark thing, out of the corner of the eye. The eye must be the camera. The dark thing must be a shape with legs, with arms, with a white-helmeted head.

Now the film speeds up.

A surprise, how light you become on film! You are very graceful. It's a suspension of gravity. The Director calls to me, yells to me: *Run, Run.* But I can't. I am too light, and then too heavy; the hand on my shoulder weighs me down. I think I am giggling. *Hurry up! Hurry up!*

The marker is a real rock.

Scream! cries The Director.

But I can't, I can't get breath. They are at me. I scramble up onto my feet. But. But I have lost hold. I can't see. The Director is very close to us, right beside us. *Turn her around, make her scream—hurry up—do it like this, like this, do it fast like this—come on—*

The film is speeded up. Too fast. I have lost hold of it, can't see. I am being driven backwards, downwards, burrowed-into, like a hammer being hammered being hammered against all at once. Do I see noseholes, eyeholes, mouthholes?

Something being pounded into flesh like meat.

IV   *A Sequel*

I was babbling, hanging onto someone's wrist. Not the doctor, who was in a hurry on his rounds, but a nurse. I said: "Did they find them? The police? Did it get in the newspapers? Was the movie shown? Was it—?"

What? What? At the important instant I lost sight of her, one adult face like another. Then it contracted into someone's regular-sized face. The ceiling above him seemed to open behind his face and to glow, fluorescent lighting as if for a stage, a studio. Why, this must be someone who knows me! He is looking at me without disgust. I don't know him. But I pretend. I ask him if they were caught, if—He says not to think about it right now. He says not to think about it. He says: "The police, they won't find them anyway . . . they don't give a damn about you . . . don't torture yourself."

But, but.

Raw reddened meat, scraped raw, hair yanked out in handfuls. A scalp bleeding and sandy. Sandy grit in my mouth. It was a jelly, a transformation. But I wanted to know. Wanted. I reached for his wrist but couldn't get it.

You can be real, but you can be stronger than real; speeded-up, lighted-up. It does take a camera. The Director helped them drag me back saying *Oh it was beautiful . . . it was beautiful . . .* and there were tears in the creases around his mouth. I strained to get free, to break the shape out of my head and into his. Strained, twisted. But there was too much noise. The back of my head was hurt and emptied out. Too much battered into me, I couldn't tell them apart, there were two of them but maybe two hundred or two thousand, I couldn't know.

But I couldn't talk right. The man tried to listen politely but here is what I said: " . . . rockhand, two of them, birdburrow, truck, toy, wheel, the arrow, the exit, the way out. . . ." Another man, also in the room, tried to interrupt. Kept asking "Who were they? How many? Five, six, a dozen? Twenty? Where did it happen? Where did you meet them? Who are you?" but I kept on talking, babbling, now I was saying saints' names that got into my head somehow . . . the names of saints like beads on a rosary, but I didn't know them, the saints had terrible names to twist my head out of shape: " . . . Saint Camarillo, Saint Oxnard, Saint . . . Saint Ventura . . . Saint Ynez . . . Saint Goleta . . . Saint Gaviota . . . Saint Jalama . . . Saint Casmalia . . . Saint Saint Saint. . . ."

V   *The Vision*

A rainy wintry day, and I crossed Carpenter Street and my eye drifted right onto someone. The Director. I stared at him and started to run after him. He turned around, staring. Didn't recognize me. Didn't know. Behind him a laundromat, some kids playing in the doorway, yelling. Too much confusion. The Director walked sideways, sideways staring at me, trying to remember. He hadn't any sunglasses now. His skin was sour-looking.

I ran up to him. I said: "Don't you remember? Don't you—?"

I laughed.

I forgave him, he looked so sick. He was about twenty-eight, thirty years old. Edgy, cautious. Creases down both sides of his mouth.

He stared at me.

Except for the rain and a bad cold, my eyes reddened, I was pretty again and recovered. I laughed but started to remember something out of the corner of my eye. Didn't want to remember. So I smiled, grinned at him, and he tried to match the way I looked.

"I'm new here, I just came here . . . I'm from. . . . I'm from up the coast, from Seattle. . . . I don't know you. . . ."

A kind of shutter clicked in his head. Showing in his eyes. He was walking sideways and I reached out for his wrist, a bony wrist, and he shook me loose. His lips were thin and chalk-colored, chalky cheesy sour-colored. One of his nostrils was bigger than the other and looked sore. That single shark tooth was greenish. He said: " . . . just in for a day, overnight, down from Seattle and . . . uh . . . I don't know you. . . . Don't remember. I'm confused. I'm not well, my feet are wet, I'm from out of town."

"What happened to the movie?" I asked.

He watched me. A long time passed. Someone walked by him on the pavement, in the rain, the way passersby walk in a movie, behind the main actors. They are not in focus and that person was not in focus either.

"Was it a real movie? Did it have film, the camera?" I asked. Beginning to be afraid. Beginning. But I kept it back, the taste in my mouth. Kept smiling to show him no harm. "Oh hey look," I said, "look, it had film, didn't it? I mean it had film? I mean you made a real movie, didn't you? I mean—"

Finally he began to see me. The creases around his mouth turned into a smile. It was like a crucial scene now; he put his hand on my shoulder and kissed my forehead, in the rain. He said: "Honey oh yeah. Yeah. Don't you ever doubt that. I mean, did you doubt that? All these months? You should never have doubted that. I mean, that's the whole thing. That's it. That's the purpose, the center, the reason behind it, all of it, the focus, the. . . . You know what I mean? The Vision?"

I knew what he meant.

So I was saved.

QUESTIONS

1. What is the antecedent of *they* in the following passage: "Later they said to me: 'What were their names? Don't you know? Can't you remember?'" What does the narrator's confusion about names tell you about her and about the event?

2. Why is the narrator unable to identify the beach? How does her vagueness about the film's setting contribute to the story's meaning?

3. Summarize the plot, showing the causal relationship among events. Assuming The Director had film in the camera, what kind of movie was he making?

4. Discuss the narrator as a character. Is she sympathetic? unsympathetic? round? flat? dynamic? static? believable? unbelievable? stereotypical? individualistic?

5. From clues provided in the story, write a short biographical sketch of the narrator. How does the girl differ from The Girl?

6. The narrator's unreliability obscures and comprises the story's meaning. Why?

7. Do the headings ("Background Material," etc.) help to clarify the action? Do they serve any other purpose?

8. Although the action concerns the making of a film, the story is about fiction-making. Why?

RICHARD BRAUTIGAN

The World War I
Los Angeles Airplane

He was found lying dead near the television set on the front room floor of a small rented house in Los Angeles. My wife had gone to the store to get some ice cream. It was an early-in-the-night-just-a-few-blocks-away store. We were in an ice-cream mood. The telephone rang. It was her brother to say that her father had died that afternoon. He was seventy. I waited for her to come home with the ice cream. I tried to think of the best way to tell her that her father was dead with the least amount of pain but you cannot camouflage death with words. Always at the end of the words somebody is dead.

She was very happy when she came back from the store.

"What's wrong?" she said.

"Your brother just called from Los Angeles," I said.

"What happened?" she said.

"Your father died this afternoon."

That was in 1960 and now it's just a few weeks away from 1970. He has been dead for almost ten years and I've done a lot of thinking about what his death means to all of us.

1. He was born from German blood and raised on a farm in South Dakota. His grandfather was a terrible tyrant who completely destroyed his three grown sons by treating them exactly the way he treated them when they were children. They never grew up in his eyes and they never grew up in their own eyes. He made sure of that. They never left the farm. They of course got married but he handled all of their domestic matters except for the siring of his grandchildren. He never allowed them to discipline their own children. He took

494

care of that for them. Her father thought of his father as another brother who was always trying to escape the never-relenting wrath of their grandfather.

2. He was smart, so he became a schoolteacher when he was eighteen and he left the farm, which was an act of revolution against his grandfather who from that day forth considered him dead. He didn't want to end up like his father, hiding behind the barn. He taught school for three years in the Midwest and then he worked as an automobile salesman in the pioneer days of car selling.

3. There was an early marriage followed by an early divorce with feelings afterward that left the marriage hanging like a skeleton in her family's closet because he tried to keep it a secret. He probably had been very much in love.

4. There was a horrible automobile accident just before the First World War in which everybody was killed except him. It was one of those automobile accidents that leave deep spiritual scars like historical landmarks on the family and friends of the dead.

5. When America went into the First World War in 1917, he decided that he wanted to be a pilot, though he was in his late twenties. He was told that it would be impossible because he was too old but he projected so much energy into his desire to fly that he was accepted for pilot training and went to Florida and became a pilot.

In 1918 he went to France and flew a De Havilland and bombed a railroad station in France and one day he was flying over the German lines when little clouds began appearing around him and he thought that they were beautiful and flew for a long time before he realized that they were German antiaircraft guns trying to shoot him down.

Another time he was flying over France and a rainbow appeared behind the tail of his plane and every turn that the plane made, the rainbow also made the same turn and it followed after him through the skies of France for part of an afternoon in 1918.

6. When the war was over he got out a captain and he was traveling on a train through Texas when the middle-aged man sitting next to him and with whom he had been talking for about three hundred miles said, "If I was a young man like you and had a little extra cash, I'd go up to Idaho and start a bank. There's a good future in Idaho banking."

7. That's what her father did.

8. He went to Idaho and started a bank which soon led to three more banks and a large ranch. It was by now 1926 and everything was going all right.

9. He married a schoolteacher who was sixteen years his junior and for their honeymoon they took a train to Philadelphia and spent a week there.

10. When the stock market crashed in 1929 he was hit hard by it and had to give up his banks and a grocery store that he had picked up along the way, but he still had the ranch, though he had to put a mortgage on it.

11. He decided to go into sheep raising in 1931 and got a big flock and was very good to his sheepherders. He was so good to them that it was a subject of gossip in his part of Idaho. The sheep got some kind of horrible sheep disease and all died.

12. He got another big flock of sheep in 1933 and added more fuel to the gossip by continuing to be so good to his men. The sheep got some kind of horrible sheep disease and all died in 1934.

13. He gave his men a big bonus and went out of the sheep business.

14. He had just enough money left over after selling the ranch to pay off all his debts and buy a brand-new Chevrolet which he put his family into and he drove off to California to start all over again.

15. He was forty-four, had a twenty-eight-year-old wife and an infant daughter.

16. He didn't know anyone in California and it was the Depression.

17. His wife worked for a while in a prune shed and he parked cars at a lot in Hollywood.

18. He got a job as a bookkeeper for a small construction company.

19. His wife gave birth to a son.

20. In 1940 he went briefly into California real estate, but then decided not to pursue it any further and went back to work for the construction company as a bookkeeper.

21. His wife got a job as a checker in a grocery store where she worked for eight years and then an assistant manager quit and opened his own store and she went to work for him and she still works there.

22. She has worked twenty-three years now as a grocery checker for the same store.

23. She was very pretty until she was forty.

24. The construction company laid him off. They said he was too old to take care of the books. "It's time for you to go out to pasture," they joked. He was fifty-nine.

25. They rented the same house they lived in for twenty-five years, though they could have bought it at one time with no down payment and monthly payments of fifty dollars.

26. When his daughter was going to high school he was working there as the school janitor. She saw him in the halls. His working as a janitor was a subject that was very seldom discussed at home.

27. Her mother would make lunches for both of them.

28. He retired when he was sixty-five and became a very careful sweet-wine alcoholic. He liked to drink whiskey but they couldn't afford to keep him in it. He stayed in the house most of the time and started drinking about ten o'clock, a few hours after his wife had gone off to work at the grocery store.

29. He would get quietly drunk during the course of the day. He always kept his wine bottles hidden in a kitchen cabinet and would secretly drink from them, though he was alone.

He very seldom made any bad scenes and the house was always clean when his wife got home from work. He did though after a while take on that meticulous manner of walking that alcoholics have when they are trying very carefully to act as if they aren't drunk.

30. He used sweet wine in place of life because he didn't have any more life to use.

31. He watched afternoon television.

32. Once he had been followed by a rainbow across the skies of France while flying a World War I airplane carrying bombs and machine guns.

33. "Your father died this afternoon."

QUESTIONS

1. Is the frame appropriate? necessary? How does it relate to the theme?

2. Is the narrator reliable? unreliable? Discuss the scope and limitations of his knowledge.

3. Is the narrator's father-in-law a sympathetic character? unsympathetic? flat? round? static? dynamic? In what sense is he a symbolic character?

4. Do the events have a causal relationship or are they ruled solely by chance and coincidence?

5. What is the effect of juxtaposing ordinary, even trivial, events with momentous occurrences?

6. What is the effect of the repetition in item 5 and item 32?

7. The narrator says that his father-in-law "has been dead for almost ten years and I've done a lot of thinking about what his death means to all of us." Does the story explain the meaning of the man's death?

8. Discuss the use of itemizing as an antimimetic device.

9. In what ways is fiction-making the subject of the story?

LE ROI
JONES

Uncle Tom's Cabin: Alternate Ending

"6½" *was* the answer. But it seemed to irritate Miss Orbach. Maybe not the answer—the figure itself, but the fact it should be there, and in such loose possession.

"OH who is he to know such a thing? That's really improper to set up such liberations. And moreso."

What came into her head next she could hardly understand. A breath of cold. She did shudder, and her fingers clawed at the tiny watch she wore hidden in the lace of the blouse her grandmother had given her when she graduated teacher's college.

Ellen, Eileen, Evelyn . . . Orbach. She could be any of them. Her personality was one of theirs. As specific and as vague. The kindly menace of leading a life in whose balance evil was a constant intrigue but grew uglier and more remote as it grew stronger. She would have loved to do something really dirty. But nothing she had ever heard of was dirty enough. So she contented herself with good, i.e., purity, as a refuge from mediocrity. But being unconscious, or largely remote from her own sources, she would only admit to the possibility of grace. Not God. She would not be trapped into *wanting* even God.

So remorse took her easily. For any reason. A reflection in a shop window, of a man looking in vain for her ankles. (Which she covered with heavy colorless woolen.) A sudden gust of warm damp air around her legs or face. Long dull rains that turned her from her books. Or, as was the case this morning, some completely uncalled-for shaking of her silent doctrinaire routines.

"6½" had wrenched her unwillingly to exactly where she was. Teaching the

5th grade, in a grim industrial complex of northeastern America; about 1942. And how the social doth pain the anchorite.

Nothing made much sense in such a context. People moved around, and disliked each other for no reason. Also, and worse, they said they loved each other, and usually for less reason, Miss Orbach thought. Or would have if she did.

And in this class sat 30 dreary sons and daughters of such circumstance. Specifically, the thriving children of the thriving urban lower middle classes. Postmen's sons and factory-worker debutantes. Making a great run for America, now prosperity and the war had silenced for a time the intelligent cackle of tradition. Like a huge grey bubbling vat the country, in its apocalyptic version of history and the future, sought now, in its equally apocalyptic profile of itself as it had urged swiftly its own death since the Civil War. To promise. Promise. And that to be that all who had ever dared to live here would die when the people and interests who had been its rulers died. The intelligent poor now were being admitted. And with them a great many Negroes . . . who would die when the rest of the dream died not even understanding that they, like Ishmael, should have been the sole survivors. But now they were being tricked. "6½" the boy said. After the fidgeting and awkward silence. One little black boy, raised his hand, and looking at the tip of Miss Orbach's nose said 6½. And then he smiled, very embarrassed and very sure of being wrong.

I would have said "No, boy, shut up and sit down. You are wrong. You don't know anything. Get out of here and be very quick. Have you no idea what you're getting involved in? My God . . . you nigger, get out of here and save yourself, while there's time. Now beat it." But those people had already been convinced. Read Booker T. Washington one day, when there's time. What that led to. The 6½'s moved for power . . . and there seemed no other way.

So three elegant Negroes in light grey suits grin and throw me through the window. They are happy and I am sad. It is an ample test of an idea. And besides "6½" is the right answer to the woman's question.

[The psychological and the social. The spiritual and the practical. Keep them together and you profit, maybe, someday, come out on top. Separate them, and you go along the road to the commonest of Hells. The one we westerners love to try to make art out of.]

The woman looked at the little brown boy. He blinked at her, trying again not to smile. She tightened her eyes, but her lips flew open. She tightened her lips, and her eyes blinked like the boy's. She said, "How do you get that answer?" The boy told her. "Well, it's right," she said, and the boy fell limp, straining even harder to look sorry. The negro in back of the answerer pinched him, and the boy shuddered. A little white girl next to him touched his hand, and he tried to pull his own hand away with his brain.

"Well, that's right, class. That's exactly right. You may sit down now Mr. McGhee."

Later on in the day, after it had started exaggeratedly to rain very hard and very stupidly against the windows and soul of her fifth-grade class, Miss Orbach became convinced that the little boy's eyes were too large. And in fact they did bulge almost grotesquely white and huge against his bony heavy-veined skull. Also, his head was much too large for the rest of the scrawny body. And he talked too much, and caused too many disturbances. He also stared out the window when Miss Orbach herself would drift off into her sanctuary of light and hygiene even though her voice carried the inanities of arithmetic seemingly without delay. When she came back to the petty social demands of twentieth-century humanism the boy would be watching something walk across the playground. OH, it just would not work.

She wrote a note to Miss Janone, the school nurse, and gave it to the boy, McGhee, to take to her. The note read: "Are the large eyes a sign of ————?"

Little McGhee, of course, could read, and read the note. But he didn't of course understand the last large word which was misspelled anyway. But he tried to memorize the note, repeating to himself over and over again its contents . . . sounding the last long word out in his head, as best he could.

Miss Janone wiped her big nose and sat the boy down, reading the note. She looked at him when she finished, then read the note again, crumpling it on her desk.

She looked in her medical book and found out what Miss Orbach meant. Then she said to the little Negro, Dr. Robard will be here in five minutes. He'll look at you. Then she began doing something to her eyes and fingernails.

When the doctor arrived he looked closely at McGhee and said to Miss Janone, "Miss Orbach is confused."

McGhee's mother thought that too. Though by the time little McGhee had gotten home he had forgotten the "long word" at the end of the note.

"Is Miss Orbach the woman who told you to say sangwich instead of sammich," Louise McGhee giggled.

"No, that was Miss Columbe."

"Sangwich, my christ. That's worse than sammich. Though you better not let me hear you saying sammich either . . . like those Davises."

"I don't say sammich, mamma."

"What's the word then?"

"Sandwich."

"That's right. And don't let anyone tell you anything else. Teacher or otherwise. Now I wonder what that word could've been?"

"I donno. It was very long. I forgot it."

Eddie McGhee Sr. didn't have much of an idea what the word could be either. But he had never been to college like his wife. It was one of the most conspicuously dealt with factors of their marriage.

So the next morning Louise McGhee, after calling her office, the Child Welfare Bureau, and telling them she would be a little late, took a trip to the school, which was on the same block as the house where the McGhees lived, to speak to Miss Orbach about the long word which she suspected might be injurious to her son and maybe to Negroes In General. This suspicion had been bolstered a great deal by what Eddie Jr. had told her about Miss Orbach, and also equally by what Eddie Sr. had long maintained about the nature of White People In General. "Oh well," Louise McGhee sighed, "I guess I better straighten this sister out." And that is exactly what she intended.

When the two McGhees reached the Center Street school the next morning Mrs. McGhee took Eddie along with her to the principal's office, where she would request that she be allowed to see Eddie's teacher.

Miss Day, the old, lady principal, would then send Eddie to his class with a note for his teacher, and talk to Louise McGhee, while she was waiting, on general problems of the neighborhood. Miss Day was a very old woman who had despised Calvin Coolidge. She was also, in one sense, exotically liberal. One time she had forbidden old man Seidman to wear his pince-nez anymore, as they looked too snooty. Center Street sold more war stamps than any other grammar school in the area, and had a fairly good track team.

Miss Orbach was going to say something about Eddie McGhee's being late, but he immediately produced Miss Day's note. Then Miss Orbach looked at Eddie again, as she had when she had written her own note the day before.

She made Mary Ann Fantano the monitor and stalked off down the dim halls. The class had a merry time of it when she left, and Eddie won an extra two Nabisco graham crackers by kissing Mary Ann while she sat at Miss Orbach's desk.

When Miss Orbach got to the principal's office and pushed open the door she looked directly into Louise McGhee's large brown eyes, and fell deeply and hopelessly in love.

QUESTIONS

1. Explain Eddie's answer, "6½", as both fact and symbol.

2. Why does the narrator advise Eddie to "get out of here and save yourself, while there's time"? Why does he advise reading Booker T. Washington?

3. What is the significance of the "three elegant Negroes in light grey suits"?

4. What illness do you think Miss Orbach's note refers to? Is this illness "injurious to her son and maybe to Negroes In General," as Louise McGhee suspects? What does Miss Orbach's incorrect diagnosis reveal about her? What does Mrs. McGhee's reaction reveal about her?

5. Discuss the story as a parable about the relationship between blacks and whites in America.

6. Discuss the story from the point of view of twentieth-century economic and political history.

7. Explain the meaning of the title.

8. Discuss the implications of the last sentence. Is the ending happy? unhappy? ambiguous?

9. Describe antimimetic devices used in this story. In what ways is fiction-making part of the story's subject?

JULIO CORTAZAR

Continuity of Parks

Translation by Paul Blackburn

He had begun to read the novel a few days before. He had put it down because of some urgent business conferences, opened it again on his way back to the estate by train; he permitted himself a slowly growing interest in the plot, in the characterizations. That afternoon, after writing a letter giving his power of attorney and discussing a matter of joint ownership with the manager of his estate, he returned to the book in the tranquillity of his study which looked out upon the park with its oaks. Sprawled in his favorite armchair, its back toward the door—even the possibility of an intrusion would have irritated him, had he thought of it—he let his left hand caress repeatedly the green velvet upholstery and set to reading the final chapters. He remembered effortlessly the names and his mental image of the characters; the novel spread its glamour over him almost at once. He tasted the almost perverse pleasure of disengaging himself line by line from the things around him, and at the same time feeling his head rest comfortably on the green velvet of the chair with its high back, sensing that the cigarettes rested within reach of his hand, that beyond the great windows the air of afternoon danced under the oak trees in the park. Word by word, licked up by the sordid dilemma of the hero and heroine, letting himself be absorbed to the point where the images settled down and took on color and movement, he was witness to the final encounter in the mountain cabin. The woman arrived first, apprehensive; now the lover came in, his face cut by the backlash of a branch. Admirably, she stanched the blood with her kisses, but he rebuffed her caresses, he had not come to perform again the ceremonies of a secret passion, protected by a world of dry leaves and furtive paths through the forest. The dagger warmed itself against his chest, and underneath liberty pounded, hidden close. A lustful, panting dialogue raced down the pages like a rivulet of snakes, and one felt it had all been decided from eternity. Even to those caresses which writhed about the lover's body, as though wishing to keep him there, to dissuade him from it; they sketched abominably the frame of that other body it was necessary to destroy. Nothing had been forgotten: alibis, unforeseen hazards, possible mistakes. From this hour on, each instant had its use minutely assigned. The cold-blooded, twice-gone-over re-examination of the details was barely broken off so that a hand could caress a cheek. It was beginning to get dark.

Not looking at one another now, rigidly fixed upon the task which awaited them, they separated at the cabin door. She was to follow the trail that led north. On the path leading in the opposite direction, he turned for a moment to watch her running, her hair loosened and flying. He ran in turn, crouching among the trees and hedges until, in the yellowish fog of dusk, he could distinguish the avenue of trees which led up to the house. The dogs were not supposed to bark, they did not bark. The estate manager would not be there at this hour, and he was not there. He went up the three porch steps and entered. The woman's words reached him over the thudding of blood in his ears: first a blue chamber, then a hall, then a carpeted stairway. At the top, two doors. No one in the first room, no one in the second. The door of the salon, and then, the knife in hand, the light from the great windows, the high back of an armchair covered in green velvet, the head of the man in the chair reading a novel.

QUESTIONS

1. Discuss the function of the setting.

2. Have you ever identified so completely with fictional characters and their situation that you imagined your actual participation, as quite possibly the man does? If the man's experiences are vicarious, what is the story's theme?

3. If the man who reads about a murder is murdered under circumstances that parallel those in the novel, the plot hinges on coincidence. Can you justify an interpretation based on the coincidence of events?

4. Can you support the contention that one of the elements of fiction, namely plot, is the subject matter of this story?

5. What questions does the story raise about the nature of fiction? of reality?

DONALD BARTHELME

Sentence

Or a long sentence moving at a certain pace down the page aiming for the bottom—if not the bottom of this page then of some other page—where it can rest, or stop for a moment to think about the questions raised by its own (temporary) existence, which ends when the page is turned, or the sentence falls out of the mind that holds it (temporarily) in some kind of an embrace, not necessarily an ardent one, but more perhaps the kind of embrace enjoyed (or endured) by a wife who has just waked up and is on her way to the bathroom in the morning to wash her hair, and is bumped into by her husband, who has been lounging at the breakfast table reading the newspaper, and didn't see her coming out of the bedroom, but, when he bumps into her, or is bumped into by her, raises his hands to embrace her lightly, transiently, because he knows that if he gives her a real embrace so early in the morning, before she has properly shaken the dreams out of her head, and got her duds on, she won't respond, and may even become slightly angry, and say something wounding, and so the husband invests in this embrace not so much physical or emotional pressure as he might, because he doesn't want to waste anything—with this sort of feeling, then, the sentence passes through the mind more or less, and there is another way of describing the situation too, which is to say that the sentence crawls through the mind like something someone says to you while you're listening very hard to the FM radio, some rock group there, with its thrilling sound, and so, with your attention or the major part of it at least already awarded, there is not much mind room you can give to the remark, especially considering that you have probably just quarreled with that person, the maker of the remark, over the radio being

504

too loud, or something like that, and the view you take, of the remark, is that you'd really rather not hear it, but if you ave to hear it, you want to listen to it for the smallest possible length of time, and during a commercial, because immediately after the commercial they're going to play a new rock song by your favorite group, a cut that has never been aired before, and you want to hear it and respond to it in a new way, a way that accords with whatever you're feeling at the moment, or might feel, if the threat of new experience could be (temporarily) overbalanced by the promise of possible positive benefits, or what the mind construes as such, remembering that these are often, really, disguised defeats (not that such defeats are not, at times, good for your character, teaching you that it is not by success alone that one surmounts life, but that setbacks, too, contribute to that roughening of the personality that, by providing a textured surface to place against that of life, enables you to leave slight traces, or smudges, on the face of human history—your mark) and after all, benefit-seeking always has something of the smell of raw vanity about it, as if you wished to decorate your own brow with laurel, or wear your medals to a cookout, when the invitation had said nothing about them, and although the ego is always hungry (we are told) it is well to remember that ongoing success is nearly as meaningless as ongoing lack of success, which can make you sick, and that it is good to leave a few crumbs on the table for the rest of your brethren, not to sweep it all into the little beaded purse of your soul but to allow others, too, part of the gratification, and if you share in this way you will find the clouds smiling on you, and the postman bringing you letters, and bicycles available when you want to rent them, and many other signs, however guarded and limited, of the community's (temporary) approval of you, or at least of its willingness to let you believe (temporarily) that it finds you not so lacking in commendable virtues as it had previously allowed you to think, from its scorn of your merits, as it might be put, or anyway its consistent refusal to recognize your basic humanness and its secret blackball of the project of your remaining alive, made in executive session by its ruling bodies, which, as everyone knows, carry out concealed programs of reward and punishment, under the rose, causing faint alterations of the status quo, behind your back, at various points along the periphery of community life, together with other enterprises not dissimilar in tone, such as producing films that have special qualities, or attributes, such as a film where the second half of it is a holy mystery, and girls and women are not permitted to see it, or writing novels in which the final chapter is a plastic bag filled with water, which you can touch, but not drink: in this way, or ways, the underground mental life of the collectivity is botched, or denied, or turned into something else never imagined by the planners, who, returning from the latest seminar in crisis management and being asked what they have learned, say they have learned how to throw up their hands; the sentence meanwhile, although not insensible of these considerations, has a festering conscience of its own, which persuades it to follow its star, and to move with all deliberate speed from one place to another, without losing any of the "riders" it may have picked up just by being there, on the page, and turning this way and that, to see what is over there, under that oddly-shaped tree, or over there, reflected in the rain barrel of the imagination, even though it is true that in our young manhood we were taught that short, punchy sentences were best (but what did he mean? doesn't "punchy" mean punch-drunk? I think he probably intended to say "short, *punching* sentences," meaning sentences that lashed out at you, bloodying your brain if possible, and looking up the word just now I came across the nearby "punkah," which is a large fan suspended from the ceiling in India, operated by an attendant pulling a rope—that is what I want for my sentence, to keep it cool!) we are mature enough now to stand the shock of learning that much of what we were taught in our youth was wrong, or improperly understood by those who were teaching it, or perhaps shaded a bit, the shading resulting from the personal needs of the teachers, who as human beings had a tendency to introduce some of their heart's blood into their work, and sometimes this may not have been of the first water, this heart's blood, and even if they thought they were moving the "knowledge" out, as the Board of Education had mandated, they could have noticed that their sentences weren't having the knockdown power of the new weapons whose bullets tumble end-over-end (but it is true that we didn't have these weapons at that time) and they might have taken into account the fundamental dubiousness of their project (but all the intelligently conceived projects have been eaten up already, like the moon and the stars) leaving us, in our best clothes, with only things to do like conducting vigorous wars of attrition against our wives, who have now thoroughly come awake, and slipped into their striped bells, and pulled sweaters over their torsi, and adamantly refused to wear any bras under the sweaters, carefully explaining the political significance of this refusal to anyone who will listen, or look, but not touch, because that has nothing to do with it, so they say; leaving us, as it were, with only things to do like floating sheets of Reynolds Wrap around the room, trying to find out how many we can keep in the air at the same time, which at least gives us a sense of participation, as though we were the Buddha, looking down at the mystery of your smile, which needs to be investigated, and I think I'll do that right now, while there's still enough light, if you'll sit down over there, in the best chair, and take off all your clothes, and put your feet in that electric toe caddy (which prevents pneumonia) and slip into this permanent press white hospital gown, to cover your nakedness—why, if you do all that, we'll be ready to begin! after I wash my hands, because you pick up an amazing amount of exuviae in this city, just by walking around in the open air, and nodding to acquaintances, and speaking to friends, and copulating with lovers, in the ordinary course (and death to our enemies! by the by)—but I'm getting a little uptight, just about washing my hands, because I can't find the soap, which somebody has used and not put back in the soap dish, all of which is extremely irritating, if you have a beautiful patient sitting in the examining room, naked inside her gown, and peering at her moles in the mirror, with her immense brown eyes following your every movement (when they are not watching the moles, expecting them, as in a Disney nature film, to exfoliate) and her immense brown head wondering what you're going to do to her, the pierced places in the head letting that question

leak out, while the therapist decides just to wash his hands in plain water, and
hang the soap! and does so, and then looks around for a towel, but all the towels
have been collected by the towel service, and are not there, so he wipes his
hands on his pants, in the back (so as to avoid suspicious stains on the front)
thinking: what must she think of me? and, all this is very unprofessional and at-
sea looking! trying to visualize the contretemps from her point of view, if she
has one (but how can she? she is not in the washroom) and then stopping,
because it is finally his own point of view that he cares about and not hers, and
with this firmly in mind, and a light, confident step, such as you might find in the
works of Bulwer-Lytton, he enters the space she occupies so prettily and, taking
her by the hand, proceeds to tear off the stiff white hospital gown (but no, we
cannot have that kind of pornographic *merde* in this majestic and high-minded
sentence, which will probably end up in the Library of Congress) (that was just
something that took place inside his consciousness, as he looked at her, and
since we know that consciousness is always consciousness *of* something, she is
not entirely without responsibility in the matter) so, then, taking her by the
hand, he falls into the stupendous white purée of her abyss, no, I mean rather
that he asks her how long it has been since her last visit, and she says a fortnight,
and he shudders, and tells her that with a condition like hers (she is an
immensely popular soldier, and her troops win all their battles by pretending to
be forests, the enemy discovering, at the last moment, that those trees they have
eaten their lunch under have eyes and swords) (which reminds me of the
performance, in 1845, of Robert-Houdin, called *The Fantastic Orange Tree,*
wherein Robert-Houdin borrowed a lady's handkerchief, rubbed it between his
hands and passed it into the center of an egg, after which he passed the egg into
the center of a lemon, after which he passed the lemon into the center of an
orange, then pressed the orange between his hands, making it smaller and
smaller, until only a powder remained, whereupon he asked for a small potted
orange tree and sprinkled the powder thereupon, upon which the tree burst into
blossom, the blossoms turning into oranges, the oranges turning into butterflies,
and the butterflies turning into beautiful young ladies, who then married
members of the audience), a condition so damaging to realtime social intercourse of any kind, the best thing she can do is give up, and lay down her arms,
and he will lie down in them, and together they will permit themselves a bit of
the old slap and tickle, she wearing only her Mr. Christopher medal, on its silver
chain, and he (for such is the latitude granted the professional classes) worrying
about the sentence, about its thin wires of dramatic tension, which have been
omitted, about whether we should write down some natural events occurring in
the sky (birds, lightning bolts), and about a possible coup d'etat within the
sentence, whereby its chief verb would be—but at this moment a messenger
rushes into the sentence, bleeding from a hat of thorns he's wearing, and cries
out: "You don't know what you're doing! Stop making this sentence, and begin
instead to make Moholy-Nagy cocktails, for those are what we really need, on
the frontiers of bad behavior!" and then he falls to the floor, and a trap door
opens under him, and he falls through that, into a damp pit where a blue narwhal

waits, its horn poised (but maybe the weight of the messenger, falling from such a height, will break off the horn)—thus, considering everything carefully, in the sweet light of the ceremonial axes, in the run-mad skimble-skamble of information sickness, we must make a decision as to whether we should proceed, or go back, in the latter case enjoying the pathos of eradication, in the former case reading an erotic advertisement which begins, *How to Make Your Mouth a Blowtorch of Excitement* (but wouldn't that overtax our mouthwashes?) attempting, during the pause, while our burned mouths are being smeared with fat, to imagine a better sentence, worthier, more meaningful, like those in the Declaration of Independence, or a bank statement showing that you have seven thousand kroner more than you thought you had—a statement summing up the unreasonable demands that you make on life, and one that also asks the question, if you can imagine these demands, why are they not routinely met, tall fool? but of course it is not that query that this infected sentence has set out to answer (and hello! to our girl friend, Rosetta Stone, who has stuck by us through thin and thin) but some other query that we shall some day discover the nature of, and here comes Ludwig, the expert on sentence construction we have borrowed from the Bauhaus, who will—"Guten Tag, Ludwig!"—probably find a way to cure the sentence's sprawl, by using the improved ways of thinking developed in Weimar—"I am sorry to inform you that the Bauhaus no longer exists, that all of the great masters who formerly thought there are either dead or retired, and that I myself have been reduced to constructing books on how to pass the examination for police sergeant"—and Ludwig falls through the Tugendhat House into the history of man-made objects; a disappointment, to be sure, but it reminds us that the sentence itself is a man-made object, not the one we wanted of course, but still a construction of man, a structure to be treasured for its weakness, as opposed to the strength of stones

QUESTIONS

1. Identify the following allusions and relate them to the story's meaning: Bulwer-Lytton, Robert-Houdin, Moholy-Nagy, Rosetta Stone, the Bauhaus.

2. Is the narrator merely a jumble of words or does he have a flesh-and-blood existence? Is he reliable? unreliable? sympathetic? unsympathetic? engaging? annoying? provocative? dull? none of these?

3. Discuss the characters with whom the narrator interacts. Are they believable either collectively or singly?

4. Discuss the relationship of the narrator to the reader. Is the reader an unspecified but interested listener or is the reader given a specific identity?

5. Does the story have a beginning, middle, and end? Or is it only a verbal collage in which "unlike things are stuck together"?

6. Describe the setting(s) of this story.

7. Do you find the story comic? Why? Why not?

8. Discuss the story as a reflection of contemporary life.

9. By calling attention to itself as artifice, the story enhances the primacy of words. Do you agree or disagree?

10. In what ways is fiction-making the subject of the story?

CHARLES NICOL

I Am Donald Barthelme

To the Editor:

   The fall 1973 number of the *Carolina Quarterly* contains a story called "Divorce" and signed with my name. As it happens, I did not write it. It is quite a worthy effort, as pastiches go, and particularly successful in reproducing my weaknesses. A second story, titled "Cannon," also signed with my name, appears in the current issue of *Voyages.* As a candidate-member of the Scandinavian Institute of Comparative Vandalism, I would rate the second item somewhat inferior to the first, but again, I am not responsible. May I say, as a sort of notice to mariners, that only manuscripts offered to editors by my agent, Lynn Nesbit, are authentic—not good or bad, but at least authentic.

Donald Barthelme
New York City
(letter in *The New York Times Book Review*
December 23, 1973)

   The Sunday *New York Times* has just gone up from seventy-five to ninety cents in Terre Haute—a little tax on living practically nowhere. On Monday or sometimes Tuesday. My own copy of *The New York Times Book Review* is borrowed from one of my wealthier and more literary baby-sitters and arrives with its black Gothic title suitably yellowed; after several more hours, days, or weeks, I comfortably settle into its faded pulp. When several issues arrive at the same time, I read them all backwards, starting with the latest letters to the editor. First I read how an author did not understand the reviewer's review, then how the reviewer did not understand the author's book, then how the book did not understand the reviewer. Sometimes I have already read the book and know they are all wrong. But who am I to say? I write a letter and file it away. Who am I indeed.

On this day an unlikely April snowfall spat on my windows. Nan was helping Paula with her taxes. As I read the pages I fed them to the fire where they darkened, curled, and shattered, hurrrying into the smoke that flowed past the living-room window before it fled for good in the pines. The snow would protect my lettuce from tonight's deep freeze. And then I read the letter and knew who I was.

I am Donald Barthelme.

I am not the Donald Barthelme, I hasten to add, who wrote "Divorce" or "Cannon." Or, as the letter seems to suggest, either of the two Barthelmes who wrote these two stories, one inferior to the other. I have not even read these stories. Nor am I the Donald Barthelme who wrote the letter and who has an agent named Lynn Nesbit (indeed, I do not intend to offer the world such unlikely names out of Dickens or Wodehouse; my comedy lies deeper). I have never written any Barthelme stories I have read—I admit this with shame, for I have recognized them often as my own. And others? There have been others, the ones I too cried were not *authentic*. And I sympathize with this other, this third (or fourth) Barthelme who cries out in the letter to *The New York Times Book Review*. Clearly he has thought himself to be Barthelme and his existence is shaken. Still more touching is his worry that the quality of spurious Barthelme is declining; it is as a critic and upholder of values that he writes. How could I not sympathize and wish to hold his hand in this time of crisis? With Baudelaire I cry, my Brother! But he is not I.

There is, I must in the interest of truth reveal here with considerable regret for my brother, no "Scandinavian Institute of Comparative Vandalism." Everywhere I look it is not listed. And if "Barthelme" was not true in that statement, where can he be trusted? In his overweening rage to impress us with his credentials he has given himself away like a swooning bride in a sweetshop. I who have given *myself* to the rigors of honest scholarship note only that a finespun web of deceit catches only fish in its net. Ah, Barthelme! Ah, humanity!

A young friend of mine . . . Karen . . . wrote her M.A. thesis on Barthelme . . . afterward she divorced her husband and changed her name . . . but she did not change it to Donald Barthelme . . . I do not think she is Donald Barthelme . . . and I know I am not she . . . reader, are you finally convinced? And why should I have read her hundred unpublished pages about Barthelme's fiction if I were not he? Who else would care?

Borges, once, argued that every man was Shakespeare I do not wish to bore you. (Borges also thought once he was not Borges somebody else was.) But I am not Borges I am not Shakespeare I am Barthelme. I used to think I was perhaps Melville or Nabokov, but now I know who they are. It was a great shock to learn who Kafka was. I have stopped eating Special K. I had recently wondered if I was Pynchon, Thomas Pynchon, but now I know I am Barthelme I know nobody is Pynchon. The field is wide open. (There was a time when Norman Mailer was young and didn't want his picture taken by *Life,* didn't want anyone to know someone had written *The Naked and the Dead;* later he decided to become Norman Mailer and did not write *The Naked and the Dead.*) (Although he had his picture taken.) I did not take his picture. I do not like Norman Mailer. I have not had my picture taken. I have kept myself available.

I grieve to hear that the third (or fourth) Barthelme is "not responsible." This explains several things. But he too showed promise in his letter. Tonight my lettuce is growing. My own taxes are due. My child is asleep. The rabbits are hopping (I have not told you about them), my calf knows who I am even while the world labors over its misconception. The dog scratches at the door. Should I answer?

QUESTIONS

1. Identify the following allusions and relate them to the story's meaning: Dickens, Wodehouse, Borges, Melville, Nabokov, Kafka, Pynchon, Mailer.

2. Identify the Barthelmes you found in this story. How many are there? Three? Four?

3. Why does the narrator admit to being Donald Barthelme but then add, "I have never written any Barthelme stories I have read—I admit this with shame, for I have recognized them often as my own"?

4. Discuss the effect of the first, second, and concluding paragraphs on your conception of the narrator.

5. Discuss this story as literary satire.

GRACE PALEY

A Conversation with My Father

My father is eighty-six years old and in bed. His heart, that bloody motor, is equally old and will not do certain jobs any more. It still floods his head with brainy light. But it won't let his legs carry the weight of his body around the house. Despite my metaphors, this muscle failure is not due to his old heart, he says, but to a potassium shortage. Sitting on one pillow, leaning on three, he offers last-minute advice and makes a request.

"I would like you to write a simple story just once more," he says, "the kind de Maupassant wrote, or Chekhov, the kind you used to write. Just recognizable people and then write down what happened to them next."

I say, "Yes, why not? That's possible." I want to please him, though I don't remember writing that way. I *would* like to try to tell such a story, if he means the kind that begins: "There was a woman . . ." followed by plot, the absolute line between two points which I've always despised. Not for literary reasons, but because it takes all hope away. Everyone, real or invented, deserves the open destiny of life.

Finally I thought of a story that had been happening for a couple of years right across the street. I wrote it down, then read it aloud. "Pa," I said, "how about this? Do you mean something like this?"

Once in my time there was a woman and she had a son. They lived nicely, in a small apartment in Manhattan. This boy at about fifteen became a junkie, which is not unusual in our neighborhood. In order to maintain her close friendship with him, she became a junkie too. She said it was part of the youth culture, with which

513

she felt very much at home. After a while, for a number or reasons, the boy gave it all up and left the city and his mother in disgust. Hopeless and alone, she grieved. We all visit her.

"O.K., Pa, that's it," I said, "an unadorned and miserable tale."

"But that's not what I mean," my father said. "You misunderstood me on purpose. You know there's a lot more to it. You know that. You left everything out. Turgenev wouldn't do that. Chekhov wouldn't do that. There are in fact Russian writers you never heard of, you don't have an inkling of, as good as anyone, who can write a plain ordinary story, who would not leave out what you have left out. I object not to facts but to people sitting in trees talking senselessly, voices from who knows where . . ."

"Forget that one, Pa, what have I left out now? In this one?"

"Her looks, for instance."

"Oh. Quite handsome, I think. Yes."

"Her hair?"

"Dark, with heavy braids, as though she were a girl or a foreigner."

"What were her parents like, her stock? That she became such a person. It's interesting, you know."

"From out of town. Professional people. The first to be divorced in their county. How's that? Enough?" I asked.

"With you, it's all a joke," he said. "What about the boy's father? Why didn't you mention him? Who was he? Or was the boy born out of wedlock?"

"Yes," I said. "He was born out of wedlock."

"For Godsakes, doesn't anyone in your stories get married? Doesn't anyone have the time to run down to City Hall before they jump into bed?"

"No," I said. "In real life, yes. But in my stories, no."

"Why do you answer me like that?"

"Oh, Pa, this is a simple story about a smart woman who came to N.Y.C. full of interest love trust excitement very up to date, and about her son, what a hard time she had in this world. Married or not, it's of small consequence."

"It is of great consequence," he said.

"O.K.," I said.

"O.K. O.K. yourself," he said, "but listen. I believe you that she's good-looking, but I don't think she was so smart."

"That's true," I said. "Actually that's the trouble with stories. People start out fantastic. You think they're extraordinary, but it turns out as the work goes along, they're just average with a good education. Sometimes the other way around, the person's a kind of dumb innocent, but he outwits you and you can't even think of an ending good enough."

"What do you do then?" he asked. He had been a doctor for a couple of decades and then an artist for a couple of decades and he's still interested in details, craft, technique.

"Well, you just have to let the story lie around till some agreement can be reached between you and the stubborn hero."

"Aren't you talking silly, now?" he asked. "Start again," he said. "It so happens I'm not going out this evening. Tell the story again. See what you can do this time."

"O.K.," I said. "But it's not a five-minute job." Second attempt:

Once, across the street from us, there was a fine handsome woman, our neighbor. She had a son whom she loved because she'd known him since birth (in helpless chubby infancy, and in the wrestling, hugging ages, seven to ten, as well as earlier and later). This boy, when he fell into the fist of adolescence, became a junkie. He was not a hopeless one. He was in fact hopeful, an ideologue and successful converter. With his busy brilliance, he wrote persuasive articles for his high-school newspaper. Seeking a wider audience, using important connections, he drummed into Lower Manhattan newsstand distribution a periodical called *Oh! Golden Horse!*

In order to keep him from feeling guilty (because guilt is the stony heart of nine tenths of all clinically diagnosed cancers in America today, she said), and because she had always believed in giving bad habits room at home where one could keep an eye on them, she too became a junkie. Her kitchen was famous for a while—a center for intellectual addicts who knew what they were doing. A few felt artistic like Coleridge and others were scientific and revolutionary like Leary. Although she was often high herself, certain good mothering reflexes remained, and she saw to it that there was lots of orange juice around and honey and milk and vitamin pills. However, she never cooked anything but chili, and that no more than once a week. She explained, when we talked to her, seriously, with neighborly concern, that it was her part in the youth culture and she would rather be with the young, it was an honor, than with her own generation.

One week, while nodding through an Antonioni film, this boy was severely jabbed by the elbow of a stern and proselytizing girl, sitting beside him. She offered immediate apricots and nuts for his sugar level, spoke to him sharply, and took him home.

She had heard of him and his work and she herself published, edited, and wrote a competitive journal called *Man Does Live By Bread Alone.* In the organic heat of her continuous presence he could not help but become interested once more in his muscles, his arteries, and nerve connections. In fact he began to love them, treasure them, praise them with funny little songs in *Man Does Live . . .*

> the fingers of my flesh transcend
> my transcendental soul
> the tightness in my shoulders end
> my teeth have made me whole

To the mouth of his head (that glory of will and determination) he brought hard apples, nuts, wheat germ, and soy-bean oil. He said to his old friends, From now on, I guess I'll keep my wits about me. I'm going on the natch. He said he was about to begin a spiritual deep-breathing journey. How about you too, Mom? he asked kindly.

His conversion was so radiant, splendid, that neighborhood kids his age began to say that he had never been a real addict at all, only a journalist along for the smell of the story. The mother tried several times to give up what had become without her son and his friends a lonely habit. This effort only brought it to supportable levels. The boy and his girl took their electronic mimeograph and moved to the bushy edge of another borough. They were very strict. They said they would not see her again until she had been off drugs for sixty days.

At home alone in the evening, weeping, the mother read and reread the seven issues of *Oh! Golden Horse!* They seemed to her as truthful as ever. We often crossed the street to visit and console. But if we mentioned any of our children who were at college or in the hospital or dropouts at home, she would cry out, My baby! My baby! and burst into terrible, face-scarring, time-consuming tears. The End.

First my father was silent, then he said, "Number One: You have a nice sense of humor. Number Two: I see you can't tell a plain story. So don't waste time." Then he said sadly, "Number Three: I suppose that means she was alone, she was left like that, his mother. Alone. Probably sick?"

I said, "Yes."

"Poor woman. Poor girl, to be born in a time of fools, to live among fools. The end. The end. You were right to put that down. The end."

I didn't want to argue, but I had to say, "Well, it is not necessarily the end, Pa."

"Yes," he said, "what a tragedy. The end of a person."

"No, Pa," I begged him. "It doesn't have to be. She's only about forty. She could be a hundred different things in this world as time goes on. A teacher or a social worker. An ex-junkie! Sometimes it's better than having a master's in education."

"Jokes," he said. "As a writer that's your main trouble. You don't want to recognize it. Tragedy! Plain tragedy! Historical tragedy! No hope. The end."

"Oh, Pa," I said. "She could change."

"In your own life, too, you have to look it in the face." He took a couple of nitroglycerin. "Turn to five," he said, pointing to the dial on the oxygen tank. He inserted the tubes into his nostrils and breathed deep. He closed his eyes and said, "No."

I had promised the family to always let him have the last word when arguing, but in this case I had a different responsibility. That woman lives across the street. She's my knowledge and my invention. I'm sorry for her. I'm not going to leave her there in that house crying. (Actually neither would Life, which unlike me has no pity.)

Therefore: She did change. Of course her son never came home again. But right now, she's the receptionist in a storefront community clinic in the East Village. Most of the customers are young people, some old friends. The head doctor has said to her, "If we only had three people in this clinic with your experiences . . ."

"The doctor said that?" My father took the oxygen tubes out of his nostrils and said, "Jokes. Jokes again."

"No, Pa, it could really happen that way, it's a funny world nowadays."

"No," he said. "Truth first. She will slide back. A person must have character. She does not."

"No, Pa," I said. "That's it. She's got a job. Forget it. She's in that storefront working."

"How long will it be?" he asked. "Tragedy! You too. When will you look it in the face?"

QUESTIONS

1. Identify the following allusions and relate them to the story's meaning: de Maupassant, Chekhov, Turgenev, Coleridge, Leary, Antonioni.

2. Are the narrator and her father believable characters? unbelievable? sympathetic? unsympathetic? flat? round? static? dynamic?

3. What insight into fiction is revealed by their disagreement about marriage?

4. Why does the narrator object to plot? Do you agree? Explain the significance of the title.

5. Compare and contrast the stories the daughter tells with the story considered as a whole. What are the father's objections to her stories? Are those objections overcome in the story as a whole?

6. At the conclusion of the second story, the father says, "'You have a nice sense of humor.'" Do you think the story is funny? What does the father mean?

7. Why does the father reject the added-on ending of the second story?

8. What does the father mean when he says, "'Tragedy! You too. When will you look it in the face?'" Is he talking only about his daughter's story, or do his remarks have a wider significance?

What a Story Is (Again)

JOHN BARTH

Lost in the Funhouse

For whom is the funhouse fun? Perhaps for lovers. For Ambrose it is *a place of fear and confusion.* He has come to the seashore with his family for the holiday, *the occasion of their visit is Independence Day, the most important secular holiday of the United States of America.* A single straight underline is the manuscript mark for italic type, *which in turn* is the printed equivalent to oral emphasis of words and phrases as well as the customary type for titles of complete works, not to mention. Italics are also employed, in fiction stories especially, for "outside," intrusive, or artificial voices, such as radio announcements, the texts of telegrams and newspaper articles, et cetera. They should be used *sparingly.* If passages originally in roman type are italicized by someone repeating them, it's customary to acknowledge the fact. *Italics mine.*

Ambrose was "at that awkward age." His voice came out high-pitched as a child's if he let himself get carried away; to be on the safe side, therefore, he moved and spoke with *deliberate calm* and *adult gravity.* Talking soberly of unimportant or irrelevant matters and listening consciously to the sound of your own voice are useful habits for maintaining control in this difficult interval. *En route* to Ocean City he sat in the back seat of the family car with his brother Peter, age fifteen, and Magda G——, age fourteen, a pretty girl, an exquisite young lady, who lived not far from them on B—— Street in the town of D——, Maryland. Initials, blanks, or both were often substituted for proper names in nineteenth-century fiction to enhance the illusion of reality. It is as if the author felt it necessary to delete the names for reasons of tact or legal liability. Interestingly, as with other aspects of realism, it is an *illusion* that is being enhanced, by purely artificial means. Is it likely, does it violate the principle of verisimilitude, that a thirteen-year-old boy could make such a sophisticated observation? A girl of fourteen is *the psychological coeval* of a boy of fifteen or sixteen; a thirteen-year-old boy, therefore, even one precocious in some other respects, might be three years *her emotional junior.*

Thrice a year—on Memorial, Independence, and Labor Days—the family visits Ocean City for the afternoon and evening. When Ambrose and Peter's father was their age, the excursion was made by train, as mentioned in the novel *The 42nd Parallel* by John Dos Passos. Many families from the same neighborhood used to travel together, with dependent relatives and often with Negro servants; schoolfuls of children swarmed through the railway cars; everyone shared everyone else's Maryland fried chicken, Virginia ham, deviled eggs, potato salad, beaten biscuits, iced tea. Nowadays (that is in 19—, the year of our story) the journey is made by automobile—more comfortably and quickly though without the extra fun though without the *camaraderie* of a general excursion. It's all part of the deterioration of American life, their father declares; Uncle Karl supposes that when the boys take *their* families to Ocean City for the holidays they'll fly in Autogiros. Their mother, sitting in the middle of the front seat like Magda in the second, only with her arms on the seat-back behind the men's shoulders, wouldn't want the good old days back again, the steaming trains and stuffy long dresses; on the other hand she can do without Autogiros, too, if she has to become a grandmother to fly in them.

Description of physical appearance and mannerisms is one of several standard methods of characterization used by writers of fiction. It is also important to "keep the senses operating"; when a detail from one of the five senses, say visual, is "crossed" with a detail from another, say auditory, the reader's imagination is oriented to the scene, perhaps unconsciously. This procedure may be compared to the way surveyors and navigators determine their positions by two or more compass bearings, a process known as triangulation. The brown hair on Ambrose's mother's forearms gleamed in the sun like. Though right-handed, she took her left arm from the seat-back to press the dashboard cigar lighter for Uncle Karl. When the glass bead in its handle glowed red, the lighter was ready for use. The smell of Uncle Karl's cigar smoke reminded one of. The fragrance of the ocean came strong to the picnic ground where they always stopped for lunch, two miles inland from Ocean City. Having to pause for a full hour almost within sound of the breakers was difficult for Peter and Ambrose when they were younger; even at their present age it was not easy to keep their anticipation, *stimulated by the briny spume,* from turning into short temper. The Irish author James Joyce, in his unusual novel entitled *Ulysses,* now available in this country, uses the adjectives *snot-green* and *scrotum-tightening* to describe the sea. Visual, auditory, tactile, olfactory, gustatory. Peter and Ambrose's father, while steering their black 1936 LaSalle sedan with one hand, could with the other remove the first cigarette from a white pack of Lucky Strikes and, more remarkably, light it with a match forefingered from its book and thumbed against the flint paper without being detached. The matchbook cover merely advertised U.S. War Bonds and Stamps. A fine metaphor, simile, or other figure of speech, in addition to its obvious "first-order" relevance to the thing it describes, will be seen upon reflection to have a second order of significance: it may be drawn from the *milieu* of the action, for example, or be particularly appropriate to the sensibility of the narrator, even hinting to the reader things of which the narrator is unaware; or it may cast futher and subtler lights upon the thing it describes, sometimes ironically qualifying the more evident sense of the comparison.

To say that Ambrose's and Peter's mother was *pretty* is to accomplish nothing; the reader may acknowledge the proposition, but his imagination is not engaged. Besides, Magda was also pretty, yet in an altogether different way. Although she lived on B——— Street she had very good manners and did better than average in school. Her figure was very well developed for her age. Her right hand lay casually on the plush upholstery of the seat, very near Ambrose's left leg, on which his own hand rested. The space between their legs, between her right and his left leg, was out of the line of sight of anyone sitting on the other side of Magda, as well as anyone glancing into the rearview mirror. Uncle Karl's face resembled Peter's—rather, vice versa. Both had dark hair and eyes, short husky statures, deep voices. Magda's left hand was probably in a similar position on her left side. The boy's father is difficult to describe; no particular feature of his appearance or manner stood out. He wore glasses and was principal of a T——— County grade school. Uncle Karl was a masonry contractor.

Although Peter must have known as well as Ambrose that the latter, because of his position in the car, would be the first to see the electrical towers of the power plant at V———, the halfway point of their trip, he leaned forward and slightly toward the center of the car and pretended to be looking for them through the flat pinewoods and tuckahoe creeks along the highway. For as long as the boys could remember, "looking for the Towers" had been a feature of the first half of their excursions to Ocean City, "looking for the standpipe" of the second. Though the game was childish, their mother preserved the tradition of rewarding the first to see the Towers with a candybar or piece of fruit. She insisted now that Magda play the game; the prize, she said, was "something hard to get nowadays." Ambrose decided not to join in; he sat far back in his seat. Magda, like Peter, leaned forward. Two sets of straps were discernible through the shoulders of her sun dress; the inside right one, a brassiere-strap, was fastened or shortened with a small safety pin. The right armpit of her dress, presumably the left as well, was damp with perspiration. The simple strategy for being first to espy the Towers, which Ambrose had understood by the age of four, was to sit on the right-hand side of the car. Whoever sat there, however, had also to put up with the worst of the sun, and so Ambrose, without mentioning the matter, chose sometimes the one and sometimes the other. Not impossibly Peter had never caught on to the trick, or thought that his brother hadn't simply because Ambrose on occasion preferred shade to a Baby Ruth or tangerine.

The shade-sun situation didn't apply to the front seat, owing to the windshield; if anything the driver got more sun, since the person on the passenger side not only was shaded below by the door and dashboard but might swing down his sunvisor all the way too.

"Is that them?" Magda asked. Ambrose's mother teased the boys for letting Magda win, insinuating that "somebody [had] a girlfriend." Peter and Ambrose's father reached a long thin arm across their mother to butt his cigarette in the dashboard ashtray, under the lighter. The prize this time for seeing the Towers first was a banana. Their mother bestowed it after chiding their father for wasting a half-smoked cigarette when everything was so scarce. Magda, to take the prize, moved her hand from so near Ambrose's that he could have touched it as though accidentally. She offered to share the prize, things like that were so hard to find; but everyone insisted it was hers alone. Ambrose's mother sang an iambic trimeter couplet from a popular song, femininely rhymed:

> "What's good is in the Army;
> What's left will never harm me."

Uncle Karl tapped his cigar ash out the ventilator window; some particles were sucked by the slipstream back into the car through the rear window on the passenger side. Magda demonstrated her ability to hold a banana in one hand and peel it with her teeth. She still sat forward; Ambrose pushed his glasses back onto the bridge of his nose with his left hand, which he then negligently let fall to the seat cushion immediately behind her. He even permitted the single hair, gold, on the second joint of his thumb to brush the fabric of her skirt. Should she have sat back at that instant, his hand would have been caught under her.

Plush upholstery prickles uncomfortably through gabardine slacks in the July sun. The function of the *beginning* of a story is to introduce the principal characters, establish their initial relationships, set the scene for the main action, expose the background of the situation if necessary, plant motifs and foreshadowings where appropriate and initiate the first complication or whatever of the "rising action." Actually, if one imagines a story called "The Funhouse," or "Lost in the Funhouse," the details of the drive to Ocean City don't seem especially relevant. The *beginning* should recount the events between Ambrose's first sight of the funhouse early in the afternoon and his entering it with Magda and Peter in the evening. The *middle* would narrate all relevant events from the time he goes in to the time he loses his way; middles have the double and contradictory function of delaying the climax while at the same time preparing the reader for it and fetching him to it. Then the *ending* would tell what Ambrose does while he's lost, how he finally finds his way out, and what everybody makes of the experience. So far there's been no real dialogue, very little sensory detail, and nothing in the way of a *theme*. And a long time has gone by already without anything happening; it makes a person wonder. We haven't even reached Ocean City yet: we will never get out of the funhouse.

The more closely an author identifies with the narrator, literally or metaphorically, the less advisable it is, as a rule, to use the first-person narrative viewpoint. Once three years previously the young people *aforementioned* played Niggers and Masters in the backyard; when it was Ambrose's turn to be Master and theirs to be Niggers Peter had to go serve his evening papers; Ambrose was afraid to punish Magda alone, but she led him to the whitewashed Torture Chamber between the woodshed and the privy in the Slaves Quarters; there she knelt sweating among bamboo rakes and dusty Mason jars, pleadingly embraced his knees, and while bees droned in the lattice as if on an ordinary summer afternoon, purchased clemency at a surprising price set by herself. Doubtless she remembered nothing of this event; Ambrose on the other hand seemed unable to forget the least detail of his life. He even recalled how, standing beside himself with awed impersonality in the reeky heat, he'd stared the while at an empty cigar box in which Uncle Karl kept stone-cutting chisels: beneath the words *El Producto,* a laureled, loose-toga'd lady regarded the sea from a marble bench; beside her, forgotten or not yet turned to, was a five-stringed lyre. Her chin reposed on the back of her right hand; her left depended negligently from the bench-arm. The lower half of scene and lady was peeled away; the words EXAMINED BY ___ were inked there into the wood. Nowadays cigar boxes are made of pasteboard. Ambrose wondered what Magda would have done, Ambrose wondered what Magda would do when she sat back on his hand as he resolved she should. Be angry. Make a teasing joke of it. Give no sign at all. For a long time she leaned forward, playing cow-poker with Peter against Uncle Karl and Mother and watching for the first sign of Ocean City. At nearly the same instant, picnic ground and Ocean City standpipe hove into view; an Amoco filling station on their side of the road cost Mother and Uncle Karl fifty cows and the game; Magda bounced back, clapping her right hand on Mother's right arm; Ambrose moved clear "in the nick of time."

At this rate our hero, at this rate our protagonist will remain in the funhouse forever. Narrative ordinarily consists of alternating dramatization and summarization. One symptom of nervous tension, paradoxically, is repeated and violent yawning; neither Peter nor Magda nor Uncle Karl nor Mother reacted in this manner. Although they were no longer small children, Peter and Ambrose were each given a dollar to spend on boardwalk amusements in addition to what money of their own they'd brought along. Magda too, though she protested she had ample spending money. The boys' mother made a little scene out of distributing the bills; she pretended that her sons and Magda were small children and cautioned them not to spend the sum too quickly or in one place. Magda promised with a merry laugh and, having both hands free, took the bill with her left. Peter laughed also and pledged in a falsetto to be a good boy. His imitation of a child was not clever. The boys' father was tall and thin, balding, fair-complexioned. Assertions of that sort are not effective; the reader may acknowledge the proposition, but. We should be much farther along than we are; something has gone wrong; not much of this preliminary rambling seems relevant. Yet everyone begins in the same place; how is it that most go along without difficulty but a few lose their way?

"Stay out from under the boardwalk," Uncle Karl growled from the side of his mouth. The boys' mother pushed his shoulder *in mock annoyance*. They were all standing before Fat May the Laughing Lady who advertised the funhouse. Larger than life, Fat May mechanically shook, rocked on her heels, slapped her thighs while recorded laughter—uproarious, female—came amplified from a hidden loudspeaker. It chuckled, wheezed, wept; tried in vain to catch its breath; tittered, groaned, exploded raucous and anew. You couldn't hear it without laughing yourself, no matter how you felt. Father came back from talking to a Coast-Guardsman on duty and reported that the surf was spoiled with crude oil from tankers recently torpedoed offshore. Lumps of it, difficult to remove, made tarry tidelines on the beach and stuck on swimmers. Many bathed in the surf nevertheless and came out speckled; others paid to use a municipal pool and only sunbathed on the beach. We would do the latter. We would do the latter. We would do the latter.

Under the boardwalk, matchbook covers, grainy other things. What is the story's theme? Ambrose is ill. He perspires in the dark passages; candied apples-on-a-stick, delicious-looking, disappointing to eat. Funhouses need men's and ladies' room at intervals. Others perhaps have also vomited in corners and corridors; may even have had bowel movements liable to be stepped in in the dark. The word *fuck* suggests suction and/or and/or flatulence. Mother and Father; grandmothers and grandfathers on both sides; great-grandmothers and great-grandfathers on four sides, et cetera. Count a generation as thirty years: in approximately the year when Lord Baltimore was granted charter to the province of Maryland by Charles I, five hundred twelve women—English, Welsh, Bavarian, Swiss—of every class and character, received into themselves the penises the intromittent organs of five hundred twelve men, ditto, in every circumstance and posture, to conceive the five hundred twelve ancestors of the two hundred fifty-six ancestors of the et cetera et cetera et cetera et cetera et cetera et cetera et cetera et cetera of the author, of the narrator, of this story, *Lost in the Funhouse*. In alleyways, ditches, canopy beds, pinewoods, bridal suites, ship's cabins, coach-and-fours, coaches-and-four, sultry toolsheds; on the cold sand under boardwalks, littered with *El Producto* cigar butts, treasured with Lucky Strike cigarette stubs, Coca-Cola caps, gritty turds, cardboard lollipop sticks, matchbook covers warning that A Slip of the Lip Can Sink a Ship. The shluppish whisper, continuous as seawash round the globe, tidelike falls and rises with the circuit of dawn and dusk.

Magda's teeth. She *was* left-handed. Perspiration. They've gone all the way, through, Magda and Peter, they've been waiting for hours with Mother and Uncle Karl while Father searches for his lost son; they draw french-fried potatoes from a paper cup and shake their heads. They've named the children they'll one day have and bring to Ocean City on holidays. Can spermatozoa properly be thought of as male animalcules when there are no female spermatozoa? They grope through hot, dark windings, past Love's Tunnel's fearsome obstacles. Some perhaps lose their way.

Peter suggested then and there that they do the funhouse; he had been through it before, so had Magda, Ambrose hadn't and suggested, his voice cracking on account of Fat May's laughter, that they swim first. All were chuckling, couldn't help it; Ambrose's father, Ambrose's and Peter's father came up grinning like a lunatic with two boxes of syrup-coated popcorn, one for Mother, one for Magda; the men were to help themselves. Ambrose walked on Magda's right; being by nature left-handed, she carried the box in her left hand. Up front the situation was reversed.

"What are you limping for?" Magda inquired of Ambrose. He supposed in a husky tone that his foot had gone to sleep in the car. Her teeth flashed. "Pins and needles?" It was the honeysuckle on the lattice of the former privy that drew the bees. Imagine being stung there. How long is this going to take?

The adults decided to forgo the pool; but Uncle Karl insisted they change into swimsuits and do the beach. "He wants to watch the pretty girls," Peter teased, and ducked behind Magda from Uncle Karl's pretended wrath. "You've got all the pretty girls you need right here," Magda declared, and Mother said: "Now that's the gospel truth." Magda scolded Peter, who reached over her shoulder to sneak some popcorn. "Your brother and father aren't getting any." Uncle Karl wondered if they were going to have fireworks that night, what with the shortages. It wasn't the shortages, Mr. M____ replied; Ocean City had fireworks from pre-war. But it was too risky on account of the enemy submarines, some people thought.

"Don't seem like Fourth of July without fireworks," said Uncle Karl. The inverted tag in dialogue writing is still considered permissible with proper names or epithets, but sounds old-fashioned with personal pronouns. "We'll have 'em again soon enough," predicted the boys' father. Their mother declared she could do without fireworks: they reminded her too much of the real thing. Their father said all the more reason to shoot off a few now and again. Uncle Karl asked *rhetorically* who needed reminding, just look at people's hair and skin.

"The oil, yes," said Mrs. M____.

Ambrose had a pain in his stomach and so didn't swim but enjoyed watching the others. He and his father burned red easily. Magda's figure was exceedingly well developed for her age. She too declined to swim, and got mad, and became angry when Peter attempted to drag her into the pool. She always swam, he insisted; what did she mean not swim? Why did a person come to Ocean City?

"Maybe I want to lay here with Ambrose," Magda teased.

Nobody likes a pedant.

"Aha," said Mother. Peter grabbed Magda by one ankle and ordered Ambrose to grab the other. She squealed and rolled over on the beach blanket. Ambrose pretended to help hold her back. Her tan was darker than even Mother's and Peter's. "Help out, Uncle Karl!" Peter cried. Uncle Karl went to seize the other ankle. Inside the top of her swimsuit, however, you could see the line where the sunburn ended and, when she hunched her shoulders and squealed again, one nipple's auburn edge. Mother made them behave themselves. "*You* should certainly know," she said to Uncle Karl. Archly. "That when

a lady says she doesn't feel like swimming, a gentleman doesn't ask questions."
Uncle Karl said excuse *him;* Mother winked at Magda; Ambrose blushed; stupid
Peter kept saying "Phooey on *feel like!*" and tugging at Magda's ankle; then even
he got the point, and cannonballed with a holler into the pool.

"I swear," Magda said, in mock *in feigned* exasperation.

The diving would make a suitable literary symbol. To go off the high board
you had to wait in a line along the poolside and up the ladder. Fellows tickled
girls and goosed one another and shouted to the ones at the top to hurry up, or
razzed them for bellyfloppers. Once on the springboard some took a great while
posing or clowning or deciding on a dive or getting up their nerve; others ran
off. Especially among the younger fellows the idea was to strike the funniest
pose or do the craziest stunt as you fell, a thing that got harder to do as you kept
on and kept on. But whether you hollered *Geronimo!* or *Sieg heil!,* held your
nose or "rode a bicycle," pretended to be shot or did a perfect jacknife or
changed your mind halfway down and ended up with nothing, it was over in two
seconds, after all that wait. Spring, pose, splash. Spring, neat-o, splash. Spring,
aw fooey, splash.

The grown-ups had gone on; Ambrose wanted to converse with Magda;
she was remarkably well developed for her age; it was said that that came from
rubbing with a turkish towel, and there were other theories. Ambrose could
think of nothing to say except how good a diver Peter was, who was showing off
for her benefit. You could pretty well tell by looking at their bathing suits and
arm muscles how far along the different fellows were. Ambrose was glad he
hadn't gone in swimming, the cold water shrank you up so. Magda pretended to
be uninterested in the diving; she probably weighed as much as he did. If you
knew your way around in the funhouse like your own bedroom, you could wait
until a girl came along and then slip away without ever getting caught, even if her
boyfriend was right with her. She'd think *he* did it! It would be better to be the
boyfriend, and act outraged, and tear the funhouse apart.

Not act; *be.*

"He's a master diver," Ambrose said. In feigned admiration. "You really
have to slave away at it to get that good." What would it matter anyhow if he
asked her right out whether she remembered, even teased her with it as Peter
would have?

There's no point in going farther; this isn't getting anybody anywhere; they
haven't even come to the funhouse yet. Ambrose is off the track, in some new or
old part of the place that's not supposed to be used; he strayed into it by some
one-in-a-million chance, like the time the roller-coaster car left the tracks in the
nineteen-teens against all the laws of physics and sailed over the boardwalk in
the dark. And they can't locate him because they don't know where to look.
Even the designer and operator have forgotten this other part, that winds around
on itself like a whelk shell. That winds around the right part like the snakes on
Mercury's caduceus. Some people, perhaps, don't "hit their stride" until their
twenties, when the growing-up business is over and women appreciate other
things besides wisecracks and teasing and strutting. Peter didn't have one-tenth

the imagination *he* had, not one-tenth. Peter did this naming-their-children thing as a joke, making up names like Aloysius and Murgatroyd, but Ambrose knew *exactly* how it would feel to be married and have children of your own, and be a loving husband and father, and go comfortably to work in the mornings and to bed with your wife at night, and wake up with her there. With a breeze coming through the sash and birds and mockingbirds singing in the Chinese-cigar trees. His eyes watered, there aren't enough ways to say that. He would be quite famous in his line of work. Whether Magda was his wife or not, one evening when he was wise-lined and gray at the temples he'd smile gravely, at a fashionable dinner party, and remind her of his youthful passion. The time they went with his family to Ocean City; the *erotic fantasies* he used to have about her. How long ago it seemed, and childish! Yet tender, too, *n'est-ce pas?* Would she have imagined that the world famous whatever remembered how many strings were on the lyre on the bench beside the girl on the label of the cigar box he'd stared at in the toolshed at age ten while she, age eleven. Even then he had felt *wise beyond his years;* he'd stroked her hair and said in his deepest voice and correctest English, as to a dear child: "I shall never forget this moment."

But though he had breathed heavily, groaned as if ecstatic, what he'd really felt throughout was an odd detachment, as though someone else were Master. Strive as he might to be transported, he heard his mind take notes upon the scene: *This is what they call* passion. *I am experiencing it.* Many of the digger machines were out of order in the penny arcades and could not be repaired or replaced for the duration. Moreover the prizes, made now in USA, were less interesting than formerly, pasteboard items for the most part, and some of the machines wouldn't work on white pennies. The gypsy fortune-teller machine might have provided a foreshadowing of the climax of this story if Ambrose had operated it. It was even dilapidateder than most: the silver coating was worn off the brown metal handles, the glass windows around the dummy were cracked and taped, her kerchiefs and silks long-faded. If a man lived by himself, he could take a department-store mannequin with flexible joints and modify her in certain ways. *However:* by the time he was that old he'd have a real woman. There was a machine that stamped your name around a white-metal coin with a star in the middle: A____. His son would be the second, and when the lad reached thirteen or so he would put a strong arm around his shoulder and tell him calmly: "It is perfectly normal. We have all been through it. It will not last forever." Nobody knew how to be what they were right. He'd smoke a pipe, teach his son how to fish and softcrab, assure him he needn't worry about himself. Magda would certainly give, Magda would certainly yield a great deal of milk, although guilty of occasional solecisms. It don't taste so bad. Suppose the lights came on now!

The day wore on. You think you're yourself, but there are other persons in you. Ambrose gets hard when Ambrose doesn't want to, *and obversely.* Ambrose watches them disagree; Ambrose watches him watch. In the funhouse mirror-room you can't see yourself go on forever, because no matter how you stand, your head gets in the way. Even if you had a glass periscope, the image of your eye would cover up the thing you really wanted to see. The police will come; there'll be a story in the papers. That must be where it happened. Unless he can find a surprise exit, an unofficial backdoor or escape hatch opening on an alley, say, and then stroll up to the family in front of the funhouse and ask where everybody's been; *he's* been out of the place for ages. That's just where it happened, in that last lighted room: Peter and Magda found the right exit; he found one that you weren't supposed to find and strayed off into the works somewhere. In a perfect funhouse you'd be able to go only one way, like the divers off the highboard; getting lost would be impossible; the doors and halls would work like minnow traps or the valves in veins.

On account of German U-boats, Ocean City was "browned out": streetlights were shaded on the seaward side; shop-windows and boardwalk amusement places were kept dim, not to silhouette tankers and Liberty-ships for torpedoing. In a short story about Ocean City, Maryland, during World War II, the author could make use of the image of sailors on leave in the penny arcades and shooting galleries, sighting through the crosshairs of toy machine guns at swastika'd subs, while out in the black Atlantic a U-boat skipper squints through his periscope at real ships outlined by the glow of penny arcades. After dinner the family strolled back to the amusement end of the boardwalk. The boys' father had burnt red as always and was masked with Noxzema, a minstrel in reverse. The grownups stood at the end of the boardwalk where the Hurricane of '33 had cut an inlet from the ocean to Assawoman Bay.

"Pronounced with a long *o*," Uncle Karl reminded Magda with a wink. His shirt sleeves were rolled up; Mother punched his brown biceps with the arrowed heart on it and said his mind was naughty. Fat May's laugh came suddenly from the funhouse, as if she'd just got the joke; the family laughed too at the coincidence. Ambrose went under the boardwalk to search for out-of-town matchbook covers with the aid of his pocket flashlight; he looked out from the edge of the North American continent and wondered how far their laughter carried over the water. Spies in rubber rafts; survivors in lifeboats. If the joke had been beyond his understanding, he could have said: *"The laughter was over his head."* And let the reader see the serious wordplay on second reading.

He turned the flashlight on and then off at once even before the woman whooped. He sprang away, heart athud, dropping the light. What had the man grunted? Perspiration drenched and chilled him by the time he scrambled up to the family. "See anything?" his father asked. His voice wouldn't come; he shrugged and violently brushed sand from his pants legs.

"Let's ride the old flying horses!" Magda cried. I'll never be an author. It's been forever already, everybody's gone home, Ocean City's deserted, the ghostcrabs are tickling across the beach and down the littered cold streets. And the empty halls of clapboard hotels and abandoned funhouses. A tidal wave; an enemy air raid; a monster-crab swelling like an island from the sea. *The inhabitants fled in terror.* Magda clung to his trouser leg; he alone knew the maze's secret. "He gave his life that we might live," said Uncle Karl with a scowl of pain, as he. The fellow's hands had been tattooed; the woman's legs, the woman's fat white legs had. *An astonishing coincidence.* He yearned to tell Peter. He wanted to throw up for excitement. They hadn't even chased him. He wished he were dead.

One possible ending would be to have Ambrose come across another lost person in the dark. They'd match their wits together against the funhouse, struggle like Ulysses past obstacle after obstacle, help and encourage each other. Or a girl. By the time they found the exit they'd be closest friends, sweethearts if it were a girl; they'd know each other's inmost souls, be bound together *by the cement of shared adventure;* then they'd emerge into the light and it would turn out that his friend was a Negro. A blind girl. President Roosevelt's son. Ambrose's former archenemy.

Shortly after the mirror room he'd groped along a musty corridor, his heart already misgiving him at the absence of phosphorescent arrows and other signs. He'd found a crack of light—not a door, it turned out, but a seam between the plyboard wall panels—and squinting up to it, espied a small old man, *in appearance not unlike* the photographs at home of Ambrose's late grandfather, nodding upon a stool beneath a bare, speckled bulb. A crude panel of toggle- and knife-switches hung beside the open fuse box near his head; elsewhere in the little room were wooden levers and ropes belayed to boat cleats. At the time, Ambrose wasn't lost enough to rap or call; later he couldn't find that crack. Now it seemed to him that he'd possibly dozed off for a few minutes somewhere along the way; certainly he was exhausted from the afternoon's sunshine and the evening's problems; he couldn't be sure he hadn't dreamed part or all of the sight. Had an old black wall fan droned like bees and shimmied two flypaper streamers? Had the funhouse operator—gentle, somewhat sad and tired-appearing, in expression not unlike the photographs at home of Ambrose's late Uncle Konrad—murmured in his sleep? Is there really such a person as Ambrose, or is he a figment of the author's imagination? Was it Assawoman Bay or Sinepuxent? Are there other errors of fact in this fiction? Was there another sound besides the little slap slap of thigh on ham, like water sucking at the chine-boards of a skiff?

When you're lost, the smartest thing to do is stay put till you're found, hollering if necessary. But to holler guarantees humiliation as well as rescue; keeping silent permits some saving of face—you can act surprised at the fuss when your rescuers find you and swear you weren't lost, if they do. What's more you might find your own way yet, *however belatedly.*

"Don't tell me your foot's still asleep!" Magda exclaimed as the three young people walked from the inlet to the area set aside for ferris wheels, carrousels, and other carnival rides, they having decided in favor of the vast and ancient merry-go-round instead of the funhouse. What a sentence, everything was wrong from the outset. People don't know what to make of him, he doesn't know what to make of himself, he's only thirteen, *athletically and socially inept,* not astonishingly bright, but there are antennae; he has . . . some sort of receivers in his head; things speak to him, he understands more than he should, the world winks at him through its objects, grabs grinning at his coat. Everybody else is in on some secret he doesn't know; they've forgotten to tell him. Through simple *procrastination* his mother put off his baptism until this year. Everyone else had it done as a baby; he'd assumed the same of himself, as had his mother, so she claimed, until it was time for him to join Grace Methodist-Protestant and the oversight came out. He was mortified, but pitched sleepless through his private catechizing, intimidated by the ancient mysteries, a thirteen year old would never say that, resolved to experience conversion like St. Augustine. When the water touched his brow and Adam's sin left him, he contrived by a strain like defecation to bring tears into his eyes—but felt nothing. There was some simple, radical difference about him; he hoped it was genius, feared it was madness, devoted himself to amiability and inconspicuousness. Alone on the seawall near his house he was seized by the terrifying transports he'd thought to find in toolshed, in Communion-cup. The grass was alive! The town, the river, himself, were not imaginary; time roared in his ears like wind; the world was *going on!* This part ought to be dramatized. The Irish author James Joyce once wrote. Ambrose M_____ is going to scream.

There is no *texture of rendered sensory detail,* for one thing. The faded distorting mirrors beside Fat May; the impossibility of choosing a mount when one had but a single ride on the great carrousel; the *vertigo attendant on his recognition* that Ocean City was worn out, the place of fathers and grandfathers, straw-boatered men and parasoled ladies survived by their amusements. Money spent, the three paused at Peter's insistence beside Fat May to watch the girls get their skirts blown up. The object was to tease Magda, who said: "I swear, Peter M_____, you've got a one-track mind! Amby and me aren't *interested* in such things." In the tumbling-barrel, too, just inside the Devil's-mouth entrance to the funhouse, the girls were upended and their boyfriends and others could see up their dresses if they cared to. Which was the whole point, Ambrose realized. Of the entire funhouse! If you looked around, you noticed that almost all the people on the boardwalk were paired off into couples except the small children; in a way, that was the whole point of Ocean City! If you had X-ray eyes and could see everything going on at that instant under the boardwalk and in all the hotel rooms and cars and alleyways, you'd realize that all that normally *showed,* like restaurants and dance halls and clothing and test-your-strength machines, was merely preparation and intermission. Fat May screamed.

Because he watched the goings-on from the corner of his eye, it was Ambrose who spied the half-dollar on the boardwalk near the tumbling-barrel. Losers weepers. The first time he'd heard some people moving through a corridor not far away, just after he'd lost sight of the crack of light, he'd decided not to call to them, for fear they'd guess he was scared and poke fun; it sounded like roughnecks; he'd hoped they'd come by and he could follow in the dark without their knowing. Another time he'd heard just one person, unless he imagined it, bumping along as if on the other side of the plywood; perhaps Peter coming back for him, or Father, or Magda lost too. Or the owner and operator of the funhouse. He'd called out once as though merrily: "Anybody know where the heck we are?" But the query was too stiff, his voice cracked, when the sounds stopped he was terrified: maybe it was a queer who waited for fellows to get lost, or a longhaired filthy monster that lived in some cranny of the funhouse. He stood rigid for hours it seemed like, scarcely respiring. His future was shockingly clear, in outline. He tried holding his breath to the point of unconsciousness. There ought to be a button you could push to end your life absolutely without pain; disappear in a flick, like turning out a light. He would push it instantly! He despised Uncle Karl. But he despised his father too, for not being what he was supposed to be. Perhaps his father hated *his* father, and so on, and his son would hate him, and so on. Instantly!

Naturally he didn't have nerve enough to ask Magda to go through the funhouse with him. With incredible nerve and to everyone's surprise he invited Magda, quietly and politely, to go through the funhouse with him. "I warn you, I've never been through it before," he added, *laughing easily;* "but I reckon we can manage somehow. The important thing to remember, after all, is that it's meant to be a *fun*house; that is, a place of amusement. If people really got lost or injured or too badly frightened in it, the owner'd go out of business. There'd even be lawsuits. No character in a work of fiction can make a speech this long without interruption or acknowledgment from the other characters."

Mother teased Uncle Karl: "There's a crowd, I always heard." But actually Ambrose was relieved that Peter now had a quarter too. Nothing was what it looked like. Every instant, under the surface of the Atlantic Ocean, millions of living animals devoured one another. Pilots were falling in flames over Europe; women were being forcibly raped in the South Pacific. His father should have taken him aside and said: "There is a simple secret to getting through the funhouse, as simple as being first to see the Towers. Here it is. Peter does not know it; neither does your Uncle Karl. You and I are different. Not surprisingly, you've often wished you weren't. Don't think I haven't noticed how unhappy your childhood has been! But you'll understand, when I tell you, why it had to be kept secret until now. And you won't regret not being like your brother and your uncle. *On the contrary!*" If you knew all the stories behind all the people on the boardwalk, you'd see that *nothing* was what it looked like. Husbands and wives often hated each other; parents didn't necessarily love their children; et cetera. A child took things for granted because he had nothing to compare his life to and everybody acted as if things were as they should be. Therefore each saw himself as the hero of the story, when the truth might turn out to be that he's the villain, or the coward. And there wasn't one thing you could do about it!

Hunchbacks, fat ladies, fools—that no one chose what he was was unbearable. In the movies he'd meet a beautiful young girl in the funhouse; they'd have hairs-breadth escapes from real dangers; he'd do and say the right things; she also; in the end they'd be lovers; their dialogue lines would match up; he'd be perfectly at ease; she'd not only like him well enough, she'd think he was *marvelous;* she'd lie awake thinking about *him,* instead of vice versa—the way *his* face looked in different lights and how he stood and exactly what he'd said— and yet that would be only one small episode in his wonderful life, among many

many others. Not a *turning point* at all. What had happened in the toolshed was nothing. He hated, he loathed his parents! One reason for not writing a lost-in-the-funhouse story is that either everybody's felt what Ambrose feels, in which case it goes without saying, or else no normal person feels such things, in which case Ambrose is a freak. "Is anything more tiresome, in fiction, than the problems of sensitive adolescents?" And it's all too long and rambling, as if the author. For all a person knows the first time through, the end could be just around any corner; perhaps, *not impossibly* it's been within reach any number of times. On the other hand he may be scarcely past the start, with everything yet to get through, an intolerable idea.

Fill in: His father's raised eyebrows when he announced his decision to do the funhouse with Magda. Ambrose understands now, but didn't then, that his father was wondering whether he knew what the funhouse was *for*—especially since he didn't object, as he should have, when Peter decided to come along too. The ticket-woman, witchlike, mortifying him when inadvertently he gave her his name-coin instead of the half-dollar, then unkindly calling Magda's attention to the birthmark on his temple: "Watch out for him, girlie, he's a marked man!" She wasn't even cruel, he understood, only vulgar and insensitive. Somewhere in the world there was a young woman with such splendid understanding that she'd see him entire, like a poem or story, and find his words so valuable after all that when he confessed his apprehensions she would explain why they were in fact the very things that made him precious to her . . . and to Western Civilization! There was no such girl, the simple truth being. Violent yawns as they approached the mouth. Whispered advice from an old-timer on a bench near the barrel: "Go crabwise and ye'll get an eyeful without upsetting!" Composure vanished at the first pitch: Peter hollered joyously, Magda tumbled, shrieked, clutched her skirt; Ambrose scrambled crabwise, tight-lipped with terror, was soon out, watched his dropped name-coin slide among the couples. Shamefaced he saw that to get through expeditiously was not the point; Peter feigned assistance in order to trip Magda up, shouted "I see Christmas!" when her legs went flying. The old man, his latest betrayer, cacked approval. A dim hall then of black-thread cobwebs and recorded gibber: he took Magda's elbow to steady her against revolving discs set in the slanted floor to throw your feet out from under, and explained to her in a calm, deep voice his theory that each phase of the funhouse was triggered either automatically, by a series of photoelectric devices, or else manually by operators stationed at peepholes. But he lost his voice thrice as the discs unbalanced him; Magda was anyhow squealing; but at one point she clutched him about the waist to keep from falling, and her right cheek pressed for a moment against his belt-buckle. Heroically he drew her up, it was his chance to clutch her close as if for support and say: "I love you." He even put an arm lightly about the small of her back before a sailor-and-girl pitched into them from behind, sorely treading his left big toe and knocking Magda asprawl with them. The sailor's girl was a string-haired hussy with a loud laugh and light blue drawers; Ambrose realized that he wouldn't have said "I love you" anyhow, and was smitten with self-contempt. How much better it would be to be that common sailor! A wiry little Seaman 3rd, the fellow squeezed a girl to each side and stumbled hilarious into the mirror room, closer to Magda in thirty seconds than Ambrose had got in thirteen years. She giggled at something the fellow said to Peter; she drew her hair from her eyes with a movement so womanly it struck Ambrose's heart; Peter's smacking her backside then seemed particularly coarse. But Magda made a pleased indignant face and cried, "All right for *you,* mister!" and pursued Peter into the maze without a backward glance. The sailor followed after, leisurely, drawing his girl against his hip; Ambrose understood not only that they were all so relieved to be rid of his burdensome company that they didn't even notice his absence, but that he himself shared their relief. Stepping from the treacherous passage at last into the mirror-maze, he saw once again, more clearly than ever, how readily he deceived himself into supposing he was a person. He even foresaw, wincing at his dreadful self-knowledge, that he would repeat the deception, at ever-rarer intervals, all his wretched life, so fearful were the alternatives. Fame, madness, suicide; perhaps all three. It's not believable that so young a boy could articulate that reflection, and in fiction the merely true must always yield to the plausible. Moreover, the symbolism is in places heavy-footed. Yet Ambrose M____ understood, as few adults do, that the famous loneliness of the great was no popular myth but a general truth—furthermore, that it was as much cause as effect.

All the preceding except the last few sentences is exposition that should've been done earlier or interspersed with the present action instead of lumped together. No reader would put up with so much with such *prolixity.* It's interesting that Ambrose's father, though presumably an intelligent man (as indicated by his role as grade-school principal), neither encouraged nor discouraged his sons at all in any way—as if he either didn't care about them or cared all right but didn't know how to act. If this fact should contribute to one of them's becoming a celebrated but wretchedly unhappy scientist, was it a good thing or not? He too might someday face the question; it would be useful to know whether it had tortured his father for years, for example, or never once crossed his mind.

In the maze two important things happened. First, our hero found a name-coin someone else had lost or discarded: *AMBROSE,* suggestive of the famous lightship and of his late grandfather's favorite dessert, which his mother used to prepare on special occasions out of coconut, oranges, grapes, and what else. Second, as he wondered at the endless replication of his image in the mirrors, second, as he *lost himself in the reflection* that the necessity for an observer makes perfect observation impossible, better make him eighteen at least, yet that would render other things unlikely, he heard Peter and Magda chuckling somewhere together in the maze. "Here!" "No, here!" they shouted to each other; Peter said, "Where's Amby?" Magda murmured. "Amb?" Peter called. In a pleased, friendly voice. He didn't reply. The truth was, his brother was a *happy-go-lucky youngster* who'd've been better off with a regular brother of his own, but who seldom complained of his lot and was generally cordial. Ambrose's throat ached; there aren't enough different ways to say that. He stood quietly while the two young people giggled and thumped through the glittering maze, hurrah'd their discovery of its exit, cried out in joyful alarm at what next beset them. Then he set his mouth and followed after, as he supposed, took a wrong turn, strayed into the pass *wherein he lingers yet.*

The action of conventional dramatic narrative may be represented by a diagram called Freitag's Triangle:

$$\underset{A \diagup \quad \diagdown C}{B}$$

or more accurately by a variant of that diagram:

$$\underset{A \underline{\quad\quad} \underset{B}{\diagup} \diagdown D}{C}$$

in which *AB* represents the exposition, *B* the introduction of conflict, *BC* the "rising action," complication, or development of the conflict, *C* the climax, or turn of the action, *CD* the dénouement, or resolution of the conflict. While there is no reason to regard this pattern as an absolute necessity, like many other conventions it became conventional because great numbers of people over many years learned by trial and error that it was effective; one ought not to forsake it, therefore, unless one wishes to forsake as well the effect of drama or has clear cause to feel that deliberate violation of the "normal" pattern can better can better effect that effect. This can't go on much longer; it can go on forever. He died telling stories to himself in the dark; years later, when that vast unsuspected area of the funhouse came to light, the first expedition found his skeleton in one of its labyrinthine corridors and mistook it for part of the entertainment. He died of starvation telling himself stories in the dark; but unbeknownst unbeknownst to him, an assistant operator of the funhouse, happening to overhear him, crouched just behind the plyboard partition and wrote down his every word. The operator's daughter, an exquisite young woman with a figure unusually well developed for her age, crouched just behind the partition and transcribed his every word. Though she had never laid eyes on him, she recognized that here was one of Western Culture's truly great imaginations, the eloquence of whose suffering would be an inspiration to unnumbered. And her heart was torn between her love for the misfortunate young man (yes, she loved him, though she had never laid though she knew him only—but how well!— through his words, and the deep, calm voice in which he spoke them) between her love et cetera and her womanly intuition that only in suffering and isolation could he give voice et cetera. Lone dark dying. Quietly she kissed the rough plyboard, and a tear fell upon the page. Where she had written in shorthand *Where she had written in shorthand* Where she had written in shorthand *Where she* et cetera. A long time ago we should have passed the apex of Freitag's

Triangle and made brief work of the *dénouement;* the plot doesn't rise by meaningful steps but winds upon itself, digresses, retreats, hesitates, sighs, collapses, expires. The climax of the story must be its protagonist's discovery of a way to get through the funhouse. But he has found none, may have ceased to search.

What relevance does the war have to the story? Should there be fireworks outside or not?

Ambrose wandered, languished, dozed. Now and then he fell into his habit of rehearsing to himself the unadventurous story of his life, narrated from the third-person point of view, from his earliest memory parenthesis of maple leaves stirring in the summer breath of tidewater Maryland end of parenthesis to the present moment. Its principal events, on this telling, would appear to have been *A, B, C,* and *D.*

He imagined himself years hence, successful, married, at ease in the world, the trials of his adolescence far behind him. He has come to the seashore with his family for the holiday: how Ocean City has changed! But at one seldom at one ill-frequented end of the boardwalk a few derelict amusements survive from times gone by: the great carrousel from the turn of the century, with its monstrous griffins and mechanical concert band; the roller coaster rumored since 1916 to have been condemned; the mechanical shooting gallery in which only the image of our enemies changed. His own son laughs with Fat May and wants to know what a funhouse is; Ambrose hugs the sturdy lad close and smiles around his pipestem at his wife.

The family's going home. Mother sits between Father and Uncle Karl, who teases him good-naturedly who chuckles over the fact that the comrade with whom he'd fought his way shoulder to shoulder through the funhouse had turned out to be a blind Negro girl—to their mutual discomfort, as they'd opened their souls. But such are the walls of custom, which even. Whose arm is where? How must it feel. He dreams of a funhouse vaster by far than any yet constructed; but by then they may be out of fashion, like steamboats and excursion trains. Already quaint and seedy: the draperied ladies on the frieze of the carrousel are his father's father's mooncheeked dreams; if he thinks of it more he will vomit his apple-on-a-stick.

He wonders: will he become a regular person? Something has gone wrong; his vaccination didn't take; at the Boy-Scout initiation campfire he only pretended to be deeply moved, as he pretends to this hour that it is not so bad after all in the funhouse, and that he has a little limp. How long will it last? He envisions a truly astonishing funhouse, incredibly complex yet utterly controlled from a great central switchboard like the console of a pipe organ. Nobody had enough imagination. He could design such a place himself, wiring and all, and he's only thirteen years old. He would be its operator: panel lights would show what was up in every cranny of its cunning of its multifarious vastness; a switch-flick would ease this fellow's way, complicate that's, to balance things out; if anyone seemed lost or frightened, all the operator had to do was.

He wishes he had never entered the funhouse. But he has. Then he wishes he were dead. But he's not. Therefore he will construct funhouses for others and be their secret operator—though he would rather be among the lovers for whom funhouses are designed.

QUESTIONS

1. In what ways do Magda and Ambrose's mother complement each other? Peter and Uncle Karl? Ambrose and his father?

2. Ambrose compares the funhouse operator to a relative. Which one? What significance does the character of the funhouse operator have to Ambrose and to the meaning of the story as a whole?

3. What advice is offered to Ambrose by the old man sitting near the tumbling-barrel? Why does Ambrose initially accept and then reject his advice?

4. Why does Ambrose despise his father "for not being what he was supposed to be"?

5. Find the many references to conventions of plot that occur in this story. Does the story itself adhere to any of these conventions? If so, which one(s)? Would you be interested in reading a story totally devoid of plot?

6. What statement about plot in conventional narrative is Barth making in this story?

7. Describe the effect of this story's being set during World War II, on Independence Day.

8. Discuss the literal and symbolic functions of the amusement park as the generalized location for the story.

9. Throughout the story, the prose shifts stylistically as Ambrose attempts to reconcile his emotional reactions to both his family and Magda, his insights into fiction writing, and his fantasies. Cite several examples to support this contention. Discuss your response to these stylistic shifts. Do you find them objectionable?

10. The story repeatedly uses the process of fiction as subject matter. Do you object to being reminded that you are reading a story—that fiction is an artifice?

11. Describe Barth's attitude toward himself as an author and to the writing of fiction. How does his choice of Ambrose as narrator influence your perception of the implied author?

ACKNOWLEDGMENTS *(continued)*

GERALD DUCKWORTH AND CO., LTD. For "Ned Softly the Poet" from *The Tatler,* Volume 3, by Joseph Addison, edited by George Aitken.

WILLIAM EASTLAKE For "The Death of Sun" by William Eastlake from *Cosmopolitan* (October 1972). Reprinted by permission of the author.

FARRAR, STRAUS & GIROUX, INC. For "Sentence" from *City Life* by Donald Barthelme, copyright © 1970 by Donald Barthelme. "Sentence" appeared originally in *The New Yorker;* for "A Conversation with My Father" from *Enormous Changes at the Last Minute* by Grace Paley, copyright © 1972 by Grace Paley; for "Old Love" from *Passions and Other Stories* by Isaac Bashevis Singer, copyright © 1975 by Isaac Bashevis Singer. "Old Love" appeared originally in *The New Yorker;* and for "Zakhar-the-Pouch" from *Stories and Prose Poems* by Alexander Solzhenitsyn, translated by Michael Glenny, German text copyright © 1970 by Hermann Luchterhand Verlag, GmbH, Neuwied und West Berlin, translation copyright © 1970, 1971 by Michael Glenny. All are reprinted with the permission of Farrar, Straus & Giroux, Inc.

GROSSMAN PUBLISHERS For "The Oranging of America" from *The Oranging of America* by Max Apple. Copyright © 1974 by Max Apple. Reprinted by permission of Grossman Publishers.

GROVE PRESS, INC. For "Theme of the Traitor and the Hero" from *Ficciones* by Jorge Luis Borges. Copyright © 1962 by Grove Press, Inc. Translated from the Spanish, copyright © 1956 by Emece Editores, S.A., Buenos Aires, Argentina; and for "Uncle Tom's Cabin: Alternate Ending" from *Tales* by LeRoi Jones. Copyright © 1967 by LeRoi Jones. Both are reprinted by permission of Grove Press, Inc.

HARCOURT BRACE JOVANOVICH, INC. For "Why I live at the P.O." by Eudora Welty. Copyright, 1941, 1969 by Eudora Welty. Reprinted from her volume *A Curtain of Green and Other Stories;* and for "Lappin and Lapinova" from *A Haunted House and Other Stories* by Virginia Woolf, copyright, 1944, 1972, by Harcourt Brace Jovanovich, Inc. Both are reprinted by permission of Harcourt Brace Jovanovich, Inc.

HARPER'S MAGAZINE COMPANY For "I Am Donald Barthelme" by Charles Nicol. Copyright © 1975 by Harper's Magazine Company. All rights reserved. Reprinted from the March 3, 1975, issue of *Bookletter* by special permission.

THE HOGARTH PRESS LTD. For "Lappin and Lapinova" from *A Haunted House and Other Stories* by Virginia Woolf. Reprinted by permission of the Author's Literary Estate and The Hogarth Press Ltd.

KENT STATE UNIVERSITY PRESS For "The Offensive Man" and "The Oligarchical Man" from *Theophrastus: The Character Sketches,* translated by Warren Anderson. Reprinted by permission.

VIRGINIA KIDD For "Nine Lives" from *The Wind's Twelve Quarters* by Ursula K. Le Guin. An earlier version appeared in *Playboy* Magazine. Reprinted by permission of the author and the author's agent, Virginia Kidd.

ALFRED A. KNOPF, INC. For "The Jewels of the Cabots" from *The World of Apples* by John Cheever. Copyright © 1972 by John Cheever; for "The Girl Who Sang with the Beatles" from *The Girl Who Sang with the Beatles and Other Stories* by Robert Hemenway. Copyright © 1969 by Robert Hemenway; and for "The Day of the Dying Rabbit" from *Museums and Women and Other Stories* by John Updike. Copyright © 1969 by John Updike. Originally appeared in *The New Yorker.* All are reprinted by permission of Alfred A. Knopf, Inc.

HAROLD MATSON COMPANY, INC. For "August 2026: There Will Come Soft Rains" by Ray Bradbury. Copyright © 1950, 1977 by Ray Bradbury. Reprinted by permission of Harold Matson Company, Inc.

McINTOSH AND OTIS, INC. For "Sanchez" by Richard Dokey. Copyright © 1967 by Richard Dokey. Appeared originally in *Southwest Review.* Reprinted by permission of the author and McIntosh and Otis, Inc.

THOMAS NELSON & SONS LIMITED For "How Odysseus Visited the Lotus-eaters and the Cyclops" from the Odyssey by Homer, translated by W. H. D. Rouse. Reprinted by permission.

OXFORD UNIVERSITY PRESS For "William Wimble" from *The Spectator,* Volume I, by Joseph Addison, edited by Donald F. Bond.

RANDOM HOUSE, INC. For "Continuity of Parks" from *End of the Game And Other Stories,* by Julio Cortazar, translated by Paul Blackburn. Copyright © 1963, 1967 by Random House, Inc. Reprinted by permission of the publisher, Pantheon Books, a Division of Random House, Inc.; and for "Spotted Horses" by William Faulkner. Copyright 1931 and renewed 1959 by William Faulkner. Reprinted from Scribner's Magazine by permission of Random House, Inc. An expanded version of this story appears as part of *The Hamlet* by William Faulkner.

PHILIP ROTH For "I Always Wanted You to Admire My Fasting; or, Looking at Kafka" by Philip Roth from *American Review,* #17 (May 1973). Reprinted by permission of the author.

SCHOCKEN BOOKS INC. For "A Hunger Artist" from *The Penal Colony* by Franz Kafka. Copyright © 1948 by Schocken Books Inc. Copyright renewed © 1975 by Schocken Books Inc. Reprinted by permission of Schocken Books Inc.

CHARLES SCRIBNER'S SONS For "Babylon Revisited" (copyright 1931 The Curtis Publishing Co.) from *Taps at Reveille* by F. Scott Fitzgerald; for "Hills Like White Elephants" (copyright 1927 Charles Scribner's Sons) from *Men Without Women* by Ernest Hemingway; for "The Middle Years" from Vol. XVI of *The Novels and Tales of Henry James,* N.Y. ed. Copyright 1909 Charles Scribner's Sons; renewal copyright 1937 Henry James; and for "The Waste Land" from *Tales from a Troubled Land* by Alan Paton. Copyright © 1961 Alan Paton. All are reprinted by permission of Charles Scribner's Sons.

LESLIE SILKO For "Lullaby" by Leslie Silko from *Chicago Review,* Vol. 26, No. 1, 1974. Reprinted by permission of the author.

SIMON & SCHUSTER, INC. For "The World War I Los Angeles Airplane" from *Revenge of the Lawn* by Richard Brautigan. Copyright 1963, 1964, 1965, 1966, 1967, 1969, 1970, 1971 by Richard Brautigan. Reprinted by permission of Simon & Schuster, Inc.

HELEN THURBER For "The Fox and the Crow" and "The Lover and His Lass" by James Thurber. Copr. © 1956 James Thurber. From *Further Fables for Our Time,* published by Simon & Schuster. Originally printed in *The New Yorker.*

VANGUARD PRESS, INC. For "The Girl" by Joyce Carol Oates. Reprinted from *The Goddess and Other Women* by Joyce Carol Oates by permission of the publisher, Vanguard Press, Inc. Copyright © 1974, 1973, 1972, 1971, 1970, 1968, 1967, 1966 by Joyce Carol Oates.

THE VIKING PRESS, INC. For "Daydreams" by Anton Chekhov from *The Portable Chekhov* edited by Avrahm Yarmolinsky. Copyright 1947, © 1975 by The Viking Press, Inc.; for "Araby" from *Dubliners* by James Joyce. Originally published by B. W. Huebsch, Inc. in 1916. Copyright © 1967 by the Estate of James Joyce. All rights reserved; for "You Were Perfectly Fine" from *The Portable Dorothy Parker.* Copyright 1929, © 1957 by Dorothy Parker. Originally appeared in *The New Yorker;* and for "The Story-Teller" from *The Short Stories of Saki* (H. H. Munro). All rights reserved. All are reprinted by permission of The Viking Press, Inc.

Chronological List of Authors

Homer (eighth century B.C.)
Aesop (late sixth century B.C.)
Theophrastus (372?–287 B.C.)
Joseph Addison (1672–1719)
The Brothers Grimm: Jacob (1785–1863); Wilhelm (1786–1859)
Nathaniel Hawthorne (1804–1864)
Edgar Allan Poe (1809–1849)
Mark Twain (1835–1910)
Henry James (1843–1916)
Arthur Conan Doyle (1859–1930)
Anton Chekhov (1860–1904)
Saki (1870–1916)
Stephen Crane (1871–1900)
James Joyce (1882–1941)
Virginia Woolf (1882–1941)
Franz Kafka (1883–1924)
Dorothy Parker (1893–1967)
James Thurber (1894–1961)
F. Scott Fitzgerald (1896–1940)
William Faulkner (1897–1962)
Ernest Hemingway (1898–1961)
Jorge Luis Borges (b. 1899)
Alan Paton (b. 1903)
Isaac Bashevis Singer (b. 1904)
Richard Wright (1908–1960)
Eudora Welty (b. 1909)
John Cheever (b. 1912)
Julio Cortazar (b. 1914)
William Eastlake (b. 1918)
Alexander Solzhenitsyn (b. 1918)
Ray Bradbury (b. 1920)
Robert Hemenway (b. 1921)
Grace Paley (b. 1922)
Ursula K. Le Guin (b. 1929)
John Barth (b. 1930)
Donald Barthelme (b. 1931)

John Updike (b. 1932)
Richard Dokey (b. 1933)
Philip Roth (b. 1933)
LeRoi Jones (b. 1934)
Richard Brautigan (b. 1935)
Joyce Carol Oates (b. 1938)
Rosellen Brown (b. 1939)
Charles Nicol (b. 1940)
Max Apple (b. 1941)
Leslie Silko (b. 1948)

Thematic Table of Contents

Selected Bibliography

Short-story collections are indicated by an asterisk.

Joseph Addison (1672–1719); English.
  The Campaign (1704)
  Cato (1713)
  Essays in *The Tatler* (1709–1711); *The Spectator* (1711–12; 1714); *Guardian* (1713);
    The Freeholder (1715–16)

Aesop (late sixth century B.C.); Greek,
  *Fables

Max Apple (b. 1941); American.
  The Oranging of America and Other Stories (1976)

John Barth (b. 1930); American.
  The Floating Opera (rev. ed. 1967)
  The End of the Road (rev. ed. 1967)
  The Sot-Weed Factor (rev. ed. 1967)
  Giles Goat-Boy (1966)
  Lost in the Funhouse (1968)
  Chimera (1972)

Donald Barthelme (b. 1931); American.
  Come Back, Dr. Caligari (1964)
  Snow White (1967)
  Unspeakable Practices, Unnatural Acts (1968)
  City Life (1970)
  Sadness (1972)

Jorge Luis Borges (b. 1899); Argentine.
  Ficciones, 1935–1944 (1962)
  Labyrinths: Selected Stories and Other Writings (1962)
  The Aleph and Other Stories 1933–1969 (1970)
  Dr. Brodie's Report (1972)

Ray Bradbury (b. 1920); American.
  Dark Carnival (1947)
  The Martian Chronicles (1950)
  The Illustrated Man (1951)
  The Golden Apples of the Sun (1953)

Fahrenheit 451 (1953)
*The October Country (1955)
*Dandelion Wine (1957)
*The Day It Rained Forever (1959)
*The Machineries of Joy (1964)
*I Sing the Body Electric! (1969)

Richard Brautigan (b. 1935); American.
A Confederate General from Big Sur (1965)
Trout Fishing in America (1967)
The Pill versus the Springhill Mine Disaster (1968)
Rommel Drives On Deep into Egypt (1970)
*Revenge of the Lawn: Stories, 1962–1970 (1971)
Sombrero Fallout: A Japanese Novel (1976)

Rosellen Brown (b. 1939); American.
Some Deaths in the Delta and Other Poems (1970)
*Street Games (1974)
The Autobiography of My Mother (1976)

John Cheever (b. 1912); American.
*The Way Some People Live (1943)
*The Enormous Radio and Other Stories (1953)
*The Housebreaker of Shady Hill (1958)
The Wapshot Chronicle (1958)
*Some People, Places, and Things That Will Not Appear in My Next Novel (1961)
*The Brigadier and the Golf Widow (1964)
The Wapshot Scandal (1964)
Bullet Park (1969)
*The World of Apples (1973)
Falconer (1977)

Anton Chekhov (1860-1904); Russian.
*The Bet and Other Stories (1915)
*The Duel and Other Stories (1916)
*The Cook's Wedding and Other Stories (1922)
*The Bishop and Other Stories (1930)

Samuel L. Clemens (Mark Twain) (1835–1910); American.
*The Celebrated Jumping Frog of Calaveras County and Other Sketches (1867)
The Adventures of Tom Sawyer (1876)
Life on the Mississippi (1883)
The Adventures of Huckleberry Finn (1885)
A Connecticut Yankee in King Arthur's Court (1889)
*The American Claimant (1892)
*The Man That Corrupted Hadleyburg and Other Stories and Essays (1900)
*The $30,000 Bequest (1906)
The Mysterious Stranger (1916)

Julio Cortazar (b. 1914); Argentine.
   The Winners (1965)
   Hopscotch (1966)
   *End of the Game and Other Stories (Pantheon, 1967, reprinted as *Blow-up and Other
      Stories,* Collier, 1968)
   62: A Model Kit (1972)
   *All Fires the Fire and Other Stories (1973)

Stephen Crane (1871–1900); American.
   Maggie: A Girl of the Streets (1893)
   The Red Badge of Courage (1895)
   The Black Riders (1895)
   *The Little Regiment (1896)
   *The Open Boat (1898)
   *The Monster (1899)
   War Is Kind (1899)
   *Wounds in the Rain (1900)
   *Whilomville Stories (1900)
   *Last Words (1902)

Richard Dokey (b. 1933); American.
   Contributor to *Southwest Review, Michigan Quarterly Review, Carolina Quarterly,* and
      other journals.

Arthur Conan Doyle (1859–1930); English.
   *The Adventures of Sherlock Holmes (1892)
   *Memoirs of Sherlock Holmes (1894)
   *The Great Kleinplatz Experiment and Other Stories (1894)
   *Round the Red Lamp (1894)
   *The Man From Archangel and Other Tales of Adventure (1898)
   The Hound of the Baskervilles (1902)
   *The Return of Sherlock Holmes (1905)
   *The Croxley Master and Other Tales of Ring and Camp (1909)
   *The Dealings of Captain Sharkey and Other Tales of the Pirates (1919)

William Eastlake (b. 1918); American.
   Go in Beauty (1956)
   The Bronc People (1958)
   Portrait of an Artist with Twenty-Six Horses (1963)
   *3 by Eastlake: Go in Beauty, The Bronc People, Portrait of an Artist with Twenty-Six
      Horses* (1970)
   Castle Keep (1965)
   Dancers in the Scalp House: A Novel (1975)
   The Long Naked Descent into Boston (1977)

William Faulkner (1897–1962); American.
   Soldiers' Pay (1926)
   Mosquitoes (1927)

Sartoris (1929)
The Sound and the Fury (1929)
As I Lay Dying (1930)
Sanctuary (1932)
*These Thirteen (1931)
Light in August (1932)
*Doctor Martino and Other Stories (1934)
Absalom, Absalom! (1936)
*The Unvanquished (1938)
The Hamlet (1940)
*Go Down, Moses and Other Stories (1942)
Intruder in the Dust (1948)
Requiem for a Nun (1951)
The Town (1957)
The Mansion (1959)
The Reivers (1962)

F. Scott Fitzgerald (1896–1940); American.
This Side of Paradise (1920)
*Flappers and Philosophers (1921)
*Tales of the Jazz Age (1922)
The Beautiful and Damned (1922)
The Great Gatsby (1925)
*All the Sad Young Men (1926)
Tender Is the Night (1934)
*Taps at Reveille (1935)
*The Pat Hobby Stories (1962)

The Brothers Grimm, Jacob (1785–1863) and Wilhelm (1786–1859); German.
*Kinder-und Hausmarchen, widely known and translated as *Grimm's Fairy Tales* (1812–
1815)

Nathaniel Hawthorne (1804–1864); American.
Fanshawe (1828)
*Twice-Told Tales (1837)
*Mosses from an Old Manse (1846)
The Scarlet Letter (1850)
The House of the Seven Gables (1851)
The Blithedale Romance (1852)
The Marble Faun (1860)

Robert Hemenway (b. 1921); American.
*The Girl Who Sang with the Beatles and Other Stories (1970)

Ernest Hemingway (1898–1961); American.
*In Our Time (1925)
The Sun Also Rises (1926)
*Men Without Women (1927)
A Farewell to Arms (1929)

*Winner Take Nothing (1933)
To Have and Have Not (1937)
For Whom the Bell Tolls (1940)
Across the River and Into the Trees (1950)
The Old Man and the Sea (1952)
Islands in the Stream (1970)

Homer (eighth century B.C.); Greek.
  Iliad
  Odyssey

Henry James (1843–1916); American.
  Roderick Hudson (1876)
  The American (1877)
  Daisy Miller (1879)
  The Europeans (1879)
  *The Madonna of the Future and Other Tales (1879)
  Washington Square (1881)
  The Portrait of a Lady (1882)
  *The Siege of London (1883)
  The Bostonians (1886)
  The Princess Casamassima (1886)
  *The Aspern Papers (1888)
  *A London Life (1889)
  *The Lesson of the Master (1892)
  *The Real Thing and Other Tales (1893)
  *The Private Life (1893)
  *The Wheel of Time (1893)
  *Terminations (1895)
  *Embarrassments (1896)
  The Spoils of Poynton (1897)

LeRoi Jones (Imamu Amiri Baraka) (b. 1934); American.
  The Dead Lecturer (1964)
  Dutchman [and] The Slave (1964)
  The System of Dante's Hell (1965)
  Home: Social Essays (1966)
  *Tales (1967)
  Black Music (1967)
  Black Magic Poetry (1969)
  Four Black Revolutionary Plays (1969)
  Poem for Black Hearts (1970)

James Joyce (1882–1941); Irish.
  *Dubliners (1914)
  A Portrait of the Artist as a Young Man (1916)
  Ulysses (1922)
  Finnegan's Wake (1939)

Franz Kafka (1883–1924); Austrian.
  The Metamorphosis (1916)
  The Penal Colony (1919)
  The Country Doctor (1919)
  The Trial (1925)
  The Castle (1926)
  Amerika (1927)
  The Great Wall of China (1933)

Ursula K. Le Guin (b. 1929); American.
  Rocannon's World (1964)
  City of Illusions (1967)
  A Wizard of Earthsea (1968)
  The Left Hand of Darkness (1969)
  The Tombs of Atuan (1971)
  The Lathe of Heaven (1971)
  The Dispossessed (1974)
  The Wind's Twelve Quarters (1975)
  The Water is Wide (1976)
  The Word for World Is Forest (1976)

Charles Nicol (b. 1940); American.
  Contributor to *Harper's, Atlantic Monthly, The New York Times Book Review, New Republic, Saturday Review,* and other journals.

Joyce Carol Oates (b. 1938); American.
  By the North Gate (1963)
  With Shuddering Fall (1964)
  Upon the Sweeping Flood and Other Stories (1966)
  A Garden of Earthly Delights (1967)
  Expensive People (1968)
  Them (1969)
  The Wheel of Love (1970)
  Wonderland (1971)
  Marriages and Infidelities (1972)
  Do With Me What You Will (1973)
  The Goddess and Other Women (1974)
  The Poisoned Kiss and Other Stories from the Portuguese (1975)
  The Assassins (1975)
  Childwold (1976)
  Crossing the Border: Fifteen Tales (1976)

Grace Paley (b. 1922); American.
  The Little Disturbances of Man (1959, 1968)
  Enormous Changes at the Last Minute (1974)

Dorothy Parker (1893–1967); American.
  Enough Rope (1926)
  Laments for the Living (1930)

Death and Taxes (1931)
Not So Deep As a Well (1936)
**Here Lies* (1939)

Alan Paton (b. 1903); South African.
  Cry, the Beloved Country (1948)
  Too Late the Phalarope (1953)
  **Tales from a Troubled Land* (1961)
  For You Departed (1969)
  Knocking On the Door: Shorter Writings (1975)

Edgar Allan Poe (1809–1849); American.
  Tamerlane and Other Poems (1827)
  The Narrative of Arthur Gordon Pym (1838)
  **Tales of the Grotesque and Arabesque* (1840)
  The Raven and Other Poems (1845)
  **Tales* (1845)
  Eureka: A Prose Poem (1848)

Philip Roth (b. 1933); American.
  **Goodbye, Columbus and Five Short Stories* (1959)
  Letting Go (1962)
  When She Was Good (1967)
  Portnoy's Complaint (1969)
  Our Gang (1971)
  The Breast (1972)
  The Great American Novel (1973)
  My Life as a Man (1974)
  Reading Myself and Others (1975)
  The Professor of Desire (1977)

Saki (H. H. Munro) (1870–1916); English.
  **Reginald* (1904)
  **Reginald in Russia* (1910)
  **The Chronicles of Clovis* (1911)
  **Beasts and Super-Beasts* (1914)
  **The Toys of Peace* (1923)
  **The Square Egg* (1924)

Leslie Silko (b. 1948); American.
  Laguna Woman (1974)
  Ceremony (1977)
  Three stories by Silko are included in *The Man to Send Rain Clouds: Contemporary Stories by American Indians* (1974)

Isaac Bashevis Singer (b. 1904); Polish/American.
  **Satan in Goray and Other Stories* (1923; 1955)
  The Family Moskat (1950)
  **Gimpel the Fool and Other Stories* (1957)

*The Spinoza of Market Street (1961)
*Short Friday (1964)
*The Seance and Other Stories (1968)
*When Shlemiel Went to Warsaw and Other Stories (1968)
*A Friend of Kafka and Other Stories (1970)
*A Crown of Feathers and Other Stories (1973)
*Passions and Other Stories (1975)

Alexander Solzhenitsyn (b. 1918); Russian.
One Day in the Life of Ivan Denisovich (1963)
For the Good of the Cause (1964)
We Never Make Mistakes (1963)
The First Circle (1968)
The Cancer Ward (1969)
*Stories and Prose Poems (1971)
Gulag Archipelago, 1918–1956 (1974)

Theophrastus (372?–287 B.C.); Greek.
The History of Plants
The Causes of Plants
*Characters

James Thurber (1894–1961); American.
The Seal in the Bedroom (1932)
My Life and Hard Times (1933)
*The Middle-Aged Man on the Flying Trapeze (1935)
*Fables for Our Time (1940)
The Male Animal (1940)
Men, Women, and Dogs (1943)
Many Moons (1943)
. . . My World—and Welcome to It (1944)
The White Deer (1945)
The Thirteen Clocks (1945)
*The Beast in Me and Other Animals (1948)
*Further Fables for Our Time (1956)

John Updike (b. 1932); American.
The Poorhouse Fair (1959)
*The Same Door (1959)
Rabbit, Run (1960)
*Pigeon Feathers (1962)
The Centaur (1963)
Of the Farm (1965)
*The Music School (1966)
Couples (1968)
Bech: A Book (1970)
Rabbit Redux (1971)
*Museums and Women and Other Stories (1972)

A Month of Sundays (1975)
Picked-Up Pieces (1975)
Marry Me: A Romance (1976)

Eudora Welty (b. 1909); American.
  *A Curtain of Green (1941)
  *The Wide Net (1943)
  Delta Wedding (1946)
  *The Golden Apples (1949)
  *The Bride of the Innisfallen (1955)
  Losing Battles (1970)
  The Optimist's Daughter (1972)

Virginia Woolf (1882–1941); English.
  The Voyage Out (1915)
  Night and Day (1919)
  Jacob's Room (1922)
  Mrs. Dalloway (1925)
  To the Lighthouse (1927)
  Orlando (1928)
  The Waves (1931)
  The Years (1937)
  Between the Acts (1941)
  *A Haunted House and Other Stories (1943)

Richard Wright (1908–1960); American.
  Native Son (1940)
  Black Boy (1945)
  The Outsider (1953)
  *Eight Men (1961)

Index

A 8
B 9
C 0
D 1
E 2
F 3
G 4
H 5
I 6
J 7